CW00944273

# Mastering
## AutoCAD® for Mac®

**Autodesk®**
Official Training Guide

**George Omura**

**Rick Graham**

WILEY

Wiley Publishing, Inc.

Senior Acquisitions Editor: Willem Knibbe
Development Editor: Candace English
Technical Editor: Lee Ambrosius
Production Editors: Rachel Gigliotti and Dassi Zeidel
Copy Editor: Judy Flynn
Editorial Manager: Pete Gaughan
Production Manager: Tim Tate
Vice President and Executive Group Publisher: Richard Swadley
Vice President and Publisher: Neil Edde
Book Designers: Maureen Forys and Judy Fung
Compositor: JoAnn Kolonick, Happenstance Type-O-Rama
Proofreader: Publication Services, Inc.
Indexer: Ted Laux
Project Coordinator, Cover: Lynsey Stanford
Cover Designer: Ryan Sneed
Cover Image: © PhotoAlto/James Hardy/Getty Images

Copyright © 2011 by Wiley Publishing, Inc., Indianapolis, Indiana
Published simultaneously in Canada

ISBN: 978-0-470-93234-6
ISBN: 978-1-118-01096-9 (ebk)
ISBN: 978-1-118-01097-6 (ebk)
ISBN: 978-1-118-01079-2 (ebk)

No part of this publication may be reproduced, stored in a retrieval system or transmitted in any form or by any means, electronic, mechanical, photocopying, recording, scanning or otherwise, except as permitted under Sections 107 or 108 of the 1976 United States Copyright Act, without either the prior written permission of the Publisher, or authorization through payment of the appropriate per-copy fee to the Copyright Clearance Center, 222 Rosewood Drive, Danvers, MA 01923, (978) 750-8400, fax (978) 646-8600. Requests to the Publisher for permission should be addressed to the Permissions Department, John Wiley & Sons, Inc., 111 River Street, Hoboken, NJ 07030, (201) 748-6011, fax (201) 748-6008, or online at http://www.wiley.com/go/permissions.

Limit of Liability/Disclaimer of Warranty: The publisher and the author make no representations or warranties with respect to the accuracy or completeness of the contents of this work and specifically disclaim all warranties, including without limitation warranties of fitness for a particular purpose. No warranty may be created or extended by sales or promotional materials. The advice and strategies contained herein may not be suitable for every situation. This work is sold with the understanding that the publisher is not engaged in rendering legal, accounting, or other professional services. If professional assistance is required, the services of a competent professional person should be sought. Neither the publisher nor the author shall be liable for damages arising herefrom. The fact that an organization or Web site is referred to in this work as a citation and/or a potential source of further information does not mean that the author or the publisher endorses the information the organization or Web site may provide or recommendations it may make. Further, readers should be aware that Internet Web sites listed in this work may have changed or disappeared between when this work was written and when it is read.

For general information on our other products and services or to obtain technical support, please contact our Customer Care Department within the U.S. at (877) 762-2974, outside the U.S. at (317) 572-3993 or fax (317) 572-4002.

Wiley also publishes its books in a variety of electronic formats. Some content that appears in print may not be available in electronic books.

Library of Congress Cataloging-in-Publication Data is available from the publisher.

TRADEMARKS: Wiley, the Wiley logo, and the Sybex logo are trademarks or registered trademarks of John Wiley & Sons, Inc. and/or its affiliates, in the United States and other countries, and may not be used without written permission. AutoCAD is a registered trademark of Autodesk, Inc. Mac is a registered trademark of Apple, Inc. All other trademarks are the property of their respective owners. Wiley Publishing, Inc., is not associated with any product or vendor mentioned in this book.

10 9 8 7 6 5 4 3 2 1

Dear Reader,

Thank you for choosing *Mastering AutoCAD for Mac*. This book is part of a family of premium-quality Sybex books, all of which are written by outstanding authors who combine practical experience with a gift for teaching.

Sybex was founded in 1976. More than 30 years later, we're still committed to producing consistently exceptional books. With each of our titles, we're working hard to set a new standard for the industry. From the paper we print on to the authors we work with, our goal is to bring you the best books available.

I hope you see all that reflected in these pages. I'd be very interested to hear your comments and get your feedback on how we're doing. Feel free to let me know what you think about this or any other Sybex book by sending me an email at nedde@wiley.com. If you think you've found a technical error in this book, please visit http://sybex.custhelp.com. Customer feedback is critical to our efforts at Sybex.

Best regards,

Neil Edde
Vice President and Publisher
Sybex, an Imprint of Wiley

To the memory of Barry Elbasani, 1941–2010:
founding member of ELS Architecture and
Urban Design
—George Omura

# Acknowledgments

Many talented and hardworking folks gave their best effort to produce *Mastering AutoCAD for Mac*. I offer my sincerest gratitude to those people who helped bring this book to you.

Heartfelt thanks go to the editorial and production teams at Sybex for their efforts. Willem Knibbe, as always, made sure things got off to a great start and was always there for support. Candace English kept a watchful eye on the progress of the book. Lee Ambrosius did an excellent job of ensuring that we didn't make any glaring mistakes and offered suggestions based on his own writing experience. On the production side, Rachel Gigliotti kept the workflow going and answered my dumb questions during the review process, and Judy Flynn made sure we weren't trying out new uses of the English language. I can't forget my son Charles, for helping with the reviews of the earlier chapters.

At Autodesk, special thanks go to Rob Maguire for taking the time from his busy schedule to write the foreword. Thanks for the kind words. Thanks also go to Denis Cadu, who has always given his steadfast support of our efforts over many projects. Jim Quanci always gives his generous and thoughtful assistance to us author types. We'd be lost without your help, Jim. Thanks also go to Barbara Vezos and Richard Lane for their assistance. As always, a big thanks to Shaan Hurley, Lisa Crounse, and the Autodesk beta team for generously allowing us to have a look at the prerelease software.

And finally, a big thank-you goes to Rick Graham for making such a huge contribution to this book as coauthor.

—*George Omura*


Thanks to my wonderful wife Melony, for putting up without me during the preparation of this book. Thanks to George Omura for a fine series of books and allowing me to be a part of this. Thanks to the AutoCAD for Mac team for all the work you've done to make this the product it is today. And last, thanks to Willem Knibbe and all the folks who work behind the scenes at Sybex to make sure what is published is the absolute best.

—*Rick Graham*

# About the Authors

**George Omura** is a licensed architect, Autodesk authorized author, and CAD specialist with more than 20 years of experience in AutoCAD and over 30 years of experience in architecture. He has worked on design projects ranging from resort hotels to metropolitan transit systems. George has written numerous other AutoCAD books for Sybex, including *Introducing AutoCAD 2010, Mastering AutoCAD 2011 and AutoCAD LT 2011,* and *Introducing AutoCAD 2009.*

**Richard (Rick) Graham** is a CAD/IT manager at James R. Holley & Associates, Inc. He has been using and supporting users of AutoCAD and other Autodesk products for over 20 years. Rick has multidiscipline experience, from architecture to civil engineering. He is currently serving as president of his local AUGI chapter and has presented various topics. He coauthored *Introducing AutoCAD Civil 3D 2010* and is involved with several blogs, including his latest, www.macacad.com. He has been using the Mac OS for many years and has long felt that the marriage between Mac and AutoCAD would happen again. Oh, happy days!

# Contents at a Glance

# Contents

# Foreword

Developing AutoCAD for Mac has been a great opportunity for Autodesk to deliver something our customers have been requesting for almost 20 years. To meet the high expectations of our customers, Autodesk had to deliver a high-quality customer experience, tailored not only for the traditional AutoCAD user, but one for the native Mac OS user as well. We needed a product that was the best of both worlds.

I was fortunate to help deliver the best of both worlds in my role as product manager for AutoCAD for Mac. After learning AutoCAD in Mechanical Engineering school and at UC Berkeley, I began working for Autodesk immediately in the QA department, and quickly transitioned to a software development role on the AutoCAD team for six years. Following a break from Autodesk, I returned to school and graduated at the top of my class with a dual Master's degree in Business Administration and Information Systems. I was in the unique position of being able to understand our technical customers, push the limits of software development, and justify the business motivation to do so. AutoCAD for Mac was the perfect project for me.

AutoCAD for Mac first and foremost is AutoCAD. We needed to make it native, so change from the Windows version was inevitable; however, we knew none of the changes could alter the customer's impression that "this is AutoCAD." After countless research sessions, customer interviews, and some numerical analysis of commands and functioned used, we had our initial scope. Next we had to understand the essence of what makes a Mac program truly native. To help us understand this, Autodesk recruited the largest pool of beta testers in the history of the company. These customers helped us guide the development of the product so that we kept the right balance of AutoCAD and Mac-native experiences.

George Omura and Rick Graham were among our most active beta testers and helped us craft the product, address issues, and understand and articulate our customers' needs. Both have had many years of AutoCAD experience under their belts, which allows them to understand both users who are new to AutoCAD, as well as those that have used it for many years. No matter what your skill level, this excellent book will help you quickly become productive with AutoCAD for Mac.

Finally, to our many users, I'd like to say that we are eternally grateful for the opportunity to provide such a great product and benefit from your constant feedback. I wish you all good luck with the product, and the AutoCAD for Mac team will eagerly await your feedback on the discussion forums.

Thank you,

—*Rob Maguire*
*Product Manager, AutoCAD for Mac*
*Platform Solutions and Emerging Business Division*
*Autodesk, Inc.*

# Introduction

Welcome to *Mastering AutoCAD for Mac*. As many readers of the original *Mastering AutoCAD* have already discovered, this book is a unique blend of tutorial and reference that includes everything you need to get started and stay ahead with AutoCAD.

## How to Use This Book

Rather than just showing you how each command works, this book shows you AutoCAD for Mac in the context of meaningful activities. You'll learn how to use commands while working on an actual project and progressing toward a goal. This book also provides a foundation on which you can build your own methods for using AutoCAD and become an AutoCAD expert. For this reason, I haven't covered every single command or every permutation of a command response. You should think of this book as a way to get a detailed look at AutoCAD as it's used on a real project. As you follow the exercises, I encourage you to also explore AutoCAD on your own, applying the techniques you learn to your own work.

Both experienced and beginning AutoCAD users will find this book useful. If you aren't an experienced user, the way to get the most out of this book is to approach it as a tutorial—chapter by chapter, at least for the first two parts of the book. You'll find that each chapter builds on the skills and information you learned in the previous one. To help you navigate, the exercises are shown in numbered steps. To address the needs of all readers worldwide, the exercises provide both Imperial (feet/inches) and metric measurements.

After you've mastered the material in Parts 1 and 2, you can follow your interests and explore other parts of the book in whatever order you choose. Part 3 takes you to a more advanced skill level. There you'll learn more about storing and sharing drawing data and how to create more complex drawings. If you're interested in 3D, check out Part 4.

You can also use this book as a ready reference for your day-to-day problems and questions about commands. Optional exercises at the end of each chapter will help you review and look at different ways to apply the information you've learned. Experienced users will also find this book a handy reference tool.

## Getting Information Fast

In each chapter, you'll find extensive tips and discussions in the form of sidebars set off from the main text. These provide a wealth of information I have gathered over years of using AutoCAD on a variety of projects in different office environments. You may want to browse through the book and read these boxes just to get an idea of how they might be useful to you.

Another quick reference you'll find yourself using often is Appendix D, "System Variables and Dimension Styles," included on the companion website, www.sybex.com/go/masteringautocadmac. It contains descriptions of all the dimension settings with comments on their uses. If you experience any problems, you can consult the section "When Things Go Wrong" in Appendix C, "Hardware and Software Tips," also included on the companion website.

## The Mastering Series

The Mastering series from Sybex provides outstanding instruction for readers with intermediate and advanced skills, in the form of top-notch training and development for those already working in their field and clear, serious education for those aspiring to become pros. Every Mastering book includes the following:

◆ Real-World Scenarios, ranging from case studies to practical information you can use now, that show how the tool, technique, or knowledge presented is applied in actual practice

◆ Skill-based instruction, with chapters organized around real tasks rather than abstract concepts or subjects

◆ Self-review test questions, so you can be certain you're equipped to do the job right

# What to Expect

*Mastering AutoCAD for Mac* is divided into four parts, each representing a milestone in your progress toward becoming an expert AutoCAD user. Here is a description of those parts and what they will show you.

## Part 1: The Basics

As with any major endeavor, you must begin by tackling small, manageable tasks. In this first part, you'll become familiar with the way AutoCAD looks and feels.

Chapter 1, "Exploring the AutoCAD Interface," shows you how to get around in AutoCAD.

Chapter 2, "Creating Your First Drawing," details how to start and exit the program and how to respond to AutoCAD commands.

Chapter 3, "Setting Up and Using AutoCAD's Drafting Tools," tells you how to set up a work area, edit objects, and lay out a drawing.

Chapter 4, "Organizing Objects with Blocks and Groups," explores some tools unique to CAD: symbols, blocks, and layers. As you're introduced to AutoCAD, you'll also get a chance to make some drawings that you can use later in the book and perhaps even in future projects of your own.

Chapter 5, "Keeping Track of Layers and Blocks," shows you how to use layers to keep similar information together and object properties such as linetypes to organize things visually.

## Part 2: Mastering Intermediate Skills

After you have the basics down, you'll begin to explore some of AutoCAD's more subtle qualities.

Chapter 6, "Editing and Reusing Data to Work Efficiently," tells you how to reuse drawing setup information and parts of an existing drawing.

Chapter 7, "Mastering Viewing Tools, Hatches, and External References," details how to use viewing tools and hatches and how to assemble and edit a large drawing file.

Chapter 8, "Introducing Printing and Layouts," shows you how to get your drawing onto hard copy.

Chapter 9, "Adding Text to Drawings," tells you how to annotate your drawing and edit your notes.

Chapter 10, "Using Fields and Tables," shows you how to add spreadsheet functionality to your drawings.

Chapter 11, "Using Dimensions," gives you practice in using automatic dimensioning (another unique CAD capability).

## Part 3: Mastering Advanced Skills

At this point, you'll be on the verge of becoming a real AutoCAD expert. Part 3 is designed to help you polish your existing skills and give you a few new ones.

Chapter 12, "Using Attributes," tells you how to attach information to drawing objects and how to export that information to database and spreadsheet files.

Chapter 13, "Copying Existing Drawings into AutoCAD," details techniques for transferring paper drawings to AutoCAD.

Chapter 14, "Advanced Editing and Organizing," is where you'll complete the apartment building tutorial. During this process you'll learn how to integrate what you've learned so far and gain some tips on working in groups.

Chapter 15, "Laying Out Your Printer Output," shows you the tools that let you display your drawing in an organized fashion.

Chapter 16, "Making 'Smart' Drawings with Parametric Tools," introduces you to parametric drawing. This feature lets you quickly modify a drawing by changing a few parameters.

Chapter 17, "Drawing Curves," gives you an in-depth look at some special drawing objects, such as splines and fitted curves.

Chapter 18, "Getting and Exchanging Data from Drawings," is where you'll practice getting information about a drawing and learn how AutoCAD can interact with other applications, such as spreadsheets and page-layout programs. You'll also learn how to copy and paste data.

## Part 4: 3D Modeling and Imaging

Although 2D drafting is AutoCAD's workhorse application, AutoCAD's 3D capabilities give you a chance to expand your ideas and look at them in a new light.

Chapter 19, "Creating 3D Drawings," covers AutoCAD's basic features for creating three-dimensional drawings.

Chapter 20, "Using Advanced 3D Features," introduces you to some of the program's more powerful 3D capabilities.

Chapter 21, "Rendering 3D Drawings," shows how you can use AutoCAD to produce lifelike views of your 3D drawings.

Chapter 22, "Editing and Visualizing 3D Solids," takes a closer look at 3D solids and how they can be created, edited, and displayed in AutoCAD.

Chapter 23, "Exploring 3D Mesh and Surface Modeling," introduces you to free-form 3D modeling using mesh and surface objects. With this latest addition to AutoCAD, there isn't anything you can't model in 3D.

## The Appendix

Finally, this book has one appendix.

Appendix A, "The Bottom Line," contains the solutions to the book's Master It review questions.

## What's on the Book's Website

The companion website, www.sybex.com/go/masteringautocadmac, contains the sample drawing files from all the exercises in this book. You can pick up an exercise anywhere you like without having to work through the book from front to back. You can also use these sample files to repeat exercises or to just explore how files are organized and put together. In addition, you'll find the following:

- Links to important resources like video demos of the new features in AutoCAD for the Mac

- A trial version of AutoCAD for the Mac

- Trial software of companion products to AutoCAD for the Mac

- Three appendices and two bonus chapters to further enhance your skills

  - Appendix B, "Installing and Setting Up AutoCAD for Mac," contains an installation and configuration tutorial. If AutoCAD isn't already installed on your system, follow the steps in this tutorial before starting Chapter 1.

  - Appendix C, "Hardware and Software Tips," provides information about hardware related to AutoCAD. It also provides tips on improving AutoCAD's performance and troubleshooting and provides more detailed information on setting up AutoCAD's plotting feature.

  - Appendix D, "System Variables and Dimension Styles," provides a reference to dimension style settings.

◆ Bonus Chapter 1, "Exploring AutoLISP," is a primer to AutoCAD's popular macro language. You'll learn how you can create custom commands built on existing ones and how you can retrieve and store locations and other data.

◆ Bonus Chapter 2, "Customizing Toolsets, Menus, Linetypes, and Hatch Patterns," shows you how to use workspaces, customize the user interface, and create custom linetypes and hatch patterns. You'll also be introduced to the Diesel macro language.

---

**THE AUTOCAD FREE TRIAL**

If you don't have AutoCAD, you can install a trial version from the companion website. Be aware that the trial is good for only 30 days—don't start to use it until you're certain you'll have plenty of free time to practice using AutoCAD.

---

## The Minimum System Requirements

This book assumes you have an Apple Macintosh computer with an Intel Core Duo or Quad Core processor running OS X Leopard v10.5.8 or later or OS X Snow Leopard v10.6 or later. Generally speaking, any Macintosh released after January 1, 2009 should work. Your computer should have a hard disk with 1 GB or more of free space (3 GB recommended) for the AutoCAD program files and about 120 MB of additional space for sample files and the workspace.

AutoCAD for Mac runs best on systems with at least 2 GB or more of RAM. Your computer should also have a high-resolution monitor and an Nvidia GeForce or ATI Radeon display processor. We also assume you're using a mouse and have the use of a printer or a plotter. You can use a trackpad, but make sure you are familiar with the click-and-drag (double-tap and drag) and right-click (two-finger tap) emulation on the trackpad. Finally, you'll need an Internet connection to take full advantage of the support offerings from Autodesk.

If you want a more detailed explanation of hardware options with AutoCAD, see Appendix C on the companion website. You'll find a general description of the available hardware options and their significance to AutoCAD.

## Doing Things in Style

Much care has been taken to see that the stylistic conventions in this book—the use of uppercase or lowercase letters, italic or boldface type, and so on—are the ones most likely to help you learn AutoCAD. On the whole, their effect should be subliminal. However, you may find it useful to be conscious of the following rules:

◆ Menu selections are shown by a series of options separated by the ➢ symbol (for example, choose File ➢ New). These are typically used to show selections from a shortcut menu or the menu bar, which you will learn about in Chapter 1.

◆ Keyboard entries are shown in boldface (for example, enter **ROTATE**↵).

◆ Command-line prompts are shown in a monospaced font (for example, `Select objects:`).

For most functions, this book describes how to select icons or tools from the different AutoCAD panels. In addition, where applicable, I include related keyboard shortcuts and command names. These command names provide continuity for readers accustomed to working at the Command prompt.

I use the standard symbols for the Mac shift, control, option and command keys. These keys are used in conjunction with letter keys to control many of AutoCAD's features. Here is a list of the symbols and the keys they represent:

⇧    Shift key

⌃    Control key

⌥    Option key

⌘    Command key

## New Features of AutoCAD for Mac

AutoCAD for Mac has a helpful interface with elements like tooltips and a Web-based help system. A Welcome screen offers short videos to help you learn basic functions. Dig a little deeper and you'll find that some features can simplify your work so you don't have to keep track of so many details. Here are some of the features covered in this book:

◆    Mac-oriented interface with support for Multi-Touch devices allow you to easily navigate your drawing.

◆    Advanced surface modeling with procedural and NURBS surface tools give you a new level of control in 3D modeling.

◆    Streamlined materials and rendering tools make it easier to produce presentation-quality renderings from diagrammatic sketches to photo-real presentations.

◆    Expanded transparency control adds transparency to any pattern or object.

◆    Multifunction grips give you expanded control over 2D and 3D objects.

◆    New selection features enable you to isolate and select similar objects quickly and easily.

## Contact the Authors

We hope that *Mastering AutoCAD for Mac* will be of benefit to you and that, after you've completed the tutorials, you'll continue to use the book as a reference. If you have comments, criticism, or ideas about how the book can be improved, you can contact us at the following addresses:

George Omura: george.omura@gmail.com.

Rick Graham: macacad@yahoo.com

Rich Graham's AutoCAD for Mac blog: www.macacad.com

If you find errors, please let the publisher know. Visit the book's web page, www.sybex.com/go/masteringautocadmac, and click the Errata link to find a form on which you can identify the problem.

And thanks for choosing *Mastering AutoCAD for Mac*.

# Part 1

# The Basics

# Chapter 1

# Exploring the AutoCAD Interface

Before you can start to use AutoCAD for Mac, you'll need to become familiar with the basics. If you're completely new to AutoCAD, you'll want to read this first chapter carefully. It introduces you to many of AutoCAD's basic operations, such as opening and closing files, getting a close-up look at part of a drawing, and changing a drawing. If you're familiar with the latest Windows version of AutoCAD, you should review this chapter anyway to get acquainted with the Macintosh version. The AutoCAD Mac interface is quite different from the Windows version, so this chapter will help you find the tools you are familiar with.

Autodesk releases new versions of AutoCAD every year. Part of this strategy is to introduce improvements that focus on a particular category of features. This latest version, AutoCAD for Mac, includes several new features that are related to curves in both 2D drafting and 3D modeling. There are also a number of enhancements that allow you to easily select similar objects in a drawing. The ability to make objects appear transparent has also been improved.

Autodesk has discovered that the number of 3D users is on the upswing, so with this version, you'll see some new 3D features that will give you more freedom to create 3D shapes. These features include some new ways to create surface forms and the editing tools that enable you to easily manipulate 3D solids and surfaces.

You'll get a chance to explore these new features and many more as you work through this book. Before you begin the exercise later in this chapter, make sure that you have loaded the sample files from this book's companion website, www.sybex.com/go/masteringautocadmac. See the introduction for details.

In this chapter, you'll learn to do the following:

◆ Use the AutoCAD application

◆ Get a closer look with the Zoom command

◆ Save a file as you work

◆ Make changes and open multiple files

## Taking a Guided Tour

In this section, you'll get a chance to familiarize yourself with the AutoCAD application and how you communicate with AutoCAD. As you do the exercises in this chapter, you'll also get a feel for how to work with this book. Don't worry about understanding or remembering everything you see in this chapter. You'll get plenty of opportunities to probe the finer details of the program as you work through the later chapters. To help you remember the material, you'll find a brief set of questions at the end of each chapter. For now, just enjoy your first excursion into AutoCAD.

### Launching AutoCAD

If you have already installed AutoCAD (see Appendix B on the book's website) and are ready to jump in and take a look, click the AutoCAD icon in the Dock. AutoCAD opens and displays a blank default document named Drawing1.dwg.

If you're using the trial version, you'll see the Product License Activation window after you click the AutoCAD icon. This window shows you the number of days you have left in the trial version. It also enables you to activate the product if you purchase a license. Click the Try button to continue to the blank default document.

Now let's look at the AutoCAD application in detail. Don't worry if it seems like a lot of information. You don't have to memorize it, but by looking at all the parts, you'll be aware of what is available in a general way.

### The AutoCAD Application

The AutoCAD program window is divided into seven parts:

♦ Menu bar

♦ Layers palette

♦ Properties Inspector palette

♦ Tool Sets palette

♦ Drawing area

♦ Command Line palette

♦ Status bar

Figure 1.1 shows a typical layout of the AutoCAD application. You can organize the AutoCAD palettes into any arrangement you want, but while you're learning AutoCAD you may want to leave the default arrangement in place.

**FIGURE 1.1**
A typical arrangement of the AutoCAD application

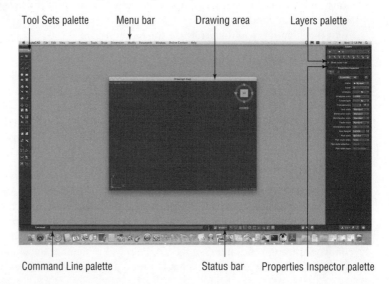

Tool Sets palette    Menu bar    Drawing area    Layers palette

Command Line palette    Status bar    Properties Inspector palette

## THE MENU BAR

Like a typical Mac application, AutoCAD displays a menu bar where you can select a command to perform a task. As you work through this book, you'll be directed to choose commands from the menu bar where appropriate. Often commands in the menu bar are repeated as tools in the Tool Sets palette, so I'll direct you to select a tool from the Tool Sets palette or a command from the menu bar and you can decide which method you prefer. You'll learn about the Tool Sets palette a bit later.

## THE LAYERS PALETTE

The Layers palette (Figure 1.2) displays the layer information in the current drawing. Layers help you organize your drawing. If you've used Photoshop or other drawing programs that employ layers, you're probably familiar with the basic concept of layers. You can separate parts of a drawing into layers and then control the display of those parts by adjusting layer properties. You'll learn more about layers in Chapter 5, "Keeping Track of Layers and Blocks."

**FIGURE 1.2**
The Layers palette

Click the disclosure triangle to expand or contract the Layers palette.

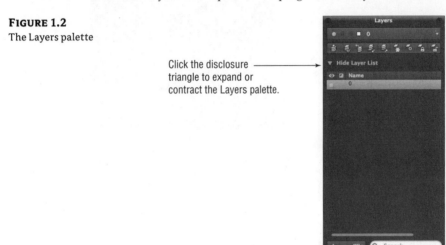

## THE PROPERTIES INSPECTOR PALETTE

The Properties Inspector palette (Figure 1.3) displays information about the layers and objects in your drawing. When you select a layer name from the Layers palette, the layer's properties are displayed in the Properties Inspector palette. When you draw lines, circles, and other objects, you can use the Properties Inspector palette to display the properties of those objects. You'll learn more about object properties in Chapter 2, "Creating Your First Drawing."

**FIGURE 1.3**
The Properties
Inspector palette

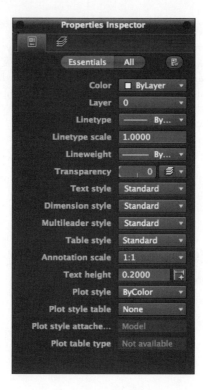

## THE TOOL SETS PALETTE

The Tool Sets palette (Figure 1.4) contains tools you'll use to create and edit your drawings. The tools in the palette give you a clue to their purpose, and you can hover the cursor over a tool to see a tooltip showing a descriptive name of the tool. The Tool Sets palette gives you a quick, one-click method for issuing commands. You'll also find that many of the tools in the Tool Sets palette duplicate commands in the menu bar.

The Tool Sets palette is organized into groups of tools that serve similar functions. Figure 1.4 shows the tool groups; some can be expanded into panels, which are described later in this section.

Though not obvious, the Tool Sets palette offers three tool sets, or *workflow panels*: Drafting, Annotation, and Modeling (see Figure 1.4). The one you see now is the Drafting workflow. You can open the other workflows by clicking the tool in the Tool Sets palette title bar. This opens a pop-up menu offering the Drafting, Annotation, and Modeling options. You'll use these other sets of tools in later chapters.

Another feature you'll want to know about is the Tool Sets palette *tool group arrow*. A tool group arrow is similar to a menu bar option because you can click a tool group arrow to expand a panel of additional options. A tool group arrow appears to the right of a group of tools that can be expanded to a tool group panel. Clicking the tool group arrow expands the palette to reveal a panel with more tools (Figure 1.5). A tool group arrow gives you access to a set of additional tools that are similar to the set of tools the tool group arrow is attached to.

**FIGURE 1.4**
The Tool Sets
palette

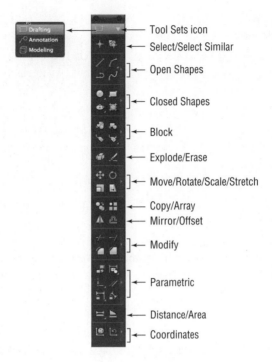

**FIGURE 1.5**
A Tool Sets tool
group and tool
group arrow

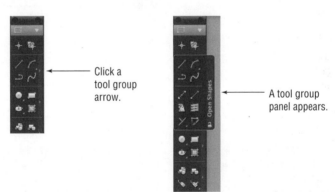

Some of the tools in the Tool Sets palette contain more than one option. For example, if you click and hold the Circle tool (labeled as Center, Radius on its help tag), you will see additional tools in a column below the tool (Figure 1.6). This set of additional tools is called a *flyout*. You can tell if a tool opens a flyout if you see a small triangle in the lower-right corner of the icon (Figure 1.6).

Flyouts offer additional ways to use a tool. For example, the Circle tool flyout lets you draw a circle by specifying a center and radius, a center and diameter, 2 points, 3 points, two tangent points and a radius, or three tangent points. The flyouts often mimic the options in the menu bar. If you click Draw ➢ Circle, you will see the same options appear in the flyout menu.

**FIGURE 1.6**
Click and hold the
circle tool to open
the flyout menu.

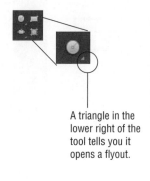

A triangle in the
lower right of the
tool tells you it
opens a flyout.

### THE DRAWING AREA

The drawing area occupies the center of the screen. Figure 1.7 shows it without the grid for clarity. (You can turn the grid off and on by pressing ⌘-G.) Everything you draw appears in this area. As you move your mouse around, crosshairs appear to move within the drawing area. This is the drawing cursor that lets you point to locations in the drawing area. You'll get your first chance to work with the drawing area later in the section "Picking Points in the Drawing Area."

**FIGURE 1.7**
The drawing area
shown without
the grid

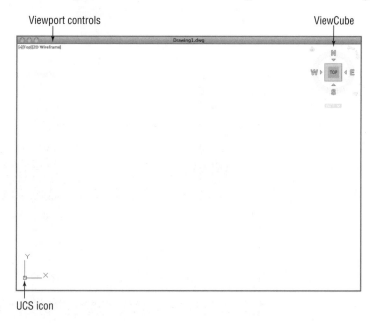

Viewport controls

ViewCube

UCS icon

Within the drawing area, you see three items. The UCS icon appears in the lower-left corner. You'll learn more about the UCS icon in a moment (see the section "Understanding the UCS Icon"). In the upper-right corner, you see the ViewCube. The ViewCube is primarily for 3D modeling, and you'll learn more about it in Chapter 19, "Creating 3D Drawings." In the upper-left corner you see the viewport controls. In Figure 1.7 they show a plus sign and the words Top, and 2D Wireframe. The plus sign offers viewport options that you'll learn about in Chapter 20, "Using Advanced 3D Features." The other two options change depending on the way your drawing is displayed. You'll get a closer look at these options a bit later in this chapter. For now, let's continue examining the parts of the AutoCAD screen.

---

**WHY DOES THE DRAWING AREA LOOK DIFFERENT ON MY SCREEN?**

You probably noticed that the drawing area shown in this book has a white background while the drawing area in your version of AutoCAD shows a dark gray background. I'm using a white background in the book to make things easier to see on a printed page. White lines on a dark background do not print very well. You can also change your drawing area background to white using the AutoCAD Application Preferences. See Appendix B on the book's website for more on the AutoCAD Application Preferences.

---

### THE COMMAND LINE PALETTE

The Command Line palette (Figure 1.8), located just below the drawing area, gives you feedback about AutoCAD's commands as you use them. You can move and resize this palette just as you move and resize other palettes and windows on the Mac. For example, you can click the disclosure triangle (more commonly called the disclosure triangle, which is the term I'll use throughout this book) on the right side to expand and contract the palette.

**FIGURE 1.8**
The expanded
Command Line
palette

◄——— Disclosure triangle

### THE STATUS BAR

To the right of the Command Line palette is the status bar (Figure 1.9). The tools in the status bar offer aids to the drafting process. You'll find tools to turn on the grid and snap functions as well as tools to help you control the scale of text and symbols.

**FIGURE 1.9**
The status bar

---

### TOOLS VS. THE KEYBOARD

Throughout this book, you'll be told to select tools from the Tool Sets palette to invoke commands. For new and experienced users alike, the Tool Sets palette offers an easy-to-remember method for accessing commands. If you're an experienced AutoCAD user, though, you can type commands directly from the keyboard. The keyboard commands you know and love still work as they do in the Windows version of AutoCAD (but with the ⌘ key used in place of the Windows Control key).

Many tools and commands have *aliases*. Aliases are one-, two-, or three-letter abbreviations of a command name. As you become more proficient with AutoCAD, you may find these aliases helpful. As you work through this book, the aliases will be identified for your reference.

Finally, in typical Mac fashion, you can find the command shortcuts in the pull-down menus of the menu bar. Shortcuts are multiple key presses that start a command or change a feature. For example, you can press ⌘-1 to open or close the Tool Sets palette. If you choose Tools ≻ Palettes, you'll see the keyboard shortcuts to the right of the command names.

---

## Picking Points in the Drawing Area

Now that you've seen the general layout of AutoCAD, take a look at the drawing cursor to get a sense of how the parts of the AutoCAD screen work together:

---

### CLICK A MOUSE OR TAP A TRACKPAD?

This book assumes that you are using a mouse. If you are using a trackpad, use the corresponding gestures to issue a click, a click-and-drag, or a right-click. For example, a mouse click is a one-finger tap on a trackpad. A right-click is a two-finger tap on a trackpad. A click-and-drag requires a one-finger double-tap and drag on the trackpad.

---

1. Place the cursor in the middle of the drawing area and click and hold. Trackpad users should use a one-finger double-tap. Move the mouse and a rectangle follows. This is a *selection window;* you'll learn more about this window in Chapter 2. You also see Specify opposite corner: in the Command Line palette (Figure 1.10).

**FIGURE 1.10**
The Command Line palette shown un-docked

2.  Release the mouse button. Trackpad users should use a one-finger tap. The window selection disappears.

3.  Try the click-and-drag motion with the mouse (or double-tap, tap gesture for trackpads) again in the drawing area. Notice that as you click and drag, a window appears, and as you release the mouse, the window disappears.

If you happen to right-click (or ⌘-click or use a two-finger tap on a trackpad), a shortcut menu appears. A right-click frequently opens a menu containing options that are *context sensitive*. This means the contents of the shortcut menu depend on the location where you right-click as well as the command that is active at the time. If there are no appropriate options at the time of the right-click, AutoCAD treats the right-click as a ↵. You'll learn more about these options as you progress through the book. For now, if you happen to open this menu by accident, press the Esc key to close it.

## Understanding the UCS Icon

In the lower-left corner of the drawing area, you see an L-shaped line (Figure 1.11). This is the *User Coordinate System (UCS)* icon, which tells you your orientation in the drawing. This icon becomes helpful as you start to work with complex 2D drawings and 3D models. The X and Y indicate the X and Y axes of your drawing. Chapter 20 discusses this icon in detail. For now, you can use it as a reference to tell you the direction of the axes.

**FIGURE 1.11**
The UCS icon

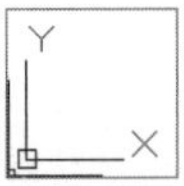

**IF YOU CAN'T FIND THE UCS ICON**

The UCS icon can be turned on and off, so if you're on someone else's system and you don't see the icon, don't panic. If you don't see the icon or it doesn't look as it does in this chapter, see Chapter 20 for more information.

## Using the Command Line Palette and the Dynamic Input Display

AutoCAD is the perfect servant: It does everything you tell it to and no more. You communicate with AutoCAD by using tools and menu bar options to invoke AutoCAD commands. A *command* is a single-word instruction you give to AutoCAD telling it to do something, such as draw a line (the Line tool in the Tool Sets palette) or erase an object (the Erase tool in the Tool Sets palette). Whenever you invoke a command, by either typing it or selecting a menu option or tool, AutoCAD responds by presenting messages to you in the Command Line palette and the Dynamic Input display or by displaying a dialog box.

The Dynamic Input display allows you to enter dimensional data of objects as you draw them. Besides echoing the Command Line palette messages, the Dynamic Input display shows temporary dimensions, coordinates, and angles of objects you're drawing and editing. As you enter coordinate or angle values through the keyboard, they appear in the Dynamic Input display, which is connected to the cursor (Figure 1.12).

**FIGURE 1.12**
A sample of how the Dynamic Input display looks

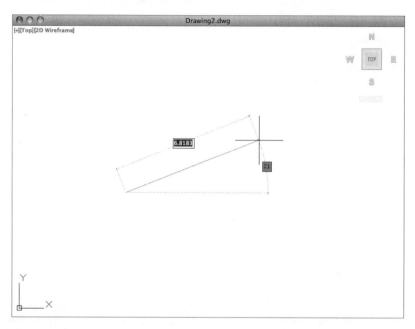

You can easily turn the Dynamic Input display on or off by clicking the Dynamic Input tool in the status bar. When the Dynamic Input display is turned off, responses to your keyboard input appear only in the Command Line palette.

The messages in the Command Line palette, or in the Dynamic Input display, often tell you what to do next. Commands may also display a list of options in the Command Line palette. A single command often presents a series of messages, which you answer to complete the command. These messages serve as an aid to new users who need a little help. If you ever get lost while using a command or forget what you're supposed to do, look at the Command Line palette for clues. As you become more comfortable with AutoCAD, you'll find that you won't need to refer to these messages as frequently.

As an additional aid, you can right-click to display a context-sensitive shortcut menu. That is, if you're in the middle of a command, the context-sensitive menu displays a list of options specifically related to that command. For example, if you right-click before picking the first point for the Rectangle command, a menu opens, displaying the same options that are listed in the Command Line palette plus some additional options.

As mentioned, the Command Line palette is located in the bottom left of the AutoCAD application. By default, it shows a single line of text. You can expand the Command Line palette by clicking the disclosure triangle, which, as mentioned earlier, is the triangle icon on the right side of the palette. The expanded Command Line palette shows several lines. The bottom line shows the current messages, and the top lines show messages that have scrolled by or, in some cases, components of the current message that don't fit in a single line. Right now, the bottom line displays the message Command (see Figure 1.8, earlier in this chapter). This *prompt* tells you that AutoCAD is waiting for your instructions. When you click a point in the drawing area, you see the message Specify opposite corner:. At the same time, the cursor starts to draw a window selection that disappears when you click another point. The same message appears in the Dynamic Input display at the cursor.

As a new user, pay special attention to messages displayed in the Command Line palette and the Dynamic Input display because this is how AutoCAD communicates with you. Besides giving you messages, the Command Line palette records your activity within AutoCAD. You can use the scroll bar to the right of the expanded Command Line palette to review previous messages. You can also resize the palette for a better view using the resizing handle in the lower-right corner of the palette. And you can close or open the Command Line palette by pressing ⌘-3 or by choosing Tools ➢ Palettes ➢ Command Line. (Chapter 2 discusses these components in more detail.)

Now, let's look at AutoCAD's window components in detail.

> ### DO I REALLY NEED THE COMMAND LINE?
>
> The Command Line palette and the Dynamic Input display allow AutoCAD to provide text feedback on your actions. You can think of these features as a chat window to AutoCAD—as you enter commands, AutoCAD responds with messages. As you become more familiar with AutoCAD, you may find you don't need to rely on the Command Line palette and Dynamic Input display for feedback. If you're an experienced Mac user, you might think of the Command Line palette as a kind of terminal window that lets you get deeper into the inner workings of AutoCAD. Experienced users can take advantage of the Command Line palette to query the program, create macros, or enter commands and command options. For new and casual users, however, the Command Line palette and Dynamic Input display can be helpful in understanding what steps to take as you work.

## Getting Familiar with AutoCAD

Now that you've been introduced to the AutoCAD application, you're ready to try using a few AutoCAD commands. First you'll open a sample file and make a few modifications to it. In the process, you'll become familiar with some common methods of operation in AutoCAD.

### Opening an Existing File

In this exercise, you'll get a chance to see and use a typical Select File dialog box.

Before you start, make sure you have installed the sample files for this book from the accompanying website. See the introduction for instructions on how to find the sample files.

To start, you'll open an existing file:

1. Click the red close button in the upper-left corner of the drawing area.

   An alert message appears, asking whether you want to save the changes you've made to the current drawing. Click No.

2. Choose File ➢ Open to open the Select File dialog box. This is a typical Finder dialog box. You can preview a drawing before you open it by switching to a column view, thereby saving time while searching for files (see Figure 1.13).

**FIGURE 1.13**

The Select File dialog box

3. In the Select File dialog box, navigate to the Chapter 01 folder of the sample files you downloaded.

4. Select clip.dwg. The Preview column now shows a thumbnail image of the file. Be aware that a thumbnail may not show for files from older releases of AutoCAD.

5. Click the Open button at the bottom of the Select File dialog box. AutoCAD opens the clip.dwg file, which is shown in Figure 1.14.

The clip.dwg file opens to display a *layout* view of the drawing. A layout is a type of view in which you lay out different views of your drawing in preparation for printing. You can tell you are in a layout view by the white area over the gray background. This white area represents your drawing on a printed page. This view is like a print preview. See the following section for more on the layout views.

**FIGURE 1.14**

The Layout1 view of the clip.dwg file

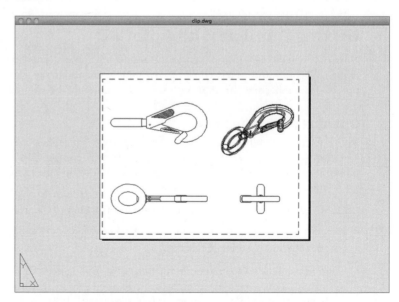

Also note that the drawing area's title bar displays the name of the drawing. This offers easy identification of the file.

This particular file contains both 2D drawings and a 3D model of a typical locking clip. The layout view shows a top, front, and right-side view as well as an isometric view.

## Using the Model Space and Layout Views

AutoCAD offers a number of ways to view your drawing. You have the typical zoom and pan tools, but you also have different modes of viewing your drawing. The two main viewing modes are *Model Space* and *layout views*. Within these two modes are options to display your model in 3D and shaded views. Try the following exercise to see these modes and view options firsthand.

You'll start by switching to a Model Space view of the drawing. The Model Space view places you in a workspace where you do most of your drawing creation and editing. Follow these steps:

1. In the status bar, click the option labeled Layout1. This opens a pop-up menu that lets you switch between layout views and the Model Space view (see Figure 1.15).

**FIGURE 1.15**
Click the Layout1 option in the status bar and select Model from the pop-up menu.

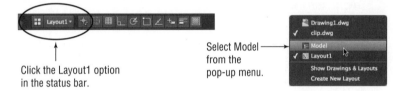

Click the Layout1 option in the status bar.

Select Model from the pop-up menu.

2. Click Model on the pop-up menu (Figure 1.15). Your view changes to show the full 3D model with the 2D representations of the model. Note the option in the upper-left corner of the drawing area that shows SW Isometric. This tells you your view orientation and offers other options, as you'll see in the next exercise.

3. Go to the ViewCube and click the part labeled Top (Figure 1.16). Your display changes to a two-dimensional view looking down on the drawing, as shown in Figure 1.17. Note that the option in the upper-left portion of the drawing area now shows "Top."

**FIGURE 1.16**
3D model with 2D representations of the model

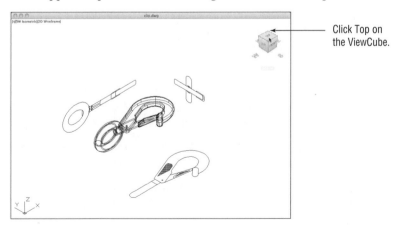

Click Top on the ViewCube.

**FIGURE 1.17**
The Top view of the drawing

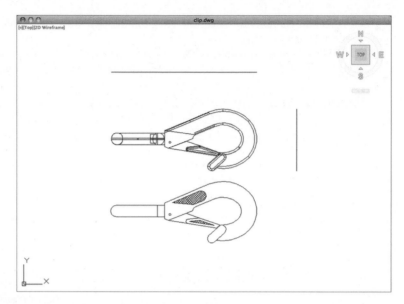

You've just seen how you can get into the Model Space view from a layout view and then switch from a 3D view to a 2D view using the ViewCube. Let's take a look at a few more ViewCube options as well as some other view-related tools. Try the following to see how you can control the AutoCAD display:

1. Click the lower-left corner of the ViewCube (Figure 1.18). The view changes back to the 3D view you saw earlier. Note that you can now see the corner of the ViewCube you clicked as the corner that intersects the left, front, and top sides of the ViewCube.

**FIGURE 1.18**
Click the lower-left corner of the ViewCube.

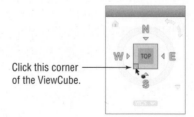

Click this corner of the ViewCube.

2. Click the 2D Wireframe option from the Viewport controls in the upper left of the drawing area. A pop-up menu appears (Figure 1.19).

3. Select Realistic from the pop-up menu. Your view changes to show the 3D part of the drawing with a more realistic shading (Figure 1.20).

4. Click the Realistic option in the upper left of the drawing area and select 2D Wireframe from the pop-up menu. The drawing changes back to the view you started with.

**FIGURE 1.19**
The 2D Wireframe
pop-up menu

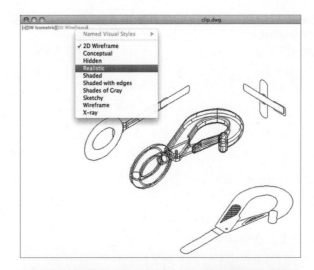

**FIGURE 1.20**
The drawing in a
shaded view

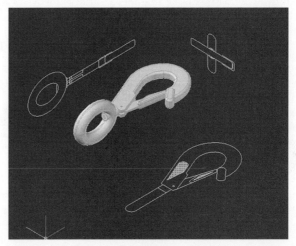

**5.** Click the SW Isometric option from the Viewport controls in the upper left of the drawing area, then select Top from the pop-up menu (Figure 1.21). The view changes to a "top-down" view of the drawing, similar to the view you saw when you selected Top from the ViewCube.

In this exercise, you used the ViewCube to change your view orientation to a 3D view called SW Isometric. You also saw how you could change your view to one that shows the 3D object in a shaded mode using the Viewport controls pop-up menu in the upper left of the drawing area. These different modes of displaying your drawing are called *Visual Styles*. You'll learn more about Visual Styles in Part 4, "Modeling and Imaging."

**FIGURE 1.21**
The SW Isometric
pop-up menu

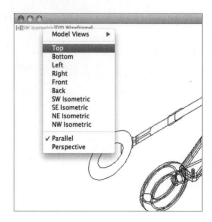

## Using Zoom and Pan

One of the most frequently used commands is Zoom, which gives you a closer look at part of your drawing. This command offers a variety of ways to control your view. In this section, you'll enlarge a portion of the clip drawing to get a more detailed look. To tell AutoCAD which area you want to enlarge, you use what is called a *zoom window*.

Now let's continue with a look at the Zoom command. Try the following exercise to get a feel for moving around in the drawing:

1. Click the Zoom tool in the status bar (Figure 1.22).

**FIGURE 1.22**
The Zoom tool in
the status bar

2. At first, the Dynamic Input display shows the Specify corner of window: prompt with some options. Move the crosshair cursor to the lower-left location shown in Figure 1.23, and then click. Now as you move the cursor, a rectangle appears with one corner fixed on the point you just picked; the other corner follows the cursor.

**FIGURE 1.23**
Placing the zoom
window around
the clip

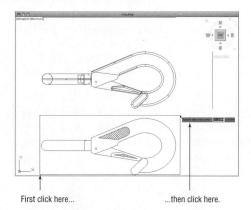

First click here...          ...then click here.

3. The Dynamic Input display now shows `Specify opposite corner:`. Position the other corner of the zoom window so it encloses the lower image of the clip, as shown in Figure 1.23, and click again. The clip enlarges to fill the screen.

In this exercise, you used a window to define an area to enlarge for your close-up view. You saw how the Dynamic Input display gave you messages to help you decide what to do. These messages are helpful for first-time users of AutoCAD. Getting a close-up view of your drawing is crucial to working accurately, but you'll often want to return to a previous view to get the overall picture. To do so, you can use the Zoom shortcut menu (Figure 1.24):

1. Click the Zoom tool in the status bar again.

2. With the cursor in the drawing area, right-click and select Previous.

**FIGURE 1.24**

The Zoom Previous option

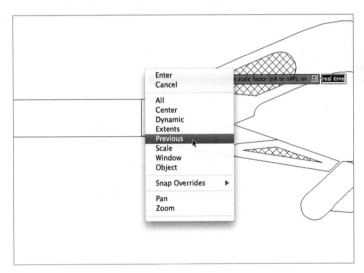

You can quickly enlarge or reduce your view by using the Zoom Realtime option of the Zoom command. Follow these steps to change your view with Zoom Realtime:

1. Right-click in the drawing area and select Zoom from the shortcut menu. You can also click the Zoom tool in the status bar then press the spacebar or ↵.

2. Place the Zoom Realtime cursor slightly above the center of the drawing area, and then click and drag downward. Your view zooms out to show more of the drawing.

3. While still holding the mouse button, move the cursor upward. Your view zooms in and enlarges. When you have a view similar to the one shown in Figure 1.25, release the mouse button. (Don't worry if you don't get *exactly* the same view as the figure. This is just for practice.)

4. You're still in Zoom Realtime mode. Click and drag the mouse again to see how you can further adjust your view. To exit, right-click and choose Exit from the shortcut menu. You can also press the Esc key.

**FIGURE 1.25**
The final view you
want to achieve in
step 3 of the
exercise

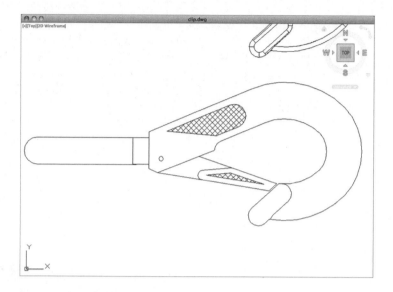

In these exercises, you used the Zoom tool on the status bar as well as the Zoom option in the right-click shortcut menu. A third option is to use the View ➤ Zoom options in the menu bar. You'll get a chance to try the Zoom menu bar options in Chapter 2.

As you can see from this exercise, you have a wide range of options for viewing your drawings, just by using a few tools. These tools are all you need to control the display of 2D drawings.

---

**USING MULTI-TOUCH TO ZOOM AND PAN**

If you are using a Magic Mouse or a Multi-Touch trackpad, you can use its Multi-Touch feature to zoom and pan over your view. On the Magic Mouse, use a one-finger vertical swipe gesture to zoom in and out or hold down the ⌘ key and use one finger to pan your view. You can also hold down the spacebar and move the mouse to pan.

On a Multi-Touch trackpad, use two fingers to pan or hold down the ⌘ key and use a two-finger vertical gesture to zoom in or out. You can also use the pinch gesture to zoom in or out.

You may want to experiment with both the Zoom tool and the Multi-Touch feature to see which works best for you. If you are using a trackpad, make sure "Tap to Click" and "Dragging" are enabled in the Trackpad settings in the System Preferences for your Mac.

If you're a new user, you may find Multi-Touch too sensitive. You can turn off the Multi-Touch Scroll and Zoom features through the mouse settings in the OS X system preferences. Be aware that this will turn off the feature for all Mac applications, so you may want to turn it back on when you exit AutoCAD.

If you're using a Magic Mouse, you can gain much finer control by installing the free MagicPrefs preference pane application. MagicPrefs can be found on the website that accompanies this book, or you can go online to the Apple website to download it.

## Saving a File as You Work

It's a good idea to save your file periodically as you work on it. You can save it under its original name (choose File ➢ Save from the menu bar) or under a different name (choose File ➢ Save As from the menu bar), thereby creating a new file.

By default, AutoCAD automatically saves your work at 10-minute intervals under a name that is a combination of the current filename plus a number and that ends with the .sv$ file-name extension; this is known as the *Automatic Save* feature. Using settings in the Application Preferences dialog box or AutoCAD system variables, you can change the name of the autosaved file and control the time between autosaves. See the section "The Look & Feel Options" in Appendix B on the accompanying website for details.

---

 **Real World Scenario**

### "I CAN'T FIND MY AUTOMATIC SAVES!"

As an IT manager at ELS Architecture and Urban Planning, one of the most common questions I get is "Where does AutoCAD put the Automatic Save files?" By default, the Automatic Save file is stored in the Macintosh HD/Private/tmp folder. You can find the exact location for your system by typing **Savefilepath**↵ in the Command Line palette. The location is displayed in the Command Line palette and in the Dynamic Input display. This file location is often set as a hidden folder, but you can get to it using the Go To Folder command. While in the Finder, press Shift-⌘-G. In the Go To Folder dialog box, enter **/tmp** and click Go. You can also specify a different location for the Automatic Save files. See Appendix B on the accompanying website for information on how to locate hidden files and specify a location for your files.

---

## Making Changes

You'll frequently make changes to your drawings. One of AutoCAD's primary advantages is the ease with which you can make changes. The following exercise shows you a typical sequence of operations involved in changing a drawing:

1. Use the Save As option in the File menu to save the current clip.dwg file under the name MyFirst. For convenience, you can save your files in the Documents folder.

2. Make sure you are in the Drafting workflow, then from the Tool Sets palette, click the Erase tool (the one with a pencil eraser touching paper). This activates the Erase command.

   Notice that the cursor has turned into a small square. This square is called the *pickbox*. You also see Select objects: in the Command Line palette and the Dynamic Input display. This message helps remind new users what to do.

3. Place the pickbox on the crosshatch pattern of the clip (see Figure 1.26) and click. The crosshatch changes in appearance to a light highlight. The pickbox and the Select objects: prompt remain, indicating that you can continue to select objects.

4. Right-click and select Enter, or press ↵ or the spacebar. The crosshatch disappears. You've just erased a part of the drawing.

**FIGURE 1.26**
Erasing a portion
of the clip

Click here.

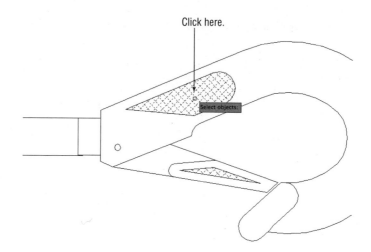

Select objects:

In this exercise, first you issued the Erase command, and then you selected an object by using a pickbox to click it. The pickbox tells you that you must select items on the screen, and it shows you what you're about to select by highlighting objects as you hover the cursor over them. Once you've clicked an object or a set of objects, press ↵ to move on to the next step. (You can also click an object or a set of objects and then press the Delete key.) This sequence of steps is common to many of the commands you'll work with in AutoCAD.

## Working with Multiple Files

You can have multiple documents open at the same time in AutoCAD. This can be especially helpful if you want to exchange parts of drawings between files or if you want another file open for reference. Try the following exercise to see how multiple documents work in AutoCAD:

1. Choose File ➢ New.

2. Make sure `acad.dwt` is selected, and then click Open.

3. Turn off the grid by pressing ⌘-G.

When you create a new file in AutoCAD, you're actually opening a copy of a *template file*, as you saw in step 1. A template file is a blank file that is set up for specific drawing types. The `acad.dwt` file is a generic template set up for Imperial measurements. Another template file, called `acadiso.dwt`, is a generic template useful for metric measurements. Other templates are set up for specific drawing-sheet sizes and measurement systems. You'll learn more about templates in Chapter 6, "Editing and Reusing Data to Work Efficiently."

Next, let's try drawing a rectangle to see how AutoCAD behaves while drawing objects:

1. Click the Rectangle tool in the Tool Sets palette, as shown in Figure 1.27.

Notice that the Dynamic Input display and Command Line palette now show the following prompt:

```
Specify first corner point or
```

AutoCAD is asking you to select the first corner for the rectangle. In the Command Line palette you see some additional text in brackets offering a few options that you can take advantage of at this point in the command. Don't worry about those options right now. You'll have an opportunity to learn about command options in Chapter 2. Note that you can view the command options at the Dynamic Input display by right-clicking or by pressing the down arrow key on your keyboard.

**FIGURE 1.27**
Click the Rectangle tool in the Tool Sets palette.

2. Click a point roughly in the lower-left corner of the drawing area, as shown in Figure 1.28. Now, as you move your mouse, a rectangle follows the cursor, with one corner fixed at the position you just selected. You also see the following prompt in the Command Line palette, with a similar prompt in the Dynamic Input display:

   `Specify other corner point or [Area/Dimensions/Rotation]:`

3. Click another point anywhere in the upper-right region of the drawing area. A rectangle appears (see Figure 1.28). You'll learn more about the different cursor shapes and what they mean in Chapter 2.

**FIGURE 1.28**
Drawing the rectangle

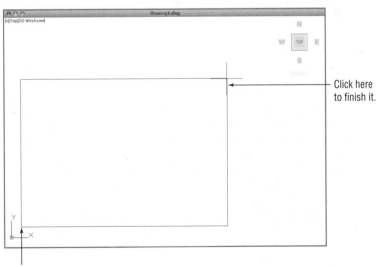

Click here to finish it.

Click here to start the rectangle.

4. Let's try copying objects between these two files. Click in the window with the clip drawing to make it active. You can also choose Window ➤ Clip.dwg.

5. Click the Zoom tool in the status bar, right-click, and select All from the shortcut menu to get an overall view of the drawing (see Figure 1.29).

**FIGURE 1.29**
The Zoom All option gives you an overall view of your drawing.

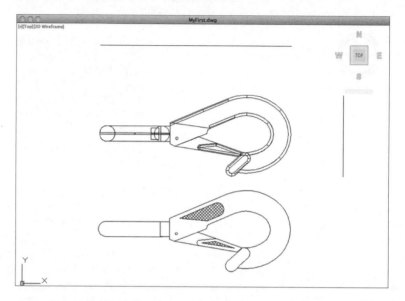

6. Click the 2D version of the clip at the bottom of the drawing to select it. A series of squares and arrows appears on the drawing. These are called *grips* (see Figure 1.30), and you'll learn more about them in the next chapter.

7. Right-click and select Clipboard ➤ Copy or press ⌘-C.

8. Click inside the other drawing window, Drawing 2.dwg, to make it active.

9. Right-click and select Clipboard ➤ Paste or press ⌘-V. The clip appears at the cursor in the new drawing.

10. Position the clip in the middle of the rectangle you drew earlier and left-click (Figure 1.31). The clip is copied into the second drawing.

11. Save the new file as My Clip and then exit AutoCAD. You don't have to save the clip.dwg file.

You can have as many files open as you want as long as your computer has adequate memory to accommodate them. You can control the individual document windows as you would any window, using the window control buttons in the upper-left corner of the document window.

This concludes your introduction to the AutoCAD application. In the next chapter, you'll try your hand at drawing a few simple shapes and using some of the other drafting tools that AutoCAD offers.

**FIGURE 1.30**
Grips shown in the 2D drawing

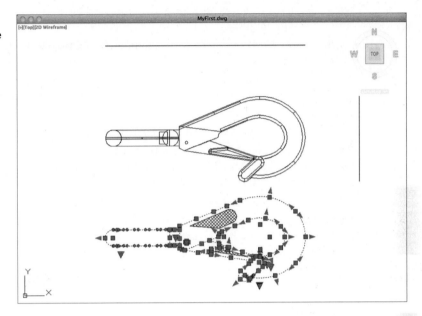

**FIGURE 1.31**
Pasting the clip drawing into the new drawing

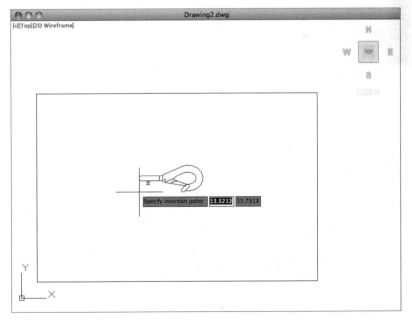

## The Bottom Line

**Use the AutoCAD application.**   AutoCAD is a typical Windows graphics program that makes use of the menu bar and tools. If you've used other graphics programs, you'll see at least a few familiar tools.

**Master It**   Name the components of the AutoCAD application you can use to select a function.

**Get a closer look with the Zoom command.**   The Zoom command is a common tool in graphics programs. It enables you to get a closer look at a part of your drawing or to expand your view to see the big picture.

**Master It**   Name at least two ways of zooming into a view.

**Save a file as you work.**   Nothing is more frustrating than having a power failure cause you to lose hours of work. It's a good idea to save your work frequently. AutoCAD offers an Automatic Save feature that can be a lifesaver if you happen to forget to save your files.

**Master It**   How often does the AutoCAD Automatic Save feature save your drawing?

**Make changes and open multiple files.**   As with other Mac applications, you can have multiple files open and exchange data between them.

**Master It**   With two drawings open, how can you copy parts of one drawing into the other?

# Chapter 2

# Creating Your First Drawing

This chapter examines some of AutoCAD's basic functions. You'll get a chance to practice with the drawing editor by building a simple drawing to use in later exercises. You'll learn how to give input to AutoCAD, interpret prompts, and get help when you need it. This chapter also covers the use of coordinate systems to give AutoCAD exact measurements for objects. You'll see how to select objects you've drawn and how to specify base points for moving and copying.

If you're not a beginning AutoCAD user, you may want to move on to the more complex material in Chapter 3, "Setting Up and Using AutoCAD's Drafting Tools." You can use the files supplied on the companion website, www.sybex.com/go/masteringautocadmac, to continue the tutorials at that point.

In this chapter, you'll learn to do the following:

- ◆ Specify distances with coordinates
- ◆ Interpret the cursor modes and understand prompts
- ◆ Select objects and edit with grips
- ◆ Use dynamic input
- ◆ Get help
- ◆ Display data in the Command Line palette
- ◆ Display the properties of an object

## Getting to Know the Tool Sets palette

Your first task in learning how to draw in AutoCAD is simply to draw a line. Since AutoCAD is designed as a precision drawing tool, you'll be introduced to methods that allow you to input exact distances. But before you begin drawing, take a moment to familiarize yourself with the feature you'll be using more than any others to create objects with AutoCAD: the Tool Sets palette.

1. Start AutoCAD just as you did in Chapter 1, "Exploring the AutoCAD Interface," by clicking the AutoCAD icon in the Dock.

2. Make sure that the Tool Sets palette is displaying the drafting tools. To do this, click the icon in the Tool Sets palette title bar and select Drafting (Figure 2.1).

3. Move the arrow cursor to the Line tool in the Tool Sets palette. As you hold the cursor over the tool, a tooltip appears (see Figure 2.2).

FIGURE 2.1

**FIGURE 2.1**
The Tool Sets palette title bar menu

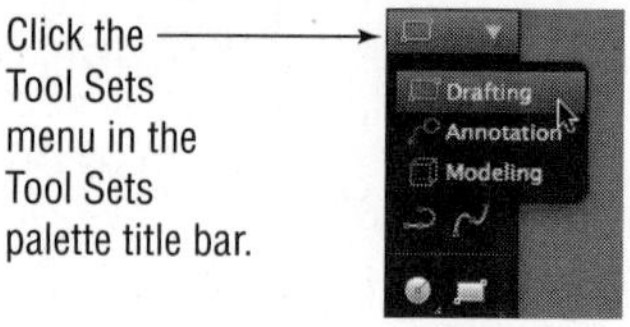

Click the ⎯⎯⎯⎯⎯
Tool Sets
menu in the
Tool Sets
palette title bar.

**FIGURE 2.2**
The tools you'll use in this chapter and the Line tool and tooltip

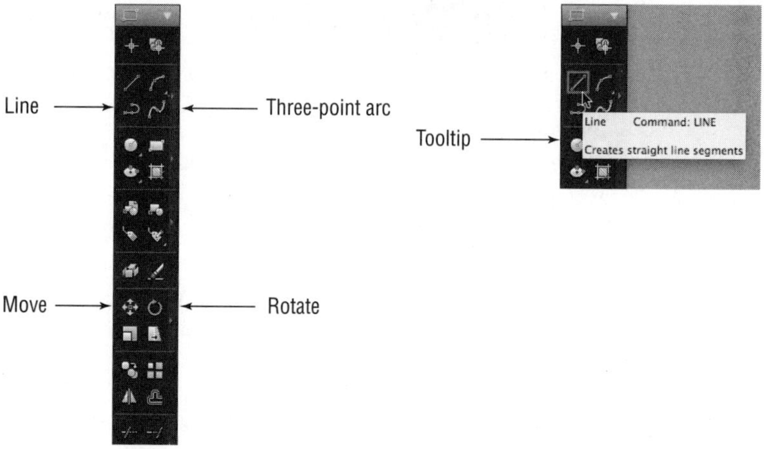

Line ⎯⎯→          ←⎯⎯ Three-point arc

Tooltip ⎯⎯→

Move ⎯⎯→          ←⎯⎯ Rotate

4. Slowly move the arrow cursor to the right over the other tools in the Tool Sets palette and read each tooltip.

In most cases, you'll be able to guess what each tool does by how it looks. The tooltips will help you identify any tools that you're not sure of. You can use Figure 2.2 to find the tools for the exercises in this chapter.

## Starting Your First Drawing

In Chapter 1, you looked at a preexisting sample drawing. This time, you'll begin to draw your own drawing by creating a door that will be used in later exercises. First, though, you must learn how to tell AutoCAD what you want, and even more important, you must understand what AutoCAD wants from you.

---

**IMPERIAL AND METRIC**

In this chapter, you'll start to see instructions for both Imperial and metric measurements. In general, you'll see the instructions for Imperial measurement first, followed by the metric instructions. You won't be dealing with inches or centimeters yet, however. You're just getting to know the AutoCAD system.

---

You'll start by setting the size of the work area, known as the drawing *limits*. These limits aren't fixed in any way, and you aren't forced to stay within the bounds of the drawing limits unless the Limits ON/OFF command line option is turned on. But limits can help to establish a starting area from which you can expand your drawing.

AutoCAD starts with a new blank file, but it's a little difficult to tell how big the drawing area is. First, you'll set up the work area so you have a better idea of the space you're working with:

1. Choose Format ➢ Drawing Limits from the menu bar.

2. At the `Specify lower left corner or` prompt, right-click and select Enter. You can also press ↵ or the spacebar. By doing this, you are accepting the default location for the lower-left corner, which is the coordinate 0,0.

3. At the `Specify upper right corner <12.0000,9.0000>:` prompt, if you use Imperial units (feet and inches), press ↵ to accept the default of 12.0000,9.0000. Metric users should enter **40,30**↵.

4. Choose View ➢ Zoom ➢ All. You can also type **Z**↵ **A**↵.

In the last step, the All option of the Zoom command uses the limits you set up in steps 2 and 3 to determine the display area. In a drawing that contains objects, the Zoom command's All option displays the limits plus the area occupied by the objects in the drawing if they happen to fall outside the limits. Now give your file a unique name:

1. Choose File ➢ Save As from menu bar or type **Saveas**↵ to open the Save Drawing As dialog box.

2. Type **Door**. As you type, the name appears in the Save As text box.

3. Save your file in the `Documents` folder, or if you prefer, save it in another folder of your choosing. Just remember where you put it because you'll use it later.

4. Click Save. You now have a file called `Door.dwg`, located in the `Documents` folder. Of course, your drawing doesn't contain anything yet. You'll take care of that next.

---

**UNDERSTANDING THE DRAWING AREA**

The new file shows a drawing area roughly 12 inches wide by 9 inches high. Metric users have a file that shows an area roughly 40 mm wide by 30 mm high. This is just the area you're given to start with, but you're not limited to it in any way. No visual clues indicate the size of the area. To check the area size for yourself, turn on the Dynamic Input display and then choose Tools ➢ Inquiry ➢ ID Point. Move the crosshair cursor to the upper-right corner of the drawing area and observe the value in the coordinate readout at the cursor. Click the upper-right corner. The coordinate is reported in the expanded Command Line palette in X, Y, and Z coordinate values. The coordinate won't show exactly $12 \times 9$ inches, or $40 \times 30$ mm for metric, because the proportions of your drawing area aren't likely to be exactly $12 \times 9$ or $40 \times 30$. AutoCAD does try to optimize the display for the drawing area when you choose the All option of the Zoom command.

You're almost ready to do some drawing. Before you begin, turn off the Dynamic Input display. The Dynamic Input display is a great tool, but while you're learning how to enter coordinates, it can be a distraction.

1. Locate the Dynamic Input tool in the status bar and click it to turn it off. You can tell it is off when it turns a light gray color (Figure 2.3).

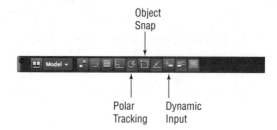

**FIGURE 2.3**
The Dynamic Input, Polar Tracking, and Object Snap tools

Object Snap

Polar Tracking   Dynamic Input

2. Locate the Polar Tracking tool in the status bar and click it to turn it on. The Polar Tracking tool should now be blue, indicating that it is on (Figure 2.3).

3. Locate the Object Snap tool in the status bar and click it to turn it off. The Object Snap tool should now be gray, indicating that it is off (Figure 2.3).

You'll get a chance to work with the Dynamic Input display and Object Snap a bit later in this chapter. I'm asking you to turn these features off for now to simplify AutoCAD's behavior.

Now you can begin to explore the drawing process. To begin a drawing, follow these steps:

1. Click the Line tool on the Tool Sets palette. You can also choose Draw ➢ Line from the menu bar or type L↵.

   You've just issued the Line command. AutoCAD responds in two ways. First, you see the message

   ```
   Specify first point:
   ```

   in the Command prompt, asking you to select a point to begin your line. Also, the cursor changes its appearance; it no longer has a square in the crosshairs. This is a clue telling you to pick a point to start a line.

2. Using the left mouse button, select a point in the drawing area near the center. After you select the point, AutoCAD changes the prompt to this:

   ```
   Specify next point or [Undo]:
   ```

   Now as you move the mouse around, notice the line with one end fixed on the point you just selected and the other end following the cursor in a *rubber-banding* motion (see the first image in Figure 2.4).

3. Move the cursor to a location directly to the left or right of the point you clicked, and you'll see a dotted horizontal line appear along with a message at the cursor. This action also occurs when you point directly up or down. Your cursor seems to jump to a horizontal or vertical position (Figure 2.5).

**FIGURE 2.4**
While drawing line segments, a rubber-banding line follows the cursor.

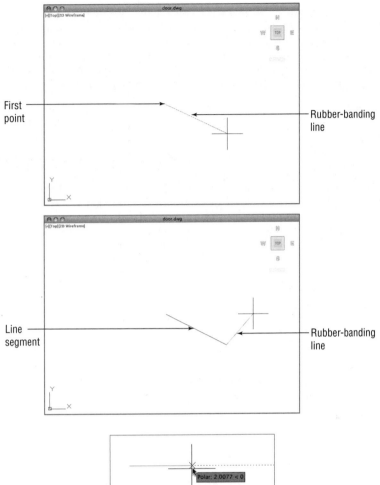

**FIGURE 2.4**
While drawing line segments, a rubber-banding line follows the cursor.

**FIGURE 2.5**
Polar Tracking

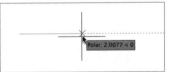

This feature is called *Polar Tracking*, and you turned it on at the beginning of this section. Like a T-square or triangle, it helps to restrict your line to an exact horizontal or vertical direction. You can turn Polar Tracking on or off by clicking the Polar Tracking tool in the status bar. You'll learn more about Polar Tracking in Chapter 3.

4. Continue with the Line command. Move the cursor to a point below and to the right of the first point you selected, and click again. You've just drawn a line segment, and a second rubber-banding line appears (see the second image in Figure 2.4).

5. If the line you drew isn't the exact length you want, you can back up during the Line command and change it. To do this, right-click and select Undo or type **U↵**. The line you drew previously rubber-bands as if you hadn't selected the second point to fix its length.

6. Right-click and select Enter. This terminates the Line command.

You've just drawn and then undrawn a line of an arbitrary length. The Line command is still active. Two onscreen clues tell you that you're in the middle of a command. If you don't see the word Command to the left of the Command Line input area, a command is still active. Also, the cursor is the plain crosshair without the box at its intersection.

From now on, I'll refer to the crosshair cursor without the small box as the Point Selection mode of the cursor. If you look ahead to Figure 2.11, you'll see all the modes of the drawing cursor.

---

### KEYBOARD ALIASES AND THE SPACEBAR

Throughout this book, you are shown the keyboard alias for commands. Long-time AutoCAD users swear by them, and even new users find they prefer command aliases over the menu bar or tools. And if you are a long-time Mac user, you know how useful keyboard shortcuts can be in a variety of situations. But if it seems awkward to hit the ↵ key to start a command, you have an alternative: Just press the spacebar. That way, you can keep one hand on the mouse while entering keyboard aliases. So whenever you see ↵, think "spacebar" instead of the Return key.

---

## Specifying Exact Distances with Coordinates

Next, you'll continue with the Line command to draw a plan view (an overhead view) of a door, to no particular scale. This will give you some practice in drawing objects to exact distances. Later, you'll resize the drawing to use in future exercises. The door will be 3.0 units long and 0.15 units thick. For metric users, the door will be 9 units long and 0.5 units thick. To specify these exact distances in AutoCAD, you can use either relative polar coordinates or Cartesian coordinates.

The Imperial and metric distances aren't equivalent in the exercises in this chapter. For example, 3 units in the Imperial-based drawing aren't equal to 9 metric units. These distances are arbitrary and based on how they appear in the figures in this chapter.

---

### GETTING OUT OF TROUBLE

Beginners and experts alike are bound to make a few mistakes. Before you get too far into the tutorial, here are some powerful but easy-to-use tools to help you recover from accidents:

**Delete** If you make a typing error, press the Delete key to back up to your error, and then retype your command or response. You can also use the Delete key to delete objects in your drawing. Just select an object or set of objects and press Delete. The Delete key is in the upper-right corner of the main keyboard area.

**Escape (Esc)** This is perhaps the single most important key on your keyboard. When you need to exit a command or a dialog box quickly without making changes, press the Esc key in the upper-left corner of your keyboard. In most cases, you need to press Esc only once, although it won't hurt to press it twice. (Press Esc before editing with grips or issuing commands through the keyboard.)

**Cancel** Another way to quit out of a command is to right-click and select Cancel from the shortcut menu. This works just like the Esc key.

⌘**-Z and U.↵**   If you accidentally change something in the drawing and want to reverse that change, you can use the standard ⌘-Z keystroke to back up one operation. You can also type **U.↵** at the Command prompt. Each time you do this, AutoCAD undoes one operation at a time, in reverse order. The last command performed is undone first, then the next-to-last command, and so on. The prompt displays the name of the command being undone, and the drawing reverts to its state prior to when that command was issued. If you need to, you can undo everything back to the beginning of an editing session.

**Undo**   If you want more control over the way Undo works, you can use the Undo command, which allows you to "bookmark" places in your editing session that you can "undo" to. Type **Undo.↵** and you'll see the Enter the number of operations to undo or [Auto/ Control/BEgin/End/Mark/Back] <1>: prompt. You can enter a number indicating the number of steps you want to "undo." Use the Mark option to "bookmark" a location; then use Back to undo your work to that "bookmark." You can use Begin and End to mark the beginning and end of a set of operations that will be undone all at once. Control offers options to control the behavior of the Undo command. Auto is an option that is on by default and causes AutoCAD to undo the action of the whole command rather than the individual actions within a command.

**Redo**   If you accidentally undo one too many commands, you can redo the last undone command by pressing ⌘-Y or by typing **Redo.↵**.

**Palette toggle**   If a palette has been turned off, you can turn it back on by choosing Tools ➢ Palettes. A list of palettes appears. Click the palette that you want to turn on.

## Specifying Polar Coordinates

To enter the exact distance of 3 (or 9 metric) units to the right of the last point you selected, do the following:

1. Click the Line tool in the Tool Sets palette, or type **L.↵**.

2. Click a point slightly to the left of the center of the drawing area to select the start point.

3. Type **@3<0**. Metric users should type **@9<0**. As you type, the letters appear at the Command prompt.

4. Press .↵. A line appears, starting from the first point you picked and ending 3 units to the right of it (see Figure 2.6). You've just entered a relative polar coordinate.

The "at" sign (@) you entered tells AutoCAD that the coordinate you're specifying is from the last point you selected. The 3 (or 9 metric) is the distance, and the less-than symbol (<) tells AutoCAD that you're designating the angle at which the line is to be drawn. The last part is the value for the angle, which in this case is 0 for 0°. This is how to use polar coordinates to communicate distances and directions to AutoCAD.

If you're accustomed to a different method for describing directions, you can set AutoCAD to use a vertical direction or downward direction as 0°. See Chapter 3 for details.

Angles are given based on the system shown in Figure 2.7, in which 0° is a horizontal direction from left to right, 90° is straight up, 180° is horizontal from right to left, and so on. You can specify degrees, minutes, and seconds of arc if you want to be that exact. I'll discuss angle formats in more detail in Chapter 3.

**FIGURE 2.6**
Notice that the rubber-banding line now starts from the last point selected. This indicates that you can continue to add more line segments.

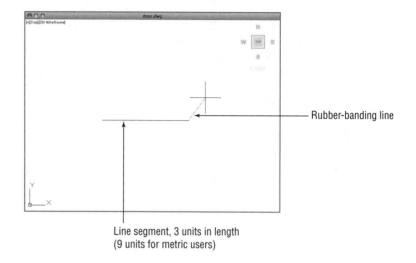

Rubber-banding line

Line segment, 3 units in length
(9 units for metric users)

**FIGURE 2.7**
AutoCAD's default system for specifying angles

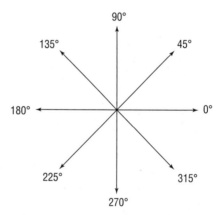

## Specifying Relative Cartesian Coordinates

For the next line segment, let's try another method for specifying exact distances:

1. Enter @0,0.15↵. Metric users should enter @0,0.5↵. A short line appears above the endpoint of the last line. Once again, @ tells AutoCAD that the coordinate you specify is from the last point picked. But in this example, you give the distance in X and Y values. The X distance, 0, is given first, followed by a comma, and then the Y distance, 0.15. This is how to specify distances in relative Cartesian coordinates.

---

**COMMAS AND PERIODS**

Step 1 indicates that metric users should enter **@0,0.5**↵ for the distance. Instead, you could enter **@0,.5** (zero comma point five). The leading zero is included for clarity. Please be aware that the comma is used as a separator between the X and Y components of the coordinate. In AutoCAD, commas aren't used for decimal points; you must use a period to denote a decimal point.

---

2. Enter **@-3,0↵**. Metric users should enter **@-9,0↵**. This distance is also in X,Y values, but here you use a negative value to specify the X distance. The result is a drawing that looks like Figure 2.8.

**FIGURE 2.8**
These three sides of the door were drawn by using the Line tool. Points are specified by using either relative Cartesian or polar coordinates.

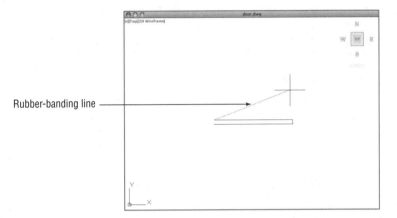

Positive values in the Cartesian coordinate system are from left to right and from bottom to top (see Figure 2.9). (You may remember this from your high school geometry class!) If you want to draw a line from right to left, you must designate a negative value. It's also helpful to know where the origin of the drawing lies. In a new drawing, the origin—or coordinate 0,0—is in the lower-left corner of the drawing.

**FIGURE 2.9**
Positive and negative Cartesian coordinate directions

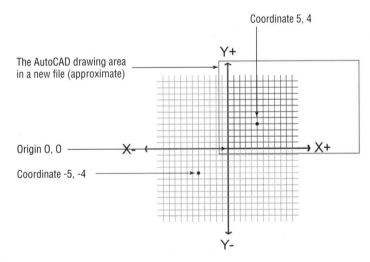

3. Type **C↵**. This C stands for the Close option. It closes a sequence of line segments. A line connecting the first and last points of a sequence of lines is drawn (see Figure 2.10), and the Line command terminates. The rubber-banding line also disappears, telling you that

AutoCAD has finished drawing line segments. You can also use the rubber-banding line to indicate direction while simultaneously entering the distance through the keyboard. See the sidebar "Other Ways to Enter Distances."

To finish drawing a series of lines without closing them, you can press Esc, ⏎, or the spacebar.

**FIGURE 2.10**
Distance and direction input for the door. Distances for metric users are shown in brackets.

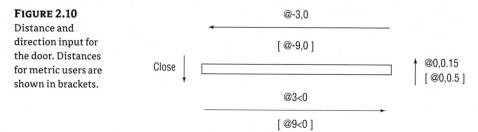

## Interpreting the Cursor Modes and Understanding Prompts

The key to working with AutoCAD successfully is understanding the way it interacts with you. The following sections will help you become familiar with some of the ways AutoCAD prompts you for input. Understanding the format of the messages in the Command Line palette and recognizing other events on the screen will help you learn the program more easily.

### Understanding Cursor Modes

As the Command Line palette aids you with messages, the cursor gives you clues about what to do. Figure 2.11 illustrates the various modes of the cursor and gives a brief description of the role of each mode. Take a moment to study this figure.

**FIGURE 2.11**
The drawing cursor's modes

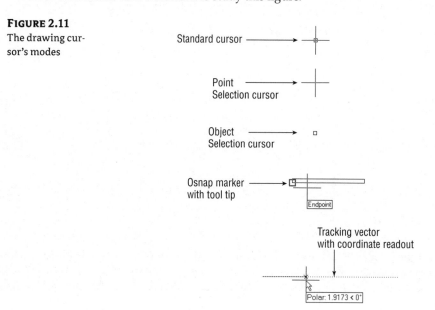

**The Standard cursor** tells you that AutoCAD is waiting for instructions. You can also edit objects by using grips when you see this cursor. *Grips* are squares, rectangles, or arrowheads that appear at endpoints and at the midpoint of objects when they're selected. (You might know them as *workpoints* from other graphics programs.)

### OTHER WAYS TO ENTER DISTANCES

A third method for entering distances is to point in a direction with a rubber-banding line and then enter the distance through the keyboard. For example, to draw a line 3 units long from left to right, click the Line tool in the Tool Sets palette, click a start point, and then move the cursor so the rubber-banding line points to the right at some arbitrary distance. With the cursor pointing in the direction you want, type **3**↵. The rubber-banding line becomes a fixed line 3 units long. Using this method, called the Direct Distance method, along with the Ortho mode or Polar Tracking described in Chapter 3, can be a fast way to draw orthogonal lines of specific lengths.

If you turn on Dynamic Input, you can also specify an exact angle along with the distance. For example, start the Line command and then pick the first point. Type **3** for the length but don't press ↵. Press the Tab key instead. The line segment will become fixed at 3 units, and as you move the cursor, the segment will rotate freely around the first point. Next type an angle in degrees, **30**↵ for example, and the line will be drawn at 30 degrees. Or, instead of typing in an angle, just adjust the angle of the line visually until you see the angle you want on the Dynamic Input temporary angle dimension, and then click the mouse.

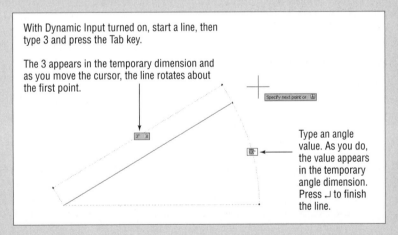

With Dynamic Input turned on, start a line, then type 3 and press the Tab key.

The 3 appears in the temporary dimension and as you move the cursor, the line rotates about the first point.

Type an angle value. As you do, the value appears in the temporary angle dimension. Press ↵ to finish the line.

If you watch the temporary dimensions as you press the Tab key, you'll see that the Tab key lets you move from the length dimension to the angle dimension and back again. You can press the Tab key at any time to shift back and forth between dimensions. A lock appears next to a dimension that you have entered, telling you that the dimension is "locked" until you tab to it again.

You'll learn more about how to enter values with the Dynamic Input's temporary dimensions later in this chapter.

**The Point Selection cursor** appears whenever AutoCAD expects point input. It can also appear in conjunction with a rubber-banding line. You can either click a point or enter a coordinate through the keyboard.

**The Object Selection cursor** tells you that you must select objects—either by clicking them or by using any of the object-selection options available.

**The Osnap (object snap) marker** appears along with the Point Selection cursor when you invoke an osnap. Osnaps let you accurately select specific points on an object, such as endpoints or midpoints.

**The tracking vector** appears when you use the Polar Tracking or Object Snap Tracking feature. Polar Tracking aids you in drawing orthogonal lines, and Object Snap Tracking helps you align a point in space relative to the geometry of existing objects. Object Snap Tracking works in conjunction with osnaps. You'll learn more about the tracking vector in Chapters 3 and 4.

If you're an experienced AutoCAD user, you may prefer to use the old-style crosshair cursor that crosses the entire screen. You can change the size of the crosshair cursor through the Cursor And Selection settings in the Application Preferences dialog box. See Appendix B on the companion website for more on the Preferences settings.

## Choosing Command Options

Many commands in AutoCAD offer several options, which are often presented to you in the Command window in the form of a prompt. This section uses the Arc command to illustrate the format of AutoCAD's prompts.

Usually, in a floor-plan drawing in the United States, an arc is drawn to indicate the direction of a door swing. Figure 2.12 shows a drawing that includes other standard symbols used in architectural-style drawings.

Here, you'll draw the arc for the door you started in the previous exercise:

1. Click the 3-Point Arc tool in the Tool Sets palette. The `Specify start point of arc or [Center]:` prompt appears, and the cursor changes to Point Selection mode.

   Examine the `Specify start point of arc or [Center]:` prompt in the Command Line palette. The start point contains two options. The default option is the one stated in the main part of the prompt. In this case, the default option is to specify the start point of the arc. If other options are available, they appear within square brackets. In the Arc command, you see the word `Center` within brackets telling you that, if you prefer, you can also start your arc by selecting a center point instead of a start point. If multiple options are available, they appear within the brackets and are separated by slashes (/). The default is the option AutoCAD assumes you intend to use unless you tell it otherwise.

2. Type **C**↵ to select the Center option. The `Specify center point of arc:` prompt appears. Notice that you had to type only the C and not the entire word `Center`.

   When you see a set of options in the Command Line palette, note their capitalization. If you choose to respond to prompts by using the keyboard, these capitalized letters are all you need to enter to select the option. In some cases, the first two letters are capitalized to differentiate two options that begin with the same letter, such as `LAyer` and `LType`.

**FIGURE 2.12**

Samples of standard symbols used in architectural drawings

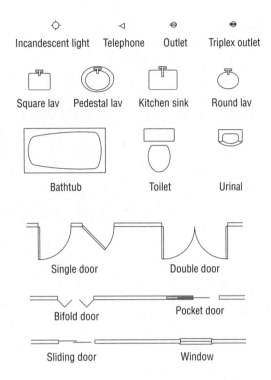

Incandescent light　Telephone　Outlet　Triplex outlet

Square lav　Pedestal lav　Kitchen sink　Round lav

Bathtub　Toilet　Urinal

Single door　Double door

Bifold door　Pocket door

Sliding door　Window

3. Pick a point representing the center of the arc near, but not too close to, the upper-left corner of the door (see the top image in Figure 2.13). The Specify start point of arc: prompt appears.

4. Type @3<0↵. Metric users should type @9<0↵. The Specify end point of arc or [Angle/chord Length]: prompt appears.

5. Move the mouse and a temporary arc appears, originating from a point 3 units to the right of the center point you selected and rotating about that center, as in the middle image in Figure 2.13. (Metric users will see the temporary arc originating 9 units to the right of the center point.)

   As the prompt indicates, you now have three options. You can enter an angle, a chord length, or the endpoint of the arc. The prompt default, to specify the endpoint of the arc, picks the arc's endpoint. Again, the cursor is in Point Selection mode, telling you it's waiting for point input. To select this default option, you only need to pick a point on the screen indicating where you want the endpoint.

6. Move the cursor so that it points in a vertical direction from the center of the arc. You'll see the Polar Tracking vector snap to a vertical position (Figure 2.14).

7. Click any location with the Polar Tracking vector in the vertical position. The arc is now fixed in place, as in the bottom image of Figure 2.13.

**FIGURE 2.13**
Using the Arc
command

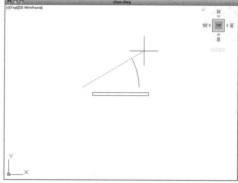

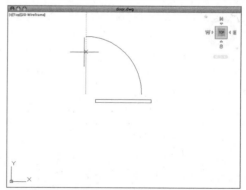

**FIGURE 2.14**
The vertical Polar
Tracking vector

This exercise has given you some practice working with AutoCAD's Command Line palette prompts and entering keyboard commands—skills you'll need when you start to use some of the more advanced AutoCAD functions.

As you can see, AutoCAD has a distinct structure in its prompt messages. You first issue a command, which in turn offers options in the form of a prompt. Depending on the option you select, you get another set of options or you're prompted to take some action, such as picking a point, selecting objects, or entering a value.

As you work through the exercises, you'll become intimately familiar with this routine. After you understand the workings of the Tool Sets palette, the Command Line palette prompts, and the dialog boxes, you can almost teach yourself the rest of the program!

### SELECTING OPTIONS FROM A SHORTCUT MENU

Now you know that you can select command options by typing them. You can also right-click at any time during the execution of a command to open a shortcut menu containing those same options. For example, in step 2 in the previous exercise, you typed **C⏎** to tell AutoCAD that you wanted to select the center of the arc. Instead of typing, you can right-click the mouse to open a shortcut menu with options that are currently applicable to the Arc command.

Notice that in addition to the options shown in the Command prompt, the shortcut menu shows you a few more: Enter, Cancel, Pan, and Zoom. The Enter option is the same as pressing ⏎. Cancel cancels the current command. Pan and Zoom let you adjust your view as you're working through the current command.

The shortcut menu is context sensitive, so you see only those options that pertain to the command or activity that is currently in progress. Also, when AutoCAD is expecting a point, an object selection, or a numeric value, right-clicking doesn't display a shortcut menu. Instead, AutoCAD treats a right-click as ⏎.

The location of your cursor when you right-click determines the contents of the shortcut list. A right-click in the Command Line palette input area displays a list of operations you can apply to the command line, such as repeating one of the last several commands you've used or copying the most recent history of command activity to the Clipboard.

A right-click in the drawing area when no command is active displays a set of basic options for editing your file, such as repeating the command most recently used, Pan, and Zoom, to name a few (see Figure 2.15).

**FIGURE 2.15**
A set of basic list options

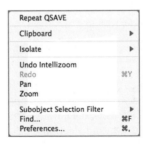

If you're ever in doubt about what to do in AutoCAD, you can right-click to see a list of options. You'll learn more about these options later in this book. For now, let's move on to the topic of selecting objects.

## Selecting Objects

In AutoCAD, you can select objects in many ways. There are two categories of selection methods: The first includes object-selection methods unique to AutoCAD, and the second includes the more common selection method used in most popular graphics programs, the Noun/Verb method. Because these two kinds of methods play a major role in working with AutoCAD, it's a good idea to familiarize yourself with them early on.

### Using a ⇧-Click and Selection Windows

With many AutoCAD commands, you'll see the `Select objects:` prompt. Along with this prompt, the cursor changes from crosshairs to a small square (look back at Figure 2.11). Whenever you see the `Select objects:` prompt and the square Object Selection cursor, you have several options while making your selection. Often, as you select objects on the screen, you'll change your mind about a selection or accidentally select an object you don't want. Let's look at most of the selection options available in AutoCAD and learn what to do when you make the wrong selection.

Before you continue, you'll turn off two features that, although extremely useful, can be confusing to new users. These features are called Object Snap and Object Snap Tracking. You'll get a chance to explore these features in depth later in this book, but for now follow these steps to turn them off:

1. Check to see if either Object Snap or Object Snap Tracking is turned on in the status bar. If they're turned on, they will be a light blue (Figure 2.16).

**FIGURE 2.16**
The Object Snap and Object Snap Tracking tools

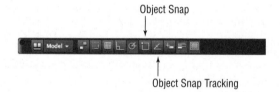

Object Snap

Object Snap Tracking

2. To turn off Object Snap or Object Snap Tracking, click the tool in the status bar. When turned off, they turn gray.

Now, let's see how to select an object in AutoCAD:

1. Click the Move tool in the Tool Sets palette. You can also choose Modify ➢ Move or type **M↵**.

2. At the `Select objects:` prompt, click each of the two horizontal lines that constitute the door (trackpad users can tap on the lines). As you know, whenever AutoCAD wants you to select objects, the cursor turns into the small Object Selection cursor. This tells you that you're in Object Selection mode. As you click an object, it's highlighted, as shown in Figure 2.17.

   If objects don't become "thicker" as you roll over them with your selection cursor, the Selection preview system variable may be turned off. You can turn it back on by entering **selectionpreview↵ 3↵**.

**3.** After making your selections, you may decide to deselect some items. Press ⌘-Z on the keyboard. Notice that one line is no longer highlighted. When you press ⌘-Z, objects are deselected, one at a time, in reverse order of selection.

**4.** You can deselect objects in another way. ⇧-click (or ⇧-tap if you use a trackpad) on the remaining highlighted line. It reverts to a solid line, showing you that it's no longer selected for editing.

**FIGURE 2.17**
Selecting the lines of the door and seeing them highlighted

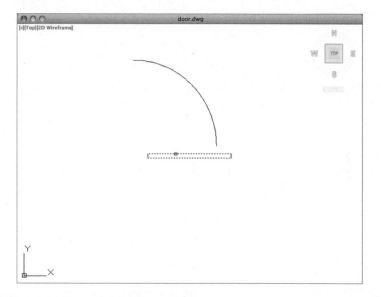

**5.** By now, you've deselected both lines. Let's try another method for selecting groups of objects. To select objects with a window selection, type **W**↵. The cursor changes to a Point Selection cursor, and the prompt changes to

```
Specify first corner:
```

**6.** Click and drag a point below and to the left of the rectangle representing the door. Trackpad users should double-tap and drag. As you move your cursor across the screen, a selection window appears and stretches across the drawing area. Also notice that the window has a blue tint.

**7.** After the selection window completely encloses the door but not the arc, release the mouse button to highlight the entire door. Trackpad users can simply move your finger from the trackpad. This window selects only objects that are completely enclosed by the window, as shown in Figure 2.18.

Don't confuse the selection window you're creating here with the zoom window you used in Chapter 1, which defines an area of the drawing you want to enlarge. Remember that the Window option works differently under the Zoom command than it does for other editing commands.

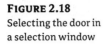

**FIGURE 2.18**

Selecting the door in a selection window

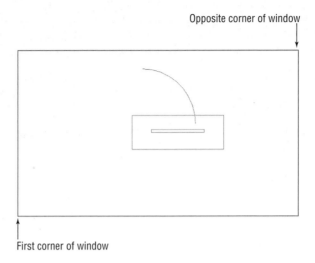

8. Press ↵. This tells AutoCAD that you've finished selecting objects. It's important to remember to press ↵ as soon as you finish selecting the objects you want to edit. A new prompt, `Specify base point or [Displacement] <Displacement>:`, appears. The cursor changes to its Point Selection mode.

Now you've seen how the selection process works in AutoCAD—but you're in the middle of the Move command. The next section discusses the prompt that's on your screen and describes how to enter base points and displacement distances.

**PROVIDING BASE POINTS**

When you move or copy objects, AutoCAD prompts you for a base point, which can be a difficult concept to grasp. AutoCAD must be told specifically *from* where and *to* where the move occurs. The *base point* is the exact location from which you determine the distance and direction of the move. After the base point is determined, you can tell AutoCAD where to move the object in relation to that point.

Follow these steps to practice using base points:

1. To select a base point, ⇧-right-click, or if you are using a trackpad, hold ⇧ down and tap with two fingers. The Snap Overrides menu appears, displaying the Object Snap options (see Figure 2.19).

   When you ⇧-right-click or use a two-finger tap with ⇧, make sure the cursor is within the AutoCAD drawing area; otherwise, you won't get the results described in this book.

2. Choose Intersection from the Snap Overrides menu. The Object Snap menu closes.

3. Move the cursor to the lower-right corner of the door. Notice that as you approach the corner, a small X-shaped graphic appears on the corner. This is called an *Osnap marker*.

4. After the X-shaped marker appears, hold the mouse motionless for a second or two. A tooltip appears, telling you the current osnap point AutoCAD has selected.

**FIGURE 2.19**

The Object Snap options

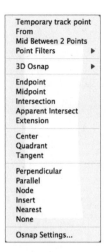

5. Click the mouse button or tap on the trackpad to select the intersection indicated by the Osnap marker. Whenever you see the Osnap marker at the point you want to select, you don't have to point exactly at the location with your cursor. Just click the mouse to select the exact osnap point (see Figure 2.20). In this case, you selected the exact intersection of two lines.

**FIGURE 2.20**

Using the Point Selection cursor and the Osnap marker

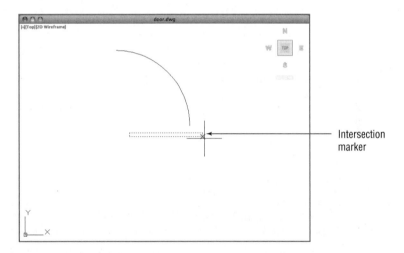

6. At the `Specify second point or <use first point as displacement>:` prompt, ⇧-right-click or press ⇧ and two-finger tap on the trackpad to open the Snap Overrides menu.

7. Click the Endpoint option in the menu.

8. Pick the lower-right end of the arc you drew earlier. (Remember that you need to move your cursor close to the endpoint just until the Osnap marker appears.) The door moves so that the corner connects exactly with the endpoint of the arc (see Figure 2.21).

As you can see, the osnap options let you select specific points on an object. You used Endpoint and Intersection in this exercise, but other options are available. You may have also noticed that the Osnap marker is different for each of the options you used. You'll learn more about osnaps and the other osnap options that are available in Chapter 3. Now, let's continue with our look at point selection.

**FIGURE 2.21**
Moving the rectangle to its new position using the Endpoint osnap

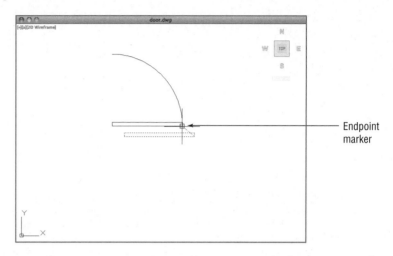

Endpoint marker

You may have noticed the statement use first point as displacement in the prompt in step 6. This means that if you press ↵ instead of clicking a point, the object will move a distance based on the coordinates of the point you selected as a base point. If, for example, the point you click for the base point is at coordinate 2,4, the object will move 2 units in the X axis and 4 units in the Y axis.

If you want to specify an exact distance and direction by typing a value, select any point on the screen as a base point. As an alternative, you can type @ followed by ↵ at the base point prompt; then, enter the second point's location in relative coordinates. Remember that @ means the last point selected. In the next exercise, you'll try moving the entire door an exact distance of 1 unit at a 45° angle. Metric users will move the door 3 units at a 45° angle. Here are the steps:

1. Click the Move tool in the Tool Sets palette.

2. Type **P**↵. The set of objects you selected in the previous exercise is highlighted. P is a selection option that selects the previously selected set of objects.

3. You're still in Object Selection mode, so click the arc to include it in the set of selected objects. The entire door, including the arc, is highlighted.

4. Press ↵ to tell AutoCAD that you've finished your selection. The cursor changes to Point Selection mode.

5. At the Specify base point or [Displacement] <Displacement>: prompt, choose a point on the screen between the door and the left side of the screen (see Figure 2.22).

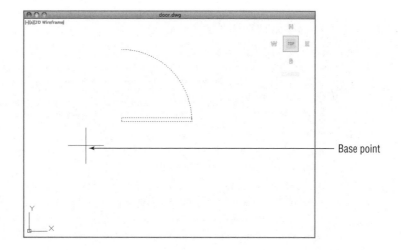

**FIGURE 2.22**
The highlighted door and the base point just to the left of the door. Note that the base point doesn't need to be on the object that you're moving.

Base point

6. Move the cursor around slowly and notice that the door moves as if the base point you selected were attached to it. The door moves with the cursor, at a fixed distance from it. This demonstrates how the base point relates to the objects you select.

7. Type @1<45↵. (Metric users should type @3<45↵.) The door moves to a new location on the screen at a distance of 1 unit (3 for metric users) from its previous location and at an angle of 45°.

If AutoCAD is idle and waiting for a command, you can repeat the last command used by pressing the spacebar or pressing ↵. You can also right-click in the drawing area and select the option at the top of the list. If you right-click the Command Line palette, a shortcut menu offers the commands most recently used.

This exercise illustrates that the base point doesn't have to be on the object you're manipulating; it can be virtually anywhere on your drawing. You also saw how to reselect a group of objects that were selected previously without having to duplicate the selection process.

## Using Noun/Verb Selection

Nearly all graphics programs today allow the Noun/Verb method for selecting objects. This method requires you to select objects before you issue a command to edit them—that is, you identify the "noun" (the object you want to work on) before you identify the "verb" (the action you want to perform on it). The following exercises show you how to use the Noun/Verb method in AutoCAD.

You've seen that when AutoCAD is waiting for a command, it displays the crosshair cursor with the small square. As mentioned, this square is an Object Selection cursor superimposed on the Point Selection cursor. It indicates that you can select objects even while the Command prompt appears at the bottom of the screen and no command is currently active. The square momentarily disappears when you're in a command that asks you to select points.

## OTHER SELECTION OPTIONS

There are several other selection options you haven't tried yet. You'll see how these options work in exercises later in this book. Or, if you're adventurous, try them now on your own. To use these options, type their keyboard shortcuts (shown in parentheses in the following list) at any Select objects: prompt.

**Add (add↵)**  Switches from Remove mode to the Add mode. See the description for Remove later in this sidebar.

**All (all↵)**  Selects all the objects in a drawing except those in frozen or locked layers. (See Chapter 5 for information on layers.)

**Box (b↵)**  Forces the standard selection window so a left-to-right selection uses a standard window and a right-to-left selection uses a crossing window.

**Crossing (c↵)**  Similar to the Window selection option (described later in this sidebar) but selects anything that is entirely within or crosses through the window that you define.

**Crossing Polygon (cp↵)**  Acts exactly like Window Polygon (see later in this sidebar), but like the Crossing selection option, selects anything that crosses through a polygon boundary.

**Fence (f↵)**  Selects objects that are crossed by a temporary line called a *fence*. This operation is like using a line to cross out the objects you want to select. After you invoke this option, you can then pick points, as when you're drawing a series of line segments. After you finish drawing the fence, press ↵, and then go on to select other objects or press ↵ again to finish your selection.

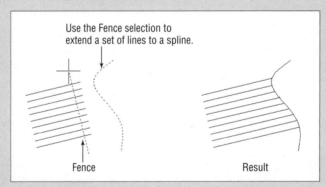

**Group (g↵)**  Allows you to select a group by name.

**Last (l↵)**  Selects the last object you created.

**Multiple (m↵)**  Lets you select several objects first, before AutoCAD highlights them. In a large file, selecting objects individually can cause AutoCAD to pause after each selection while it locates and highlights each object. The Multiple option can speed things up by letting you first select all the objects quickly and then highlight them all by pressing ↵. This has no menu equivalent.

**Previous (p↵)**  Selects the last object or set of objects that was edited or changed.

**Remove (r↵)**  Switches to a selection mode whereby the objects you click are removed from the selection set.

**Window (w.↵)**   Forces a standard window selection. This option is useful when your drawing area is too crowded to use the Autoselect feature to place a window around a set of objects. (See the Auto entry later in this sidebar.) It prevents you from accidentally selecting an object with a single pick when you're placing your window.

**Window Polygon (wp↵)**   Lets you select objects by enclosing them in an irregularly shaped polygon boundary. When you use this option, you see the `First polygon point:` prompt. You then pick points to define the polygon boundary. As you pick points, the `Specify endpoint of line or [Undo]:` prompt appears. Select as many points as you need to define the boundary. You can undo boundary line segments as you go by pressing **U**↵. With the boundary defined, press ↵. The bounded objects are highlighted and the `Select objects:` prompt returns, allowing you to use more selection options.

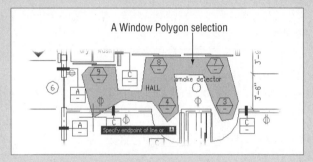

A Window Polygon selection

The following two selection options are also available but are seldom used. They're intended for use in creating custom menu options or custom tools:

**Auto (au↵)**   Forces the standard automatic window or crossing window when a point is picked and no object is found. (See the section "Using Autoselect" later in this chapter.) A standard window is produced when the two window corners are picked from left to right. A crossing window is produced when the two corners are picked from right to left. After this option is selected, it remains active for the duration of the current command. Auto is intended for use on systems on which the Autoselect feature has been turned off.

**Single (si↵)**   Forces the current command to select only a single object. If you use this option, you can pick a single object and the current command acts on that object as if you had pressed ↵ immediately after selecting it. This has no menu equivalent.

Try moving objects by first selecting them and then using the Move command:

1. Press the Esc key twice to make sure AutoCAD isn't in the middle of a command you might have accidentally issued. Then click the arc you drew earlier. The arc is highlighted, and you may also see squares and arrowheads appear at various points on the arc. As stated earlier, these squares and arrowheads are handles that are called *grips* in AutoCAD. You'll get a chance to work with them later.

2. Choose Move from the Tool Sets palette. The cursor changes to Point Selection mode. Notice that the grips on the arc disappear but the arc is still selected.

3. At the Specify base point or [Displacement] <Displacement>: prompt, pick any point on the screen. The following prompt appears:

```
Specify second point or
<use first point as displacement>:
```

4. Type @1<0.↵. Metric users should type @3<0.↵. The arc moves to a new location 1 unit (3 units for metric users) to the right.

In this exercise, you picked the arc *before* issuing the Move command. Then, when you clicked the Move tool, you didn't see the Select objects: prompt. Instead, AutoCAD assumed you wanted to move the arc that you selected and went directly to the Specify base point or [Displacement] <Displacement>: prompt.

### USING AUTOSELECT

Next you'll move the rest of the door in the same direction by using the Autoselect feature:

1. Click and drag (or double-tap and drag) from a point just above and to the left of the rectangle representing the door. Be sure not to pick the door itself. A selection window appears that you can drag across the screen as you move the cursor. If you move the cursor to the left of the last point selected, the window outline appears dotted with a green tint inside the window (see the first image in Figure 2.23). If you move the cursor to the right of that point, the outline appears solid with a blue tint inside (see the second image in Figure 2.23).

2. While still holding the mouse button, move the cursor to a point below and to the right of the door so that the door is completely enclosed by the window but not the arc, as shown in the second image in Figure 2.23.

**FIGURE 2.23**
The dotted window (first image) indicates a crossing selection; the solid window (second image) indicates a standard selection window.

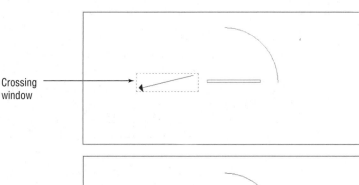

Crossing window

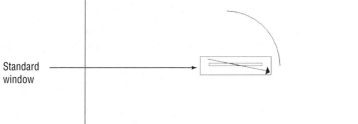

Standard window

3. Release the mouse button. The door is highlighted (and again, you may see grips appear at the lines' endpoints and midpoints).

4. Click the Move tool again. Just as in the preceding exercise, the `Specify base point or [Displacement] <Displacement>:` prompt appears.

5. Pick any point on the screen; then enter @1<0↵. Metric users should enter @3<0↵. The door joins with the arc.

The two selection windows you've just seen—the blue solid one and the dotted green one—represent a standard window and a crossing window. If you use a *standard window*, anything completely within the window is selected. If you use a *crossing window*, anything that crosses through the window is selected. These two types of windows start automatically when you click any blank portion of the drawing area with a Standard cursor or a Point Selection cursor; hence the name *Autoselect*.

Next, you'll select objects with an automatic crossing window:

1. Click and drag (or double-tap and drag) from a point below and to the right of the door. As you move the cursor left, the crossing (dotted) window appears.

2. Position the cursor so that the window encloses the door and part of the arc (see Figure 2.24); then release the mouse button (or tap the trackpad). The entire door, including the arc, is highlighted.

**FIGURE 2.24**
The door
enclosed by a
crossing window

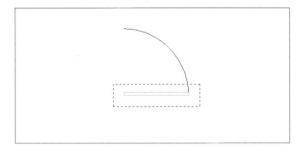

3. Click the Move tool.

4. Pick any point on the screen; then enter @1<180↵. Metric users should type @3<180↵. The door moves back to its original location.

You'll find that, in most cases, the Autoselect standard and crossing windows are all you need when selecting objects. They really save you time, so you'll want to become familiar with these features.

Before continuing, choose File ➤ Save from the menu bar to save the Door.dwg file. You won't want to save the changes you make in the next section, so saving now stores the current condition of the file on your hard disk for safekeeping.

**RESTRICTIONS ON NOUN/VERB OBJECT SELECTION**

For many of the modifying or construction-oriented commands, the Noun/Verb selection method is inappropriate because for those commands, you must select more than one set of objects. You'll know whether a command accepts the Noun/Verb selection method right away. Commands that don't accept the Noun/Verb selection method clear the selection and then ask you to select an object or set of objects.

If you'd like to take a break, now is a good time to do so. If you want, exit AutoCAD, and return to this point in the tutorial later. When you return, start AutoCAD and open the Door.dwg file.

AutoCAD offers selection options in addition to Noun/Verb selection. See Appendix B on the companion website to learn how you can control object-selection methods. That appendix also describes how to change the size of the Standard cursor.

# Editing with Grips

Earlier, when you selected the door, grips appeared at the endpoints, center points, and midpoints of the lines and arcs. You can use grips to make direct changes to the shape of objects or to move and copy them quickly.

If you didn't see grips on the door in the previous exercise, your version of AutoCAD may have the Grips feature turned off. To turn them on, refer to the information on grips in Appendix B on the companion website.

So far, you've seen how operations in AutoCAD have a discrete beginning and ending. For example, to draw an arc, you first issue the Arc command and then go through a series of operations, including answering prompts and picking points. When you're finished, you have an arc and AutoCAD will be ready for the next command.

The Grips feature, on the other hand, plays by a different set of rules. Grips offer a small yet powerful set of editing functions that don't conform to the lockstep command/prompt/input routine you've seen so far. As you work through the following exercises, it's helpful to think of grips as a subset of the standard method of operation in AutoCAD. If you've used other graphics programs, grip editing will be familiar to you.

To practice using the Grips feature, you'll make some temporary modifications to the door drawing.

## Stretching Lines by Using Grips

In this exercise, you'll stretch one corner of the door by grabbing the grip points of two lines:

1. Use the Zoom tool in the status bar to adjust your view so the size of the door is similar to what is shown in Figure 2.25.

2. Press the Esc key to make sure you're not in the middle of a command. Click and drag (or double-tap and drag) from a point below and to the left of the door to start a selection window.

3. Move the cursor above and to the right of the rectangular part of the door and then release the mouse to place the selection window around the door and select it.

4. Place the cursor on the lower-left corner grip of the rectangle, *but don't press the mouse button yet*. Notice that the cursor jumps to the grip point and that the grip changes color.

**FIGURE 2.25**

Stretching lines by using hot grips. The first image shows the rectangle's corner being stretched upward. The second image shows the new location of the corner at the top of the arc.

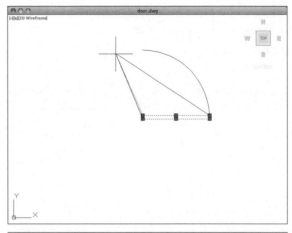

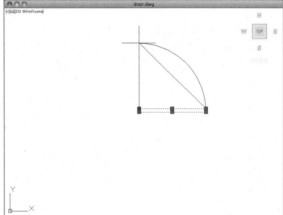

5. Move the cursor to another grip point. Notice again how the cursor jumps to it. When placed on a grip, the cursor moves to the exact center of the grip point. This means, for example, that if the cursor is placed on an endpoint grip, it's on the exact endpoint of the object.

6. Move the cursor to the upper-left corner grip of the rectangle and click. The grip becomes a solid color and is now a *hot grip*. The prompt displays the following message:

```
**STRETCH**
Specify stretch point or [Base point/Copy/Undo/eXit]:
```

This prompt tells you that Stretch mode is active. Notice the options in the prompt. As you move the cursor, the corner follows and the lines of the rectangle stretch (see Figure 2.25).

You can control the size and color of grips by using the Cursor and Selection settings in the Application Preferences dialog box; see Appendix B on the companion website for details.

7. Move the cursor upward toward the top end of the arc and click that point. The rectangle deforms, with the corner placed at your pick point (see Figure 2.25).

Here you saw that a command called Stretch is issued by clicking a grip point. As you'll see in these next steps, a handful of other hot-grip commands are also available:

1. Notice that the grips are still active. Click the grip point that you moved before to make it a hot grip again.

2. Right-click (or two-finger tap if you use a trackpad) to open a shortcut menu that contains a list of grip edit options (see Figure 2.26).

**FIGURE 2.26**

A list of grip edit options

When you click the joining grip point of two contiguous line segments, AutoCAD selects the overlapping grips of two lines. When you stretch the corner away from its original location, the endpoints of both lines follow.

3. Choose Base Point from the list, and then click a point to the right of the hot grip. Now as you move the cursor, the hot grip moves relative to the cursor.

4. Right-click again, choose Copy from the shortcut menu, and enter @1<-30↵. (Metric users should enter @3<-30↵.) Instead of the hot grip moving and the lines changing, copies of the two lines are made with their endpoints 1 unit (or 3 units for metric users) below and to the right of the first set of endpoints.

5. Pick another point just below the last. More copies are made.

6. Press ↵ or enter X↵ to exit Stretch mode. You can also right-click again and choose Exit from the shortcut menu.

In this exercise, you saw that you can select a base point other than the hot grip. You also saw how you can specify relative coordinates to move or copy a hot grip. Finally, you saw that with grips selected on an object, right-clicking the mouse opens a shortcut menu that contains grip edit options.

## Moving and Rotating with Grips

As you've just seen, the Grips feature is an alternative method for editing your drawings. You've already seen how you can stretch endpoints, but you can do much more with grips. The next exercise demonstrates some other options. You'll start by undoing the modifications you made in the preceding exercise:

1. Press ⌘-Z or type U↵. The copies of the stretched lines disappear.

2. Press ↵. The deformed door snaps back to its original form.

Pressing ↵ at the Command prompt causes AutoCAD to repeat the last command entered—in this case, ⌘-Z or U.

3. You are going to select the entire door. First click and drag (or double-tap and drag) from a blank area below and to the right of the door.

4. Move the cursor to a location above and to the left of the rectangular portion of the door and release the mouse button or tap the trackpad. Because you went from right to left, you created a crossing window. Recall that the crossing window selects anything enclosed and crossing through the window.

5. Click the lower-left grip of the rectangle to turn it into a hot grip. Just as before, as you move your cursor, the corner stretches.

6. Right-click (or two-finger tap) and choose Move from the shortcut menu. The Command Line palette displays the following:

```
**MOVE**
Specify move point or [Base point/Copy/Undo/eXit]
```

Now as you move the cursor, the entire door moves with it.

7. Position the door near the center of the screen and click. The door moves to the center of the screen. Notice that the Command prompt returns but the door remains highlighted, indicating that it's still selected for the next operation.

8. Click the lower-left grip again, right-click, and choose Rotate from the shortcut menu. The Command Line palette displays the following:

```
**ROTATE**
Specify rotation angle or [Base point/Copy/Undo/Reference/eXit]:
```

As you move the cursor, the door rotates about the grip point.

9. Position the cursor so that the door rotates approximately 180° (see Figure 2.27). Then ⌃-click the mouse (hold down ⌃ and press the left mouse button). A copy of the door appears in the new rotated position, leaving the original door in place.

10. Press ↵ to exit Grip Edit mode.

You've seen how the Move command is duplicated in a modified way as a hot-grip command. Other hot-grip commands (Stretch, Rotate, Scale, and Mirror) have similar counterparts in the standard set of AutoCAD commands. You'll see how those work in Chapters 11 and 13, "Using Dimensions" and "Copying Existing Drawings into AutoCAD."

After you complete any operation by using grips, the objects are still highlighted with their grips active. To clear the grip selection, press the Esc key.

In this exercise, you saw how hot-grip options appear in a shortcut menu. Several other options are available in that menu, including Exit, Base Point, Copy, and Undo.

You can access many of these grip edit options by pressing the spacebar or ↵ while a grip is selected. With each press, the next option becomes active. The options then repeat if you continue to press ↵. ⌃ acts as a shortcut to the Copy option. You have to use it only once; then, each time you click a point, a copy is made.

**FIGURE 2.27**
Rotating and copy-ing the door by using a hot grip. Notice that more than one object is affected by the grip edit, even though only one grip is hot.

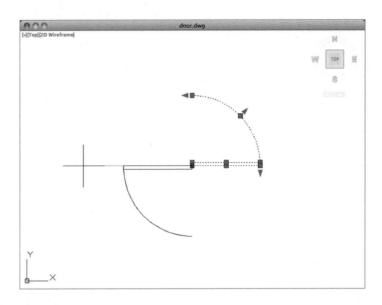

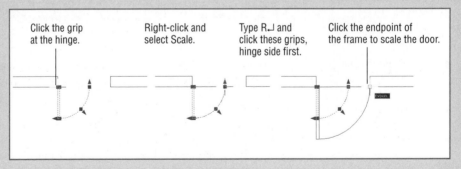

### Real World Scenario

#### SCALING WITH GRIPS

Grips can be used to scale an object graphically to fit between two other objects. For example, a door can be scaled to fit within a door frame. Place the door so its hinge side is at the door frame and the door is oriented properly for the frame. With the door selected, click the grip at the hinge side. Right-click and select Scale. Type **R**↵, and then click the grip at the hinge again. Click the grip at the end of the arc representing the door swing. Finally, click the opposite side of the door frame.

Click the grip at the hinge.

Right-click and select Scale.

Type R↵ and click these grips, hinge side first.

Click the endpoint of the frame to scale the door.

## Using Rotate Reference to Align Objects

You can use the Rotate command's Reference option to graphically align a set of objects to another object. For example, suppose you want to rotate a set of circles inside a hexagon to align with the corner of the hexagon.

To do this, you can use the Rotate command's Reference option as follows:

1. Open the `Circlehex.dwg` file from the sample files on this book's accompanying website. You'll use this file to practice using the Reference option.

2. Click the Rotate tool in the Tool Sets palette, select the circles inside the hexagon, and press ⏎.

3. At the `Specify base point:` prompt, use the Center osnap to select the center of the hexagon as represented by the central circle (Figure 2.28). Once you do this, the objects rotate around the selected point as you move your cursor.

**FIGURE 2.28**
Rotate using the Reference option.

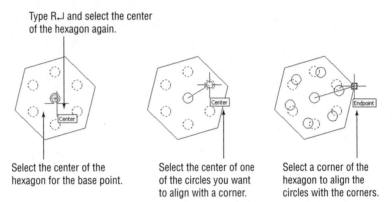

Type R⏎ and select the center of the hexagon again.

Select the center of the hexagon for the base point.

Select the center of one of the circles you want to align with a corner.

Select a corner of the hexagon to align the circles with the corners.

4. At the `Specify rotation angle or [Copy/Reference]:` prompt, enter **R⏎**.

5. At the `Specify the reference angle <0>:` prompt, use the Center osnap to select the center of the hexagon again. You can also enter **@⏎** since the last point you selected was the center.

6. At the `Specify second point:` prompt, use the Center osnap to select the center of one of the circles you want to align with the hexagon. Now as you move the cursor, the circle whose center you selected is aligned with the cursor angle.

7. At the `Specify the new angle or [Points] <0>:` prompt, use the Endpoint osnap to select one of the corners of the hexagon. The circles align with the corners.

8. Close `Circlehex.dwg` without saving it.

You can also use grips to align objects. Here's how:

1. Select the object or set of objects and then click a grip. The grip you select becomes the rotation point, so select this first grip carefully.

2. Right-click and select Rotate.

3. Type **R⏎** and select the grip you just selected and another point to determine the reference angle.

4. Finally, select the new angle for the object or set of objects. If you want to rotate about a point other than the first grip, use the grip's Base right-click option.

**A QUICK SUMMARY OF THE GRIPS FEATURE**

The exercises in this chapter include only a few of the grips options. You'll get a chance to use other hot-grip options in later chapters. Meanwhile, here is a summary of the Grips feature:

◆ Clicking endpoint grips stretches those endpoints.

◆ Clicking the midpoint grip of a line moves the entire line.

◆ If two objects meet end to end and you click their overlapping grips, both grips are selected simultaneously.

◆ You can select multiple grips by holding down ⇧ and clicking the desired grips.

◆ When a hot grip is selected, the Stretch, Move, Rotate, Scale, and Mirror options are available to you; right-click the mouse.

◆ You can cycle through the Stretch, Move, Rotate, Scale, and Mirror options by pressing ↵ while a hot grip is selected.

◆ All the hot-grip options let you make copies of the selected objects by either using the Copy option or holding down ^ while selecting points.

◆ All the hot-grip options let you select a base point other than the originally selected hot grip.

## Using Dynamic Input

Earlier in this chapter, you turned off the Dynamic Input display so you could get an uncluttered view of what was going on in AutoCAD's display. In this section, you'll get a chance to explore the Dynamic Input display through grip editing.

You'll start by going back to the original version of the Door.dwg drawing that you saved earlier:

1. Click the Close icon in the upper-left corner of the drawing area.

2. When you're asked if you want to save changes, click No.

3. Choose File ➢ Open, and then locate and select the Door.dwg file you saved earlier. You can also open the doorsample.dwg file from the sample files you installed from this book's companion website.

4. The door appears in the condition you left it when you last saved the file.

5. Click the Dynamic Input tool in the status bar to turn it on (Figure 2.29). It should be a light blue color.

6. Click the arc to expose its grips.

**FIGURE 2.29**
The Dynamic Input
tool in the status bar

**7.** Place the cursor on the outward-pointing arrow grip at the middle of the arc, but don't click it. (This is called *hovering* over a grip.) You see the dimensions of the arc appear. This feature is useful when you need to check the size of objects you've drawn (see Figure 2.30).

**8.** Click the arrow you're hovering over. The Command prompt appears at the cursor, and the radius dimension changes to a text box.

**9.** Move the cursor toward the upper-right corner of the drawing area. The radius dimension changes as you move the cursor.

**FIGURE 2.30**
Hovering over
a grip

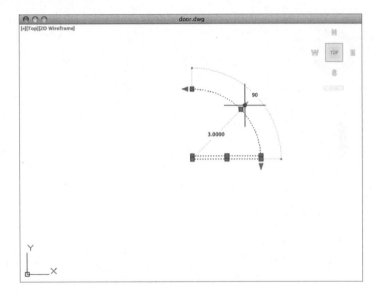

**10.** Enter **4**↵. Metric users enter **130**↵. As you type, the new value appears in the radius dimension. When you press ↵, the arc changes to the new radius.

**11.** Press ⌘-Z to revert to the original arc size.

Here you saw the basic methods for using the Dynamic Input display. You can hover over an object's grip to display its dimensions. Click the grip and, if available, those dimensions can be edited directly through the keyboard. In this example, you were able to change the radius of the arc to an exact value. Depending on the grip you click, you can change a dimension through direct keyboard input. For example, if you want to change the degrees the arc covers instead of its radius, you can click the arrow grip at either end of the arc.

---

### SELECTING MULTIPLE GRIPS AND DYNAMIC DISPLAY

You can make more than one grip "hot" by holding down the shift key while clicking grips. But you may find this a little difficult to do when Dynamic Display is turned on. If you are having problems selecting multiple grips, make sure you don't hover over the first grip too long before you ⇧-click. Hold down the shift key and click the grips as quickly as possible.

Next, try Dynamic Input display on a line:

1. Click the bottommost line of the door, as shown in Figure 2.31; hover over the rightmost grip on the selected line. Just as with the arc, you can see the dimensions of the line, including its length and directional angle.

**FIGURE 2.31**
Selecting a line on the door

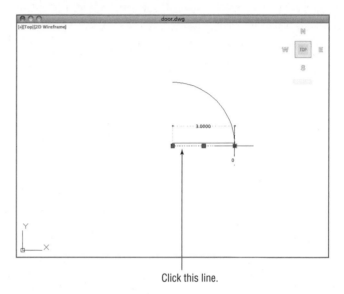

Click this line.

2. Click the grip you're hovering over, and then move the cursor upward and to the right. You see two dimensions: One indicates the overall length and the other shows the change in length of the line. You also see the Command prompt at the cursor. Notice that the dimension indicating the change in length is highlighted (see Figure 2.32).

**FIGURE 2.32**
The overall length dimension and the change in length dimension

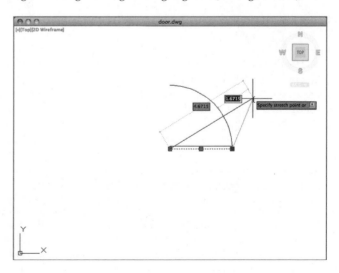

3. Enter **1** and press the Tab key to increase the length of the line by 1 unit. Metric users should enter **30** and press the Tab key. Now as you move the cursor, the line is locked at a new length that is 1 or 30 units longer than its original length. Also notice that the overall dimension is highlighted. You also see a lock icon on the length dimension (see Figure 2.33).

**FIGURE 2.33**
The line locked at a new length

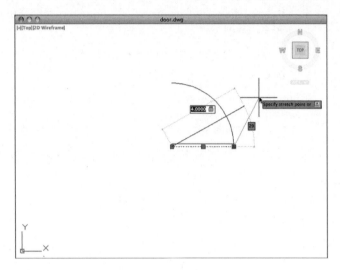

4. Press the Tab key again. The angle value is highlighted.

5. Enter **45** and press the Tab key to lock the angle of the line at 45°.

6. Make sure the cursor isn't too close to the locked endpoint of the line and then click the left mouse button. The line is now in its new orientation with a length of 4 (130 for metric users) and an angle of 45°, as shown in Figure 2.34.

**FIGURE 2.34**
The line's new length and orientation

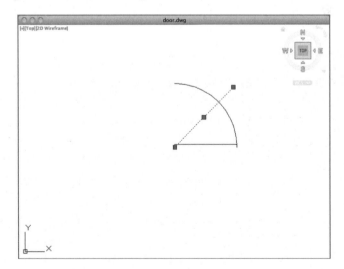

You can see that the Dynamic Input display lets you enter specific dimensions for the selected object, making possible precise changes in an object's size.

You can also use the Dynamic Input display while using other grip-editing features. Try the following exercise to see how the Dynamic Input display works while moving objects:

1. Click and drag from a point above and to the right of the door drawing to start a crossing selection window.

2. Release the mouse button below and to the left to select the entire door drawing.

3. Click the middle grip of the arc.

4. Right-click (or two-finger tap) and choose Move. You see the Command prompt at the cursor with the distance value highlighted. As you move the cursor, you can see the distance and angle values in the Dynamic Input display change (see Figure 2.35).

**FIGURE 2.35**
The Dynamic Input display

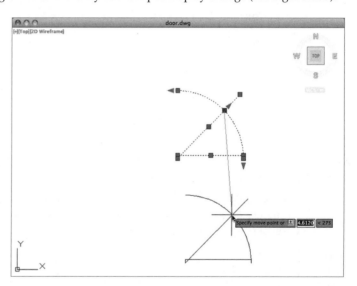

5. Enter **4**, and then press the Tab key. As you move the cursor, the distance from the original location of the arc's midpoint is locked at 4 units. The angle value is now highlighted and available for editing.

6. Enter **225**, and then press the Tab key to lock the angle at 225°.

7. Click a location away from the door drawing. The door moves to its new location, exactly 4 units from its original location.

As you can see from these exercises, the Dynamic Input display adds some helpful methods for editing objects. To summarize, here is a rundown of the basic Dynamic Input display features:

◆ You can easily turn the Dynamic Input display on or off by clicking the Dynamic Input tool in the status bar.

◆ You can quickly check the dimensions of an object by selecting it and then hovering over a grip.

◆ You can alter an object's dimensions by entering values into the highlighted dimensions of the Dynamic Input display.

◆ To highlight a different dimension, press the Tab key.

◆ To accept any changes you've made using Dynamic Input display, click the mouse at a location away from the grip you're editing. You can also press ↵ or the spacebar.

Not all grips offer dimensions that can be edited. If you click the midpoint grip on the line, for example, you won't see the dimensions of the line, although you'll see the Command prompt and you'll be able to enter a new coordinate for the midpoint.

As you've seen in the arc and line examples, each object offers a different set of dimensions. If you like the way the Dynamic Input display works, you can experiment on other types of objects.

---

**TYPING COORDINATES WITH DYNAMIC INPUT**

When entering coordinates through the keyboard while Dynamic Input is on, you have to use a slightly different notation for relative and absolute coordinates. If you're entering relative coordinates, you can leave off the @ sign, so instead of typing **@12,9**↵, you can simply type **12,9**↵. If you are entering absolute coordinates, you need to precede your coordinate list with a # sign. So instead of entering **1,1**↵ to specify a point at coordinate 1,1, you would need to enter **#1,1**↵.

---

# Getting Help

Eventually, you'll find yourself somewhere without documentation and you'll have a question about an AutoCAD feature. AutoCAD provides an online help facility that gives you information on nearly any topic related to AutoCAD. Here's how to find help:

1. Choose Help ➢ AutoCAD Help from the menu bar to open the AutoCAD Mac Help website (Figure 2.36).

2. Take a moment to see what is offered on this website. On the left is a column of topics that act like tabs. User's Guide is at the top followed by Command Reference, Customization Guide, and so on.

3. Click Command Reference. The middle of the page changes to show Commands, Command Modifiers, System Variables, and Glossary along with a section labeled Basics And Tutorials.

4. Click Commands. An alphabetical index appears.

5. Click M Commands under "Topics in the section" and you see a list of command names that start with *M*.

You also have the Home and Index options in the upper-left corner of the page as well as a search box in the upper right.

**FIGURE 2.36**
The AutoCAD Mac
Help website

## Using Context-Sensitive Help

AutoCAD also provides *context-sensitive help* to give you information related to the command you're currently using. To see how this works, try the following:

1. Close or minimize the Help window, and return to the AutoCAD window.

2. Click the Move tool in the Home tab's Modify panel to start the Move command.

3. Hold down the Function key (fn) and press the F1 key to open the Help window. A description of the Move command appears in the AutoCAD Mac Help website.

4. Press the Esc key to exit the Move command.

## Finding Additional Sources of Help

The AutoCAD Mac Help website is the main online source for reference material, but you can also find answers to your questions through the other options in the Help menu bar menu. Here is a brief description of the Help options:

**AutoCAD Help**   Opens the AutoCAD Mac Help website.

**Welcome screen**   In a new installation of AutoCAD, you will see a welcome screen that offers information on how to use AutoCAD. If you're totally new to AutoCAD, you may want to take advantage of the basic tutorials on how to draw. You'll also find information on other learning resources.

**Getting Started Videos**   The Getting Started videos offer instructions on the basic features of AutoCAD and how to use them.

**Send Feedback**   The product feedback web page enables you to send comments to Autodesk. The Send Feedback option takes you directly to this page.

**Customer Involvement Program**   The Customer Involvement Program is really a way for Autodesk to monitor the condition of AutoCAD by allowing its customers to send comments about program errors or crashes. This voluntary program lets you participate anonymously, or you can provide contact information for follow-up contacts.

You can also obtain general information about your version of AutoCAD by choosing AutoCAD ➢ About AutoCAD. This opens the About window. Click the Product Information button to find your serial number, product key, and other license information.

## Displaying Data in the Command Line Palette

You may have noticed that as you work in AutoCAD, the activity displayed in the Command Line palette scrolls up. Sometimes, it's helpful to view information that has scrolled past the view shown in the Command Line palette. For example, you can review the command activity from your session to check input values or to recall other data-entry information. Try the following exercise to see how scrolling in the Command Line palette might be helpful:

1. Choose Tools ➢ Inquiry ➢ List from the menu bar or type **LIST**↵.

2. At the `Select objects:` prompt, click the arc and press ↵. Information about the arc is displayed in the AutoCAD Command Line palette. Figure 2.37 shows the Command Line palette stretched to show all of the information from the List command. Toward the bottom is the list of the arc's properties. Don't worry if the meaning of some listed properties isn't obvious yet; as you work through this book, you'll learn what the properties of an object mean.

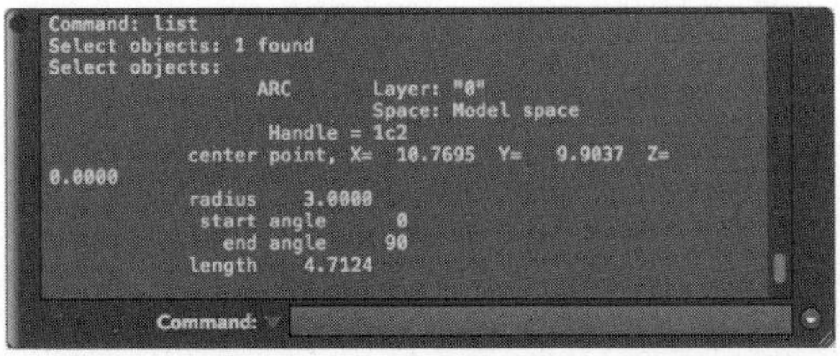

**FIGURE 2.37**

The stretched Command Line palette showing the data displayed by the List command

3. Expand the Command Line palette using the disclosure triangle at the right of the palette. Use the scroll bar to the right of the Command Line palette to scroll up the contents of the palette.

The scroll bar to the right of the Command Line palette lets you scroll to earlier events. You can even have AutoCAD record the Command Line palette information in a text file.

When you have more than one document open, the Command Line palette displays a listing for the drawing that is currently active.

## Displaying the Properties of an Object

While we're on the subject of displaying information, you'll want to know about the Properties Inspector palette. In the preceding exercise, you saw how the List command showed some information regarding the properties of an object, such as the location of an arc's center and end-points. You can also select an object to display its properties in the Properties Inspector palette.

To see how the Properties Inspector palette works firsthand, try the following exercise:

1. Select the arc in the drawing. The Properties Inspector palette displays a list of the arc's properties. Don't worry if many of the items in this palette are undecipherable; you'll learn more about this palette as you work through the early chapters of this book. For now, just be aware that you can select an object to display its properties. You can also use the Properties Inspector palette to modify many of the properties listed (see Figure 2.38).

**FIGURE 2.38**
The Properties
Inspector palette

2. Click and drag the scroll bar to the right to see more of the object's properties.

3. You're finished with the door drawing, so choose File ➤ Close from the menu bar.

4. In the Save Changes dialog box, click the No button. (You've already saved this file just as you want it, so you don't need to save it again.)

You may notice the Essential and All options in the upper-right side of the Properties Inspector. These two options enable you to choose the level of information displayed in the palette. The Essential option limits the number of properties displayed to a few of the basic ones like layer and linetype. The All option displays a complete set of properties.

## The Bottom Line

**Specify distances with coordinates.** One of the most basic skills you need to learn is how to indicate exact distances through the keyboard. AutoCAD uses a simple annotation system to indicate distance and direction.

**Master It** What would you type to indicate a relative distance of 14 units at a 45° angle?

**Interpret the cursor modes and understand prompts.** AutoCAD's cursor changes its shape depending on the command that is currently active. These different cursor modes can give you a clue regarding what you should be doing.

 **Master It** Describe the Point Selection cursor and the Object Selection cursor.

**Select objects and edit with grips.** Grips are small squares or arrowheads that appear at key points on the object when they're selected. They offer a powerful way to edit objects.

 **Master It** How do you select multiple grips?

**Use Dynamic Input.** Besides grips, objects display their dimensional properties when selected. These dimensional properties can be edited to change an object's shape.

 **Master It** How do you turn on Dynamic Input? And once it's on, what key lets you shift between the different dimensions of an object?

**Get help.** AutoCAD's Help window is thorough in its coverage of AutoCAD's features. New and experienced users alike can often find answers to their questions through the Help window, so it pays to become familiar with it.

 **Master It** What keyboard key do you press for context-sensitive help?

**Display data in the Command Line palette.** AutoCAD offers the Command Line palette, which keeps a running account of the commands you use. This can be helpful in retrieving input that you've entered when constructing your drawing.

 **Master It** Name a command that displays its results in the Command Line palette.

**Display the properties of an object.** The Properties Inspector palette is one of the most useful sources for drawing information. Not only does it list the properties of an object, it lets you change the shape, color, and other properties of objects.

 **Master It** How do you open the Properties Inspector palette for a particular object?

# Chapter 3

# Setting Up and Using AutoCAD's Drafting Tools

Chapters 1 and 2, "Exploring the AutoCAD Interface" and "Creating Your First Drawing," covered the basic information you need to understand the workings of AutoCAD. Now you'll put this knowledge to work. In this architectural tutorial, which begins now and continues through Chapter 14, "Advanced Editing and Organizing," you'll draw an apartment building composed of studios. The tutorial illustrates how to use AutoCAD commands and gives you a solid understanding of the basic AutoCAD package. With these fundamentals, you can use AutoCAD to its fullest potential regardless of the kinds of drawings you intend to create or the enhancement products you may use in the future.

In this chapter, you'll start drawing an apartment's bathroom fixtures. In the process, you'll learn how to use AutoCAD's basic tools. You'll also be introduced to the concept of drawing scale and how the size of what you draw is translated into a paper sheet size.

In this chapter, you'll learn to do the following:

- Set up a work area
- Explore the drawing process
- Plan and lay out a drawing
- Use the AutoCAD modes as drafting tools

## Setting Up a Work Area

Before beginning most drawings, you should set up your work area. To do this, determine the *measurement system*, the *drawing sheet size*, and the *scale* you want to use. The default work area is roughly 16″ × 9″ at full scale, given a decimal measurement system in which 1 unit equals 1 inch. Metric users will find that the default area is roughly 550 mm × 300 mm, in which 1 unit equals 1 mm. If these are appropriate settings for your drawing, you don't have to do any setting up. It's more likely, however, that you'll make drawings of various sizes and scales. For example, you might want to create a drawing in a measurement system in which you can specify feet, inches, and fractions of inches at 1″ = 1′ scale and print the drawing on an 8½″-×-11″ sheet of paper.

In the following sections, you'll learn how to set up a drawing exactly the way you want.

## Specifying Units

You'll start by creating a new file called Bath. Then you'll set up the unit type.
Use these steps to create the file:

1. If you haven't done so already, start AutoCAD. If AutoCAD is already running, select File ➢ New from the menu bar.

2. In the Select Template dialog box, select acad.dwt and click Open. Metric users should select acadiso.dwt and then click Open.

3. Choose View ➢ Zoom ➢ All from the menu bar or type **Z**⏎ **A**⏎.

4. Choose File ➢ Save As from the menu bar.

5. In the Save Drawing As dialog box, enter **Bath** for the filename.

6. Check to make sure you're saving the drawing in the Documents folder or in the folder where you've chosen to store your exercise files, and then click Save.

---

### USING THE IMPERIAL AND METRIC EXAMPLES

Many of the exercises in this chapter are shown in both the metric and Imperial measurement systems. Be sure that if you start with the Imperial system, you continue with it throughout this book.

The metric settings described in this book are only approximations of their Imperial equivalents. For example, the drawing scale for the metric example is 1:10, which is close to the 1″ = 1′-0″ scale used in the Imperial example. In the grid example, you're asked to use a 30-unit grid, which is close to the 1′ grid of the Imperial example. Dimensions of objects are similar, but not exact. For example, the Imperial version of the tub measures 2′-8″ × 5′-0″ and the metric version of the tub is 81 cm × 152 cm. The actual metric equivalent of 2′-8″ × 5′-0″ is 81.28 cm × 152.4 cm. Measurements in the tub example are rounded to the nearest centimeter.

Metric users should also be aware that AutoCAD uses a period as a decimal point instead of the comma used in most European nations, South Africa, and elsewhere. Commas are used in AutoCAD to separate the X, Y, and Z components of a coordinate.

---

The next thing you want to tell AutoCAD is the *unit type* you intend to use. So far, you've been using the default, which is a generic decimal unit. This unit can be interpreted as inches, centimeters, feet, kilometers, or light years. When it comes time to print your drawing, you can tell AutoCAD how to convert these units into a meaningful scale.

If you are a U.S. user, decimal units typically represent inches. If you want to be able to enter distances in feet, you must change the unit type to one that accepts feet as input. You'll do this through the Drawing Units dialog box shown in Figure 3.1.

If you're a civil engineer, you should know that the Engineering unit type lets you enter feet and decimal feet for distances. For example, the equivalent of 12´-6″ is 12.5´. If you use the Engineering unit type, you'll ensure that your drawings conform to the scale of drawings created by your architectural colleagues.

**FIGURE 3.1**

The Drawing Units dialog box

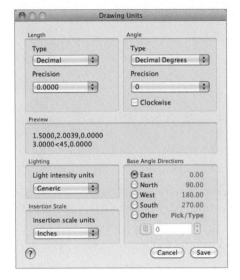

Follow these steps to set a unit type:

1. Choose Format ➢ Units from the menu bar or type **Un**⏎ to open the Drawing Units dialog box.

2. Let's look at a few of the options available. In the upper left, click the Type pop-up list in the Length group. It currently shows Decimal. Notice the unit types in the list.

3. Click Architectural from the list. The Preview section of the dialog box shows you what the Architectural type looks like in AutoCAD. Metric users should keep this setting as Decimal.

---

**SHORTCUT TO SETTING UNITS**

You can also control the Drawing Units settings by using several system variables. To set the unit type, you can type **'lunits.**⏎ at the Command prompt. (The apostrophe lets you enter this command while in the middle of other commands.) At the Enter new value for LUNITS <2>: prompt, enter **4** for Architectural. See Appendix C, "Hardware and Software Tips," on the accompanying website, www.sybex.com/go/masteringautocadmac for other settings.

4. Click the Precision pop-up list just below the Type pop-up list. Notice the options available. You can set the smallest unit AutoCAD will display in this drawing. For now, leave this setting at its default value of 0'-0 ¹⁄₁₆″. Metric users will keep the setting at 0.0000.

5. Take a look at the Base Angle Directions group. This group lets you set the direction for the 0° angle. For now, don't change these settings—you'll read more about them in a moment.

6. Click the pop-up list in the Insertion Scale group. The list shows various units of measure.

7. Click Inches; if you're a metric user, choose Centimeters. This option lets you control how AutoCAD translates drawing scales when you import drawings from outside the current drawing.

8. Click Save in the Drawing Units dialog box to return to the drawing.

If you use the Imperial system of measurement, you selected Architectural measurement units for this tutorial, but your work may require a different unit type. You saw the unit types available in the Drawing Units dialog box. Table 3.1 shows examples of how the distance 15.5 is entered in each of these styles.

**TABLE 3.1:** Measurement systems available in AutoCAD

| MEASUREMENT SYSTEM | AUTOCAD'S DISPLAY OF MEASUREMENT |
| --- | --- |
| Scientific | 1.55E+01 (inches or metric) |
| Decimal | 15.5000 (inches or metric) |
| Engineering | 1'-3.5″ (input as 1'3.5″) |
| Architectural | 1'-3½″ (input as 1'3-½″) |
| Fractional | 15½″ (input as 15-½″) |

In the previous exercise, you needed to change only two settings. Let's look at the other Drawing Units settings in more detail. As you read, you may want to refer to Figure 3.1.

## Fine-Tuning the Measurement System

Most of the time, you'll be concerned only with the Length and Angle settings of the Drawing Units dialog box. But as you saw in the preceding exercise, you can control many other settings related to the input and display of units.

---

**TAKING MEASUREMENTS**

To measure the distance between two points, click Tools ➤ Inquiry ➤ Distance from the menu bar, or type **Di**↵, and then click the two points. (*Di* is the shortcut for entering **Dist**↵.) If this command doesn't give you an accurate distance measurement, examine the Precision setting in the Drawing Units dialog box. If it's set too high, the value returned by the Dist command may be rounded to a value greater than your tolerances allow even though the distance is drawn accurately.

---

The Precision pop-up list in the Length group lets you specify the smallest unit value that you want AutoCAD to display in the status bar and in the prompts. If you choose a measurement system that uses fractions, the Precision pop-up list includes fractional units. You can also control this setting with the Luprec system variable. (You can find out more about system variables on the AutoCAD Mac Help website.)

The Angle group lets you set the style for displaying angles. You have a choice of five angle styles: Decimal Degrees, Degrees/Minutes/Seconds, Grads, Radians, and Surveyor's Units. In the Angle group's Precision pop-up list, you can specify the degree of accuracy you want AutoCAD to display for angles. You can also control these settings with the Aunits and Auprec system variables. Go to the AutoCAD Mac Help website and select the Command Reference option in the left column of the page, and then select the first letter of a system variable name from the System Variable listing.

You can tell AutoCAD which direction is positive, either clockwise or counterclockwise. The default, which is counterclockwise, is used in this book. The Base Angle Directions group lets you set the direction of the 0 base angle. The default base angle (and the one used throughout this book) is a direction from left to right. However, at times you may want to designate another direction as the 0 base angle. You can also control these settings with the Angbase and Angdir system variables.

The Insertion scale units setting in the Drawing Units dialog box lets you control how blocks are scaled as they're inserted into your current drawing. A *block* is a collection of drawing objects that form a single object. Blocks are frequently used to create standard symbols. You'll learn more about blocks in Chapter 4, "Organizing Objects with Blocks and Groups." The Insertion Scale setting lets you compensate for drawings of different scales by offering an automatic scale translation when importing blocks from an external file. The Insunits system variable also controls the Insertion Scale setting.

The Light intensity units setting relates to the 3D rendering feature discussed in Chapter 21, "Rendering 3D Drawings."

If you're new to AutoCAD, don't worry about the Insertion Scale setting right now. Make a mental note of it. It may come in handy in your work in the future.

## Setting Up the Drawing Limits

One of the big advantages of using AutoCAD is that you can draw at full scale; you aren't limited to the edges of a piece of paper the way you are in manual drawing. But you may find it difficult to start drawing without knowing the drawing boundaries. You can set up some arbitrary boundaries using the Limits feature. You got a taste of the Limits feature in Chapter 2. You'll use it again here to set up a work area for your next drawing.

 **Real World Scenario**

### THINGS TO WATCH FOR WHEN ENTERING DISTANCES

When you're using Architectural units, you should be aware of two points:

◆ Use hyphens only to distinguish fractions from whole inches.

◆ You can't use spaces while specifying a dimension. For example, you can specify eight feet, four and one-half inches as 8′4-½″ or 8′4.5, but not as 8′-4½″.

These idiosyncrasies are a source of confusion to many architects and engineers new to AutoCAD because the program often displays architectural dimensions in the standard architectural format but doesn't allow you to enter dimensions that way.

Here are some tips for entering distances and angles in unusual situations:

◆ When entering distances in inches and feet, you can omit the inch (″) sign. If you're using the Engineering unit type, you can enter decimal feet and forgo the inch sign entirely.

◆ You can enter fractional distances and angles in any format you like, regardless of the current unit type. For example, you can enter a distance as **@½<1.5708r**, even if your current unit system is set for decimal units and decimal degrees (1.5708r is the radian equivalent of 90°).

◆ If you have your angle units set to degrees, grads, or radians, you don't need to specify *d*, *g*, or *r* after the angle. You do have to specify d, g, or r, however, if you want to use these units when they aren't the current default angle system.

◆ If your current base angle is set to something other than horizontal from left to right, you can use a double less-than symbol (<<) in place of the single less-than symbol (<) to override the current base angle . The << assumes the base angle of 0° to be a direction from left to right and the positive direction to be counterclockwise.

◆ If your current angle system uses a different base angle and direction and you want to specify an angle in the standard base direction, you can use a triple less-than symbol (<<<) to indicate angles. Note that this works only if Dynamic Input is turned off.

◆ You can specify a denominator of any size when specifying fractions. However, be aware that the value you've set for the maximum number of digits to the right of decimal points (under the Precision setting in the Length group of the Drawing Units dialog box) restricts the fractional value AutoCAD reports. For example, if your units are set for a maximum of two digits of decimals and you give a fractional value of ⁵⁄₃₂, AutoCAD rounds this value to ³⁄₁₆. Note that this doesn't affect the accuracy of the actual drawing dimensions.

◆ You can enter decimal feet for distances in the Architectural unit type. For example, you can enter 6′-6″ as **6.5′**.

You'll be drawing a bathroom that is roughly 8´ × 5´ (230 cm × 150 cm for metric users). You'll want to give yourself some extra room around the bathroom, so your drawing limits should be a bit larger than that actual bathroom size. You'll use an area of 11´ × 8´-6˝ for the limits of your drawing. Metric users will use an area 297 cm × 210 cm. These sizes will accommodate your bathroom with some room to spare.

Now that you know the area you need, you can use the Limits command to set up the area:

1. Choose Format ➤ Drawing Limits or type **Limits**↵.

2. At the `Specify lower left corner or [ON/OFF] <0´-0˝,0´-0˝>:` prompt, specify the lower-left corner of your work area. Press ↵ to accept the default.

3. At the `Specify upper right corner <1´-0˝,0´-9˝>:` prompt, specify the upper-right corner of your work area. (The default is shown in brackets.) Enter **132,102**. Or if you prefer, you can enter **11´,8´6** because you've set up your drawing for architectural units. Metric users should enter **297,210**.

4. Choose View ➤ Zoom ➤ All from the menu bar, or type **Z**↵ **A**↵. Although it appears that nothing has changed, your drawing area is now set to a size that will enable you to draw your bathroom at full scale.

5. To check the area, turn on the Dynamic Input display in the status bar, and then choose Tools ➤ Inquire ➤ ID Point.

6. Move the cursor to the upper-right corner of the drawing area and watch the coordinate readout at the cursor. Notice that now the upper-right corner has a Y coordinate of approximately 8´-6˝, or 210 for metric users. The X coordinate depends on the proportion of your drawing window. The coordinate readout also displays distances in feet and inches.

7. Click a point to finish the ID command and turn off the Dynamic Input display.

8. Press ⌘-Z or click the Grid Display tool in the status bar to turn off the grid.

In step 6, the coordinate readout shows you that your drawing area is larger than before. The background grid can help you visualize the area you're working with. You can control the grid using the Grid Display tool in the status bar. Grid Display shows a background grid that helps you visualize distances and can also show you the limits of your drawing. It can also be a bit distracting for a new user, so I've asked you to turn it off for now.

## Looking at an Alternative to Limits

As an alternative to setting up the drawing limits, you can draw a rectangle that outlines the same area used to define the drawing limits. For example, in the previous exercise, you could use the Rectangle tool to draw a rectangle that has its lower-left corner at coordinate 0,0 and its upper-right corner at 132,102 (297,210 for metric users). You can set up the rectangle to be visible without printing using the Layer feature. You'll learn more about layers in Chapter 5, "Keeping Track of Layers and Blocks."

**COORDINATING WITH PAPER SIZES**

At this point, you may have questions about how your full-scale drawing will fit onto standard paper sizes. AutoCAD offers several features that give you precise control over the scale of your drawing. These features offer industry-standard scales to match your drawing with any paper size you need. You'll learn more about these features as you work through the chapters of this book. However, if you're anxious to find out about them, look at the sections on layouts in Chapters 8 and 15 and also check out the Annotation Scale feature in Chapter 9.

## Understanding Scale Factors

When you draft manually, you work on the final drawing directly with pen and ink or pencil. With a CAD program, you're a few steps removed from the finished product. Because of this, you need a deeper understanding of your drawing scale and how it's derived. In particular, you need to understand *scale factors*. For example, one of the most common uses of scale factors is translating the size of a graphic symbol, such as a section symbol in an architectural drawing, to the final printed text size. When you draw manually, you draw your symbol at the size you want. In a CAD drawing, you need to translate the desired final symbol size to the drawing scale.

When you start adding graphic symbols to your drawing (see Chapter 4), you have to specify a symbol height. The scale factor helps you determine the appropriate symbol height for a particular drawing scale. For example, you may want your symbol to appear ½″ high in your final print. But if you draw your symbol to ½″ in your drawing, it appears as a dot when printed. The symbol has to be scaled up to a size that, when scaled back down at print time, appears ½″ high. For a ¼″-scale drawing, you multiply the ½″ text height by a scale factor of 48 to get 24″. Your symbol should be 24″ high in the CAD drawing in order to appear ½″ high in the final print.

Where did the number 48 come from? The scale factor for fractional inch scales is derived by multiplying the denominator of the scale by 12 and then dividing by the numerator. For example, the scale factor for ¼″ = 1′-0″ is (4 × 12) / 1, or 48/1. For ³⁄₁₆″ = 1′-0″ scale, the operation is (16 × 12) / 3, or 64. For whole-foot scales such as 1″ = 10′, multiply the feet side of the equation by 12. Metric scales require simple decimal conversions.

You can also use scale factors to determine your drawing limits. For example, if you have a sheet size of 11″ × 17″ and you want to know the equivalent full-scale size for a ¼″ scale drawing, you multiply the sheet measurements by 48. In this way, 11″ becomes 528″ (48 × 11″), and 17″ becomes 816″ (48 × 17″). Your work area must be 528″ × 816″ if you intend to have a final output of 11″ × 17″ at ¼″ = 1′. You can divide these inch measurements by 12″ to get 44′ × 68′.

Table 3.2 shows scale factors as they relate to standard drawing scales. These scale factors are the values by which you multiply the desired final printout size to get the equivalent full-scale size. If you're using the metric system, you can use the drawing scale directly as the scale factor. For example, a drawing scale of 1:10 has a scale factor of 10, a drawing scale of 1:50 has a scale factor of 50, and so on. Metric users need to take special care regarding the base unit. Centimeters are used as a base unit in the examples in this book, which means that if you enter a distance as 1, you can assume the distance to be 1 cm.

**TABLE 3.2:**     Scale conversion factors

| SCALE FACTOR FOR ENGINEERING DRAWING SCALES | DRAWING SCALE | | | | | | | |
|---|---|---|---|---|---|---|---|---|
| $n = 1''$ | 10´ | 20´ | 30´ | 40´ | 50´ | 60´ | 100´ | 200´ |
| Scale factor | 120 | 240 | 360 | 480 | 600 | 720 | 1200 | 2400 |
| **SCALE FACTORS FOR ARCHITECTURAL DRAWING SCALES** | **DRAWING SCALE** | | | | | | | |
| $n = 1´\text{-}0''$ | ¹⁄₁₆″ | ⅛″ | ¼″ | ½″ | ¾″ | 1″ | 1½″ | 3″ |
| Scale factor | 192 | 96 | 48 | 24 | 16 | 12 | 8 | 4 |

In older drawings, scale factors were used to determine text height and dimension settings. Chances are you will eventually have to work with drawings created by older AutoCAD releases, so understanding scale factors will pay off later. Printing to a particular scale is also easier with an understanding of scale factors.

## Using Polar Tracking

In this section, you'll draw the first item in the bathroom: the toilet. It's composed of a rectangle representing the tank and a truncated ellipse representing the seat. To construct the toilet, you'll use Polar Tracking, which is one of the most versatile drafting tools. Polar Tracking helps you align your cursor to exact horizontal and vertical angles, much like a T-square and triangle.

In this exercise, you'll use Polar Tracking to draw a rectangular box:

1. Start a line at the coordinate 5´-7″,6´-3″ by entering **L**↵ **5´7″,6´3″**↵. Metric users should enter **L**↵ **171,189**↵ as the starting coordinate. This starting point is somewhat arbitrary, but by entering a specific starting location, you're coordinated with the figures and instructions in this book. You can also use the Line tool in the Tool Sets palette to start the line.

2. Make sure Polar Tracking is on (the Polar Tracking tool in the status bar should be blue), and then point the cursor directly to the right of the last point. The Polar Tracking cursor appears along with the Polar Tracking readout.

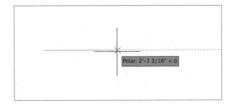

3. With the cursor pointing directly to the right, enter **1´-10″**↵. Metric users should enter **56**↵. You can use the spacebar in place of the ↵ key when entering distances in this way.

4. Point the cursor downward, enter **9**↵ for 9″, and click this point. Metric users should enter **23**↵.

5. Continue drawing the other two sides of the rectangle by using Polar Tracking. After you've completed the rectangle, press ↵ or the Esc key to exit the Line tool. You should have a drawing that looks like Figure 3.2.

**FIGURE 3.2**
A plan view of the toilet tank

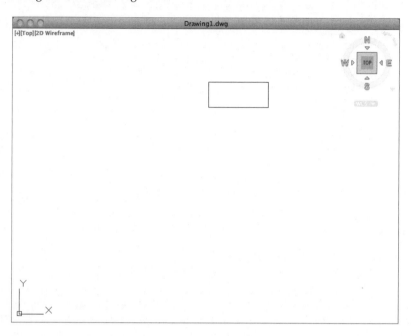

As you can see from the exercise, you can use Polar Tracking to restrain your cursor to horizontal and vertical positions, just as you would use a T-square and triangle. Later, you'll learn how you can set up Polar Tracking to set the angle to any value you want in a way similar to an adjustable triangle.

In some situations, you may find that you don't want Polar Tracking on. You can turn it off by clicking the Polar Tracking tool in the status bar.

Although this exercise tells you to use the Line tool to draw the tank, you can also use the Rectangle tool. The Rectangle tool creates what is known as a *polyline*, which is a set of line or arc segments that act like a single object. You'll learn more about polylines in Chapter 17, "Drawing Curves."

By using the Snap modes in conjunction with the coordinate readout and Polar Tracking, you can locate coordinates and measure distances as you draw lines. This is similar to the way you draw when using a scale. The smallest distance registered by the coordinate readout and Polar Tracking readout depends on the area you've displayed on your screen. For example, if you're displaying an area the size of a football field, the smallest distance you can indicate with your cursor may be 6″, or 15 cm. On the other hand, if your view is enlarged to show an area of only one square inch or centimeter, you can indicate distances as small as $\frac{1}{1000}$ of an inch or centimeter by using your cursor.

## Setting the Polar Tracking Angle

You've seen how Polar Tracking lets you draw exact vertical and horizontal lines. You can also set Polar Tracking to draw lines at other angles, such as 30° or 45°. To change the angle Polar Tracking uses, you use the Polar Tracking tab in the Drafting Settings dialog box (see Figure 3.3).

**FIGURE 3.3**

The Polar Tracking tab in the Drafting Settings dialog box

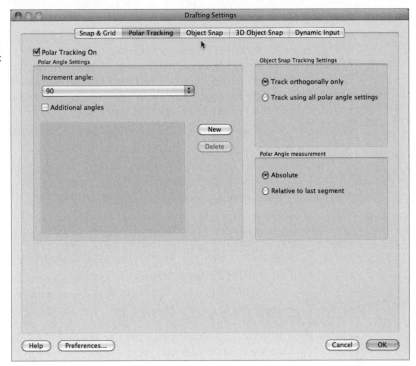

Right-click the Polar Tracking tool in the status bar, and then choose Settings from the shortcut menu to open the Drafting Settings dialog box. As an alternative, you can type **DS↵** and then click the Polar Tracking tab.

To change the Polar Tracking angle, enter an angle in the Increment Angle text box or select a predefined angle from the pop-up list. You can do this while drawing a series of line segments, for example, so that you can set angles on the fly.

---

### ORTHO MODE

Besides using Polar Tracking mode, you can restrain the cursor to a vertical or horizontal direction by using Ortho mode. To use Ortho mode, hold down ⇧ while drawing. You can also click Ortho Mode in the status bar to keep Ortho mode on while you draw. When you move the cursor around while drawing objects, the rubber-banding line moves only vertically or horizontally. With Ortho mode turned on, Polar Tracking is automatically turned off.

Numerous other settings are available in the Polar Tracking tab. Here is a listing of their functions for your reference:

**Additional Angles**   This setting lets you enter a specific angle for Polar Tracking. For example, if you want Polar Tracking to snap to 12°, click the New button next to the Additional Angles list box and enter 12. The value you enter appears in the list box, and when the Additional Angles check box is selected, Polar Tracking snaps to 12°. To delete a value from the list box, highlight it and click the Delete button.

The Additional Angles option differs from the Increment Angle setting in that the latter causes Polar Tracking to snap to every increment of its setting, whereas Additional Angles snaps only to the angle specified. You can enter as many angles as you want in the Additional Angles list box. As a shortcut, you can use the Polarang system variable (**Polarang.**↵) to set the incremental angle without using the dialog box.

**Object Snap Tracking Settings**   These settings let you control whether Object Snap Tracking uses strictly orthogonal directions (0°, 90°, 180°, and 270°) or the angles set in the Polar Angle Settings group in this dialog box. (See the section "Aligning Objects by Using Object Snap Tracking" later in this chapter.)

**Polar Angle Measurement**   These radio buttons let you determine the zero angle on which Polar Tracking bases its incremental angles. The Absolute option uses the current AutoCAD setting for the 0° angle. The Relative To Last Segment option uses the last drawn object as the 0° angle. For example, if you draw a line at a 10° angle and the Relative To Last Segment option is selected with Increment Angle set to 90°, Polar Tracking snaps to 10°, 100°, 190°, and 280°, relative to the actual 0° direction.

## Exploring the Drawing Process

The following sections present some of the most common AutoCAD commands and show you how to use them to complete a simple drawing. As you draw, watch the prompts and notice how your responses affect them. Also notice how you use existing drawing elements as reference points.

While drawing with AutoCAD, you create simple geometric forms to determine the basic shapes of objects, and you can then modify the shapes to fill in detail.

AutoCAD offers a number of basic 2D drawing object types; lines, arcs, circles, text, dimensions, traces, polylines, points, ellipses, elliptical arcs, spline curves, regions, hatches, and multiline text are the most common. All drawings are built on at least some of these objects. In addition, there are several 3D solids and meshes, which are three-dimensional shapes. You're familiar with lines and arcs; these, along with circles, are the most commonly used objects. As you progress through the book, you'll learn about the other objects and how they're used. You'll also learn about 3D objects in Part 4, "Modeling and Imaging."

### Locating an Object in Reference to Others

To define the toilet seat, you'll use an ellipse. Follow these steps:

1. Click the Center Ellipse tool in the Tool Sets palette, or type **El.**↵.

2. At the Specify center of ellipse: prompt, pick the midpoint of the bottom horizontal line of the rectangle. To do this, ⇧-right-click to open the Snap Overrides

shortcut menu and select Midpoint; then move the cursor toward the bottom line. (Remember, ⇧-two finger tap opens the Snap Overrides menu on a trackpad.) When you see the Midpoint Osnap marker on the line, left-click.

3. At the `Specify other endpoint of axis:` prompt, point the cursor downward and enter **1′-10″**↵. Metric users should enter **55**↵.

4. At the `Specify distance to other axis or [Rotation]:` prompt, point the cursor horizontally from the center of the ellipse and enter **8″**↵. Metric users should enter **20**↵. Your drawing should look like Figure 3.4.

**FIGURE 3.4**

The ellipse added to the tank

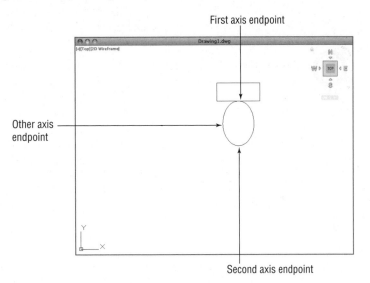

## Getting a Closer Look

During the drawing process, you'll often want to enlarge areas of a drawing to edit its objects. In Chapter 1, you saw how to use the Zoom capability for this purpose. Follow these steps to enlarge the view of the toilet:

1. Choose View ➢ Zoom ➢ Window from the menu bar, or type **Z**↵ **W**↵.

2. At the `Specify first corner:` prompt, pick a point below and to the left of your drawing, at or near coordinate 5′-0″,3′-6″. Metric users should use the coordinate 150.0000,102.0000.

3. At the `Specify opposite corner:` prompt, pick a point above and to the right of the drawing, at or near coordinate 8′-3″,6′-8″ (246.0000,195.0000 for metric users). The toilet should be completely enclosed by the zoom window. You can also use the Zoom tool in conjunction with the Pan tool on the status bar. The toilet enlarges to fill more of the screen. Your view should look similar to Figure 3.5 in the following section.

If you have a mouse with a scroll wheel, you can avoid using the Zoom command altogether. Just place the cursor on the toilet and turn the wheel to zoom into the image. For Magic Mouse users, use a one-finger vertical gesture on the Multi-Touch area of the mouse. Trackpad users can hold down ⌥ and use a two-finger vertical gesture.

## Modifying an Object

Now let's see how editing commands are used to construct an object. To define the back edge of the seat, let's put a copy of the line defining the front of the toilet tank 3″ (7 cm for metric users) toward the center of the ellipse:

1. Click the Copy tool in the Tool Sets palette, or type **CO**↵.

2. At the Select objects: prompt, pick the horizontal line that touches the top of the ellipse. The line is highlighted. Press ↵ to complete your selection.

3. At the Specify base point or [Displacement/mOde] <Displacement>: prompt, pick a base point near the line. Then point the cursor down and enter **3″**↵, or **7**↵ if you're a metric user.

4. Press ↵ to exit the Copy command. Your drawing should look like Figure 3.5.

**FIGURE 3.5**
The line
copied down

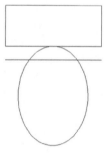

Notice that the Copy command acts exactly like the Move command you used in Chapter 2 except that Copy doesn't alter the position of the objects you select and you must press ↵ to exit Copy.

### TRIMMING AN OBJECT

Now you must delete the part of the ellipse that isn't needed. You'll use the Trim command to trim off part of the ellipse:

1. Click the Trim tool in the Tool Sets palette. You can also type **TR**↵. You'll see this prompt:

```
Current settings: Projection=UCS Edge=None
Select cutting edges ...
Select objects or <select all>:
```

2. Click the line you just created—the one that crosses through the ellipse—and press ↵ to finish your selection.

3. At the `Select object to trim or shift-select to extend or [Fence/Crossing/ Project/Edge/eRase/Undo]:` prompt, pick the topmost portion of the ellipse above the line. This trims the ellipse back to the line.

4. Press ↵ to exit the Trim command.

In step 1 of the preceding exercise, the Trim command produces two messages in the prompt. The first message, `Select cutting edges...`, tells you that you must first select objects to define *the edge to which you want to trim an object*. In step 3, you're again prompted to select objects, this time to select the *object to trim*. Trim is one of a handful of AutoCAD commands that asks you to select two sets of objects: The first set defines a boundary, and the second is the set of objects you want to edit. The two sets of objects aren't mutually exclusive. You can, for example, select the cutting-edge objects as objects to trim. The next exercise shows how this works.

First, you'll undo the trim you just did. Then, you'll use the Trim command again in a slightly different way to finish the toilet:

1. Press ⌘-Z or type **U**↵ to undo the last action. The top of the ellipse reappears.

2. Start the Trim tool again by clicking it in the Tool Sets palette.

3. At the `Select objects or <select all>:` prompt, click the ellipse and the line crossing through the ellipse. (See the first image in Figure 3.6.)

4. Press ↵ to finish your selection.

5. At the `Select object to trim or shift-select to extend or [Fence/Crossing/ Project/Edge/eRase/Undo]:` prompt, click the top portion of the ellipse, as you did in the previous exercise. The ellipse trims back.

6. Click a point near the left end of the trim line, outside the ellipse. The line trims back to the ellipse.

7. Click the other end of the line. The right side of the line trims back to meet the ellipse. Your drawing should look like the second image in Figure 3.6.

8. Press ↵ to exit the Trim command.

9. Choose File ➢ Save from the menu bar to save the file in its current state, but don't exit the file. You may want to get in the habit of doing this every 20 minutes.

Here you saw how the ellipse and the line are both used as trim objects as well as the objects to be trimmed. The Trim options you've seen so far—Fence, Crossing, Project, Edge, eRase, and Undo—are described in the next section in this chapter. Also note that by holding down ⇧ in step 4, you can change from trimming an object to extending an object.

**FIGURE 3.6**
Trimming the
ellipse and the line

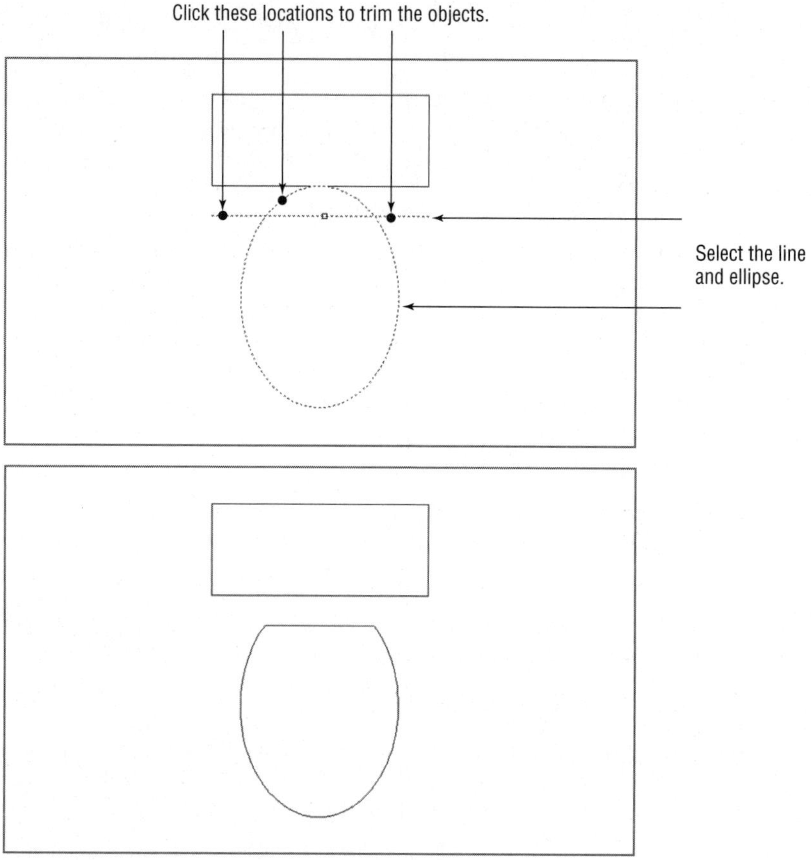

Click these locations to trim the objects.

Select the line
and ellipse.

### EXPLORING THE TRIM OPTIONS

AutoCAD offers six options for the Trim command: Fence, Crossing, Project, Edge, eRase, and Undo. As described in the following list, these options give you a higher degree of control over how objects are trimmed:

**Fence/Crossing [F or C]** Lets you use a fence or crossing window to select objects.

**Project [P]** Useful when you're working on 3D drawings. It controls how AutoCAD trims objects that aren't coplanar. Project offers three options: None, UCS, and View. The None option causes Trim to ignore objects that are on different planes so that only coplanar objects are trimmed. If you choose UCS, the Trim command trims objects based on a plan view of the current UCS and then disregards whether the objects are coplanar. (See the middle of Figure 3.7.) View is similar to UCS but uses the current view's "line of sight" to determine how non-coplanar objects are trimmed. (See the bottom of Figure 3.7.)

**FIGURE 3.7**

The Trim command's options

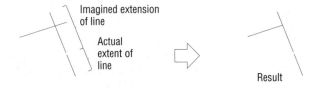

With the Extend option, objects will trim even if the trimmed object doesn't actually intersect with the object to be trimmed.

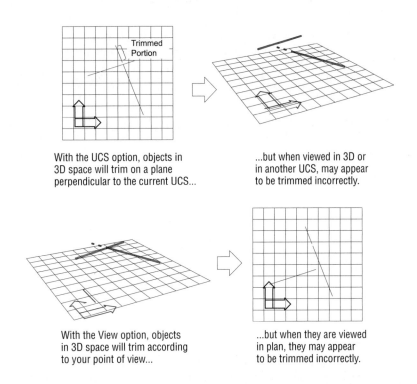

With the UCS option, objects in 3D space will trim on a plane perpendicular to the current UCS...

...but when viewed in 3D or in another UCS, may appear to be trimmed incorrectly.

With the View option, objects in 3D space will trim according to your point of view...

...but when they are viewed in plan, they may appear to be trimmed incorrectly.

**Edge [E]**   Lets you trim an object to an apparent intersection, even if the cutting-edge object doesn't intersect the object to be trimmed (see the top of Figure 3.7). Edge offers two options: Extend and No Extend. You can also set these options by using the Edgemode system variable.

**eRase [R]**   Allows you to erase an object while remaining in the Trim command.

**Undo [U]**   Causes the last trimmed object to revert to its original length.

You've just seen one way to construct the toilet. However, you can construct objects in many ways. For example, you can trim only the top of the ellipse, as you did in the first trim exercise, and then use the Grips feature to move the endpoints of the line to meet the endpoints of the ellipse. As you become familiar with AutoCAD, you'll start to develop your own ways of working, using the tools best suited to your style.

If you'd like to take a break, now is a good time. You can exit AutoCAD and then come back to the Bath drawing file when you're ready to proceed.

## Planning and Laying Out a Drawing

For the next object, the bathtub, you'll use some new commands to lay out parts of the drawing. This will help you get a feel for the kind of planning you must do to use AutoCAD effectively. You'll begin the bathtub by using the Line command to draw a rectangle 2'-8" × 5'-0" (81 cm × 152 cm for metric users) on the left side of the drawing area. For a change this time, you'll use a couple of shortcut methods built into AutoCAD: the Line command's keyboard shortcut and the Direct Distance method for specifying distance and direction.

First, though, you'll go back to the previous view of your drawing and arrange some more room to work. Follow these steps:

1. Return to your previous view, shown in Figure 3.8. A quick way to do this is to type **Z↵ P↵**. Your view returns to the one you had before the last Zoom command.

**FIGURE 3.8**
The view of the finished toilet after typing **Z↵ P↵**. You can also obtain this view by using View ➤ Zoom ➤ Previous or View ➤ Zoom ➤ All.

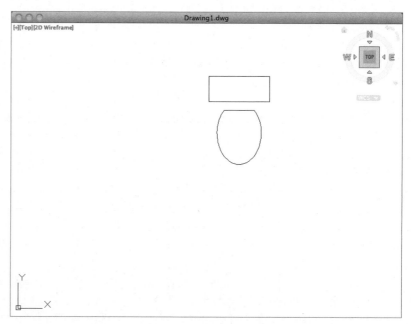

2. Type **L↵**, and then enter **9,10↵** to start the line at the 0'-9",0'-10" coordinate. Metric users should enter **24,27↵** for the coordinate 24.0000,27.0000.

3. Place your cursor to the right of the last point selected, so that the rubber-banding line is pointing directly to the right, and type **2'8"**. Then press ↵ for the first side of the tub. Metric users should enter **81↵**.

4. Point the rubber-banding line upward toward the top of the screen and type **5'**. Then press ↵ for the next side. Metric users should enter **152↵**.

5. Point the rubber-banding line directly to the left of the last point and type **2'8"** (**81** for metric users). Then press ↵ for the next side.

6. Type **C↵** to close the rectangle and exit the Line command.

Instead of pressing ↵ during the Direct Distance method, you can press the spacebar, or you can right-click and choose Enter from the shortcut menu.

Now you have the outline of the tub. Notice that you don't have to enter the at sign (@) or angle specification. Instead, you use the Direct Distance method to specify direction and distance. You can use this method for drawing lines or moving and copying objects at right angles. The Direct Distance method is less effective if you want to specify exact angles other than right angles.

---

**BE CAREFUL WITH HYPHENS**

When you enter feet and inches in the Command window, you must avoid hyphens or spaces. Thus, 2 feet 8 inches is typed as **2´8˝**. But be aware that hyphens are allowed when using the Direct Distance method.

---

The keyboard aliases for some of the tools or commands you've used in this chapter are CO (Copy), E (Erase), EL (Ellipse), F (Fillet), M (Move), O (Offset), and TR (Trim). Remember that you can enter keyboard aliases only when the Command prompt is visible in the Command Line palette.

## Making a Preliminary Sketch

In this section, you'll see how planning ahead will make your use of AutoCAD more efficient. When drawing a complex object, you'll often have to do some layout before you do the actual drawing. This is similar to drawing an accurate pencil sketch using construction lines that you later trace over to produce a finished drawing. The advantage of doing this in AutoCAD is that your drawing doesn't lose any accuracy between the sketch and the final product. Also, AutoCAD enables you to use the geometry of your sketch to aid in drawing. While you're planning your drawing, think about what you want to draw, and then decide which drawing elements will help you create that object.

You'll use the Offset command to establish reference lines to help you draw the inside of the tub. This is where the Osnap overrides are useful. (See the sidebar "The Osnap Options" later in this chapter.)

You can use the Offset tool on the Tool Sets palette to make parallel copies of a set of objects, such as the lines forming the outside of your tub. Offset is different from the Copy command; while Offset allows only one object to be copied at a time, it can remember the distance you specify. The Offset option doesn't work with all types of objects. Only lines, arcs, circles, ellipses, splines, and 2D polylines can be offset.

Standard lines are best suited to the layout of the bathtub in this situation. In Chapter 6, "Editing and Reusing Data To Work Efficiently," you'll learn about two other objects, construction lines and rays, that are specifically designed to help you lay out a drawing. In this exercise, you'll use standard lines:

1.  Click the Offset tool in the Tool Sets palette, or type **O**↵.

2.  At the `Specify offset distance or [Through/Erase/Layer] <Through>:` prompt, enter **3**↵. This specifies the distance of 3˝ as the offset distance. Metric users should enter **7** for 7 cm, which is roughly equivalent to 3˝.

**3.** At the `Select object to offset or [Exit/Undo] <Exit>:` prompt, click the bottom line of the rectangle you just drew.

**4.** At the `Specify point on side to offset or [Exit/Multiple/Undo]:` prompt, pick a point inside the rectangle. A copy of the line appears. You don't have to be exact about where you pick the side to offset; AutoCAD only wants to know on which side of the line you want to make the offset copy.

**5.** The prompt `Select object to offset or [Exit/Undo] <Exit>:` appears again. Click another side to offset. Then click again on a point inside the rectangle.

**6.** Continue to offset the other two sides. Then offset these four new lines inside the rectangle toward the center. You'll have a drawing that looks like Figure 3.9.

**7.** When you're done, exit the Offset command by pressing ↵.

**FIGURE 3.9**
The completed layout

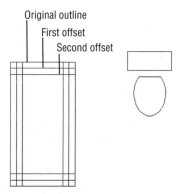

**Using the Layout**

Now you'll begin to draw the inside of the tub, starting with the narrow end. You'll use your offset lines as references to construct the arcs that make up the tub. Also in this exercise, you'll set up some of the osnap options to be available automatically whenever AutoCAD expects a point selection. Here are the steps:

**1.** Right-click the Object Snap tool in the status bar and select Settings from the shortcut menu. You can also type **OS**↵.

**2.** Click the Clear All button to turn off any options that may be selected.

Look at the graphic symbols next to each of the osnap options in the Object Snap tab. These are the Osnap markers that appear in your drawing as you select osnap points. Each osnap option has its own marker symbol. As you use the osnaps, you'll become more familiar with how they work.

**3.** Click the Endpoint, Midpoint, and Intersection check boxes so that a check mark appears in each box, and make sure the Object Snap On option is selected. Click OK (see Figure 3.10).

**FIGURE 3.10**

The Object Snap tab in the Drafting Settings dialog box

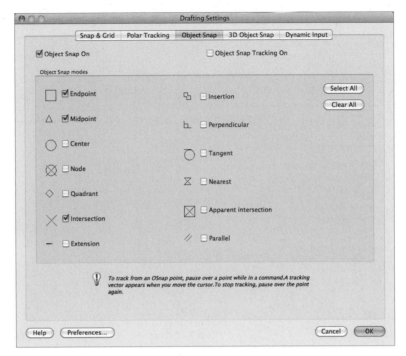

You've just set up the Endpoint, Midpoint, and Intersection osnaps to be on by default. This is called a *Running Osnap*; AutoCAD automatically selects the nearest osnap point without your intervention. Now let's see how a Running Osnap works:

1. First, turn off Dynamic Input in the status bar. This will help you see the osnap markers more easily.

2. Click the 3-Point Arc tool in the Tool Sets palette or type **A↵**. See Figure 3.11 for other Arc options available from the Draw menu on the menu bar.

3. For the first point of the arc, move the cursor toward the intersection of the two lines as indicated in the top image in Figure 3.12. Notice that the Intersection Osnap marker appears on the intersection.

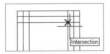

4. With the Intersection Osnap marker on the desired intersection, left-click.

5. Move the cursor to the midpoint of the second horizontal line near the top. When the Midpoint Osnap marker appears at the midpoint of the line, left-click.

**6.** Use the Intersection Osnap marker to locate and select the intersection of the two lines at the upper-left side of the bathtub.

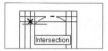

The top image in Figure 3.12 shows the sequence I just described.

**FIGURE 3.11**
The Draw ➤ Arc submenu on the menu bar offers several ways to draw an arc.

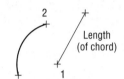

Center, Start, Length

Center, Start, Angle

Start, End, Direction

Center, Start, End

Start, End, Radius

Start, Center, Angle

Start, Center, Length
(of chord)

Start, Center, Angle

3-point

Start, Center, End

**FIGURE 3.12**
Drawing the top, left side, and bottom of the tub

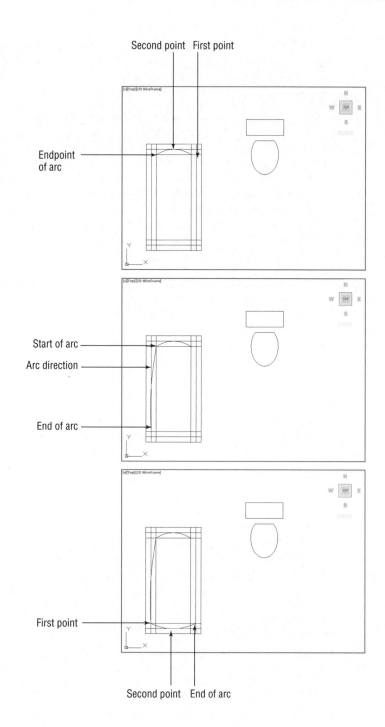

If you have several Running Osnap modes on (Endpoint, Midpoint, and Intersection, for example), pressing the Tab key cycles through those osnap points on the object. This feature can be especially useful in a crowded area of a drawing.

Next, you'll draw an arc for the left side of the tub:

1. Click the Arc tool in the Tool Sets palette again.

2. Type @↵ to select the last point you picked as the start of the next arc.

It's easy for new users to select points inadvertently. If you accidentally select additional points after the last exercise and prior to step 1, you may not get the results described here. If this happens, issue the Arc command again; then, use the Endpoint osnap and select the endpoint of the last arc.

3. Type E↵ to tell AutoCAD that you want to specify the other end of the arc instead of the next point. As another option, you can right-click anywhere in the drawing area and choose End from the shortcut menu.

4. At the Specify end point of arc: prompt, use the Intersection osnap to pick the intersection of the two lines in the lower-left corner of the tub. See the middle image in Figure 3.12 for the location of this point.

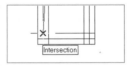

5. Type D↵ to select the Direction option. You can also right-click anywhere in the drawing area and then choose Direction from the shortcut menu. The arc drags as you move the cursor along with a rubber-banding line from the starting point of the arc.

Here, the rubber-banding line indicates the direction of the arc. Be sure Ortho mode is off because Ortho mode forces the rubber-banding line and the arc in a direction you don't want. Check the status bar; if the Ortho tool is blue (on), click it to turn off Ortho mode.

6. Turn off Object Snap and then move the cursor to the left of the dragging arc until it touches the middle line on the left side of the tub. When the arc looks like the arc shown in the middle image in Figure 3.12, click the mouse to fix the arc in place.

7. Turn Object Snap back on. You turned Object Snap off in step 6 because the lines are so crowded you might accidentally select a midpoint on one of the vertical lines representing the side of the tub.

Now, you'll draw the bottom of the tub:

1. Click the Arc tool in the Tool Sets palette again. You can also press ↵ to replay the last command.

2. Using the Endpoint Osnap marker, pick the endpoint of the bottom of the arc just drawn.

3. Using the Midpoint Osnap marker, pick the middle horizontal line at the bottom of the tub.

4. Pick the intersection of the two lines in the lower-right corner of the tub. (See the image at the bottom in Figure 3.12.)

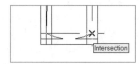

Next, create the right side of the tub by mirroring the left side:

1. Click the Mirror tool on the Tool Sets palette. You can also choose Modify ➤ Mirror from the menu bar or enter **MI**↵ at the Command prompt.

2. At the `Select objects:` prompt, pick the long arc on the left side of the tub to highlight the arc. Press ↵ to indicate that you've finished your selection.

3. At the `Specify first point of mirror line:` prompt, pick the midpoint of the top horizontal line. By now, you should know how to use the automatic osnap modes you set up earlier.

4. At the `Specify second point of mirror line:` prompt, use Polar Tracking mode to pick a point directly below the last point selected.

5. At the `Erase source objects? [Yes/No] <N>:` prompt, press ↵ to accept the Mirror command's default `Erase source objects` option (No) and exit the Mirror command. A mirror image of the arc you picked appears on the right side of the tub. Your drawing should look like Figure 3.13.

**FIGURE 3.13**
The inside of the tub completed with the layout lines still in place

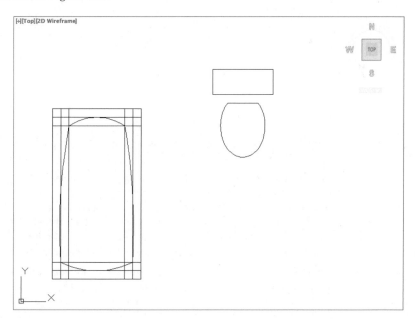

In this exercise, you were able to use osnaps in a Running Osnap mode. You'll find that you'll use osnaps constantly as you create your drawings. For this reason, you may want Running Osnaps on all the time. Even so, at times Running Osnaps can get in the way. For example, they may be a nuisance in a crowded drawing when you want to use a zoom window. The osnaps can cause you to select an inappropriate window area by automatically selecting osnap points.

Fortunately, you can toggle Running Osnaps on and off easily by clicking the Object Snap tool in the status bar. If you don't have any Running Osnaps set, clicking the Object Snap tool opens the Object Snap settings in the Drafting Settings dialog box, enabling you to select your osnaps. Or you can right-click the Object Snap tool and select Settings from the shortcut menu that appears.

---

### THE OSNAP OPTIONS

Earlier, you made several of the osnap settings automatic so they're available without having to select them from the Osnap shortcut menu. Another way to invoke the osnap options is to type their keyboard equivalents while selecting points or to ⇧-right-click (or ⇧-two-finger-tap on a trackpad) and select the osnap option you want to use from the Snap Overrides menu.

The following is a summary (in alphabetic order) of all the available osnap options, including their keyboard aliases. You've already used many of these options in this chapter and in the previous chapter. Pay special attention to those options you haven't yet used in the exercises but may find useful to your style of work. The full name of each option is followed by its keyboard shortcut name in parentheses. To use these options, you can enter either the full name or the abbreviation at any point prompt. You can also select these options from the pop-up menu obtained by ⇧-clicking the right mouse button.

**3D Osnaps**    Offers additional osnaps for 3D modeling. With these osnap options, you can select a vector that is perpendicular to a surface or find the midpoint of an edge of a 3D object.

**Apparent Intersection (app)**    Selects the apparent intersection of two objects. This is useful when you want to select the intersection of two objects that don't actually intersect. You'll be prompted to select the two objects.

**Center (cen)**    Selects the center of an arc or a circle. You must click the arc or circle itself, not its apparent center.

**Endpoint (endp or end)**    Selects the endpoints of lines, polylines, arcs, curves, and 3D Face vertices.

**Extension (ext)**    Selects a point that is aligned with an imagined extension of a line. For example, you can pick a point in space that is aligned with an existing line but isn't on that line. To use that point, type **EXT**↵ during point selection or select Extension from the Osnap pop-up menu. Then move the cursor to the line whose extension you want to use and hold it there until you see a small, cross-shaped marker on the line. The cursor also displays a tooltip with the word *extension*, letting you know that the Extension osnap is active.

**From (fro)**    Selects a point relative to a picked point. For example, you can select a point that is 2 units to the left and 4 units above a circle's center. This option is usually used in conjunction with another osnap option, such as From Endpoint or From Midpoint.

**Insert (ins)**   Selects the insertion point of text, blocks, Xrefs (see Chapters 4 and 7), and overlays.

**Intersection (int)**   Selects the intersection of objects.

**Mid Between 2 Points (m2p)**   Selects a point that is midway between two other points.

**Midpoint (mid)**   Selects the midpoint of a line or an arc. In the case of a polyline, it selects the midpoint of the polyline segment.

**Nearest (nea)**   Selects a point on an object nearest the pick point.

**Node (nod)**   Selects a point object.

**None (non)**   Temporarily turns off Running Osnaps for a single point selection.

**Parallel (par)**   Lets you draw a line segment that is parallel to another existing line segment. To use this option, type **PAR.⏎** during point selection, or select Parallel from the Osnap pop-up menu. Then move the cursor to the line you want to be parallel to and hold it there until you see a small, cross-shaped marker on the line. The cursor also displays a tool tip with the word *parallel*, letting you know that the Parallel osnap is active.

**Perpendicular (per)**   Selects a position on an object that is perpendicular to the last point selected.

**Point filters**   Not really object snaps, but point-selection options that let you filter X, Y, or Z coordinate values from a selected point. (See Chapter 19, "Creating 3D Drawings," for more on point filters.)

**Quadrant (qua)**   Selects the nearest cardinal (north, south, east, or west) point on an arc or a circle.

**Tangent (tan)**   Selects a point on an arc or a circle that represents the tangent from the last point selected.

**Temporary Track Point**   Provides an alternate method for using the Object Snap Tracking feature described later in this chapter.

Sometimes you'll want one or more of these osnap options available as the default selection. Remember that you can set Running Osnaps to be on at all times. Type **DS.⏎**, and then click the Object Snap tab. You can also right-click the Object Snap tool in the status bar and choose Settings from the shortcut menu to open the Drafting Settings dialog box, or just select osnap options directly from the shortcut menu.

## Erasing the Layout Lines

Next, you'll erase the layout lines you created using the Offset command. But this time, you'll try selecting the lines *before* issuing the Erase command.

Follow these steps:

1. Click each internal layout line individually.

   If you have problems selecting just the lines, try using a selection window to select single lines. (Remember, a window selects only objects that are completely within it.)

**2.** After all the inner layout lines are highlighted, enter **E↵** to use the keyboard command alias for the Erase command, or right-click and choose Erase from the shortcut menu. Your drawing will look like Figure 3.14.

If you right-clicked to use the shortcut menu in step 2, you'll notice that you have several options besides Erase. You can move, copy, scale, and rotate the objects you selected. These options are similar to the tools on the Tool Sets palette in the way they act. But be aware that they act somewhat differently from the hot-grip options described in Chapter 2.

If you need more control over the selection of objects, you'll find the Add/Remove Selection Mode setting useful. This setting lets you deselect a set of objects within a set of objects you've already selected. While in Object Selection mode, enter **R↵**, then proceed to use a window or other selection method to remove objects from the selection set. Enter **A↵** to continue to add options to the selection set. Or, if you need to deselect only a single object, ⇧-click it.

**FIGURE 3.14**

The drawing after erasing the layout lines

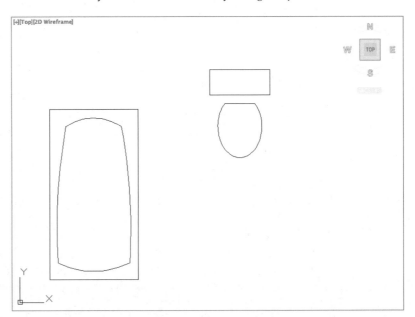

## Putting On the Finishing Touches

The inside of the tub still has some sharp corners. To round out these corners, you can use the versatile Fillet tool on the Tool Sets palette. Fillet enables you to join lines and arcs end to end, and it can add a radius where they join so there is a smooth transition from arc to arc or line to line. Fillet can join two lines that don't intersect, and it can trim two crossing lines back to their point of intersection.

Another tool, called Chamfer, performs a similar function, but instead of joining lines with an arc, Chamfer joins lines with another line segment. Since they perform similar functions, Fillet and Chamfer are next to each other on the Tool Sets palette.

Fillet ——→  ←—— Chamfer

Continue with your tutorial by following these steps:

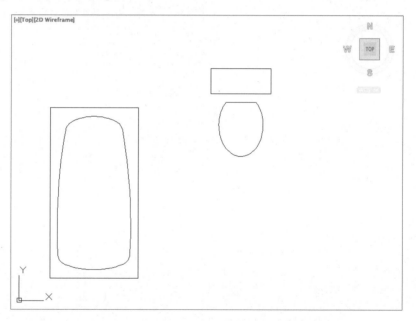

1. Click the Fillet tool on the Tool Sets palette, or type **F↵**.

2. At the prompt

   ```
   Current settings: Mode = TRIM, Radius = 0´-0 0˝
   Select first object or [Undo/Polyline/Radius/Trim/Multiple]:
   ```

   enter **R↵**, or right-click and choose Radius from the shortcut menu.

3. At the Specify fillet radius <0´-0˝>: prompt, enter **4↵**. This tells AutoCAD that you want a 4˝ radius for your fillet. Metric users should enter **10↵**.

4. Pick two adjacent arcs. The fillet arc joins the two larger arcs.

5. Press ↵ again, and fillet another corner. Repeat until all four corners are filleted. Your drawing should look like Figure 3.15.

**FIGURE 3.15**
A view of the fin-
ished toilet and
tub with the tub
corners filleted

## Aligning Objects by Using Object Snap Tracking

You saw how to use lines to construct an object such as the bathtub. In many situations, using these *construction lines* is the most efficient way to draw, but they can also be a bit cumbersome. AutoCAD offers another tool that helps you align locations in your drawing to existing objects without having to draw intermediate construction lines. The tool is called *Object Snap Tracking*, or *Osnap Tracking*.

Osnap Tracking is like an extension of object snaps that enables you to *align* a point to the geometry of an object instead of just selecting a point on an object. For example, with Osnap Tracking, you can select a point that is exactly at the center of a rectangle.

In the following exercises, you'll draw a plan view of a bathroom sink as an introduction to the Osnap Tracking feature. This drawing will be used as a symbol in later chapters.

### GETTING SET UP

First, as a review, you'll create a new file. Because this drawing will be used as a symbol for insertion in other CAD drawings, don't worry about setting it up to conform to a sheet size. Chances are you won't be printing individual symbols. Here are the steps:

1. Choose File ➤ New from the menu bar to create a new drawing for your bathroom sink.

2. As before, choose `acad.dwt` from the Select Template dialog box (Figure 3.16) or select `acadiso.dwt` if you are using the metric system.

**FIGURE 3.16**
The Select Template dialog box

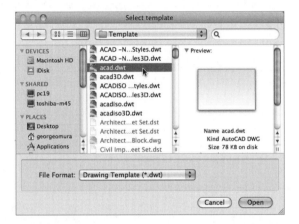

3. Click Open to open the new file.

4. Choose Format ➤ Units from the menu bar.

5. In the Drawing Units dialog box, choose Architectural from the Type pop-up list and then click Save. Metric users can use the default Decimal option.

6. Choose Format ➤ Drawing Limits from the menu bar.

7. Press ↵ to accept the origin of the drawing as the lower-left corner of the drawing limits.

8. Enter **48,36**↵ for the upper-right corner. Metric users should enter **122,92**↵.

9. Type **Z**↵ **A**↵ to display the overall area of the drawing set by the limits.

10. Choose File ➤ Save As from the menu bar to save the file under the name `Sink`.

If you find that you use the same drawing setup over and over, you can create template files that are already set up to your own, customized way of working. Templates are discussed in Chapter 6.

### DRAWING THE SINK

You're ready to draw the sink. First, you'll draw the sink countertop. Then, you'll make sure Running Osnaps and Osnap Tracking are turned on. Finally, you'll draw the bowl of the sink.
Here are the steps for drawing the outline of the sink countertop:

1. If the grid is on, click the Grid tool in the status bar to turn it off.

2. Click the Rectangle tool in the Tool Sets palette, or type **rec↵**.

3. At the prompt

   ```
   Specify first corner point or [Chamfer/Elevation/Fillet/Thickness/Width]:
   ```

   enter **0,0↵**. This places one corner of the rectangle in the origin of the drawing.

4. At the `Specify other corner point or [Area/Dimensions/Rotation]:` prompt, enter **@2´4,1´6↵** to place the other corner of the rectangle. Metric users should enter **@71,46↵**. This makes the rectangle 2´-4″ wide and 1´-6″ deep, or 71 cm wide and 46 cm deep for metric users. The rectangle appears in the lower half of the drawing area.

5. Click View ➢ Zoom ➢ Extents from the menu bar or type **Z↵ E↵**. This enlarges the view of the sink outline so it fits in the drawing area.

6. Use the Zoom tool in the status bar to adjust your view so it looks similar to the one shown in Figure 3.17. You can also enter **Z↵↵** to start the real-time zoom feature or just use your scroll wheel or Multi-Touch feature on your Magic Mouse or trackpad.

**FIGURE 3.17**
The view of the sink countertop after you've made some adjustments

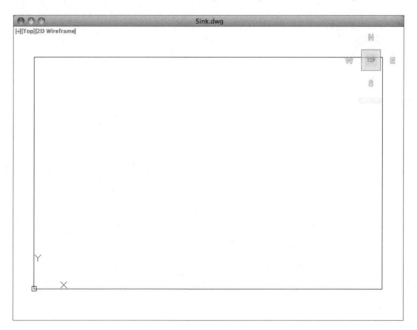

When you draw the bowl of the sink, the bowl will be represented by an ellipse. You want to place the center of the ellipse at the center of the rectangle you've just drawn. To do this, you'll use the midpoint of two adjoining sides of the rectangle as alignment locations. This is where the Osnap Tracking tool will be useful.

You need to make sure that both the Object Snap tool and the Midpoint Object Snap option are turned on. Then you'll make sure Osnap Tracking is turned on. Use these steps:

1. Right-click the Object Snap Tracking tool in the status bar and choose Settings from the shortcut menu to open the Drafting Settings dialog box at the Object Snap tab (see Figure 3.18).

2. Make sure the Midpoint check box in the Object Snap Modes group is selected.

3. Also make sure Object Snap On and Object Snap Tracking On are both selected. Click OK. You'll notice that the Object Snap and Object Snap Tracking tools in the status bar are now in the on position.

**FIGURE 3.18**

The Object Snap tab in the Drafting Settings dialog box

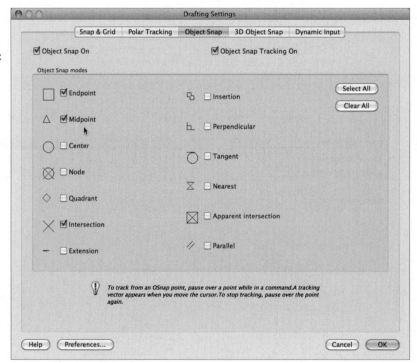

Finally, you're ready to draw the ellipse:

1. Click the Center Ellipse tool in the Tool Sets palette. You can also choose Draw ➢ Ellipse ➢ Center from the menu bar or enter **EL⏎ C⏎**.

2. Move your cursor to the top, horizontal edge of the rectangle until you see the Midpoint tool tip.

3. Move the cursor directly over the Midpoint Osnap marker. Without clicking the mouse, hold the cursor there for a second until you see a small cross appear. Look carefully, because the cross is small. This is the Object Snap Tracking marker (see Figure 3.19).

**FIGURE 3.19**

The Object Snap Tracking marker

Alternatively, you can insert and remove the Object Snap Tracking marker by passing the cursor over the Osnap marker.

4. As you move the cursor downward, a dotted line appears, emanating from the midpoint of the horizontal line. The cursor also shows a small X following the dotted line as you move it (see Figure 3.20).

**FIGURE 3.20**

A vertical dotted line appears.

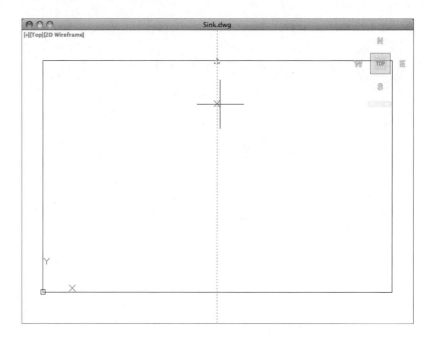

**FIGURE 3.20**

A vertical dotted line appears.

5. Move the cursor to the midpoint of the left vertical side of the rectangle. Don't click, but hold it there for a second until you see the small cross. Now as you move the cursor away, a horizontal dotted line appears with an *X* following the cursor (see Figure 3.21).

**FIGURE 3.21**

A horizontal dotted line appears.

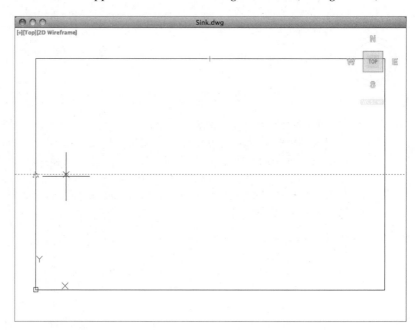

6. Move the cursor to the center of the rectangle. The two dotted lines appear simultaneously and a small *X* appears at their intersection (see Figure 3.22).

**FIGURE 3.22**
The vertical and horizontal dotted lines appear simultaneously.

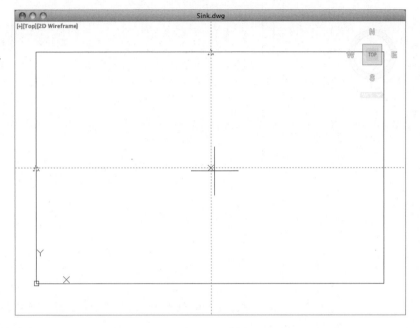

7. With the two dotted lines crossing and the *X* at their intersection, left-click to select the exact center of the rectangle.

8. Point the cursor to the right, and enter **8.**↵ to make the width of the bowl 16˝. Metric users should enter **20.**↵ for a bowl 40 cm wide.

9. Point the cursor downward, and enter **6.**↵ to make the length of the bowl 12˝. Metric users should enter **15.**↵ for a bowl with a length of 30 cm. The basic symbol for the sink is complete (see Figure 3.23).

10. Choose File ➢ Save from the menu bar and close the current file. You can also save and close the Bath file and exit AutoCAD.

In this exercise, you saw how Object Snap Tracking enables you to align two locations to select a point in space. Although you used only the Midpoint osnap setting in this exercise, you aren't limited to one osnap setting. You can use as many as you need to select the appropriate geometry. You can also use as many alignment points as you need, although in this exercise you used only two. If you like, erase the ellipse and repeat this exercise until you get the hang of using the Object Snap Tracking feature.

As with all the other tools in the status bar, you can turn Object Snap Tracking on or off by clicking the Object Snap Tracking tool.

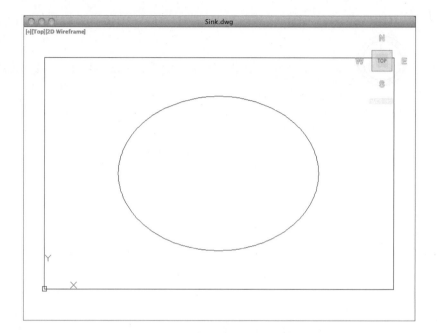

**FIGURE 3.23**
The completed bathroom sink

## Using the AutoCAD Modes as Drafting Tools

Before you finish this chapter, you'll want to know about a few of the other drafting tools that are common to drawing programs. These tools may be compared to a background grid (*Grid mode*) and the ability to "snap" to grid points (*Snap modes*). These drawing modes can be indispensable tools under certain conditions. Their use is fairly straightforward. You can experiment with them on your own using the information in the following sections.

### Using Grid Mode as a Background Grid

Using Grid mode is like having a grid under your drawing to help you with layout, as shown in Figure 3.24. In this figure, the grids are set to a 1′ spacing with major grid lines at 5′. The grid also shows, in darker lines, the X and Y axes that start at the origin of the drawing.

Grids will not print in your final output. They are a visual aid to help you gauge distances. In AutoCAD, Grid mode can also let you see the limits of your drawing because the grid can be set to display only within the limits setting of your drawing. Grid mode can help you visually determine the distances with which you're working in any given view. In this section, you'll learn how to control the grid's appearance. You can also click the Grid Display tool in the status bar.

**FIGURE 3.24**
A sample drawing showing the grids turned on

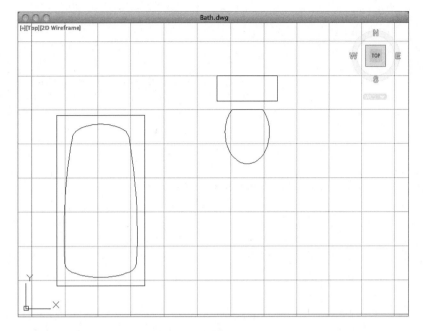

## USING OBJECT SNAP TRACKING AND POLAR TRACKING TOGETHER

In addition to selecting as many tracking points as you need, you can use different angles besides the basic orthogonal angles of 0°, 90°, 180°, and 270°. For example, you can have AutoCAD locate a point that is aligned vertically to the top edge of the sink and at a 45° angle from a corner.

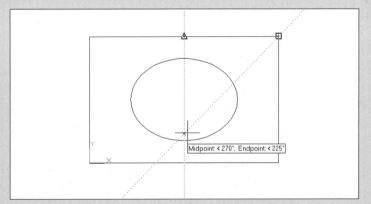

This can be accomplished by using the settings in the Polar Tracking tab of the Drafting Settings dialog box. (See the section "Setting the Polar Tracking Angle" earlier in this chapter.) If you set the increment angle to 45° and turn on the Track Using All Polar Angle Settings option, you'll be able to use 45° in addition to the orthogonal directions. You'll see firsthand how this works in Chapter 6.

To set up the grid spacing, follow these steps:

1. Right-click the Grid Display tool in the status bar and select Settings (or type **DS↵**) to open the Drafting Settings dialog box, showing all the mode settings.

2. Click the Snap & Grid tab if it isn't already selected. You see six groups: Snap Spacing, Grid Style, Polar Spacing, Grid Spacing, Snap Type, and Grid Behavior. Notice that the Grid X Spacing text box contains a value of 1/2″. Metric users see a value of 10 (see Figure 3.25).

3. Enter the grid spacing you want in the Grid X Spacing and Grid Y Spacing input boxes.

4. Click the Grid On check box to make the grid visible. Click OK to dismiss the Drafting Settings dialog box and save your settings.

If you prefer, you can use the Gridunit system variable to set the grid spacing. Enter **Gridunit↵**, and at the Enter new value for GRIDUNIT <0´-0 ″,0´-0 ″>: prompt, enter a grid spacing in X,Y coordinates. You must enter the Gridunit value as an X,Y coordinate.

There are several other grid options in the Drafting Settings dialog box. The Grid Style group lets you display the grid as a series of dots instead of the graph-paper-style lines. Place a check by the view name where you want to display dots instead of grid lines.

**FIGURE 3.25**
The Snap & Grid tab of the Drafting Settings dialog box

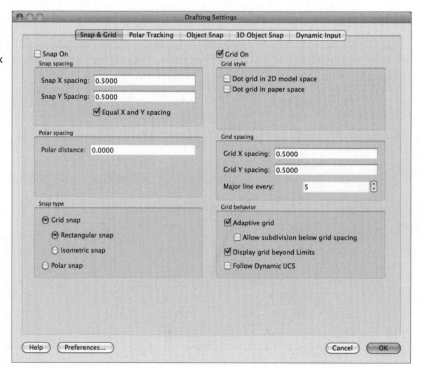

In the Grid Spacing group, the Major Line Every option lets you control how frequently the major grid lines (lines that appear darker than the others) appear.

In the Grid Behavior group, the Adaptive Grid option adjusts the grid spacing depending on how much of the view is displayed. If you zoom out to a point where the grid becomes too dense to view the drawing, the grid automatically increases its interval. The Display Grid Beyond Limits check box lets you determine whether the grid displays outside the limits of the drawing.

Once you've set up your grid, you can press ⌘-G to turn the grid on and off.

## Using the Snap Modes

The *Snap modes* force the cursor to move in steps of a specific distance. Snap modes are useful when you want to select points on the screen at a fixed interval. Two snap modes are available in AutoCAD: *Grid Snap* and *Polar Snap*. You can click the Snap tool in the status bar to turn the Snap mode on and off. Follow these steps to access the Snap modes:

1. Right-click the Grid Display tool in the status bar and select Settings (or type **DS**↵) to open the Drafting Settings dialog box.

2. In the Snap Spacing group of the dialog box, double-click the Snap X Spacing text box and enter a value for your snap spacing. Then press the Tab key to move to the next option. AutoCAD assumes you want the X and Y snap spacing to be the same unless you specifically ask for a different Y setting.

3. You can click the Snap On check box to turn on Snap mode from this dialog box.

4. Click OK to save your settings and close the dialog box.

With Snap mode on, the cursor seems to move in steps rather than in a smooth motion. The Snap Mode tool in the status bar appears blue, indicating that Snap mode is on. Click the Snap Mode tool in the status bar to turn Snap mode on or off.

Note that you can use the Snapunit system variable to set the snap spacing. Enter **Snapunit**↵. Then, at the `Enter new value for SNAPUNIT <0´0˝,0´0˝>:` prompt, enter a snap distance value as an X,Y coordinate.

Take a moment to look at the Drafting Settings dialog box in Figure 3.25. The other option in the Snap Spacing group enables you to force the X and Y spacing to be equal (Equal X and Y Spacing).

In the Snap Type group, you can change the snap and grid configuration to aid in creating 2D isometric drawings by clicking the Isometric Snap radio button. The Polar Snap option enables you to set a snap distance for the Polar Snap feature. When you click the Polar Snap radio button, the Polar Distance option at the middle left of the dialog box changes from gray to black and white to allow you to enter a Polar Snap distance.

You can also set up the grid to follow the snap spacing automatically. To do this, set Grid X Spacing and Grid Y Spacing to 0 in the Snap Spacing group.

## The Bottom Line

**Set up a work area.** A blank AutoCAD drawing offers few clues about the size of the area you're working with, but you can get a rough idea of the area shown in the drawing window.

**Master It** Name two ways to set up the area of your work.

**Explore the drawing process.** To use AutoCAD effectively, you'll want to know how the different tools work together to achieve an effect. The drawing process often involves many cycles of adding objects and then editing them.

**Master It** Name the tool that causes the cursor to point in an exact horizontal or vertical direction.

**Plan and lay out a drawing.** If you've ever had to draw a precise sketch with just a pencil and pad, you've probably used a set of lightly drawn guidelines to lay out your drawing first. You do the same thing in AutoCAD, but instead of lightly drawn guidelines, you can use any object you want. In AutoCAD, objects are easily modified or deleted, so you don't have to be as careful when adding guidelines.

**Master It** What is the name of the feature that lets you select exact locations on objects?

**Use the AutoCAD modes as drafting tools.** The main reason for using AutoCAD is to produce precise technical drawings. AutoCAD offers many tools to help you produce a drawing with the precision you need.

**Master It** What dialog box lets you set both the grid and snap spacing?

# Chapter 4

# Organizing Objects with Blocks and Groups

Drawing the tub, toilet, and sink in Chapter 3, "Setting Up and Using AutoCAD's Drafting Tools," may have taken what seemed to you an inordinate amount of time. As you continue to use AutoCAD, however, you'll learn to draw objects more quickly. You'll also need to draw fewer of them because you can save drawings as symbols and then use those symbols like rubber stamps, duplicating drawings instantaneously wherever they're needed. This saves a lot of time when you're composing drawings.

To make effective use of AutoCAD, begin a *symbol library* of drawings you use frequently. A mechanical designer might have a library of symbols for fasteners, cams, valves, or other parts used in their application. An electrical engineer might have a symbol library of capacitors, resistors, switches, and the like. A circuit designer will have yet another unique set of frequently used symbols.

In Chapter 3, you drew three objects—a bathtub, a toilet, and a sink—that architects often use. In this chapter, you'll see how to create symbols from those drawings.

In this chapter, you'll learn to do the following:

◆ Create and insert a block

◆ Modify a block

◆ Understand the annotation scale

◆ Group objects

## Creating a Block

In word processors, the term *block* refers to a group of words or sentences selected for moving, saving, or deleting. You can copy a block of text elsewhere within the same file, to other files, or to a separate location on a server or USB storage device for future use. AutoCAD uses blocks in a similar fashion. In a file, you can turn parts of your drawing into blocks that can be saved and recalled at any time. You can also use existing drawing files as blocks.

You'll start by opening the file you worked on in the previous chapter and selecting the objects that will become a block:

1. Start AutoCAD, and open the existing Bath file. Use the one you created in Chapter 3, or open the 04-bath.dwg sample file from this book's companion website, www.sybex.com/go/masteringautocadmac. Metric users can use the 04-bath-metric.dwg file. The drawing appears just as you left it in the last session.

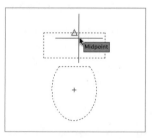

2. In the Tool Sets palette, click the Create icon, which starts the Block command. You can also choose Draw ➤ Block ➤ Make or type **B**↵, the keyboard alias for the Block command. This opens the Define Block dialog box (see Figure 4.1).

3. In the Name text box, type **Toilet**.

4. In the Base Point group, click the Pick Point button. This option enables you to select a base point for the block by using your cursor. (The *insertion base point* of a block is a point of reference on the block that is used like a grip.) When you've selected this option, the Define Block dialog box temporarily closes.

   Notice that the Define Block dialog box gives you the option to specify the X, Y, and Z coordinates for the base point instead of selecting a point.

5. Using the Midpoint Osnap, pick the midpoint of the back of the toilet as the base point. Remember that you learned how to set up Running Osnaps in Chapter 3; all you need to do is point to the midpoint of a line to display the Midpoint Osnap marker and then left-click.

   After you've selected a point, the Define Block dialog box reappears. Notice that the X, Y, and Z values in the Base Point group now display the coordinates of the point you picked. For two-dimensional drawings, the Z coordinate should remain at 0.

   Next, you need to select the objects you want as part of the block.

6. Click the Select Objects icon in the Source Objects group. Once again, the dialog box momentarily closes. You now see the familiar Select objects: prompt in the Command Line palette, and the cursor becomes an Object Selection cursor. Click and drag from a point below and to the left of the toilet. Use the selection window to select the entire toilet. The toilet is now highlighted.

7. Press ↵ to confirm your selection. The Define Block dialog box opens again.

8. Select Inches from the Block Unit pop-up list. Metric users should select Centimeters.

FIGURE 4.1
The Define Block
dialog box

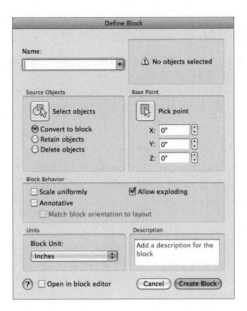

9. Click the Description list box, and enter **Standard Toilet**.

10. Make sure the Retain Objects radio button in the Source Objects group is selected, and then click Create Block. The toilet drawing is now a block with the name Toilet.

11. Repeat the blocking process for the tub, but this time use the upper-left corner of the tub as the insertion base point and give the block the name Tub. Enter **Standard Tub** for the description.

   You can press ↵ or right-click and choose Repeat BLOCK from the shortcut menu to start the Block command again.

When you turn an object into a block, it's stored in the drawing file, ready to be recalled at any time. The block remains part of the drawing file even when you end the editing session. When you open the file again, the block is available for your use. In addition, you can access blocks from other drawings by using the AutoCAD Content palette, which you'll learn about later in this chapter.

A block acts like a single object, even though it's really made up of several objects. One unique characteristic of a block is that when you modify it, all instances of it are updated to reflect the modifications. For example, if you insert several copies of the toilet into a drawing and then later decide the toilet needs to be a different shape, you can edit the Toilet block and all the other copies of the toilet are updated automatically.

You can modify a block in a number of ways after it has been created. In this chapter, you'll learn how to make simple changes to individual blocks by modifying the block's properties. For more detailed changes, you'll learn how to redefine a block after it has been created. Later in this chapter, you'll learn how to use the Block Editor to make changes to blocks.

**MAKE SURE YOU SELECT OBJECTS WHEN CREATING BLOCKS**

Make sure you use the Select Objects option in the Define Block dialog box to select the objects you want to turn into a block. AutoCAD lets you create a block that contains no objects, but if you try to proceed without selecting objects, you'll get a warning message. This can cause confusion and frustration, even for an experienced user.

## Understanding the Define Block Dialog Box

The Define Block dialog box offers several options that can help make using blocks easier. If you're interested in these options, take a moment to review the Define Block dialog box as you read the descriptions. If you prefer, you can continue with the tutorial and come back to this section later.

You've already seen how the Name option lets you enter a name for your block. AutoCAD doesn't let you complete the block creation until you enter a name.

You've also seen how to select a base point for your block. The base point is like the grip of the block: it's the reference point you use when you insert the block back into the drawing. In the exercise, you used the Pick Point option to indicate a base point, but you also have the option to enter X, Y, and Z coordinates just below the Pick Point option. In most cases, however, you'll want to use the Pick Point option to indicate a base point that is on or near the set of objects you're converting to a block.

The Source Objects group of the Define Block dialog box lets you select the objects that make up the block. You use the Select Objects button to visually select the objects you want to include in the block you're creating. Once you select a set of objects for your block, you'll see a thumbnail preview of the block's contents near the top center of the Define Block dialog box.

Other options in the Source Objects group and Block Behavior group let you specify what to do with the objects you're selecting for your block. Table 4.1 shows a list of the options and what they mean.

**TABLE 4.1:** The Define Block dialog box options

| OPTION | PURPOSE |
| --- | --- |
| **Source Objects group** | |
| Select Objects | Lets you select the objects for the block after you click Create Block. |
| Convert To Block | Converts the objects you select into the block you're defining. The block then acts like a single object after you've completed the Block command. |
| Retain Objects | Keeps the objects you select for your block as they are, unchanged. |

**TABLE 4.1:**     The Define Block dialog box options     *(CONTINUED)*

| OPTION | PURPOSE |
| --- | --- |
| Delete Objects | Deletes the objects you selected for your block. You may also notice that a warning message appears at the bottom of the Source Objects group. This warning appears if you haven't selected objects for the block. After you've selected objects, the warning changes to tell you how many objects you've selected. |
| **Base Point group** | |
| Pick Point | Lets you select the base point for the block before you click Create Block to dismiss the dialog box. |
| X, Y, and Z input boxes | Enable you to enter exact coordinates for the block's base point. |
| **Block Behavior group** | |
| Scale Uniformly | By default, blocks can have a different X, Y, or Z scale. This means they can be stretched in any of the axes. You can lock the X, Y, and Z scale of the block by selecting this option. That way, the block will always be scaled uniformly and can't be stretched in one axis. |
| Allow Exploding | By default, blocks can be exploded or reduced to their component objects. You can lock a block so that it can't be exploded by turning off this option. You can always turn on this option later through the Properties Inspector palette if you decide that you need to explode a block. |
| Annotative | Turns on the Annotative scale feature for blocks. This feature lets you use a single block for different scale views of a drawing. With this feature turned on, AutoCAD can be set to adjust the size of the block to the appropriate scale for the drawing. |
| Match Block Orientation To Layout | With the Annotative option turned on, this option is available. This option causes a block to appear always in its normal orientation regardless of the orientation of the layout view. |
| Block Unit | Lets you determine how the object is to be scaled when it's inserted into the drawing using the Content palette. By default, this value is the same as the current drawing's Insert value. |
| Description | Lets you include a brief description or keyword for the block. This option is helpful when you need to find a specific block in a set of drawings. |
| Open In Block Editor | If you turn on this option, the block is created and then opened in the Block Editor, described later in this chapter. |

## Inserting a Symbol

You can recall the Tub and Toilet blocks at any time, as many times as you want. In this section, you'll draw the interior walls of the bathroom first, and then you'll insert the tub and toilet. Follow these steps to draw the walls:

1. Delete the original tub and toilet drawings. Click the Erase icon in the Tool Sets palette, and then enter **All**⏎ to erase the entire visible contents of the drawing. (Doing so has no effect on the blocks you created previously.)

2. Draw a rectangle 7′-6″ × 5′. Metric users should draw a 228 cm × 152 cm rectangle. Orient the rectangle so the long sides go from left to right and the lower-left corner is at coordinate 1′-10″,1′-10″ (or coordinate 56.0000,56.0000 for metric users).

If you use the Rectangle icon to draw the rectangle, make sure you explode it by using the Explode command (Modify ➤ Explode from the menu bar). This is important for later exercises. (See the section "Unblocking and Redefining a Block" later in this chapter if you aren't familiar with the Explode command.) Your drawing should look like Figure 4.2.

**FIGURE 4.2**
The interior walls
of the bathroom

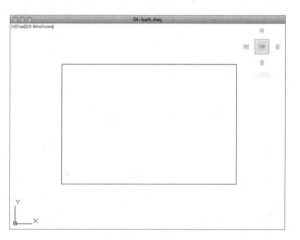

Now you're ready to place your blocks. Start by placing the tub in the drawing:

1. In the Tool Sets palette, click the Insert icon. You can also choose Insert ➤ Block from the menu bar or type **I**⏎ to open the Insert Block dialog box (see Figure 4.3).

**FIGURE 4.3**
The Insert Block
dialog box

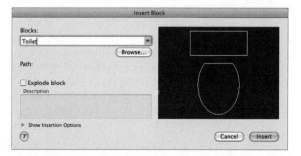

2. Click the Blocks pop-up list to display a list of the available blocks in the current drawing.

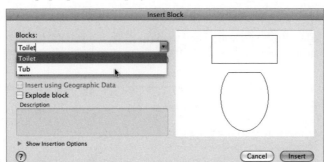

3. Click the block name Tub.

4. Click Insert and you will see a preview image of the tub attached to the cursor. The upper-left corner you picked for the tub's base point is now on the cursor intersection.

5. At the Specify insertion point or [Basepoint/Scale/X/Y/Z/Rotate]: prompt, pick the upper-left intersection of the room as your insertion point. The tub should look like the one in Figure 4.4.

**FIGURE 4.4**

The bathroom, first with the tub and then with the toilet inserted

Tub insertion point at corner of room

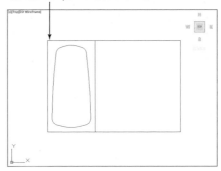

Toilet insertion point at coordinates 5'-8", 6'-10" [170,208 metric]

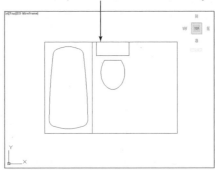

You've got the tub in place. Now place the Toilet block in the drawing:

1. Open the Insert Block dialog box again, but this time select Toilet in the Blocks pop-up list.

2. Click the Insert button and then place the toilet at the location on the line along the top of the rectangle representing the bathroom wall, as shown in the bottom image in Figure 4.4.

 **Real World Scenario**

### SYMBOLS FOR PROJECTS LARGE AND SMALL

A symbol library was a crucial part of the production of the San Francisco Main Library construction documents. Shown here is a portion of an AutoCAD floor plan of the library in which some typical symbols were used.

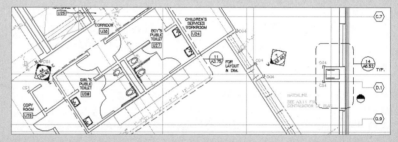

Notice the familiar symbols, such as the symbol for the door you created in Chapter 2, "Creating Your First Drawing." And yes, there are even toilets in the lower half of the plan in the public restrooms. Symbol use isn't restricted to building components. Room-number labels, diamond-shaped interior elevation reference symbols, and the hexagonal column grid symbols are all common to an architectural drawing, regardless of the project's size. As you work through this chapter, keep in mind that all the symbols used in the library drawing were created using the tools presented here.

## Scaling and Rotating Blocks

When you insert the tub, you have the option to scale or rotate the block before you place it in the drawing. After you have closed the Insert Block dialog box and before you click a location for the block, you can enter **S↵** and enter a scale value or enter **R↵** and enter a rotation angle. In addition, if you don't like the point on the block that is used for the insertion, you can change it by entering **B↵** and selecting a new insertion point.

You aren't limited to scaling or rotating a block when it's being inserted into a drawing. You can always use the Scale or Rotate icon or modify an inserted block's properties to stretch it in one direction or another. This exercise shows you how this is done:

1. Click the Toilet block to select it.

2. In the Properties Inspector palette, click the All button. Take a moment to study the properties that appear. Toward the bottom, under the Geometry heading, you see a set of labels that show *Position* and *Scale*.

**3.** Let's try making some changes to the toilet properties. Click the Scale X text box just to the right of the Scale X label.

**4.** Enter **1.5↵**. Notice that the toilet changes in width as you do this.

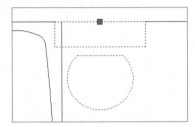

**5.** You don't really want to change the width of the toilet, so click in the Scale X text box and enter **1↵** to change the Scale X value back to 1. Press the Esc key to clear the selection.

If a block is created with the Scale Uniformly option turned on in the Define Block dialog box, you can't scale the block in just one axis as shown in the previous exercise. You can only scale the block uniformly in all axes.

You've just seen how you can modify the properties of a block by using the Properties Inspector palette. In the exercise, you changed the X scale of the Toilet block, but you could have just as easily changed the Y value. You may have noticed other properties available in the Properties Inspector palette. You'll learn more about those properties as you work through this chapter.

You've seen how you can turn a drawing into a symbol, known as a block in AutoCAD. Now you'll see how you can use an existing drawing file as a symbol.

## Using an Existing Drawing as a Symbol

You need a door into the bathroom. Because you've already drawn a door and saved it as a file, you can bring the door into this drawing file and use it as a block:

**1.** In the Tool Sets palette, click the Insert icon, or type **I↵**.

**2.** In the Insert Block dialog box, click the Browse button to open the Select Drawing File dialog box.

**3.** This is a standard file browser dialog box. Locate the Door file and double-click it. If you didn't create a door file, you can use the door file from the Chapter 4 project files on this book's companion website.

You can also browse your hard disk by looking at thumbnail views of the drawing files in a folder.

**4.** When you return to the Insert Block dialog box, click Insert. As you move the cursor around, notice that the door appears above and to the right of the cursor intersection, as in Figure 4.5.

**5.** At this point, the door looks too small for this bathroom. This is because you drew it 3 units long, which translates to 3″. Metric users drew the door 9 cm long.

**FIGURE 4.5**

The door drawing
being inserted in
the Bath file

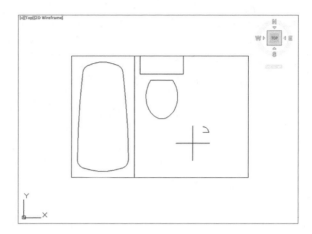

**FIGURE 4.5**

The door drawing
being inserted in
the Bath file

As mentioned earlier, you can specify a smaller or larger size for an inserted object. In this case, you want a 3´ door. Metric users want a 90 cm door. To get 3´ from a 3˝ door (or 90 cm from a 9 cm door), you need an X scale factor of 12, or 10 for metric users. (You may want to review "Understanding Scale Factors" in Chapter 3 to see how this is determined.)

6. At the `Specify insertion point or [Basepoint/Scale/X/Y/Z/Rotate]:` prompt, enter **S↵ 12↵**. Metric users should enter **S↵ 10↵**.

7. Pick a point between the bottom of the toilet and the lower wall of the bathroom so that the door is placed in the lower-right corner of the room.

You would expect to see the door, but nothing seems to happen to the drawing. This is because when you enlarged the door, you also enlarged the distance between the base point and the object. This brings up another issue to be aware of when you're considering using drawings as symbols: All drawings have base points. The default base point is the absolute coordinate 0,0, otherwise known as the *origin*, which is located in the lower-left corner of any new drawing. When you drew the door in Chapter 2, you didn't specify the base point. When you try to bring the door into this drawing, AutoCAD uses the origin of the door drawing as its base point (see Figure 4.6).

**FIGURE 4.6**

By default, a drawing's origin is also its insertion point. You can change a drawing's insertion point by using the Base command.

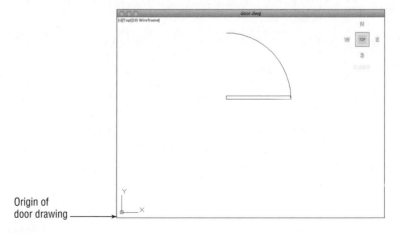

Origin of
door drawing

Because the door appears outside the bathroom, you must first choose View ➢ Zoom ➢ All from the menu bar to show more of the drawing and then use the Move icon in the Tool Sets palette to move the door to the right-side wall of the bathroom. Let's do this now:

1. Choose View ➢ Zoom ➢ All from the menu bar to display the area set by the limits of your drawing plus any other objects that are outside those limits. You can also enter **Z⌐ A⌐**. The view of the room shrinks and the door is displayed. Notice that it's now the proper size for your drawing (see Figure 4.7).

**FIGURE 4.7**
The enlarged door

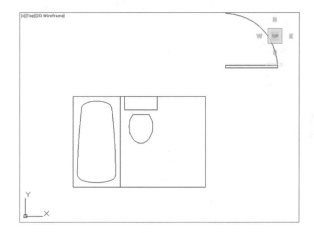

2. Choose the Move icon from the Tool Sets palette, or type **M⌐**.

3. To pick the door you just inserted, at the `Select objects:` prompt, click a point any-where on the door and press ⌐. Notice that now the entire door is highlighted. This is because a block is treated like a single object, even though it may be made up of several lines, arcs, and so on.

4. At the `Specify base point or [Displacement] <Displacement>:` prompt, turn on Running Osnaps, and pick the lower-left corner of the door. Remember that pressing Function-F3 or clicking Object Snap in the status bar toggles Running Osnaps on or off.

5. At the `Specify second point or <use first point as displacement>:` prompt, right-click and choose Snap Override ➢ Nearest and then position the door along the right wall so that your drawing looks like Figure 4.8.

Because the door is an object that you'll use often, it should be a common size so you don't have to specify an odd value every time you insert it. It would also be helpful if the door's insertion base point were in a more convenient location; that is, a location that would let you place the door accurately within a wall opening. Next you'll modify the Door block to better suit your needs.

**FIGURE 4.8**
The door on the
right-side wall of
the bathroom

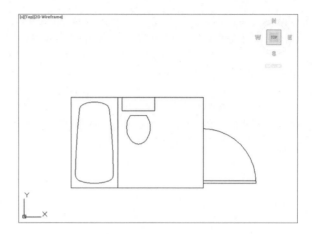

## Modifying a Block

You can modify a block in three ways. One way is to completely redefine it. In earlier releases of AutoCAD, this was the only way to make changes to a block. A second way is to use the Block Editor.

In the following sections, you'll learn how to redefine a block by making changes to the door symbol. Later you'll see how the Block Editor lets you easily edit a block.

To edit most objects, you can either use their grips or use the Properties Inspector palette. A few other objects will offer additional editing tools when you double-click on them. If you double-click a block, the Block Editor appears, which enables you to edit a block directly without having to redefine it. First you'll learn how you can redefine a block.

### Unblocking and Redefining a Block

One way to modify a block is to break it down into its components, edit them, and then turn them back into a block. This is called *redefining* a block. If you redefine a block that has been inserted in a drawing, each occurrence of that block in the current file changes to reflect the new block definition. You can use this block-redefinition feature to make rapid changes to a design.

To separate a block into its components, use the Explode command:

1. Click Explode in the Tool Sets palette. You can also choose Modify ➤ Explode from the menu bar or type **X↵** to start the Explode command.

2. Click the door, and press ↵ to confirm your selection.

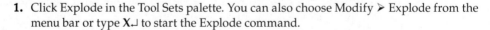

> **INSERT AND EXPLODE AT THE SAME TIME**
>
> You can simultaneously insert and explode a block by clicking the Explode Block check box in the Insert Block dialog box.

Now you can edit the individual objects that make up the door, if you desire. In this case, you want to change only the door's insertion point because you've already made it a more convenient size. You'll turn the door back into a block, this time using the door's lower-left corner for its insertion base point:

1. In the Tool Sets palette, click the Create icon. You can also choose Draw ➢ Block ➢ Make from the menu bar or type **B**↵.

2. In the Define Block dialog box, select Door from the Name pop-up list.

3. Click the Pick Point button, and pick the lower-left corner of the door.

4. Click the Select Objects button, and select the components of the door. Press ↵ when you've finished making your selection.

5. Select the Convert To Block option in the Source Objects group to automatically convert the selected objects in the drawing into a block.

6. Select Inches (or Centimeters for metric users) from the Block Unit pop-up list, and then enter **Standard door** in the Description box.

7. Click Create Block. You see a warning message that reads, The block definition has changed. Do you want to redefine it? You don't want to redefine an existing block accidentally. In this case, you know you want to redefine the door, so click the Redefine button to proceed.

In step 7, you received a warning message that you were about to redefine the existing Door block. But originally you inserted the door as a file, not as a block. Whenever you insert a drawing file by using the Insert icon, the inserted drawing automatically becomes a block in the current drawing. When you redefine a block, however, you don't affect the drawing file you imported. AutoCAD changes only the block in the current file.

You've just redefined the door block. Now place the door in the wall of the room:

1. Click the Erase icon in the Tool Sets palette, and then click the door. Notice that the entire door is one object instead of individual lines and an arc. Had you not selected the Convert To Block option in step 5 of the previous exercise, the components of the block would have remained individual objects.

2. Press ↵ to erase the door.

3. Insert the Door block again by using the Insert icon on the Tool Sets palette. This time, use the Nearest Snap override on the right-click shortcut menu, and pick a point on the right-side wall of the bathroom, near coordinate 9′-4″,2′-1″. Metric users should insert the door near 284,63.4.

4. Use the Grips feature to mirror the door, using the wall as the mirror axis so that the door is inside the room. To mirror an object using grips, select the objects to mirror, click a grip, and right-click. Select Mirror from the shortcut menu; then, indicate a mirror axis with the cursor. Press Esc to clear your selection.

Your drawing will look like Figure 4.9.

**FIGURE 4.9**
The bathroom floor
plan thus far

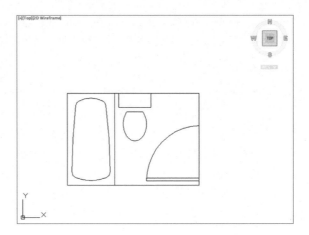

Next you'll see how you can update an external file with a redefined block.

## Exploring the Block Editor

The Block Editor offers an easy way to make changes to existing blocks. It is especially useful if you just need to make a minor change to a block or if you want to create a new block that is a variation of an existing one. The Block Editor offers a safer way to edit blocks that are inserted at different scales in your drawing because you can't accidentally resize the original size of the block components.

As an introduction to the Block Editor, you'll make changes to the Toilet block. Open the 04b-bath.dwg file, and double-click the toilet in the plan to open the Block Editor. You see an enlarged view of the toilet in the drawing area with a light gray background (Figure 4.10). The gray background tells you that you're in the Block Editor. You'll also see the Block Editor options along the top of the drawing area.

**FIGURE 4.10**
The Block Editor
with the Toilet
block opened

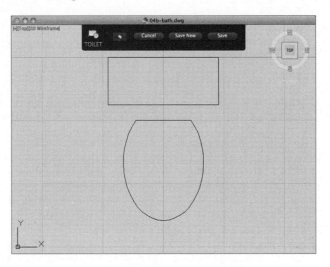

The Block Editor lets you edit a block using all the standard AutoCAD editing tools. In the following exercise, you'll modify the toilet and save your changes to the drawing:

**1.** Add the two lines shown in Figure 4.11.

**FIGURE 4.11**
The toilet with
lines added

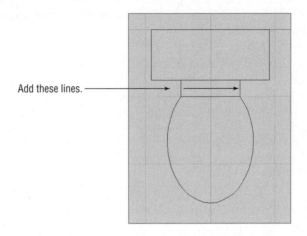

Add these lines. ──────────→

**2.** Click Save New from the Block Editor options. The Save Block Definition As dialog box appears (Figure 4.12).

**FIGURE 4.12**
The Save Block
Definition As
dialog box.

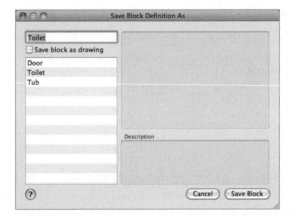

At this dialog box, you have the option to save the block as an external drawing file by checking the Save Block As Drawing check box. You can also replace an existing block by selecting the name of the block from the list to the left. Or you can enter an entirely different name in the text box at the top left to create a new block.

**3.** Click Toilet from the list to replace the existing block.

**4.** Click Save Block.

**5.** A message appears asking if you want to redefine the Toilet block. Click the Redefine block option.

6. Click Cancel from the Block Editor menu. Now the Toilet block appears with the added lines.

7. After reviewing the changes, close the 04b-bath.dwg file without saving it.

As you can see, editing blocks with the Block Editor is simple and straightforward. In this example, you added some lines to the Toilet block, but you can perform any type of drawing or editing to modify the block.

## Saving a Block as a Drawing File

You've seen that, with little effort, you can create a symbol and place it anywhere in a file. Suppose you want to use this symbol in other files. When you create a block by using the Block command, the block exists in the current file only until you specifically instruct AutoCAD to save it as a drawing file on disk. When you have an existing drawing that has been brought in and modified, such as the door, the drawing file on disk associated with that door isn't automatically updated. To update the Door file, you must take an extra step and choose File ➢ Export on the menu bar. Let's see how this works.

Start by turning the Tub and Toilet blocks into individual files on disk:

1. Press the Esc key to make sure nothing is selected and no command is active.

2. From the menu bar, choose File ➢ Export to open the Export Data dialog box, which is a simple file dialog box.

3. Open the File Format pop-up list, and select Block (*.dwg).

4. Double-click the Save As text box and enter **Tub**.

5. Click the Save button to close the Export Data dialog box.

6. At the Enter name of existing block or [= (block=output file)/* (whole drawing)] <define new drawing>: prompt, enter the name of the block you want to save to disk as the tub file—in this case, **Tub** ↵.

   The Tub block is now saved as a file.

7. Repeat steps 1 through 6 for the Toilet block. Give the file the same name as the block.

## Replacing Existing Files with Blocks

The Wblock command does the same thing as choosing File ➢ Export, but output is limited to AutoCAD DWG files. Let's try using the Wblock command this time to save the Door block you modified:

1. Issue the Wblock command by typing **WBLOCK**↵, or use the keyboard shortcut by typing **w**↵. This opens the Write Block dialog box (see Figure 4.13).

2. In the Save Location group, click the Block radio button.

**FIGURE 4.13**

The Write Block
dialog box

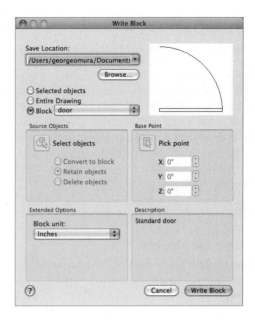

3. Select Door from the pop-up list to the right of the Block radio button.

4. In this case, you want to update the door you drew in Chapter 2. Click the Browse button just below the Save Location pop-up list.

5. Locate and select the original Door.dwg file that you inserted earlier. Click Save.

6. A warning message appears: "Door.dwg" already exists. Do you want to replace it? Click Replace.

7. Click Write Block. A warning message tells you that the Door.dwg file already exists. Go ahead and click the "Replace the existing...." option to confirm that you want to over-write the old door drawing with the new door definition.

In this exercise, you typed the Wblock command at the Command prompt instead of choosing File ➢ Export. The results are the same regardless of which method you use. If you're in a hurry, the Wblock command is a quick way to save part of your drawing as a file. The File ➢ Export option might be easier for new users because it is a little easier to remember and follows the standard method for exporting files.

### UNDERSTANDING THE WRITE BLOCK DIALOG BOX OPTIONS

The Write Block dialog box offers a way to save parts of your current drawing as a file. As you can see from the dialog box shown in the previous exercise, you have several options.

In that exercise, you used the Block option of the Save Location group to select an existing block as the source object to be exported. You can also export a set of objects by choosing the Selected Objects option. If you choose this option, the Base Point and Source Objects groups become available. These options work the same way as their counterparts in the Define Block dialog box, which you saw earlier when you created the Tub and Toilet blocks.

The other option in the Save Location group, Entire Drawing, lets you export the whole drawing to its own file. This may seem to duplicate the Save As option in the File menu on the menu bar, but saving the entire drawing from the Write Block dialog box performs some additional operations, such as stripping out unused blocks or other unused components. This has the effect of reducing file size. You'll learn more about this feature later in this chapter.

## Other Uses for Blocks

So far you've used the Create icon to create symbols, and you've used the Export and Wblock commands to save those symbols to disk. As you can see, you can create symbols and save them at any time while you're drawing. You've made the tub and toilet symbols into drawing files that you can see when you check the contents of your current folder.

However, creating symbols isn't the only use for the Block, Export, and Wblock commands. You can use them in any situation that requires grouping objects. You can also use blocks to stretch a set of objects along one axis by using the Properties Inspector palette. Export and Wblock also enable you to save a part of a drawing to disk. You'll see instances of these other uses of the Block, Export, and Wblock commands throughout the book.

Block, Export, and Wblock are extremely versatile commands, and if used judiciously, they can boost your productivity and simplify your work. If you aren't careful, however, you can get carried away and create more blocks than you can track. Planning your drawings helps you determine which elements will work best as blocks and recognize situations in which other methods of organization are more suitable.

Another way of using symbols is to use AutoCAD's external reference capabilities. External reference files, known as *Xrefs*, are files inserted into a drawing in a way similar to how blocks are inserted. The difference is that Xrefs don't become part of the drawing's database. Instead, they're loaded along with the current file at startup time. It's as if AutoCAD opens several drawings at once: the main file you specify when you start AutoCAD and the Xrefs associated with the main file.

By keeping the Xrefs independent from the current file, you make sure that any changes made to the Xrefs automatically appear in the current file. You don't have to update each inserted copy of an Xref. For example, if you use the Insert ➤ DWG Reference option on the menu bar to insert the tub drawing and later you make changes to the tub, the next time you open the Bath file, you'll see the new version of the tub.

Xrefs are especially useful in workgroup environments, where several people are working on the same project. One person might be updating several files that have been inserted into a variety of other files. Before Xrefs were available, everyone in the workgroup had to be notified of the changes and had to update all the affected blocks in all the drawings that contained them. With Xrefs, the updating is automatic. Many other features are unique to these files. They're discussed in more detail in Chapters 7 and 14.

## Understanding the Annotation Scale

One common use for AutoCAD's block feature is creating *reference symbols*. These are symbols that refer the viewer to other drawings or views in a set of drawings. An example would be a building-section symbol on a floor plan that directs the viewer to look at a location on another sheet to see a cross-section view of a building. Such a symbol is typically a circle with two numbers: One is the drawing sheet number and the other is the view number on the sheet (examples appear a little later, in Figure 4.18).

In the past, AutoCAD users had to insert a reference symbol block multiple times to accommodate different scales of the same view. For example, the same floor plan might be used for a ¼″ = 1′-0″ scale view and a ⅛″ = 1′-0″ view. An elevation symbol block that works for the ¼″ = 1′-0″ scale view would be too small for the ⅛″ = 1′-0″ view, so two copies of the same block were inserted, one for each scale. The user then had to place the two blocks on different layers to control their visibility. In addition, if sheet numbers changed, the user had to make sure every copy of the elevation symbol block was updated to reflect the change.

The annotation scale feature does away with this need for redundancy. You can now use a single instance of a block even if it must be displayed in different scale views. To do this, you must take some additional steps when creating and inserting the block. Here's how you do it:

1. Draw your symbol at the size it should appear when plotted. For example, if the symbol is supposed to be a ¼″ circle on a printed sheet, draw the symbol as a ¼″ circle.

2. Open the Define Block dialog box by choosing the Create icon from the Tool Sets palette.

3. Turn on the Annotative option in the Block Behavior section of the Define Block dialog box. You can also turn on the Match Block Orientation To Layout option if you want the symbol to appear always in a vertical orientation (see Figure 4.14).

**FIGURE 4.14**
The Define Block dialog box's Block Behavior group with the Annotative option turned on

4. Select the objects that make up the block, and indicate an insertion point as usual.

5. Give the block a name, and then click Create Block.

After you've followed these steps, you need to apply an annotation scale to the newly created block:

1. Click the new block to select it.

2. Right-click and choose Annotative Object Scale ➢ Add/Delete Scales. The Annotation Object Scale List dialog box appears (see Figure 4.15).

**FIGURE 4.15**
The Annotation
Object Scale List
dialog box

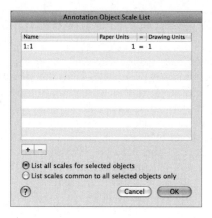

**3.** Click the Add button, which looks like a plus sign at the bottom of the list box. The Add Scales To Object dialog box appears (see Figure 4.16).

**FIGURE 4.16**
The Add Scales To
Object dialog box

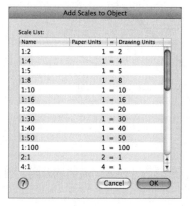

**4.** Select from the list the scale you'll be using with this block. You can ⌘-click to select multiple scales. When you're finished selecting scales, click OK. The selected scales appear in the Annotation Object Scale List dialog box.

**5.** Click OK to close the Annotation Object Scale List dialog box.

At this point, the block is ready to be used in multiple scale views. You need only to select a scale from the Model view's Annotation Scale pop-up list or the layout view's Viewport Scale pop-up list (see Figure 4.17), which are both in the lower-right corner of the status bar.

**FIGURE 4.17**
The Model Space
Annotation Scale
(left) and layout
view's Viewport
Scale (right)
pop-up lists

The Annotation Scale pop-up list appears in model view, and the Viewport Scale pop-up list appears in layout view and when a viewport is selected. (See Chapter 15, "Laying Out Your Printer Output," for more about layouts and viewports.) In layout view, you can set the Viewport Scale value for each individual viewport so the same block can appear at the appropriate size for different scale viewports (see Figure 4.18).

**FIGURE 4.18**
A single block is used to create building section symbols of different sizes in these layout views. Both views show the same floor plan displayed at different scales.

The size of the block adjusts to the viewport scale so its size remains constant.

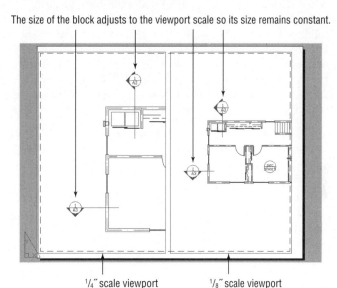

¼" scale viewport          ⅛" scale viewport

Note that if you want to use several copies of a block that is using multiple annotation scales, you should insert the block and assign the additional annotation scales, and then make copies of the block. If you insert a new instance of the block, the block acquires only the annotation scale that is current for the drawing. You'll have to assign additional annotation scales to each new insertion of the block.

If you're uncertain whether an annotation scale has been assigned to a block, you can click the block and you'll see the different scale versions of the block as ghosted images. Also, if you hover over a block, triangular symbols appear next to the cursor for blocks that have been assigned annotative scales.

Annotative Scale symbol

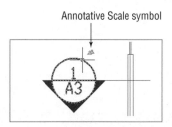

If you need to change the position of a block for a particular layout viewport scale, go to Model view, select the appropriate scale from the Annotation Scale pop-up list, and then adjust the position of the block.

## Grouping Objects

Blocks are extremely useful tools, but for some situations, they're too restrictive. At times, you'll want to group objects so they're connected but can still be edited individually.

For example, consider a space planner who has to place workstations on a floor plan. Although each workstation is basically the same, some slight variations in each station could make the use of blocks unwieldy. For instance, one workstation might need a different configuration to accommodate special equipment, and another workstation might need to be slightly larger than the standard size. You would need to create a block for one workstation and then, for each variation, explode the block, edit it, and create a new block. A better way is to draw a prototype workstation and turn it into a group. You can copy the group into position and then edit it for each individual situation without losing its identity as a group.

The following exercise demonstrates how grouping works:

1. Save the Bath file, and then open the drawing Office1.dwg from the sample files from this book's companion website. Metric users should open Office1-metric.dwg.

2. Use the Zoom command to enlarge just the view of the workstation, as shown in the first image in Figure 4.19.

**FIGURE 4.19**
A workstation in
an office plan

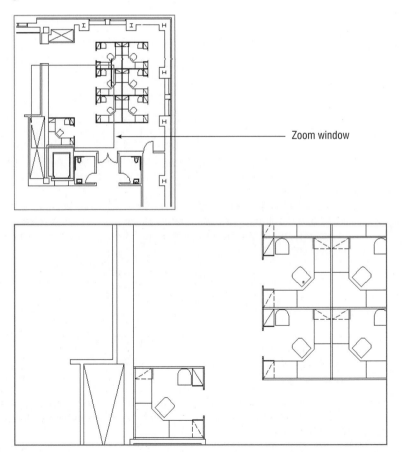

Zoom window

3. Type **G↵** or **Group↵**.

4. Type **C↵** to use the Create option.

5. Type **Station1↵** for the group name and then press ↵ at the Description prompt.

6. At the `Select objects:` prompt, use a window to select the entire workstation in the lower-left corner of the plan, and press ↵. You've just created a group.

Now whenever you want to select the workstation, you can click any part of it to select the entire group. At the same time, you can still modify individual parts of the group—the desk, partition, and so on—without losing the grouping of objects (see the following section).

## Modifying Members of a Group

Next you'll make copies of the original group and modify the copies. Figure 4.20 is a sketch of the proposed layout that uses the new workstations. Look carefully and you'll see that some of the workstations in the sketch are missing a few of the standard components that exist in the Station1 group. One pair of stations has a partition removed; another station has one fewer chair.

**FIGURE 4.20**
A sketch of the new office layout

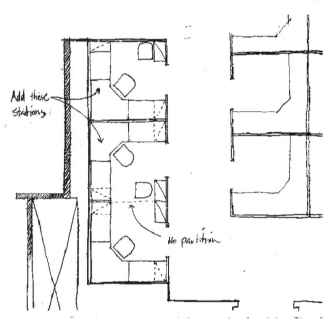

The exercises in this section show you how to complete your drawing to reflect the design requirements of the sketch.

Start by making a copy of the workstation:

1. Click the Copy icon on the Tool Sets palette, or type **CO↵**, and click the Station1 group you just created. Notice that you can click any part of the station to select the entire station. If only a single object is selected, press ⇧-^-A and try clicking another part of the group.

2. Press ↵ to finish your selection.

3. At the `Specify base point or [Displacement/mOde] <Displacement>:` prompt, enter @↵. Then enter **@8′2″<90** to copy the workstation 8′-2″ vertically. Metric users should enter **@249<90**. Press ↵ to exit the Copy command.

   You can also use the Direct Distance method by typing **@↵** and then pointing the rubber-banding line 90° and typing **8′2″↵**. Metric users should type **249↵**.

4. Issue the Copy command again, but this time click the copy of the workstation you just created. Notice that it, too, is a group.

5. Copy this workstation 8′-2″ (249 cm for the metric users) vertically, just as you did the original workstation. Press ↵ to exit the Copy command.

Next you'll use grips to mirror the first workstation copy:

1. Click the middle workstation to highlight it, and notice that grips appear for all the entities in the group.

2. Click the grip in the middle-left side, as shown in Figure 4.21.

**FIGURE 4.21**
Mirroring the new group by using grips

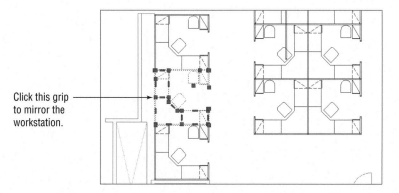

Click this grip to mirror the workstation.

3. Right-click, and choose Mirror from the shortcut menu. Notice that a temporary mirror image of the workstation follows the movement of your cursor.

4. Turn on Ortho mode, and pick a point directly to the right of the hot grip you picked in step 2. The workstation is mirrored to a new orientation.

5. Press the Esc key to clear the grip selection. Also, turn off Ortho mode.

Now that you've got the workstations laid out, you need to remove some of the partitions between the new workstations. If you had used blocks for the workstations, you would first need to explode the workstations that have partitions you want to edit. Groups, however, let you make changes without undoing their grouping.

Use these steps to remove the partitions:

1. At the Command prompt, press ⇧-⌃-A. You should see the <Group off> message in the command line. If you see the <Group on> message instead, press ⇧-⌃-A until you see <Group off>. This turns off groupings so you can select and edit individual objects within a group.

2. Erase the partition that divides the two copies of the workstations, as shown in Figure 4.22. Since you made a mirror copy of the original workstation, you'll need to erase two partitions, the original and the copy.

**FIGURE 4.22**

Remove the partitions between the two workstations.

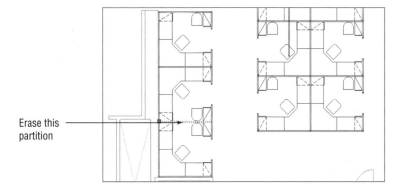

Erase this partition

3. Press ⇧-⌃-A again to turn groupings back on.

4. To check your workstations, click one of them to see whether all its components are highlighted together.

5. Close the file when you're finished. You don't need to save your changes.

## Working with the Group Options

Each group has a unique name, and you can also attach a brief description of a group while you are creating it. When you copy a group, AutoCAD assigns an arbitrary name to the newly created group. Copies of groups are considered unnamed.

Objects in a group aren't bound solely to that group. One object can be a member of several groups, and you can have nested groups (groups with groups).

Figure 4.23 shows the Group options in the Command Line palette and Table 4.2 gives a rundown of the options available in the Group command.

**FIGURE 4.23**

The Group options in the Command Line palette

**TABLE 4.2:** Group options

| OPTION | PURPOSE |
| --- | --- |
| Add | Use this option to add objects to a group. While you're using this option, grouping is temporarily turned off to allow you to select objects from other groups. |
| Create | This option creates a group. You are prompted for a name and description. |
| Explode | Use this option to separate a group into its individual components. |
| Order | Use this option to change the order of objects in a group. The order refers to the order in which you selected the objects to include in the group. You can change this selection order for special purposes such as tool-path machining. |
| Remove | This option removes objects from a group. |
| Rename | Use this option to rename a group. |
| Selectable | Use this option to turn individual groups on and off. When a group is selectable, it can be selected only as a group. When a group isn't selectable, the individual objects in a group can be selected, but not the group. |

If a group is selected, you can remove individual items from the selection with a shift-click. In this way, you can isolate objects within a group for editing or removal without having to turn off groups temporarily.

You've seen how you can use groups to create an office layout. You can also use groups to help you keep sets of objects temporarily together in a complex drawing. Groups can be especially useful in 3D modeling when you want to organize complex assemblies together for easy selection.

## The Bottom Line

**Create and insert a block.** If you have a symbol that you use often in a drawing, you can draw it once and then turn it into an AutoCAD block. A block can be placed in a drawing multiple times in any location, like a rubber stamp. A block is stored in a drawing as a block definition, which can be called up at any time.

**Master It** Name the dialog box used to create a block from objects in a drawing, and also name the tool to open this dialog box.

**Modify a block.** Once you've created a block, it isn't set in stone. One of the features of a block is that you can change the block definition and all the copies of the block are updated to the new definition.

**Master It** What is the name of the tool used to "unblock" a block?

**Understand the annotation scale.** In some cases, you'll want to create a block that is dependent on the drawing scale. You can create a block that adjusts itself to the scale of your drawing through the annotation scale. When the annotation scale feature is turned on for a block, the block can be set to appear at the correct size depending on the scale of your drawing.

**Master It** What setting in the Define Block dialog box turns on the annotation scale feature, and how do you set the annotation scale of a block?

**Group objects.** Blocks can be used as a tool to group objects together, but blocks can be too rigid for some grouping applications. AutoCAD offers groups, which are collections of objects that are similar to blocks but aren't as rigidly defined.

**Master It** How are groups different from blocks?

# Chapter 5

# Keeping Track of Layers and Blocks

Imagine a filing system that has only one category into which you put all your records. For only a handful of documents, such a filing system might work. However, as soon as you start to accumulate more documents, you would want to start separating them into meaningful categories, perhaps alphabetically or by their use, so you could find them more easily.

The same is true for drawings. If you have a simple drawing with only a few objects, you can get by without using layers. But as soon as your drawing gets the least bit complicated, you'll want to start sorting your objects into layers to keep track of what's what. Layers don't restrict you when you're editing objects such as blocks or groups, and you can set up layers so that you can easily identify which object belongs to which layer.

In this chapter, you'll learn how to create and use layers to keep your drawings organized. You'll learn how color can play an important role while you're working with layers, and you'll also learn how to include linetypes such as dashes and center lines through the use of layers.

In this chapter, you'll learn to do the following:

◆ Organize information with layers

◆ Control layer visibility

◆ Keep track of blocks and layers

## Organizing Information with Layers

You can think of layers as overlays on which you keep various types of information (see Figure 5.1). In a floor plan of a building, for example, you want to keep the walls, ceiling, plumbing fixtures, wiring, and furniture separate so that you can display or plot them individually or combine them in different ways. It's also a good idea to keep notes and reference symbols, as well as the drawing's dimensions, on their own layers. As your drawing becomes more complex, you can turn the various layers on and off to allow easier display and modification.

For example, one of your consultants might need a plot of just the dimensions and walls, without all the other information; another consultant might need only a furniture layout. Using manual drafting, you would have to redraw your plan for each consultant or use overlay drafting techniques, which can be cumbersome. With AutoCAD, you can turn off the layers you don't need and plot a drawing containing only the required information. A carefully planned layering scheme helps you produce a document that combines the types of information needed in each case.

Using layers also lets you modify your drawings more easily. For example, suppose you have an architectural drawing with separate layers for the walls, the ceiling plan, and the floor plan. If any change occurs in the wall locations, you can turn on the ceiling plan layer to see where the new wall locations will affect the ceiling and then make the proper adjustments.

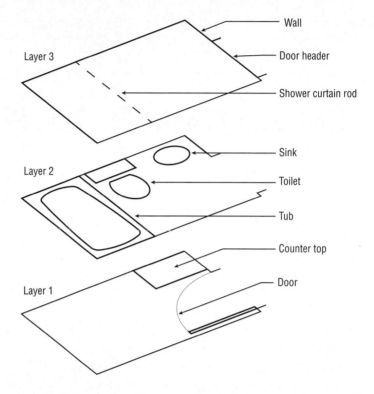

**FIGURE 5.1**
Placing drawing elements on separate layers

Layer 3

Layer 2

Layer 1

Wall

Door header

Shower curtain rod

Sink

Toilet

Tub

Counter top

Door

AutoCAD allows an unlimited number of layers, and you can name each layer anything you want using any characters with the exception of these: < > / \ " " : ; ? * | , = ' '.

## Creating and Assigning Layers

You'll start your exploration of layers by using the Layers palette and the Properties Inspector palette to create a new layer, giving it a name, and assigning it a color. Then, you'll look at alternate ways of creating a layer through the command line. Next, you'll assign the new layer to the objects in your drawing. Start by getting familiar with the Layers palette:

1. Open the Bath file you created in Chapter 4, "Organizing Objects with Blocks and Groups." (If you didn't create one, use either 04b-bath.dwg or 04b-bath-metric.dwg, available on the book's website, www.sybex.com/go/masteringautocadmac.)

   Take a look at the Layers palette. It shows you at a glance the status of your layers. Right now, you have only one layer, a layer named 0, but as your work expands, so will the number of layers. You'll then find this palette indispensable (Figure 5.2).

2. Click the plus icon at the bottom left of the palette.

   A new layer named Layer1 appears in the list box. Notice that the name is highlighted. This tells you that, by typing, you can change the default name to something better suited to your needs.

**FIGURE 5.2**
The Layers palette

3. Type **Wall**↵. As you type, your entry replaces the Layer1 name in the list box.

4. Click the name Wall to select it.

5. Take a look at the Properties Inspector palette. You'll see the properties of the selected layer.

6. In the Properties Inspector palette, click and hold the Color list to open the pop-up list of colors (Figure 5.3).

**FIGURE 5.3**
The Properties
Inspector palette
showing the Color
option and pop-up list

7. Choose the Select Color option at the bottom of the list and release the mouse button.

   The Color Palette dialog box opens (Figure 5.4).

8. In the row of standard colors to the left of the ByLayer button, click the green square, and then click OK. Notice that the color swatch in the Wall layer listing is now green.

**FIGURE 5.4**
The Color Palette
dialog box

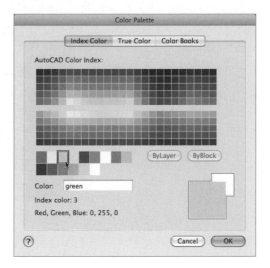

You could have selected a color from the Color pop-up list, but by using the Select Color option, you were introduced to the Color Palette dialog box.

From this point on, any object assigned to the Wall layer will appear green unless the object is specifically assigned a different color.

I'd like to point out another method for setting layer colors. In addition to using the Properties Inspector palette, you can set the layer color using the Color column in the Layers palette. The Color column is the one with the square icon (Figure 5.5).

**FIGURE 5.5**
The layer color
can be set in the
Color column of
the Layers
palette.

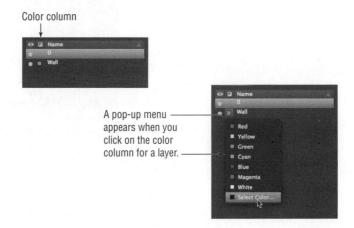

When a layer is assigned a color other than white, the color is displayed in this column. You can click this column to open a pop-up menu that offers the same color options you saw in the Properties Inspector palette.

### USING THE PROPERTIES INSPECTOR PALETTE TO SET LAYER OPTIONS

Now let's take a closer look at how the Properties Inspector palette interacts with the Layers palette. In Chapter 4, you saw how the Properties Inspector palette displays information about objects in your drawing. When you click on a layer in the Layers palette, the Properties Inspector palette displays the properties of the selected layer. Try the following to see firsthand how this works:

1. In the Layers palette, click the layer 0 under the Name column and watch what happens in the Properties Inspector palette. You see detailed information about layer 0.

2. Click the Wall layer under the Name column in the Layers palette. Now information about the Wall layer is displayed in the Properties Inspector palette (Figure 5.6).

**FIGURE 5.6**
The Properties Inspector palette displays information about a selected layer.

The Properties Inspector palette offers several pop-up lists that enable you to change the layer properties such as color, linetype, and line weight. Layer transparency can be controlled with a slider. You used the Color pop-up list to select a color for the Wall layer in the previous exercise.

You'll also want to know about the two icons in the upper-left corner of the Properties Inspector palette. They are labeled Current and Layer (Figure 5.7). These icons enable you to switch between displaying the properties of an object in the drawing and the current layer.

You'll get a chance to use some of the other settings later in this chapter. Let's continue with a closer look at some other layer features.

**FIGURE 5.7**
The Current and Layer icons in the Properties Inspector palette

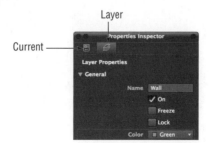

### USING TRUE OR PANTONE COLORS

In an earlier exercise, you chose a color from the Index Color tab of the Color Palette dialog box. Most of the time, you'll find that the Index Color tab includes enough colors to suit your needs. But if you're creating a presentation drawing in which color selection is important, you can choose colors from either the True Color tab or the Color Books tab of the Color Palette dialog box.

The True Color tab offers a full range of colors through a color palette similar to the one found in Adobe Photoshop and other image editing programs (Figure 5.8).

**FIGURE 5.8**
The True Color tab

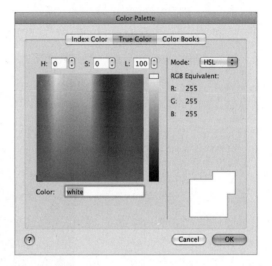

You have the choice of using hue, saturation, and luminance, which is the HSL color mode, or you can use the RGB (red, green, blue) color mode. You can select HSL or RGB from the Mode drop-down list in the upper-right corner of the dialog box (Figure 5.9).

**FIGURE 5.9**
The Mode drop-
down list

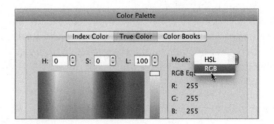

You can also select from PANTONE, RAL, and DIC *color books* by using the Color Books tab (Figure 5.10). Color books are "books" that contain color samples with their corresponding number code. If you've ever gone to a paint store to select a color, chances are you've used one. In AutoCAD, the color books are displayed as a list of colors and codes.

**FIGURE 5.10**
The Color Books tab

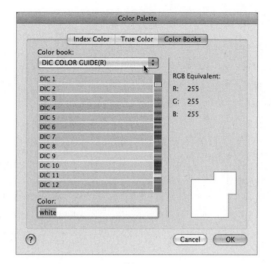

Let's continue with our look at layers in AutoCAD.

## UNDERSTANDING THE LAYERS PALETTE

The most prominent feature of the Layers palette is the layer list box, as you saw in the preceding exercise. As you add them, the list box begins to fill up with layers. Notice that the bar at the top of the list of layers offers several buttons for the various layer properties. You can adjust the width of the Name column in the list of layers by clicking and dragging either side of the column head. You can also sort the layer list based on the name at the top of the list. And just as with other Mac list boxes, you can also click names to select a block of layer names, or you can ⌘-click individual names to select multiple layers that don't appear together. These features will become helpful as your list of layers grows.

You've already seen how the New Layer icon works. To delete layers, you select a layer or group of layers and then click the Delete Layer icon, which looks like a minus sign. Be aware that you can't delete layer 0, locked layers, or layers that contain objects. You can also see at a glance which layer is the current drawing layer by the gray highlighted row in the layer list. Right now, layer 0 is highlighted in gray (Figure 5.11). This is the layer on which objects will be placed when you're drawing in the drawing area.

**FIGURE 5.11**
The current drawing layer is highlighted in gray

Note that just clicking on a layer does not make it the current drawing layer. When you click on a layer to set its properties, it is highlighted in blue. If you click on the Wall layer, it will be highlighted in blue while layer 0 will continue to be highlighted in gray.

Another way to create or delete layers is to select a layer or set of layers from the list box and then right-click. A menu appears, offering additional options that you can apply to selected layers (Figure 5.12). Table 5.1 describes the function of these options.

**FIGURE 5.12**
A shortcut menu appears when you right-click a layer name in the Layers palette.

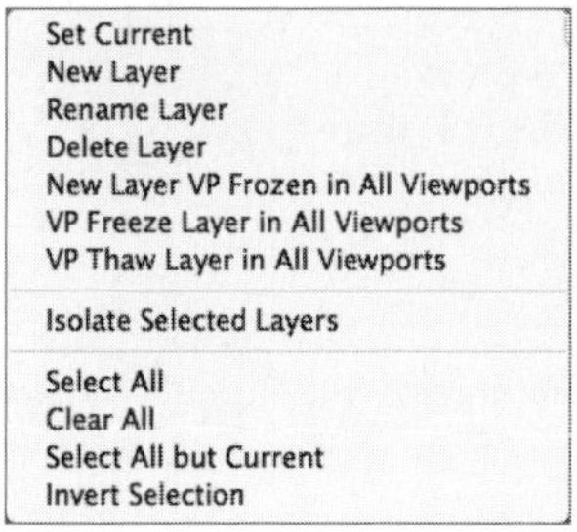

| Set Current |
| New Layer |
| Rename Layer |
| Delete Layer |
| New Layer VP Frozen in All Viewports |
| VP Freeze Layer in All Viewports |
| VP Thaw Layer in All Viewports |
| Isolate Selected Layers |
| Select All |
| Clear All |
| Select All but Current |
| Invert Selection |

**TABLE 5.1:**     The Layers palette shortcut menu options

| OPTION NAME | FUNCTION |
| --- | --- |
| Set Current | Sets the selected layer to be the current drawing layer |
| New Layer | Creates a new layer |
| Rename Layer | Renames the selected layer |
| Delete Layer | Deletes the selected layer(s) with the option to delete its contents when objects are present on the layer |
| New Layer VP Frozen In All Viewports | Creates a new layer that is frozen in all viewports |
| VP Freeze Layer In All Viewports | Freezes selected layer(s) in all viewports |
| VP Thaw Layer In All Viewports | Thaws selected layers in all viewports |
| Isolate Selected Layers | Hides (turns off) all but the selected layer(s) in the drawing |
| Select All | Selects all the layers that are displayed in the layer list |
| Clear All | Clears the selection of layers in the layer list |
| Select All But Current | Selects all but the current layer |
| Invert Selection | Inverts the selection of layers in the list |

You'll also notice another set of icons at the top of the Layers palette. Those icons offer features to control and manage layers. You'll get a closer look at them a little later in this chapter in the section "Using Objects to Control Layers."

### CONTROLLING LAYERS THROUGH THE LAYER COMMAND

You've seen how the Layers palette makes it easy to view and edit layer information and how you can easily select layer colors from the Color Palette dialog box. But you can also control layers through the Command prompt.

Use these steps to control layers through the Command prompt:

1. Press the Esc key to make sure any current command is canceled.

2. At the Command prompt, enter **–Layer**↵. Make sure you include the minus sign in front of the word *Layer*. The following prompt appears:

```
Enter an option
[?/Make/Set/New/Rename/ON/OFF/Color/Ltype/LWeight/TRansparency/MATerial/
Plot/Freeze/Thaw/LOck/Unlock/stAte/
Description/rEconcile]:
```

If the Dynamic Input display is on, you'll see these options appear at the cursor as a list. You'll learn about many of the options in this prompt as you work through this chapter.

3. Enter **N**↵ to select the New option.

4. At the `Enter name list for new layer(s):` prompt, enter **Wall2**↵. The `[?/Make/Set/New/Rename/ON/OFF/Color/Ltype/LWeight/TRansparency/MATerial/Plot/Freeze/Thaw/LOck/Unlock/stAte/rEconcile]:` prompt appears again.

5. Enter **C**↵.

6. At the `New color [Truecolor/COlorbook]:` prompt, enter **Yellow**↵. Or, you can enter **2**↵, the numeric equivalent of the color yellow in AutoCAD.

7. At the `Enter name list of layer(s) for color 2 (yellow) <0>:` prompt, enter **Wall2**↵. The `[?/Make/Set/New/Rename/ON/OFF/Color/Ltype/LWeight/TRansparency/MATerial/Plot/Freeze/Thaw/LOck/Unlock/stAte/rEconcile]:` prompt appears again.

8. Press ↵ to exit the Layer command.

Each method of controlling layers has its own advantages. The Layers palette offers more information about your layers at a glance. On the other hand, the Layer command offers a quick way to control and create layers if you're in a hurry. Also, if you intend to write custom macros and scripts, you'll want to know how to use the Layer command as opposed to using the Layers palette because palettes can't be controlled through custom macros or scripts.

### ASSIGNING LAYERS TO OBJECTS

When you create an object, that object is assigned to the current layer. Until now, only one layer has existed—layer 0—and it contains all the objects you've drawn so far. Now that you've created some new layers, you can reassign objects to them by using the Properties Inspector palette:

1. Select the four lines that represent the bathroom walls. If you have trouble singling out the wall to the left, use a window (click and drag from left to right) to select the wall line.

**2.** Make sure the Current icon is highlighted in the upper-left corner of the Properties Inspector palette. This causes the Properties Inspector palette to display the properties of the selected object or set of objects.

**3.** Click the Layer option on in the Properties Inspector palette. The list expands to show the current set of layers available.

**4.** Select the Wall layer from the list. Notice that the wall lines you selected change to a green color. This tells you that the objects have been assigned to the Wall layer. (Remember that you assigned a green color to the Wall layer.)

**5.** Press the Esc key to clear the selection so you can see the wall more clearly.

The bathroom walls are now on the new layer called Wall, and the walls are changed to green. Layers are more easily distinguished from one another when you use colors to set them apart.

Next, you'll practice the commands you learned in this section and try some new ones by creating new layers and changing the layer assignments of the rest of the objects in your bathroom:

**1.** Use the Layers palette to create a new layer called Fixture, and give it the color blue. Remember that after you create the layer, you need to select it in the Layers palette list before you can set its color in the Properties Inspector palette.

If you need to change the name of a layer in the Layers palette, select the layer name that you want to change and click it again so that the name is highlighted. You can then rename the layer. This works in the same way as renaming a file or folder in the Finder.

**2.** Click the Tub and Toilet blocks to select them, and then make sure that the Current icon is selected in the Properties Inspector palette.

**3.** In the Properties Inspector palette, click the disclosure triangle in the Layer option and select Fixture from the pop-up list that appears.

**4.** Press the Esc key to clear your selection.

For blocks, you can change the color assignment and linetype of only those objects that are on layer 0 within a block. See the sidebar "Controlling Colors and Linetypes of Blocked Objects" later in this chapter.

Continue by creating new layers and assigning objects to them:

1. Create a new layer for the door, name the layer Door, and make it red.

2. Just as you've done with the walls and fixtures, use the Properties Inspector palette to assign the door to the Door layer.

3. Use the Layers palette to create three more layers, one for the ceiling, one for the door jambs, and one for the floor. Create these layers, and set their colors as indicated (remember that you can open the Color Palette dialog box by selecting the Select Color option in the expanded Color option in the Properties Inspector palette):

| Layer Name | Color |
| --- | --- |
| Ceiling | Magenta (6) |
| Jamb | Green (3) |
| Floor | Cyan (4) |

---

### UNDERSTANDING OBJECT PROPERTIES

It helps to think of the components of an AutoCAD drawing as having properties. For example, a line has geometric properties, such as its length and the coordinates that define its endpoints. An arc has a radius, a center, and beginning and ending coordinates. Even though a layer isn't an object you can grasp and manipulate, it can have properties such as color, linetypes, and line weights.

By default, objects take on the color, linetype, and line weight of the layer to which they're assigned, but you can also assign these properties directly to individual objects. These general properties can be manipulated through the Properties Inspector palette.

Although many of the options in the Properties Inspector palette may seem cryptic, don't worry about them at this point. As you work with AutoCAD, these properties will become more familiar. You'll find that you won't be too concerned with the geometric properties because you'll be manipulating them with the standard editing tools in the Tool Sets palette or the menu bar. The other properties will be explained in the rest of this chapter and in other chapters.

---

In step 2 of the previous exercise, you used the Properties Inspector palette, which offered several options for modifying the block. The options displayed in the Properties Inspector palette depend on the objects you've selected. With only one object selected, AutoCAD displays options that apply specifically to that object. With several objects selected, you'll see a more limited set of options because AutoCAD can change only those properties that are common to all the objects selected.

## Working on Layers

So far, you've created layers and then assigned objects to them. In this section, you'll continue to use the Layer pop-up list in the Properties Inspector palette to assign layers to objects. In the process, you'll make some additions to the drawing.

---

### CONTROLLING COLORS AND LINETYPES OF BLOCKED OBJECTS

Layer 0 has special importance to blocks. When objects assigned to layer 0 are used as parts of a block and that block is inserted on another layer, those objects take on the characteristics of their new layer. On the other hand, if those objects are on a layer other than layer 0, they maintain their original layer characteristics even if you insert or change that block to another layer. For example, suppose the tub is drawn on the Door layer instead of on layer 0. If you turn the tub into a block and insert it on the Fixture layer, the objects the tub is composed of will maintain their assignment to the Door layer even though the Tub block is assigned to the Fixture layer.

It may help to think of the block function as a clear plastic bag that holds together the objects that make up the tub. The objects inside the bag maintain their assignment to the Door layer even while the bag itself is assigned to the Fixture layer. This may be a bit confusing at first, but it should become clearer after you use blocks for a while.

AutoCAD also enables you to have more than one color or linetype on an object. For example, you can use the Color and Linetype pop-up lists in the Properties Inspector palette to alter the color or linetype of an object on layer 0. That object then maintains its assigned color and linetype—no matter what its layer assignment. Likewise, objects specifically assigned a color or linetype aren't affected by their inclusion in blocks.

---

The current layer is still layer 0, and, unless you change the current layer, every new object you draw will be on layer 0. Here's how to change the current layer:

1. First press the Esc key to clear any selections.

2. Click the Jamb layer name in the Layers palette, right-click, and select Set Current from the shortcut menu. The Jamb layer in the layer list is highlighted indicating that Jamb is now the current layer.

   You can also use the Layer command to reset the current layer. To do this here, enter **–Layer.↵ S.↵** and then enter **Jamb.↵↵**.

3. Zoom in on the door, and draw a 5″ line; start at the lower-right corner of the door and draw toward the right. Metric users should draw a 13 cm line.

4. Draw a similar line from the top-right end of the arc. Your drawing should look like Figure 5.13.

   Because you assigned the color green to the Jamb layer, the two lines you just drew to represent the door jambs are green. This gives you immediate feedback about which layer you're on as you draw.

**FIGURE 5.13**
Door at wall with
door jambs added

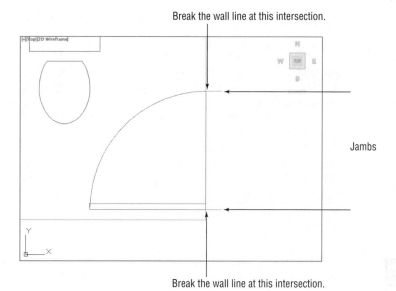

Break the wall line at this intersection.

Jambs

Break the wall line at this intersection.

Now you'll use the part of the wall between the jambs as a line representing the door header (the part of the wall above the door). To do this, you'll have to cut the line into three line segments and then change the layer assignment of the segment between the jambs:

1. Click the disclosure triangle to open the Modify panel (Figure 5.14).

2. Click the Break At Point icon in the Modify panel.

3. At the `Select object:` prompt, click the wall between the two jambs.

**FIGURE 5.14**
Open the
Modify panel.

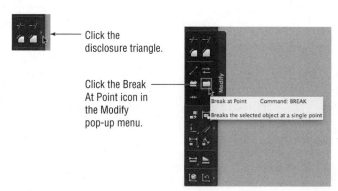

Click the
disclosure triangle.

Click the Break
At Point icon in
the Modify
pop-up menu.

4. At the `Specify first break point:` prompt, use the Endpoint Osnap override to pick the endpoint of the door's arc that is touching the wall, as shown previously in Figure 5.13.

5. Click Break At Point on the Modify panel again, and then repeat steps 2 and 3, this time using the jamb near the door hinge location to locate the break point (see Figure 5.13).

Although it may not be obvious, you've just broken the right-side wall line into three line segments: one at the door opening and two more on either side of the jambs. You can also use the Break tool (to the left of the Break At Point tool) to produce a gap in a line segment.

The Break At Point icon won't work on a circle. You can, however, use the Break tool, also on the Modify panel, to place a small gap in the circle. If you create a small enough gap, the circle will still look like a full circle.

Next you'll change the Layer property of the line between the two jambs to the Ceiling layer. But instead of using the Properties Inspector palette as you've done in earlier exercises, you'll use a shortcut method:

1. Click the line between the door jambs to highlight it. Notice that the layer listing in the Layers palette changes to highlight the Wall layer and the Properties Inspector palette shows the Wall layer for the selected line. Whenever you select an object to expose its grips, the Color, Linetype, Lineweight, and Plot Style listings in the Properties Inspector palette change to reflect those properties of the selected object.

2. Click the Layer option in the Properties Inspector palette to open the Layer pop-up list.

3. Select the Ceiling layer. The list closes and the line you selected changes to the magenta color, showing you that it's now on the Ceiling layer. Also notice that the Color pop-up list in the Properties Inspector palette changes to reflect the new color for the line.

4. Press the Esc key to clear the grip selection. Notice that the layer returns to Jamb, the current layer.

5. Choose View ➤ Zoom ➤ Previous from the menu bar, or you can enter **Z↵ P↵**.

In this exercise, you saw that when you select an object with no command active, the object's properties are immediately displayed in the Properties Inspector palette under Color, Linetype, and Lineweight. Using this method, you can also change an object's color, linetype, and line weight independent of its layer. Just as with the Properties Inspector palette, you can select multiple objects and change their layers through the Layer pop-up list.

Now, you'll finish the bathroom by adding a sink to a layer named Casework:

1. In the Layers palette, create a new layer called Casework.

2. With the Casework layer selected in the Layers palette, right-click and select Set Current.

3. In the Properties Inspector palette, click the Color option for Casework, and then select Blue from the pop-up list. Notice that the Layer list in the Layers palette indicates that the current layer is Casework.

   Next you'll add the sink. As you draw, the objects will appear in blue, the color of the Casework layer.

4. Choose View ➤ Zoom ➤ All from the menu bar, or type **Z↵ A↵**.

5. Click the Insert icon on Tool Sets palette, and then click the Browse button in the Insert Block dialog box to open the Select Drawing File dialog box.

6. Locate the `sink.dwg` file, and double-click it.

7. In the Insert dialog box, click Insert.

8. Place the sink roughly in the upper-right corner of the bathroom plan, and then use the Move command to place it accurately in the corner, as shown in Figure 5.15.

**FIGURE 5.15**
The bathroom with sink and countertop added

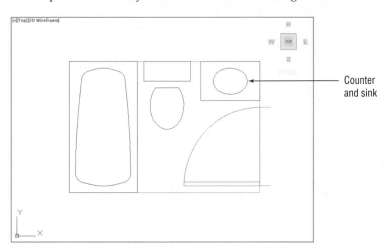

Counter and sink

## Controlling Layer Visibility

I mentioned earlier that you'll sometimes want to display only certain layers to work with in a drawing. In this bathroom is a door header that would normally appear only in a reflected ceiling plan. To turn off a layer so that it becomes invisible, you click the On/Off icon in the Layers palette, as shown in these steps:

1. Click the Ceiling layer in the layer list.

2. Click the On/Off icon to the far left end of the Ceiling layer name. It looks like a white dot. If you don't see the On/Off icon, use the scroll bar at the bottom of the Layers palette to scroll all the way to the left. Once you click the On/Off icon, it changes from a solid white dot to a black dot to indicate that the layer is off.

With the Ceiling layer off, the line representing the door header disappears.

**Real World Scenario**

### GETTING MULTIPLE USES FROM A DRAWING USING LAYERS

Layering lets you use a single AutoCAD drawing for multiple purposes. A single drawing can show both the general layout of the plan and more detailed information such as equipment layout or floor-paving layout.

The following two images are reproductions of the San Francisco Main Library's lower level and show how one floor plan file was used for two purposes. The first view shows the layout of furnishings, and the second view shows a paving layout. In each case, the same floor plan file was used, but in the first panel, the paving information is on a layer that is turned off. Layers also facilitate the use of differing scales in the same drawing. Frequently, a small-scale drawing of an overall plan will contain the same data for an enlarged view of other portions of the plan, such as a stairwell or an elevator core. The detailed information, such as notes and dimensions, might be on a layer that is turned off for the overall plan.

There are a few other icons and corresponding columns that appear with each of the layers in the layer list but they may be hidden from view. Use the scroll bar at the bottom of the Layer palette to scroll the list to the left. You'll see three more icons. These are Freeze/Thaw, Lock/Unlock, Plot/No Plot (Figure 5.16).

The Freeze/Thaw column controls the visibility of layers in a way similar to the On/Off icon. The Lock/Unlock column locks a layer to prevent accidental edits to objects on the layer. The Plot/No Plot column enables you to control whether a layer appears in printed output or if it only appears in the drawing on the computer screen. All of these columns at the top of the layer list are duplicated in the Properties Inspector palette and the properties they control can be set in both places.

**FIGURE 5.16**

The Freeze/Thaw, Lock/Unlock/, Plot/No Plot, and VP icons

Freeze/Thaw | Plot/No Plot

Lock/Unlock

## Adding Control Features to the Layer List

As mentioned earlier, the Properties Inspector palette duplicates some of the settings found in the layer list of the Layers palette. You can include more of the layer properties in the layer list by using the Layers palette's Display Settings icon. Click the Display Settings icon to view the pop-up menu (Figure 5.17). You'll see a list of options, some of which have a check mark next to them. The options with the check mark are the ones that already appear in the layer list.

**FIGURE 5.17**

The Display Settings icon found in the lower-left corner of the Layers palette

You can select an unchecked option to include it in the layer list. For example, if you select Status, a triangle marker appears in the layer list indicating the current layer.

The VP Freeze, VP Color, and VP Lineweight options are used when multiple *viewports* (VPs) are present. You'll learn more about viewports in Chapter 8, "Introducing Printing and Layouts," Chapter 15, "Laying Out Your Printer Output," and Chapter 20, "Using Advanced 3D Features." Viewports interact with layers in a unique way. A viewport is like a custom view of your drawing. You can have multiple viewports in a layout, each showing a different part of your drawing. Layer properties can be controlled for each viewport independently, so you can set up different linetypes, colors, and layer visibility for each viewport.

Toward the bottom of the list, you see three options that control the overall appearance of the list. Optimize All Columns compresses the columns to their smallest size, enabling you to see as many columns as possible within the layer list. Optimize Column adjusts the width of the columns so they fit comfortably within the width of the Layers palette. Restore All Columns To Defaults sets the columns to their default widths.

## Finding the Layers You Want

With only a handful of layers, it's fairly easy to find the layer you want to turn off. It becomes much more difficult, however, when the number of layers exceeds 20 or 30. The Layers palette offers some useful tools to help you find the layers you want quickly.

Suppose you have several layers whose names begin with C, such as C-lights, C-header, and C-pattern, and you want to find those layers quickly. You can click the Name button at the top of the layer list to sort the layer names in alphabetic order. (You can click the Name button again to reverse the order.) To select those layers for processing, click the first layer name that starts with C, and then scroll down the list until you find the last layer of the group and ⇧-click it. All the layers between those layers are selected. If you want to deselect some of those layers, hold down the ⌘ key while clicking the names of the layers you don't want to include in your selection. Another option is to ⌘-click the names of other layers you want selected.

The Color and On/Off column icons at the top of the list let you sort the list by virtue of the color or linetype assignments of the layers. Other column icons sort the list by virtue of status: Freeze/Thaw, Lock/Unlock, and so forth. (See the sidebar "Freeze, Lock, Transparency, and Other Layer Options" later in this chapter.)

Now try changing the layer settings again by turning off all the layers except Wall and Ceiling, leaving just a simple rectangle. In this exercise, you'll get a chance to experiment with the On/Off options of the Layers palette:

1. Click layer 0 in the layer list; then right-click and select Set Current.

2. Click the top layer name in the list box; then ⇧-click the last layer name. All the layer names are highlighted.

   Another way to select all the layers at once in the Layers palette is to right-click the layer list and then choose the Select All option from the shortcut menu. If you want to clear your selections, right-click the layer list and choose Clear All.

3. ⌘-click the Wall and Ceiling layers to deselect them and thus exempt them from your next action.

4. Click the On/Off column icon of any of the highlighted layers.

5. A message appears, asking if you want the current layer on or off. Select Keep The Current Layer On in the message box. The On/Off column icons turn black to show that the selected layers have been turned off.

6. The drawing now appears with only the Wall and Ceiling layers displayed. It looks like a simple rectangle of the room outline.

7. Select all the layers as you did in step 2, and then click any of the black On/Off column icons to turn on all the layers at once.

In this exercise, you turned off a set of layers by clicking the On/Off column icon. You can freeze/thaw, lock/unlock, or change the color of a group of layers in a similar manner by clicking the appropriate layer column icon. For example, clicking a color column icon of one of the selected layers opens the Color Palette dialog box, in which you can set the color for all the selected layers.

---

**FREEZE, LOCK, TRANSPARENCY, AND OTHER LAYER OPTIONS**

You were briefly introduced to the Freeze/Thaw icon in the Layers palette. This icon is similar to the On/Off icon. However, Freeze/Thaw not only makes layers invisible, it also tells AutoCAD to ignore the contents of those layers during selection and display operations. Freezing layers can save time when you issue a command that regenerates a complex drawing. This is because AutoCAD ignores objects on frozen layers during regen. You'll get firsthand experience with Freeze and Thaw in Chapter 7, "Mastering Viewing Tools, Hatches, and External References."

Another Layers palette option, Lock/Unlock, offers functionality similar to Freeze/Thaw. If you lock a layer, you can view and snap to objects on that layer, but you can't edit those objects. This feature is useful when you're working on a crowded drawing and you don't want to accidentally edit portions of it. You can lock all the layers except those you intend to edit and then proceed to work without fear of making accidental changes. Locked layers will dim slightly to help you distinguish them from unlocked layers.

The Properties Inspector palette offers a Transparency slider that allows you to control the transparency of layers. The slider does not affect printer output unless you turn on the Plot option just below the Transparency slider.

Three more Properties Inspector palette options—Lineweight, Plot Style, and Plot—offer control over the appearance of printer output. Lineweight lets you control the width of lines in a layer. Plot Style lets you assign plotter configurations to specific layers. (You'll learn more about plot styles in Chapter 8.) Plot lets you determine whether a layer gets printed in hard-copy output. This can be useful for setting up layers you may use for layout purposes only. The Linetype option lets you control line patterns, such as dashed or center lines.

---

## NAMING LAYERS TO STAY ORGANIZED

If you name layers carefully, you can use them as a powerful layer-management tool. For example, suppose you have a drawing whose layer names are set up to help you easily identify floor-plan data versus ceiling-plan data, as in the following list:

- A-FP-WALL-JAMB
- A-FP-WIND-JAMB
- A-CP-WIND-HEAD
- A-CP-DOOR-HEAD
- L-FP-CURB
- C-FP-ELEV

The first character in the layer name designates the discipline related to that layer: *A* for architectural, *L* for landscape, *C* for civil, and so on. In this example, layers with names containing the two characters *FP* signify floor-plan layers. *CP* designates ceiling-plan information.

These layer name examples are loosely based on a layer naming convention devised by the American Institute of Architects (AIA). As you can see from this example, careful naming of layers can help you manage them.

### FILTERING LAYERS BY THEIR NAMES

Once you start to use a layer-naming system, you can use the Layers palette's Search text box to isolate layers that you want to work on. For example, if you want to isolate only those layers that have to do with floor plans, regardless of their discipline, enter **-FP** in the Layers palette's Search text box. Once you do this, the layer list changes to display only layers with FP in their names. In addition, if you press ↵ after typing -FP, -FP becomes an option in the Search text box pop-up list, which can be opened by clicking the magnifying glass icon to the left of the list. (Figure 5.18).

**FIGURE 5.18**
Enter **-FP** in the Layers palette's Search text box and the name becomes an option in the search list.

Click the magnifying glass icon to display previous searches.

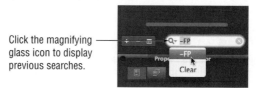

Once you've filtered your layer list using the Search text box, you can turn off all of the remaining layers in the list, change their color assignment, or change other settings quickly without having to wade through a long list of layers you don't want to touch. You can add more Search options to the Search text box list. AutoCAD keeps these options for future use until you delete them by selecting Clear from the Search text box pop-up menu.

As the number of layers in a drawing grows, you'll find the Search text box an indispensable tool. But bear in mind that the successful use of the Search text box can depend on a careful layer-naming convention. If you're producing architectural plans, you may want to consider the AIA layer-naming guidelines.

## Assigning Linetypes to Layers

You'll often want to use different linetypes to show hidden lines, center lines, fence lines, or other noncontinuous lines. You can assign a color and a linetype to a layer. You then see International Organization for Standardization (ISO) and complex linetypes, including lines that can be used to illustrate gas and water lines in civil work or batt insulation in a wall cavity.

AutoCAD comes with several linetypes, as shown in Figure 5.19. ISO linetypes are designed to be used with specific plotted line widths and linetype scales. For example, if you're using a pen width of 0.5 mm, set the linetype scale of the drawing to 0.5 as well. (See Chapter 15 for more information on plotting and linetype scale.) You can also create your own linetypes (see Bonus Chapter 2 on the book's companion website).

Linetypes that contain text, such as the gas-line sample at the bottom of Figure 5.19, use the current text height and font to determine the size and appearance of the text displayed in the line. A text height of zero displays the text properly in most cases. See Chapter 9, "Adding Text to Drawings," for more on text styles.

AutoCAD stores linetype descriptions in an external file named Acad.lin, or Acadiso.lin for metric users. You can edit this file in a text editor like Notepad to create new linetypes or to modify existing ones. You'll see how this is done in Bonus Chapter 2 on the book's companion website.

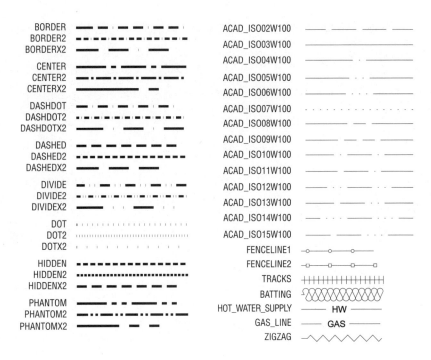

**FIGURE 5.19**

Standard, ISO, and complex AutoCAD linetypes

## Adding a Linetype to a Drawing

To see how linetypes work, you'll add a DASHDOT line in the bathroom plan to indicate a shower curtain rod:

1. In the Layers palette, click the plus icon in the lower-left corner to create a new layer, and then type **Pole**↵ to give the new layer a unique name.

2. Select the Pole layer in the list, and then in the Properties Inspector palette, click the Linetype option to open the pop-up menu.

   If you're in a hurry, you can simultaneously load a linetype and assign it to a layer by using the Layer command. In this exercise, you enter **-Layer**↵ at the Command prompt. Then enter **L**↵, **DASHDOT**↵, and **pole**↵, and press ↵ to exit the Layer command.

3. Select Manage from the pop-up list. The Select Linetype dialog box appears (see Figure 5.20).

4. The Select Linetype dialog box offers a list of linetypes to choose from. In a new file such as the Bath file, only one linetype is available by default. You must load any additional linetypes you want to use. Click the Load button at the bottom of the dialog box to open the Load Or Reload Linetypes dialog box. You can sort the names alphabetically or by description by clicking the Linetype or Description heading at the top of the list (see Figure 5.21).

**FIGURE 5.20**
The Select Linetype dialog box

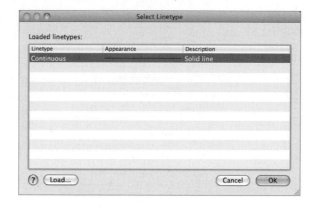

**FIGURE 5.21**
The Load Or Reload Linetypes dialog box

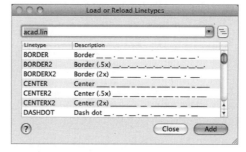

5. In the list of linetypes, scroll down to locate the DASHDOT linetype, click it, and then click Add.

6. Notice that the DASHDOT linetype is added to the linetypes available in the Select Linetype dialog box.

7. Click DASHDOT to highlight it; then click OK. DASHDOT appears in the Linetype option in the Properties Inspector palette.

8. Back in the Layers palette, make sure Pole is still highlighted, and then right-click and select Set Current from the shortcut menu.

9. Turn off Object Snap mode; then, draw a line representing the shower curtain rod across the opening of the tub area as shown later in Figure 5.23.

### CONTROLLING LINETYPE SCALE

Although you've designated this as a DASHDOT line, it appears solid. Zoom in to a small part of the line and you'll see that the line is indeed as you specified.

Because your current drawing is at a scale of 1″ = 1′, you must adjust the scale of your linetypes accordingly. This is accomplished in the Linetype Manager dialog. Here are the steps:

1. Choose Format ➤ Linetype from the menu bar. You can also enter **LT**↵. The Linetype Manager dialog box opens (see Figure 5.22).

**FIGURE 5.22**

The Linetype
Manager dialog box

Linetype Manager

Linetype filters: Show all linetypes

| Linetype | Appearance | Description |
|---|---|---|
| ByBlock | ———————— | |
| ▶ ByLayer | – – – – – – – | |
| Continuous | ———————— | Solid line |
| DASHDOT | – · – · – · – · – · | Dash dot _ . _ . _ . _ .... |

\+ −

Details

Name: No Selection

Description: No Selection

Global scale factor: 1.0000

Current object scale: 1.0000

ISO pen width: 1.0 mm

☑ Use paperspace units for scaling

? Cancel Save

The Linetype Manager dialog box offers plus and minus buttons below the Linetypes list that let you load or delete a linetype directly without having to go through a particular layer's linetype setting.

2. Double-click the Global Scale Factor text box, and then type **12** (metric users type **30**). This is the scale conversion factor for a 1″ = 1′ scale. (See the section "Understanding Scale Factors" in Chapter 3, "Setting Up and Using AutoCAD's Drafting Tools.")

3. Click Save. The shower curtain rod is displayed in the linetype and at the scale you designated.

4. Choose View ➢ Zoom ➢ All or type **Z↵ A↵** so your drawing looks like Figure 5.23.

You can also use the Ltscale system variable to set the linetype scale. Type **LTS↵**, and at the `Enter new linetype scale factor <1.0000>:` prompt, enter **12↵**.

**FIGURE 5.23**

The completed
bathroom

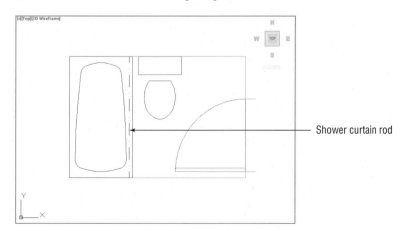

Shower curtain rod

### LINETYPES TROUBLESHOOTING

If you change the linetype of a layer or an object but the object remains a continuous line, check the Ltscale system variable. It should be set to your drawing scale factor. If this doesn't work, set the Viewres system variable to a higher value (see Appendix D on the book's companion website). (Viewres can also be set by the Arc And Circle Smoothness option in the Document Settings option of the Application Preferences dialog box.) The behavior of linetype scales depends on whether you're in Model Space or in a drawing layout. If your efforts to control linetype scale have no effect on your linetype's visibility, you may be in a drawing layout. See Chapter 15 for more on Model Space and layouts.

Remember that if you assign a linetype to a layer, everything you draw on that layer will be of that linetype. This includes arcs, polylines, circles, and traces. As explained in the sidebar "Assigning Colors, Linetypes, and Linetype Scales to Individual Objects" later in this chapter, you can also assign different colors and linetypes to individual objects rather than relying on their layer assignment to define color and linetype. However, you may want to avoid assigning colors and linetypes directly to objects until you have some experience with AutoCAD and a good grasp of your drawing's organization.

In the previous exercise, you changed the global linetype scale setting. This affects all noncontinuous linetypes within the current drawing. You can also set the default linetype scale for all new objects with the Celtscale system variable (type **CELTSCALE**↵ and enter the desired scale factor).

When individual objects are assigned a linetype scale, they're still affected by the global linetype scale set by the Ltscale system variable. For example, say you assign a linetype scale of 2 to the curtain rod in the previous example. This scale is then multiplied by the global linetype scale of 12, for a final linetype scale of 24.

You can also set the default linetype scale for individual objects by using the Celtscale system variable. After it's set, only newly created objects are affected. You must use the Properties Inspector palette to change the linetype scale of individual existing objects.

### LINETYPES IN LAYOUTS

A system variable called Psltscale affects how layout viewports display linetypes. When the Psltscale system variable is set to 1, layout viewports display linetypes at the Ltscale setting, which is usually incorrect for the 1-to-1 scale of the layout. When Psltscale is set to 0, linetypes appear in layout viewports in the same way they appear in the Model Space.

### ADDING THE FINAL DETAIL

If you're working through the tutorial, your final task is to set up an insertion point for the current drawing to facilitate its insertion into other drawings in the future. Follow these steps:

1. Type **BASE**↵.

2. At the `Enter base point <0'-0",0'-0",0'-0">:` prompt, use the Endpoint object snap to pick the upper-left corner of the bathroom. The bathroom drawing is complete.

3. Choose File ➢ Save to save the current drawing.

### Controlling Line Weights

You may have noticed a Lineweight option in the Properties Inspector palette. If you click this option for a given layer or object, a pop-up list that enables you to control the plotted thickness of your lines appears. Plotted line weights can be assigned directly to an object or to layers. You can view line weights as they will appear in your final plot by making setting changes in the Lineweights Settings dialog box, which you'll learn about in Chapter 15.

With the Lineweight option and Lineweight Settings dialog box, you have greater control over the look of your drawings. This can save time because you don't have to print your drawing just to check for line weights. You'll be able to see how thick or thin your lines are as you edit your drawing.

## Using Objects to Control Layers

You've seen the various tools used to control the layers in a drawing. AutoCAD also offers a set of icons that can help streamline many of the layer operations. You may have already noticed the row of icons at the top of the Layers palette. These icons enable you to set layer properties through the objects in your drawing.

For example, suppose you want to turn off the layer of a particular object in the drawing. You can select the object and then check the Properties Inspector palette to find its layer. Once you know the layer name, you can turn it off. But the Turn Off Object's Layer icon in the Layers palette turns off an object's layer with a single click, saving a few steps.

Figure 5.24 shows you the tooltip name of each icon and Table 5.2 describes how each tool is used. Keep these icons in mind as you work with AutoCAD. You'll find they can be real timesavers.

**FIGURE 5.24**
The Layers
palette icons

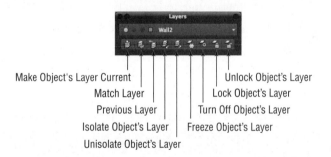

Make Object's Layer Current

Match Layer

Previous Layer

Isolate Object's Layer

Unisolate Object's Layer

Unlock Object's Layer

Lock Object's Layer

Turn Off Object's Layer

Freeze Object's Layer

**TABLE 5.2:** The Layers palette icons

| ICON NAME | USE |
|---|---|
| Make Object's Layer Current | Click this icon, and then select an object to make its layer current. |
| Match Layer | Click this icon, select an object or objects whose layer assignment you want to change, press ⏎, and then select an object whose layer you want to change to. |
| Previous Layer | Click this icon to switch to the previous current layer. |

**TABLE 5.2:** The Layers palette icons *(CONTINUED)*

| ICON NAME | USE |
|---|---|
| Isolate Object's Layer | Click this icon, and then select an object to turn off all layers except the selected object's layer. |
| Unisolate Objects Layer | Click this option to undo the action of the Isolate Object's Layer icon. |
| Freeze Object's Layer | Click this icon, and then select an object to freeze its layer. |
| Turn Off Object's Layer | Click this icon, and then select an object to turn off its layer. |
| Lock Object"s Layer | Click this icon, and then select an object to lock its layer. |
| Unlock Object's Layer | Click this icon, and then select an object to unlock its layer. |

## Keeping Track of Blocks and Layers

The Insert Block dialog box and the Layers palette let you view the blocks and layers available in your drawing by listing them in a window. The Layers palette also includes information about the status of layers. However, you may forget the layer on which an object resides. You've seen how the Properties Inspector palette shows you the properties of an object or layer. The List option menu bar also enables you to get information about individual objects.

Use these steps to see an alternate way to view the properties of a block:

1. Choose Tools ➢ Inquiry ➢ List. You can also type **LIST**↵.

2. At the Select objects: prompt, click the Tub block, and then press ↵.

3. In the Command Line palette, a listing appears that shows not only the layer the tub is on, but also its space, insertion point, name, rotation angle, and scale. You may need to expand the Command Line palette to view the information (click the disclosure triangle on the right side of the palette).

The information in the Command Line palette, except the handle listing, is duplicated in the Properties Inspector palette when you select an object. But having the data in the Command Line palette gives you the flexibility to record it in a text file in case you need to store data about parts of your drawing. You can also use the Command Line palette to access and store other types of data regarding your drawings.

The Space property listed for the Tub block designates whether the object resides in Model Space or Paper Space. You'll learn more about these spaces in Chapters 8 and 15.

### Getting a Text File List of Layers or Blocks

With complex drawings, it can be helpful to get a text file that lists the layers or blocks in your drawing. You can do this by using the log-file feature in AutoCAD. At the Command prompt, enter **LOGFILEMODE**↵, and then enter **1**↵. Type **-LA**↵ **?**↵↵ (don't forget the minus sign at the beginning of the LA command). Your list of layers appears in the Command Line palette. For a list of blocks, enter **-Insert**↵ **?**↵↵. When you've obtained your list, close the log-file feature by typing **LOGFILEMODE**↵ **0**↵.

Once the log-file feature is closed, you can use any text editor to open the AutoCAD log. To find the location of the log file, enter **LOGFILENAME**↵. The name and location of the log file appears in the Command Line palette. Typically, the location would look similar to the following:

```
/Users/user name/Library/Application Support/
Autodesk/local/AutoCAD Mac/R18.1/English/
```

The log file may be in a hidden folder, but you can get to it using the Go To Folder command. While in Finder, press ⇧-⌘-G. In the Go To Folder dialog box, enter the location of the log file, and click Go.

With the log-file feature, you can record virtually anything that appears at the Command prompt. You can even record an entire AutoCAD session. The log file can also be helpful in constructing script files to automate tasks. (See Bonus Chapter 1 on the book's companion website for more information on scripts.) If you want a hard copy of the log file, print it from an application such as TextEdit or your favorite word processor.

---

### ASSIGNING COLORS, LINETYPES, AND LINETYPE SCALES TO INDIVIDUAL OBJECTS

If you prefer, you can set up AutoCAD to assign specific colors and linetypes to objects instead of having objects take on the color and linetype settings of the layer on which they reside. Normally, objects are given a default color and linetype called ByLayer, which means each object takes on the color or linetype of its assigned layer. (You've probably noticed the word *ByLayer* in the Properties Inspector palette and in various dialog boxes.)

Use the Properties Inspector palette to change the color or linetype of existing objects. For new objects, choose Format ➤ Color or enter **COLOR**↵ to open the Color Palette dialog box. This enables you to set the current default color to red (for example) instead of ByLayer. Then everything you draw will be red regardless of the current layer color.

For linetypes, you can use the Linetype Manager (Format ➤ Linetype) to select a default linetype for all new objects. To set the default linetype in the Linetype Manager, double-click on the linetype name so that the "current" triangle to the far left points to the linetype. The list in the Linetype Manager shows only linetypes that have already been loaded into the drawing, so if a desired linetype does not appear in the list, you must use the Load icon (plus sign) to load additional linetypes.

Another possible color and linetype assignment is ByBlock, which you also set with the Properties Inspector palette. ByBlock color makes everything you draw white until you turn your drawing into a block and then insert the block on a layer with an assigned color. The objects then take on the color of that layer. This behavior is similar to that of objects drawn on layer 0. The ByBlock linetype and the ByBlock color work similarly.

Finally, if you want to set the linetype scale for each individual object instead of relying on the global linetype scale (the Ltscale system variable), you can use the Properties Inspector palette to modify the linetype scale of individual objects. In place of using the Properties Inspector palette, you can set the Celtscale system variable to the linetype scale you want for new objects.

As mentioned earlier, stay away from assigning colors and linetypes to individual objects until you're comfortable with AutoCAD; even then, use color and linetype assignments carefully. Other users who work on your drawing may have difficulty understanding your drawing's organization if you assign color and linetype properties indiscriminately.

## The Bottom Line

**Organize information with layers.** Layers are perhaps the most powerful feature in AutoCAD. They help to keep drawings well organized, and they give you control over the visibility of objects. They also let you control the appearance of your drawing by setting colors, line weights, and linetypes.

**Master It** Describe the process of creating a layer.

**Control layer visibility.** When a drawing becomes dense with information, it can be difficult to edit. If you've organized your drawing using layers, you can reduce its complexity by turning off layers that aren't important to your current session.

**Master It** Describe two methods for hiding a layer.

**Keep track of blocks and layers.** At times, you may want a record of the layers or blocks in your drawing. You can create a list of layers using the log-file feature in AutoCAD.

**Master It** How do you turn on the log-file feature?

# Part 2

# Mastering Intermediate Skills

# Chapter 6

# Editing and Reusing Data to Work Efficiently

At least five AutoCAD commands are devoted to duplicating objects—10 if you include the grips options. Why so many? If you're an experienced drafter, you know that you frequently have to draw the same item several times in many drawings. AutoCAD offers a variety of ways to reuse existing geometry, thereby automating much of the repetitive work usually associated with manual drafting.

In this chapter, as you finish drawing the studio apartment unit, you'll explore some of the ways to exploit existing files and objects while constructing your drawing. For example, you'll use existing files as prototypes for new files, eliminating the need to set up layers, scales, and paper sizes for similar drawings. With AutoCAD, you can also duplicate objects in multiple arrays. In Chapter 3, "Setting Up and Using AutoCAD's Drafting Tools," you saw how to use the Object Snap (Osnap) overrides on objects to locate points for drawing complex forms. This chapter describes other ways of using lines to aid your drawing.

Because you'll begin to use the Zoom command more in the exercises in this chapter, you'll review this command as you go along. You'll also discover the Pan command—another tool to help you get around in your drawing.

You're already familiar with many of the commands you'll use to draw the apartment unit. So, rather than going through every step of the drawing process, the exercises will sometimes ask you to copy the drawing from a figure and, using notes and dimensions as guides, put objects on the indicated layers. If you have trouble remembering a command you've already learned, go back and review the appropriate section of the book.

In this chapter, you'll learn to do the following:

- ◆ Create and use templates
- ◆ Copy an object multiple times
- ◆ Develop your drawing
- ◆ Find an exact distance along a curve
- ◆ Change the length of objects
- ◆ Create a new drawing by using parts from another drawing

## Creating and Using Templates

Most programs today include what are called templates. A *template* is a file that is already set up for a specific application. For example, in your word processor, you might want to set up a document with a logo, a return address, and a date so you don't have to add these elements each time you create a letter. You might also want to create a template for invoices to maintain consistent formatting. You can set up a different template for each type of document to meet its specific needs. That way, you don't have to spend time reformatting each new document you create.

Similarly, AutoCAD offers templates, which are drawing files that contain custom settings designed for a particular function. You can also create your own templates for your particular style and method of drawing.

If you find that you use a particular drawing setup frequently, you can turn one or more of your typical drawings into a template. For example, you might want to create a set of drawings with the same scale and paper size as an existing drawing. By turning a frequently used drawing into a template, you can save a lot of setup time for subsequent drawings.

### Creating a Template

The following exercise guides you through creating and using a template drawing for your studio's kitchenette. Because the kitchenette will use the same layers, settings, scale, and paper size as the bathroom drawing, you can use the Bath file as a prototype. Follow these steps:

1.  Start AutoCAD in the usual way.

2.  Choose File ➢ Open from the menu bar, or press ⌘-O to open the Select File dialog box.

3.  Locate the Bath file you created in the last chapter. You can also use the file 06-bath.dwg, which is included on the companion website for this book, www.sybex.com/go/masteringautocadmac.

4.  Click the Erase tool on the Tool Sets palette, choose Modify ➢ Erase from the menu bar, or enter E↵; then type ALL↵↵. This erases all the objects that make up the bathroom, but other elements, such as layers, linetypes, and stored blocks, remain in the drawing.

5.  Choose File ➢ Save As from the menu bar, or type ⇧-⌘-S to open the Save Drawing As dialog box. Open the File Format pop-up menu, and select AutoCAD Drawing Template (*.dwt). The file list window changes to display the current template files in the \Template\ folder.

---

**LOCATING THE** Template Folder

When you choose the AutoCAD Drawing Template option in the Save Drawing As dialog box, AutoCAD automatically opens the folder containing the template files. The standard AutoCAD installation creates the folder named Template to contain the template files. If you want to place your templates in a different folder, you can change the default template location by using the Application Preferences dialog box (right-click on the drawing area and choose Preferences, or press ⌘-,). Click the Application tab in the sidebar, and in the Files area, double-click to expand Template Settings and then double-click Drawing Template File Location in the list. Double-click the folder name that appears just below Drawing Template File Location; then select a new location from the Browse For Folder dialog box that appears.

6. In the Save As text box, enter the name **ARCH8x11H**. If you're a metric user, enter the name **A4PLAN**.

7. Click Save.

8. At the Enter Template Measurement [English/Metric] <English>: prompt, enter **E⏎** (English) or **M⏎** (metric) depending on the unit system you're using.

9. Enter the following description: **ARCHITECTURAL ONE INCH SCALE DRAWING ON 8.5 by 11 INCH MEDIA**. Metric users should enter the description **ARCHITECTURAL 1 to 10 SCALE DRAWING ON A4 MEDIA**.

10. The template file you saved becomes the current file. (Choosing File ➤ Save As from the menu bar also makes the saved file current.) This exercise shows that you can edit template files just as you would regular drawing files.

11. Close the template file.

## Using a Template

Now let's see how a template is used. You'll use the template you just created as the basis for a new drawing you'll work on in this chapter:

1. Choose File ➤ New from the menu bar, or press ⌘-N to open the Select Template dialog box. This is a typical file dialog box that you should be familiar with by now.

2. In the Select Template list box, select the filename Arch8x11h.dwt. Metric users should select the filename A4plan.dwt. Because this file is blank, you won't see anything in the preview window.

3. Click Open. It may not be obvious, but your new file is set up with the same architectural units and drawing limits as the bathroom drawing. It also contains the Door, Sink, Toilet, and Tub blocks.

4. You need to give your new file a name. Select Save As to open the Save Drawing As dialog box. Enter **KITCHEN** for the filename, and select the folder in which to save your new Kitchen file.

5. Click Save to create the Kitchen file and close the dialog box.

You've created and used your own template file. Later, when you've established a comfortable working relationship with AutoCAD, you can create a set of templates that are custom made to your particular needs.

However, if you're in a hurry, you don't need to create a template every time you want to reuse settings from another file. You can use an existing file as the basis or prototype for a new file without creating a template. Open the prototype file, and choose Save As to create a new version of the file under a new name. You can then edit the new version without affecting the original prototype file.

## Copying an Object Multiple Times

Let's explore the tools that let you quickly duplicate objects. In this section, you'll begin to draw parts of a small kitchen. The first exercise introduces the Array command, which you can use to draw the gas burners of a range top.

As you'll see, an array can be either in a circular pattern, called a *polar array*, or a matrix of columns and rows, called a *rectangular array*.

### Making Circular Copies

To start the range top, first set the layer on which you want to draw, and then draw a circle representing the edge of one burner:

1. Set the current layer to Fixture by right-clicking on the Fixture layer from the Layers palette and selecting Set Current.

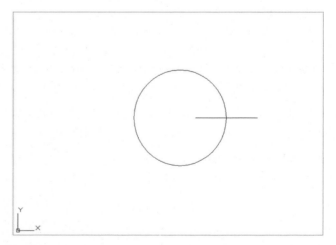

2. Click the Center, Radius Circle tool on the Tool Sets palette. You can also choose Draw ➤ Circle ➤ Center, Radius from the menu bar, or type **C↵**.

3. At the Specify center point for circle or [3P/2P/Ttr (tan tan radius)]: prompt, pick a point at coordinate 4′,4′. Metric users should pick a point at coordinate 120,120.

4. At the Specify radius of circle or [Diameter]: prompt, enter **3↵**. Metric users should enter **7.6↵**. The circle appears.

Now you're ready to use the Array command to draw the burner grill. You'll first draw one line representing part of the grill and then use the Array command to create the copies:

1. Zoom into the circle you just drew and then make sure the Snap mode is off by checking the Snap Mode button in the status bar.

2. Draw a 4″ line starting from the coordinate 4′-1″,4′-0″ and ending to the right of that point. Metric users should draw a 9 cm line starting at coordinate 122,120 and ending to the right of that point.

3. Adjust your view so it looks similar to Figure 6.1.

**FIGURE 6.1**
A close-up of the circle and line

You've got the basic parts needed to create the burner grill. You're ready to make multiple copies of the line. For this part, you'll use the Array dialog box.

1. Click the Array tool on the Tool Sets palette. You can also choose Modify ➤ Array from the menu bar or type **AR**↵ to open the Array dialog box (see Figure 6.2).

**FIGURE 6.2**
The Array
dialog box

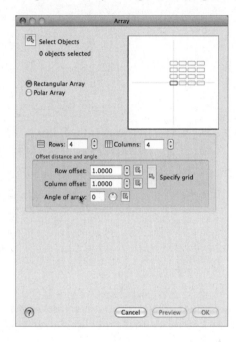

2. Click the Select Objects button. The dialog box temporarily closes, enabling you to select objects.

3. Type **L**↵ to select the last object drawn, or click the object you want to array.

4. Press ↵ to confirm your selection. The Array dialog reopens.

5. Click the Polar Array radio button near the top of the dialog box to tell AutoCAD you want a circular array. The Array dialog box displays the Polar Array options (see Figure 6.3).

6. Click the Pick Center Point button to temporarily close the Array dialog box.

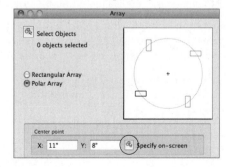

**FIGURE 6.3**
The Polar Array
options

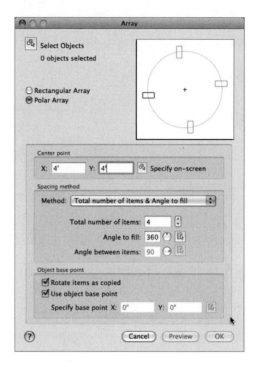

7. Right-click and select Snap Overrides ➤ Center, and then place the cursor on the circle. When you see the circular Osnap marker at the center of the circle, click the mouse. This selects the circle's exact center for the center of the polar array. After you've clicked, the Array dialog box returns.

Remember that to access osnaps other than those set up as Running Osnaps, you right-click and then select Snap Overrides and the osnap you want to use from the resulting menu.

At this point, you've selected an object to array, and you've indicated the center location of the array. If you've selected the wrong object or the wrong center point, you can go back and specify these options again.

Now to complete the process, tell AutoCAD the number of copies in the array and the extent of the array through the circle:

1. In the Array dialog box, enter **8** in the Total Number Of Items text box. This tells AutoCAD to make eight copies including the original.

2. Accept the default of 360 for the Angle To Fill text box. This tells AutoCAD to spread the copies evenly over the full 360 degrees of the circle. Of course, you can enter other values here. For example, if you enter 180, the array will fill half the circle.

   You can click the Pick Angle To Fill button to the right of the Angle To Fill text box to graphically select an angle in the drawing. You can also use the circular slider control as shown in Figure 6.4.

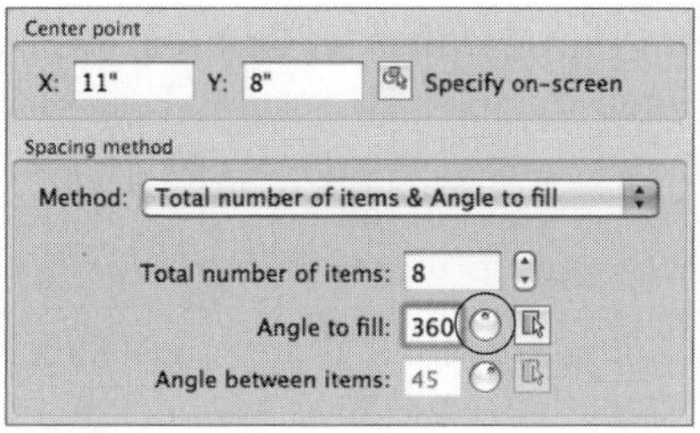

**FIGURE 6.4**

The circular slider

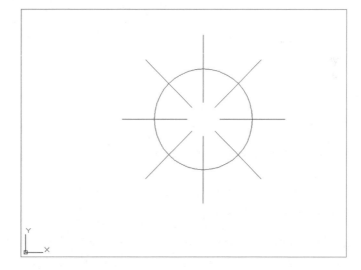

Center point

X: 11"    Y: 8"    Specify on-screen

Spacing method

Method: Total number of items & Angle to fill

Total number of items: 8

Angle to fill: 360

Angle between items: 45

3. Make sure the Rotate Items As Copied check box in the lower-left corner of the dialog box is selected. This ensures that the arrayed object is rotated about the array center. If you clear this option, the copies will all be oriented in the same direction as the original object.

4. Click the Preview button. AutoCAD shows you the results of your array settings.

5. Right-click to accept the array. The circular array appears in the drawing, as shown in Figure 6.5.

In step 5, you could click to return to the Array dialog box and change settings before committing to a final array pattern. You could also press Esc. The Array dialog box gives you a lot of leeway in creating your array copies.

If you're a veteran AutoCAD user and you prefer the command-line version of the Array command, you can type **-ARRAY↵** or **-AR↵** at the Command prompt and then answer the prompts as you would in earlier releases of AutoCAD.

**FIGURE 6.5**

The completed gas burner

## Making Row and Column Copies

Now you'll draw the other three burners of the gas range by creating a rectangular array from the burner you just drew. You'll first zoom back a bit to get a view of a larger area. Then you'll proceed with the Array command.

Follow these steps to zoom back:

1. Click Zoom from the status bar and then type **S↵**. You can also choose View ➢ Zoom ➢ Scale from the menu bar or type **Z↵ S↵**.

2. Enter **0.5x↵**. Your drawing will look like Figure 6.6.

**FIGURE 6.6**
The preceding view reduced by a factor of 0.5

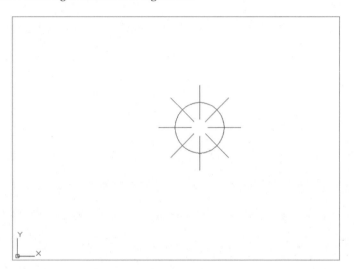

If you're not too fussy about the amount you want to zoom out, you can move the center mouse wheel up or down to reduce your view quickly.

Entering 0.5x for the Zoom Scale factor tells AutoCAD you want a view that reduces the width of the current view to fill half the display area, enabling you to see more of the work area. If you specify a scale value greater than 1 (5, for example), you'll magnify your current view. If you leave off the *x*, your new view will be in relation to the drawing limits rather than the current view.

Next you'll finish the range top. You'll get a chance to use the Rectangular Array option to create three additional burners:

1. Start the Array command to open the Array dialog box.

2. Click the Select Objects button to close the Array dialog box temporarily.

3. Select the entire burner, including the lines and the circle, and then press ↵ to confirm your selection.

4. In the Array dialog box, click the Rectangular Array radio button.

5. Change both the Rows and Columns text boxes to **2**.

**6.** Change the Row Offset text box value to **1´-2″** (**35.5** for metric users) and the Column Offset text box value to **1´-4″** (**40.6** for metric users). See Figure 6.7.

**FIGURE 6.7**
Changes to the
Row Offset text
box value and the
Column Offset text
box value

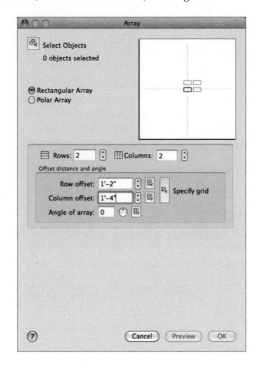

**7.** Click OK. Your screen will look similar to Figure 6.8.

**FIGURE 6.8**
The burners
arrayed

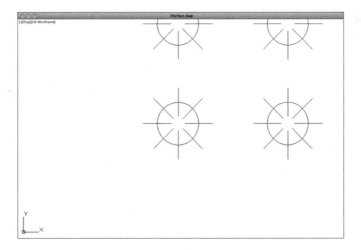

AutoCAD usually draws a rectangular array from bottom to top and from left to right. You can reverse the direction of the array by giving negative values for the distance between columns and rows.

At times, you may want to create a rectangular array at an angle. To accomplish this, enter the desired angle in the Angle Of Array text box in the Array dialog box. You can also select the angle graphically by clicking the Pick Angle Of Array button or using the circular slider to the right of the Angle Of Array text box.

If you need to indicate an array cell graphically, you can do so by using options in the Offset Distance And Angle group of the Array dialog box (see the bottom image in Figure 6.9). An *array cell* is a rectangle defining the distance between rows and columns (see the top image in Figure 6.9). You may want to use this option when objects are available to use as references from which to determine column and row distances. For example, you might draw a crosshatch pattern, as on a calendar, within which you want to array an object. You use the intersections of the hatch lines as references to define the array cell, which is one square in the hatch pattern.

In the Offset Distance And Angle group, the Pick Both Offsets tool lets you indicate the row and column distance by placing an array cell graphically in the drawing, as shown in the bottom image in Figure 6.9. You can also indicate a row or column distance graphically by using the Pick Row Offset button or the Pick Column Offset button to the right of the Pick Both Offsets button. Clicking the circular slider to the right of the offset text boxes allows you to incrementally change the distance up or down.

**FIGURE 6.9**
An array cell and the Array dialog box tool that let you graphically indicate array cells

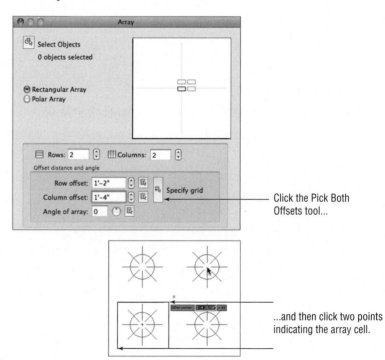

Click the Pick Both Offsets tool...

...and then click two points indicating the array cell.

## Fine-Tuning Your View

Back in Figure 6.8, you may have noticed that parts of the burners don't appear on the display. To move the view over so you can see all the burners, use the Pan command. Pan is similar to Zoom in that it changes your view of the drawing. However, Pan doesn't alter the magnification of the view the way Zoom does. Rather, Pan maintains the current magnification while moving your view across the drawing, just as you would pan a camera across a landscape.

To activate the Pan command, follow these steps:

1.  Click Pan from the status bar. You can also choose View ➢ Pan ➢ Realtime from the menu bar or type **P**↵ You can also right-click and choose Pan from the shortcut menu or hold down the spacebar while moving the mouse or swiping on the trackpad. A small hand-shaped cursor appears in place of the AutoCAD cursor.

2.  Place the hand cursor in the center of the drawing area, and then click and drag it downward and to the left. The view follows the motion of your mouse.

3.  Continue to drag the view until it looks similar to Figure 6.10; then release the mouse button.

4.  To finish the kitchen, you want a view that shows more of the drawing area. Right-click to open the Zoom/Pan shortcut menu, and then choose Zoom. The cursor changes to the Zoom Realtime cursor. The Zoom/Pan shortcut menu also appears when you right-click during the Zoom Realtime command.

5.  Place the cursor close to the top of the screen, and click and drag the cursor downward to zoom out until your view looks like Figure 6.11. You may need to click and drag the Zoom Realtime cursor a second time to achieve this view.

**FIGURE 6.10**
The panned view
of the range top

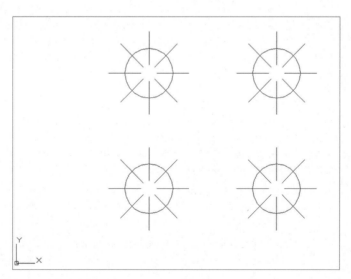

**FIGURE 6.11**

The final view of the finished kitchen. Metric dimensions are shown in brackets.

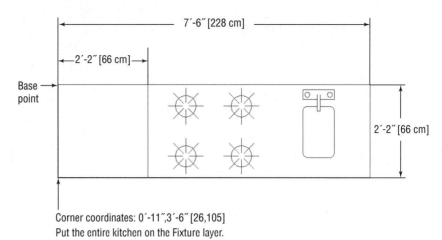

Corner coordinates: 0´-11˝,3´-6˝ [26,105]
Put the entire kitchen on the Fixture layer.

6. Right-click again, and choose Exit from the shortcut menu. You're now ready to add more information to the kitchen drawing.

You can also exit the Pan or Zoom Realtime command without opening the shortcut menu; just press the Esc key.

This exercise showed how you can fine-tune your view by easily switching between Pan and Zoom Realtime. After you get the hang of these two tools working together, you'll be able to access the best view for your needs quickly. The other options in the shortcut menu—Zoom Window, Zoom Original, and Zoom Extents—perform the same functions as the options in the Zoom flyout (choose View ➢ Zoom from the menu bar or in the Status Bar).

The Zoom Window option in the Zoom/Pan shortcut menu functions in a slightly different way from the standard Zoom Window option. Instead of clicking two points, you click and drag a window across your view.

## Finishing the Kitchenette

Before you save and close the Kitchen file, you need to do one more thing. You'll be using this drawing as a symbol and inserting it into the overall plan of the studio apartment unit. To facilitate accurate placement of the kitchen, you'll change the location of the base point of this drawing to the upper-left corner of the kitchen. This will then be the drawing's grip:

1. Complete the kitchenette as indicated earlier in Figure 6.11. As the figure indicates, make sure you put the kitchenette on the Fixture layer. This will help you control the visibility of the kitchenette in future edits of this file. Draw the sink roughly as shown in the figure.

2. Choose Draw ➢ Block ➢ Base from the menu bar or type **BASE**↵. You can also expand the Block panel on the Tool Sets palette and click the Set Base Point icon.

3. At the Enter base point: prompt, pick the upper-left corner of the kitchen, as indicated in Figure 6.11. The kitchen drawing is complete.

4. Choose File ➢ Save from the menu bar, or press ⌘-S, or type **SAVE**↵ and then exit the file.

# Developing Your Drawing

As mentioned briefly in Chapter 3, when you're using AutoCAD, you first create the basic geometric forms used in your drawing, and then you refine them. In the following sections, you'll create two drawings—the studio apartment unit and the lobby—that demonstrate this process in more detail.

First, you'll construct a typical studio apartment unit by using the drawings you've created thus far. In the process, you'll explore the use of lines as reference objects.

You'll also further examine how to use existing files as blocks. In Chapter 4, "Organizing Objects with Blocks and Groups," you inserted a file into another file. The number of files you can insert is limitless, and you can insert files of any size. As you may already have guessed, you can also *nest* files and blocks; that is, you can insert blocks or files in other blocks or files. Nesting can help reduce your drawing time by enabling you to build one block out of smaller blocks. For example, you can insert your door drawing into the bathroom plan. In turn, you can insert the bathroom plan into the studio unit plan, which also contains doors. Finally, you can insert the unit plan into the overall floor plan for the studio apartment building.

## Importing Settings

In this exercise, you'll use the Bath file as a prototype for the studio unit plan. However, you must make a few changes to it first. After the changes are made, you'll import the bathroom and thereby import the layers and blocks contained in the bathroom file.

As you go through this exercise, observe how the drawings begin to evolve from simple forms to complex, assembled forms.

Use these steps to modify the Bath file:

1. Open the Bath file. If you skipped drawing the Bath file in Chapter 5, "Keeping Track of Layers and Blocks," use the file 05c-bath.dwg (or 05c-bath-metric.dwg), which can be obtained from the companion website.

2. Start the Base command using one of the previously mentioned methods. Select the upper-left corner of the bathroom as the new base point for this drawing so you can position the Bath file more accurately.

3. Save the Bath file. If you use the file from the website, choose Save As and save it as Bath in the Documents folder.

4. Click the red Close button in the upper-left corner of the drawing window, choose File ➢ Close from the menu bar, or press ⌘-W to close the bath drawing.

Next you'll create a new file:

1. Click File ➢ New to open the Select Template dialog box.

2. Locate and select the acad.dwt template file. Metric users should locate the acadiso.dwt template file.

3. Click Open to open the new file.

4. If you're using Imperial (English) measurements, choose Format ➢ Units from the menu bar; then in the Drawing Units dialog box, select Architectural from the Length group's Type pop-up menu and click Save. Metric users, use the default Decimal length type.

5. Choose Format ➢ Drawing Limits or type **LIMITS**⏎. At the Specify lower left corner or [ON/OFF] <0'-0",0'-0">: prompt, press ⏎ to accept the default drawing origin for the lower-left corner.

6. If you're using Imperial measurements, enter **528,408**⏎ at the next prompt. These are the appropriate dimensions for a drawing that's 8½″ × 11″ at 1/4″ = 1′-0 ″ scale. Metric users should enter **1485,1050**. This is the work area for a 1:50 scale drawing on an A4 sheet.

7. Choose View ➢ Zoom ➢ All from the menu bar or type **Z**⏎ **A**⏎.

Let's continue by laying out a typical studio unit. You'll discover how importing a file also imports a variety of drawing items such as layers and linetypes. Follow these steps:

1. Begin the unit by drawing two rectangles, one 14′ long by 24′ wide and the other 14′ long by 4′ wide. Metric users should make the rectangles 426 cm wide by 731 cm long and 426 cm wide by 122 cm long. Place them as shown in Figure 6.12. The large rectangle represents the interior of the apartment unit, and the small rectangle represents the balcony. The size and location of the rectangles are indicated in the figure.

**FIGURE 6.12**
The apartment unit interior and balcony. Metric locations and dimensions are shown in brackets.

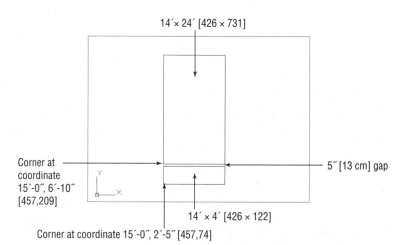

14′× 24′ [426 × 731]

Corner at coordinate 15′-0″, 6′-10″ [457,209]

5″ [13 cm] gap

14′ × 4′ [426 × 122]

Corner at coordinate 15′-0″, 2′-5″ [457,74]

---

**IF YOU USED THE RECTANGLE TOOL TO DRAW THE INTERIOR AND BALCONY...**

...of the apartment unit, make sure you use the Explode tool on the Tool Sets palette to explode the rectangles. The Rectangle command draws a polyline rectangle instead of simple line segments, so you need to explode the rectangle to reduce it to its component lines. You'll learn more about polylines in Chapter 17, "Drawing Curves."

**2.** Click the Insert tool on the Tool Sets palette, choose Insert ➢ Block from the menu bar, or enter **I**↵ to open the Insert Block dialog box.

**3.** Click the Browse button, and locate and select the bathroom drawing (`Bath.dwg`) by using the Select Drawing File dialog box. Then click Open. If you haven't saved a bathroom drawing from earlier exercises, you can use `05c-bath.dwg`.

**4.** If you're using the `05c-bath.dwg` file, do the following: After selecting `05c-bath.dwg` in step 3, change the name that appears in the Name text box to `Bath` instead of `05c-bath` before you click Insert in step 5. This gives the inserted file a block name of `Bath`, even though its originating filename is `05c-bath`.

**5.** Click Insert in the Insert Block dialog box, and then click the upper-left corner of the unit's interior as the insertion point (see Figure 6.13). You can use the Endpoint osnap to place the bathroom accurately. Use a scale factor of 1.0 and a rotation angle of 0°.

**FIGURE 6.13**
The unit after the bathroom is inserted

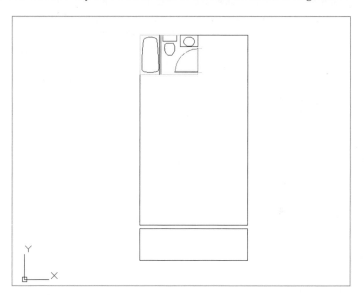

**6.** If Running Osnaps haven't been set up, you need to use the Osnap shortcut menu (right-click and choose Snap Overrides) to access the Endpoint osnap. You can set up Running Osnaps to take advantage of AutoCAD's AutoSnap functions by right-clicking the Object Snap button in the status bar. Set the Running Osnaps as described in Chapter 3.

**7.** Assign the two rectangles that you drew earlier to the Wall layer. To do this, select the lines that make up the rectangles so they're highlighted, and then in the Properties Inspector palette, choose the Layers pop-up menu and select Wall. Press the Esc key to clear the selection.

By inserting the bathroom, you imported the layers and blocks contained in the Bath file. You were then able to move previously drawn objects to the imported layers. If you're in a hurry, this can be a quick way to duplicate layers that you know exist in another drawing. This method is similar to using an existing drawing as a template, but it lets you start work on a drawing before deciding which template to use.

---

**INSERTED DRAWING AND LAYER BEHAVIOR**

If you insert a drawing and the same layers already exist in the current drawing, the inserted drawing layers will be ignored. Therefore, any layer properties in the inserted drawing are not picked up.

---

## Using Osnap Tracking to Place Objects

You'll draw lines in the majority of your work, so it's important to know how to manipulate lines to your best advantage. In the following sections, you'll look at some of the most common ways to use and edit these fundamental drawing objects. The following exercises show you the process of drawing lines rather than just how individual commands work. While you're building walls and adding doors, you'll get a chance to become more familiar with Polar Tracking and Osnap Tracking.

### ROUGHING IN THE LINE WORK

The bathroom you inserted in the preceding section has only one side of its interior walls drawn. (Walls are usually shown by double lines.) In this next exercise, you'll draw the other side. Rather than trying to draw the wall perfectly the first time, you'll sketch in the line work and then clean it up in the next section, in a way similar to manual drafting.

Use these steps to rough in the wall lines:

1.  Zoom in to the bathroom so that the entire bathroom and part of the area around it are displayed, as in Figure 6.14.

**FIGURE 6.14**
The enlarged view
of the bathroom

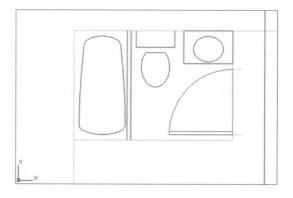

2.  Right-click the layer Wall in the Layers palette. From the menu, click Set Current.

3. Make sure that the Object Snap Tracking and Object Snap buttons on the status bar are turned on.

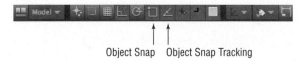

Object Snap     Object Snap Tracking

4. Click the Line tool on the Tool Sets palette; choose Draw ➤ Line from the menu bar, or enter **L**↵.

5. At the `Specify first point:` prompt, hover your cursor over the lower-right corner of the bathroom so that the Endpoint Osnap marker appears, but don't click it.

6. Now move the cursor downward; as you do, the tracking vector appears. (If the tracking vector doesn't appear at first, hover your cursor over the corner again until it does appear.)

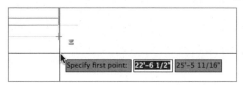

Remember that a little cross appears at the osnap location, telling you that Osnap Tracking has "locked on" to that location.

7. With the tracking vector visible, point the cursor directly downward from the corner, and then type **5**↵. Metric users should type **13**↵. A line starts 5″ (or 13 cm) below the lower-right corner of the bathroom. This is known as *direct distance*.

8. Continue the line horizontally to the left, to cross the left wall of the apartment unit slightly, as illustrated in the top image in Figure 6.15. Press ↵.

9. Draw another line upward from the endpoint of the top door jamb to meet the top wall of the unit (see the bottom image in Figure 6.15). Use the Perpendicular osnap to pick the top wall of the unit. This causes the line to end precisely on the wall line in a perpendicular position, as in the bottom image in Figure 6.15.

   You can also use the Perpendicular Osnap override to draw a line perpendicular to a non-orthogonal line—one at a 45° angle, for instance.

---

**SMOOTHING THE ARC**

You may notice that some of the arcs in your bathroom drawing aren't smooth. Don't be alarmed; this is how AutoCAD displays arcs and circles in enlarged views. The arcs will be smooth when they're printed. If you want to see them now as they're stored in the file, you can regenerate the drawing by typing **REGEN**↵ at the Command prompt. Chapter 7, "Mastering Viewing Tools, Hatches, and External References," discusses regeneration in more detail.

**FIGURE 6.15**

The first wall line and the wall line by the door

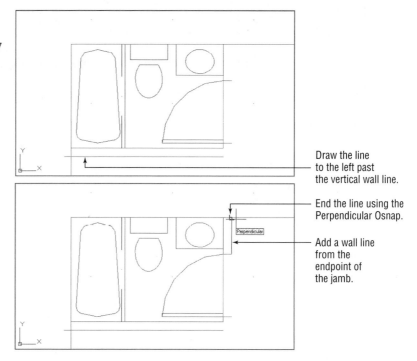

Draw the line to the left past the vertical wall line.

End the line using the Perpendicular Osnap.

Add a wall line from the endpoint of the jamb.

**10.** Draw a line connecting the two door jambs. Then assign that line to the Ceiling layer. (See the top panel in Figure 6.16.)

**11.** Draw a line 6″ downward from the endpoint of the door jamb nearest the corner. Assign that line to the Wall layer. (See the top panel in Figure 6.16.)

In the previous exercise, Osnap Tracking mode enabled you to specify a starting point of a line at an exact distance from the corner of the bathroom. In step 7, you used the Direct Distance method for specifying distance and direction.

---

**SELECTING POINTS FROM A KNOWN LOCATION**

Instead of using a tracking vector in step 6 of the previous exercise, you can choose From on the Osnap shortcut menu and then open the shortcut menu again and select Endpoint. Select the corner and enter a polar coordinate such as **@5<-90** to accomplish the same task as this exercise.

**FIGURE 6.16**
The corner of the bathroom wall and the filleted wall around the bathroom

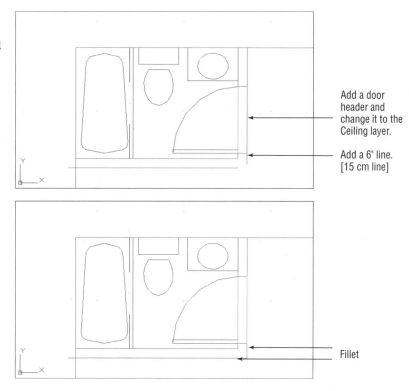

Add a door header and change it to the Ceiling layer.

Add a 6" line. [15 cm line]

Fillet

## CLEANING UP THE LINE WORK

You've drawn some of the wall lines, approximating their endpoint locations. Next you'll use the Fillet command to join lines exactly end to end and then import the kitchen drawing.

---

### UNDERSTANDING THE OSNAP TRACKING VECTOR

The Osnap Tracking vector comes into play only after you've placed an Osnap marker on a location—in this case, the corner of the bathroom. It won't appear at any other time. If you have both Running Osnaps and Osnap Tracking turned on, you'll get the tracking vector every time the cursor lands on an osnap location. This can be confusing to novice users, so you may want to use Osnap Tracking sparingly until you become more comfortable with it.

Because Polar Tracking also uses a tracking vector, you may get the two confused. Remember that Polar Tracking lets you point the cursor in a specific direction while selecting points. If you're an experienced AutoCAD user, you can think of it as a more intelligent Ortho mode. On the other hand, Osnap Tracking lets you align points to osnap locations. Experienced AutoCAD users can think of Osnap Tracking as a more intelligent XYZ filter option.

Follow these steps to join the lines:

1. Click the Fillet tool on the Tool Sets palette, choose Modify ➤ Fillet from the menu bar, or enter **F↵**.

2. Type **R↵ 0↵** to make sure the fillet radius is set to zero.

---

**CHAMFER VS. FILLET**

The Chamfer command performs a function similar to the function the Fillet command performs, but unlike Fillet, it enables you to join two lines with an intermediate beveled line rather than with an arc. Chamfer can be set to join two lines at a corner in exactly the same manner as Fillet.

---

3. Fillet the two lines by picking the vertical and horizontal lines, as indicated in the bottom panel in Figure 6.16 shown earlier in this chapter. Notice that these points lie on the portion of the line you want to keep. Your drawing will look like the bottom panel in Figure 6.16.

4. Fillet the bottom wall of the bathroom with the left wall of the unit, as shown in Figure 6.17. Make sure the points you pick on the wall lines are on the side of the line you want to keep, not on the side you want trimmed.

5. Fillet the top wall of the unit with the right-side wall of the bathroom, as shown in Figure 6.17.

**FIGURE 6.17**
The cleaned-up
wall intersections

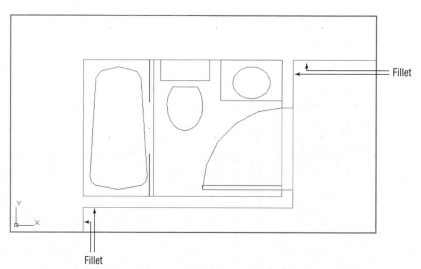

You can select two lines at once for the fillet operation by using a crossing window; to do so, type **C↵** at the `Select first object or ...:` prompt. The two endpoints closest to the fillet location are trimmed.

Where you select the lines affects how the lines are joined. As you select objects to fillet, the side of the line where you click is the side that remains when the lines are joined. Figure 6.18 illustrates how the Fillet command works and shows what the Fillet options do.

**FIGURE 6.18**
Where you click the object to select it determines which part of an object gets filleted.

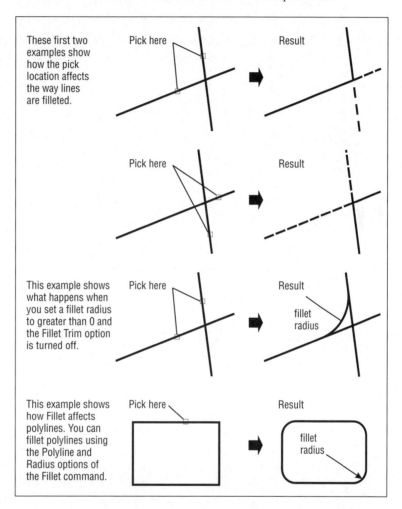

These first two examples show how the pick location affects the way lines are filleted.

Pick here            Result

Pick here            Result

This example shows what happens when you set a fillet radius to greater than 0 and the Fillet Trim option is turned off.

Pick here            Result
                     fillet radius

This example shows how Fillet affects polylines. You can fillet polylines using the Polyline and Radius options of the Fillet command.

Pick here            Result
                     fillet radius

If you select two parallel lines during the Fillet command, the two lines are joined with an arc.

Now import the kitchen plan you drew earlier in this chapter:

1. Insert the kitchen drawing using one of the previously mentioned methods. In the Insert Block dialog box, click the Browse button to locate the kitchen drawing you created earlier in this chapter. Make sure you leave the Specify On-Screen check box unselected under the Scale and Rotation groups; click the Show Insertion Options disclosure triangle if you do not see the options.

2. Place the kitchen drawing at the wall intersection below the bathtub. (See the top image in Figure 6.19.)

   If you didn't complete the kitchen earlier in this chapter, you can insert the `06a-kitchen.dwg` file. Metric users can insert `06 kitchen-metric.dwg`.

3. Adjust your view with Pan and Zoom so that the upper portion of the apartment unit is centered in the drawing area, as illustrated in the top image in Figure 6.19.

**FIGURE 6.19**
The view after using Pan and Zoom, with the door inserted and the jamb and header added

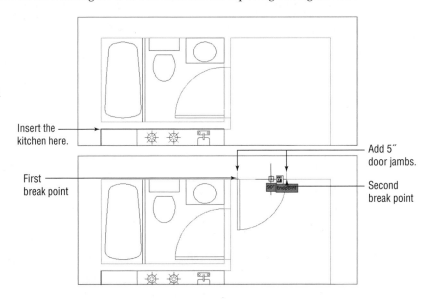

Insert the kitchen here.

Add 5″ door jambs.

First break point

Second break point

## PLACING THE DOOR ACCURATELY

The next step is to add the entry door shown in the bottom image in Figure 6.19. In doing that, you'll use a number of new tools together to streamline the drawing process.

In this exercise, you'll practice using the Osnap Tracking feature and the From Osnap option to place the entry door at an exact distance from the upper corner of the floor plan:

1. Make sure the Door layer is current. Right-click in the Command window, and choose Insert from the shortcut menu to open the Insert Block dialog box. The shortcut menu displays the last three commands used, but if you choose More Commands, you can see additional commands you previously used.

2. Select Door from the Name pop-up menu.

3. Make sure the Specify On-Screen option is checked in the Rotation group but not in the Scale group, and then click Insert. You'll see the door follow the cursor in the drawing window. You may need to click the Show Insertion Options disclosure triangle to view the scale and rotate options.

4. Right-click the mouse, and choose Snap Overrides ➤ From.

**5.** Make sure the Object Snap and Object Snap Tracking buttons on the status bar are on; then use the Endpoint Running Osnap to pick the corner where the upper horizontal wall line meets the bathroom wall.

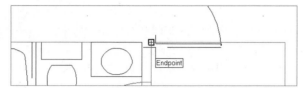

**6.** Move the cursor over the Osnap marker so that the Osnap Tracking vector appears from the corner. Now move the cursor to the right, and you'll see the Osnap Tracking vector extend from the corner.

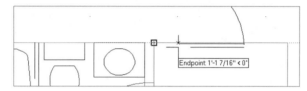

**7.** Continue to move the cursor to the right so that the tracking vector readout shows roughly 6″, or 15 cm for metric users.

**8.** With the cursor in this position, enter **5.↵**. Metric users should enter **13.↵**. The door is placed exactly 5 (or 13) units to the right of the corner.

**9.** At the `Specify rotation angle <0>:` prompt, enter **270.↵**. Or, if you prefer, turn on Polar Tracking to orient the door so that it's swinging *into* the studio. You've now accurately placed the entry door in the studio apartment.

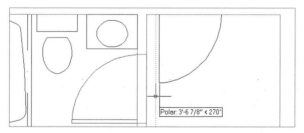

**10.** Make sure the door is on the Door layer.

Next, add the finishing touches to the entry door:

**1.** Add 5″ (13 cm for metric users) door jambs as shown in the bottom image in Figure 6.19, and change their Layer property to the Jamb layer.

2. Click the arrow from the Tool Sets palette to expand the Modify panel on the Tool Sets palette and then click the Break tool. You can also choose Modify ➢ Break from the menu bar or enter **BR**⏎. Select the line over the entry door. (See the bottom image in Figure 6.19.)

3. Type **F**⏎ to use the first-point option; then select the endpoint of one of the door jambs.

4. At the `Specify second break point:` prompt, select the endpoint of the other jamb, as shown in the bottom image in Figure 6.19.

5. Draw the door header on the Ceiling layer, as shown in Figure 6.20.

**FIGURE 6.20**
The other side
of the wall

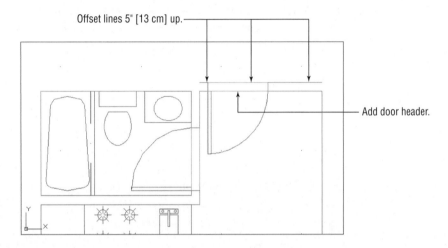

6. Click the arrow from the Tool Sets palette to expand the Block panel and click the Set Base Point tool, or enter **BASE**⏎. Offset the top wall lines of the unit and the door header up 5″ (13 cm for metric users) so they connect with the top end of the door jamb, as shown in Figure 6.20. Don't forget to include the short wall line from the door to the bathroom wall.

7. Choose File ➢ Save to save your file as `Unit`.

### USING POLAR AND OBJECT SNAP TRACKING AS CONSTRUCTION LINE TOOLS

So far, you've been using existing geometry to place objects in the plan accurately. In this section, you'll use the Polar and Object Snap Tracking tools to extend the upper wall line 5″ (13 cm for metric users) beyond the right-side interior wall of the unit. You'll also learn how to use the Construction Line tool to locate door jambs accurately near the balcony.

## OTHER METHODS FOR USING THE BREAK COMMAND

In the exercise for finishing the unit plan, you used the Break command to place a gap in a line accurately over the entry door. In Chapter 5, you broke a line at a single point to create multiple, contiguous line segments.

Earlier in this chapter, you used the Break command's F option, which allows you to specify the first point of a break. You can also break a line without the F option, but with a little less accuracy. When you don't use the F option, the point at which you select the object is used as the first break point. If you're in a hurry, you can dispense with the F option and place a gap in an approximate location. You can then later use other tools to adjust the gap.

In addition, you can use locations on other objects to select the first and second points of a break. For example, you might want to align an opening with another opening some distance away. After you've selected the line to break, you can then use the F option and select two points on the existing opening to define the first and second break points. The break points will align in an orthogonal direction to the selected points.

Start by changing the Polar Tracking setting to include a 45° angle:

1. Right-click the Polar Tracking button in the status bar, and choose Settings to open the Drafting Settings dialog box at the Polar Tracking tab (see Figure 6.21).

**FIGURE 6.21**
The Polar Tracking tab in the Drafting Settings dialog box

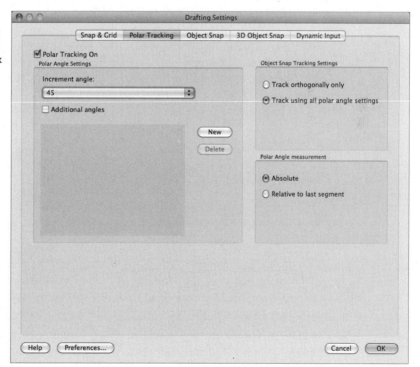

2. Select 45 from the Increment Angle pop-up menu in the upper-left corner of the dialog box.

3. In the Object Snap Tracking Settings group, make sure the Track Using All Polar Angle Settings option is selected and click OK.

You're ready to extend the wall line. For this operation, you'll use grip editing:

1. Click the wall line at the top of the plan and to the right of the door to select the line and expose its grips.

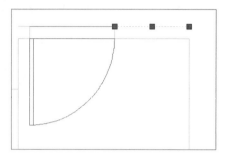

2. Click the Ortho Mode button in the status bar to turn on Ortho mode. This keeps the wall line straight as you edit it.

3. Click the rightmost grip of the line to make it hot.

4. Place the cursor on the upper-right corner of the plan until you see the Endpoint Osnap marker; then move the cursor away from the corner at a 45° angle. The Osnap Tracking vector appears at a 45° angle. Notice the small X that appears at the intersection of the Osnap Tracking vector and the line (see Figure 6.22).

**FIGURE 6.22**
The Osnap Tracking vector

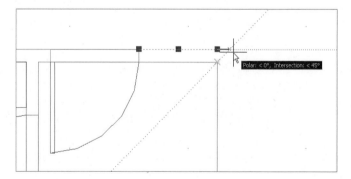

With the Osnap Tracking vector and the line intersecting, click the mouse button. The line changes to extend exactly 5 units beyond the vertical interior wall of the plan.

5. Press the Esc key to clear your selection. Then repeat steps 1 through 4 for the horizontal wall line to the left of the door to extend that line to the left corner (Figure 6.23).

**FIGURE 6.23**
Extend the wall line using the Osnap Tracking vector.

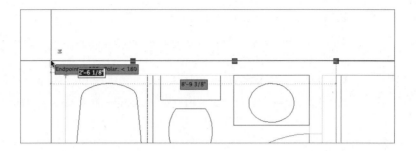

**6.** Click Zoom All or type **Z.↵ A.↵** to view the entire drawing, which should look like Figure 6.24.

**FIGURE 6.24**
The studio unit so far

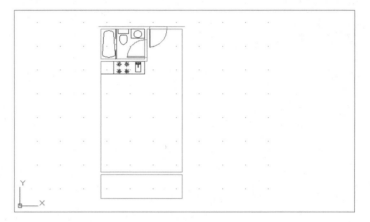

With Polar Tracking set to 45° and Osnap Tracking turned on in a crowded drawing, you may find that you're selecting points you don't really want to select. Just remember that if a drawing becomes too crowded, you can turn off these options temporarily by clicking the Object Snap Tracking or Polar Tracking button in the status bar.

In this exercise, you used Polar Tracking and Ortho mode to position the two lines used for the exterior walls of the studio unit accurately. This shows how you can take advantage of existing geometry with a combination of tools in the status bar.

Now you'll finish the balcony by adding a sliding-glass door and a rail. This time, you'll use lines for construction as well as for parts of the drawing. First, you'll add the door jamb by drawing a construction line. A *construction line* is a line that has an infinite length, but unlike a ray, it extends in both directions. After drawing the construction line, you'll use it to position the door jambs quickly.

Follow these steps:

**1.** Zoom in to the balcony area, which is the smaller rectangle at the bottom of the drawing.

Click the arrow from the Tool Sets palette to expand the Open Shapes panel and then select the Construction Line tool. You can also choose Draw ➤ Construction Line from the menu bar, or enter **XL.↵**. You'll see this prompt:

```
Specify a point or [Hor/Ver/Ang/Bisect/Offset]:
```

2. Type **O↵** to select Offset.

3. At the `Specify offset distance or [Through] <0´-5˝>:` prompt, type **4↵**. Metric users should type **122↵**.

4. At the `Select a line object:` prompt, click the wall line at the right of the unit.

5. At the `Specify side to offset:` prompt, click a point to the left of the wall to display the construction line. (See the top image of Figure 6.25.)

6. At the `Select a line object:` prompt, click the left wall line and then click to the right of the selected wall to create another construction line and press ↵. Your drawing should look like the top image in Figure 6.25.

**FIGURE 6.25**
Drawing the door
opening

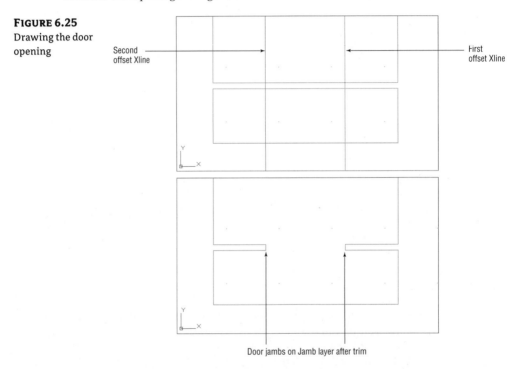

Second offset Xline

First offset Xline

Door jambs on Jamb layer after trim

Next you'll edit the construction lines to form the jambs.

7. Click Trim on the Tool Sets palette, choose Modify ➢ Trim, or type **TR↵**.

8. Select the construction lines and the two horizontal lines representing the wall between the unit and the balcony, and press ↵. You can either use a crossing window or select each line individually. You've just selected the objects to trim to.

You can also use the Fence selection option to select the lines to be trimmed.

9. Click the horizontal lines at any point between the two construction lines. Then click the construction lines above and below the horizontal lines to trim them. Your drawing now looks like the bottom image in Figure 6.25.

10. Assign the trimmed construction lines to the Jamb layer.

11. Add lines on the Ceiling layer to represent the door header.

12. Draw lines between the two jambs (on the Door layer) to indicate a sliding-glass door (see Figure 6.26).

The wall facing the balcony is now complete. To finish the unit, you need to show a handrail and the corners of the balcony wall:

1. Offset the bottom line of the balcony 3″ toward the top of the drawing. Metric users should offset the line 7.6 units.

2. Create a new layer called F-rail, and assign this offset line to it.

3. Add a 5″ (13 cm for metric users) horizontal line to the lower corners of the balcony, as shown in Figure 6.26.

**FIGURE 6.26**
Finishing the
sliding-glass door
and the railing

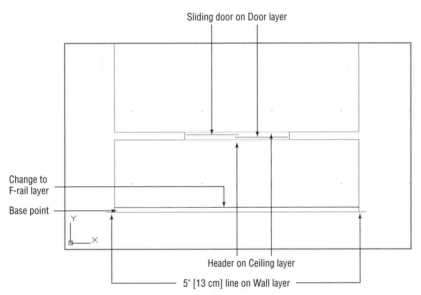

4. Click the arrow from the Tool Sets palette to expand the Block panel and then click the Set Base Point tool. Set the base point at the lower-left corner of the balcony, at the location shown in Figure 6.26.

5. Zoom back to the previous view. Your drawing should now look like Figure 6.27.

6. Choose File ➢ Save to save the drawing, and then close the file.

Your studio apartment unit plan is now complete. The exercises you've just completed demonstrate a typical set of operations you'll perform while building your drawings. In fact, nearly 80 percent of what you'll do in AutoCAD is represented here.

Now, to review the drawing process and to create a drawing you'll use later, you'll draw the apartment building's lobby. As you follow the steps, refer to Figure 6.28.

**FIGURE 6.27**
The completed
studio apartment
unit

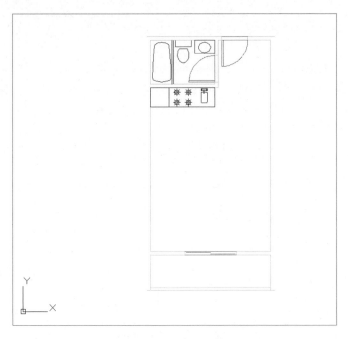

**FIGURE 6.28**
Drawing the
lobby plan. Metric
dimensions are
shown in brackets.

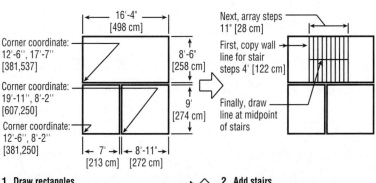

Corner coordinate:
12'-6'', 17'-7''
[381,537]

Corner coordinate:
19'-11'', 8'-2''
[607,250]

Corner coordinate:
12'-6'', 8'-2''
[381,250]

16'-4"
[498 cm]

8'-6"
[258 cm]

9'
[274 cm]

7'
[213 cm]

8'-11"
[272 cm]

Next, array steps
11" [28 cm]

First, copy wall
line for stair
steps 4' [122 cm]

Finally, draw
line at midpoint
of stairs

**1. Draw rectangles
on Wall layer.**

**2. Add stairs
on Floor layer.**

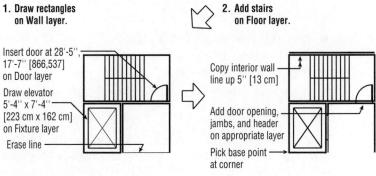

Insert door at 28'-5'',
17'-7'' [866,537]
on Door layer

Draw elevator
5'-4'' x 7'-4''
[223 cm x 162 cm]
on Fixture layer

Erase line

Copy interior wall
line up 5'' [13 cm]

Add door opening,
jambs, and header
on appropriate layer

Pick base point
at corner

**3. Add door and elevator.**

**4. Add door openings.**

---

### THE CONSTRUCTION LINE OPTIONS

There is more to the Construction Line tool than you've seen in the exercises in this chapter. Here is a list of the Construction Line options and their uses:

**Hor**   Draws horizontal construction lines as you click points

**Ver**   Draws vertical construction lines as you click points

**Ang**   Draws construction lines at a specified angle as you pick points

**Bisect**   Draws construction lines bisecting an angle or a location between two points

**Offset**   Draws construction lines offset at a specified distance from an existing line

---

As is usual in floor plans, the elevator shaft is indicated by the box with the large X through it, and the stair shaft is indicated by the box with the row of vertical lines through it. If you're in a hurry, use the finished version of this file, called Lobby.dwg (Lobby-metric.dwg for metric users).

To draw the apartment building lobby, follow these steps:

1. Create a new file called Lobby, using the Unit file as a prototype. (Open the Unit file, choose File ➢ Save As from the menu bar, and enter **Lobby** for the new filename.)

2. Erase the entire unit (click the Erase tool from the Tool Sets palette, and then type **ALL**↵).

3. Draw the three main rectangles that represent the outlines of the stair shaft, the elevator shaft, and the lobby.

4. To draw the stairs, copy or offset the stair shaft's left wall to the right a distance of 4′ (122 cm). This creates the first line representing the steps.

5. Array this line in one row of 10 columns, using 11″ (28 cm) column offset.

6. Draw the center line dividing the two flights of stairs.

7. Draw the elevator, insert the door, and assign the door to the Door layer. Practice using construction lines here.

8. Draw the door jambs. Edit the door openings to add the door jambs and headers.

9. Use the Base command to set the base point of the drawing. Your plan should resemble the one in Figure 6.28, step 4.

10. Save the Lobby file and close it.

---

### USING RAYS

If you like the Construction Line tool but you would like to have one endpoint, you can use a ray (click Ray in the expanded Open Shapes panel on the Tool Sets palette). A *ray* is like a line that starts from a point you select and continues off to an infinite distance. You specify the start point and angle of the ray. You can place a ray at the corner at a 45° angle and then fillet the ray to the horizontal wall line to shorten or lengthen the line to the appropriate length.

## Finding an Exact Distance along a Curve

To find an exact distance along a curve or to mark off specific distance increments along a curve, do the following:

1. Open a new drawing. Click the arrow from the Tool Sets palette to expand the Open Spaces panel and then click the Point Style tool. You can also click Format ➤ Point Style from the menu bar or enter **DDPTYPE**↵ to open the Point Style dialog box (Figure 6.29).

**FIGURE 6.29**
The Point Style dialog box

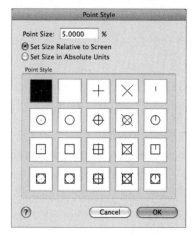

2. Click the X icon in the top row. Also be sure the Set Size Relative To Screen radio button is selected. Then click OK.

   You can also set the point style by setting the Pdmode system variable to 3.

3. Click the Measure tool from the Tool Sets palette, choose Draw ➤ Point ➤ Measure from the menu bar, or type **ME**↵.

---

**THE DIFFERENCE BETWEEN DIVIDE AND MEASURE**

Divide (choose Draw ➤ Point ➤ Divide from the menu bar) marks off a line, an arc, or a curve into equal divisions as opposed to divisions of a length you specify. You might use Divide to divide an object into 12 equal segments, for example. Aside from this difference in function, Divide works exactly the same way as Measure.

---

4. At the Select object to measure: prompt, click the end of the curve that you want to use as the starting point for your distance measurement.

5. At the Specify length of segment or [Block]: prompt, enter the distance you want. A series of Xs appears on the curve, marking off the specified distance along the curve. You can select the exact location of the Xs by using the Node Osnap override (see Figure 6.30).

**FIGURE 6.30**

Finding an exact distance along a spline curve by using points and the Measure command

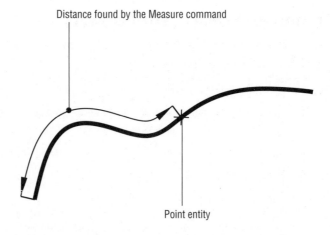

Distance found by the Measure command

Point entity

---

**USING BLOCKS INSTEAD OF POINTS**

The Block option of the Measure command enables you to specify a block to be inserted at the specified segment length in place of the Xs on the arc. You can align the block with the arc as it's inserted. (This is similar to the polar array's Rotate Items As Copied option.)

---

The Measure command also works on most objects, including arcs and polylines. You'll get a more detailed look at the Measure command in Chapter 17.

As you work with AutoCAD, you'll find that constructing temporary geometry such as the circle and points in the two previous examples will help you solve problems in new ways. Don't hesitate to experiment! Remember, you've always got the Save and Undo commands to help you recover from mistakes.

---

 **Real World Scenario**

**DIVIDE AND MEASURE AS AUTOLISP CUSTOMIZATION TOOLS**

Divide and Measure are great tools for gathering information about objects in a drawing. A colleague of mine found Measure to be an excellent way to find the length of a complex object while working on an AutoLISP macro. In AutoLISP, you have to write some elaborate code just to find the length of a complex polyline. After struggling with his program code, he realized that he could use the Measure command to mark off known distances along a polyline and then count the points to find the overall length of the polyline. For more on AutoLISP, see the Bonus Chapter 1 on the accompanying website.

## Changing the Length of Objects

Suppose that, after finding the length of an arc, you realize you need to lengthen the arc by a specific amount. The Lengthen tool in the expanded Modify panel on the Tool Sets palette lets you lengthen or shorten arcs, lines, polylines, splines, and elliptical arcs. As an example, here's how to lengthen an arc:

1. Click the arrow from the Tool Sets palette to expand the Modify panel and then click the Lengthen tool. You can also choose Modify ➢ Lengthen from the menu bar or enter **LEN**↵

2. At the `Select an object or [DElta/Percent/Total/DYnamic]:` prompt, type **T**↵.

3. At the `Specify total length or [Angle] <1.0000)>:` prompt, enter the length you want for the arc.

4. At the `Select an object to change or [Undo]:` prompt, click the arc you want to change. Be sure to click at a point nearest the end you want to lengthen. The arc increases in length to the size you specified.

The Lengthen command also shortens an object if it's currently longer than the value you enter. In this short example, you've learned how to change an object to a specific length. You can use other criteria to change an object's length, using these options available for the Lengthen command:

**DElta** Lengthens or shortens an object by a specific length. To specify an angle rather than a length, use the Angle suboption.

**Percent** Increases or decreases the length of an object by a percentage of its current length.

**Total** Specifies the total length or angle of an object.

**DYnamic** Lets you graphically change the length of an object using your cursor.

## Creating a New Drawing by Using Parts from Another Drawing

This section explains how to use the Export command. Export can be used to turn parts of a drawing into a separate file in a way similar to the Wblock command described in Chapter 4. Here you'll use the Export command to create a separate staircase drawing by using the staircase you've already drawn for the lobby.

Follow these steps:

1. If you closed the Lobby file, open it now. If you didn't create the lobby drawing, open the Lobby.dwg (or Lobby-metric.dwg) file.

2. Choose File ➢ Export from the menu bar, press ⌘-E, or type **Export**↵ to open the Export Data dialog box.

3. Enter **stair** in the Save As text box, and select Block (*.dwg) from the File Format pop-up menu. Click Save.

4. At the `Enter name of existing block or [= (block=output file)/* (whole drawing)] <define new drawing>:` prompt, press ↵. When you export to a DWG format, AutoCAD assumes you want to export a block. Bypassing this prompt by pressing ↵ tells AutoCAD that you want to create a file from part of the drawing rather than from a block.

5. At the `Specify insertion base point:` prompt, pick the lower-right corner of the stair shaft. This tells AutoCAD the base point for the new drawing.

6. At the `Select objects:` prompt, use a window to select the stair shaft, as shown in Figure 6.31.

**FIGURE 6.31**
A selection window enclosing the stair shaft

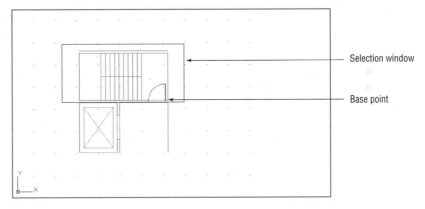

Selection window

Base point

7. When the stair shaft, including the door, is highlighted, press ↵ to confirm your selection. The stairs disappear.

8. Because you want the stairs to remain in the lobby drawing, right-click and choose Undo Export to bring them back. Undo doesn't affect any files you might export by choosing File ➢ Export from the menu bar, by using Wblock, or by using the Block tool.

## Eliminating Unused Blocks, Layers, Linetypes, Shapes, Styles, and More

A template can contain blocks and layers you don't need in your new file. For example, the lobby you just completed contains the Bathroom block because you used the Unit file as a prototype. Even though you erased this block, it remains in the drawing file's database. It's considered unused because it doesn't appear as part of the drawing. Such extra blocks can slow you down by increasing the amount of time needed to open the file. They also increase the size of your file unnecessarily. You can eliminate unused elements from a drawing by using the Purge command.

### SELECTIVELY REMOVING UNUSED ELEMENTS

You use the Purge command to remove unused individual blocks, layers, linetypes, shapes, text styles, and other drawing elements from a drawing file. To help keep the file size small and to make layer maintenance easier, you should purge your drawing of unused elements. Bear in mind, however, that the Purge command doesn't delete certain primary drawing elements—namely, layer 0, the Continuous linetype, and the Standard text style.

Use these steps to practice using the Purge command:

1. Choose File ➢ Open from menu bar, and open the Lobby.dwg sample file.

2. Type **PURGE**↵ (or **PU**↵) to see a listing of drawing components that can be purged.

3. At the Enter type of unused objects to purge: prompt, type **B**↵.

4. At the Enter name(s) to purge <*>: prompt, type **BATH**↵↵.

5. Type **N**↵ to dismiss verification of names. The Bath block has been deleted from the drawing.

### REMOVING ALL UNUSED ELEMENTS

In the preceding exercise, you selected a single block for removal from the Lobby file. If you want to clear all the unused elements from a file at once, you can select the All option.

Here are the steps:

1. Type **PURGE**↵ (or **PU**↵) to see a listing of drawing components that can be purged.

2. At the Enter type of unused objects to purge: prompt, type **A**↵.

3. Press ↵ at the Enter name(s) to purge <*>: prompt. This will select all names.

4. Press ↵ at the Verify each name to be purged? [Yes/No] <Y>: prompt. You can continue to type **Y**↵ and AutoCAD will display the next unused element still in the drawing.

5. Close and save the Lobby file, and exit AutoCAD.

The Lobby file is now trimmed down to the essential data it needs and nothing else.

---

#### PURGING ZERO-LENGTH GEOMETRY AND BLANK TEXT

One of the purge options is to "purge zero-length geometry and empty text objects." This has long been on the wish list of AutoCAD users, and it does just what it says: It purges objects that have no length as well as text objects that do not contain any text.

---

## The Bottom Line

**Create and use templates.**   If you find that you're using the same settings repeatedly when you create a new drawing file, you can set up an existing file the way you like and save it as a template. You can then use your saved template for any new drawings you create.

**Master It**   Describe the method for saving a file as a template.

**Copy an object multiple times.**   Many tools in AutoCAD allow you to create multiple copies. The Array command offers a way to create circular copies or row and column copies.

**Master It**   What names are given to the two types of arrays in the Array dialog box?

**Develop your drawing.**   When laying down simple line work, you'll use a few tools frequently. The exercises in the early part of this book showed you some of these commonly used tools.

**Master It**   What tool can you use to join two lines end to end?

**Find an exact distance along a curve.**   AutoCAD offers some tools that allow you to find an exact distance along a curve.

**Master It**   Name the two tools you can use to mark off exact distances along a curve.

**Change the length of objects.**   You can accurately adjust the length of a line or arc in AutoCAD using a single command.

**Master It**   What is the command alias for the command that changes the length of objects?

**Create a new drawing by using parts from another drawing.**   You can save a lot of time by reusing parts of drawings. The Export command can help.

**Master It**   True or false: The Export command saves only blocks as drawing files.

# Chapter 7

# Mastering Viewing Tools, Hatches, and External References

Now that you've created drawings of a typical apartment unit and the apartment building's lobby and stairs, you can assemble them to complete the first floor of the apartment building. In this chapter, you'll take full advantage of AutoCAD's features to enhance your drawing skills as well as to reduce the time it takes to create accurate drawings.

As your drawing becomes larger, you'll find that you need to use the Zoom and Pan commands more often. Larger drawings also require some special editing techniques. You'll learn how to assemble and view drawings in ways that will save you time and effort as your design progresses. Along the way, you'll see how you can enhance the appearance of your drawings by adding hatch patterns.

In this chapter, you'll learn to do the following:

◆ Assemble the parts

◆ Take control of the AutoCAD display

◆ Use hatch patterns in your drawings

◆ Understand the boundary hatch options

◆ Use external references

## Assembling the Parts

One of the best timesaving features of AutoCAD is its ability to duplicate repetitive elements quickly in a drawing. In this section, you'll assemble the drawings you've been working on into the complete floor plan of a fictitious apartment project. This will demonstrate how you can quickly and accurately copy your existing drawings in a variety of ways.

---

**DON'T SEE THE STATUS BAR?**

In this chapter, you'll be asked to use the Zoom and Pan buttons on the status bar frequently. If you don't see the status bar, choose Tools ➤ Palettes ➤ Status Bar from the menu bar, or press ⌘-6.

---

Start by creating a new file for the first floor:

1. Create a new file named `Plan` to contain the drawing of the apartment building's first floor. This is the file you'll use to assemble the unit plans into an apartment building. If you want to use a template file, use `acad.dwt`. Metric users can use the `acadiso.dwt` template file. (These are AutoCAD template files that appear in the Select Template dialog box when you choose File ➢ New from the menu bar.)

2. Set the Units style to Architectural (choose Format ➢ Units from the menu bar). Metric users can leave the unit style as decimal but change the Insertion scale to centimeters.

3. Set up the drawing for a 1/8″ = 1′-0″ scale on a 24″-×-18″ drawing area (you can use the Limits command for this). Such a drawing requires an area 2,304 units wide by 1,728 units deep. Metric users should set up a drawing at 1:100 scale on an A2 sheet size. Your drawing area should be 5940 cm × 4200 cm.

4. Create a layer called Plan1, and make it the current layer.

5. Right-click the Snap Mode button in the status bar and select Settings.

6. Set Snap Spacing to 1.

7. Choose View ➢ Zoom ➢ All from the menu bar or type **Z**↵ **A**↵ to get an overall view of the drawing area.

Now you're ready to start building a floor plan of the first floor from the unit plan you created in the previous chapter. You'll start by creating a mirrored copy of the apartment plan:

1. Make sure the Object Snap button is turned off, and then insert the `07a-unit.dwg` drawing (which is available on the book's companion website, `www.sybex.com/go/mastering autocadmac`) at coordinate 31′-5″,43′-8″. Metric users should insert the `07a-unit-metric.dwg` drawing at coordinate 957,1330. Accept the Insert defaults. `07a-unit` and `07a-unit-metric` are the same drawings as the `Unit.dwg` file you were asked to create in earlier chapters.

   If you prefer, you can specify the insertion point in the Insert Block dialog box by removing the check mark from the Specify On-Screen check box. The Input options in the dialog box then become available to receive your input.

2. Zoom in to the apartment unit plan.

3. Click Mirror on the Tool Sets palette, select the unit plan, and press ↵.

4. At the `Specify first point of the mirror line:` prompt, right-click the mouse, and choose Snap Overrides ➢ From from the shortcut menu.

5. Right-click again, and choose Snap Overrides ➢ Endpoint from the shortcut menu.

6. Select the endpoint of the upper-right corner of the apartment unit, as shown in Figure 7.1.

7. Enter **@2.5<0**↵. Metric users should enter **@6.5<0**↵. A rubber-banding line appears, indicating the mirror axis.

8. Turn on the Ortho Mode button and select any point to point the mirror axis in a vertical orientation. You can also hold down the ⇧ key as you make your point selection to temporarily turn on the Ortho mode.

**9.** At the `Erase Source Objects? [Yes/No] <N>:` prompt, press ↵. You'll get a 5″ wall thickness between two studio units. Your drawing should be similar to Figure 7.1.

**FIGURE 7.1**

The unit plan mirrored

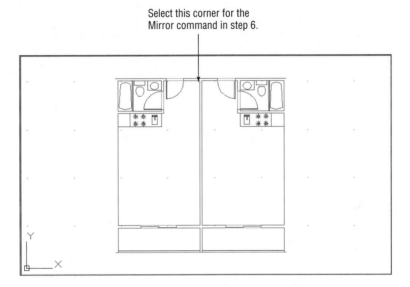

Select this corner for the Mirror command in step 6.

You now have a mirror-image copy of the original plan in the exact location required for the overall plan. Next, make some additional copies for the opposite side of the building:

**1.** Press ↵ to reissue the Mirror command and select both units.

**2.** Use the From osnap option again, and using the Endpoint osnap, select the same corner you selected in step 6 of the preceding set of steps.

**3.** Enter **@24<90** to start a mirror axis 24″ directly above the selected point. Metric users should enter **@61<90**.

**4.** With Ortho mode on, select a point so that the mirror axis is exactly horizontal.

**5.** At the `Erase source objects? [Yes/No] <N>:` prompt, press ↵ to keep the two unit plans you selected in step 1 and complete the mirror operation.

With the tools you've learned about so far, you've quickly and accurately set up a fairly good portion of the floor plan. Continue with the next few steps to "rough in" the main components of the floor:

**1.** Click the Zoom button from the status bar and then type **E↵**, or type **Z↵ E↵** to get a view of the four plans. The Extents option forces the entire drawing to fill the screen at the center of the display area. Your drawing will look like Figure 7.2.

If you happen to insert a block in the wrong coordinate location, you can use the Properties Inspector palette to change the insertion point for the block.

**2.** Copy the four units to the right at a distance of 28′-10″ (878 cm for metric users), which is the width of two units from center line to center line of the walls.

**FIGURE 7.2**
The unit plan,
duplicated four
times

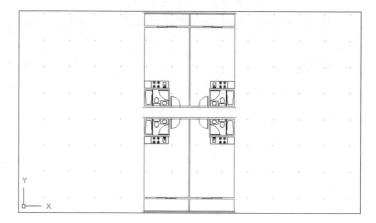

**FIGURE 7.2**
The unit plan,
duplicated four
times

3. Insert the lobby.dwg file at coordinate 89´-1˝,76´-1˝ (the Lobby-metric.dwg file at coordinate 2713,2318 for metric users).

4. Copy all the unit plans to the right 74´-5˝ (2267 cm for metric users), the width of four units plus the width of the lobby.

5. Click the Zoom button from the status bar and then type **A↲**, or type **Z↲ A↲** to view the entire drawing, which should look like Figure 7.3.

**FIGURE 7.3**
The Plan drawing

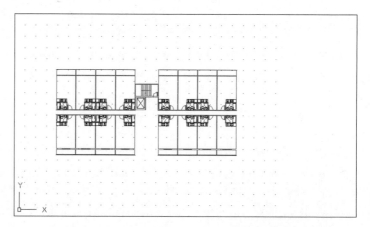

6. Choose File ➢ Save on the menu bar, or press ⌘-S to save this Plan.dwg file to disk.

## Taking Control of the AutoCAD Display

By now, you should be familiar with the Pan and Zoom functions in AutoCAD. Many other tools can also help you get around in your drawing. In the following sections, you'll get a closer look at the ways you can view your drawing.

## Understanding Regeneration and Redrawing

AutoCAD uses two commands for refreshing your drawing display: Regen (drawing regeneration) and Redraw. Each command serves a particular purpose, although it may not be clear to a new user.

To better understand the difference between Regen and Redraw, it helps to know that AutoCAD stores drawing data in two ways:

♦ In a database of highly accurate coordinate information that is part of the properties of objects in your drawing

♦ In a simplified database used just for the display of the objects in your drawing

As you draw, AutoCAD starts to build an accurate, core database of objects and their properties. At the same time, it creates a simpler database that it uses just to display the drawing quickly. AutoCAD uses this second database to allow quick manipulation of the display of your drawing. For the purposes of this discussion, I'll call this simplified database the *virtual display* because it's like a computer model of the overall display of your drawing. This virtual display is in turn used as the basis for what is shown in the drawing area. When you issue a Redraw command, you're telling AutoCAD to reread this virtual display data and display that information in the drawing area. A Regen command, on the other hand, tells AutoCAD to rebuild the virtual display based on information from the core drawing database.

You may notice that the Pan Realtime and Zoom Realtime commands don't work beyond a certain area in the display. When you reach a point where these commands seem to stop working, you've come to the limits of the virtual display data. To go beyond these limits, AutoCAD must rebuild the virtual display data from the core data; in other words, it must regenerate the drawing. You can usually do this by zooming out to the extents of the drawing.

Sometimes, when you zoom in to a drawing, arcs and circles may appear to be faceted instead of smooth curves. This faceting is the result of AutoCAD's virtual display simplifying curves to conserve memory. You can force AutoCAD to display smoother curves by typing **RE↵**, which is the shortcut for the Regen command.

---

### CONTROLLING DISPLAY SMOOTHNESS WITH VIEWRES

As you work in AutoCAD, you may notice that linetypes sometimes appear continuous even when they're supposed to be dotted or dashed. You may also notice that arcs and circles occasionally appear to be segmented lines although they're always plotted as smooth curves. A command called Viewres controls how smoothly linetypes, arcs, and circles are displayed in an enlarged view. The lower the Viewres value, the fewer the segments and the faster the redraw and regeneration. However, a low Viewres value causes noncontinuous linetypes, such as dashes or center lines, to appear as though they're continuous, especially in drawings that cover very large areas (for example, civil site plans).

Finding a Viewres value that best suits the type of work you do will take some experimentation. The default Viewres setting is 1000. You can try increasing the value to improve the smoothness of arcs and see if a higher value works for you. Enter **VIEWRES↵** at the Command prompt to change the value. If you work with complex drawings, you may want to keep the value at 1000; then when you zoom in close to a view, use the Regen command to display smooth arcs and complete linetypes.

---

**CREATING MULTIPLE VIEWS**

So far, you've looked at ways to help you get around in your drawing while using a single view window. You can also set up multiple views of your drawing, called *viewports*. With viewports, you can display more than one view of your drawing at one time in the AutoCAD drawing area. For example, one viewport can display a close-up of the bathroom, another viewport can display the overall plan view, and yet another can display the unit plan.

When viewports are combined with AutoCAD's Paper Space feature, you can print multiple views of your drawing. Paper Space is a display mode that lets you paste up multiple views of a drawing, much like a page-layout program. To find out more about viewports and Paper Space, see Chapter 14, "Advanced Editing and Organizing."

## Saving Views

Another way to control your views is by saving them. You might think of saving views as a way of creating a bookmark or a placeholder in your drawing.

For example, a few walls in the Plan drawing aren't complete. To add the lines, you'll need to zoom in to the areas that need work, but these areas are spread out over the drawing. AutoCAD lets you save views of the areas you want to work on and then jump from saved view to saved view. This technique is especially helpful when you know you'll often want to return to a specific area of your drawing.

You'll see how to save and recall views in the following set of exercises. We'll save a view of the elevator lobby:

1. Click the Zoom button from the status bar and then type **W↵**, or type **Z↵ W↵** and put a window around the elevator lobby, as shown in Figure 7.4.

2. Type **V↵** at the command line.

**FIGURE 7.4**
Select this area for your saved view.

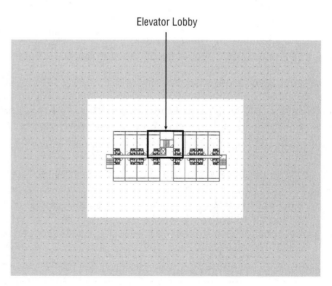

Elevator Lobby

---

**MANAGING SAVED VIEWS**

In the View options on the command line, you can call up an existing view (Restore), create a new view (Save), or get detailed information about a view. You can also select from a set of predefined views that include orthographic and isometric views of 3D objects. You'll learn more about these options in Chapter 19, "Creating 3D Drawings."

---

**3.** Type **S↵** at the command line.

**4.** At the Enter view name to save: prompt, type **Elevator Lobby↵**. The view is saved.

Let's see how to recall the view that you've saved.

**1.** Click the Zoom button from the status bar and then type **A↵**, or type **Z↵ A↵** to view the entire plan.

**2.** Type **V↵** at the command line.

**3.** Type **R↵** to initiate the restore subfunction.

**4.** At the Enter view name to restore: prompt, type **Elevator Lobby↵**.

Your view changes to a close-up of the area you selected earlier.

If you need to make adjustments to a view after you've created it, you can do so by following these steps: Zoom to the view you want to save, and type **V↵** and then **S↵**. Type the name exactly as you did before. Allow the new view to overwrite the old view.

**5.** Save the Plan file to disk.

---

**REPEAT THE LAST COMMAND**

Remember that when no command is active, you can right-click the command line and then select one of the recent commands at the top of the shortcut menu to repeat it. You can also right-click the drawing area when AutoCAD is idle and repeat the last command.

---

## Understanding the Frozen Layer Option

As mentioned earlier, you may want to turn off certain layers to print a drawing containing only selected layers. But even when layers are turned off, AutoCAD still takes the time to redraw and regenerate them. The Layers palette offers the Freeze option; this acts like the Off option, except that Freeze causes AutoCAD to ignore frozen layers when redrawing and regenerating a drawing. By freezing layers that aren't needed for reference or editing, you can reduce the time AutoCAD takes to perform regens. This can be helpful in large, multi-megabyte files.

Be aware, however, that the Freeze option affects blocks in an unusual way. Try the following exercise to see firsthand how the Freeze option makes entire blocks disappear:

**1.** Close the Plan file, and open the 07b-plan.dwg file from the book's companion website. Metric users should open 07b-plan-metric.dwg. This file is similar to the Plan file you created but with a few additional walls and stairs added to finish off the exterior.

2. In the Layers palette, set the current layer to 0.

3. Click the on/off icon in the Plan1 layer listing to turn off that layer. Nothing changes in your drawing. Even though you turned off the Plan1 layer, the layer on which the unit blocks were inserted, the unit blocks remain visible.

4. Right-click in the layer list, choose Select All from the shortcut menu, and then click an on/off icon (not the one you clicked in step 3). You see a message warning you that the current layer will be turned off. Click Turn The Current Layer Off. Now everything is turned off, including objects contained in the unit blocks.

5. Click the on/off icon next to any layer to turn all of the layers back on.

6. Right-click in the layer list, and choose Clear All from the shortcut menu. All layers are now deselected.

7. Click the Plan1 layer's Freeze/Thaw column. (You can't freeze the current layer.) A gray snowflake appears, indicating that the layer is now frozen (Figure 7.5). Only the unit blocks disappear.

**FIGURE 7.5**
Freezing the
Plan1 layer

Even though none of the objects in the unit blocks were drawn on the Plan1 layer, the entire contents of the blocks assigned to the Plan1 layer are frozen when Plan1 is frozen.

You don't really need the Plan1 layer frozen. You froze it to see the effects of Freeze on blocks. Do the following to thaw the Plan1 layer:

1. Thaw layer Plan1 by going back to the Layers palette and clicking the snowflake icon in the Plan1 layer listing.

2. Turn off the Ceiling layer.

The previous exercise showed the effect of freezing on blocks. When a block's layer is frozen, the entire block is made invisible regardless of the layer assignments of the objects contained in the block.

Keep in mind that when blocks are on layers that aren't frozen, the individual objects that are part of the block are still affected by the status of the layer to which they're assigned. This means that if some objects in a block are on a layer called Wall and the Wall layer is turned off or frozen, then those objects become invisible. Objects within the block that aren't on the layer that is off or frozen remain visible.

# Using Hatch Patterns in Your Drawings

To help communicate your ideas to others, you'll want to add graphic elements that represent types of materials, special regions, or textures. AutoCAD provides hatch patterns for quickly placing a texture over an area of your drawing. In the following sections, you'll add a hatch pattern to the floor of the studio apartment unit, thereby instantly enhancing the appearance of one drawing. In the process, you'll learn how to update all the units in the overall floor plan quickly to reflect the changes in the unit.

## Placing a Hatch Pattern in a Specific Area

It's always a good idea to provide a separate layer for hatch patterns. By doing so, you can turn them off if you need to. For example, the floor paving pattern might be displayed in one drawing but be turned off in another so it won't distract from other information.

In the following exercises, you'll set up a layer for a hatch pattern representing floor tile and then add that pattern to your drawing. This will give you the opportunity to learn the different methods of creating and controlling hatch patterns.

Follow these steps to set up the layer:

1. Open the 07a-unit.dwg file. Metric users should open 07a-unit-metric.dwg. These files are similar to the Unit drawing you created in earlier chapters and are used to create the overall plan in the 07b-plan and 07b-plan-metric files. Remember that you also still have the 07b-plan or 07b-plan-metric file open.

2. Zoom in to the bathroom and kitchen area.

3. Create a new layer called Flr-pat.

4. Make Flr-pat the current layer.

Now that you've set up the layer for the hatch pattern, you can place the pattern in the drawing:

1. Click the Hatch tool on the Tool Sets palette, or type **H**↵. The Hatch And Gradient dialog box appears (Figure 7.6).

2. In the Type pop-up menu (see Figure 7.6), select User Defined. The User Defined option lets you define a simple crosshatch pattern by specifying the line spacing of the hatch and whether it's a single- or double-hatch pattern.

3. Highlight the value in the Spacing input box, and enter **6** (metric users should enter **15**). This tells AutoCAD you want the hatch's line spacing to be 6 inches, or 15 cm. Leave the Angle value at 0 because you want the pattern to be aligned with the bathroom.

**FIGURE 7.6**
The Hatch And
Gradient dialog box

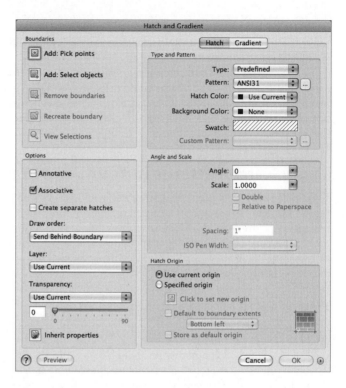

4. Click the Double check box. This tells AutoCAD that you want the hatch pattern to run both vertically and horizontally.

5. Click the Add: Pick Points button. The Hatch And Gradient dialog box disappears. Back in your drawing, hover the cursor over different parts of the bathroom layout but don't click anything. You will see a preview of your hatch pattern appear in each area that you hover over.

6. Click inside the area representing the bathroom floor. The floor area is now highlighted. Notice that the area inside the door swing is not highlighted. This is because the door swing area is not a contiguous part of the floor.

---

### HATCHING AROUND TEXT

If you have text in the hatch boundary, AutoCAD will avoid hatching over it unless the Ignore option is selected in the Island Display Style options of the Advanced Hatch settings. See the section "Controlling Hatch Behavior" later in this chapter for more on the Ignore setting.

---

7. Click inside the door swing to place the hatch pattern.

8. Press ↵ twice to exit the Hatch command.

As you saw from the exercise, AutoCAD gives you a preview of your hatch pattern before you place it in the drawing. In the previous steps, you set up the hatch pattern first by selecting the User Defined option, but you can reverse the order if you like. You can click in the areas you want to hatch first and then select a pattern; then you can adjust the scale and apply other hatch options.

---

**INHERITING HATCH PROPERTIES**

Say you want to add a hatch pattern that you've previously inserted in another part of the drawing. With the Inherit Properties button in the Hatch And Gradient dialog box, you can select a previously created hatch pattern as a prototype for the current hatch pattern. However, this feature doesn't work with exploded hatch patterns.

---

## Adding Predefined Hatch Patterns

In the previous exercise, you used the User Defined option to create a simple crosshatch pattern. You also have a number of predefined hatch patterns to choose from. You can also find other hatch patterns on the Internet, and if you can't find the pattern you want, you can create your own (see Bonus Chapter 2, "Customizing Toolsets, Menus, Linetypes, and Hatch Patterns," found on the book's companion website).

Try the following exercise to see how you can add one of the predefined patterns available in AutoCAD:

1. Pan your view so that you can see the area below the kitchenette. Using the Rectangle tool in the Tool Sets palette, draw the 3′-0″-×-8′-0″ outline of the floor tile area, as shown in Figure 7.7. Metric users should create a rectangle that is 91 cm × 228 cm. You can also use a closed polyline.

**FIGURE 7.7**
The area below the kitchen, showing the outline of the floor tile area

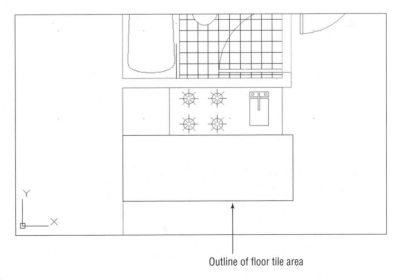

Outline of floor tile area

**2.** Click the Hatch tool in the Tool Sets palette.

**3.** In the Hatch And Gradient dialog box, change the Type from User Defined to Predefined.

**4.** Select the ellipsis button next to Pattern, and the Hatch Pattern Palette appears (Figure 7.8). This list has a scroll bar to the right that lets you view additional patterns.

**5.** Scroll down the list and locate and select AR-PARQ1 (Figure 7.8).

**FIGURE 7.8**
The Hatch Pattern
Palette

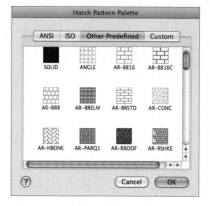

**6.** Click OK to dismiss the Hatch Pattern Palette.

**7.** Click the Add: Pick Points button and then click inside the rectangle you just drew.

**8.** Press ↵ twice to exit the Hatch command.

The predefined patterns with the *AR* prefix are architectural patterns that are drawn to full scale. In general, you should leave their Scale setting at 1. You can adjust the scale after you place the hatch pattern by using the Properties Inspector palette, as described later in this chapter.

---

### ADDING SOLID FILLS

With Type set to Predefined, you can select Solid from the Pattern pop-up menu in the Hatch And Gradient dialog box. The Hatch Color pop-up menu lets you set the color of your solid fill.

---

## Positioning Hatch Patterns Accurately

In the previous hatch pattern exercise, you may have noticed that the hatch pattern fit neatly into the 8′ × 3′ rectangle. The AR-PARQ1 pattern is made up of 1′ squares so they will fit exactly in an area that is of even 1′ increments. In addition, AutoCAD places the origin of the pattern in the bottom-left corner of the area being filled by default.

You won't always have a hatch pattern fit so easily in an area. If you've ever laid tile in a bathroom, for example, you know that you have to carefully select the starting point for your tiles to get them to fit in an area with pleasing results. If you need to fine-tune the position of a hatch pattern within an enclosed area, you can do so by first clicking the Specified Origin radio button in the Hatch And Gradient dialog. This will enable other options below, including the Click To Set New Origin button.

Click To Set New Origin lets you specify an origin point for your hatch pattern. You can also use the **HPORIGIN** system variable to accomplish this, or click the Default To Boundary Extents check box to select from a set of predefined origin locations. These locations are bottom left, bottom right, top left, top right, and center. The Use Current Origin option refers to the X,Y origin of the drawing.

If you are hatching an irregular shape, these origin locations are applied to the *boundary extents* of the shape. An imaginary rectangle represents the outermost boundary, or the boundary extents of the shape, as shown in Figure 7.9.

**FIGURE 7.9**
The origin options shown in relation to the boundary extents of an irregular shape

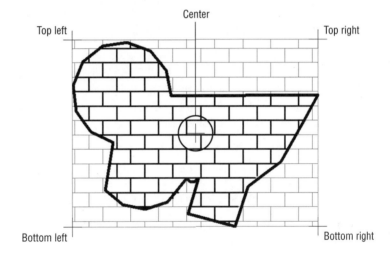

The Store As Default Origin option lets you save your selected origin as the default origin for future hatch patterns in the current drawing.

Now that you've learned how to add a hatch pattern, let's continue with a look at how your newly edited plan can be used. In the next exercise, you'll use this updated 07a-unit file to update all the units in the Plan file.

## Updating a Block from an External File

As you progress through a design project, you make countless revisions. With traditional drafting methods, revising a drawing such as the studio apartment floor plan takes a good deal of time. If you change the bathroom layout, for example, you have to erase every occurrence of the bathroom and redraw it 16 times. With AutoCAD, on the other hand, revising this drawing can be a quick operation. You can update the studio unit you just modified throughout the overall plan drawing by replacing the current Unit block with the updated Unit file. AutoCAD can update all occurrences of the Unit block. The following exercise shows how this is accomplished.

For this exercise, remember that the blocks representing the units in the 07b-plan and 07b-plan-metric files are named 07a-unit and 07a-unit-metric:

1. Make sure you've saved the 07a-unit (07a-unit-metric for metric users) file with the changes, and then return to the 07b-plan file that is still open.

---

**YOU CAN'T UPDATE EXPLODED BLOCKS**

Exploded blocks won't be updated when you update blocks from an external file. If you plan to use this method to update parts of a drawing, don't explode the blocks you plan to update. See Chapter 4, "Organizing Objects with Blocks and Groups."

---

2. Click the Insert tool on the Tool Sets palette.

3. Click the Browse button. In the Select Drawing File dialog box, double-click the 07a-unit filename (07a-unit-metric for metric users).

4. Click Insert in the Insert Block dialog box. A warning message tells you that a block already exists with the same name as the file. You can cancel the operation or redefine the block in the current drawing.

5. Click Redefine Block. The drawing regenerates.

6. At the Specify insertion point or [Basepoint/Scale/X/Y/Z/Rotate]: prompt, press the Esc key. You do this because you don't want to insert the Unit file into your drawing; you're just using the Insert feature to update an existing block.

7. Zoom in to one of the units. The floor tile appears in all the units as you drew it in the Unit file (see Figure 7.10).

**FIGURE 7.10**
The Plan drawing with the tile pattern

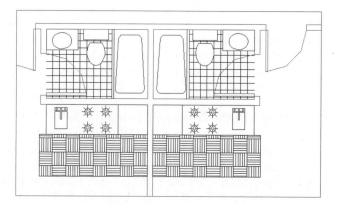

Nested blocks must be updated independently of the parent block. For example, if you modified the Toilet block while editing the 07a-unit file and then updated the 07a-unit drawing in the 07b-plan file, the old Toilet block wouldn't be updated. Even though the toilet is part of the

07a-unit file, it's still a unique, independent block in the Plan file, and AutoCAD won't modify it unless specifically instructed to do so. In this situation, you must edit the original Toilet block and then update it in both the Plan and Unit files.

### REPLACING BLOCKS

If you want to replace one block with another in the current file, type **–Insert**↵. (Don't forget the minus sign in front of *Insert*.) At the *Block name:* prompt, enter the block name followed by an equal sign (=), and then enter the name of the new block or the filename. Don't include spaces between the name and the equal sign.

Also, block references and layer settings of the current file take priority over those of the imported file. For example, if a file to be imported has layers of the same name as the layers in the current file but those layers have color and linetype assignments that are different from the current file's, the current file's layer color and linetype assignments determine those of the imported file. This doesn't mean, however, that the imported file on disk is changed; only the inserted drawing is affected.

### SUBSTITUTING BLOCKS

In the preceding example, you updated a block in your Plan file by using the Browse button in the Insert Block dialog box. In that exercise, the block name and the filename were the same. You can also replace a block with another block or a file of a different name. Here's how to do that:

1. Open the Insert Block dialog box.

2. Click the Browse button next to the Name input box, locate and select the file you want to use as a substitute, and then click Open to return to the Insert Block dialog box.

3. Change the name in the Name input box to the name of the block you want replaced.

4. Click Insert. A warning message appears, telling you that a block with this name already exists. Click Redefine Block to proceed with the block substitution.

You can use this method of replacing blocks if you want to see how changing one element of your project can change your design. You might, for example, draw three different apartment unit plans and give each plan a unique name. You could then generate and print three apartment building designs in a fraction of the time it would take you to do so by hand.

Block substitution can also reduce a drawing's complexity and accelerate regenerations. To substitute blocks, you temporarily replace large, complex blocks with schematic versions. For example, you might replace the Unit block in the Plan drawing with another drawing that contains just a single-line representation of the walls and bathroom fixtures. You would still have the wall lines for reference when inserting other symbols or adding mechanical or electrical information, but the drawing would regenerate much faster. When you did the final print, you would reinsert the original Unit block showing every detail.

## Changing the Hatch Area

You may have noticed the Associative option in the Hatch And Gradient dialog box. When this check box is selected, AutoCAD creates an associative hatch pattern. *Associative* hatches adjust their shapes to any changes in their associated boundary, hence the name (see the section "Controlling Hatch Behavior" later this chapter). The following exercise demonstrates how this works.

Suppose you want to enlarge the tiled area of the kitchen by one tile. Here's how it's done:

1. Choose Window ➢ 07a-Unit.dwg file from the menu bar.

2. Click the outline border of the hatch pattern you created earlier. Notice the grips that appear around the hatch-pattern area.

3. Click the grip in the bottom center of the hatch area.

---

**SELECTING HATCH GRIPS**

If the boundary of the hatch pattern consists of line segments, you can use a crossing window or polygon-crossing window to select the corner grips of the hatch pattern.

---

4. Enter @12<–90↵ (@30<–90 for metric users) to widen the hatch pattern by 1′, or 30 cm for metric users. The hatch pattern adjusts to the new size of the hatch boundary.

5. Press the Esc key to clear any grip selections.

6. Choose File ➢ Save from the menu bar or press ⌘-S to save the Unit file.

7. Return to the Plan file using the menu bar, and repeat the steps in the section "Updating a Block from an External File" earlier in this chapter to update the units again.

The Associative feature of hatch patterns can save time when you need to modify your drawing, but you need to be aware of its limitations. A hatch pattern can lose its associativity when you do any of the following:

◆ Erase or explode a hatch boundary

◆ Erase or explode a block that forms part of the boundary

◆ Move a hatch pattern away from its boundary

These situations frequently arise when you edit an unfamiliar drawing. Often, boundary objects are placed on a layer that is off or frozen, so the boundary objects aren't visible. Also, the hatch pattern might be on a layer that is turned off and you proceed to edit the file not knowing that a hatch pattern exists. When you encounter such a file, take a moment to check for hatch boundaries so you can deal with them properly.

## Modifying a Hatch Pattern

Like everything else in a project, a hatch pattern may eventually need to be changed in some way. Hatch patterns are like blocks in that they act like single objects. You can explode a hatch pattern to edit its individual lines. The Properties Inspector palette contains most of the settings you'll need to make changes to your hatch patterns. But the most direct way to edit a hatch pattern is to use the Hatch Edit dialog box.

### EDITING HATCH PATTERNS FROM THE HATCH EDIT DIALOG BOX

Follow these steps to modify a hatch pattern by using the Hatch Edit dialog box (Figure 7.11):

1. Return to the Unit drawing using the menu bar.

2. Press the Esc key to clear any grip selections that may be active from earlier exercises.

3. Double-click the hatch pattern in the kitchen to open the Hatch Edit dialog box. It's the same as the Hatch And Gradient dialog box.

4. In the Pattern pop-up menu, select the pattern named AR-BRSTD. It's the pattern that looks like a brick wall.

5. Click OK. The AR-BRSTD pattern appears in place of the original parquet pattern.

6. Exit and save your file.

**FIGURE 7.11**
The Hatch Edit dialog box

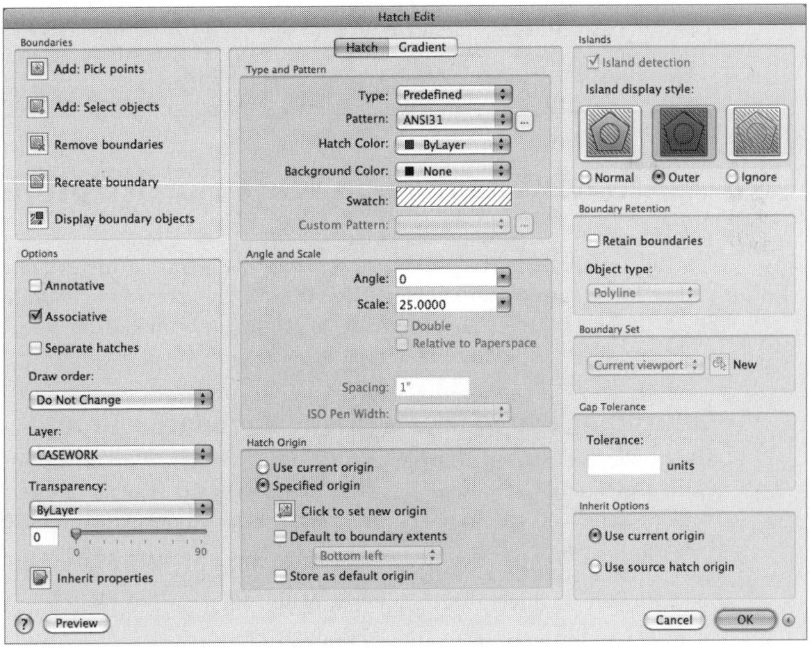

In this exercise, you were able to change the hatch just by double-clicking it. Although you changed only the pattern type, other options are available. You can, for example, change a pre-defined pattern to a user-defined one by selecting User Defined from the Type pop-up menu in the Hatch Edit dialog box.

You can then enter angle and scale values for your hatch pattern in the options provided in the Angle and Scale group in the Hatch Edit dialog box.

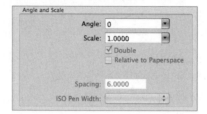

The other items in the Hatch Edit dialog box are duplicates of the options in the Hatch And Gradient dialog box. They let you modify the individual properties of the selected hatch pattern. The upcoming section, "Understanding the Boundary Hatch Options," describes these other properties in detail.

---

**TAKE A BREAK**

If you're working through the tutorial in this chapter, this would be a good place to take a break or stop. You can pick up the next exercise in the section "Attaching a Drawing as an External Reference" at another time.

---

## Understanding the Boundary Hatch Options

The Hatch And Gradient dialog box and Hatch Edit dialog box offer many other options that you didn't explore in the previous exercises. For example, instead of clicking in the area to be hatched, you can select the objects that bound the area you want to hatch by clicking the Add: Select Objects button in the Boundaries group. You can use the Add: Select Objects button to add boundaries to existing hatch patterns as well.

### Controlling Boundaries with the Boundaries Group

The previous exercises in this chapter have just touched on the options in the Boundaries group of the Hatch and Gradient dialog box. Options in the Boundaries group are Add: Pick Points, Add: Select Objects, Remove Boundaries, Recreate Boundary, and View Selections.

**Add: Pick Points**   Lets you select an area to be hatched based on a closed boundary.

**Add: Select Objects**   Lets you select objects to define a hatch boundary.

**Remove Boundaries**   Lets you remove a bounded area, or *island*, in the area to be hatched. An example is the toilet seat in the bathroom. This option is available only when you select a hatch area by using the Add: Pick Points option and an island has been detected.

**Recreate Boundary**   Draws a region or polyline around the current hatch pattern. You're then prompted to choose between a region or a polyline and to specify whether to reassociate the pattern with the re-created boundary. (See the Associative Hatch Patterns sidebar, discussed later in this chapter.)

**View Selections**   After you have selected boundaries to hatch, clicking this tool will temporarily close the Hatch And Gradient dialog box and highlight the areas that you have selected.

## Fine-Tuning the Boundary Behavior

The Boundary Hatch feature is view dependent; that is, it locates boundaries based on what is visible in the current view. If the current view contains a lot of graphic data, AutoCAD can have difficulty or be slow in finding a boundary. If you run into this problem, or if you want to single out a specific object for a point selection boundary, you can use the Boundary Set options found in the expanded Hatch And Gradient dialog box to further limit the area that AutoCAD uses to locate hatch boundaries:

**View Selections in the Boundaries Group**   This highlights the objects that have been selected as the hatch boundary by AutoCAD.

**Retain Boundary Objects under the Boundary Retention Group**   This retains outlines used to create the hatch pattern. This can be helpful if you want to duplicate the shape of the boundary for other purposes. Typically this is set to Don't Retain Boundaries, but you can use two other settings: Retain Boundaries – Polyline and Retain Boundaries – Region. The Retain Boundaries – Polyline option retains the boundaries as polylines. The Retain Boundaries – Regions option retains the boundaries as regions.

---

**HATCH BOUNDARIES WITHOUT THE HATCH PATTERN**

The Boundary command creates a polyline outline or region in a selected area. It works much like the Retain Boundaries – Polyline option but doesn't add a hatch pattern.

---

**Select New Boundary Set under the Boundary Set Group**   This lets you select the objects you want AutoCAD to use to determine the hatch boundary instead of searching the entire view. The screen clears and lets you select objects. This option discards previous boundary sets. It's useful for hatching areas in a drawing that contains many objects that you don't want to include in the hatch boundary.

**Use Current Viewport under the Boundary Set Group**   This uses the current viewport extents to define the boundary set.

The Boundary Set options are designed to give you more control over the way a point selection boundary is created. These options have no effect when you use the Add: Select Objects button to select specific objects for the hatch boundary.

### BOUNDARY RETENTION

The Hatch command can also create an outline of the hatch area by using one of two objects: 2D regions, which are like 2D planes, or polyline outlines. Hatch creates such a polyline boundary temporarily to establish the hatch area. These boundaries are automatically removed after the hatch pattern is inserted. If you want to retain the boundaries in the drawing, make sure the Retain Boundaries – Polyline option is selected. Retaining the boundary can be useful if you know you'll be hatching the area more than once or if you're hatching a fairly complex area.

Retaining a hatch boundary is useful if you want to know the hatched area's dimensions in square inches or feet because you can find the area of a closed polyline by using the List command. See Chapter 2, "Creating Your First Drawing," for more on the List command.

## Controlling Hatch Behavior

The Hatch And Gradient dialog box offers a set of tools that control some additional features of the Hatch command. These features affect the way a hatch pattern fills a boundary area as well as how it behaves when the drawing is edited. Note that the Gap Tolerance and Island Detection options are on the expanded dialog box. You can find these by clicking on the disclosure triangle located on the lower-right side of the dialog box. The following gives you a brief description of the options in the Options, Islands, Gap Tolerance, and Inherit Options groups:

**Annotative** Allows the hatch pattern to adjust to different scale views of your drawing. With this option turned on, a hatch pattern's size or spacing adjusts to the annotation scale of a viewport layout or Model Space view. See Chapter 4 for more on the annotation scale.

### ANNOTATIVE HATCH PATTERNS

In Chapter 4, you learned about a feature called the *annotation scale*. With this feature, you can assign several scales to certain types of objects and AutoCAD displays the object to the proper scale of the drawing. You can take advantage of this feature to allow hatch patterns to adjust their spacing or pattern size to the scale of your drawing. The Annotative option in the Hatch And Gradient dialog box turns on the annotation scale feature for hatch patterns. Once this feature is turned on for a hatch pattern, you can set up the drawing scales that you want to apply to the hatch pattern using the same methods described for blocks in Chapter 4.

**Associative** Allows the hatch pattern to adjust to changes in its boundary. With this option turned on, any changes to the associated boundary of a hatch pattern cause the hatch pattern to flow with the changes in the boundary.

**Create Separate Hatches** Creates separate and distinct hatches if you select several enclosed areas while selecting hatch areas. With this option off, separate hatch areas behave as a single hatch pattern.

**Draw Order** Allows you to specify whether the hatch pattern appears on top of or underneath its boundary. This is useful when the boundary is of a different color or shade and must read clearly or when the hatch pattern must cover the boundary. The options in this list are self-explanatory and are Do Not Assign, Send To Back, Bring To Front, Send Behind Boundary, and Bring In Front Of Boundary. See "Overlapping Objects with Draw Order" later in this chapter.

**Layer**    Allows you to select a layer that the hatch will be drawn on. By default, the hatch will be drawn on the current layer.

**Transparency**    Contains four options for transparency:

> **Use Current**    Will use the current object transparency setting.
>
> **ByLayer**    Will use the current layer transparency setting.
>
> **ByBlock**    If the hatch object is contained in a block, it will use the current block transparency setting.
>
> **Specify Value**    You can choose a transparency value by either entering it into the text box or using the slider.

**Inherit Properties**    The Inherit Properties icon allows you to select a hatch on the drawing area. All properties associated with the selected hatch will be passed to the new hatch area.

**Islands Detection**    Controls how islands within a hatch area are treated. Islands are enclosed areas that are completely inside a hatch boundary. When the Island Detection checkbox is selected, there are three options in this list:

> **Normal Island Detection**    This causes the hatch pattern to alternate between nested boundaries. The outer boundary is hatched; if there is a closed object within the boundary, it isn't hatched. If *another* closed object is inside the first closed object, *that* object is hatched. This is the default setting.
>
> **Outer Island Detection**    This applies the hatch pattern to an area defined by the outermost boundary and a closed object within that boundary. Any boundaries nested in that closed object are ignored.
>
> **Ignore Island Detection**    This supplies the hatch pattern to the entire area within the outermost boundary, ignoring any nested boundaries.

**Gap Tolerance**    This group lets you hatch an area that isn't completely enclosed. The Gap Tolerance value sets the maximum gap size in an area you want to hatch. You can use a value from 0 to 5000.

**Inherit Options**    This group allows you to use an existing hatch pattern when inserting additional hatch patterns into a drawing. Select the Use Current Origin button and then select the hatch on the drawing screen that you wish to use. All properties of the selected hatch will be copied to the newly created hatch.

## Using Gradient Shading

We have discussed the Solid option in the Pattern pop-up menu. The solid hatch pattern lets you apply a solid color instead of a pattern to a bounded area. AutoCAD also offers a set of gradient patterns that let you apply a color gradient to an area.

You can apply a gradient to an area by using the Gradient tab on the Hatch And Gradient dialog box. When you select the Gradient tab, you'll see a slight change. The Type And Pattern group changes to show a set of different gradient patterns. The Origin group also changes to the Orientation group (Figure 7.12).

**FIGURE 7.12**
The Gradient tab of
the Hatch And Gra-
dient dialog box

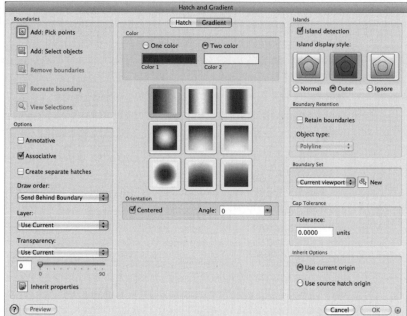

### CHOOSING A GRADIENT COLOR

Instead of offering hatch patterns, the Gradient tab offers a variety of gradient patterns. If you wish to change a color, you can click the color swatch to open the Color Palette dialog box. This dialog box lets you choose from Index, True Color, or Color Books colors (Figure 7.13).

**FIGURE 7.13**
The Color Palette
dialog box

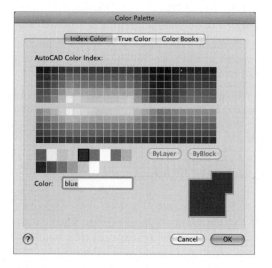

### Choosing between a Single Color and Two Colors

You can choose a gradient that transitions between shades of a single color by clicking the One Color radio button. This turns on the Shade And Tint slider and disables the Color 2 swatch. When you select the Two Color radio button, the Shade And Tint slider is disabled and the Color 2 swatch is displayed.

### Selecting Gradient Patterns

As mentioned earlier, you can choose from a set of gradient patterns from the Color option. The Angle pop-up menu gives you further control over the gradient pattern by allowing you to rotate the angle of the pattern. The pop-up menu is set to 15-degree increments; however, you can type in a value in the text box. The Centered option places the center of the gradient at the center of the area selected for the pattern. This option is a toggle that is either on or off.

To place a gradient pattern, select a set of objects or a point in a bounded area, just as you would for a hatch pattern.

## Tips for Using Hatch

Here are a few tips on using the Hatch feature:

- Watch out for boundary areas that are part of a large block. AutoCAD examines the entire block when defining boundaries. This can take time if the block is large. Use the Select New Boundary Set option in the Boundary Set option group to focus in on the set of objects you want AutoCAD to use for your hatch boundary. If you desire, you can turn off the preview by using the **HPQUICKPREVIEW** system variable. ON turns the preview on, and OFF turns it off. You may want to turn this off if you are doing a lot of hatching in large areas.

- The Hatch feature is view dependent; that is, it locates boundaries based on what is visible in the current view. To ensure that AutoCAD finds every detail, zoom in to the area to be hatched.

- If the area to be hatched is large yet requires fine detail, first outline the hatch area by using a polyline. (See Chapter 17, "Drawing Curves," for more on polylines.) Then use the Add: Select Objects option in the Boundaries group to select the polyline boundary manually instead of depending on Hatch to find the boundary for you.

- Consider turning off layers that might interfere with AutoCAD's ability to find a boundary.

- Hatch works on nested blocks as long as the nested block entities are parallel to the current UCS.

## Space Planning and Hatch Patterns

Suppose you're working on a plan in which you're constantly repositioning equipment and furniture or you're in the process of designing the floor covering. You might be a little hesitant to place a hatch pattern on the floor because you don't want to have to rehatch the area each time you move a piece of equipment or change the flooring. You have two options in this situation: You can use Hatch's associative capabilities to include the furnishings in the boundary set, or you can use the Draw Order feature.

### USING ASSOCIATIVE HATCH

Associative Hatch is the most straightforward method. Make sure the Associative option is selected in the Options group, and include your equipment or furniture in the boundary set. You can do this by using the Add: Select Objects option in the Boundaries options.

After the hatch pattern is in place, it automatically adjusts to its new location when you move the furnishings in your drawing. One drawback, however, is that AutoCAD attempts to hatch the interior of your furnishings if they cross the outer boundary of the hatch pattern. Also, if any boundary objects are erased or exploded, the hatch pattern no longer follows the location of your furnishings. To avoid these problems, you can use the method described in the next section.

### OVERLAPPING OBJECTS WITH DRAW ORDER

The Draw Order feature lets you determine how objects overlap. In the space-planning example, you can create furniture by using a solid hatch to indicate horizontal surfaces (see Figure 7.14).

**FIGURE 7.14**
Using Draw Order to create an overlapping effect over a hatch pattern

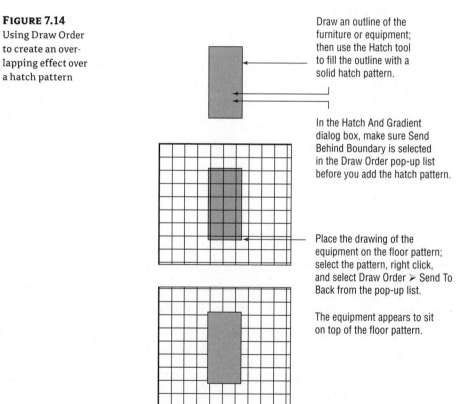

Draw an outline of the furniture or equipment; then use the Hatch tool to fill the outline with a solid hatch pattern.

In the Hatch And Gradient dialog box, make sure Send Behind Boundary is selected in the Draw Order pop-up list before you add the hatch pattern.

Place the drawing of the equipment on the floor pattern; select the pattern, right click, and select Draw Order ➢ Send To Back from the pop-up list.

The equipment appears to sit on top of the floor pattern.

### How to Match a Hatch Pattern and Other Properties Quickly

Another tool to help you edit hatch patterns is Match Properties, which is similar to Format Painter in the Microsoft Office system. This tool lets you change an existing hatch pattern to match another existing hatch pattern. Here's how to use it:

1. Type **MA**↵.

2. Click the source hatch pattern you want to copy.

3. Click the target hatch pattern you want to change. The target pattern changes to match the source pattern.

The Match Properties tool transfers other properties as well, such as layer, color, and linetype settings. You can select the properties that are transferred by opening the Match Properties Settings dialog box.

To open this dialog box, type **S**↵ after selecting the source object in step 2, or right-click and choose Settings from the shortcut menu. You can then select the properties you want to transfer from the options shown. All the properties are selected by default. You can also transfer text and dimension style settings. You'll learn more about text and dimension styles in Chapter 9, "Adding Text to Drawings," and Chapter 11, "Using Dimensions."

You can then place the furniture on top of a floor-covering pattern and the pattern will be covered and hidden by the furniture. Here's how to do that. (These steps aren't part of the regular exercises of this chapter. They're shown here as general guidelines when you need to use the Draw Order feature.)

1. Draw the equipment outline, and make sure the outline is a closed polygon.

2. Start the Hatch tool described earlier in this chapter and place a solid hatch pattern inside the equipment outline.

3. In the Hatch And Gradient dialog box, make sure Send To Back is selected in the Draw Order pop-up menu.

4. Turn the outline and solid hatch into a block, or use the Group command to group them.

5. Move your equipment drawing into place over the floor pattern.

6. Double-click on the floor hatch pattern, and then in the Hatch Edit dialog box, select Send To Back from the Draw Order pop-up menu. (See the middle panel in Figure 7.14.)

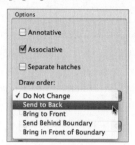

After you take these steps, the equipment will appear to rest on top of the pattern. (See the bottom panel in Figure 7.14.) You also change the display order of objects relative to other objects in the drawing using the Draw Order options in the right-click menu.

The Draw Order options are all part of the Draworder command. As an alternative to the menus, you can type **DR↵** at the Command prompt, select an object, and then enter an option at the prompt:

```
Enter object ordering option
[Above objects/Under objects/Front/Back] <Back>:
```

For example, the equivalent of choosing the Send To Back tool from the Draw Order option is entering **DR↵ B↵**. You can also select the object you want to edit, right-click, and then choose Draw Order from the shortcut menu.

## Using External References

AutoCAD allows you to import drawings in a way that keeps the imported drawing independent from the current one. A drawing imported in this way is called an *external reference* (*Xref*). Unlike drawings that have been imported as blocks, Xref files don't become part of the drawing's database. Instead, they're loaded along with the current file at startup time. It's as if AutoCAD were opening several drawings at once: the currently active file you specify when you start AutoCAD and any file inserted as an Xref.

If you keep Xref files independent from the current file, any changes you make to the Xref automatically appear in the current file. You don't have to update the Xref file manually as you do blocks. For example, if you use an Xref to insert the Unit file into the Plan file and you later make changes to the Unit file, you will see the new version of the Unit file in place of the old one the next time you open the Plan file. If the Plan file was still open while edits were made, AutoCAD will notify you that a change has been made to an Xref.

---

**BLOCKS AND XREFS CAN'T HAVE THE SAME NAME**

You can't use an Xref file if the file has the same name as a block in the current drawing. If this situation occurs but you still need to use the file as an Xref, you can rename the block of the same name by using the Rename command. You can also use Rename to change the name of various objects and named elements.

---

Another advantage of Xref files is that because they don't become part of a drawing's database, drawing size is kept to a minimum. This results in more efficient use of your hard disk space.

Xref files, like blocks, can be edited only by using special tools. You can, however, use osnaps to snap to a location in an Xref file, or you can freeze or turn off the Xref file's insertion layer to make it invisible.

## Attaching a Drawing as an External Reference

The next exercise shows how to use an Xref in place of an inserted block to construct the studio apartment building. You'll first create a new unit file by copying the old one. Then you'll bring a new feature, the Reference Manager palette, to the screen. Follow these steps to create the new file:

1. Choose Window ➤ 07a-unit.dwg from the menu bar to return to the 07a-unit file.

2. Choose File ➤ Save As from the menu bar or press ⇧-⌘-S to save it under the name unitxref.dwg, and then close the unitxref.dwg file. This will make a copy of the 07a-unit.dwg file for the following steps. Or, if you prefer, you can use the unitxref.dwg file for the following steps.

3. In the 07b-plan file, choose Save As, and save the file under the name Planxref. The current file is now Planxref.dwg.

4. Erase all the unit plans. In the next step, you'll purge the unit plans from the file. (By completing steps 2 through 4, you save yourself from having to set up a new file.)

5. Type **PURGE**↵ **ALL**↵ ↵ **N**↵. This purges blocks that aren't in use in the drawing.

Now you're ready to use the External References palette:

1. Type **XR**↵ to open the Reference Manager palette (see Figure 7.15).

2. Click the Attach Reference button in the upper-left corner of the palette to open the Select Reference File dialog box. This is a typical file navigation dialog box.

3. Locate and select the unitxref.dwg file, and then click Open to open the Attach External Reference dialog box (see Figure 7.16). Notice that this dialog box looks similar to the Insert Block dialog box. It offers the same options for insertion point, scale, and rotation.

**FIGURE 7.15**
The Reference
Manager palette

**FIGURE 7.16**
The Attach External Reference dialog box

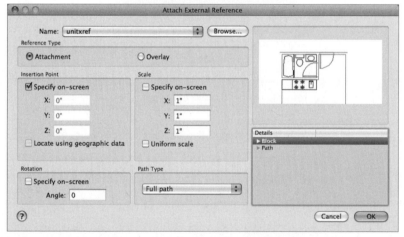

4. You'll see a description of the options presented in this dialog box in the Options in the Reference Manager Palette section later this chapter. For now, click OK.

5. Enter **31′-5″,43′-8″**↵ (metric users enter **957,1330**) for the insertion point.

6. The inserted plan may appear faded. If it does, type **XDWGFADECTL**↵ **0**↵ (that is a zero). This will give the plan a more solid appearance.

7. After the `unitxref.dwg` file is inserted, re-create the same layout of the floor plan you created in the first section of this chapter by copying and mirroring the `Unitxref.dwg` external reference.

8. Save the `Planxref` file.

You now have a drawing that looks like the `07b-plan.dwg` file you worked with earlier in this chapter, but instead of blocks that are detached from their source file, you have a drawing composed of Xrefs. These Xrefs are the actual `unitxref.dwg` file, and they're loaded into AutoCAD at the same time that you open the `Planxref.dwg` file.

---

**FADING XREFS**

In step 6 of the previous exercise, you saw the Xref Fading feature. This tool is an aid to help you visualize which objects in your drawing are Xrefs. You can also use the XRefs slider in the Application Preferences dialog box.

1. Right-click on an open area of the drawing.

2. From the right-click menu, select Preferences. You can also press ⌘-, (comma). The Application Preferences dialog box will open.

3. Click the Look & Feel tab.

4. Click the XRefs slider. When the slider is all the way over to the left, there will not be any fading. When the slider is all the way to the right, the maximum fading is in effect.

5. Click OK.

The Xref fading option affects only the appearance of the Xref in the drawing. It does not cause the Xref to fade in your printed output.

---

Next, you'll modify the `unitxref.dwg` file and see the results in the `Planxref.dwg` file:

1. To open the `Unitxref.dwg` file, from the current `Planxref` file, open the Reference Manager palette, right-click the `Unitxref` file, and choose Open File from the shortcut menu. You can also enter **XOPEN**↵ at the Command prompt and then select the unit plan Xref.

2. Erase the hatch pattern and kitchen outline for the floors, and save the `unitxref.dwg` file.

3. Choose Window ➢ `Planxref.dwg` in the menu bar to return to the `Planxref.dwg` file.

4. Notice that the units in the Planxref drawing have not been updated to include the changes you made to the `Unitxref` file. Click the Refresh Content button near the top of the Reference Manager palette to reload all Xrefs.

You can also select the Xref that needs to be updated, right-click, and choose the Reload option from the shortcut menu to reload the selected Xref. Multiple Xrefs can be selected if more than one needs updating.

Another option found on the right-click shortcut menu is the Relink option. When you select this option, the Select Dwg File To Relink dialog box opens. Here, you can choose a different file to put in place of the original Xref file. In the case of the plans, it would be handy if you had multiple versions that you needed to try out. To bring the original Xref file back, select Relink and choose that file.

Here you saw how an Xref file is updated in a different way than a block. Because Xrefs are loaded along with the drawing file that contains them, the containing file, which in this case was the Planxref file, automatically displays any changes made to the Xref when it's opened. Also, you avoid having to update nested blocks because AutoCAD updates nested Xrefs as well as non-nested Xrefs.

## Other Differences between External References and Blocks

Here are a few other differences between Xrefs and inserted blocks that you'll want to keep in mind:

- Any new layers, text styles, or linetypes brought in with Xref files don't become part of the current file. If you want to import any of these items, you can use the Bind External References (Xbind) command (described in Chapter 14, "Advanced Editing and Organizing").

- A way to ensure that layer settings for Xrefs are retained is to enter **VISRETAIN**⏎ at the Command prompt. At the `New value for VISRETAIN <0>:` prompt, enter **1**.

- To segregate layers in Xref files from layers in the current drawing, AutoCAD prefixes the names of the Xref file's layers with their file's name. A vertical bar separates the file-name prefix and the layer name when you view a list of layers in the Layers palette (as in unitxref | wall).

- You can't explode Xrefs. You can, however, convert an Xref into a block and then explode it. To do this, select the Xref in the Reference Manager palette, then right-click and choose Bind or Bind-Insert to convert the Xref into a block. See the section "Other External Reference Options" later in this chapter for more information.

- If an Xref is renamed or moved to another location on your hard disk, AutoCAD won't be able to find that file when it opens other files to which the Xref is attached. If this happens, right-click on the missing Xref name in the Reference Manager palette and from the short-cut menu select Relink File.

- Take care when relinking an Xref. It can assign a file of a different name to an existing Xref as a substitution.

- Xref files are especially useful in workgroup environments in which several people are working on the same project. For example, one person might be updating several files that are inserted into a variety of other files. With Xref files, however, the updating is automatic; you avoid confusion about which files need their blocks updated.

> **IMPORTING BLOCKS, LAYERS, AND OTHER NAMED ELEMENTS FROM EXTERNAL FILES**
>
> You can use the Xbind command to import blocks and other named elements from another file. First, use the Reference Manager palette to cross-reference a file; then type **XBIND** at the Command prompt. In the Bind External Definitions dialog box, click the disclosure triangle next to the Xref filename and select the Block option. Locate the name of the block you want to import, click the Add button, and click OK.
>
> Finally, in the Reference Manager palette, select the Xref filename from the list, and click the Detach Referenced File button along the top of the palette. You can also right-click and select Detach to remove the Xref file. The imported block remains as part of the current file. (See Chapter 14 for details on importing named elements.)
>
> The Content palette gives you access to your frequently used blocks. You can open the Content palette by choosing Tools ➢ Palettes ➢ Content from the menu bar or by pressing ⌘-2.

## Other External Reference Options

Many other features are unique to external reference files. Let's briefly look at the other options in the External References palette and the Attach External Reference dialog box.

### OPTIONS IN THE REFERENCE MANAGER PALETTE

The tools located at the top of the Reference Manager palette offer some options for Xrefs, as shown in Figure 7.17.

**FIGURE 7.17**
The tools on the Reference Manager palette

Attach Reference
Toggle References State
Detach Referenced File
Relink File
Refresh Content
Show Details

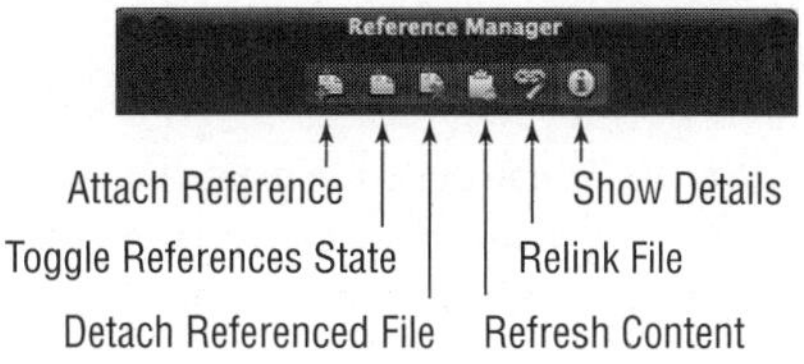

**Attach Reference**   Opens the Select Reference File dialog box.

**Toggle References State**   Toggles the Xref between loaded and unloaded.

**Detach Referenced File**   Removes the Xref file from the drawing.

**Refresh Content**   Reloads all Xrefs in the drawing.

**Relink File**   Allows another Xref file to be loaded in place of the present one, or loads an Xref file that has lost its linked state.

**Show Details**   Displays or hides the Details panel located below the list of referenced files.

Several options are also available when you right-click an external reference name listed in the Reference Manager palette, shown in Figure 7.15 earlier in this chapter. Some of them are duplicated with the row of buttons shown in Figure 7.17. You saw the Reload and Relink File options in earlier exercises. The following other options are available:

**Show In Model**   Zooms to the location of the Xref in the drawing.

**Open File**   Lets you open an Xref. Select the Xref from the list, and then click Open File. The Xref opens in a new drawing window.

**Show Details**   Opens a panel at the bottom of the Reference Manager palette. It's similar to the Properties Inspector palette in that it displays the properties of a selected external reference and also allows you to modify some of those properties. For example, the Reference Name option in the Details panel lets you give the external reference a name that is different from the Xref filename. Table 7.1 gives you a rundown of the options in the Details panel.

**TABLE 7.1:**   Options in the Details panel of the Reference Manager palette

| OPTION | FUNCTION |
| --- | --- |
| Reference Name | Lets you give the Xref a name that is different from the Xref's filename. This can be helpful if you want to use multiple external references of the same file. A caution will appear alerting you of the consequences of renaming the file. |
| Status | Tells you whether the Xref is loaded, unloaded, or not found. (Read-only.) |
| Size | Gives you the file size information. (Read-only.) |
| Type | Shows you which attachment method is set for the Xref. (Read-only.) |
| Date | Gives you the date and time the file was last saved. (Read-only.) |
| Saved Path | Tells you where AutoCAD expects to find the Xref file. (Read-only.) |
| Found At | Lets you select the location of the Xref file. You can click the ellipsis button to locate a lost Xref or use a different file from the original attached Xref. |
| Block Unit | Gives you the unit of the Xref block. (Read-only.) |
| Unit Factor | Displays the unit factor based on the INSUNITS system variable value of the Xref. INSUNITS is a value for scaling of blocks, images, and Xrefs. (Read-only.) |

**Reveal In Finder**   While not an AutoCAD command, this will open the Mac OS Finder utility and show you the location of the Xref file.

**Attach**   Toggles the attachment type to Attach if it is currently set to Overlay.

**Overlay**   Tells AutoCAD to ignore other Xref attachments that are nested in the selected file. This avoids multiple attachments of other files and eliminates the possibility of circular references (referencing the current file into itself through another file).

**Unload**   Removes an Xref from the current file, but maintains a link to the Xref file so that it can be quickly reattached. This has an effect similar to freezing a layer and can reduce redraw, regeneration, and file-loading times.

**Reload**   Restores an unloaded Xref.

**Relink File**   Opens the Select Dwg File To Relink dialog box. Works the same as the Relink File option mentioned previously.

**Bind**   Converts an Xref into a block. This option maintains the Xref's named elements (layers, linetypes, and text and dimension styles) by creating new layers in the current file with the Xref's filename prefix (discussed again in Chapter 14).

**Bind-Insert**   The Bind-Insert option is similar to the Bind option. Bind-Insert doesn't maintain the Xref's named elements but merges them with named elements of the same name in the current file. For example, if both the Xref and the current file have layers of the same name, the objects in the Xref are placed in the layers of the same name in the current file.

**Detach**   Detaches an Xref from the current file. The file is then completely disassociated from the current file.

### The Attach External Reference Dialog Box

The Attach External Reference dialog box, shown in Figure 7.16 earlier in this chapter, offers these options:

**Browse**   Opens the Select Reference File dialog box to enable you to change the file you're importing as an Xref.

**Path Type**   Offers options for locating Xrefs. Xref files can be located anywhere on your system, including network servers. For this reason, you can easily lose links to Xrefs either by moving them or by rearranging file locations. To help you manage Xrefs, the Path Type option offers three options: Full Path, Relative Path, and No Path. Full Path retains the current full path. Relative Path maintains paths in relation to the current drawing. The current drawing must be saved before using the Relative Path option. The No Path option is for drawings in which Xrefs are located in the same folder as the current drawing or in the path specified in Support File Search Path in the Application tab of the Application Preferences dialog box. Remember, you can press ⌘-, (comma) to open the Application Preferences dialog box.

**Specify On-Screen**   Appears in three places. It gives you the option to enter insertion point, scale factors, and rotation angles in the dialog box or at the Command prompt, in a way similar to inserting blocks. If you clear this option for any of the corresponding parameters, the parameters change to allow input. If they're selected, you're prompted for those parameters after you click OK to close the dialog box. With all three Specify On-Screen check boxes cleared, the Xref is inserted in the drawing using the settings indicated in the dialog box.

**Attachment**   Tells AutoCAD to include other Xref attachments that are nested in the selected file.

**Overlay**   Tells AutoCAD to ignore other Xref attachments that are nested in the selected file. This avoids multiple attachments of other files and eliminates the possibility of circular references (referencing the current file into itself through another file).

**Details**   Displays or hides the path information for the selected Xref file.

### OTHER XREF FEATURES AVAILABLE

In addition to those mentioned, there are two other options that are used in Xref editing:

**Visretain**   Instructs AutoCAD to remember any layer color or visibility settings of Xrefs from one editing session to the next. In the standard AutoCAD settings, this option is on by default. Visretain has two settings: 0 – Off and 1 – On.

**XEdit System Variable**   Allows editing the drawing in place. XEdit has two settings: 0 – No and 1 – Yes.

## Clipping Xref Views and Improving Performance

Xrefs are frequently used to import large drawings for reference or backgrounds. Multiple Xrefs, such as a floor plan, column grid layout, and site-plan drawing, might be combined into one file. One drawback to multiple Xrefs in earlier releases of AutoCAD was that the entire Xref was loaded into memory even if only a small portion of it was used for the final printed output. For computers with limited resources, multiple Xrefs could slow the system to a crawl.

AutoCAD offers two tools that help make display and memory use more efficient when using Xrefs: the Xclip command and the Demand Load feature.

### CLIPPING VIEWS WITH XCLIP

The Xclip command lets you clip the display of an Xref or a block to any shape you want, as shown in Figure 7.18. For example, you might want to display only an L-shaped portion of a floor plan to be part of your current drawing. Xclip lets you define such a view. To access the command, type **XCLIP**↵.

You can clip blocks and multiple Xrefs as well. You can also specify a front and back clipping distance so that the visibility of objects in 3D space can be controlled. You can define a clip area by using polylines or spline curves, although curve-fitted polylines revert to decurved polylines. (See Chapter 17 for more on polylines and spline curves.)

**FIGURE 7.18**
The first panel shows a polyline outline of the area to be isolated with Xclip. The second panel shows how the Xref appears after Xclip is applied. The last panel shows a view of the plan with the polyline's layer turned off.

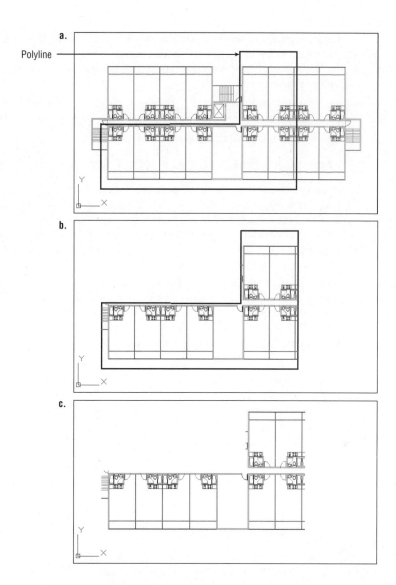

## CONTROLLING XREF SETTINGS VIA THE XLOADCTL SYSTEM VARIABLE

The Xloadctl system variable offers three settings: 0 – Disabled, 1 – Enabled, and 2 – Enabled With Copy. Xloadctl (also known as Demand Loading) is set to Enabled With Copy by default in the standard AutoCAD setup. In addition to reducing the amount of memory an Xref consumes, it prevents other users from editing the Xref while it's being viewed as part of your current drawing. This helps aid drawing version control and drawing management. The Enabled With Copy option creates a copy of the source Xref file and then uses the copy, thereby enabling other AutoCAD users to edit the source Xref file.

Demand loading improves performance by loading only the parts of the referenced drawing that are needed to regenerate the current drawing. You can set the location for the Xref copy in the Application tab of the Application Preferences dialog box under Temporary External Reference File Location.

 **Real World Scenario**

### EXTERNAL REFERENCES IN THE SAN FRANCISCO MAIN LIBRARY PROJECT

Although the exercises in this chapter demonstrate how Xrefs work, you aren't limited to using them in the way shown here. Perhaps one of the most common ways of using Xrefs is to combine a single floor plan with different title block drawings, each with its own layer settings and title block information. In this way, single-drawing files can be reused in several drawing sheets of a final construction document set. This helps keep data consistent across drawings and reduces the number of overall drawings needed.

This is exactly how Xrefs were used in the San Francisco Main Library drawings. One floor-plan file contained most of the main information for that floor. The floor plan was then used as an Xref in another file that contained the title block as well as additional information such as furnishings or floor finish reference symbols. Layer visibility was controlled in each title block drawing so only the data related to that drawing appeared.

Multiple Xref files were also used by segregating the structural column grid layout drawings from the floor-plan files. In other cases, portions of plans from different floors were combined into the single drawing shown here by using Xrefs.

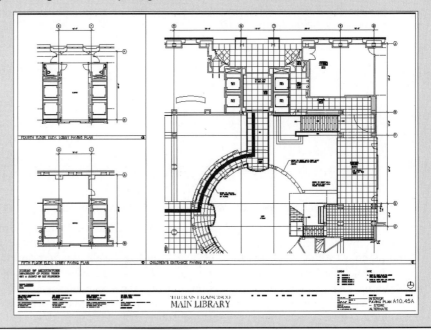

### CREATE UNIQUE LAYER, STYLE, AND BLOCK NAMES

When you make a copy of a block from an Xref, AutoCAD needs to assign that block a name. The Create Unique Layer, Style, And Block Names option tells AutoCAD to use the original block name and append a $#$ prefix to the name (# is a numeric value starting with zero). If you were to import the Bath block, for example, it would become $0$bath in the current drawing. This ensures that the block maintains a unique name when it's imported even if there is a block with the same name in the current drawing. If you use the **BINDTYPE** system variable and then type **1**, the original name is maintained. If the current drawing contains a block of the same name, the imported block uses the current file's definition of that block.

## The Bottom Line

**Assemble the parts.**    Technical drawings are often made up of repetitive parts that are drawn over and over. AutoCAD makes quick work of repetitive elements in a drawing, as shown in the first part of this chapter.

**Master It**    What is the object used as the basic building block for the unit plan drawing in the beginning of this chapter?

**Take control of the AutoCAD display.**    Understanding the way the AutoCAD display works can save you time, especially in a complex drawing.

**Master It**    Name the command used to save views in AutoCAD. Describe how to recall a saved view.

**Use hatch patterns in your drawings.**    Patterns can convey a lot of information at a glance. You can show the material of an object, or you can indicate a type of view, like a cross section, by applying hatch patterns.

**Master It**    How do you open the Hatch And Gradient dialog box?

**Understand the boundary hatch options.**    The boundary hatch options give you control over the way hatch patterns fill an enclosed area.

**Master It**    Describe an island as it relates to boundary hatch patterns.

**Use external references.**    External references are drawing files that you've attached to the current drawing to include as part of the drawing. Because external references aren't part of the current file, they can be worked on at the same time as the referencing file.

**Master It**    Describe how drawing files are attached as external references.

# Chapter 8

# Introducing Printing and Layouts

Getting hard-copy output from AutoCAD is something of an art. You'll need to be intimately familiar with both your output device and the settings available in AutoCAD. You'll probably spend a good deal of time experimenting with AutoCAD's print settings and with your printer or plotter to get your equipment set up just the way you want.

With the huge array of output options available, this chapter can provide only a general discussion of plotting and printing. As a rule, the process for using a plotter isn't much different from that for using a printer; you just have more media-size options with plotters. Still, every output device is different. It's up to you to work out the details and fine-tune the way you and AutoCAD together work with your particular plotter or printer. This chapter describes the features available in AutoCAD and discusses some general rules and guidelines to follow when setting up your plots and printouts.

We'll start with an overview of the printing/plotting features in AutoCAD and then delve into the finer details of setting up your drawing and controlling your plotter or printer.

In this chapter, you'll learn to do the following:

◆ Print a plan

◆ Understand the print settings

◆ Use layout views for WYSIWYG printing

◆ Examine output-device settings

◆ Understand plot styles

---

### PRINTER OR PLOTTER?

In this chapter and throughout the book, you will find references to printing and plot styles.

For the most part in AutoCAD for Mac, the output device is referred to as a printer. Some AutoCAD commands still reference plot. Both are technically correct. For example, typing either **PLOT.⏎** or **PRINT.⏎** will open the Print dialog. The names of the dialog boxes and commands will match those on the AutoCAD for Mac interface.

## Print a Plan

To see firsthand how the Print command works, you'll plot the Plan file by using the default settings on your system. You'll start by getting a preview of your plot, before you commit to printing your drawing. As an introduction, you'll plot from the model view of an AutoCAD drawing, but be aware that typically you should plot from a layout view. Layout views give you a greater degree of control over how your output will look. You'll be introduced to layout views later in this chapter. Now let's get started!

First, try plotting your drawing to no particular scale:

1. Be sure your printer or plotter is connected to your computer and is turned on.

2. Start AutoCAD, and open the Plan.dwg (Plan-metric.dwg for metric users) file. These can be obtained from www.sybex.com/go/masteringautocadmac.

3. Click the Zoom button on the status bar and then type **A↵**. You can also type **Z↵ A↵** to display the entire drawing.

4. Choose File ➢ Print from the menu bar or press ⌘-P to open the Print dialog box (see Figure 8.1).

**FIGURE 8.1**

The Print dialog box

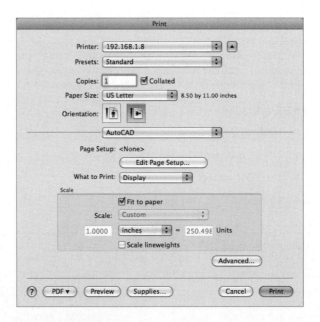

---

**MODEL SPACE LAYOUT WARNING**

You may see a warning screen regarding the Model Space layout. Click Continue, or if you want to suppress this message, click the check box next to Do Not Show This Message Again and then click Continue.

5. If the Printer pop-up menu shows None, click the pop-up menu and select your current system printer.

6. Click the disclosure triangle on the right to expand the Print dialog box.

7. In the What To Print pop-up menu, make sure the Display option is selected (see Figure 8.2). This tells AutoCAD to plot the drawing as it looks in the drawing window. You can choose to print the extents of a drawing, have the option to plot the limits of the drawing, select a saved view, or select an area to plot with a window.

**FIGURE 8.2**
Choose the Display option.

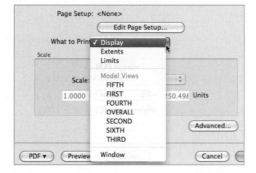

8. Make sure the Fit To Paper check box is checked in the Scale group.

9. Click the Preview button in the lower-left corner of the dialog box. AutoCAD works for a moment and then displays a sample view of how your drawing will appear when printed. The default Mac OS viewer is called Preview.

10. Close the Preview by clicking the Close button. Back in the Print dialog, click the Print button. AutoCAD sends the drawing to your printer.

11. Your plotter or printer prints the plan to no particular scale.

You've just plotted your first drawing. You used the minimal settings to ensure that the complete drawing appears on the paper. You may notice that a message appears on your screen (see Figure 8.3). If you click the text that reads *Click to view plot and publish details*, the Print Details dialog box opens to display some detailed information about your plot.

**FIGURE 8.3**
Click the message text to open the Print Details dialog.

As you become more experienced with AutoCAD and your projects become more demanding, the information presented in the Print Details dialog box may be useful to you. For now, make a mental note that this information is available should you need it.

---

**SET THE APPROPRIATE UNITS**

It's important to make sure you use the appropriate unit settings in this chapter. If you've been using the metric measurements for previous exercises, make sure you use the metric settings in the exercises of this chapter; otherwise, your results won't coincide.

---

Next, try plotting your drawing to an exact scale. This time, you'll expand the Print dialog box to show a few more options:

1. In the status bar, click the Annotation Scale pop-up menu and select ¹⁄₁₆″ = 1′-0″. Metric users can select 1:20

2. Select File ➤ Print from the menu bar again to open the Print dialog box.

3. If your last printout wasn't oriented on the paper correctly, select the Landscape option in the Orientation group.

---

**PRINT PREVIEW DEPENDENCIES**

The appearance of the print preview depends on the type of output device you chose when you set up your page (described in the section "WYSIWYG Printing Using Layout Views" later in this chapter). This example shows a typical preview view using the default system printer in landscape mode.

---

4. In the Scale group, clear the Fit To Paper check box. Then, select ¹⁄₁₆″ = 1′-0″ from the Scale pop-up menu. Metric users should select 1:20. As you can see, you have several choices for the scale of your output.

5. For the paper size, select Letter. Metric users should select A4. The options in this pop-up menu depend on your system printer or the output device you configured for AutoCAD.

6. In the What To Print pop-up menu, select Limits. This tells AutoCAD to use the limits of your drawing to determine which part of your drawing to plot.

7. Click the Preview button again to get a preview of your plot.

8. Close the Preview. From the Print dialog, click Print. This time, your printout is to scale.

Here, you were asked to specify a few more settings in the Print dialog box. Several settings work together to produce a drawing that is to scale and that fits properly on your paper. This is where it pays to understand the relationship between your drawing scale and your paper's size, discussed in Chapter 3, "Setting Up and Using AutoCAD's Drafting Tools." You also saw how you can expand the options in the Print dialog box.

The following sections don't contain any exercises. If you prefer to continue with the exercises in this chapter, skip to the section "WYSIWYG Printing Using Layout Views." However, be sure to come back and read the following sections while the previous exercises are still fresh in your mind.

## Understanding the Print Settings

In the following sections, you'll explore all the settings in the Print dialog box. These settings give you control over the size and orientation of your image on the paper. They also let you control which part of your drawing gets printed.

---

**AUTOCAD REMEMBERS PRINT SETTINGS**

AutoCAD relies mainly on the system printer configuration instead of any custom drivers. However, it does remember printer settings that are specific to AutoCAD, so you don't have to adjust your printer settings each time you use AutoCAD. This gives you more flexibility and control over your output. Be aware that you'll need to understand the system printer settings in addition to those offered by AutoCAD.

---

## Paper Size

You can select a paper size from the Paper Size pop-up menu. These sizes are derived from the sizes available from your currently selected system printer. You'll find out how to select a different printer later in this chapter.

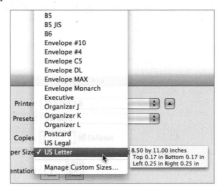

AutoCAD offers sheet sizes in both Imperial and metric measurements in the Paper Size pop-up menu.

## Drawing Orientation

When you used the Preview button in the first exercise in this chapter, you saw your drawing as it would be placed on the paper. In that example, it was placed in a *landscape orientation*, which places the image on the paper so that the width of the paper is greater than its height. You can rotate the image on the paper 90° into a *portrait orientation* by clicking the Portrait button. There is one more option, Plot Upside Down, which will be covered in the section "The Advanced Printing Options" later in this chapter. It lets you change the orientation further by turning the landscape or portrait orientation upside down. These three settings let you print the image in any one of four orientations on the sheet.

In AutoCAD, the preview displays the paper in the orientation it's in when it leaves the printer. For most small-format printers, if you're printing in the portrait orientation, the image appears in the same orientation you see when you're editing the drawing. If you're using the landscape orientation, the preview image is turned sideways. For large-format plotters, the preview may be oriented in the opposite direction. The graphic in the Orientation group displays a graphic on a sheet showing the orientation of your drawing on the paper output.

## Plot Area

The What To Print pop-up menu lets you specify which part of your drawing you want to print. You may notice some similarities between these settings and the Zoom command options. The Print pop-up options are described next. Most of these options are used only in a model view. Typically, when printing from a layout view, you'll use the Layout option. You will learn about this in the Setting Print Scale in the Layout viewports section later this chapter.

**Display**   Display is the default option; it tells AutoCAD to print what is currently displayed on the screen. If you let AutoCAD fit the drawing onto the sheet (that is, you select the Fit To Paper check box from the Scale group), the print is exactly the same as what you see on your screen, adjusted for the width and height proportions of your display.

**Extents**   The Extents option uses the extents of the drawing to determine the area to print. If you let AutoCAD fit the drawing onto the sheet (by selecting the Fit To Paper check box in the Scale group), the printout displays exactly the same image that you would see on the screen if you chose Zoom Extents.

**Limits**   The Limits option (available in Model Space only) uses the limits of the drawing to determine the area to print.

---

**GETTING A BLANK PRINT?**

Do you get a blank printout even though you selected Extents or Display? Chances are the Fit To Paper check box isn't selected or the Inches = Units (mm = Units for metric users) setting is inappropriate for the sheet size and scale of your drawing. If you don't care about the scale of the drawing, make sure the Fit To Paper option is selected. Otherwise, make sure the Scale settings are set correctly. The next section describes how to set the scale for your prints.

---

**Window**   The Window option enables you to use a window to indicate the area you want to print. Nothing outside the window prints. To use this option, select it from the pop-up menu. The Print dialog box temporarily closes to allow you to select a window. After you've done this the first time, a Window button appears next to the pop-up menu. You can click the Window button and then indicate a window in the drawing area or AutoCAD will use the last indicated window. If you use the Fit To Paper option in the Scale group to let AutoCAD fit the drawing onto the sheet, the printout displays exactly the same thing that you enclose in the window.

The descriptions of several What To Print options indicate that the Fit To Paper option can be selected. Bear in mind that when you instead apply a scale factor to your print, it changes the results of the What To Print settings and some problems can arise. This is where most new users have difficulty.

For example, the apartment plan drawing fits nicely on the paper when you use Fit To Paper. But if you try to print the drawing at a scale of 1″ = 1′, you'll probably get a blank piece of paper because at that scale, hardly any of the drawing fits on your paper. AutoCAD will tell you that it's printing and then tell you that the print is finished. You won't have a clue as to why your sheet is blank.

If an image is too large to fit on a sheet of paper because of improper scaling, the print image is placed on the paper differently, depending on whether the printer uses the center of the image or the lower-left corner for its origin. Keep this in mind as you specify scale factors in this area of the dialog box.

### SCALE

You can select a drawing scale from a set of predefined scales in the Scale pop-up menu. These options cover the most common scales you'll need to use.

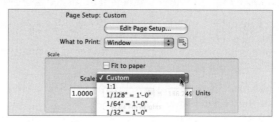

You've already seen how the Fit To Paper option enables you to avoid giving a scale and forces the drawing to fit on the sheet when you're printing from the model view. This works fine if you're printing illustrations that aren't to scale. If you select another option, such as ⅛″ = 1′-0″, the inches and units input boxes change to reflect this scale. The Inches = input box changes to 0.125, and the Units input box changes to 12.

If you're plotting from a layout, you'll use the 1:1 scale option or perhaps a 1:2 scale if you're plotting a half-size drawing. In a layout, the drawing scale is typically set up through the view-port. While you're printing from a layout, AutoCAD automatically determines the area to print based on the printer and sheet size you select. For more information, see "WYSIWYG Printing Using Layout Views" later in this chapter.

### CUSTOM SCALE

In some cases, you may need to set up a nonstandard scale (not shown in the pop-up menu) to print your drawing. If you can't find the scale you want in the Scale pop-up menu, you can select Custom and then enter custom values in the Inches or mm and Unit input boxes.

Through these input boxes, you can indicate how the drawing units in your drawing relate to the final printed distance in inches or millimeters. For example, if your drawing is of a scale factor of 96, follow these steps:

1. In the Scale group of the Print dialog box, double-click in the Inches (or mm) input box and enter **1**; then press the Tab key.

2. In the Unit input box, enter **96** and press the Tab key.

   Metric users who want to plot to a scale of 1:10 should enter **1** in the mm input box and **10** in the Units input box.

If you're more used to the Architectural unit style in the Imperial measurement system, you can enter a scale as a fraction. For example, for a ⅛″ scale drawing, do this:

1. Double-click the Inches input box, enter ⅛, and press the Tab key.

2. Enter **12** in the Unit input box and press the Tab key.

If you specify a different scale than the one you chose while setting up your drawing, AutoCAD prints your drawing to that scale. You aren't restricted in any way as to scale, but entering the correct scale is important: If it's too large, AutoCAD will think your drawing is too large to fit on the sheet, although it will attempt to print your drawing anyway. See Chapter 3 for a discussion of unit styles and scale factors.

---

### DON'T FORGET YOUR ANNOTATION SCALE

You may see a message saying that the "annotation scale is not equal to the print scale" when you attempt to print your drawing. You can click Continue at the message and your drawing will still be printed to the scale you specify. If you are using any text or blocks that use the annotation scale feature, those items will be printed at the Annotation Scale setting for the model view or layout you are trying to print. See Chapter 4, "Organizing Objects with Blocks and Groups," for more on the annotation scale.

---

If you print to a scale that is different from the scale you originally intended, objects and text appear smaller or larger than is appropriate for your print. You'll need to edit your text size to match the new scale. You can do so by using the Properties Inspector palette. Select the text whose height you want to change, and then change the Height (or Paper/Model Text Height) setting in the Properties Inspector palette.

### ADDING A CUSTOM SCALE TO THE SCALE POP-UP MENU

If you use a custom scale frequently, you may find it annoying to have to input the scale every time you print. AutoCAD offers the ability to add your custom scale to the Scale pop-up menu shown earlier. You can then easily select your custom scale from the list instead of entering it through the input box.

Here are the steps you use to add a custom scale to the Scale pop-up menu:

1. Click on the Annotation Scale pop-up menu on the status bar.

2. Select the Edit Scale List option from the menu. The Edit Drawing Scales dialog box opens. (See Figure 8.4.)

3. In the Edit Drawing Scales dialog box, click the + button.

**4.** Enter a name for your custom scale in the Name input box, and then press the Tab key to enter the appropriate values in the Paper Units and Drawing Units input boxes as shown on Figure 8.4.

**5.** Click OK to close the dialog box.

**FIGURE 8.4**
The Edit Drawing
Scales dialog

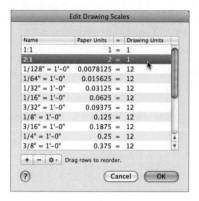

There are several other options in the Edit Drawing Scales dialog box. Clicking the – (minus) button deletes an item or a set of items from the list. Clicking on the action menu will give you two more options: the Edit button, which lets you edit an existing scale in the list, and the Reset button, which restores the list to its default condition and removes any custom items you may have added. You can also click-drag a list to move an item up and down the list. This lets you change its location on the list. Finally, you can type the command **SCALELISTEDIT** to get to the Edit Drawing Scales dialog box.

### SCALE LINEWEIGHTS

AutoCAD offers the option to assign line weights to objects either through their layer assignments or by directly assigning a line weight to individual objects. The Scale Lineweights option, however, doesn't have any meaning until you specify a scale for your drawing. Click this check box if you want the line weight assigned to layers and objects to appear correctly in your prints. You'll get a closer look at line weights and printing later in this chapter.

## The Advanced Printing Options

In addition to the standard Print dialog box, there are printing options available to give you further control over your printing. The Advanced button will open the Print – Advanced dialog box shown in Figure 8.5.

**FIGURE 8.5**
The Print –
Advanced
dialog box

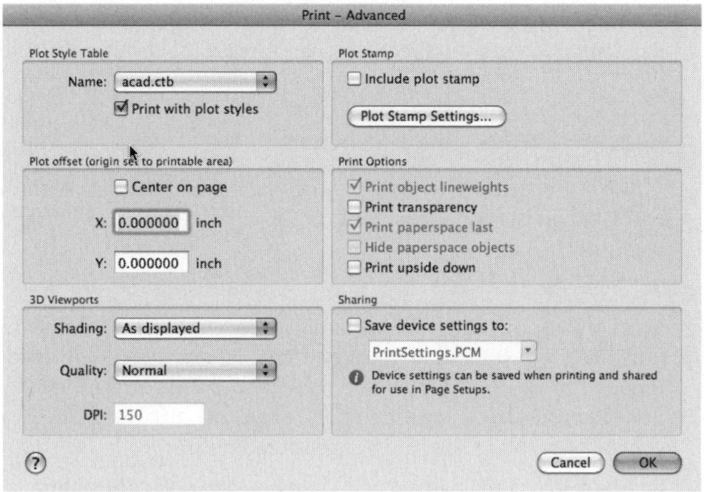

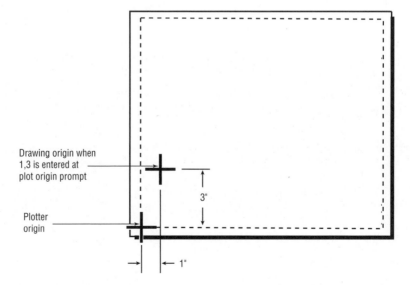

## PLOT STYLE TABLE

Plot styles give you a high degree of control over your drawing output. You can control whether your output is in color or black and white, and you can control whether filled areas are drawn in a solid color or a pattern. You can even control the way lines are joined at corners.

## PLOT OFFSET

Sometimes, your first print of a drawing shows the drawing positioned incorrectly on the paper. You can fine-tune the location of the drawing on the paper by using the Plot Offset group. To adjust the position of your drawing on the paper, enter the location of the view origin in relation to the printer origin in X and Y coordinates (see Figure 8.6).

**FIGURE 8.6**
Adjusting the
image location
on a sheet

For example, suppose you print a drawing and then realize that it needs to be moved 1″ to the right and 3″ up on the sheet. You can reprint the drawing by making the following changes:

1. Double-click the X input box, type **1**, and press the Tab key.

2. Type **3**, and press the Tab key.

Now proceed with the rest of the print configuration. With the preceding settings, the image is shifted on the paper exactly 1″ to the right and 3″ up when the print is done.

### 3D VIEWPORTS

Most of your printing will probably involve 2D technical line drawings, but occasionally you may need to print a shaded or rendered 3D view. You may need to include such 3D views combined with 2D or 3D wireframe views. AutoCAD offers the 3D Viewports group that enables you to print shaded or rendered 3D views of your AutoCAD drawing. These options give you control over the quality of your rendered output.

**Shading**   The Shading pop-up menu lets you control how a model view or layout is printed. You can choose from the following options:

**As Displayed** plots the model view as it appears on your screen.

**Legacy Wireframe** plots the model view of a 3D object as a wireframe view.

**Legacy Hidden** plots your model view with hidden lines removed.

**Conceptual/Hidden/Realistic** plots the model view using one of several visual styles. These selections override the current model view visual style. See Chapter 19, "Creating 3D Drawings," for more on visual styles.

**Rendered** renders your model view before printing (see Chapter 21, "Rendering 3D Drawings," for more on rendered views).

**Draft/Low/Medium/High/Presentation** sets the quality of the print.

The Shading options aren't available if you're printing from a layout view. You can control the way each layout viewport is printed through the viewport's Properties Inspector palette settings. You'll learn more about layout viewport properties in the section "WYSIWYG Printing Using Layout Views" later in this chapter.

**Quality and DPI**   The Quality pop-up menu determines the dots per inch (dpi) setting for your output. These options aren't available if you select Legacy Wireframe or Legacy Hidden from the Shading pop-up menu:

**Draft** prints 3D views as wireframes.

**Preview** offers 75 dpi resolution.

**Normal** offers 150 dpi resolution.

**Presentation** offers 300 dpi resolution.

**Maximum** defers dpi resolution to the current output device's settings.

**Custom** lets you set a custom dpi setting. When Custom is selected, the DPI input box is made available for your input.

If some of the terms discussed for the 3D Viewports group are unfamiliar, don't be alarmed. You'll learn about 3D shaded and rendered views in Part 4 of this book. When you start to explore 3D modeling in AutoCAD, come back and review the 3D Viewports group.

### PLOT STAMP

The Plot Stamp feature lets you place pertinent data on the drawing in a location you choose. This includes the drawing name, date and time, scale, and other data. Click the Include Plot Stamp check box to turn this feature on.

Click the Plot Stamp Settings button to gain access to the Plot Stamp Settings dialog box (see Figure 8.7). This dialog box offers many controls for the plot stamp. It is a fairly extensive tool, so rather than fill this chapter with a description of all its features, I've included a complete rundown of the Plot Stamp options in Appendix C, "Hardware and Software Tips," on the book's companion website.

**FIGURE 8.7**

The Plot Stamp dialog

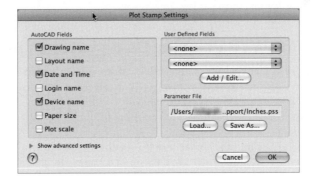

### PRINT OPTIONS

The Print Options group contains additional options that will affect the printed output. The options can be activated via check boxes.

**Print Object Lineweights**   As mentioned earlier, AutoCAD lets you assign line weights to objects either through their layer assignment or by assigning them directly. If you use this feature in your drawing, this option lets you turn line weights on or off in your output.

**Print Transparency**   You can apply a transparency of objects and layers in your drawing. This option lets you control whether transparency is used when your drawing is printed.

**Print Paperspace Last**   When you're using a layout view, otherwise known as Paper Space, this option determines whether objects in Paper Space are printed before or after objects in Model Space. You'll learn more about Model Space and Paper Space later in this chapter.

**Hide Paperspace Objects**   This option pertains to 3D models in AutoCAD. When you draw in 3D, you can view your drawing as a *wireframe view*. In a wireframe view, your drawing looks like it's transparent even though it's made up of solid surfaces. Using hidden-line removal, you can view and print your 3D drawings so that solid surfaces are opaque. To view a 3D drawing in the drawing area with hidden lines removed, use the Hide command or use one of the visual styles other than wireframe. To print a 3D drawing with hidden lines removed, choose the Hidden option or a visual style from the Shading pop-up menu in the 3D Viewports group.

Hide Paperspace Objects doesn't work for views in the layout viewport described in the section "WYSIWYG Printing Using Layout Views." Instead, you need to set the viewport's Shade Plot property to Hidden. (Click the viewport, right-click, and choose Shade Plot ➤ Hidden from the shortcut menu.)

**Print Upside Down**   This option does exactly what it says. It adjusts the printout to print upside down.

### Sharing

The Sharing group features a Save Device Settings To option. When this option is turned on, the changes you make to Print dialog box settings are saved to a specified file. You'll learn more about layouts in the following section.

## WYSIWYG Printing Using Layout Views

So far you've done all your work in the model view, also known as Model Space. There are other views to your drawing that are specifically geared toward printing. The *layout* views enable you to control drawing scale, add title blocks, and set up layer settings that are different from those in the model view. You can think of the layout views as page-layout spaces that act like a desktop-publishing program.

This section introduces you to layout views as they relate to printing. You'll learn more about layout views in Chapter 15, "Laying Out Your Printer Output."

You can have as many layout views as you like, each set up for a different type of output. You can, for example, have two or three layout views, each set up for a different scale drawing or with different layer configurations for reflected ceiling plans, floor plans, or equipment plans. You can even set up multiple views of your drawing at different scales in a single layout view. In addition, you can draw and add text and dimensions in layout views just as you would in Model Space.

To get familiar with the layout views, try the following exercise:

Model ▾

1. With the Plan file open, click the Model/Layout tool in the status bar (see Figure 8.8) and then select Layout1 from the pop-up menu. The Model/Layout tool now indicates that it is set to Layout1.

**FIGURE 8.8**
Choose Layout1
from the pop-up
menu.

**2.** Click in the drawing area. A view of your drawing appears on a gray background, as shown in Figure 8.9. This is a view of your drawing as it will appear when printed on your current default printer. The white area represents the current paper size.

**FIGURE 8.9**
A view of Layout1

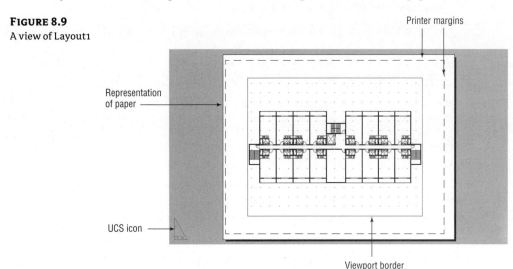

Printer margins

Representation of paper

UCS icon

Viewport border

**3.** Try zooming in and out using the Zoom button or the scroll wheel of your mouse or a single finger swipe on the Magic Mouse or trackpad. Notice that the entire image zooms in and out, including the area representing the paper.

Layout views give you full control over the appearance of your drawing printouts. You can print a layout view just as you did the view in Model Space.

Let's take a moment to look at the elements in the Layout1 view. As mentioned previously, the white area represents the paper on which your drawing will be printed. The dashed line immediately inside the edge of the white area represents the limits of your printer's margins. Finally, the solid rectangle that surrounds your drawing is the outline of the viewport border. A *viewport* is an AutoCAD object that works like a window into your drawing from the layout view. Also notice the triangular symbol in the lower-left corner of the view: This is the UCS icon for the layout view. It tells you that you're currently in layout view space. You'll see the significance of this icon in the following exercise:

**1.** Try using a selection window to select the lobby area of your drawing. Nothing is selected.

**2.** Click the viewport border, which is the rectangle surrounding the drawing, as shown in Figure 8.9. This is the viewport into Model Space. Notice that you can select it.

**3.** You can see from the Properties Inspector palette that the viewport is just like any other AutoCAD object with layer, linetype, and color assignments. You can even hide the viewport outline by turning off its layer.

**4.** With the viewport still selected, click the Erase tool in the Tool Sets palette. The view of your drawing disappears with the erasure of the viewport. Remember that the viewport is like a window into the drawing you created in the model view. After the viewport is erased, the drawing view goes with it.

**5.** Type **U**↵, choose Edit ➤ Undo from the menu bar, or press ⌘-Z to restore the viewport.

---

**CREATING NEW VIEWPORTS**

You can create new viewports using the Vports command (the New Viewport option in the View ➤ Viewports on the menu bar). See the section "Creating New Paper Space Viewports" in Chapter 15 for more information.

---

**6.** Double-click anywhere within the viewport's boundary. Notice that the UCS icon you're used to seeing appears in the lower-left corner of the viewport. The Layout UCS icon disappears. The Viewport label menus and ViewCube also appear inside the viewport.

**7.** Click the lobby in your drawing. You can now select parts of your drawing.

**8.** Try zooming and panning your view. Changes in your view take place only within the boundary of the viewport.

**9.** Click Zoom from the status bar and then type **A**↵, or type **Z**↵ **A**↵ to display the entire drawing in the viewport.

**10.** To return to Paper Space, double-click an area outside the viewport. You can also type **PS**↵ to return to Paper Space or **MS**↵ to access Model Space within the viewport.

This exercise shows you the unique characteristics of layout viewports. The objects in the viewport are inaccessible until you double-click the interior of the viewport. You can then move about and edit your drawing in the viewport, just as you would while in the model view.

Layout views can contain as many viewports as you like, and each viewport can hold a different view of your drawing. You can size and arrange each viewport any way you like, or you can create multiple viewports, giving you the freedom to lay out your drawing as you would a page in a page-layout program. You can also draw in the layout view or import Xrefs and blocks for title blocks and borders.

## Setting Print Scale in the Layout Viewports

In the first part of this chapter, you plotted your drawing from the model view. You learned that to get the print to fit on your paper, you had to either use the Fit To Paper option in the Print dialog box or indicate a specific drawing scale, print area, and drawing orientation.

The layout view works in a different way: It's designed to enable you to print your drawing at a 1-to-1 scale. Instead of specifying the drawing scale in the Print dialog box, as you did when you printed from Model Space, you let the size of your view in the layout viewport determine the drawing scale. You can set the viewport view to an exact scale by making changes to the properties of the viewport.

To set the scale of a viewport in a layout, try the following exercise:

1. Press the Esc key to clear any selections. Then, click the viewport border to select it. You'll see the Viewport Scale pop-up menu appear in the status bar.

2. Click the Viewport Scale pop-up, and a list of common drawing scales appears (see Figure 8.10).

**FIGURE 8.10**

Choose a viewport scale.

3. Select ¹⁄₁₆″ = 1′ (metric users should select 1:20). The view in the viewport changes to reflect the new scale. Now most of the drawing fits into the viewport, and it's to scale. The scale of ¹⁄₁₆″ = 1′ is similar to the metric 1:200 scale, but because you used centimeters instead of millimeters as the base unit for the metric version of the Plan file, you drop the second 0 in 200. The metric scale becomes 1:20.

4. Use the viewport grips to enlarge the viewport enough to display all of the drawing, as shown in Figure 8.11. As you move a corner grip, notice that the viewport maintains a rectangular shape.

**FIGURE 8.11**

The enlarged viewport

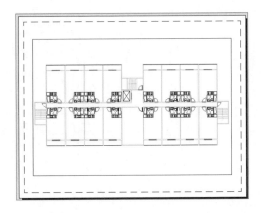

5. Choose File ➢ Print from the menu bar, type **PLOT**↵, or press ⌘-P, and in the Print dialog box (see Figure 8.12), click the Edit Page Setup button. The Page Setup – Layout1 dialog opens (see Figure 8.13). Make sure your system printer is selected in the Printer/Plotter group and the Scale pop-up menu in the Scale group is set to 1:1; then click OK. Your drawing is printed as it appears in the Layout view, and it's printed to scale.

6. After reviewing your print, close the drawing without saving it.

**FIGURE 8.12**
The Print
dialog box

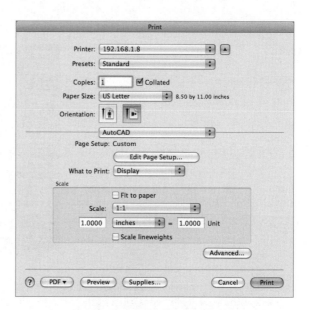

**FIGURE 8.13**
The Page Setup
dialog

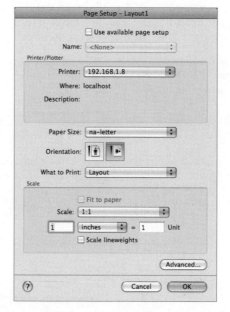

In step 2, you saw that you can select a scale for a viewport by selecting it from the Viewport Scale pop-up menu in the status bar. If you look just below the Viewport Scale pop-up menu, you see the Custom Scale options. Both options work like their counterparts, the options in the Scale group in the Print dialog box.

Layout views and viewports work in conjunction with your printer settings to give you a better idea of how your prints will look. There are numerous printer settings that can dramatically change the appearance of your layout view and your prints. In the next section, you'll learn how some of the printer settings can enhance the appearance of your drawings. You'll also learn how layout views can display those settings, letting you see on your computer screen exactly what will appear on your paper output.

## Examining Output-Device Settings

As mentioned already, you can set up AutoCAD for more than one output device. You can do this even if you have only one printer connected to your computer. You might want multiple printer configurations in AutoCAD for many reasons. For instance, you might want to set up your system so that you can print to a remote location over a network or the Internet.

---

**SETTING UP NEW PRINTERS**

As was mentioned, AutoCAD for Mac uses the system printer for printing. It is beyond the scope of this book to provide instruction on how to install a printer. Each printer installation routine can vary.

---

### Adding a Printer Configuration File

You may already have a printer configuration file (PCM, with the filename extension .pcm) that works for your printer and wish to incorporate that into AutoCAD for Mac. The default location for printer configuration files can be found in the Computer/Users/{Username}/Library/ Application Support/Autodesk/roaming/AutoCAD/R18.1/enu/Plotters folder. You can change the location that AutoCAD for Mac will search for these files, which will be covered in the section "Changing the Default Printer Configuration File Location" later in this chapter.

---

**WHAT IS A PCM FILE?**

A file with the filename extension of .pcm is a printer configuration file. It is a compressed file (you cannot view it with a text editor) that contains information pertaining to a particular printer. It contains the available paper sizes and characteristics for your printer.

---

**PRINTING TO PDF**

The PDF drop-down list, as shown here, is not an AutoCAD function; rather it is part of the Mac OS. It will give you basic PDF output. When you click the Save As PDF option in the drop-down list, a Save dialog box opens. Clicking the disclosure triangle to the right of the Save As input box will give you the option of saving to a specific location. When you click Save, it will go through the print routine and save the file at the specified location.

If you use Adobe Acrobat, you can save the PDF with more options, such as layers.

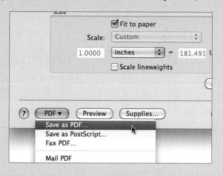

## Changing the Default Printer Configuration File Location

As was shown earlier, the file location for the printer configuration file is buried deep inside the Mac folders. You can modify this location via the Application Preferences dialog box. To get to the Application Preferences dialog box, press ⌘-, (comma). You can also right-click anywhere in the drawing area and choose Preferences from the shortcut menu, choose AutoCAD ➢ Preferences from the menu bar, or type **OP**↵.

In the Application Preferences dialog box, select the Application tab on the left side. Click the disclosure triangles as shown on Figure 8.14. Here you can see the path that AutoCAD uses to locate the configuration files.

**FIGURE 8.14**

The default printer configuration search path

Let's change the location to make it easier to access the files:

1. First, create the folder for your configuration files. For this example, I created a folder called CAD Configs within the Documents folder. Next copy the PCM files to this new location.

2. Make sure the path is highlighted as shown on Figure 8.14. This will ensure that you are changing the correct parameter.

3. Click the action menu and choose Change Path. The Browse For Folder dialog box appears.

4. Select the CAD Configs folder and click Open. The new path is now displayed, as shown on Figure 8.15.

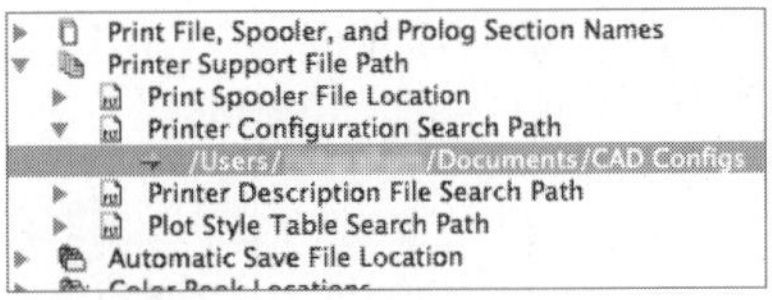

**FIGURE 8.15**
The printer con-
figuration search
path revised.

```
▶  🗋  Print File, Spooler, and Prolog Section Names
▼  🗐  Printer Support File Path
   ▶  🗐  Print Spooler File Location
   ▼  🗐  Printer Configuration Search Path
          ↳  /Users/          /Documents/CAD Configs
   ▶  🗐  Printer Description File Search Path
   ▶  🗐  Plot Style Table Search Path
▶  🗀  Automatic Save File Location
        Color Book Locations
```

# Understanding Plot Styles

To gain full control over the appearance of your output, you'll want to know about plot styles.
By using plot styles, you can control aspects of how the printer draws each object in a drawing.

If you don't use plot styles, your printer will produce output as close as possible to what you
see in the drawing editor, including colors. With plot styles, you can force all the colors to print
as black, and you can also assign a color to a fill pattern or a screen. This can be useful for charts
and maps that require area fills of different gradations. You can use multiple plot styles to produce prints that fit the exact requirements of your project.

I will show you firsthand how you can use plot styles to enhance your printer output. You'll
look at how to adjust the line weight of the walls in the Plan file and make color changes to your
printer output.

## Choosing between Color-Dependent and Named Plot Style Tables

You can think of a plot style as a virtual pen that has the attributes of color, width, shape, and
screen percentage. A typical drawing may use several different line widths, so you use a different
plot style for each line width. Multiple plot styles are collected into *plot style tables* that allow you to
control a set of plot styles from one file. AutoCAD offers two types of plot styles: color and named.

*Color plot style tables* (.ctb) enable you to assign plot styles to the individual AutoCAD colors.
For example, you can assign a plot style with a 0.50 mm width to the color red so that anything
that is red in your drawing is plotted with a line width of 0.50 mm. You can, in addition, set
the plot style's color to black so that everything that is red in your drawing is plotted in black.
AutoCAD's out-of-the-box setting is color plot style tables.

*Named plot styles* (.stb) let you assign plot styles directly to objects in your drawing instead of
assigning them in a more general way through a color. Named plot styles also enable you to assign
plot styles directly to layers. For example, with named plot styles, you can assign a plot style that is
black and has a 0.50 mm width to a single circle or line in a drawing, regardless of its color.

Named plot styles are more flexible than color plot styles, but if you already have a library of
AutoCAD drawings set up for a specific set of printer settings, the color plot styles are a better
choice when you're opening files that were created in AutoCAD R14 and earlier. This is because
using color plot styles is more similar to the older method of assigning AutoCAD colors to plotter pens. You may also want to use color plot style tables with files that you intend to share with
an individual or an office that is still using earlier versions of AutoCAD.

The type of plot style assigned to the new default Drawing1 depends on the value of the
PSTYLEPOLICY system variable.

Here's how to set up the plot style for new files:

1. Choose File ➢ Page Setup Manager from the menu bar. You can also press ⇧-⌘-P. From
   the Page Setup Manager palette, click the action menu and choose Edit.

2. In the Page Setup – Layout1 dialog, select the Advanced button.

**3.** From the Page Setup – Advanced dialog, click the pop-up menu next to Name in the Plot Style Table group (see Figure 8.16).

**FIGURE 8.16**
The Plot Style
Table pop-up menu

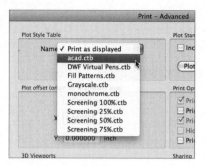

**4.** Select Grayscale.ctb. The Question dialog box appears asking if you wish to use assign the plot style to all layouts. Clicking No will assign it for the current layout. Clicking Yes will make the assignment for all layouts in the drawing. Click Yes.

**5.** Click the Print With Plot Styles check box. This will print the drawing with the associated plot style applied.

**6.** Click the Display Plot Styles check box. This will allow you to see what your printed output will look like without clicking the Preview button.

**7.** Click OK to close the Page Setup – Advanced dialog box. Then click OK to close the Page Setup – Layout1 dialog box. And finally, click Close to close the Page Setup Manager.

Now let's see how plot styles affect your drawing. You're going to change the wall so that it appears and plots thicker by changing the Line Width property of the Color 3 (green) plot style. Remember that green is the color assigned to the Wall layer of your Plan drawing. Follow these steps:

**1.** In the Layers palette, click the Wall layer.

**2.** Now, in the Properties Inspector palette, click the Lineweight drop-down list and select 0.50 mm. You may have to scroll down the list to find 0.5000 mm.

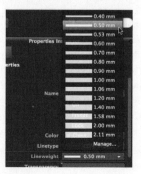

**3.** Zoom in to the plan to enlarge the view of a unit bathroom and entrance.

## Making Your Plot Styles Visible

You won't see any changes in your drawing yet. You need to make one more change to your drawing options:

1. Type **LW⏎** to open the Lineweight Settings dialog box (see Figure 8.17). You can also right-click the Show/Hide Lineweight button on the status bar and select Settings from the menu. The Lineweight Settings dialog box lets you control the appearances of line weights in the drawing. If line weights aren't showing up, this is the place to go to make them viewable.

**FIGURE 8.17**
Check the line weight settings.

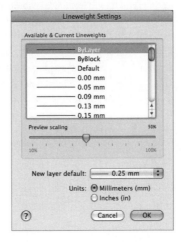

2. Just above the Units options, click the New Layer Default drop-down list and select 0.09 mm. This makes any unassigned or default line weight a very fine line.

3. Click OK.

4. Click the Show/Hide Lineweights button on the status bar. The layout displays the drawing with the line weight assignments you set up earlier (see Figure 8.18).

**FIGURE 8.18**
The drawing with new line weight assignments

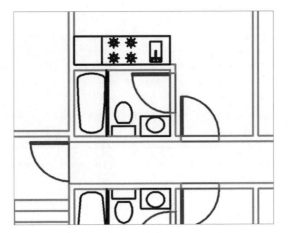

If your view doesn't reflect the Plot Style settings, make sure you have the Display Plot Styles option selected in the Plot Style Table group of the Page Setup dialog box.

### Real World Scenario

#### COLORS AND LINE WEIGHTS IN THE SAN FRANCISCO MAIN LIBRARY

Technical drawings can have a beauty of their own, but they can also be deadly boring. What really sets a good technical drawing apart from a poor one is the control of line weights. Knowing how to vary and control line weights in both manual and CAD drawings can make a huge difference in the readability of the drawing.

In the San Francisco Main Library project, the designers at SMWM Associates were especially concerned with line weights in the reflected ceiling plan. The following image shows a portion of the reflected ceiling plan from the library drawings.

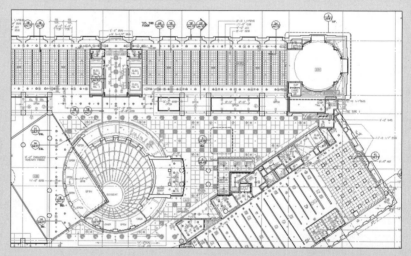

As you can see, it contains a good deal of graphical information, which, without careful line weight control, could become confusing. (Although you can't see it in the black-and-white print, a multitude of colors were used to vary the line weight.) When the electronic drawings were plotted, colors were converted into lines of varying thickness. Bolder lines were used to create emphasis in components such as walls and ceiling openings, and fine lines were used to indicate ceiling-tile patterns.

By emphasizing certain lines over others, you avoid visual monotony and the various components of the drawing can be seen more easily.

# Printer Hardware Considerations

Before you face a deadline with hundreds of prints to produce, you may want to create some test prints and carefully refine your printer settings so that you have AutoCAD set up properly for those rush jobs.

As part of the setup process, you'll need to understand how your particular printer works. Each device has its own special characteristics, so a detailed description of printer hardware setup is beyond the scope of this discussion. The following sections include a few guidelines.

## Understanding Your Printer's Limits

If you're familiar with a word processing or page-layout program, you know that you can set the margins of a page, thereby telling the program exactly how far from each edge of the paper you want the text to appear. With AutoCAD, you don't have that luxury. To place a print on your paper accurately, you must know the printer's hard clip limits. The *hard clip limits* are like built-in margins, beyond which the printer won't print. These limits vary from printer to printer (see Figure 8.19).

**FIGURE 8.19**
The hard clip limits of a printer

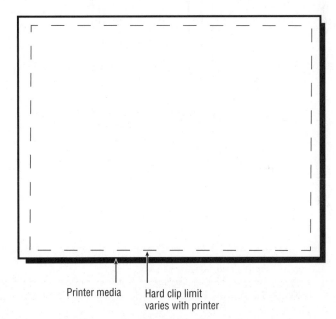

Printer media    Hard clip limit
varies with printer

It's crucial that you know your printer's hard clip limits in order to place your drawings accurately on the sheet. Take some time to study your printer manual and find out exactly what these limits are. Then make a record of them and store it somewhere in case you or someone else needs to format a sheet in a special way.

Hard clip limits for printers often depend on the software that drives them. You may need to consult your printer manual or use the trial-and-error method of printing several samples to see how they come out.

## Knowing Your Printer's Origin

Another important consideration is the location of your printer's origin. For example, on some printers, the lower-left corner of the print area is used as the origin. Other printers use the center of the print area as the origin. When you print a drawing that is too large to fit the sheet on a printer that uses a corner for the origin, the image is pushed toward the top and to the right of the sheet (see Figure 8.20). When you print a drawing that is too large to fit on a printer that uses the center of the paper as the origin, the image is pushed outward in all directions from the center of the sheet.

**FIGURE 8.20**
Printing an over-sized image on a printer that uses the lower-left corner for its origin

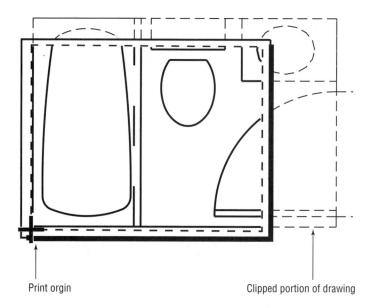

Print orgin          Clipped portion of drawing

In each situation, the origin determines a point of reference you can use to relate your drawing in the computer to the physical output. After you understand this, you're better equipped to place your electronic drawing accurately on the physical medium.

---

### OUTPUTTING IMAGE FILES AND CONVERTING 3D TO 2D

If your work involves producing manuals, reports, or similar documents, you may want to output to raster image files. Drawing files can be output to a wide range of raster file formats, including JPEG, PNG, TIFF, and BMP. You can then import your drawings into documents that accept bitmap images. Images can contain as many colors as the file format allows.

To convert your 3D wireframe models into 2D line drawings, use the Flatshot tool described in Chapter 19. You can then include your 2D line drawings with other 2D drawings for printing.

# The Bottom Line

**Print a plan.**   Unlike other types of documents, AutoCAD drawings can end up on nearly any size sheet of paper. To accommodate the range of paper sizes, the AutoCAD printer settings are fairly extensive and give you a high level of control over your output.

**Master It**   Name a few of the settings available in the Print dialog box.

**Understanding the print settings.**   The print settings in AutoCAD offer a way to let you set up how a drawing will be printed.

**Master It**   Where would you find the setting to print upside down?

**Use layout views for WYSIWYG printing.**   The layout views show you what your print output will look like before you actually print.

**Master It**   True or false: Layout views give you limited control over the appearance of your drawing printouts.

# Chapter 9

# Adding Text to Drawings

One of the most tedious drafting tasks is applying notes to your drawing. AutoCAD makes this job faster by enabling you to type your notes, insert text from other sources, and copy notes that repeat throughout a drawing, and it helps you to create notes that are more professional looking using a variety of fonts, type sizes, and type styles.

In this chapter, you'll add notes to your apartment building plan. In the process, you'll explore some of AutoCAD's text-creation and text-editing features. You'll learn how to control the size, slant, type style, and orientation of text and how to import text files. You'll start by working through some exercises that show you the process of preparing a drawing for text. You'll then add a few lines of text to the drawing and learn how text size and drawing scale interrelate. The rest of the chapter shows you the tools available for formatting text to fit your application.

In this chapter, you'll learn to do the following:

- ◆ Prepare a drawing for text
- ◆ Set the annotation scale and add text
- ◆ Explore text formatting in AutoCAD
- ◆ Add simple single-line text objects
- ◆ Use the Check Spelling feature
- ◆ Find and replace text

## Preparing a Drawing for Text

In these first sections, you'll go through the process of adding text to a drawing that currently has no text. By doing this, you'll gain firsthand experience in using all the tools you'll need for adding text to a drawing. Start by setting up a drawing to prepare it for the addition of text:

1. Start AutoCAD, and open the Unit file. If you haven't created the Unit file, you can use the file called 9a-unit.dwg found on www.sybex.com/go/masteringautocadmac. Metric users should use 9a-unit-metric.dwg. After the file is open, use the Saveas command to save the Unit drawing to a file called Unit.dwg.

2. Create a layer called Notes, and make it the current layer. Notes is the layer on which you'll keep all your text information.

3. If it is on, turn off the Flr-pat layer. Otherwise, the floor pattern you added previously will obscure the text you enter during the exercises in this chapter.

**4.** Set up your view so it looks similar to the top image in Figure 9.1.

**FIGURE 9.1**
The top image shows the points to pick to place the text boundary window. The bottom image shows the completed text.

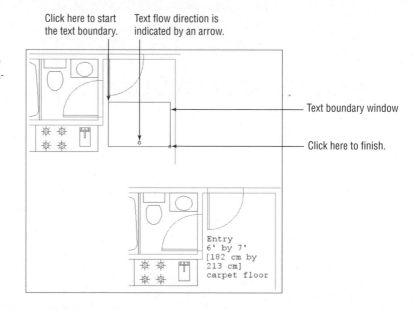

Click here to start the text boundary.

Text flow direction is indicated by an arrow.

Text boundary window

Click here to finish.

Entry
6' by 7'
[182 cm by
213 cm]
carpet floor

---

### ORGANIZE TEXT WITH LAYERS

It's a good idea to keep your notes on a separate layer so you can plot drawings containing only the graphics information or freeze the Notes layer to save redraw/regeneration time.

## Organizing Text by Styles

Before you begin to add text to your drawing, you should set up a text style or two. You can think of text styles as a tool to store your most common text formatting. Styles store text height and font information so you don't have to set these options every time you enter text. Generally, you'll need only a few text styles.

Even if you started to add text without creating your own text style, you would still be using a text style. That's because every text object must have a style, so AutoCAD includes the Standard text style in every new drawing. The Standard style uses an AutoCAD font called Txt and includes numerous other settings that you'll learn about in this section. These other settings include width factor, oblique angle, and default height.

---

### SET UP DEFAULT FONTS IN TEMPLATES

If you don't like the way the AutoCAD default style is set up, open the acad.dwt template file and change the Standard text style settings to your liking. You can also add other styles that you use frequently. Remember, AutoCAD files that use the .dwt filename extension are just AutoCAD DWG files with a slightly different extension to set them apart.

In this next exercise, you'll create a text style called Note1, which you'll use to add notes to the Unit plan you've been working on:

1. Choose Format ➤ Text Style from the menu bar, or type **ST**↵. This opens up the Text Style dialog box (Figure 9.2).

**FIGURE 9.2**
The Text Style
dialog box

2. Click the + (plus) button at the bottom left of the dialog to add a new style.

3. Type **Note1** for the name of your new style.

4. In the Family panel that is in the center of the dialog, scroll until you find the Courier New TrueType font. The Filter List input box can be helpful in reducing the number of fonts listed. Enter the first few letters of a font in the Filter List input box and select the font to use. Click the X button in the input box to clear your filter text string.

5. Click the Annotative button. When you select this button, notice that the Paper Text Height input box has now replaced the Text Height input box and the Note1 name now has an Annotative symbol in front of it.

6. In the Paper Text Height input box, enter **0.1** and press Enter. You'll see your input change to ⅛″ if you are using the architectural unit style. Metric users should enter **0.15**.

7. Right-click the Note1 style and select Set Current.

8. Click the Apply button and then click Close.

The Annotative option you turned on in step 5 is an important feature for keeping your text at the proper size for your drawing scale. You'll see how it works firsthand in the following section's exercises.

---

**MAKING A STYLE THE DEFAULT**

Once you've created a style, it becomes your default style. You can modify this by selecting it from the Text Style pop-up menu in the Properties Inspector palette while no object is selected.

## Setting the Annotation Scale and Adding Text

You've got a text style set up and ready to use. Now you'll add some text to your unit plan. Before you begin, you should determine a drawing scale. This is important because, with the Annotative feature turned on, AutoCAD needs to know the drawing scale in order to set the size of the text. Follow these steps:

1. In the right side of the status bar, click the Annotation Scale pop-up menu.

2. Select ¼″ = 1′-0″. Metric users, select 1:100.

You've just set the drawing scale for Model Space. This isn't a permanent setting; you can change it at any time, as you'll see later. The settings you used for the annotation scale are somewhat arbitrary for the purposes of demonstrating the Annotative Scale feature.

Finally, you can begin to add text:

1. Turn off the Object Snap button in the status bar.

2. Click the top icon in the Tool Sets palette. This icon will expand to show all available palettes. Click Annotation.

3. Click the Multiline Text icon in the Tool Sets palette. You can also type **MT**↵. You see a prompt that tells you the current text style and height:

```
Current text style: "Note1" Text height: 6"
Annotative: Yes
Specify first corner:
```

4. Click the first point indicated in the top image in Figure 9.1 to start the text boundary window. This boundary window indicates the area in which to place the text. Notice the arrow near the bottom of the window: It indicates the direction of the text flow. You don't have to be too precise about where you select the points for the boundary because you can adjust the location and size later.

5. At the `Specify opposite corner or [Height/Justify/Line spacing/Rotation/Style/Width/Columns]:` prompt, click the second point indicated in the top image in Figure 9.1. The Text Editor visor appears, with the text editor superimposed over the area you just selected (Figure 9.3).

6. Click the text editor and type **Entry**. As you type, the word appears in the text editor just as it will appear in your drawing.

7. Press ↵ to advance one line; then enter **6′ by 7′**.

FIGURE 9.3

The text editor
visor floats over
the selected area.

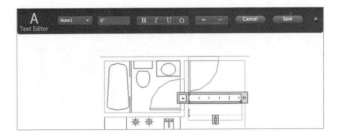

8. Press ↵ to advance another line, and enter **[182 cm by 213 cm]**.

9. Press ↵ again to advance another line, and enter **carpet floor**.

10. Click Save in the Text Editor visor. The text appears in the drawing just as it did in the text editor. (See the bottom image in Figure 9.1.)

After you've added text, if the text doesn't quite fit in the area you've indicated, you can make adjustments to the text boundary. Click the text to expose the text boundary, including the boundary grips. Then click and drag the grips to resize the boundary. AutoCAD's word-wrap feature automatically adjusts the text formatting to fit the text boundary.

You may have noticed that the Text Editor visor and text editor work like many other text editors; if you make a typing error, you can highlight the error and retype the letter or word. You can perform other word processing functions too, such as using search and replace, importing text, and changing fonts.

You also saw that the text editor shows how your text will appear in the location you selected using the text boundary. If your view of the drawing is such that the text is too small to be legible, the text editor enlarges the text so you can read it clearly. Likewise, if you're zoomed in too closely to see the entire text, the text editor adjusts the text to enable you to see all of it.

---

**MAKING TEXT READABLE OVER HATCH PATTERNS**

If text is included in a selection where a hatch pattern is to be placed, AutoCAD automatically avoids hatching over the text. If you add text over a hatched area, you can use the Background Mask option in the text editor shortcut menu to make the text more readable. Another option is to use the Add: Select Objects button in the Hatch Edit dialog box to add text to a hatch selection.

---

## Exploring Text and Scale

Even though your text height is 0.1″, or 0.15 cm, it appears at the appropriately enlarged size for the current scale. If the text were drawn to the size of 0.1″, it would be very small and barely visible. However, the Annotative Scale feature makes the adjustment to your text size based on the Annotation Scale setting.

You can see firsthand how the Annotation Scale setting affects your text:

1. First, make sure the Annotative Visibility button is turned on in the status bar, or type **ANNOALLVISIBLE↵ 1↵**.

2. Click the Automatically Add Scales To Annotative Objects When the Scale Changes setting.

**3.** Select ½″ = 1′-0″ from the pop-out menu. Metric users should select 1:50. The text changes to the appropriate size for the selected scale.

**4.** Select the Add/Delete Scales icon from the Tool Sets palette. You can also choose Modify ➤ Annotative Object Scale ➤ Add/Delete Scales in the menu bar or type **OBJECTSCALE**↵.

**5.** At the Select annotative objects: prompt, select the text, and press ↵. You see the Annotation Object Scale List dialog box (Figure 9.4) listing the two annotation scales you have used for this drawing.

**FIGURE 9.4**
The Annotation Object Scale List dialog box

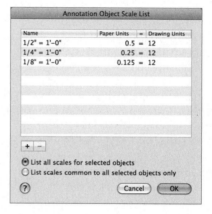

**6.** You can add additional scales to your text object by clicking the + (plus) button, which opens the Add Scales To Object dialog box (Figure 9.5).

**FIGURE 9.5**
The Add Scales To Object dialog box

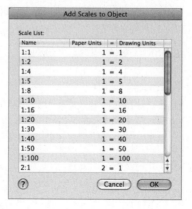

**7.** Click OK and then click OK again at the Annotation Object Scale List dialog box.

Now test your settings by changing the Annotation Scale value back to the previous setting: In the status bar, click the Annotation Scale pop-up menu, and select ¼″ = 1′-0″. Metric users should select 1:100. The text changes back to its original size.

In steps 4 through 6, you added a new annotation scale to the text. This is necessary for the text to be aware of the new annotation scale you want to use. Each time you include a new scale for your drawing, you need to add an annotation scale to the text in your drawing.

If you prefer, you can turn on the Automatically Add Scale To Annotative Objects in the status bar, which does just what its name says. The keyboard entry for this setting is **ANNOAUTOSCALE**⏎ **4**⏎. Once a scale is added, you can quickly change between scales by selecting a scale from the Annotation Scale pop-up menu.

### Real World Scenario

#### TEXT AND SCALE IN LEGACY DRAWINGS

AutoCAD for Mac offers the Annotative Scale feature to automate the scaling of text and other objects to their proper size based on the drawing's annotation scale. But there is a good chance you'll encounter drawings that were created before the Annotative Scale feature was available. For that reason, you should have a basic understanding of scale factors as they apply to text.

As you know by now, AutoCAD lets you draw at full scale; that is, you can represent distances as values equivalent to the actual size of the object. When you later print the drawing, you tell AutoCAD the scale at which you want to print and the program reduces the drawing accordingly. This gives you the freedom to enter measurements at full scale and not worry about converting them to various scales every time you enter a distance. Unfortunately, in earlier releases of AutoCAD, this feature created problems when users entered text and dimensions. You had to make the text height very large in order for it to be readable when scaled down.

To illustrate this point, imagine you're drawing the Unit plan at full size on a very large sheet of paper. When you're finished with this drawing, it will be reduced to a scale that enables it to fit on an 8.5″-X-11″ sheet of paper. So you have to make your text large to keep it legible after it's reduced. If you want text to appear ⅛″ high when the drawing is printed, you must convert it to a considerably larger size when you draw it. To do this, you multiply the desired height of the final printed text by a scale conversion factor. (See Chapter 3 for more on scale conversion factors.)

For example, if your drawing is at a ⅛″ = 1′-0″ scale, you multiply the desired text height, ⅛″, by the scale conversion factor of 96 to get a height of 12″. This is the height you must make your text to get ⅛″-high text in the final print.

With AutoCAD for Mac, you don't have to work through the math to get the right text size for your drawing. But if you encounter a drawing that was created in an earlier release of AutoCAD and you notice that the text size is very large, you'll know why.

So far, you've only used a single multiline text object. However, if you have many notes distributed throughout a drawing, you'll need to add an annotation scale to all of them before they can automatically adjust themselves to the different scales you'll use with your drawing. If you have Automatically Add Scale To Annotative Objects turned on in the status bar, this happens automatically. Otherwise, you'll have to add the scales to each annotative object. This is easy to do because you have the option to select as many objects as you need when adding annotation scales.

## Understanding the Text Style Dialog Box Options

You've just taken nearly all the steps you'll need to know to add text to any drawing. Now let's take a step back and look more closely at some of the finer points of adding text, starting with text styles. The following sections give you more detailed information about the text style settings in the Text Style dialog box (Figure 9.6) you saw in the early part of this chapter. They explain those settings and their purposes. Some of them, such as Width Factor, can be quite useful. Others, such as the Backwards and Vertical options, are rarely used. Take a moment to study these settings to become familiar with what is available and make a mental note of these items for future reference.

**FIGURE 9.6**

The Text Style dialog box

### Effects

The Effects group offers settings relating to text size, scale, and orientation.

**Annotative**   Causes the text size to automatically adjust to the current annotation scale setting.

**Match Text Orientation To Layout**   Causes the text orientation to match the orientation of a layout view. This option is available only when the Annotative option is on.

**Upside Down**   Displays text upside down.

**Backwards**   Displays text backward.

**Vertical**   Displays text in a vertical column.

**Text Height/Paper Text Height**   Lets you enter a font size. With the Annotative option turned off, this option is named *Text Height* and will set the absolute height of the text. With the Annotative group turned on, it shows *Paper Text Height* and will set the height of the text when printed. A 0 height has special meaning when you use the Text command to enter text, as described later in this chapter, or when using the text style with a dimension style.

**Width Factor**   Adjusts the width and spacing of the characters in the text. A value of 1 keeps the text at its normal width. Values greater than 1 expand the text, and values less than 1 compress the text.

This is the Simplex font expanded by 1.4
This is the simplex font using a width factor of 1
This is the simplex font compressed by .6

**Oblique Angle**   Skews the text at an angle. When this option is set to a value greater than 0, the text appears italicized. A value of less than 0 (-12, for example) causes the text to lean to the left.

This is the simplex font
using a 12—degree oblique angle

## Styles

In the Styles list box you'll see a list showing the current style. This list also contains other styles that may be present in the drawing. The pop-up menu below the Styles list box lets you control whether all styles are listed or just those that are being used in the drawing. In addition, when you right-click on a style, you have the Set Current, Rename, and Delete options. You can also click and then click again to rename the style.

### Set Current/New/Delete

The + (plus) button lets you create a new text style. Right-clicking the style name will give you the Set Current option, which makes the selected style the current one. You can also double-click the leftmost portion of the style in the list to set it to current—as indicated by a triangle. The – (minus) button lets you delete the selected style. You can also select Delete from the right-click option.

The Delete option isn't available for the Standard style.

## Font

In the Font group, you have the following options:

**Style**   Displays the list of styles that are in the drawing.

**Family**   Lets you select a font from a list of available fonts. The list is derived from the font resources available to the Mac OS plus the standard AutoCAD fonts.

**Typeface**   Offers variations of a font, such as italic or bold, when they're available.

When an AutoCAD font (SHX) file is selected, the Typeface option will be replaced with the Asian set option. This is applicable to Asian fonts.

**RENAMING A TEXT STYLE OR OTHER NAMED OBJECT**

If you need to rename a text style or other named object in AutoCAD, you can do so using the Rename command. Choose Format ➢ Rename from the menu bar or enter **REN**⏎ at the Command prompt to open the Rename dialog box. In the Named Objects list box to the left, choose Text Styles. Click the name of the style you want to change from the Items list on the right, click and click again to change the name, and then click OK.

# Exploring Text Formatting in AutoCAD

You've seen how you can set up a style and make scale adjustments. AutoCAD also offers a wide range of text-formatting options that are typical of most word processing programs. You can control fonts, text height, justification, line spacing, and width. You can even include special characters such as degree symbols or stacked fractions. With these additional formatting tools, you can make adjustments to the text style with which you started.

## Adjusting the Text Height and Font

To get some firsthand experience using the text-formatting tools in AutoCAD, try the following exercise. You'll create multiline text again, but this time you'll get to try out some of its other features.

In this exercise, you'll see how you can adjust the size and font of text in the editor:

1. Pan your view so the kitchen is just at the top of the drawing, as shown in the first image in Figure 9.7.

2. In the status bar, set the Annotation Scale setting back to ¼″ = 1′-0″ (1:100 for metric users).

3. Click the Multiline Text icon on the Tool Sets palette, and then specify a text boundary window, as shown in the first image in Figure 9.7.

4. In the text editor, type the following:

   `Living Room`
   `14´-0˝ by 16´-5˝ [427 cm by 500 cm]`

   Make sure you press ⏎ after `Living Room`, but make the rest of the text a continuous string. As you type, the words wrap. AutoCAD uses word wrap to fit the text inside the text boundary area.

5. Highlight the text `14´-0˝ by 16´-5˝ [427 cm by 500 cm]` as you would in any word processor.

6. In the Text Editor visor, click in the Text Height text box and enter **3**. Metric users, enter **2.34**. The highlighted text changes to a smaller size.

7. Highlight the words `Living Room`.

**FIGURE 9.7**
Placing the text boundary window for the living room label and the final label

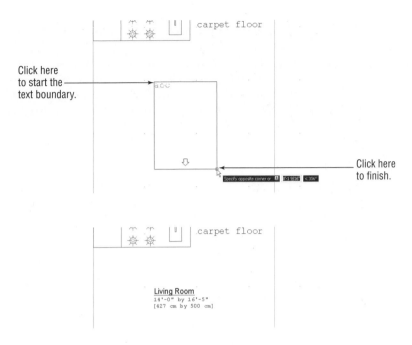

Click here to start the text boundary.

Click here to finish.

8. Click the disclosure triangle on the right side of the Text Editor visor, and click the Font pop-up menu to display a list of font options.

9. Scroll the list until you find Arial, and select it. The text in the Text Editor visor changes to reflect the new font.

10. With the words `Living Room` still highlighted, click the Underline button.

11. Click Save in the Text Editor visor. The label appears in the area you indicated in step 3 (see the bottom image in Figure 9.7).

12. To see how you can go back to the Text Editor visor, double-click the text. The Text Editor visor and text editor appear, enabling you to change the text.

13. Click Save in the Text Editor visor.

While using the Multiline Text tool, you may have noticed the `Specify opposite corner or [Height/Justify/Line spacing/Rotation/Style/Width/Columns]:` prompt immediately after you picked the first point of the text boundary. You can use any of these options to make on-the-fly modifications to the height, justification, line spacing, rotation style, or width of the multiline text.

For example, after clicking the first point for the text boundary, you can type **R↵** and then specify a rotation angle for the text window, either graphically with a rubber-banding line or by entering an angle value. After you've entered a rotation angle, you can resume selecting the text boundary.

## Understanding Text Formatting with the Text Editor Visor

You've just experimented with a few of the text formatting features of the Text Editor visor. A variety of additional formatting tools are available. Table 9.1 describes their uses. They're fairly straightforward, and if you've used other word processing programs, you should find them easy to use. Most are common to the majority of word processors, although a few—such as Symbol, Background Mask, and Oblique Angle—are unique to AutoCAD. Look at Table 9.1 and see if there are any tools you think you'll find useful.

**TABLE 9.1:**        Text-formatting tools

| TOOL | USE |
| --- | --- |
| Text Style | Select a text style. |
| Text Height | Set the paper text height of text currently being entered or edited. |
| Bold/Italic/ Underline/Overline | Select text, and then select one of these options to add bold, italic, underline, or overline to the text. |
| Color | Select text, and then choose a color from this pop-up menu. |
| Font | Select a font different from the font for the current text style. |
| Background Mask | Available through the right-click menu, this tool gives you control over the background mask feature, which places a background behind text to make it more readable when placed over hatch patterns. |
| Change Case | Available through the right-click menu, changes the case of text. |
| Paragraph | Available through the right-click menu, displays the Paragraph dialog box. Lets you set up paragraph formatting, including tabs, indents, and line and paragraph spacing. You can also set line spacing in the Properties Inspector palette for an Mtext object. (See "Setting Indents and Tabs" later in this chapter.) |
| Bullets And Lists | Available through the right-click menu; select a text list, click this tool, and then select Lettered, Numbered, or Bulleted to add letters, numbers, or bullets to the list. |
| Default/Left/ Center/Right / Justify/Distribute | Click the appropriate tool to align the text to the left, center, or right side of the text boundary. Justify adds space between words to force left and right alignment. Distribute adds space between letters to force left and right alignment. |
| Columns | Available through the right-click menu, indicates the number of columns and how the columns are set up. |
| Symbol | Place the cursor at a location for the symbol, and then click the Symbol tool to find and add a symbol. (See Figure 9.8, later in this chapter, for the available symbols.) |
| Insert Field | Click to open the Insert Field dialog box where you can add a text field. See "Adding Formulas to Cells," in Chapter 10, for more about fields. |
| Character Set | Available through the right-click menu, Character Set offers foreign-language characters such as Cyrillic or Greek, for example. |

## Adding Symbols and Special Characters

The Text Editor visor also offers a tool called Insert Symbols. This tool lets you add special symbols common to technical drawing and drafting. Figure 9.8 shows the symbols that are offered in the Symbol tool in the form of a pop-up menu.

**FIGURE 9.8**
Symbols offered by the Symbol option. (See Symbol in Table 9.1 for information about how to use these symbols.)

| | | | |
|---|---|---|---|
| Degree | $x^{\circ}$ | Identity | ≡ |
| Plus/Minus | ± | Initial Length | ⌒ |
| Diameter | ⌀ | Monument Line | ₥ |
| Almost Equal | ≈ | Not Equal | ≠ |
| Angle | ∠ | Ohm | Ω |
| Boundary Line | ℞ | Omega | Ω |
| Center Line | ℄ | Property Line | ℞ |
| Delta | Δ | Subscript 2 | $x_2$ |
| Electrical Phase | Φ | Squared | $x^2$ |
| Flow Line | ℉ | Cubed | $x^3$ |

At the bottom of the Symbol pop-up menu is an option called Other. By clicking the Other option, you open the Characters dialog box (Figure 9.9). Characters such as the trademark (™) and copyright (©) symbols are often available in the fonts offered in the Characters dialog box. The contents of the Symbol pop-up menu depend on the font currently selected.

**FIGURE 9.9**
The Characters dialog box

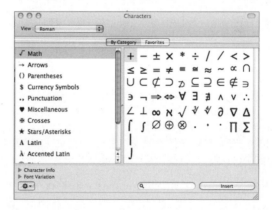

Finally, in case your application requires music, math, astronomy, Greek, or other symbols, AutoCAD offers a set of fonts with special symbols. You can set up text styles with these fonts or call them up directly from the Text Editor visor's Font pop-up menu.

### TEXT JUSTIFICATION AND OSNAPS

You may have noticed that multiline text has three center justification options: Top Center (TC), Middle Center (MC), and Bottom Center (BC). All three of these options have the same effect on the text's appearance, but they each have a different effect on how osnaps act on the text. Figure 9.10 shows where the osnap point occurs on a text boundary depending on which justification option is selected. A multiline text object has only one insertion point on its boundary, which you can access with the Insertion osnap.

**FIGURE 9.10**
The location of the Insertion osnap point on a text boundary, based on its justification setting

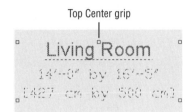

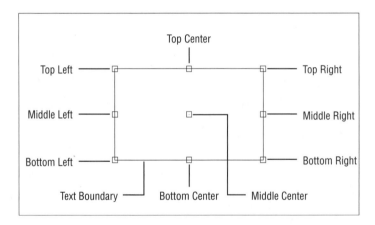

The osnap point also appears as an extra grip point on the text boundary when you click the text. If you click the text you just entered, you'll see that a grip point now appears at the top center of the text boundary.

Knowing where the osnap points occur can be helpful when you want to align the text with other objects in your drawing. In most cases, you can use the grips to align your text boundary, but the Top Center and Middle Center justification options enable you to use the center and middle portions of your text to align the text with other objects.

## Setting Indents and Tabs

You should also know about the indent and tab features of the text editor. You may have noticed the ruler at the top of the text editor. Figure 9.11 shows that ruler, including tab and indent markers.

The indent markers let you control the indention of the first line and the rest of the paragraph. The tab markers give you control over tab spacing. For new text, the tab markers don't appear until you add them by clicking the ruler. The following exercises will demonstrate the use of these markers more clearly.

**FIGURE 9.11**

The ruler at the top
of the text editor
lets you quickly set
tabs and indents
for text.

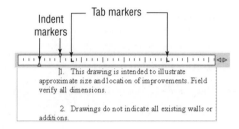

Start by practicing with the indent markers:

1. Save the Unit drawing, and then open the `indent.dwg` file, which can be obtained from this book's companion website. This file contains some text you'll experiment with.

2. Double-click the text at the top of the drawing to open the Text Editor visor.

3. Press ⌘-A to highlight all the text in the text editor. This is necessary to indicate the text group to be affected by your indent settings.

4. Click and drag the top indent marker two spaces to the right. The indent of the first line moves with the marker. Notice that the text at the first tab remains at its starting location.

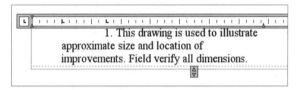

5. Click and drag the bottom indent marker two spaces to the left. The rest of the paragraph moves with the marker.

6. Click Save in the Text Editor visor to exit.

Here you see how you can control the indents of the selected text with the indent markers. You can set paragraphs of a single multiline text object differently, giving you a wide range of indent-formatting possibilities. Just select the text you want to set, and then adjust the indent markers.

Now try the tab markers. For this exercise, you'll try the text-import feature to import a tab-delimited text file:

1. Click the Multiline Text icon on the Tool Sets palette.

2. For the first corner of the text boundary, click the upper-left corner of the large rectangle in the drawing, just below the paragraph.

3. For the opposite corner of the text boundary, click the lower-right corner of the rectangle.

4. Right-click in the text editor, and select Import Text.

5. In the Select File dialog box, locate and select the `tabtest.txt` file and then click Open. The contents of the `tabtest.txt` file are displayed in the text editor.

This file contains tabs to align the columns of information. You can adjust those tabs in the text editor, as you'll see in the next set of steps.

Now use the tab markers to adjust the tab spacing of the columns of text:

1. Press ⌘-A to select all the text.

2. Click the ruler at a point that is at the 12th mark from the left (that's three of the taller tick marks in the ruler). An L-shaped marker appears, and the first tab column of text moves to this position.

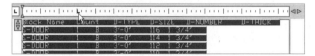

3. Click the ruler again at the 20th mark. The second tab column aligns to this position.

4. Continue to click the ruler to add more tab markers so the text looks similar to Figure 9.12. Don't worry about being exact; this is just for practice. After you've placed a marker, you can click and drag it to make adjustments.

**FIGURE 9.12**
Add tab markers so your text looks similar to this figure.

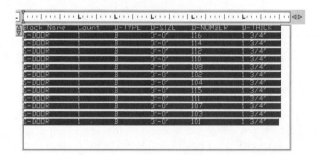

5. Click Save in the Text Editor visor. The text appears in the drawing as a door schedule.

Here you saw how you can create a table or a schedule from an imported text file. You can also create a schedule from scratch by composing it directly in the text editor of the Multiline Text (Mtext) command. AutoCAD also offers the Table feature, which is specifically designed for creating tables (see Chapter 10). Still, this example offers a way to demonstrate the tab feature of Multiline Text, and you may encounter a file in which a table is formatted in the way described here.

In addition to using the indent and tab markers on the ruler, you can control indents and tabs through the Paragraph dialog box. Do the following to get a firsthand look:

1. Double-click the text at the top of the indent.dwg drawing (the one you edited in the first part of this section), and then press ⌘-A to select all the text.

2. Right-click the ruler above the text editor, and select Paragraph to open the Paragraph dialog box (Figure 9.13). The Paragraph dialog box also lets you set other paragraph options, such as alignment, spacing between paragraphs, and line spacing in the paragraph.

**FIGURE 9.13**

The Paragraph dialog box

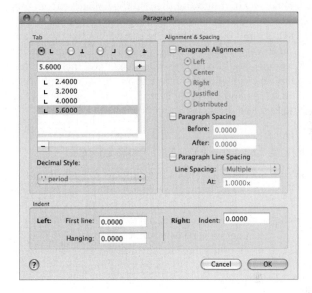

3. In the Left Indent section, change the value of the First Line input box to **1.5** and the Hanging input box to **2.2**.

4. Double-click the tab position input box in the upper-left corner, just below the row of tab symbols in the Tab group. Enter **2.2**, and click the Add button.

5. Click OK. The text now appears with the text indented from the numbers.

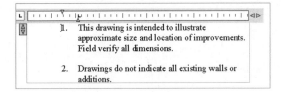

6. Click Save in the Text Editor visor. The text in the drawing is now formatted as it appeared in the text editor.

7. Exit but do not save the `indent.dwg` file.

In this exercise, you used the Paragraph dialog box to set the paragraph indent and the first tab marker to be the same value. This causes the text portion of the list to be aligned at a distance of 2.2 drawing units from the left text boundary, leaving the list number extended farther to the left. This gives the list a more professional appearance.

The Paragraph dialog box gives you fine control over the formatting of your text. It lets you delete tabs by highlighting them in the list and clicking the Remove button. You can also add tabs at specific distances from the left margin of the text boundary by entering new tab locations in the tab input box and clicking the Add button.

You specify distances in drawing units. If your drawing is set up to use architectural units, for example, you can enter values in feet and inches or just inches. In the First Line and Hanging input boxes, you enter a numeric value for paragraph indents. As you've just seen, you can use the First Line and Hanging input boxes to create a numbered list by setting the Hanging input box value to be the same as the first tab stop position.

## What Do the Fonts Look Like?

You've already seen a few of the fonts available in AutoCAD. Chances are you're familiar with the TrueType fonts available in the Mac OS. You have some additional AutoCAD fonts from which to choose. You may want to stick with the AutoCAD fonts for all but your presentation drawings because other fonts can consume more memory.

Figure 9.14 shows the basic AutoCAD text fonts. The Romans font is perhaps the most widely used because it offers a reasonable appearance while consuming little memory.

**FIGURE 9.14**
Some of the standard AutoCAD text fonts

|  |  |
|---|---|
| This is Txt | |
| This is Monotxt | |
| This is Simplex | (Old version of Roman Simplex) |
| This is Complex | (Old version of Roman Complex) |
| *This is Italic* | (Old version of Italic Complex) |
| This is Romans | (Roman Simplex) |
| This is Romand | (Roman double stroke) |
| This is Romanc | (Roman Complex) |
| **This is Romant** | (Roman triple stroke) |
| *This is Scripts* | (Script Simplex) |
| *This is Scriptc* | (Script Complex) |
| *This is Italicc* | (Italic Complex) |
| *This is Italict* | (Italic triple stroke) |
| Τηισ ισ Γρεεκσ | (This is Greeks - Greek Simplex) |
| Τηισ ισ Γρεεκχ | (This is Greekc - Greek Complex) |
| 𝔗his is 𝔊othice | (Gothic English) |
| 𝔗hif if 𝔊othicg | (Gothic German) |
| 𝔘his is 𝔊othici | (Gothic Italian) |

**IMPORTING TEXT FILES**

With multiline text objects, AutoCAD enables you to import ASCII text or Rich Text format (RTF) files. RTF files can be exported from Microsoft Word and most other word processing programs and retain most of their formatting in AutoCAD. Here's how you import text files:

1. With the Multiline Text editor open, right-click in the text area, and choose Import Text.

2. In the Select File dialog box, locate a valid text file. It must be a file in either a raw text (ASCII) format (.txt) or RTF (.rtf). RTF files can store formatting information such as boldface and varying point sizes.

3. After you've highlighted the file you want, double-click it or click Open. The text appears in the text editor.

4. Click Save in the Text Editor visor, and the text appears in your drawing.

In the following sections, you'll work with some of the AutoCAD fonts. You can see samples of all the fonts, including TrueType fonts, in the preview window of the Text Style dialog box. If you use a word processor, you're probably familiar with at least some of the TrueType fonts available in the Mac OS and AutoCAD.

**THE TEXTFILL SYSTEM VARIABLE**

Unlike the standard sticklike AutoCAD fonts, TrueType and PostScript fonts have filled areas. These filled areas take more time to generate, so if you use these fonts for a lot of text, your redraw and regen times will increase. To help reduce redraw and regen times, you can set AutoCAD to display and plot these fonts as outline fonts while still printing them as solid fonts.

To change this setting, type **TEXTFILL**↵, and then type **0**↵. Doing so turns off text fill for PostScript and TrueType fonts. (This is the same as setting the Textfill system variable to 0.)

## Adding Simple Single-Line Text Objects

You might find that you're entering a lot of single words or simple labels that don't require all the bells and whistles of the Multiline Text editor. AutoCAD offers the *single-line text object*, which is simpler to use and can speed text entry if you're adding only small pieces of text.

Continue the tutorial on the Unit.dwg file by trying the following exercise:

1. Adjust your view so you see the part of the drawing shown in Figure 9.15.

**FIGURE 9.15**
Adjust your view to look like this.

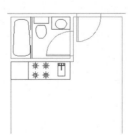

2. Make sure Note1 is the current text style and then choose Draw ➤ Text ➤ Single Line Text from the menu bar, or enter **DT**↵.

3. At the `Specify start point of text or [Justify/Style]:` prompt, pick the starting point for the text you're about to enter, just below the kitchen at coordinate 17′-2″,22′-5″ (490,664 for metric users). Note that the prompt offers the Justify and Style options.

4. At the `Specify rotation angle of text <0>:` prompt, press ↵ to accept the default, 0. You can specify any angle you like at this prompt (for example, if you want your text aligned with a rotated object). You see a text I-beam cursor at the point you picked in step 3.

5. Type **Kitchenette**. As you type, the word appears directly in the drawing.

---

**PASTING TEXT FROM OTHER SOURCES**

You can cut and paste text from the Clipboard into the cursor location by using the ⌘-V keyboard shortcut or by right-clicking in the drawing area to access the shortcut menu.

---

6. You can press ↵ to move the cursor down to start a new line below the one you just entered.

7. This time, you want to label the bathroom. Pick a point to the right of the door swing; you can approximate the location since you can always adjust the text location later. The text cursor moves to that point.

8. Type **Bathroom**↵. Figure 9.16 shows how your drawing should look now.

9. Press ↵ again to exit the Text command.

**FIGURE 9.16**
Adding simple labels to the kitchen and bath by using the Text command

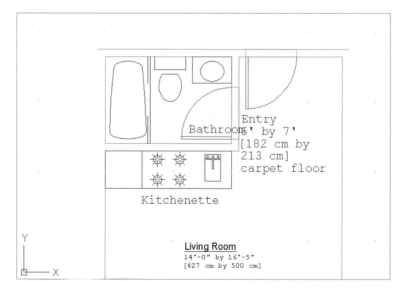

**CONTINUING WHERE YOU LEFT OFF**

If for some reason you need to stop entering single-line text objects to do something else in AutoCAD, you can continue the text where you left off by starting the Text command and then pressing ↵ at the `Specify start point of text or [Justify/Style]:` prompt. The text continues immediately below the last line of text entered.

Here you were able to add two single lines of text in different parts of your drawing fairly quickly. The Text command uses the current default text style settings.

To edit single-line text, you can double-click the text. The text is highlighted, and you can begin typing to replace it all, or you can click a location in the text to make single word or character changes.

This is the end of the tutorial section of this chapter. The rest of this chapter offers additional information about text.

## Justifying Single-Line Text Objects

Justifying single-line text objects is slightly different from justifying multiline text. For example, if you change the justification setting to Center, the text moves so the center is placed at the text-insertion point. In other words, the insertion point stays in place while the text location adjusts to the new justification setting. Figure 9.17 shows the relationship between single-line text and the insertion point based on different justification settings.

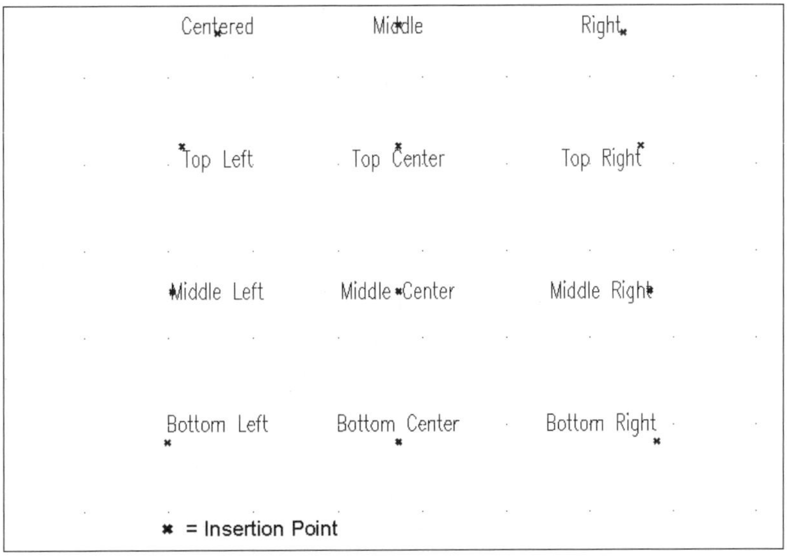

**FIGURE 9.17**
Text inserted using the various justification options

To set the justification of text as you enter it, you must enter **J**↵ at the `Specify start point of text or [Justify/Style]:` prompt after issuing the Text command. You can also change the current default style by entering **S**↵ and then the name of the style at the `Specify start point of text or [Justify/Style]:` prompt.

After you've issued Text's Justify option, you get the following prompt:

```
Enter an option
[Align/Fit/Center/Middle/Right/TL/TC/TR/ML/MC/MR/BL/BC/BR]:
```

Here are descriptions of each of the options.

**Align and Fit**   With the Align and Fit justification options, you must specify a dimension in which the text is to fit. For example, suppose you want the word *Refrigerator* to fit in the 26″-wide box representing the refrigerator. You can use either the Fit or the Align option to accomplish this. With Fit, AutoCAD prompts you to select start and end points and then stretches or compresses the letters to fit within the two points you specify. You use this option when the text must be a consistent height throughout the drawing and you don't care about distorting the font. Align works like Fit, but instead of maintaining the current text style height, the Align option adjusts the text height to keep it proportional to the text width without distorting the font. Use this option when it's important to maintain the font's shape and proportion. Figure 9.18 demonstrates how Fit and Align work.

**FIGURE 9.18**
The word *Refrigerator* as it appears normally and with the Fit and Align options selected

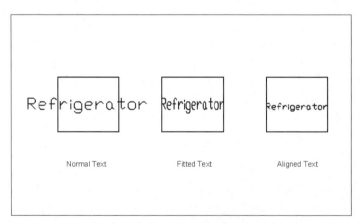

Center   Middle   Right

**Center**   Centers the text on the start point with the baseline on the start point.

**Middle**   Centers the text on the start point with the baseline slightly below the start point.

**Right**   Justifies the text to the right of the start point with the baseline on the start point.

**TL, TC, and TR**   TL, TC, and TR stand for Top Left, Top Center, and Top Right. When you use these justification styles, the text appears entirely below the start point, justified left, center, or right, depending on which option you choose.

**ML, MC, and MR**   ML, MC, and MR stand for Middle Left, Middle Center, and Middle Right. These styles are similar to TL, TC, and TR except that the start point determines a location midway between the baseline and the top of the lowercase letters of the text.

**BL, BC, and BR**   BL, BC, and BR stand for Bottom Left, Bottom Center, and Bottom Right. These styles too are similar to TL, TC, and TR, but here the start point determines the bottommost location of the letters of the text (the bottom of letters that have descenders, such as *p*, *q*, and *g*).

---

### KEEPING TEXT FROM MIRRORING

At times, you'll want to mirror a group of objects that contain some text. This operation causes the mirrored text to appear backward. You can change a setting in AutoCAD to make the text read normally even when it's mirrored:

1. At the Command prompt, enter **MIRRTEXT**↵.

2. At the Enter new value for MIRRTEXT <1>: prompt, enter **o**↵.

Now any mirrored text that isn't in a block will read normally. The text's position, however, will still be mirrored, as shown in the following example. Mirrtext is set to 0 by default.

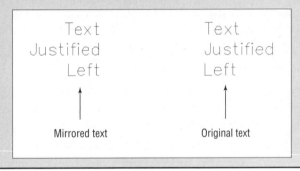

---

## Using Special Characters with Single-Line Text Objects

Just as with multiline text, you can add a limited set of special characters to single-line text objects. For example, you can place the degree symbol (°) after a number, or you can *underscore* (underline) text. To accomplish this, you use double percent signs (%%) in conjunction with a special code. For example, to underscore text, you enclose that text with %% followed by the letter *u*, which is the underscore code. So to create the text, "This is underscored text," you enter the following at the prompt:

```
This is %%uunderscored%%u text.
```

*Overscoring* (putting a line above the text) operates in the same manner. To insert codes for symbols, you place the codes in the correct positions for the symbols they represent. For example, to enter 100.5°, you type **100.5%%d**. Table 9.2 shows some other examples of special-character codes.

**TABLE 9.2:** Special-character codes

| CODE | RESULT |
|------|--------|
| %%o | Toggles overscore on and off. |
| %%u | Toggles underscore on and off. |
| %%c | Places a diameter symbol (ø) where the code occurs. |
| %%d | Places a degree sign (°) where the code occurs. |
| %%p | Places a plus/minus sign (±)where the code occurs. |
| %%% | Forces a single percent sign (%). This is useful when you want a double percent sign to appear or when you want a percent sign in conjunction with another code. |
| %%nnn | Allows the use of extended characters or Unicode characters when these characters are available for a given font. nnn is the three-digit value representing the ASCII extended character code. |

---

**USING THE CHARACTERS DIALOG BOX TO ADD SPECIAL CHARACTERS**

You can add special characters to a single line of text in the same way you add special characters to multiline text. You may recall that to access special characters, you use the Characters dialog box.

The easiest way to accomplish this is to activate the Characters dialog box from the Mac OS and have it appear in the Mac OS menu bar.

1. Open System Preferences
2. On the Mac OS menu bar, click Edit ➤ Special Characters.

## Using the Check Spelling Feature

Although AutoCAD is primarily a drawing program, you'll find that some of your drawings contain more text than graphics. Autodesk recognizes this fact and has been including a spelling checker since AutoCAD Release 14. If you've ever used the spelling checker in a typical word processor, the AutoCAD spelling checker's operation will be familiar to you. These steps show you how it works:

1. Click the Check Spelling icon in the Annotate toolset on the Tool Sets palette. You can also type **SP**↵. The Check Spelling dialog box appears (Figure 9.19).

2. You can click the Start button to check the spelling in the entire drawing. Or, if you prefer, you can be more selective of the text you want to check by choosing an option from the Where To Check pop-up menu. You can select a mixture of multiline and single-line text as well as dimension text, attributes, and text in Xrefs.

When the spelling checker finds a word it doesn't recognize, the Check Spelling dialog box shows you the word along with a suggested spelling. If the spelling checker finds more than one spelling, a list of suggested alternate words appears below the input box. You can then highlight the desired replacement and click the Change button to change the misspelled word, or you can click Change All to change all occurrences of the word in the selected text. If the suggested word is inappropriate, choose another word from the replacement list (if any) or enter your own spelling in the Suggestions text box. Then click Change or Change All.

**FIGURE 9.19**

The Check Spelling dialog

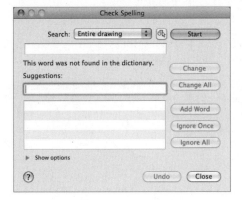

Here is a list of the options available in the Check Spelling dialog box:

**Add Word**   Adds the word in question to the current dictionary.

**Ignore Once**   Skips the word.

**Ignore All**   Skips all occurrences of the word in the text being checked.

**Change**   Changes the word in question to the word you've selected from (or entered into) the Suggestions text box.

**Change All**   Changes all occurrences of the current word when there are multiple instances of the misspelling.

**Show Options**   Clicking the Show Options disclosure triangle will expand and show the check spelling options.

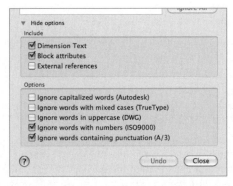

The Check Spelling feature includes types of notations that are likely to be found in technical drawings. It also checks the spelling of text that is included in block definitions.

# Finding and Replacing Text

One of the most time-consuming tasks in drafting is replacing text that appears repeatedly throughout a drawing. Fortunately, you have a Find And Replace tool to help simplify this task. AutoCAD's Find And Replace works like any other find-and-replace tool in a word processing program. Here's how it works:

1. Click the Find Text icon in the Tool Sets palette. You can also type **FIND**⏎.

2. Enter the text you want to locate in the Find And Replace dialog box (Figure 9.20), and then click the Find button.

**FIGURE 9.20**
Using Find And Replace

3. Enter the replacement text in the Replace With text box.

4. When you've made certain that this is the text you want to change, click Replace. If you want to replace all occurrences of the text string in the drawing, click Replace All.

5. If you want to skip over the found text, click the Find button to locate the next instance of the text string in your drawing. If the text string is not found, AutoCAD returns to your original view.

---

### MAKING SUBSTITUTIONS FOR MISSING FONTS

When text styles are created, the associated fonts don't become part of the drawing file. Instead, AutoCAD loads the needed font file at the same time the drawing is loaded. If a text style in a drawing requires a particular font, AutoCAD looks for the font in the AutoCAD search path; if the font is there, it's loaded. Usually this isn't a problem if the drawing file uses the standard fonts that come with AutoCAD or the operating system. But occasionally, you'll encounter a file that uses a custom font.

In earlier releases of AutoCAD, you saw an error message when you attempted to open such a file. This missing-font message often sent new AutoCAD users into a panic.

Fortunately, AutoCAD automatically substitutes an existing font for the missing font in a drawing. By default, AutoCAD substitutes the simplex.shx font, but you can specify another font by using the Fontalt system variable. Type **FONTALT**⏎ at the Command prompt, and then enter the name of the font you want to use as the substitute.

You can also select an alternate font through the Application tab of the Application Preferences dialog box. Locate the Text Editor, Dictionary, And Font File Names item, and then click the symbol at the left. Locate the Alternate Font File item, and click the symbol at the left. The current alternate is listed. You can double-click the font name to select a different font through the Select Alternate Font dialog box.

Be aware that the text in your drawing will change in appearance, sometimes radically, when you use a substitute font. If the text in the drawing must retain its appearance, substitute a font that looks as similar to the original font as possible.

You can also limit your find-and-replace operation to a specific set of objects in your drawing by choosing Select Objects from the Where To Check pop-up menu.

When you click the Select Objects button, the Find And Replace dialog box closes temporarily to enable you to select a set of objects or a region of your drawing. Find And Replace then limits its search to those objects or the region you select.

You can further control the types of objects that Find And Replace looks for by clicking the disclosure triangle in the lower-left corner of the Find And Replace dialog box. The dialog box expands to show more options (Figure 9.21).

**FIGURE 9.21**
More extensive options for Find And Replace

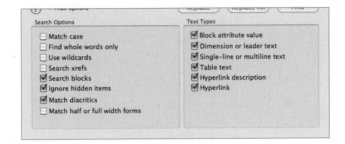

With this dialog box, you can refine your search by limiting it to blocks, dimension text, standard text, or hyperlink text. You can also specify whether to match the case and find whole words only.

---

**SPEEDING UP AUTOCAD WITH QTEXT**

If you need to edit a large drawing that contains a lot of text but you don't need to edit the text, you can use the Qtext command to help accelerate redraws and regenerations when you're working on the drawing. Qtext turns lines of text into rectangular boxes, saving AutoCAD from having to form every letter. This enables you to see the note locations so you don't accidentally draw over them. To use it, enter **QTEXT**↵ at the Command prompt and enter **On**↵ or select the On option from the Dynamic Input display. Regenerate your drawing to see only the boundary boxes for all text objects.

---

**CREATE PARAGRAPH COLUMNS**

You can format Mtext into multiple columns. This can be useful for long lists or to create a newspaper column appearance for your text. Text formatted into columns will automatically flow between columns as you add or remove text.

To format text into columns, do the following:

**1.** Create the text using the Mtext command as usual.

2. Click and drag the double-headed arrow at the bottom of the text upward. As you do this, a second column appears.

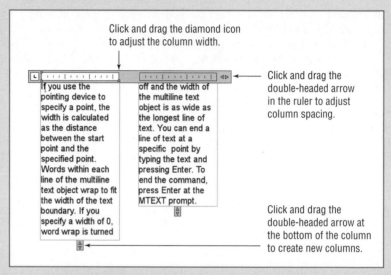

Click and drag the diamond icon to adjust the column width.

Click and drag the double-headed arrow in the ruler to adjust column spacing.

Click and drag the double-headed arrow at the bottom of the column to create new columns.

3. If you want to create another column, click and drag the double-headed arrow below the second column upward.

4. To adjust the column width, click and drag the diamond icon that appears just to the right of the first column in the ruler. All the columns will adjust to the width of the first column.

Once you've set up your columns, click Save on the Text Editor visor. You can adjust the column width and spacing by using grips that appear when you click on the text.

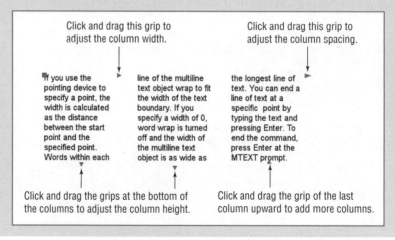

Click and drag this grip to adjust the column width.

Click and drag this grip to adjust the column spacing.

Click and drag the grips at the bottom of the columns to adjust the column height.

Click and drag the grip of the last column upward to add more columns.

To adjust the column width of existing multiline text, click and drag the arrow grip above and to the right of the first column. To adjust the width between columns, click and drag the arrow grip in the above and to the right of the group of columns. The grips at the bottom of each column allow you to adjust the height of the columns.

You can manually set column features through the Column Settings dialog box. To open it, double-click on the multiline text and then right-click in the text editor and choose Columns ➤ Column Settings.

The Dynamic Columns option is the default for the Column Type group and it allows you to adjust the column size using grips.

## The Bottom Line

**Prepare a drawing for text.**    AutoCAD offers an extensive set of features for adding text to a drawing, but you need to do a little prep work before you dive in.

> **Master It**    Name two things you need to do to prepare a drawing for text.

**Set the annotation scale and add text.**    Before you start to add text, you should set the annotation scale for your drawing. Once this is done, you can begin to add text.

> **Master It**    In a sentence or two, briefly describe the purpose of the annotation scale feature. Name the tool you use to add text to a drawing.

**Explore text formatting in AutoCAD.**    Because text styles contain font and text-size settings, you can usually set up a text style and then begin to add text to your drawing. For those special cases where you need to vary text height and font or other text features, you can use the Text Editor visor of the text editor.

> **Master It**    What text formatting tool can you use to change text to boldface type?

**Add simple single-line text objects.**   In many situations, you need only a single word or a short string of text. AutoCAD offers the single line text object for these instances.

**Master It**   Describe the methods for starting the single-line text command.

**Use the Check Spelling feature.**   It isn't uncommon for a drawing to contain the equivalent of several pages of text, and the likelihood of having misspelled words can be high. AutoCAD offers the Check Spelling feature to help you keep your spelling under control.

**Master It**   What option do you select in the Check Spelling dialog box when it finds a misspelled word and you want to accept the suggestion it offers?

**Find and replace text.**   A common activity when editing technical drawings is finding and replacing a word throughout a drawing.

**Master It**   True or false: The Find And Replace feature in AutoCAD works very differently than the find-and-replace feature in other programs.

# Chapter 10

# Using Fields and Tables

Adding text to a set of drawings can become a large part of your work. You'll find that you're editing notes and labels almost as frequently as you're editing the graphics in your drawings. To make some of those editing tasks easier, AutoCAD provides a few special text objects.

In this chapter, you'll look at fields and tables, two features that can help automate some of the common tasks in AutoCAD. Fields are a special type of text that can automatically update to reflect changes in a drawing. The Table feature helps to automate the process of creating and editing tables and schedules. Tables are a common part of technical drawings and are similar to spreadsheets. In fact, AutoCAD tables behave much like spreadsheets, giving you the ability to add formulas to cells.

In this chapter, you'll learn to do the following:

♦ Use fields to associate text with drawing properties

♦ Add tables to your drawing

♦ Edit the table line work

♦ Add formulas to cells

♦ Export tables

## Using Fields to Associate Text with Drawing Properties

The text labels you worked with in Chapter 9, "Adding Text to Drawings," are static and don't change unless you edit them by using the tools described there. Another type of text object, called a *field*, behaves in a more dynamic way than the multiline text. A field can be linked to the properties of other objects and updates itself automatically as the associated properties change. For example, you can create a field that is associated with a block name. If the block name changes, the field text automatically changes as well.

Try the following exercise to see how this works:

1. Open the 10c-unit.dwg file. This file is similar to the drawing you worked on in Chapter 9. (10c-unit.dwg can be downloaded from www.sybex.com/go/masteringautocadmac.)

2. Double-click the Kitchen text to highlight it and make it available for editing.

3. Right-click the highlighted Kitchen text, and then choose Insert Field to open the Insert Field dialog box (Figure 10.1). A list on the left shows the types of fields available.

**FIGURE 10.1**
Choose the field to insert.

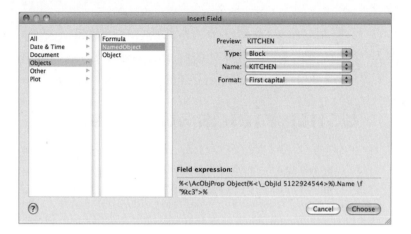

4. In the Field Category list (left column), select Objects. This limits the display of field types to object fields.

5. In the Field Names list (right column), select NamedObject.

6. Make sure Block is selected in the Type pop-up menu on the right side of the dialog box, and for the Name pop-up menu, select Kitchen. This associates the field with the Kitchen block name.

7. In the Format pop-up menu, select First Capital. This causes the field text to be lowercase with a capital first letter, regardless of how the block name is actually treated. It will work only when more than one word is present in the name; e.g., Large Kitchen). Your settings should look like Figure 10.1.

8. Click Choose to exit the Insert Field dialog box, and then press ↵ twice to return to the Command prompt.

When you return to the drawing, the text appears with a gray background. This tells you that the text is a field rather than an Mtext or Text object. The gray background is just a device to help you keep track of field text; it doesn't print.

You've converted existing text into a field that is linked to a block name. Now you'll see how the field works:

1. Enter **REN**↵ at the Command prompt to open the Rename dialog box.

2. Make sure Blocks is selected in the Named Objects list, and then select Kitchen from the Items list.

3. Double-click to edit the name. Type **Kitchenette**.

4. Click OK to close the Rename dialog box.

5. Type **RE**↵ to regenerate the drawing. The field you created changes to reflect the new block name.

Fields can be associated with a wide variety of properties. You've just seen how a block name can be associated with a field. In this exercise, you'll use a field to display the area of an object:

1. Click View ➤ Zoom ➤ Extents from the menu bar or type **Z↵ E↵** to view the entire plan.

2. Place a rectangle in the living room area so that it fills the area, as in Figure 10.2.

**FIGURE 10.2**

Place a rectangle that fills the living room.

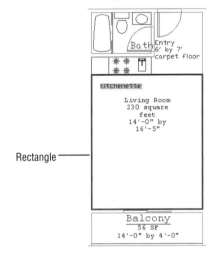

Rectangle

3. Double-click the Living Room text to open the Text Editor visor and the in-place text editor.

4. Highlight the text that reads 230 square feet. Right-click the selected text, and choose Insert Field from the shortcut menu.

5. In the Insert Field dialog box, select Objects from the Field Category list. In the Field Names list, select Object.

6. Click the Select Object button next to the Type pop-up menu at the top of the Insert Field dialog box (Figure 10.3). The Insert Field dialog box momentarily closes to enable you to select an object.

7. Select the rectangle you just added. The Insert Field dialog box returns.

8. In the Property pop-up menu, just below the Type pop-up menu, select Area.

9. Select Architectural from the Format pop-up menu. In the Precision pop-up menu, select 0.00 (see Figure 10.3).

10. Click Choose. The field you just added appears in the drawing as the area of the rectangle.

11. Click Save in the Text Editor visor.

**FIGURE 10.3**

Click the Select
Object button.

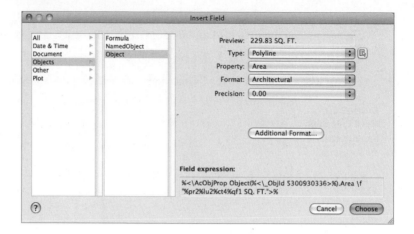

Next you'll alter the rectangle to see how it affects the field:

**1.** Click the rectangle to expose its grips (Figure 10.4). Then select the top middle grip of the rectangle, and move it upward so the top edge aligns with the bathroom wall.

**FIGURE 10.4**

Expose the grips.

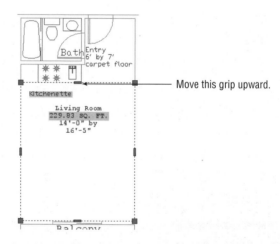

Move this grip upward.

**2.** Clear the selected objects and then type **RE↵**. The field you just added updates to reflect the new area of the rectangle.

**3.** After reviewing the results, close the 10c-unit.dwg file.

In previous exercises, you changed existing text into fields. You can create new fields in either the Text or Mtext command by selecting Insert Field from the shortcut menu whenever you're typing the text content.

In this exercise you used a rectangle, but you can use any closed polyline to create an area field.

You've touched on just two of the many possible uses for fields. You can associate other types of properties, including the current layer, the drawing name, linetypes, and more. Fields can also be used in AutoCAD's Table feature, described in the next section, which enables you to create tables and schedules quickly.

For most of your work, the standard text objects will work just fine, but you may find fields useful when you know a label has to be associated with specific types of data in your drawing. In later chapters, you'll have more opportunities to work with fields.

# Adding Tables to Your Drawing

One of the most common text-related tasks you'll do for your drawings is to create schedules, such as door and window schedules or parts schedules. Such schedules are tables used to provide detailed information regarding the elements in your design.

You can use tables to help you generate schedules more quickly. Tables allow you to format the columns and rows of text automatically, similar to formatting in spreadsheet programs.

## Creating a Table

The first step in creating a table is to determine the number of rows and columns you want. Don't worry if you aren't certain of the exact number of rows and columns; you can add or subtract them at any time. In this exercise, you'll create a table that contains 12 rows and 9 columns, as shown in Figure 10.5.

**FIGURE 10.5**

A sample table created with the Table tool

| Number | Room | Finish | | | | Ceiling Ht. | Area | Remarks |
|---|---|---|---|---|---|---|---|---|
| | | Floor | Base | Wall | Ceiling | | | |
| 110 | Lobby | B | 1 | A | 1 | 10'-0" | 200sf | |
| 111 | Office | A | 1 | B | 2 | 8'-0" | 96sf | |
| 112 | Office | A | 1 | B | 2 | 8'-0" | 96sf | |
| 113 | Office | A | 1 | B | 2 | 8'-0" | 96sf | |
| 114 | Meeting | C | 1 | B | 2 | 8'-0" | 150sf | |
| 115 | Breakout | C | 1 | B | 2 | 8'-0" | 150sf | |
| 116 | Womens | D | 2 | C | 3 | 8'-0" | 50sf | |
| 117 | Mens | D | 2 | C | 3 | 8'-0" | 50sf | |

(Room Finish Schedule)

Start by creating the basic table layout:

1. Click File ➢ New from the menu bar, or press ⌘-N. Use the standard acad.dwt drawing template.

2. Click on the Tool Sets button and select Annotation (Figure 10.6).

**FIGURE 10.6**

The Tool Sets button on the Workflow toolbar

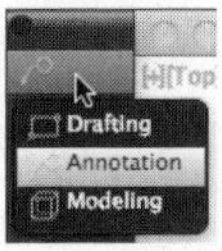

3. Click on the Table tool on the Tool Sets palette. You can also choose Draw ➢ Table from the menu bar or type **TB**↵.

4. At the `Specify first corner:` prompt, type **8.453** and press the Tab key. Now type **21.815** and press ↵.

5. At the `Specify second corner:` prompt, type **30.953** and press the Tab key. Now type **17.402** and press ↵.

6. The table is drawn with 9 columns and 12 rows and the cursor in the top cell. You also see the Text Editor visor (Figure 10.7).

**FIGURE 10.7**
The drawn table

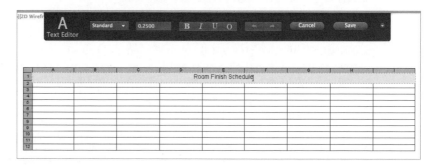

7. Enter **Room Finish Schedule** and press ↵. The cursor moves to the next cell.

8. Click Save on the Text Editor visor.

## Adding Cell Text

You've just created a table and added a title. Now let's start to add some more text to the table:

1. Adjust your view so the table fills most of the drawing area.

2. Double-click in the first cell at the top left, just below the Room Finish Schedule label (see Figure 10.8). The cell turns gray, and the Text Editor visor appears. You also see labels across the top and left side showing the row and column addresses.

3. Enter **Number** for the room number column at the far left, and then press the Tab key to advance to the next cell to the right.

4. Enter **Room**, and press the Tab key again.

**FIGURE 10.8**
Double-click
the cell shown
selected here.

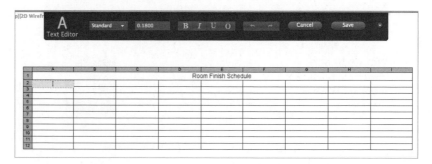

5. Enter **Finish**, and press the Tab key four times to advance four columns. You do this because the Finish heading (refer back to Figure 10.5) will have four columns under it: Floor, Base, Wall, and Ceiling. In the next exercise, you'll learn how to format those four columns under the single heading.

6. Enter **Ceiling Ht.**, and press the Tab key again.

7. Enter **Area**, press the Tab key, and enter **Remarks**.

8. Click Save in the Text Editor visor.

You have the column headings in place. Now you need to do a little extra formatting. In step 5, you left four cells blank because four of the columns will be combined under one heading: the Finish heading covers the Floor, Base, Wall, and Ceiling columns. Next you'll combine the blank cells with the Finish heading:

1. Click in the center of Finish label's cell to select it.

2. Click in the third cell to the right of the Finish cell to select all four cells (Figure 10.9).

**FIGURE 10.9**
Select a group of four cells.

3. On the Table Cell visor, select the Merge Cells flyout and then choose Merge All from the drop-down list. The four selected cells merge into a single cell with the word *Finish*.

Now you need to add the subheads under the Finish header:

1. Double-click in the leftmost cell below the Finish cell. The Text Editor visor appears (Figure 10.10).

**FIGURE 10.10**
Double-click this cell and the Text Editor visor appears.

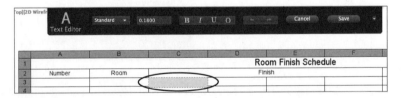

2. Enter **Floor**, and press the Tab key.

3. Enter **Base**, **Wall**, and **Ceiling**, respectively, in the following three columns. Remember that the Tab key advances you to the next cell to the right. Your table should look like Figure 10.11.

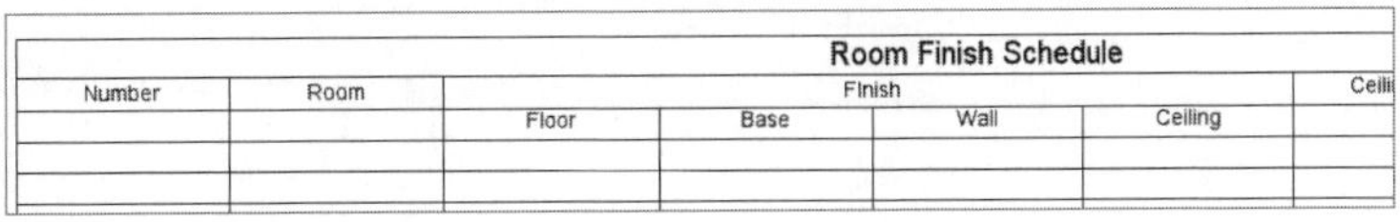

**FIGURE 10.11**
The table so far

| | | Room Finish Schedule | | | | |
|---|---|---|---|---|---|---|
| Number | Room | | Finish | | | Ceili |
| | | Floor | Base | Wall | Ceiling | |
| | | | | | | |
| | | | | | | |

4. Click Save in the Text Editor visor.

## Adjusting Table Text Orientation and Location

You now have the basic layout of the table, with one difference. The Floor, Base, Wall, and Ceiling labels you just added are oriented horizontally, but you want them oriented vertically, as in Figure 10.5. The following steps will show you how to rotate a set of labels in a table so they appear in the orientation you want:

1. Click the cell labeled Floor to select it. The Table Cell palette appears.

2. Click in the cell labeled Ceiling to select all four of the cells below the Finish heading. The combined cells have four grips, one on each side of the group.

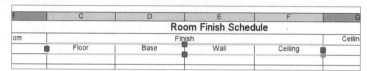

3. Click the grip at the bottom of the selected group, and move it down about four rows. Click to "fix" the row height in place. The entire row becomes taller. This provides room for the text when you rotate it.

4. In the Properties Inspector palette, click the Text Rotation input box under the Content category.

5. Enter 90↵ for a 90-degree rotation of the text. The text rotates into a vertical orientation. You can also use the circular slider located to the right of the text input box to set the rotation.

   With the text in this orientation, the columns are too wide, so you'll change the cell width for the selected cells.

6. Move the right grip to the left to decrease the width of the cells.

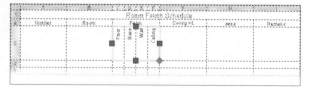

**7.** For the final touch, you'll center the text in the cells. In the Properties Inspector palette, click the Bottom Center tool next to Alignment under the Cell category. The text becomes centered in the cells and aligned at the bottom of the cells.

In the last exercise, you learned how you can adjust the text orientation through the Properties Inspector palette. You can also use it to adjust the width of cells. If you prefer, you can adjust the width of multiple cells by adjusting the grip location of selected cells.

Now continue to add text to the cells and adjust their sizes:

**1.** Double-click in the cell in the Number column just below the row that contains the Floor, Base, Wall, and Ceiling cells. A text cursor appears in the cell, and the Text Editor visor appears.

**2.** Enter **110**, and press ↵. Instead of advancing to the next cell to the right, you advance to the next cell below.

**3.** Enter **111**, and press ↵ again. Continue to enter each room number in this way until you reach room number 117. When you've finished entering the room numbers, click Save in the Text Editor visor.

Next you'll reduce the width of the column to fit the text a bit better.

**4.** Click in the cell with the Number text label. It's the first column heading in the table.

**5.** Click in the bottom cell of the Number column to select the entire column.

**6.** Click the grip to the left of the column, and move the grip to the right so the column width is approximately half the width of the Room column. You can zoom in on the column to allow more control over the positioning of the grip.

**7.** Press Esc to exit the selection and view your table so far (Figure 10.12).

 **Real World Scenario**

### AUTO-FILLING CELLS

In the previous exercise, you may have noticed that the room numbers were sequential. There is a time-saver that will allow you to auto-fill values. Follow these steps:

1. Type the number in the cell and press ↵.

2. Reclick in the cell to show the grips.

3. On the lower-right corner is a lighter-colored diamond grip. This is the auto-fill grip.

4. Click the diamond grip and drag downward. You will see a tooltip showing the incremented number.

5. When the tool tip displays 117, click again.

6. The numbers are automatically shown incremented.

Auto-fill will work in a horizontal or vertical configuration.

**FIGURE 10.12**

The table with the columns resized

| Room Finish Schedule | | | | | | | |
|---|---|---|---|---|---|---|---|
| Number | Room | Finish | | | | Ceiling Ht. | Area | Remarks |
| | | Floor | Base | Wall | Ceiling | | | |
| 110 | | | | | | | | |
| 111 | | | | | | | | |
| 112 | | | | | | | | |
| 113 | | | | | | | | |
| 114 | | | | | | | | |
| 115 | | | | | | | | |
| 116 | | | | | | | | |
| 117 | | | | | | | | |
| | | | | | | | | |

Now, suppose you want to delete the extra row of cells at the bottom of the table or add a new row. Here's what to do:

1. Click the bottom-left cell of the table to select it.

2. Select the Delete Row tool in the Table Cell visor. The row disappears.

3. To add a row, select a cell, and click either the Insert Row Above or Insert Row Below tool, depending on where you want the new row.

Insert Row Above

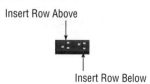

Insert Row Below

You may also notice the Insert Column Left, Insert Column Right, and Delete Column options in the Table Cell visor. These tools let you add or delete columns. These options function in a way that's similar to how the Delete Row and Insert Row options function.

## Editing the Table Line Work

So far, you've concentrated on how you can format text and cells in a table, but you'll also want some control over the lines in the table. Typically, heavier lines are used around the border of the table and between the title and the rest of the table.

The Border Style option lets you modify the outline of the border. When you select this option, the Cell Border Properties dialog box opens (Figure 10.13).

You can use this dialog box to fine-tune the appearance of the line work of the table. Try the following exercise to see firsthand how this dialog box works:

1. Turn on the display of line weights by clicking on the Show/Hide Lineweights tool on the Status Bar palette.

2. Click in the title cell at the top of the table to select the cell, and then in the Properties Inspector palette, choose Border Style in the Cell category to open the Cell Border Properties dialog box shown on Figure 10.13.

**FIGURE 10.13**
Setting border properties

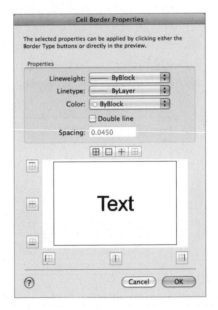

3. Click the Lineweight pop-up list, and select 0.30 mm.

4. Click the Outside Borders button that appears just above the preview to change the borders of the cell to the selected line weight (Figure 10.14).

5. Click OK. The title cell is now outlined in a heavier line. To see it clearly, press the Esc key.

**FIGURE 10.14**
Click to display
outside borders.

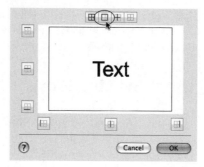

You can also adjust the line weights that encircle a group of cells, as in the following exercise:

1. Click the Number cell (in the upper-left corner).

2. Click the cell in the lower-right corner of the table so that all the cells from the second-from-the-top row down are selected.

3. In the Properties Inspector palette, choose Border Style in the Cell category to open the Cell Border Properties dialog box.

4. Select 0.30 mm from the Lineweight pop-up list. Then click the Outside Borders button as you did in step 4 of the previous exercise.

5. Click OK and press Esc. The outlines of the selected cells are given the new line weight setting (Figure 10.15).

6. Save this file as Room Finish Schedule.dwg for future reference.

**FIGURE 10.15**
The updated
borders

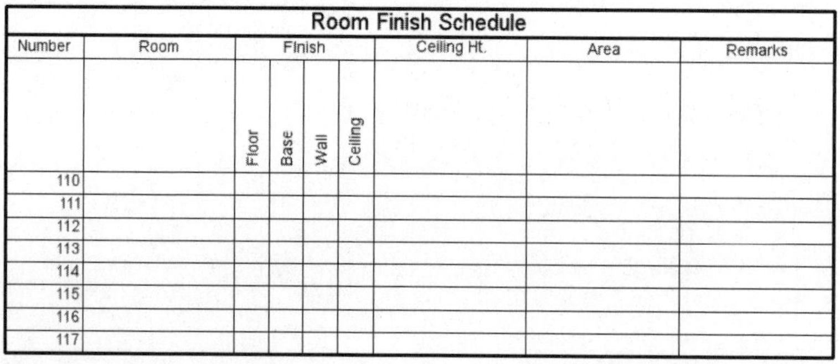

| Number | Room | Finish | | | | Ceiling Ht. | Area | Remarks |
|---|---|---|---|---|---|---|---|---|
| | | Floor | Base | Wall | Ceiling | | | |
| 110 | | | | | | | | |
| 111 | | | | | | | | |
| 112 | | | | | | | | |
| 113 | | | | | | | | |
| 114 | | | | | | | | |
| 115 | | | | | | | | |
| 116 | | | | | | | | |
| 117 | | | | | | | | |

Room Finish Schedule

**CHANGING THE BACKGROUND COLOR**

In addition to the table borders, you can change the background color for the cells of the table through the Background Fill drop-down list in the Properties Inspector palette.

The Cell Border Properties dialog box also lets you set the line colors by selecting a color from the Color pop-up menu. In addition, there are several buttons around the preview panel (Figure 10.16) that let you select the lines that are affected by the Cell Border Properties settings.

You can also use the preview to select individual borders by clicking the sample border in the preview panel. The sample changes to show you which border lines are affected.

**FIGURE 10.16**
Setting the borders that will be affected

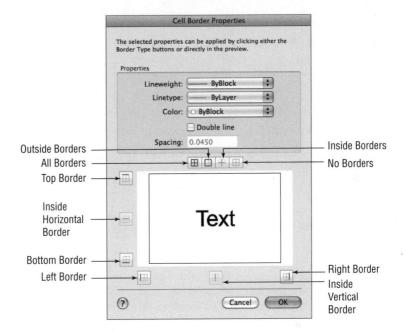

## Adding Formulas to Cells

In the beginning of this chapter, I mentioned that you can include formulas in table cells. This can be a great timesaver because you can set up a table with quantities that automatically adjust to changes in values in the table. You don't have to calculate the changes manually.

You may recall that formulas are actually a type of field and that a field can be linked with objects in a drawing so that the field displays the linked object's properties. The formula field can be linked to several numeric text values.

Although fields are the tools you use for formulas, you don't have to choose consciously to add a field to a cell every time you want to add a formula. The exercise in the following section will demonstrate how you can add a formula by typing directly in a cell. AutoCAD takes care of converting your input into a field.

## Using Formulas Directly in Cells

The simplest way to add a formula to a cell is to double-click the cell and then, when the Text Editor visor appears, enter the formula directly in the cell with the addition of an equal sign (=) at the beginning. Try the following exercise to see how it works:

1. Open the FieldSample.dwg file, which can be found on the book's companion website.

2. Double-click in the cell, as shown in Figure 10.17, to select the location for your formula.

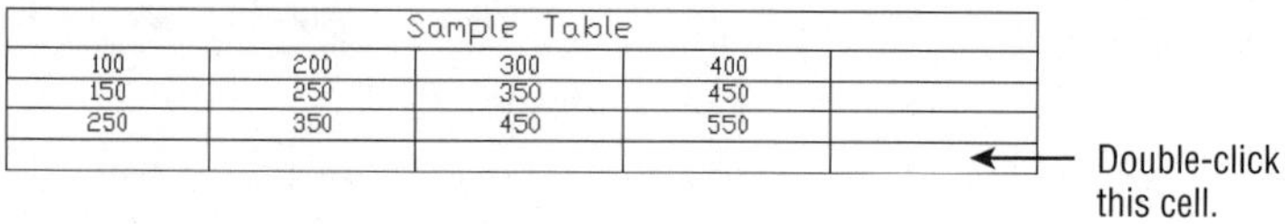

**FIGURE 10.17**

Selecting the cell for your formula

| Sample Table | | | | |
|---|---|---|---|---|
| 100 | 200 | 300 | 400 | |
| 150 | 250 | 350 | 450 | |
| 250 | 350 | 450 | 550 | |
| | | | | |

← Double-click this cell.

3. Enter **=A2+D4** in the cell to add the values in cell A2 and cell D4.

4. Press ↵ after you enter the formula. The value of A2 plus D4 appears in the cell (Figure 10.18).

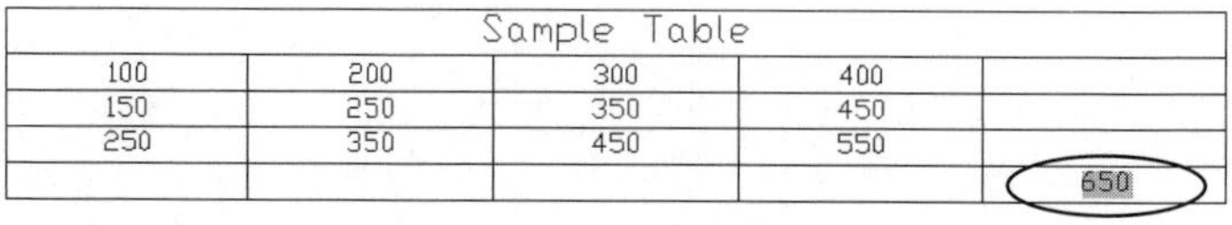

**FIGURE 10.18**

A cell showing the sum of two other cells

| Sample Table | | | | |
|---|---|---|---|---|
| 100 | 200 | 300 | 400 | |
| 150 | 250 | 350 | 450 | |
| 250 | 350 | 450 | 550 | |
| | | | | 650 |

In step 3, the equal sign tells AutoCAD to convert the text into a formula field. You may have noticed that when you start to edit a cell in a table, the row and column labels appear along the top and left side of the table. You can use these labels to determine the cell addresses for your formula.

In typical spreadsheet fashion, you can change the formula in a cell at any time. Double-click the cell containing the formula, and then edit the formula values and operators.

When a table cell is selected, you can also use the Formula drop-down list from the Table Cell visor to select from a set of predefined math operations (Figure 10.19).

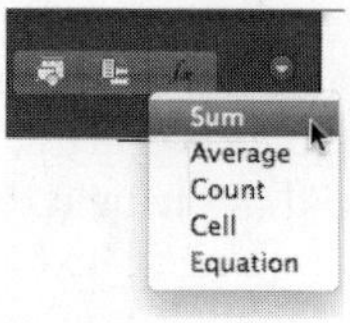

**FIGURE 10.19**

The Formula drop-down list on the Table Cell visor

Click in the cell where you want to place the formula; then, in the Table Cell visor, click the Formula drop-down list. A list opens; select the operation you want to use. Next, place a selection window around the cells you want to include in the formula. Click in the first cell that you want to include in the formula, and then click in the second cell. As you do this, a selection window appears. All the cells that are included in the selection window are included in the formula.

## Using Other Math Operations

In the previous exercise, you used the plus sign to add the value of two cells. You can string together several cells' addresses to add multiple cells, as follows:

```
=A2+A3+A4...
```

You can also subtract, multiply, or divide by using the – (subtract or minus), * (multiply or asterisk), or / (divide or slash) sign. To perform multiple operations on several cells, you can group operations within parentheses in a way similar to how you would in a typical spreadsheet formula. For example, if you want to add two cells together and then multiply their sum by another cell's value, use the following format:

```
=(A2+A3)*A4
```

The Average, Sum, and Count options that appear in the Formula drop-down list on the Table Cell visor give you quick access to these frequently used functions. You can add to a cell the average value of a set of cells, the sum of a set of cells, or the count of the number of cells. When you click one of these options after selecting a cell, you're prompted to select several cells with a selection window. Once you've selected a set of cells, you see the appropriate formula in the selected cells. Clicking the Average option, for example, produces a formula similar to the following:

```
=Average(A1:B5)
```

Clicking the Sum option produces a formula like the following:

```
=Sum(A1:B5)
```

In both cases, a range of cells is indicated by a colon, as in A1:B5. You can use this format when entering formulas manually. You can also include a formula in a single cell with a range by using a comma, as in B5,C6:

```
=Sum(A1:B5,C6)
```

# Exporting Tables

Some day, you might want to export your AutoCAD table to a spreadsheet program or database. Follow these steps:

1.  Select the table. The entire table is highlighted and the Table visor opens.

2.  Click the Export tool on the Table visor. The Export Data dialog box opens.

3.  Specify a name and location for your exported table data, and click Save.

The file is saved with a .csv filename extension. This type of file is a comma-delimited file and can be read by most spreadsheet programs, including Microsoft Excel. Unfortunately, the CSV file doesn't retain the AutoCAD table formatting.

To open the exported file from Microsoft Excel, choose File ➢ Open in the Excel menu bar (or press ⌘-O); then, in the Open dialog box, select All Files in the Files Of Type pop-up menu. You can then locate the exported table and open it.

**ADDING GRAPHICS TO TABLE CELLS**

One of the most interesting features of the Table tool is its ability to include blocks in a cell. This can be useful if you want to include graphic elements in your table. Adding a block to a cell is a simple process. Here are the steps:

1. Click in a cell to select it.

2. On the Table Cell visor, click the Insert Block tool. The Insert Block In Table Cell dialog box opens.

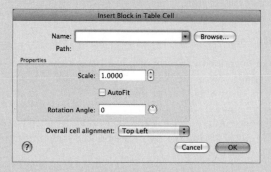

3. Select a block name from the Name drop-down list. You can also click the Browse button to the right of the list to open the Select Drawing File dialog box that enables you to select a drawing file for import to the cell.

4. After you've selected a block and specified the settings in the Properties group of the dialog box, click OK. The block appears in the cell you've selected.

The Properties Inspector palette enables you to specify the alignment and size of the inserted block. By default, the Auto-Fit option under the Blocks In Cell category is turned on. This option adjusts the size of the block to make it fit in the current cell size.

# The Bottom Line

**Use fields to associate text with drawing properties.** Fields are a special type of text object that can be linked to object properties. They can help to automate certain text-related tasks.

> **Master It** Name two uses for fields that you learned about in the first part of this chapter.

**Add tables to your drawing.** The Tables feature can help you make quick work of schedules and other tabular data that you want to include in a drawing.

> **Master It** What is the name of the visor that appears when you click the Table tool?

**Edit the table line work.** Because tables include line work to delineate their different cells, AutoCAD gives you control over table borders and lines.

> **Master It** How do you get to the Cell Border Properties dialog box?

**Add formulas to cells.**    Tables can function like spreadsheets by allowing you to add formulas to cells.

   **Master It**   What type of text object lets you add formulas to cells?

**Export tables.**   The Table feature allows you to export the text from a table to a CSV file that can be imported into a Microsoft Excel spreadsheet.

   **Master It**   Describe how to export a table from AutoCAD into an Excel spreadsheet.

# Chapter 11

# Using Dimensions

Before you determine the dimensions of a project, your design is in flux and many questions may be unanswered. After you begin dimensioning, you'll start to see whether things fit or work together. Dimensioning can be crucial to how well a design works and how quickly it develops. The dimensions answer questions about code conformance if you're an architect; they answer questions about tolerances, fit, and interference if you're involved in mechanical applications. After you and your design team reach a design on a schematic level, communicating even tentative dimensions to others on the team can accelerate design development. Dimensions represent a point from which you can develop your ideas further.

With AutoCAD, you can easily add tentative or final dimensions to any drawing. AutoCAD gives you an accurate dimension without your having to take measurements. You pick the two points to be dimensioned and the dimension line location, and AutoCAD does the rest. AutoCAD's *associative dimensioning* capability automatically updates dimensions whenever the size or shape of the dimensioned object changes. These dimensioning features can save you valuable time and reduce the number of dimensional errors in your drawings.

In this chapter, you'll learn to do the following:

- ◆ Understand the components of a dimension
- ◆ Create a dimension style
- ◆ Draw linear dimensions
- ◆ Edit dimensions
- ◆ Dimension non-orthogonal objects
- ◆ Add a note with a leader arrow
- ◆ Apply ordinate dimensions
- ◆ Add tolerance notation

## Understanding the Components of a Dimension

Before you start the exercises in this chapter, it will help to know the names of the parts of a dimension. Figure 11.1 shows a sample of a dimension with the parts labeled. The *dimension line* is the line that represents the distance being dimensioned. It's the horizontal line with the diagonal tick marks on either end. The *extension lines* are the lines that originate from the object being dimensioned. They show you the exact location from which the dimension is taken. The *dimension text* is the dimension value, usually shown inside or above the dimension line.

**FIGURE 11.1**
The components of a dimension

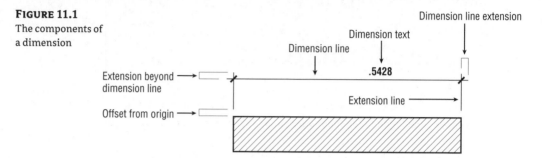

Another component of a dimension line is the *dimension line extension*. This is the part of the dimension line that extends beyond the extension line. Dimension line extensions are usually used only on architectural dimensions. The extension lines usually extend beyond the dimension lines in all types of dimensions. The extension line *offset from origin* is the distance from the beginning of the extension line to the object being dimensioned. The *extension beyond dimension line* is the distance the dimension line extends past the extension line.

You can control each of these components by creating or editing dimension styles. *Dimension styles* are the settings that determine the look of your dimensions. You can store multiple styles in a single drawing. The first exercise in this chapter will show you how to create a dimension style.

---

 **Real World Scenario**

### DIMENSIONING STANDARDS

In addition to the components of a dimension, you should know about the standards that govern the placement and style of dimensions in a drawing. Each industry has a different set of standards for text size, text style, arrow style, dimension placement, and general dimensioning methods. These issues are beyond the scope of this book; however, we urge you to become familiar with the standards associated with your industry. Many resources are available to you if you want to find out more about dimension standards. Here are a few resources on the subject:

◆ For mechanical drafting in the United States, check the American Society of Mechanical Engineers (ASME) website: www.asme.org.

◆ For European standards, see the International Organization for Standardization (ISO) website: www.iso.org.

◆ For architectural standards in the United States, see the American Institute of Architects (AIA) website: www.aia.org.

# Creating a Dimension Style

Dimension styles are similar to text styles. They determine the look of your dimensions as well as the size of dimensioning features, such as the dimension text and arrows. You can set up a dimension style to have special types of arrows, for instance, or to position the dimension text above or in line with the dimension line. Dimension styles also make your work easier by enabling you to store and duplicate your most common dimension settings.

AutoCAD gives you several default dimension styles, including *ISO-25* and *Standard*, depending on whether you use the metric or Imperial (also called English) measurement system. You'll probably add many other styles to suit the types of drawings you're creating. You can also create variations of a general style for those situations that call for only minor changes in the dimension's appearance.

In this section, you'll learn how to set up your own dimension style based on the Standard dimension style (see Figure 11.2). For metric users, the settings are different, but the overall methods are the same.

**FIGURE 11.2**
AutoCAD's Standard dimension style compared with an architectural-style dimension

A dimension using the Standard default settings

A dimension set up for architectural drawings

A sample of other arrows

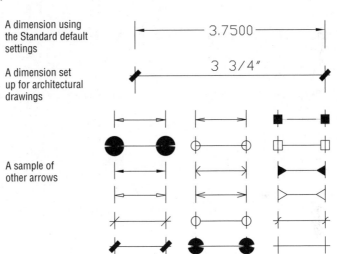

Follow these steps to create a dimension style:

1. Open the 11a-unit.dwg file and rename it Unit.dwg. Metric users should open 11a-unit-metric.dwg and rename it Unit.dwg. These files are the same as the Unit file you used in the previous chapter before the exercises.

2. Choose View ➢ Zoom ➢All from the menu bar or type **Z⏎A⏎** to display the entire floor plan.

3. Choose Format ➢ Dimension Style from the menu bar. You can also type **D⏎** at the Command prompt to open the Dimension Style Manager.

4. Select Standard from the Styles list box. Metric users should select ISO-25. See Figure 11.3.

5. Click New (the plus button) to open the Create New Dimension Style dialog box (Figure 11.4).

6. With the Copy Of Standard or ISO-25 name highlighted in the New Style Name input box, enter **My Architectural**.

7. Click Continue to open the detailed New Dimension Style dialog box (Figure 11.5).

**FIGURE 11.3**
The Dimension
Style Manager

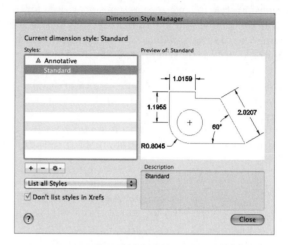

**FIGURE 11.4**
The Create New
Dimension Style
dialog box

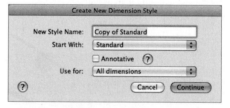

**FIGURE 11.5**
The New
Dimension Style
dialog box

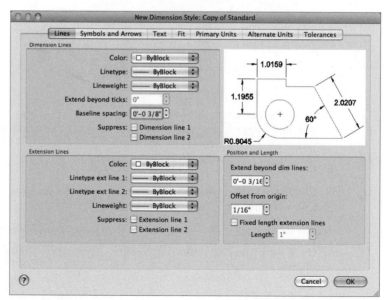

You've just created a dimension style called My Architectural, but at this point it's identical to the Standard style on which it's based. Nothing has happened to the Standard style; it's still available if you need to use it.

Nothing has been mentioned regarding the Tolerances tab of the New Dimension Style dialog box. This will be covered later in this chapter, in the section "Adding Tolerance Notation."

## Setting Up the Primary Unit Style

Now you need to set up your new dimension style so that it conforms to the U.S. architectural style of dimensioning. Let's start by changing the unit style for the dimension text. Just as you changed the overall unit style of AutoCAD to a feet-and-inches style for your bath drawing in Chapter 3, "Setting Up and Using AutoCAD's Drafting Tools," you must change your dimension styles. Setting the overall unit style doesn't automatically set the dimension unit style. Follow these steps:

1.  In the New Dimension Style dialog box, click the Primary Units tab (see Figure 11.6).

**FIGURE 11.6**
The Primary Units options

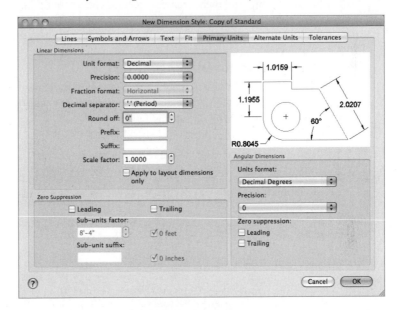

2.  In the Linear Dimensions group, open the Unit Format pop-up menu and choose Architectural. Notice that this pop-up menu contains the same unit styles as the main Drawing Units dialog box (choose Format ➤ Units from the menu bar). Metric users can skip this option.

---

**USING COMMAS OR PERIODS FOR DECIMALS**

The Decimal Separator option a few settings below the Unit Format option lets you choose between a period and a comma for decimal points. Metric users often use the comma for a decimal point, and U.S. users use a period. This option doesn't have any meaning for measurements other than decimal, so it's disabled when the Architectural unit format is selected.

---

**3.** Select 0´-0 ¼˝ from the Precision pop-up menu, just below the Unit Format option. Metric users should select 0.00. The Precision option enables you to set the level of precision that is displayed in the dimension text. It doesn't limit the precision of AutoCAD's drawing database. This value is used to limit only the display of dimension text values.

**4.** Just below the Precision pop-up menu, open the Fraction Format pop-up menu and select Diagonal. Notice what happens to the preview: The fractional dimensions change to show how your dimension text will look. Metric users can skip this step because it isn't available when the Decimal unit format is selected.

**5.** In the Zero Suppression group in the lower-left corner, click 0 Inches to deselect this check box. If you leave it turned on, indications of 0 inches will be omitted from the dimension text. (In architectural drawings, 0 inches is shown as in this dimension: 12´-0˝.) Metric users can ignore this option.

If you use the Imperial measurement system, you've set up My Architectural's dimension unit style to show dimensions in feet and inches, the standard method for U.S. construction documents. Metric users have changed the Precision value and kept the Decimal unit system.

## Setting the Height for Dimension Text

Along with the unit style, you should adjust the size of the dimension text. The Text tab of the New Dimension Style dialog box lets you set a variety of text options, including text location relative to the dimension line, style, and height.

Follow these steps to set the height of your dimension text:

**1.** Click the Text tab to display the text options (Figure 11.7).

**2.** Use the up/down arrows (known as a stepper control) to the right of the Text Height input box to make the text ⅛˝ high. Metric users should use **0.3** for the text height.

**FIGURE 11.7**
The Text options

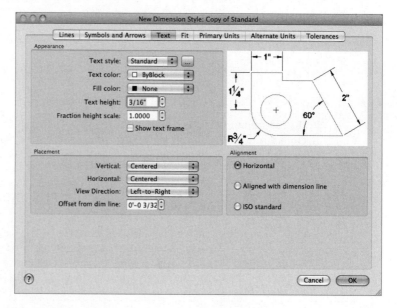

Unlike with the text you created in Chapter 9, "Adding Text to Drawings," you specify the text height by its final print size. You then specify an overall dimension scale factor that affects the sizing of all dimensioning settings, such as text and arrows.

If you want to use a specific text style for your dimensions, select a text style in the Text Style pop-up menu in the Text tab. If the style you select happens to have a height specification greater than 0, that height will override any text height settings you enter in the Text tab.

## Setting the Location and Orientation of Dimension Text

AutoCAD's default setting for the placement of dimension text puts the text in line with the dimension line, as shown in the example at the top of Figure 11.2 earlier in this chapter. However, you want the new My Architectural style to put the text above the dimension line, as is done in the center of Figure 11.2. To do that, you'll use the Placement and Alignment options in the Text tab of the New Dimension Style dialog box:

1. In the Alignment group in the lower-right corner of the dialog box, click the Aligned With Dimension Line radio button.

2. In the Placement group, open the Vertical pop-up menu, and select Above. The appearance of the preview image changes to show how your new settings will look.

3. Again in the Placement group, change the Offset From Dim Line value to ¹⁄₁₆″. This setting controls the size of the gap between the dimension line and the dimension text.

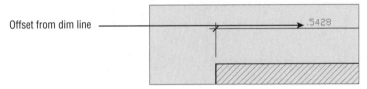

Offset from dim line ————— .5428

Each time you change a setting, the preview gives you immediate feedback about how your changes will affect your dimension style.

---

### FITTING TEXT AND ARROWS IN TIGHT PLACES

Every now and then, you'll need to dimension a small gap or a small part of an object in which dimension text won't fit. The Fit tab (covered later in this chapter) includes a few other settings that control how dimensions act when the extension lines are too close.

The Fit Options group lets you control how text and arrows are placed when there isn't enough room for both between the extension lines.

The Text Placement group contains three options to place the text in tight situations:

**Beside The Dimension Line**  Places text next to the extension line but close to the dimension line. You'll see how this affects your dimension later.

**Over Dimension Line, With Leader**  Places the dimension text farther from the dimension line, and includes an arrow or a leader from the dimension line to the text.

**Over Dimension Line, Without Leader**  Does the same as the previous setting, but doesn't include the leader.

## Choosing an Arrow Style and Setting the Dimension Scale

Next, you'll specify a different type of arrow for your new dimension style. For linear dimensions in architectural drawings, a diagonal line, or *tick* mark, is typically used instead of an arrow.

In addition, you want to set the scale for the graphical components of the dimension, such as the arrows and text. Recall from Chapter 9 that text must be scaled up in size in order to appear at the proper size in the final output of the drawing. Dimensions too must be scaled so they look correct when the drawing is plotted. The arrows are controlled by settings in the Symbols And Arrows tab, and the overall scale of the dimension style is set in the Fit tab.

Here are the steps for specifying the arrow type and scale:

1. Click the Symbols And Arrows tab to display the options for controlling the arrow style and dimension line extensions (Figure 11.8).

**FIGURE 11.8**
The Symbols And Arrows options

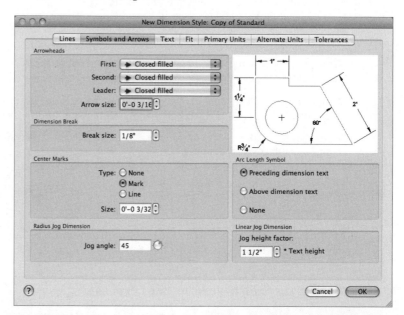

2. In the Arrowheads group, open the First pop-up menu and choose Architectural Tick. The graphic next to the arrowhead name shows you what the arrowhead looks like. Note that the Second pop-up menu automatically changes to Architectural Tick to maintain symmetry on the dimension.

3. In the Arrowheads group, change the Arrow Size setting to ⅛″. Metric users should enter **0.3**.

Next, you need to set the behavior of the dimension line and extension lines:

1. Click the Lines tab to display the options for controlling the dimension and extension lines (Figure 11.9).

**FIGURE 11.9**

The Lines options, for controlling the dimension and extension lines

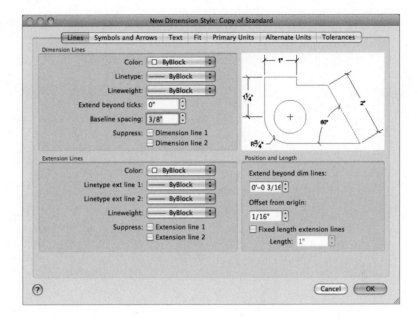

2. In the Extension Lines group, change the Extend Beyond Dim Lines setting to ⅛″. Metric users should change this to **0.3**. This setting determines the distance the extension line extends past the dimension line.

3. Again in the Position and Length group, change the Offset From Origin setting to ⅛″. Metric users should change this to **0.3**. This sets the distance from the point being dimensioned to the beginning of the dimension extension line.

4. Click the Fit tab to display the options for overall dimension scale and miscellaneous settings (Figure 11.10).

**FIGURE 11.10**

The Fit options

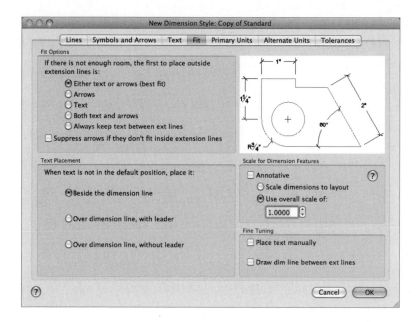

5. Turn on the Annotative option in the Scale For Dimension Features group. You may recall from Chapter 9 that the Annotative option allows AutoCAD to scale an object automatically to the drawing's annotation scale.

6. Click OK to close the New Dimension Style dialog box. The Dimension Style Manager dialog box appears again.

---

**CREATE CUSTOM ARROWHEADS**

See Appendix D, "System Variables and Dimension Styles," for details on how you can create your own arrowheads. AutoCAD also lets you set up a separate arrow style for leaders. You'll find Appendix D on this book's website, www.sybex.com/go/masteringautocadmac.

---

**USING THE LAYOUT VIEWPORT SCALE FOR DIMENSIONS**

If you use the Scale Dimensions To Layout option in the Scale For Dimension Features group of the Fit tab, AutoCAD uses the layout viewport scale to size the dimension components. See Chapter 8, "Introducing Printing and Layouts," for more information about viewport scale settings. This can be useful if you have a drawing that you want to print at multiple scales.

## Setting Up Alternate Units

You can use the Alternate Units tab of the New Dimension Style dialog box to set up AutoCAD to display a second dimension value in centimeters or millimeters. Likewise, if you're a metric user, you can set up a second dimension value to display feet and inches. The following exercise shows you how to set up alternate dimensions. You don't have to do this exercise now; it's here for your information. If you like, come back later and try it to see how it affects your dimensions. You can pick up the tutorial in the next section, "Setting the Current Dimension Style."

If you decide later that you don't want the alternate units to be displayed, you can turn them off by returning to the New Dimension Style dialog box and clearing the Display Alternate Units check box on the Alternate Units tab.

Here are the steps for setting up alternate dimensions:

1. In the Dimension Style Manager, select a style and then click the Options action menu (gear icon). From the menu, click Modify. Or, if you want to create a new style, click New (plus symbol).

2. In the Modify Dimension Style dialog box, click the Alternate Units tab (Figure 11.11). This is virtually identical to the New Dimension Style dialog box you've been working with.

3. Click the Display Alternate Units check box. The options in the tab become available for your input.

**FIGURE 11.11**
The Alternate Units options

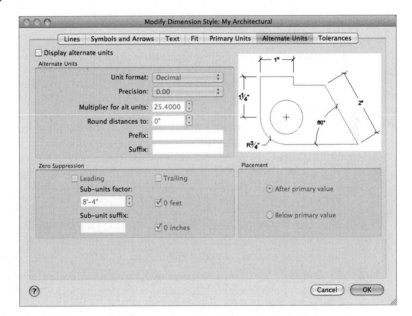

4. Select the appropriate option from the Unit Format pop-up menu. If you're a U.S. user, you should select Decimal if you want to show metric alternate units. Metric users should select Architectural.

5. Select an appropriate precision value from the Precision pop-up menu.

6. Enter a scale factor for your alternate dimension in the Multiplier For Alt Units input box. For U.S. users, the default value is 25.4. This value converts feet-and-inch dimensions to millimeters. In our metric examples, you've been using centimeters, so change this setting to **2.54**. Metric users should enter **0.3937** to convert centimeters to feet and inches.

7. In the Placement group, select where you want the alternate dimension to appear in relation to the main dimension.

8. You don't really want to display alternate units now, so turn off the Display Alternate Units setting.

9. Click OK to close the Modify Dimension Style dialog box. The Dimension Style Manager appears again.

## Setting the Current Dimension Style

Before you can begin to use your new dimension style, you must make it the current default:

1. Click My Architectural in the Styles list box in the Dimension Style Manager dialog box.

2. Click the Options action menu (gear icon), and click Set Current from the menu.

3. Click Close to exit the Dimension Style Manager.

You can also select a dimension style from the Dimension Style pop-up menu under the Annotation category of the Properties Inspector palette. You're now ready to use your new dimension style.

In the next set of exercises, you'll use the My Architectural style you just created. To switch to another style, open the Dimension Style Manager dialog, select the style you want from the Styles list, and click Set Current from the Options action menu, as you did in the previous exercise.

---

**SCALE FOR DIMENSIONS IN LEGACY DRAWINGS**

Drawings created prior to AutoCAD 2008 relied on scale factors to determine the scaling of dimensions. Because it's likely that you'll run into legacy drawing files, here is some information about the settings used for those earlier dimensions.

Instead of the Annotative option, the Use Overall Scale Of option is used in the Scale For Dimension Features group. You select the Use Overall Scale Of radio button and enter a drawing scale factor in the Use Overall Scale Of input box.

All the values you enter for the options in the New Dimension Style dialog box are multiplied by this Use Overall Scale Of value to obtain the final size of the dimension components. For example, the text height you entered earlier, ⅛″, is multiplied by 48 for a dimension text height of 6″. For metric users, the text height of 0.3 is multiplied by 50 for a text height of 15 cm. For more on the scaling of text and other objects in AutoCAD, see Chapter 3.

### Modifying a Dimension Style

To modify an existing dimension style, open the Dimension Style Manager, highlight the style you want to edit, and then click Modify from the Options action menu to open the Modify Dimension Style dialog box. You can then make changes to the different components of the selected dimension style. When you've finished making changes and closed both dialog boxes, all the dimensions associated with the edited style update automatically in your drawing. For example, if you're not using the Annotative Scale feature and you decide you need to change the dimension scale of a style, you can open the Modify Dimension Style dialog box and change the Use Overall Scale Of value in the Scale For Dimension Features group of the Fit tab.

So far, you've been introduced to the various settings that let you determine the appearance of a dimension style. We didn't discuss every option; to learn more about the other dimension style options, consult Appendix D found on the book's companion website. There you'll find descriptions of all the items in the New Dimension Style and Modify Dimension Style dialog boxes, plus reference material covering the system variables associated with each option.

If your application is strictly architectural, you may want to make these same dimension-style changes to the `acad.dwt` template file or create a set of template files specifically for architectural drawings of different scales.

## Drawing Linear Dimensions

The most common type of dimension you'll be using is the *linear dimension*. The linear dimension is an orthogonal dimension measuring the width and length of an object. AutoCAD provides three dimensioning tools for this purpose: Linear (Dimlinear), Continue (Dimcontinue), and Baseline (Dimbaseline). These options are readily accessible from the Tool Sets palette.

In the following set of exercises, you'll see figures displaying dimensions in both Imperial and metric units. I've included both measurements so that both Imperial and metric users can more easily follow the tutorial. But in your own drawing, you'll see only one dimension value displayed above the dimension line.

### Understanding the Dimensions Tool Group

Before you apply any dimension, you should study the Annotation tool set's Dimensions tool group (Figure 11.12). This panel contains nearly all the tools necessary to draw and edit your dimensions.

**FIGURE 11.12**
Dimensions on the Tool Sets palette.

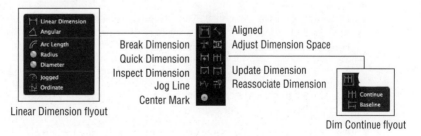

Linear Dimension flyout

Dim Continue flyout

## Placing Horizontal and Vertical Dimensions

Let's start by looking at the basic dimensioning tool, Linear. The Linear Dimension flyout (the Dimlinear command) on the Annotation tool set's Dimensions tool group accommodates both the horizontal and vertical dimensions.

In this exercise, you'll add a vertical dimension to the right side of the Unit plan:

1. Before you start to dimension your drawing, you need to set its scale. Select ¼″ = 1′-0″ from the Annotation Scale pop-up menu on the Status Bar palette. Metric users should select 1:50.

2. To start either a vertical or horizontal dimension, click Linear Dimension from the Tool Sets palette or enter **DLI**↵ at the Command prompt.

3. The `Specify first extension line origin or <select object>:` prompt asks you for the first point of the distance to be dimensioned. An extension line connects the object being dimensioned to the dimension line. Use the Endpoint Osnap override, and pick the upper-right corner of the entry, as shown in Figure 11.13.

**FIGURE 11.13**
The dimension line added to the Unit drawing

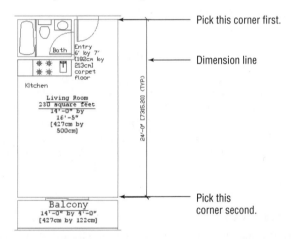

---

### SELECTING OBJECTS TO BE DIMENSIONED

The prompt in step 3 gives you the option of pressing ↵ to select an object. If you do this, you're prompted to pick the object you want to dimension rather than the distance to be dimensioned. This method is discussed later in this chapter.

---

4. At the `Specify second extension line origin:` prompt, pick the lower-right corner of the living room, as shown in Figure 11.13.

5. At the next prompt, `Specify dimension line location or [Mtext/Text/Angle/Horizontal/Vertical/Rotated]:`, the dimension line indicates the direction of the dimension and contains the arrows or tick marks. Move your cursor from left to right to display a temporary dimension. This enables you to select a dimension-line location visually.

**6.** Enter **@4´<0↵** to tell AutoCAD you want the dimension line to be 4´ to the right of the last point you selected. Metric users should enter **@122<0↵**. (You could pick a point by using your cursor, but this doesn't let you place the dimension line as accurately.) After you've done this, the dimension is placed in the drawing, as shown in Figure 11.13.

### Continuing a Dimension

You'll often want to enter a group of dimensions strung together in a line. For example, you may want to continue dimensioning the balcony and align the continued dimension with the dimension you just entered.

To do this, use the Continue option found in the Dimensions tool group's Continue/Baseline flyout:

**1.** Click the Continue tool on the Dimensions tool group, or enter **DCO↵**.

**2.** At the `Specify a second extension line origin or [Undo/Select] <Select>:` prompt, pick the upper-right corner of the balcony. (See the top image in Figure 11.14.)

**FIGURE 11.14**
The dimension string, continued and completed

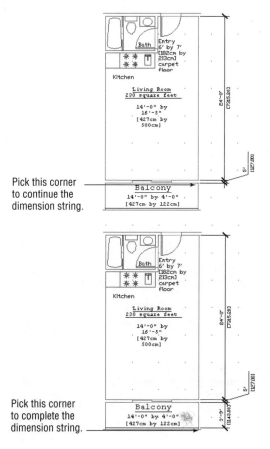

Pick this corner to continue the dimension string.

Pick this corner to complete the dimension string.

3. Pick the right end of the rail on the balcony. See the bottom image in Figure 11.14 for the results.

4. Press ↵ twice to exit the command.

If you select the wrong location for a continued dimension, you can choose Edit ➢ Undo from the menu bar or type **U**↵ to back up your dimension.

The Continue tool adds a dimension from where you left off. The last-drawn extension line is used as the first extension line for the continued dimension. AutoCAD keeps adding dimensions as you continue to pick points, until you press ↵.

You probably noticed that the 5″ dimension is placed away from the dimension line with a leader line pointing to it. This is the result of the 5″ dimension's text not having enough space to fit between the dimension extension lines. Later this chapter, in the section "Changing Style Settings of Individual Dimensions," you'll learn about dimension style settings that can remedy this problem. For now, let's continue adding dimensions to the plan.

### CONTINUING FROM AN OLDER DIMENSION

If you need to continue a string of dimensions from an older linear dimension instead of the most recently added one, press ↵ at the `Specify a second extension line origin or [Undo/Select] <Select>:` prompt you saw in step 2 of the previous exercise. Then, at the `Select continued dimension:` prompt, click the extension line from which you want to continue.

## Drawing Dimensions from a Common Base Extension Line

Another way to dimension objects is to have several dimensions originate from the same extension line. To accommodate this, AutoCAD provides the Baseline tool on the Dimensions tool group and the Dim Continue flyout, as was shown in the rightmost image in Figure 11.12.

To see how this works, you'll start another dimension—this time a horizontal one—across the top of the plan:

1. Click Linear Dimension from the Tool Sets palette. Or, as you did for the vertical dimension, type **DLI**↵ to start the horizontal dimension.

2. At the `Specify first extension line origin or <select object>:` prompt, use the Endpoint osnap to pick the upper-left corner of the bathroom, as shown in Figure 11.15.

3. At the `Specify second extension line origin:` prompt, pick the upper-right corner of the bathroom, as shown in Figure 11.15.

4. At the `Specify dimension line location or [Mtext/Text/Angle/ Horizontal/ Vertical/Rotated]:` prompt, pick a point above the Unit plan, like the 7′-6″ dimension in Figure 11.15. If you need to, pan your view downward to fit the dimension in.

---

#### USE OSNAPS WHILE DIMENSIONING

Because you usually pick exact locations on your drawing as you dimension, you may want to turn on Running Osnaps to avoid the extra step of selecting osnaps from the Object Snap shortcut menu.

---

**FIGURE 11.15**

The bathroom with horizontal dimensions

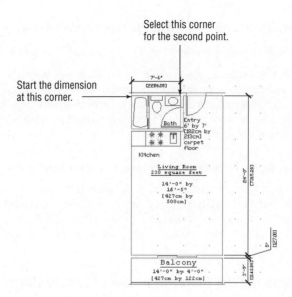

Select this corner for the second point.

Start the dimension at this corner.

5. You're set to draw another dimension continuing from the first extension line of the dimension you just drew. Click the Baseline tool from the Continue/Baseline flyout. Or, type **DBA↵** at the Command prompt to start a baseline dimension.

6. At the `Specify a second extension line origin or [Undo/Select] <Select>:` prompt, click the upper-right corner of the entry, as shown in Figure 11.16.

**FIGURE 11.16**

The overall width dimension

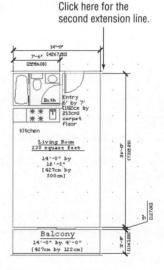

Click here for the second extension line.

**7.** Press ↵ twice to exit the Baseline command.

**8.** Pan your view down so it looks similar to Figure 11.16.

In this example, you see that the Baseline tool is similar to the Continue tool except that the Baseline tool enables you to use the first extension line of the previous dimension as the base for a second dimension. The distance between the two horizontal dimension lines is controlled by the Baseline Spacing setting in the Lines tab of the New Dimension Style and Modify Dimension Style dialog boxes.

### CONTINUING DIMENSIONING FROM A PREVIOUS DIMENSION

You may have noticed in step 7 that you had to press ↵ twice to exit the command. As with Continue, you can draw the baseline dimension from a previous dimension by pressing ↵ at the `Specify a second extension line origin [Undo/Select] <Select>:` prompt. You then get the `Select base dimension:` prompt, at which you can either select another dimension or press ↵ again to exit the command.

## Adjusting the Distance between Dimensions

As you work toward a deadline, you may find that you cut a few corners, or someone else does, when adding dimensions and a set of parallel dimension lines isn't accurately placed.

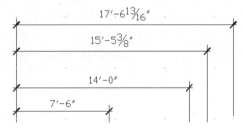

You can quickly adjust the spacing between dimension lines using the Adjust Dimension Space tool in the Dimensions tool group:

**1.** Click the Adjust Dimension Space tool on the Tool Sets palette or type **DIMSPACE**↵.

**2.** At the `Select base dimension:` prompt, click the dimension closest to the feature being dimensioned.

**3.** At the `Select dimensions to space:` prompt, click the next dimension.

**4.** Continue to select the other parallel dimensions. When you're finished with your selections, press ↵.

**5.** You see the `Enter a value or [Auto] <Auto>:` prompt. Enter a value for the distance between the dimension lines. This value should be in full-scale distances. You can also press ↵ and AutoCAD will adjust the distance between dimensions for you.

# Editing Dimensions

As you add more dimensions to your drawings, you'll find that AutoCAD occasionally places the dimension text or line in an inappropriate location or that you may need to modify the dimension text. In the following sections, you'll take an in-depth look at how you can modify dimensions to suit those special circumstances that always crop up.

## Appending Data to Dimension Text

So far in this chapter, you've been accepting the default dimension text. You can append information to the default dimension value or change it entirely if you need to. At the point when you see the temporary dimension dragging with your cursor, enter **T↵**. Then, using the less-than and greater-than (< and >) symbols, you can add text either before or after the default dimension or replace the symbols entirely to replace the default text. The Properties Inspector palette lets you modify the existing dimension text in a similar way (see Chapter 2, "Creating Your First Drawing," for more on the Properties Inspector palette). You can open the Properties Inspector palette for a dimension by double-clicking on the dimension.

Let's see how this works by changing an existing dimension's text in your drawing:

1. Type **ED↵**. This starts the Ddedit command.

2. Click the last horizontal dimension you added to the drawing at the top of the screen. The in-place text editor and Text Editor visor appears. (Figure 11.17).

**FIGURE 11.17**
The in-place text editor and Text Editor visor

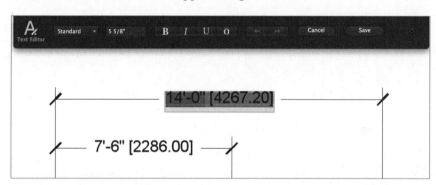

3. Place the cursor at the end of the 14´-0˝ text, and then type **to face of stud** beginning with a space. The space is to ensure that the dimension doesn't run into the text.

4. Click Save on the Text Editor visor, and then press ↵ to exit the Ddedit command. The dimension changes to read 14´-0˝ `to face of stud`.

5. Because you don't need the new appended text for the tutorial, choose Edit ➢ Undo on the menu bar to remove the appended text, or type **U↵**.

**EDITING MULTIPLE DIMENSIONS**

In this exercise, you were able to edit only a single dimension. To append text to several dimensions at once, you need to use the Dimension Edit tool. See the sidebar "Making Changes to Multiple Dimensions" later in this chapter for more on this tool.

If you need to restore the original dimension text for a dimension whose value has been completely replaced, you can use the steps shown in the previous exercise. However, in step 3, replace the text with the <> bracket symbols.

You can also have AutoCAD automatically add a dimension suffix or prefix to all dimensions instead of just a chosen few by using the Suffix or Prefix option in the Primary Units tab of the New Dimension Style or Modify Dimension Style dialog box. See Appendix D on the book's companion website for more on this feature.

AutoCAD provides the associative dimensioning capability to update dimension text automatically when a drawing is edited. Objects called *definition points* determine how edited dimensions are updated.

The definition points are located at the same points you pick when you determine the dimension location. For example, the definition points for linear dimensions are the extension line origins. The definition points for a circle diameter are the points used to pick the circle and the opposite side of the circle. The definition points for a radius are the points used to pick the circle plus the center of the circle.

Definition points are point objects. They're difficult to see because they're usually covered by the feature they define. You can, however, see them indirectly by using grips. The definition points of a dimension are the same as the dimension's grip points. You can see them by clicking a dimension. Try the following:

1. Make sure the Grips feature is turned on. (See Chapter 2 to refresh your memory on the Grips feature.)

2. Click the longest of the three vertical dimensions you drew in the earlier exercise. You'll see the grips of the dimension, as shown in Figure 11.18.

**FIGURE 11.18**
The grip points are the same as the definition points on a dimension.

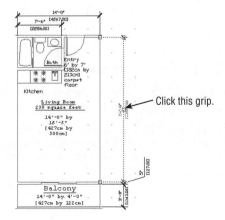

## Using Grips to Make Minor Adjustments to Dimensions

The definition points, whose location you can see through their grips, are located on their own unique layer called *Defpoints*. Definition points are displayed regardless of whether the Defpoints layer is on or off. To get an idea of how these definition points work, try the following exercises, which show you how to manipulate the definition points directly.

In this exercise, you'll use coordinates to move a dimension line:

1. With the grips visible, click the grip near the dimension text.

2. Move the cursor around. When you move the cursor vertically, the text moves along the dimension line. When you move the cursor horizontally, the dimension line and text move together, keeping their parallel orientation to the dimensioned floor plan. Here the entire dimension line, including the text, moves. In a later exercise, you'll see how you can move the dimension text independently of the dimension line.

3. Enter @9´<0↵. Metric users should enter @275<0↵. The dimension line, text, and dimension extensions stretch to the new location to the right of the text (see Figure 11.19).

**FIGURE 11.19**

Moving the dimension line by using its grip

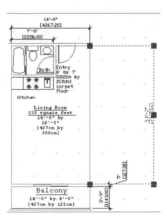

In step 3 of the previous exercise, you saw that you can specify an exact distance for the dimension line's new location by entering a relative polar coordinate. Cartesian coordinates work just as well. You can even use object snaps to relocate dimension lines.

---

### MAKING CHANGES TO MULTIPLE DIMENSIONS

You can use the Dimension Edit tool to edit existing dimensions quickly. This tool gives you the ability to edit more than one dimension's text at one time. One common use for the Dimension Edit tool is to change a string of dimensions to read Equal instead of showing the actual dimensioned distance. The following example shows an alternative to using the Properties Inspector palette for appending text to a dimension:

1. Type **DED↵**.

2. At the prompt

   ```
   Enter type of dimension editing [Home/New/Rotate/Oblique]<Home>:
   ```

   type **N↵** to use the New option. The in-place text editor and Text Editor visor opens, showing 0 in the text box.

3. Use the arrow keys to move the cursor behind or in front of the 0, and then enter the text you want to append to the dimension. You can remove the 0 and replace the dimension with your text as an alternative.

4. Click Save on the Text Editor visor.

5. At the Select objects: prompt, pick the dimensions you want to edit. The Select objects: prompt remains, enabling you to select several dimensions.

6. Press ↵ to finish your selection. The dimension changes to include your new text or to replace the existing dimension text.

The Dimension Edit tool is useful in editing dimension text, but you can also use this tool to make graphical changes to the text. Here is a list of the other Dimension Edit tool options:

**Home**  Moves the dimension text to its standard default position and angle.

**Rotate**  Rotates the dimension text to a new angle.

**Oblique**  Skews the dimension extension lines to a new angle. (See the section "Skewing Dimension Lines" later in this chapter.)

Next, try moving the dimension line back by using the Perpendicular osnap:

1. Click the grip at the bottom of the dimension line you just edited.

2. Type **PERP↵** at the command line.

3. Place the cursor on the vertical dimension line that dimensions the balcony and click it.

4. Click View ➢ Zoom ➢ All from the menu bar (or type **Z ↵ A↵**) and then choose File ➢ Save from the menu bar (or type **QSAVE↵**) to save this file in its current state.

The selected dimension line moves to align with the other vertical dimension, back to its original location.

## Changing Style Settings of Individual Dimensions

In some cases, you have to change an individual dimension's style settings in order to edit it. For example, if you try to move the text of a typical linear dimension, you may find that the text and dimension lines are inseparable. You need to make a change to the dimension style setting that controls how AutoCAD locates dimension text in relation to the dimension line. This section describes how you can change the style settings of individual dimensions to facilitate changes in the dimension.

You've seen how dimension text is attached to the dimension line so that when the text is moved, the dimension line follows. You may encounter situations in which you want to move the text independently of the dimension line. The following steps show how you can separate dimension text from its dimension line. These steps also show how you can change a single dimension's style settings:

1. Click the dimension you want to edit to expose its grips.

2. On the Properties Inspector palette, scroll down the list of properties until you see the Fit category. If you don't see a list of options under Fit, click the disclosure triangle next to Fit.

3. Scroll farther down the list until you see the Text Movement option to the left of the Text Movement listing, and then click this option.

4. Click the arrow that appears next to Keep Dim Line With Text listing to open the pop-up menu; then select the Move Text, Add Leader option (Figure 11.20).

**FIGURE 11.20**
Select the Move Text, Add Leader option.

In the Properties Inspector palette, the Move Text, Add Leader option in the Text Movement listing of the Fit category lets you move the dimension text independently of the dimension line. It also draws a leader from the dimension line to the text. Another option—Move Text, No Leader—does the same thing but doesn't include a leader. You can also set these options for a dimension style by using the Text Placement options in the Fit tab of the New Dimension Style or Modify Dimension Style dialog box.

As you can see from these steps, the Properties Inspector palette gives you access to many of the settings you saw for setting up dimension styles. The main difference here is that the Properties Inspector affects only the dimensions you've selected.

---

### PLACING DIMENSIONS OVER HATCH PATTERNS

If a hatch pattern or solid fill completely covers a dimension, you can use the TEXTTOFRONT command to have AutoCAD draw the dimension over the hatch or solid fill.

**MODIFYING THE DIMENSION STYLE SETTINGS BY USING OVERRIDE**

You just used the Properties Inspector palette to facilitate moving the dimension text. You can choose Dimension ➢ Override in the menu bar (Dimoverride command) to accomplish the same thing. You can also click the Override tool on the Tool Sets palette when the Dimensions tool group is expanded. The Override tool enables you to change an individual dimension's style settings. Here's an example that shows how you can use the Override option:

1. Press the Esc key twice to make sure you aren't in the middle of a command. Then choose Dimension ➢ Override in the menu bar.

2. At the following prompt, type **DIMFIT**↵:

   ```
   Enter dimension variable name to override or [Clear overrides]:
   ```

3. At the `Enter new value for dimension variable <3>:` prompt, enter **4**↵. This has the same effect as selecting Move Text, Add Leader from the Fit category of the Properties Inspector palette.

4. The `Enter dimension variable name to override:` prompt appears again, enabling you to enter another dimension variable. Press ↵ to move to the next step.

5. At the `Select objects:` prompt, select the dimension you want to change. You can select a set of dimensions if you want to change several dimensions at once. Press ↵ when you've finished with your selection. The dimension settings change for the selected dimensions.

As you can see from this example, the Dimoverride command requires that you know exactly which dimension variable to edit in order to make the desired modification. In this case, setting the Dimfit variable to 4 lets you move the dimension text independently of the dimension line. If you find the Dimoverride command useful, consult Appendix D to determine which system variable corresponds to the Dimension Style dialog box settings. You can find Appendix D on the book's companion website.

In a previous exercise, you changed the format setting of a single dimension *after* it was placed. These settings can be made a standard part of your My Architectural dimension style by using the Modify button in the Dimension Style Manager dialog box.

If you have multiple dimension styles and you want to change an existing dimension to the current dimension style, use the Update Dimension tool. Choose Update Dimension on the Dimensions tool group or type **-DIMSTYLE**↵ **A**↵. Then select the dimensions you want to change and press ↵. The selected dimensions will be converted to the current style.

**ROTATING AND POSITIONING DIMENSION TEXT**

Once in a while, dimension text works better if it's kept in a horizontal orientation, even if the dimension itself isn't horizontal. To rotate dimension text, choose Dimension ➢ Align Text ➢ Angle from the menu bar, select the dimension text, and then enter an angle or select two points to indicate an angle graphically. You can also enter **0**↵ to return the dimension text to its default angle.

If you need to move the dimension text to the left, center, or right of the dimension line, you can use the Left, Center, or Right tool in the Align Text submenu.

## Editing Dimensions and Other Objects Together

It's helpful to be able to edit a dimension directly by using its grips. But the key feature of AutoCAD's dimensions is their ability to adjust themselves *automatically* to changes in the drawing.

To see how this works, try moving the living room closer to the bathroom wall. You can move a group of lines and vertices by using the Stretch command and the Crossing option:

1. Make sure the Annotation tool set is current on the Tool Sets palette by clicking and holding down the Tool Sets button.

2. Click the Stretch tool in the Tool Sets palette, or type **S↵** and then **C↵**. You'll see the following prompts:

   ```
   At the Select objects to stretch by crossing-window or crossing-polygon...
   Select objects: C
   Specify first corner:
   ```

3. Pick and drag a crossing window, as illustrated in Figure 11.21, and then press ↵ to confirm your selection.

**FIGURE 11.21**

The Stretch crossing window

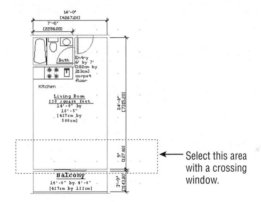

Select this area with a crossing window.

4. At the Specify base point or [Displacement] <Displacement>: prompt, pick any point on the screen.

5. At the Specify second point or <use first point as displacement>: prompt, enter **@2′<90↵** to move the wall 2′ in a 90° direction. The wall moves, and the dimension text changes to reflect the new dimensions, as shown in Figure 11.22.

6. After viewing the result of using the Stretch tool, choose Edit ➢ Undo from the menu bar or type **U↵** to change the drawing back to its previous state.

You can also use the Mirror, Rotate, and Stretch commands with dimensions. The polar arrays also work, and you can use Extend and Trim with linear dimensions.

When you're editing dimensioned objects, be sure to select the dimension associated with the object being edited. As you select objects, using the crossing window (C) or crossing polygon (CP) selection option helps you include the dimensions. For more on these selection options, see Chapter 2.

**FIGURE 11.22**
The moved wall,
with the updated
dimensions

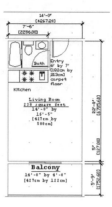

## Associating Dimensions with Objects

You've seen how dimensions and the objects they're associated with can move together so that the dimension remains connected to the object. When you're in the process of editing a drawing, dimensions may lose their association with objects, so you may need to re-create an association between a dimension and an object. The following steps show you how this is done:

1. Click Reassociate Dimension from the Tool Sets palette. You can also type **DRE**↵ at the Command prompt.

2. At the following prompt, select the dimension that you want to reassociate with an object, and then press ↵:

   ```
   Select dimensions to reassociate
   Select Objects:
   ```

3. At the Specify first extension line origin or [Select object] <next>: prompt, an X appears at one of the dimension's definition points.

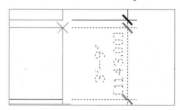

4. Use the Endpoint osnap, and click the end of the object you want to have connected to the definition point indicated in step 3.

5. An X appears at the dimension's other definition point. Use the Endpoint osnap again, and click the other endpoint of the object you want associated with the dimension. You now have the dimension associated with the endpoints of the object. You may have to adjust the location of the dimension line at this point.

In step 3, you see an X at the location of a dimension definition point. If the definition point is already associated with an object, the X appears with a box around it. The box is a reminder that the definition point is already associated with an object and that you'll be changing its association. In this situation, you can press ↵ to switch to the dimension's other definition point.

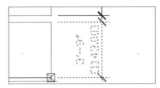

Also in step 3, you have the option to select an object. This option enables you to associate the dimension with an entire object instead of with just one endpoint. If you type **S**↵ at that prompt in step 3, you can then select the object you want to associate with the dimension. The dimension changes so that its definition points coincide with the endpoints of the object. The dimension remains in its original orientation. For example, a vertical dimension remains vertical even if you associate the dimension with a horizontal line. In this situation, the dimension dutifully dimensions the endpoints of the line but shows a distance of zero.

---

**REMOVING DIMENSION ASSOCIATIONS**

You can remove a dimension's association with an object by using the Dimdisassociate command. Type **DIMDISASSOCIATE**↵ at the Command prompt, select the dimension(s), and then press ↵.

---

## Adding a String of Dimensions with a Single Operation

AutoCAD provides a method for creating a string of dimensions by using a single operation. The Qdim command lets you select a set of objects instead of having to select points. The following exercise demonstrates how the Qdim command works:

1. If you haven't done so already, zoom out so you have an overall view of the Unit floor plan.

2. Click Quick Dimension on the Dimensions tool group of the Tool Sets palette.

3. At the `Select geometry to dimension:` prompt, place a selection window around the entire left-side wall of the unit.

4. Press ↵ to finish your selection. The following prompt appears:

```
Specify dimension line position, or
[Continuous/Staggered/Baseline/Ordinate/Radius/Diameter/
datumPoint/Edit/seTtings] <Continuous>:
```

**5.** Click a point to the left of the wall to place the dimension. A string of dimensions appears, displaying all the dimensions for the wall (Figure 11.23).

**FIGURE 11.23**
The dimensions for
the wall

**6.** When you've finished reviewing the results of this exercise, exit the file without saving it.

The prompt in step 4 indicates several types of dimensions you can choose from. For example, if you want the dimensions to originate from a single baseline, you can enter **B↵** in step 4 to select the Baseline option.

The Qdim command can be a time-saver when you want to dimension a wall quickly. It may not work in all situations, but if the object you're dimensioning is fairly simple, it can be all you need.

In this exercise, you used a simple window to select the wall. For more complex shapes, try using a crossing polygon selection window. See Chapter 2 for more on crossing polygons.

## Adding or Removing the Alternate Dimensions

You may eventually encounter a drawing that contains alternate dimensions, as shown in some of the figures earlier in this chapter. You can remove those alternate dimensions by turning off the alternate dimension features. Here's how it's done:

**1.** Choose Format ➤ Dimension Style on the menu bar or enter **D↵** to open the Dimension Style Manager.

**2.** Select the style that uses the alternate units. Below the Styles list box, click the Options action menu and choose Modify.

**3.** Click the Alternate Units tab.

**4.** Click the Display Alternate Units check box to remove the check mark.

**5.** Click OK, and then click Close to close the Dimension Style Manager.

The dimensions that use the style you just edited change to remove the alternate dimensions. You can also perform the reverse operation and add alternate dimensions to an existing set of dimensions. Follow the steps shown here, but instead of removing the check mark in step 4, add it, and make the appropriate setting changes to the rest of the Alternate Units tab.

---

**USING OBJECT SNAP WHILE DIMENSIONING**

When you pick intersections and endpoints frequently, as you do during dimensioning, it can be inconvenient to use the Object Snap shortcut menu. If you know you'll be using certain osnaps frequently, you can use Running Osnaps. (See the sidebar "The Osnap Options" in Chapter 3 for more on setting up Running Osnaps.)

After you've designated your Running Osnaps, the next time you're prompted to select a point, the selected osnap modes are automatically activated. You can still override the default settings by using the Object Snap shortcut menu (Right-click the right mouse button).

There is a drawback to setting the Running Osnaps mode: When your drawing gets crowded, you can end up picking the wrong point by accident. However, you can easily toggle the Running Osnaps mode off by right-clicking Object Snap in the Status Bar palette.

---

## Dimensioning Non-orthogonal Objects

So far, you've been reading about how to work with linear dimensions. You can also dimension non-orthogonal objects, such as circles, arcs, triangles, and trapezoids. In the following sections, you'll practice dimensioning a non-orthogonal object.

For the following exercises, you'll use a drawing of a hexagonal-shaped window. Open the 11a-wind.dwg file from the sample files; metric users should open the 11a-wind-metric.dwg file. You can use this file to follow along.

### Dimensioning Non-orthogonal Linear Distances

Now you'll dimension the window. The unusual shape of the window prevents you from using the horizontal or vertical dimensions you've used already. However, choosing Aligned in the Dimensions tool group enables you to dimension at an angle:

1. Click the Aligned tool in the Tool Sets palette. You can also enter **DAL**↵ to start the aligned dimension.

2. At the Specify first extension line origin or <select object>: prompt, press ↵. You could pick extension line origins as you did in earlier examples, but pressing ↵ shows you firsthand how the Select Object option works.

3. At the Select object to dimension: prompt, pick the upper-right face of the hexagon. As the prompt indicates, you can also pick an arc or a circle for this type of dimension.

4. At the Specify dimension line location or [Mtext/Text/Angle]: prompt, pick a point. The dimension appears in the drawing similar to Figure 11.24.

Just as with linear dimensions, you can enter **T**↵ in step 4 to enter alternate text for the dimension.

**FIGURE 11.24**
The aligned dimension of a non-orthogonal line

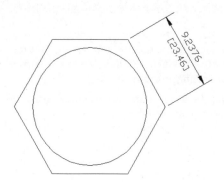

Next, you'll dimension a face of the hexagon. Instead of its actual length, however, you'll dimension a distance at a specified angle—the distance from the center of the face:

1. Click the Linear Dimension tool from the Tool Sets palette or type **DLI**↵.

2. At the Specify first extension line origin or <select object>: prompt, press ↵.

3. At the Select object to dimension: prompt, pick the lower-right face of the hexagon.

4. At the Specify dimension line location or [Mtext/Text/Angle/Horizontal/ Vertical/Rotated]: prompt, type **R**↵ to select the Rotated option.

5. At the Specify angle of dimension line <0>: prompt, enter **30**↵.

6. At the Specify dimension line location or [Mtext/Text/Angle/Horizontal/ Vertical/Rotated]: prompt, pick a point so it will appear as shown in Figure 11.25.

**FIGURE 11.25**
A linear dimension using the Rotated option

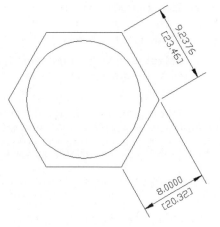

## Dimensioning Radii, Diameters, and Arcs

To dimension circular objects, you use another set of options from the Dimensions tool group or Dimension menu:

1. Click the Linear Dimension flyout on the Tool Sets palette to reveal the Angular tool. You can also type **DAN**↵.

2. At the Select arc, circle, line, or <specify vertex>: prompt, pick the upper-left face of the hexagon.

3. At the Select second line: prompt, pick the top face so that it will look like Figure 11.26.

4. At the Specify dimension arc line location or [Mtext/Text/Angle]: prompt, notice that as you move the cursor around the upper-left corner of the hexagon, the dimension changes, as shown in the top images of Figure 11.26.

5. Pick a point as shown in the bottom image of Figure 11.26. The dimension is fixed in the drawing.

**FIGURE 11.26**
The angular dimension added to the window frame

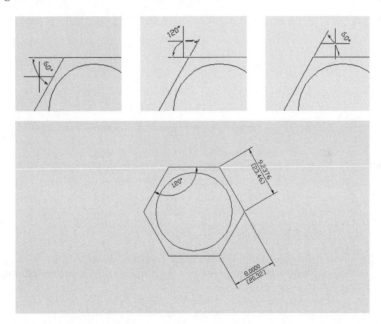

If you need to make subtle adjustments to the dimension line or text location, you can do so using grips after you place the angular dimension.

Now try the Diameter tool, which shows the diameter of a circle:

1. Click the Linear Dimension flyout on the Tool Sets palette to reveal the Diameter tool. You can also enter **DDI**↵ at the Command prompt.

2. At the Select arc or circle: prompt, pick the circle.

3. At the Specify dimension line location or [Mtext/Text/Angle]: prompt, you see the diameter dimension drag along the circle as you move the cursor. If you move the cursor outside the circle, the dimension line and text also move outside the circle. (See the top image in Figure 11.27.)

**FIGURE 11.27**
Dimension showing the diameter of a circle

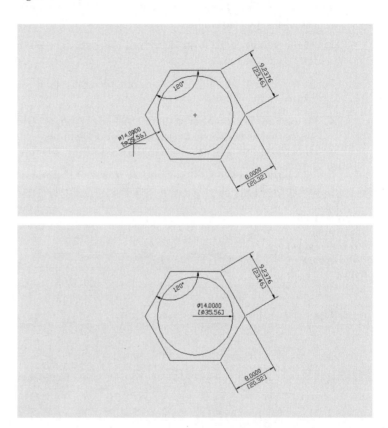

If the dimension text can't fit in the circle, AutoCAD gives you the option to place it outside the circle as you drag the temporary dimension to a horizontal position.

4. Place the cursor inside the circle so the dimension arrow points in a horizontal direction, as shown in the bottom image of Figure 11.27.

5. With the text centered, click the mouse.

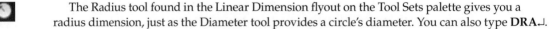

The Radius tool found in the Linear Dimension flyout on the Tool Sets palette gives you a radius dimension, just as the Diameter tool provides a circle's diameter. You can also type **DRA**↵.

Figure 11.28 shows a radius dimension on the inside of the circle, but you can place it outside in a manner similar to how you place the diameter dimension. The Center Mark tool on the expanded Dimensions tool group places a cross mark in the center of the selected arc or circle.

**Jogged**

**FIGURE 11.28**
A radius dimension shown on the inside of the circle

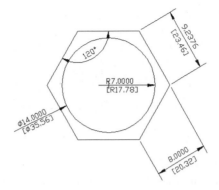

If you need to dimension an arc or a circle whose center isn't in the drawing area, you can use the jogged dimension. Here are the steps:

1. Click the Jogged tool from the Linear Dimension flyout on the Annotation tool set's Dimensions tool group, or enter **DJO**↵.

2. At the Select arc or circle: prompt, select the object you want to dimension.

3. At the Specify center location override: prompt, select a point that indicates the general direction to the center of the arc or circle. A dimension line appears and follows the movement of your cursor.

4. Position the dimension line where you want it, and then click.

5. Position the dimension line jog where you want it, and then click. The jogged dimension is placed in the drawing (Figure 11.29).

Arc lengths can also be given a dimension using the Arc Length tool. Choose the Arc Length tool from the Linear Dimension flyout on the Dimensions tool group, or enter **DAR**↵ at the Command prompt. At the Select Arc or polyline arc segment: prompt, select the arc you want to dimension. It can be either a plain arc or a polyline arc. Once you've selected the arc, the arc dimension appears and moves with the cursor. You can then select the location for the dimension.

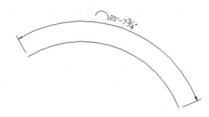

**FIGURE 11.29**
The jogged dimension in the drawing

## Skewing Dimension Lines

At times, you may need to force the extension lines to take on an angle other than 90° to the dimension line. This is a common requirement of isometric drawings, in which most lines are at 30° or 60° angles instead of 90°. To facilitate non-orthogonal dimensions like these, AutoCAD offers the Oblique option:

1.  Choose Dimension ➢ Oblique from the menu bar, or type **DED⏎ O⏎**.

2.  At the Select objects: prompt, pick the aligned dimension in the upper-right portion of the drawing, and press ⏎ to confirm your selection.

3.  At the Enter obliquing angle (press ENTER for none): prompt, enter **60⏎** for 60°. The dimension will skew so that the extension lines are at 60° (Figure 11.30).

**FIGURE 11.30**
The extension lines at 60°

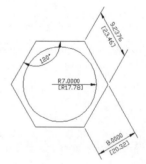

## Adding a Note with a Leader Arrow

One type of dimension is something like a text-dimension hybrid. The Multileader tool lets you add a text note combined with an arrow that points to an object in your drawing. Multileaders are easy to use and offer the same text-formatting tools as the Mtext tool. Try the following exercise to get familiar with multileaders:

1.  Click the Multileader tool in the Tool Sets palette (see Figure 11.31), select Dimension ➢ Multileader on the menu bar, or enter **MLD⏎**.

**FIGURE 11.31**
The Leaders panel

Multileader        Add Leader
Align Leaders       Remove Leader
Collect Leaders

2. At the Specify leader arrowhead location or [leader Landing first/Content first/Options] <Options>: prompt, pick a point near the top-left edge of the hexagon.

3. At the Specify leader landing location: prompt, enter @6<110↵. Metric users should enter @**15<110**↵. The Text Editor visor appears, along with the in-place text editor at the note location.

4. Enter **Window Frame** for the note, and then click Save in the Text Editor visor. Your note appears with the leader arrow similar to the one in Figure 11.32.

**FIGURE 11.32**
The leader with a
note added

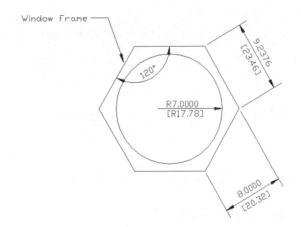

The text in the note is in the current text style unless you specify another style in the Text tab of the New Dimension Style or Modify Dimension Style dialog box. (For more information, see the section "The Text Tab" in Appendix D on the book's companion website.)

**SETTING THE SCALE OF LEADERS**

Multileaders have an Annotative option that allows them to automatically adjust to the scale of the drawing. You can find the Annotative option setting in the properties for a specific multileader in the drawing or in the multileader style setting. See the Scale option in Table 11.2, later in this chapter, under Leader Structure tab.

The Multileader tool offers a lot of options that aren't obvious when you're using it. In step 1 of the previous example, after clicking Multileader, you can press ↵ to modify the behavior of the Multileader tool. You'll see the following prompt:

```
Enter an option [Leader type/leader lAnding/Content
  type/Maxpoints/First angle/Second angle/eXit options]
  <eXit options>:
```

Table 11.1 gives you a rundown of these options and their functions.

**TABLE 11.1:** The Multileader options

| OPTION | FUNCTION |
| --- | --- |
| Leader type | Allows you to choose between straight-line leaders, curved leaders, or no leaders. |
| Leader lAnding | Determines whether a leader landing is used. The *leader landing* is the short line that connects the arrow to the note. Also lets you set landing distance. |
| Content type | Lets you select between Mtext or a block for the leader note. You also have the option to choose None. |
| Maxpoints | Lets you set the number of points you select for the leader. The default is 2. |
| First angle | Lets you constrain the angle of the leader line to a fixed value. |
| Second angle | Lets you constrain the angle of the arrow's second line segment if you're using more than two points for the Maxpoints option. |
| eXit options | Lets you return to the main part of the Multileader command to draw the leader. |

## Creating Multileader Styles

Besides using the options shown in Table 11.1, you can create multileader styles to control the appearance of multileaders. Multileader styles are similar in concept to text and dimension styles. They allow you to set up the appearance of the leader under a name that you can call up anytime. For example, you may want to have one type of leader that uses a block instead of text for the note and another leader that uses a dot in place of an arrowhead. Alternatively, you may want to set up a style that uses curved lines instead of straight ones for the leader line. You can create a multileader style for each of these types of leader features and then switch between the leader styles, depending on the requirements of your leader note.

To set up or modify a multileader style, click Format ➤ Multileader Style from the menu bar or type **MLS**⏎ at the Command prompt. This opens the Multileader Style Manager, shown in Figure 11.33. From here, you can select an existing style from the list on the left and click the Options action menu and choose Modify to edit it, or you can click New (plus symbol) to create a new one. If you click New, you're asked to select an existing style as a basis for your new style.

When you create a multileader style, the Create New Multileader Style dialog box appears. And when you Modify a multileader, the Modify Multileader Style dialog box opens (Figure 11.34).

Table 11.2 describes the options in each of the tabs of the Modify Multileader Style dialog box. Some of these options are the same as those for the Multileader command.

**FIGURE 11.33**
The Multileader
Style Manager

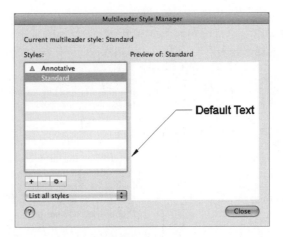

**FIGURE 11.34**
The Modify
Multileader
Style dialog box

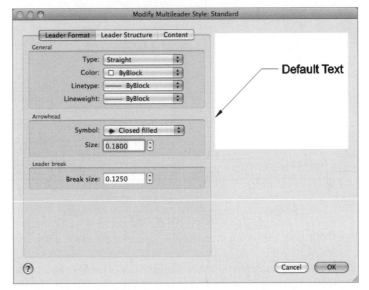

**TABLE 11.2:** The Modify Multileader Style dialog box options

| TAB AND PANEL | FUNCTION |
|---|---|
| **Leader Format tab** | |
| General | Lets you set the leader line to straight or curved. You can also set the color, linetype, and line weight for the leader line. |
| Arrowhead | Controls the arrowhead type and the arrowhead size. |

**TABLE 11.2:** The Modify Multileader Style dialog box options *(CONTINUED)*

| TAB AND PANEL | FUNCTION |
|---|---|
| Leader Break | Controls the size of the gap in a leader line when the Leaderbreak command is applied. Leaderbreak places a break on a leader line where two leader lines cross. |
| **Leader Structure tab** | |
| Constrain | Determines the number of line segments in the leader line. You can also apply angle constraints to the leader-line segments. |
| Landing | Controls the leader-line landing segment. This is the last line segment that points to the note. |
| Scale | Lets you control the scale of the leader components. You can either apply a fixed scale or use the Annotative option to have the drawing annotation scale apply to the leader. |
| **Content tab** | |
| Multileader Type | Lets you select the type of object that will be used for the leader note. The options are Mtext, Block, and None. |
| Text Options | Gives you control over the way the leader note appears. You can control color, text style, size, justification, and orientation. |
| Leader Connection | Determines the position between the leader line and the note. |

Once you've set up a multileader style, you can make it the default style by selecting it from the Multileader Style pop-up menu in the Annotation category on the Properties Inspector palette.

The selected style will be applied to any new multileader you add to your drawing. You can also change the style of an existing multileader. To do this, click Format ➤ Multileader Style from the menu bar to open the Multileader Style Manager, and then select the multileader style you want from the Styles group as was shown in Figure 11.33.

## Editing Multileader Notes

If you need to make changes to the note portion of a multileader, you can do so by double-clicking the note. This brings up the in-place text editor and the Text Editor visor, allowing you to make changes as you would in a word processor.

At other times, you may want to change the leader line, arrows, or other graphic features of the multileader. For example, you may want to have all the notes aligned vertically for a neater appearance. As another option, you may want to add more leader arrows so the note points to several objects in the drawing instead of just one.

The Leaders panel on the Tool Sets palette offers several tools that let you make these types of changes to your leader notes (refer back to Figure 11.31). The Add Leader and Remove Leader tools let you add or remove leaders from a multileader. The Add Leader tool is a handy tool if you want a single note to point to several objects. The Align Leaders tool lets you align the note portion of several multileaders. Finally, the Collect Leaders tool lets you collect several multileaders that use blocks for notes into a single note.

### Breaking a Dimension Line for a Leader

In a crowded drawing, your multileader arrow may have to cross over a dimension line. In many drafting conventions, when a leader line crosses over a dimension line, the dimension line must be shown with a gap.

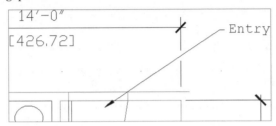

You can apply a gap to a dimension line using the Break Dimension tool. Here's how it works:

1. Click Dimension Break from the Tool Sets palette.

2. At the `Select dimension to add/remove break or [Multiple]:` prompt, select a dimension line, or enter **M⏎** and select multiple dimension lines.

3. When you're finished with your selection, press ⏎. Note that this ⏎ is necessary only when using the Multiple option.

4. At the `Select object to break dimensions or [Auto/Remove] <Auto>:` prompt, press ⏎. A gap appears wherever a leader line or other dimension line crosses over the selected dimension line.

If you prefer to indicate a break manually, enter **M⏎** at the prompt in step 4. This allows you to select two points on the dimension, indicating where the gap is to occur. If additional dimension or leader lines are added that cross over the dimension line, repeat your use of the Break Dimension tool. To remove an existing break, use the Remove option in step 4 by entering **R⏎**.

## Applying Ordinate Dimensions

In mechanical drafting, *ordinate dimensions* are used to maintain the accuracy of a machined part by establishing an origin on the part. All major dimensions are described as X coordinates or Y coordinates of that origin. The origin is usually an easily locatable feature of the part, such as a machined bore or two machined surfaces.

Figure 11.35 shows a typical application of ordinate dimensions. In the lower-right corner, note the two dimensions whose leaders are jogged. Also note the origin location in the center circle.

**FIGURE 11.35**
A drawing using
ordinate dimensions

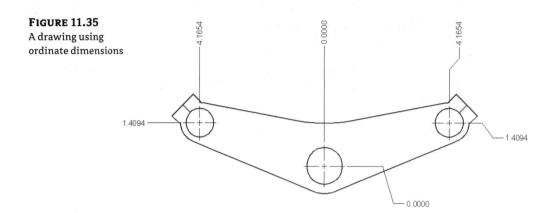

To use the Dimordinate command, perform the following steps:

1. On the Drafting tool set of the Tool Sets palette, expand the Coordinates tool group and click Set UCS Origin, or type **UCS↵ OR↵**.

2. At the `Specify new origin point <0,0,0>:` prompt, click the exact location of the origin of your part.

3. Toggle Ortho Mode on in the Status Bar palette.

4. Choose Dimension ➤ Ordinate on the menu bar. You can also enter **DOR↵** or click Ordinate from the Linear Dimension flyout on the Dimensions tool group to start the ordinate dimension.

5. At the `Specify feature location:` prompt, click the item you want to dimension. The direction of the leader determines whether the dimension will be of the Xdatum or the Ydatum.

6. At the `Specify leader endpoint or [Xdatum/Ydatum/Mtext/Text/Angle]:` prompt, indicate the length and direction of the leader. Do this by positioning the rubber-banding leader perpendicular to the coordinate direction you want to dimension and then clicking that point.

In steps 1 and 2, you used the UCS feature to establish a second origin in the drawing. The Ordinate tool then uses that origin to determine the ordinate dimensions. You'll get a chance to work with the UCS feature in Chapter 20, "Using Advanced 3D Features."

You may have noticed options in the command line for the Ordinate tool. The Xdatum and Ydatum options force the dimension to be of the X or Y coordinate no matter what direction the leader takes. The Mtext option displays the in-place text editor and Text Editor visor, enabling you to append or replace the ordinate dimension text. The Text option lets you enter replacement text directly through the Command prompt.

If you turn off Ortho mode, the dimension leader is drawn with a jog to maintain the orthogonal (look back at Figure 11.35).

# Adding Tolerance Notation

In mechanical drafting, *tolerances* are a key part of a drawing's notation. They specify the allowable variation in size and shape that a mechanical part can have. To help facilitate tolerance notation, AutoCAD provides the Tolerance command, which offers common ISO tolerance symbols together with a quick way to build a standard feature-control symbol. *Feature-control symbols* are industry-standard symbols used to specify tolerances. If you're a mechanical engineer or drafter, AutoCAD's tolerance notation options will be a valuable tool. However, a full discussion of tolerances requires a basic understanding of mechanical design and drafting and is beyond the scope of this book.

To use the Tolerance command, click Tolerance from the expanded Dimensions tool group, choose Dimension ➤ Tolerance on the menu bar, or type **TOL**↵ at the Command prompt to open the Geometric Tolerance dialog box (Figure 11.36).

**FIGURE 11.36**
The Geometric Tolerance dialog box

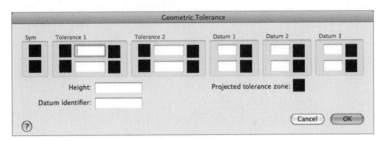

This is where you enter tolerance and datum values for the feature-control symbol. You can enter two tolerance values and three datum values. In addition, you can stack values in a two-tiered fashion.

Click a box in the Sym group to open the Symbol dialog box.

The top portion of Figure 11.37 shows what each symbol in the Symbol dialog box represents. The bottom image shows a sample drawing with a feature symbol used on a cylindrical object. The symbols in the sample drawing show that the upper cylinder needs to be parallel within 0.003″ of the lower cylinder. Note that mechanical drawings often use measurements in thousandths, so 0.3 means 0.003.

In the Geometric Tolerance dialog box, you can click a box in any of the Datum groups or a box in the right side of the Tolerance groups to open the Material Condition dialog box. This dialog box contains standard symbols relating to the maximum and minimum material conditions of a feature on the part being dimensioned.

**FIGURE 11.37**
The tolerance symbols

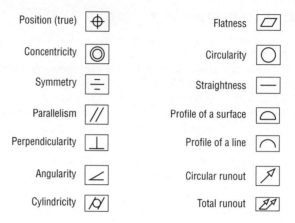

| | |
|---|---|
| Position (true) ⊕ | Flatness ▱ |
| Concentricity ◎ | Circularity ○ |
| Symmetry ⌱ | Straightness — |
| Parallelism // | Profile of a surface ⌓ |
| Perpendicularity ⊥ | Profile of a line ⌒ |
| Angularity ∠ | Circular runout ⌁ |
| Cylindricity ⌭ | Total runout ⌁⌁ |

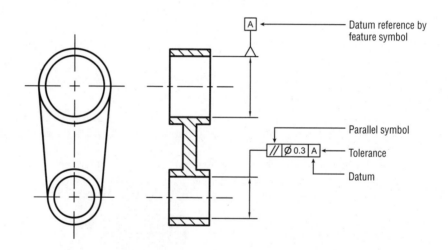

Datum reference by feature symbol

Parallel symbol

// ⌀ 0.3 A

Tolerance

Datum

## Adding Inspection Dimensions

Another type of dimension related to tolerances is the inspection dimension. This is a type of dimension notation that indicates how often the tolerances of a dimension should be checked.

To add an inspection dimension, first add a regular linear dimension as described in the early part of this chapter. Next, follow these steps:

1. Click Inspect Dimension from Tool Sets palette, choose Dimension ➢ Inspection from the menu bar, or type **DIMINSPECT**↵. The Inspection Dimension dialog box appears (Figure 11.38).

**FIGURE 11.38**
The Inspection
Dimension
dialog box

2. Click the Select Dimensions tool. The dialog box temporarily closes to allow you to select a dimension.

3. Select a shape option from the Shape group.

4. Enter values for the Label and Inspection Rate input boxes, and then click OK.

The dimension appears with the additional changes from the dialog box (Figure 11.39).

**FIGURE 11.39**
The dimension
with the addi-
tional changes

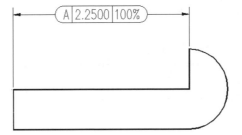

# The Bottom Line

**Understand the components of a dimension.** Before you start to dimension with AutoCAD, it helps to become familiar with the different parts of a dimension. This will help you set up your dimensions to fit the style of dimensions that you need.

**Master It** Name a few of the dimension components.

**Create a dimension style.** As you become more familiar with technical drawing and drafting, you'll learn that there are standard formats for drawing dimensions. Arrows, text size, and even the way dimension lines are drawn are all subject to a standard format. Fortunately, AutoCAD offers dimension styles that let you set up your dimension format once and then call up that format whenever you need it.

**Master It** What is the name of the dialog box that lets you manage dimension styles, and how do you open it?

**Draw linear dimensions.**   The most common dimension you'll use is the linear dimension. Knowing how to place a linear dimension is a big first step in learning how to dimension in AutoCAD.

**Master It**   Name the three locations you're asked for when placing a linear dimension.

**Edit dimensions.**   Dimensions often change in the course of a project, so you should know how to make changes to dimension text or other parts of a dimension.

**Master It**   How do you start the command to edit dimension text?

**Dimension non-orthogonal objects.**   Not everything you dimension will use linear dimensions. AutoCAD offers a set of dimension tools for dimensioning objects that aren't made up of straight lines.

**Master It**   Name some of the types of objects for which a linear dimension isn't appropriate.

**Add a note with a leader arrow.**   In addition to dimensions, you'll probably add lots of notes with arrows pointing to features in a design. AutoCAD offers the multileader for this purpose.

**Master It**   What two types of objects does the multileader combine?

**Apply ordinate dimensions.**   When accuracy counts, ordinate dimensions are often used because they measure distances that are similar to coordinates from a single feature.

**Master It**   What AutoCAD feature that isn't strictly associated with dimensions do you use for ordinate dimensions?

**Add tolerance notation.**   Mechanical drafting often requires the use of special notation to describe tolerances. AutoCAD offers some predefined symbols that address the need to include tolerance notation in a drawing.

**Master It**   How do you open the Geometric Tolerance dialog box?

# Part 3

# Mastering Advanced Skills

# Chapter 12

# Using Attributes

Early in this book, you learned how to create blocks, which are assemblies of AutoCAD objects. Blocks enable you to form parts or symbols that can be easily reproduced. Furniture, bolts, doors, and windows are a few common items that you can create with blocks. Whole rooms and appliances can also be made into blocks. There is no limit to a block's size.

AutoCAD also offers a feature called *attributes* that allows you to store text information as a part of a block. For example, you can store the material specifications for a bolt or other mechanical part that you've converted into a block. If your application is architecture, you can store the material, hardware, and dimensional information for a door or window that has been converted into a block. You can then quickly gather information about that block that may not be obvious from the graphics. By using attributes, you can keep track of virtually any object in a drawing or maintain textual information in the drawing that can be queried.

Keeping track of objects is just one way to use attributes. You can also use them in place of text objects when you must keep text and graphic items together. In this chapter, you'll use attributes for one of their common functions: maintaining lists of parts. In this case, the parts are doors. This chapter also describes how to import these attributes into a database-management program. As you go through the exercises, think about the ways attributes can help you in your particular application.

In this chapter, you'll learn to do the following:

◆ Create attributes

◆ Edit attributes

## Creating Attributes

Attributes depend on blocks. You might think of an attribute as text information attached to a block. The information can be a description of the block or some other pertinent text. For example, you can include an attribute definition with the Door block you created in Chapter 4, "Organizing Objects with Blocks and Groups." Subsequently, every time you insert the Door block, you'll be prompted for a value associated with that door. The value can be a number, a height or width value, a name, or any type of text information you want. After you enter a value, it's stored as part of the Door block in the drawing database. This value can be displayed as text attached to the Door block, or it can be invisible. You can change the value at any time. You can even specify the prompts for the attribute value.

However, suppose you don't have the attribute information when you design the Door block. As an alternative, you can add the attribute to a *symbol* that is later placed by the door when you know enough about the design to specify what type of door goes where. Figure 12.1 shows a sample door symbol and a table to which the symbol refers. The standard door-type symbol suits this purpose nicely because it's an object that you can set up and use as a block independent of the Door block.

**FIGURE 12.1**

A door symbol tells you what type of door goes in the location shown. Usually, the symbol contains a number or a letter that is keyed to a table that shows more information about the door.

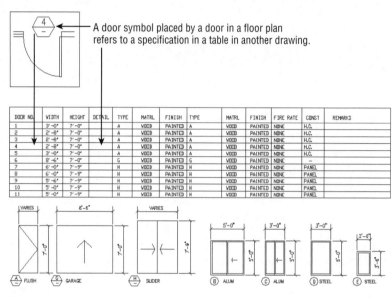

A door symbol placed by a door in a floor plan refers to a specification in a table in another drawing.

DOOR AND WINDOW SCHEDULE

## Adding Attributes to Blocks

In the following exercise, you'll create a door-type symbol, which is commonly used to describe the size, thickness, and other characteristics of any given door in an architectural drawing. The symbol is usually a circle, a hexagon, or a diamond with a number in it. The number is generally cross-referenced to a schedule that lists all the door types and their characteristics.

You'll create a new block containing attribute definitions in the file for which the block is intended: the Plan.dwg file. You may also use the 12a-plan.dwg file. You'll create the block in the file so you can easily insert it where it belongs in the plan.

First, you open the Plan.dwg file and set up a view appropriate for creating the block with the attribute:

1. Open the 12a-plan.dwg file, which can be found on the companion website, www.sybex .com/go/masteringautocadmac. Metric users can use the file 12a-plan-metric.dwg. These are similar to the Plan.dwg file you've created on your own, with a few additions to facilitate the exercises in this chapter.

2. Choose View ➢ Zoom ➢ Window from the menu bar, or click the Zoom tool on the status bar and then type **W⏎**. You can also type **Z⏎ W⏎**.

3. At the Specify first corner: prompt, enter **0,0⏎**.

**4.** At the `Specify opposite corner:` prompt, enter **12,9 (30.5,22.8** for metric users). This causes your view to zoom in to a location near the origin of the drawing in a 12″-×-9″ area.

You zoom in to this small area because you'll draw the block at its paper size of ¼″ (or 0.6 cm for metric users). Now you're ready to create the block and attribute. You'll start by drawing the graphics of the block, and then you'll add the attribute definition:

**1.** Draw a circle with its center at coordinate 7,5 (15,11 for metric users) and a diameter of 0.25 (0.6 for metric users). The circle is automatically placed on layer 0, which is the current layer. Remember that objects in a block on layer 0 take on the color and linetype assignment of the layer on which the block is inserted.

**2.** Zoom in to the circle so it's about the same size as that shown in Figure 12.2.

**3.** If the circle looks faceted, type **RE↵** to regenerate your drawing.

**FIGURE 12.2**
The attribute definition inserted in the circle

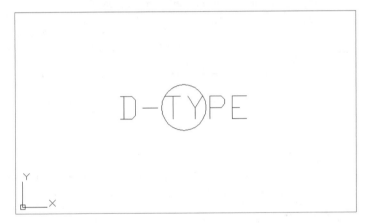

**4.** Click the Define Attributes tool from the Tool Sets palette, or type **ATT↵** to open the Attribute Definition dialog box (Figure 12.3).

**5.** In the Attribute group, click the Tag input box, and enter **D-TYPE**.

**FIGURE 12.3**
The Attribute Definition dialog box

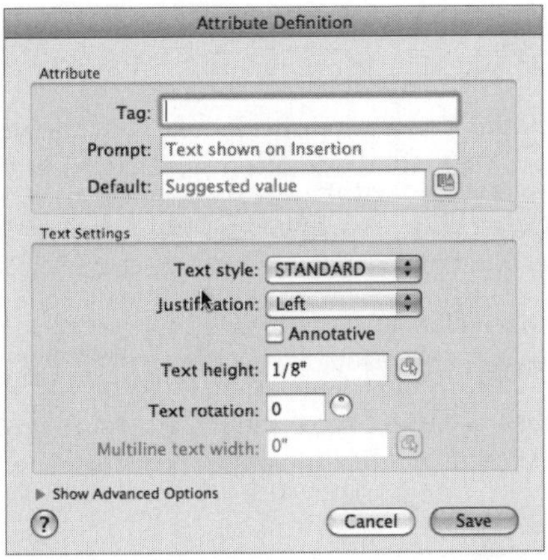

### UNDERSTANDING THE ATTRIBUTE TAG

The attribute tag is equivalent to a field name in a database. You can also think of the tag as the attribute's name or ID. It can help to identify the purpose of the attribute. The tag can be a maximum of 255 characters but can't contain spaces. If you plan to use the attribute data in a database program, check that program's documentation for other restrictions on field names.

6. Press the Tab key or click the Prompt input box, and enter **Door type**. This is the text for the prompt that will appear when you insert the block containing this attribute. Often the prompt is the same as the tag, but it can be anything you like. Unlike the tag, the prompt can include spaces and other special characters.

### GIVE YOUR PROMPTS MEANINGFUL NAMES

Use a prompt that gives explicit instructions so the user will know exactly what is expected. Consider including an example in the prompt. (Enclose the example in square brackets to imitate the way AutoCAD prompts often display defaults.)

7. Click the Default input box, and enter a hyphen (-). This is the default content for the door-type prompt.

### MAKE YOUR DEFAULTS USEFUL

If an attribute is to contain a number that will later be used for sorting in a database, use a default attribute value such as 000 to indicate the number of digits required. The zeros can also serve to remind the user that values less than 100 must be preceded by a leading zero, as in 099.

8. Click the Justification pop-up list, and select Middle Center. This enables you to center the attribute on the circle's center. The Text Settings group includes several other options. Because attributes appear as text, you can apply the same settings to them as you would to single-line text.

9. In the Text Height input box, change the value to **0.125**. (Metric users should enter **0.3**.) This makes the attribute text 0.125″ (0.3 cm) high.

10. Click the Annotative check box. This allows the attribute to adjust in size automatically according to the annotation scale of the drawing.

▶ Show Advanced Options  11. Click the Show Advanced Options disclosure triangle to reveal more options. In the Insertion Point group, make sure the Specify On-Screen radio button is selected.

12. Click Save to close the dialog box.

13. Using the Center osnap, pick the center of the circle. You need to place the cursor on the circle's circumference, not in the circle's center, to obtain the center by using the osnap. The attribute definition appears at the center of the circle (see Figure 12.2).

You've just created your first attribute definition. The attribute definition displays its tag in all uppercase letters to help you identify it. When you later insert this file into another drawing, the tag turns into the value you assign to it when it's inserted. If you want only one attribute, you can stop here and save the file. The next section shows how you can quickly add several more attributes to your drawing.

## Copying and Modifying Attribute Definitions

Next, you'll add a few more attribute definitions, but instead of using the Attribute Definition dialog box, you'll make an arrayed copy of the first attribute and then edit the attribute definition copies. This method can save you time when you want to create several attribute definitions that have similar characteristics. By making copies and modifying them, you'll also get a chance to see firsthand how to change an attribute definition.

Follow these steps to make copies of the attribute:

1. Click Array on the Tool Sets palette or type **AR**↵ to open the Array dialog box.

2. Click the Rectangular Array radio button.

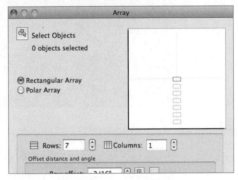

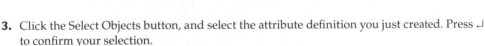

3. Click the Select Objects button, and select the attribute definition you just created. Press ↵ to confirm your selection.

4. In the Rows input box, enter **7**; in the Columns input box, enter **1**.

5. Enter **-0.18** in the Row Offset input box (**-0.432** for metric users) and **0** in the Column Offset input box. The Row Offset value is approximately 1.5 times the height of the attribute text height. The minus sign in the Row Offset value causes the array to be drawn downward.

6. Notice that the preview to the right shows an approximation of what your array will look like. If you want to see what it actually looks like on the screen, click the Preview button. To close the preview, you can press Esc to return to the array dialog box for further editing, or press ↵ to accept the edits. Press ↵ to exit the Array dialog box.

Now you're ready to modify the copies of the attribute definitions:

1. Press Esc twice to clear any selections or commands, and click the attribute definition just below the original.

2. Click on the All option in the Properties Inspector palette.

> **DOUBLE-CLICK TO EDIT ATTRIBUTE DEFINITIONS**
>
> You can double-click an attribute definition to change its Tag, Prompt, or Default value in the Edit Attribute Definition dialog box. However, this dialog box doesn't let you change an attribute definition's visibility mode.

**3.** Scroll down the list of properties until you see the Invisible option in the Misc category.

**4.** Click the check box next to the Invisible option.

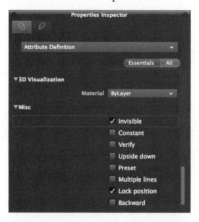

**5.** Scroll back up the list of properties and locate the Tag option in the Text category.

**6.** Highlight the Tag value to the right, and type **D-SIZE**↵. The attribute changes to reflect the change in the Tag value.

**7.** While still in the Text category, highlight the Prompt value, and type **Door Size**↵.

**8.** In the Contents field, type **3′-0″**↵. Metric users should type **90**↵.

Make sure you press ↵ after entering a new value for the properties in the Properties Inspector palette. Pressing ↵ confirms your new entry.

You've just learned how to edit an attribute definition. Now you'll make changes to the other attribute definitions:

1. Press Esc twice so that no attribute is selected, and then click the next attribute down so you can display its properties in the Properties Inspector palette.

2. Continue to edit this and the rest of the attribute definition properties by using the attribute settings listed in Table 12.1. To do this, repeat steps 4 through 8 of the preceding exercise for each attribute definition, replacing the Tag and Prompt values with those shown in Table 12.1. Also, make sure all but the original attributes have the Invisible option set to Yes.

3. When you've finished editing the attribute definition properties, close the Properties Inspector.

**TABLE 12.1:**     Attributes for the door-type symbol

| TAG | PROMPT | CONTENT VALUE |
|---|---|---|
| D-NUMBER | Door number | - |
| D-THICK | Door thickness | - |
| D-RATE | Fire rating | - |
| D-MATRL | Door material | - |
| D-CONST | Door construction | - |

*Make sure the Invisible option is selected for the attributes in this table.*

When you later insert a file or a block containing attributes, the attribute prompts will appear in the order that their associated definitions were created. If the order of the prompts at insertion time is important, you can control it by editing the attribute definitions so their creation order corresponds to the desired prompt order. You can also control the order by using the Block Attribute Manager, which you'll look at later in this chapter.

---

**ORDER DOES MATTER**

The order in which you select the attributes may not necessarily be the order in which the attribute prompts will appear when you insert the block with attributes. If you select the attributes with a window and start from the bottom up, your attribute order will start at the bottom. So it is best practice to pick the attributes one by one in the order you want them to be displayed. There are methods of changing the order and they will be discussed later in this chapter.

## Turning the Attribute Definitions into a Block

You need to perform one more crucial step before these attribute definitions can be of any use. You need to turn the attribute definitions into a block, along with the circle:

1. Click the Create tool in the Tool Sets palette, or enter **B**↲.

2. In the Define Block dialog box, enter **S-DOOR** for the name.

3. In the Base Point group, click Pick Point, and then use the Center osnap to select the center of the circle.

4. In the Source Objects group, click Select Objects, and select the circle and all the attributes from the top to the bottom. Press ↲ when you've completed your selection.

5. In the Block Behavior group, click the Annotative check box. This ensures that the block is scaled to the appropriate size for the scale of the drawing into which it's inserted.

6. Click Create Block. When the Edit Attribute dialog box opens, click Confirm to close it.

7. The attributes and the circle are now a block called S-DOOR. You can delete the S-DOOR block on your screen.

---

### UNDERSTANDING ATTRIBUTE DEFINITION MODES

The Attribute Definition dialog box includes several choices in the Attribute Options group; you've used one of these modes to see what it does. You won't use any of the other modes in this chapter, but here is a list describing all the modes for your reference:

**Invisible**   Controls whether the attribute is shown as part of the drawing.

**Constant**   Creates an attribute that doesn't prompt you to enter a value. Instead, the attribute has a constant, or fixed, value you give it during creation. Constant mode is used when you know you'll assign a fixed value to an object. After constant values are set in a block, you can't change them by using the standard set of attribute-editing commands.

**Verify**   Causes AutoCAD to review the attribute values you enter at insertion time and to ask you whether they're correct. This option appears only when the Edit Attribute dialog box is turned off (the Attdia system variable is set to 0).

**Preset**   Causes AutoCAD to assign the default value to an attribute automatically when its block is inserted. This saves time because a preset attribute won't prompt you for a value. Unlike attributes created in Constant mode, a preset attribute can be edited.

**Lock Location**   Prevents the attribute from being moved from its original location in the block when you're grip editing.

**Multiple Lines**   Allows the attribute to contain multiple lines of text, similar to Mtext objects. When this option is turned on, you can specify a text boundary width.

Later in this chapter, you'll see how to make an invisible attribute visible.

---

Once you've created the block, you can place it anywhere in the drawing using the Insert command or the Insert tool on the Tool Sets palette. You'll insert this block in another location in the drawing. If you want to use the block in other drawings, you can use the Wblock command to save the block as a drawing file.

## Inserting Blocks Containing Attributes

Earlier in this chapter, you created a door-type symbol at the desired size for the printed symbol. This size is known as the *paper size*. Because you turned on the Annotative option for the attribute and block, you can use the Annotation Scale setting to have the block insert at the appropriate size for the scale of the drawing. The following steps demonstrate the process of inserting a block that contains attributes. First, set up your view and annotation scale in preparation to insert the blocks:

1. Turn on Attribute Dialog mode by entering **ATTDIA↵ 1↵** at the Command prompt. This enables you to enter attribute values through a dialog box in the next exercise. Otherwise, you'd be prompted for the attribute values in the Command Line palette.

2. Select 1/8″=1′-0″ (1:100 for metric users) from the Annotation Scale pop-up list in the status bar. This ensures that the block appears at the proper size for the drawing scale.

3. Type **V↵ R↵ FIRST↵**. This is a view that has been saved in this drawing. (See "Taking Control of the AutoCAD Display" in Chapter 7 for more on saving views.)

4. Be sure the Ceiling and Flr-pat layers are off. Normally, in a floor plan, the door headers aren't visible anyway and their appearance will interfere with the placement of the door-reference symbol.

5. Finally, you can begin to place the blocks in the drawing. Click the Insert tool on the Tool Sets palette or type **I↵** to open the Insert Block dialog box.

6. Select S-DOOR from the Blocks pop-up list.

7. Click the Show Insertion Options disclosure triangle. In the Insertion Point group, and make sure the Specify On-Screen option is turned on.

8. In the Rotation group, make sure the Input angle option is selected and the angle is 0 (zero).

9. In the Scale group, make sure the Uniform Scale check box is selected; then click Insert.

   Now you're ready to place the block in your drawing in the appropriate locations and enter the attribute values.

10. AutoCAD is waiting for you to select a location for the symbol. To place the symbol, click in the doorway of the lower-left unit, near coordinate 41′-3″,72′-4″. Metric users should use coordinate 1256,2202. When you click the location, the Edit Attributes dialog box opens (Figure 12.4).

11. In the Door Type input box, enter **A** and press the Tab key. Note that this is the prompt you created. Note also that the default value is the hyphen you specified. Attribute data is case sensitive, so any text you enter in all capital letters is stored in all capital letters.

12. In the Door Number input box, change the hyphen to **116**. Continue to change the values for each input box as shown in Table 12.2.

**FIGURE 12.4**
The Edit Attributes
dialog box

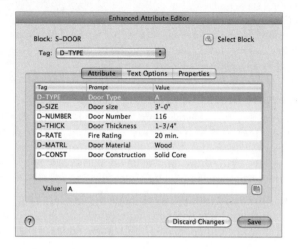

**TABLE 12.2:** Attribute values for the typical studio entry door

| PROMPT | VALUE |
| --- | --- |
| Door Type | A |
| Door Size | 3′-0″ (90 cm for metric) |
| Door Number | (Same as room number; see Figure 12.6.) |
| Door Thickness | 1¾″ (4 cm for metric) |
| Fire Rating | 20 min. |
| Door Material | Wood |
| Door Construction | Solid core |

**13.** When you're finished changing values, click Confirm and the symbol appears. The only attribute you can see is the one you selected to be visible: the door type.

**14.** Add the rest of the door-type symbols for the apartment entry doors by copying or arraying the door symbol you just inserted. You can use the previously saved views found in the 3D Navigation drop-down list in the View tab's Views panel to help you get around the drawing quickly. Don't worry that the attribute values aren't appropriate for each unit; you'll see how to edit the attributes in the next section.

In addition to the S-DOOR block, you'll need a block for the room number. To save some time, I've included a block called S-APART that contains a rectangle and a single attribute definition for the room number (see Figure 12.5).

**FIGURE 12.5**
The room-number symbol

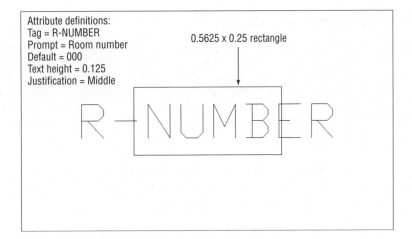

Attribute definitions:
Tag = R-NUMBER
Prompt = Room number
Default = 000
Text height = 0.125
Justification = Middle

0.5625 x 0.25 rectangle

R-NUMBER

Do the following to insert the room-number block:

1. Click the Insert tool from the Tool Sets palette, and select S-APART from the Name pop-up list.

2. Make sure the Specify On-Screen setting is turned on only for the insertion point, and then click Insert.

3. Insert the S-APART block into the lower-left unit. Give the attribute of this block the value **116**.

4. Copy or array the S-APART block so there is one S-APART block in each unit. You'll learn how to modify the attributes to reflect their proper values in the following section. Figure 12.6 shows what the view should look like after you've entered the door symbols and the apartment numbers.

**FIGURE 12.6**
An overall view of the plan with door symbols and apartment numbers added

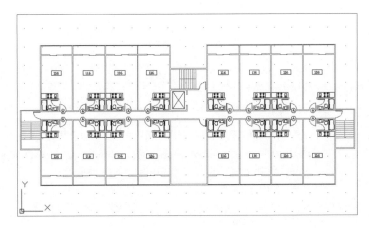

# Editing Attributes

Because drawings are usually in flux even after construction or manufacturing begins, you'll eventually have to edit previously entered attributes. In the example of the apartment building, many things can change before the final set of drawings is completed.

Attributes can be edited individually or *globally*—you can edit several occurrences of a particular attribute tag all at one time. In the following sections, you'll use both individual and global editing techniques to make changes to the attributes you've entered so far. You'll also practice editing invisible attributes.

## Editing Attribute Values One at a Time

AutoCAD offers an easy way to edit attributes one at a time through a dialog box. The following exercise demonstrates this feature:

1. Type **V↵ R↵ FIRST↵** to restore the First view.

2. Double-click the apartment number attribute in the unit just to the right of the first unit in the lower-left corner to open the Enhanced Attribute Editor (Figure 12.7).

**FIGURE 12.7**
The Enhanced Attribute Editor

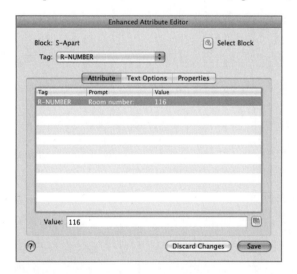

3. Change the value in the Value input box to **112**, and click Save to make the change.

4. Do this for each room, using Figure 12.8 as a reference for assigning room numbers.

5. Go back and edit the door number attribute for the S-DOOR blocks. Give each door the same number as the room number it's associated with. Again, see Figure 12.8 for the room numbers.

**FIGURE 12.8**

Apartment numbers for one floor of the studio apartment building

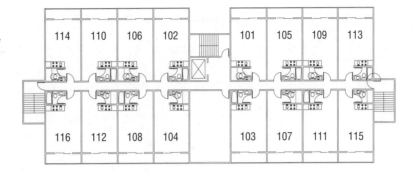

## Editing Attribute Text Formats and Properties

You may have noticed that the Enhanced Attribute Editor in the preceding exercise has three tabs: Attribute, Text Options, and Properties. When you double-click a block containing attributes, the Enhanced Attribute Editor dialog box opens at the Attribute tab. You can use the other two tabs to control the size, font, color, and other properties of the selected attribute.

The Text Options tab (Figure 12.9) lets you alter the attribute text style, justification, height, rotation, width factor, and oblique angle. (See Chapter 9, "Adding Text to Drawings," for more on these text options.)

**FIGURE 12.9**

The Enhanced Attribute Editor's Text Options tab

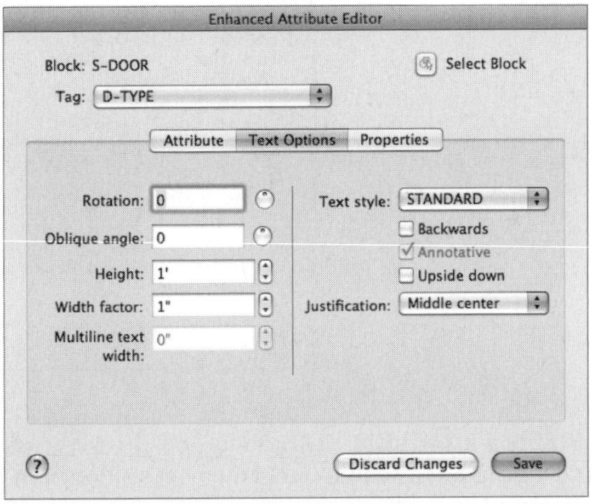

The Properties tab (Figure 12.10) lets you alter the attribute's layer, linetype, color, line weight (effective only on AutoCAD fonts), and plot style assignments.

In the previous exercise, you edited a block containing a single attribute. Double-clicking a block that contains multiple attributes, such as the S-DOOR block, opens the Enhanced Attribute Editor dialog box at the Attribute tab. This tab displays all the attributes regardless of whether they're visible, as shown in Figure 12.11. You can then edit the value, formats, and properties of the individual attributes by highlighting the attribute in the Attribute tab and using the other tabs to make changes. The changes you make affect only the attribute you've highlighted in the Attribute tab.

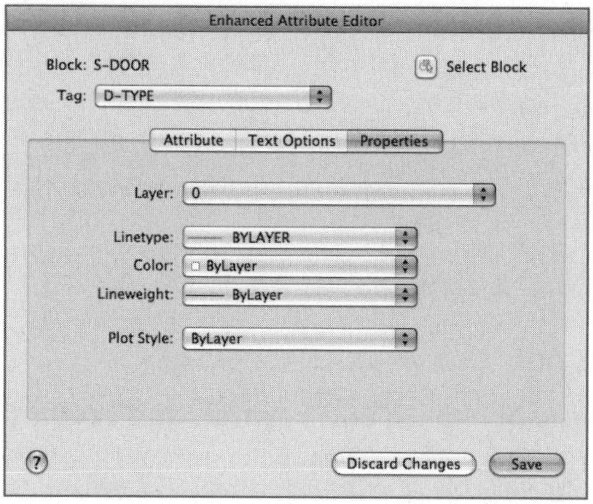

**FIGURE 12.10**
The Enhanced
Attribute Editor's
Properties tab

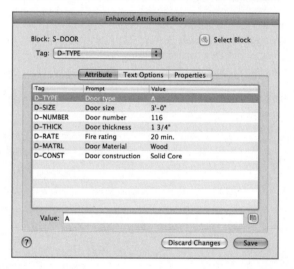

**FIGURE 12.11**
The Enhanced
Attribute Editor
showing the con-
tents of a block that
contains several
attributes

The Enhanced Attribute Editor lets you change attribute values, formats, and properties one block at a time, but as you'll see in the next section, you can also make changes to several attributes at once.

---

### MOVING THE LOCATION OF ATTRIBUTES

If you want to change the location of individual attributes in a block, you can move attributes by using grips. Click the block to expose the grips, and then click the grip connected to the attribute. Or, if you've selected several blocks, click the attribute grips, and then move the attributes to their new location. They are still attached to their associated blocks. If you don't see grips appear for the attributes, then the attribute definition has its Lock Position property turned on. This is a setting that is available when you create the attribute in the Attribute Definition dialog box.

## Making Global Changes to Attribute Values

At times, you'll want to change the value of several attributes in a file so they're all the same value. You can use the Edit Multiple Attributes option to make global changes to attribute values.

Suppose you decide you want to change all the entry doors to a type designated as B rather than A. Perhaps door type A was an input error or type B happens to be better suited for an entry door. The following exercise demonstrates how this is done:

1. Type **V.┘ R.┘ FOURTH.┘**. This restores a saved view in the drawing called Fourth. (Views are covered in Chapter 7, "Mastering Viewing Tools, Hatches, and External References.") Pan your view down so you can see the eight door-reference symbols for this view.

2. Click Multiple from the Edit Attribute flyout on the Tool Sets palette, or type **-ATTEDIT.┘** at the Command prompt. (Alternatively, you can type in **-ATE**.) Make sure you include the hyphen at the beginning.

3. At the `Edit Attributes one at a time? [Yes/No] <Y>:` prompt, enter **N.┘** for No. You see the message `Performing global editing of attribute values`. This tells you that you're in Global Edit mode.

4. At the `Edit only attributes visible on screen? [Yes/No] <Y>:` prompt, press ┘. As you can see from this prompt, you have the option to edit all attributes, including those out of the view area. You'll get a chance to work with this option in the next exercise.

5. At the `Enter block name specification <*>:` prompt, press ┘. Optionally, you can enter a block name to narrow the selection to specific blocks.

6. At the `Enter attribute tag specification <*>:` prompt, press ┘. Optionally, you can enter an attribute tag name to narrow your selection to specific tags.

7. At the `Enter attribute value specification <*>:` prompt, press ┘. Optionally, you can narrow your selection to attributes containing specific values.

8. At the `Select Attributes:` prompt, select the door-type symbol's attribute value for units 103 to 115. You can use a window to select the attributes if you prefer. Press ┘ when you've finished your selection.

9. At the `Enter string to change:` prompt, enter **A.┘**.

10. At the `Enter new string:` prompt, enter **B.┘**. The door-type symbols all change to the new value.

In step 8, you were asked to select the attributes to be edited. AutoCAD limits the changes to those attributes you select. If you know you need to change every attribute in your drawing, you can do so by answering the series of prompts in a slightly different way, as in the following exercise:

1. Try the same procedure again, but this time enter **N** for the first prompt and **N** again at the `Edit only attributes visible on screen? [Yes/No] <Y>:` prompt (step 4 in the previous exercise). The message `Drawing must be regenerated afterwards` appears.

2. Once again, you're prompted for the block name, the tag, and the value (steps 5, 6, and 7 in the previous exercise). Respond to these prompts as you did earlier.

3. You then get the message `128 attributes selected`. This tells you the number of attributes that fit the specifications you just entered.

4. At the `Enter string to change:` prompt, enter **A** to indicate you want to change the rest of the A attribute values.

5. At the `Enter new string:` prompt, enter **B**. A series of *B*s appears, indicating the number of strings that were replaced.

In the previous exercise, AutoCAD skipped the `Select Attribute:` prompt and went directly to the `String to change:` prompt. AutoCAD assumes that you want it to edit every attribute in the drawing, so it doesn't bother asking you to select specific attributes.

## Making Invisible Attributes Visible

You can globally edit invisible attributes, such as those in the door-reference symbol, by using the tools just described. You may, however, want to be more selective about which invisible attribute you want to modify. Optionally, you may want to make invisible attributes temporarily visible for other editing purposes.

This exercise shows how you can make invisible attributes visible:

1. Type **ATTDISP** **ON**. Your drawing looks like Figure 12.12.

**FIGURE 12.12**
The drawing with all the attributes visible. (Door-type symbols are so close together that they overlap.)

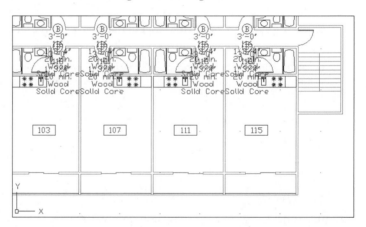

2. At this point, you could edit the invisible attributes individually, as in the first attribute-editing exercise. For now, set the attribute display back to Normal. Type **ATTDISP** **N**.

You've seen the results of the On and Normal options. The Off option makes all attributes invisible regardless of the mode used when they were created.

Because the attributes weren't intended to be visible, they appear to overlap and cover other parts of the drawing when they're made visible. Remember to turn them back off when you're done reviewing them.

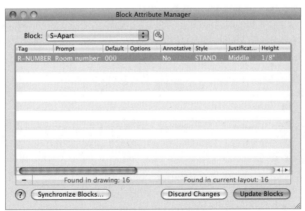

> ### Real World Scenario
>
> #### USING SPACES IN ATTRIBUTE VALUES
>
> At times, you may want the default value to begin with a blank space. This enables you to specify text strings more easily when you edit the attribute globally. For example, suppose you have an attribute value that reads 3334333. If you want to change the first 3 in this string of numbers, you have to specify 3334 when prompted for the string to change. Then, for the new string, you enter the same set of numbers again, but with the first 3 changed to the new number. If you only specify 3 for the string to change, AutoCAD will change all the 3s in the value. If you start with a space, as in _3334333 (I'm using an underscore here only to represent the space; it doesn't mean you type an underscore character), you can isolate the first 3 from the rest by specifying _3 as the string to change (again, type a space instead of the underscore).
>
> You must enter a backslash character (\) before the space in the default value to tell AutoCAD to interpret the space literally rather than as a press of the spacebar (which is equivalent to pressing ↵).

## Making Global Format and Property Changes to Attributes

While we're on the subject of global editing, you should know how to make global changes to the format and properties of attributes. Earlier you saw how to make format changes to individual attributes by using the Enhanced Attribute Editor dialog box. Let's use the Edit Attributes tool to make global changes:

Follow these steps to make the global changes:

1. Click the arrow next to Attributes on the Tool Sets palette to reveal the Block panel. Choose the Manage Attributes tool. The Block Attribute Manager dialog box will open. You can also enter **BATTMAN**↵.

2. Select S-Apart from the Block pop-up list at the top of the dialog box. This list displays all the blocks that contain attributes. The only attribute defined for the selected block is displayed in the list box below it.

**3.** Double-click an attribute value to open the Attribute Editor dialog box. The Attribute Editor dialog box is nearly identical to the Enhanced Attribute Editor you saw earlier.

**4.** Click the Properties tab, select Red from the Color pop-up list, and click OK.

**5.** Click Update Blocks to exit the Block Attribute Manager dialog box.

The Attribute Editor dialog box you saw in this exercise offers a slightly different set of options from those in the Enhanced Attribute Editor dialog box. In the Attribute tab of the Attribute Editor dialog box, you can change some of the mode settings for the attribute, such as visibility and the Verify and Preset modes. You can also change the Tag, Prompt, and Default values. In contrast, the Attribute tab in the Enhanced Attribute Editor dialog box enables you to change the attribute value but none of the other attribute properties.

### OTHER BLOCK ATTRIBUTE MANAGER OPTIONS

The Block Attribute Manager dialog box includes a few other options that weren't covered in the exercises. Here's a rundown of the Remove (–) and Synchronize Blocks buttons as well as the option to move attribute names up or down:

**Remove**   The Remove button looks like a minus sign (–). Clicking this button removes the selected attribute from the block. If you didn't mean to click this button, click the Discard Changes button.

**Synchronize Blocks**   This option updates attribute properties such as order, text formatting, mode, and so on. It can also be used to globally update blocks that have had new attribute definitions added or deleted. It doesn't affect the individual attribute values.

**Move up and move down**   It's not a true button, but you can click on an attribute name and while depressing the mouse button, drag it to a new location. If you move an item down the list, the item changes its position when viewed using the Edit Attribute dialog box (Ddatte command) or when you're viewing the attribute's properties in the Enhanced Attribute Editor dialog box (Eattedit command). Of course, this has an effect only on blocks containing multiple attributes.

## Redefining Blocks Containing Attributes

Attributes act differently from other objects when they're included in redefined blocks. Normally, blocks that have been redefined change their configuration to reflect the new block definition. But if a redefined block contains attributes, the attributes maintain their old properties, including their position in relation to other objects in the block. This means the old attribute position, style, and so on don't change even though you may have changed them in the new definition.

Fortunately, AutoCAD offers a tool that's specifically designed to let you update blocks with attributes. The following steps describe how to update attribute blocks:

1. Before you use the command to redefine an attribute block, you must create the objects and attribute definitions that will make up the replacement attribute block. The simplest way to do this is to explode a copy of the attribute block you want to update (the Explode command is covered in Chapter 4, "Organizing Objects with Blocks and Groups"). This ensures that you have the same attribute definitions in the updated block.

2. Make your changes to the exploded attribute block.

---

### EXPLODE ATTRIBUTE BLOCKS AT A 1-TO-1 SCALE

Before you explode the attribute block copy, be sure it's at a 1-to-1 scale. This is important because if you don't use the original size of the block, you could end up with all your new attribute blocks at the wrong size. Also be sure you use a marker device, such as a line, to locate the insertion point of the attribute block before you explode it. This will help you locate and maintain the original insertion point for the redefined block.

---

3. Type **AT↵**.

4. At the `Enter name of block you wish to redefine:` prompt, enter the appropriate name.

5. At the `Select objects:` prompt, select all the objects, including the attribute definitions, that you want to include in the revised attribute block.

6. At the `Specify insertion base point of new Block:` prompt, pick the same location used for the original block.

After you pick the insertion point, AutoCAD takes a few seconds to update the blocks. The amount of time depends on the complexity of the block and the number of times the block occurs in the drawing. If you include a new attribute definition with your new block, it too is added to all the updated blocks, with its default value. Attribute definitions that are deleted from your new definition are removed from all the updated blocks.

## The Bottom Line

**Create attributes.**   Attributes are a great tool for storing data with drawn objects. You can include as little or as much data as you like in an AutoCAD block.

**Master It**   What is the name of the object you must include in a block to store data?

**Edit attributes.**   The data you include in a block is easily changed. You may have several copies of a block, each of which must contain its own unique sets of data.

**Master It**   What is the simplest way to gain access to a block's attribute data?

# Chapter 13

# Copying Existing Drawings into AutoCAD

At times, you'll want to turn an existing drawing into an AutoCAD drawing file. The original drawing may be hand drawn, or it might be a PDF from another source. You may be modifying a design that someone else created or converting your library of older, hand-drafted drawings for AutoCAD use. Perhaps you want to convert a hand-drawn sketch into a formal drawing? This chapter discusses ways to import existing drawings into AutoCAD through tracing, scaling, and scanning.

In this chapter, you'll learn to do the following:

◆ Convert paper drawings into AutoCAD files

◆ Import a raster image

◆ Work with a raster image

## Methods for Converting Paper Drawings to AutoCAD Files

*Scaling* a drawing is the most flexible method for converting paper drawings into AutoCAD files because you don't need a graphics tablet to do it, and generally, you're faced with fewer cleanups afterward. Scaling also facilitates the most accurate input of orthogonal lines because you can read dimensions directly from the drawing and enter them into AutoCAD. The main drawback with scaling is that if the hand-drafted drawing does not contain written dimensions, it would be difficult to produce an accurate copy. In addition, you must constantly look at the hand-drafted drawing and measure distances with a scale, and irregular curves are difficult to scale accurately. Programs are available that automatically convert an image file into an AutoCAD drawing file consisting of lines and arcs. These programs may offer some help, but they require some editing and checking for errors.

*Tracing* with a digitizing tablet used to be the only way to enter a hand-drafted drawing into AutoCAD. However, a traced drawing usually requires some cleanup and reorganization.

*Scanning*, much like tracing, is best used for drawings that are difficult to scale, such as complex topographical maps containing more contours than are practical to trace on a digitizer or nontechnical line art such as letterhead and logos.

The simplest method for converting paper drawings, and the method covered in this chapter, is to scan your drawings as image files to be used as a background in AutoCAD. You can import your image files into AutoCAD and then trace directly over them. This technique allows you to see the original drawing in the AutoCAD window, preventing you from diverting your attention to other areas of your workstation.

**DIGITIZERS ON AUTOCAD FOR THE MAC**

Digitizers are not supported in AutoCAD for Mac.

## Importing a Raster Image

If you have a scanner and you'd like to use it to import drawings and other images into AutoCAD, you can take advantage of AutoCAD's ability to import raster images. There are many reasons you may want to import a scanned image. In architectural plans, a vicinity map is frequently used to show the location of a project. With the permission of its creator, you can scan a map into AutoCAD and incorporate it into a cover sheet. That cover sheet can also contain other images, such as photographs of the site, computer renderings and elevations of the project, and company logos. In architectural projects, scans of older drawings can be used as backgrounds for renovation work. This can be especially useful for historical buildings where the building's owner wishes to keep the original architectural detail.

Another reason for importing a scanned image is to use the image as a reference to trace over. You can trace a drawing with greater accuracy by using a scanned image. Now that the price of a scanner has fallen below $100, it has become a cost-effective tool for creating a wide variety of graphic material. In this section, you'll learn firsthand how you can import an image as a background for tracing.

Choose Tools ➤ Palettes ➤ Reference Manager on the menu bar, or press ⌘-7 to open the Reference Manager palette (Figure 13.1), which lets you import a full range of raster image files.

**FIGURE 13.1**
The Reference
Manager palette
allows you to
import raster
images.

You can also type **XR**↵. The Reference Manager palette should look familiar from Chapter 7, "Mastering Viewing Tools, Hatches, and External References." It's the same palette you used to manage external references. Just like external references (Xrefs), raster images are loaded when the current file is open, but they aren't stored as part of the current file when the file is saved. This helps keep file sizes down, but it also means that you need to keep track of inserted raster files. You must make sure they're kept together with the AutoCAD files in which they're inserted. For example, you might want to keep image files in the same folder as the drawing file to which they're attached.

Another similarity between Xrefs and imported raster images is that you can clip a raster image so that only a portion of the image is displayed in your drawing. Portions of a raster file that are clipped aren't stored in memory, so your system won't get bogged down, even if the raster file is huge.

The following exercise gives you step-by-step instructions for importing a raster file. It also lets you see how scanned resolution translates into an image in AutoCAD. This is important if you're interested in scanning drawings for the purpose of tracing over them. Here are the steps:

1. Create a new file called `Rastertrace`.

2. Set up the file as an architectural drawing with a 1/4″=1′ scale on an 8½″-x-11″ sheet (set the Limits settings to 0,0 for the lower-left corner and 528,408 for the upper-right corner). Make sure the drawing units type is set to Architectural. Metric users should set up their drawing at a 1:50 scale on an A4 size sheet. (The Limits settings for metric users should be 0,0 for the lower-left corner and 1480,1050 for the upper-right corner.)

3. Click the Zoom tool from the status bar and then type **A**↵. You can also press **Z**↵ **A**↵ to make sure the entire drawing limits are displayed on the screen.

4. Draw a line across the screen from coordinates 0,20′ to 64′,20′. Metric users should draw the line from 0,600 to 1820,600. You'll use this line in a later exercise.

5. Click the line you just drew, and then select Red from the Color pop-up list in the Properties Inspector palette. This helps make the line more visible.

6. Press ⌘-7 to open the Reference Manager palette.

7. Click the Attach Reference tool from the Reference Manager palette.

   From the Select Reference File dialog box, click the File Format pop-up list and select All Image Files. From the dialog box, locate and select the `raster1.jpg` project file, which can be obtained from the book's companion website, `www.sybex.com/go/masteringautocad-mac`. You can see a preview of the file on the right side of the dialog box.

8. Click Open to open the Attach Image dialog box (Figure 13.2).

9. Uncheck the Specify On-Screen option in the Insertion Point group to accept the 0,0,0 coordinates.

10. Click OK, and then at the `Specify scale factor <1>:` prompt, use the cursor to scale the image so it fills about half the screen, as shown in Figure 13.3. The `raster1.jpg` file-name appears in the External References palette.

**FIGURE 13.2**
The Attach Image
dialog box

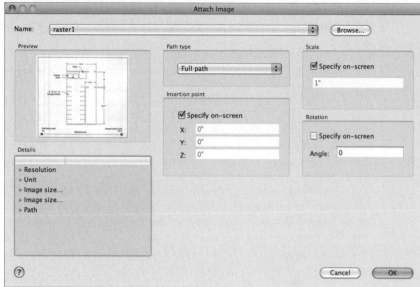

**FIGURE 13.3**
Manually scaling
the raster image

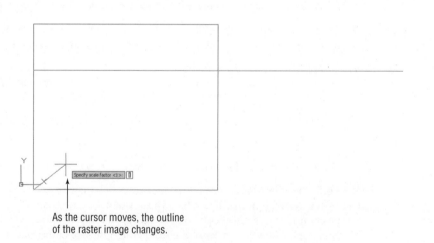

As the cursor moves, the outline
of the raster image changes.

## Working with a Raster Image

Once you've imported a raster image, you can begin to work with it in a variety of ways. You can resize the image to suit your needs and even adjust its size to a particular scale. Raster images can be made to overlap AutoCAD objects, or you can have raster images appear in the background. There are also rudimentary controls for brightness, contrast, and transparency. In the following sections, you'll continue to use the image you attached to your drawing to explore some of these options.

## Real World Scenario

### TIPS FOR IMPORTING RASTER IMAGES

When you scan a document into your computer, you get a raster image file. Unlike AutoCAD files, *raster image files* are made up of a matrix of colored pixels that form a picture, which is why raster images are also sometimes called *bitmaps*. *Vector files*, like those produced by AutoCAD, are made up of instructions to draw lines, arcs, curves, and circles. The two formats, raster and vector, are so different that it's difficult to convert one format to the other accurately. It's easier to trace a raster file in AutoCAD than it is to try to use a computer program to make the conversion for you.

But even tracing a raster image file can be difficult if the image is of poor quality. After having worked with scanned images in AutoCAD for a variety of projects, we've discovered that you can make your work a lot easier by following a few simple rules:

◆ Scan in your drawing using a grayscale or color scanner, or convert your black-and-white scanned image to grayscale using your image editing software. This will give you more control over the appearance of the image once it's in AutoCAD.

◆ Use an image editing program such as Adobe Photoshop or your scanner software to clean up unwanted gray or spotted areas in the file before importing it into AutoCAD.

◆ If your scanner software or image editing program has a "de-speckle" or "de-spot" feature, use it. It can help clean up your image and ultimately reduce the raster image's file size.

◆ Scan at a reasonable resolution. Scanning at 150 dpi to 200 dpi may be more than adequate.

◆ If you plan to make heavy use of raster imports, upgrade your computer to the fastest processor and with as much memory as you can afford.

The raster-import commands can incorporate paper maps or plans into 3D AutoCAD drawings for presentations. We know of one architectural firm that produces impressive presentations with little effort by combining 2D scanned images with 3D massing models for urban-design studies. (A *massing model* shows only the rough outline of buildings without giving too much detail, thus showing the general scale of a project without being too fussy.)

## Scaling a Raster Image

The raster1.jpg file was scanned as a grayscale image at 100 dpi. This shows that you can get a reasonable amount of detail at a fairly low scan resolution.

Now suppose you want to trace over this image to start an AutoCAD drawing. The first thing you should do is to scale the image to the appropriate size. You can scale an image file to full size. Try the following steps to see how you can begin the process:

1. Press **Z↵ E↵** to zoom extents.

2. Click the Scale tool on the Tool Sets palette.

3. Click the edge of the raster image to select it.

4. Press ↵ to finish your selection.

5. At the Specify base point: prompt, click the X in the lower-left corner of the image.

6. At the `Specify scale factor or [Copy/Reference]:` prompt, enter **R**↵ to use the Reference option.

7. At the `Specify reference length <1>:` prompt, type **@**↵. This tells AutoCAD that you want to use the last point selected as one end of the reference length. After you enter the @ symbol, you'll see a rubber-banding line emanating from the X.

8. At the `Specify second point:` prompt, click the X at the lower-right corner of the image.

9. At the `Specify new length or [Points]:` prompt, enter **44'**↵. Metric users should enter **1341**↵. The image enlarges. Remember that this reference line is 44' or 1341 cm in length.

The image is now scaled properly for the plan it portrays. You can proceed to trace over the image. You can also place the image on its own layer and turn it off from time to time to check your trace work. Even if you don't trace the scanned floor plan line for line, you can read the dimensions of the plan from your computer monitor instead of having to go back and forth between measuring the paper image and drawing the plan on the computer.

## Controlling Object Visibility and Overlap with Raster Images

With the introduction of raster-image support, AutoCAD inherited a problem that's fairly common to programs that use such images: Raster images obscure other objects that were placed previously. The image you imported in the previous exercise, for example, obscures the line you drew when you first opened the file. In most cases this overlap isn't a problem, but in some situations you'll want AutoCAD vector objects to overlap an imported raster image. An example is a civil-engineering drawing showing an AutoCAD drawing of a new road superimposed over an aerial view of the location for the road.

Paint and page-layout programs usually offer a "to front/to back" tool to control the overlap of objects and images. AutoCAD offers the Draworder command. Here's how it works:

1. Press **Z**↵ **E**↵ to get an overall view of the image.

2. Click on the red colored line you drew when you first created the file. You can select other objects if you wish.

3. Right-click and select Draw Order ➤ Bring Above Objects from the shortcut menu.

4. At the `Select reference objects:` prompt, click the edge of the raster image of the utility room, and then press ↵.

The drawing regenerates and the entire line appears, no longer obscured by the raster image.

---

**MASKING AN AREA OF AN IMAGE**

You can mask out areas of an imported raster image by creating a solid hatch area and using the Draworder command to place the solid hatch on top of the raster image. Such masks can be helpful as backgrounds for text that must be placed over a raster image. You can also use the Wipeout command (choose Draw ➤ Wipeout from the menu bar) to mask areas of a drawing.

The Draw Order tool you just used has four options in the right-click menu:

**Bring To Front**   Places an object or a set of objects at the top of the draw order for the entire drawing. The effect is that the objects are completely visible.

**Send To Back**   Places an object or a set of objects at the bottom of the draw order for the entire drawing. The effect is that other objects in the drawing may obscure those objects.

**Bring Above Objects**   Places an object or a set of objects above another object in the draw order. This has the effect of making the first set of objects appear above the second selected object.

**Send Under Objects**   Places an object or a set of objects below another object in the draw order. This has the effect of making the first set of objects appear underneath the second selected object.

You can also use the **DR** keyboard shortcut to issue the Draworder command. If you do this, you see these prompts:

```
Select objects:
Enter object ordering option [Above objects/Under objects/Front/Back]<Back>:
```

You must then select the option by typing the capitalized letter of the option.

Although this section discussed the Draworder tool's options in relation to raster images, they can also be invaluable in controlling visibility of line work in conjunction with hatch patterns and solid fills. See Chapter 7 for a detailed discussion of the Draworder tools and hatch patterns.

## Clipping a Raster Image

In Chapter 7, you saw how you can clip an external-reference object so that only a portion of it appears in the drawing. You can clip imported raster images in the same way. Just as with Xrefs, you can create a closed outline of the area you want to clip, or you can specify a simple rectangular area.

---

**IMAGES AND THE EXTERNAL REFERENCES PALETTE**

The Reference Manager palette you saw in Chapter 7 helps you manage your imported image files. It's especially helpful when you have a large number of images in your drawing. You can control imported images in a way similar to how you control Xrefs; you can temporarily unload images (to help speed up the editing of AutoCAD objects) and reload, detach, and relocate raster image files. See Chapter 7 for a detailed description of these options.

---

In the following exercise, you'll try the Clip command to control the display of the raster image:

1. Type **IMAGECLIP**↵. You can also choose Modify ➢ Clip ➢ Image from the menu bar.

2. At the Select object to clip: prompt, click the edge of the raster image.

3. At the Enter image clipping option [ON/OFF/Delete/New boundary]<New>: prompt, press ↵ to create a new boundary.

**4.** At the `Specify clipping boundary or select invert option: [Select polyline/ Polygonal/Rectangular/Invert clip] <Rectangular>:` prompt, enter **P**↵ to draw a polygonal boundary.

**5.** Select the points shown in the top image in Figure 13.4 and then press ↵. The raster image is clipped to the boundary you created, as shown in the second image in Figure 13.4.

As the prompt in step 3 indicates, you can turn the clipping off or on, or you can delete an existing clipping boundary with the Imageclip command.

After you clip a raster image, you can adjust the clipping boundary by using its grips:

**1.** Click the boundary edge of the raster image to expose its grips.

**2.** Click a grip in the upper-right corner, as shown in the final image in Figure 13.4.

**FIGURE 13.4**
Adjusting the boundary of a clipped image

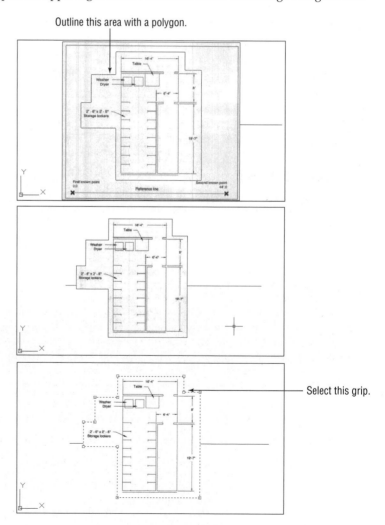

3. Drag the grip up and to the right, and then click a point. The image adjusts to the new boundary.

In addition to hiding portions of a raster image that are unimportant to you, clipping an image file reduces the amount of RAM the raster image uses during your editing session. AutoCAD loads only the visible portion of the image into RAM and ignores the rest.

## Adjusting Brightness, Contrast, and Fade

AutoCAD offers a tool that enables you to adjust the brightness, contrast, and strength of a raster image. Try making some adjustments to the raster image of the utility room in the following exercise:

1. Click the edge of the raster image.

2. In the Properties Inspector palette, navigate to the Image Adjust options. Drag the Fade slider to the right so that it's near the middle of the slider scale. The sample image fades to the AutoCAD background color as you move the slider.

3. Press the Esc key to un-select the raster image.

4. Save the file as `Rasterimport.dwg`.

You can adjust the brightness and contrast by using the other two sliders in the Adjust options of the Properties Inspector palette.

By using the Image tab in conjunction with image clipping, you can create special effects. Figure 13.5 shows an aerial view of downtown San Francisco with labels. This view consists of two copies of the same raster image. One copy serves as a background, which was lightened using this exercise. The second copy is the darker area of the image with a roughly triangular clip boundary applied. You might use this technique to bring focus to a particular area of a drawing you're preparing for a presentation.

If the draw order of objects is incorrect after you open a file or perform a Pan or Zoom, enter RE⏎ to recover the correct draw-order view.

**FIGURE 13.5**
Two copies of the same image can be combined to emphasize a portion of the drawing.

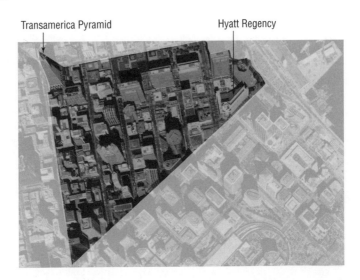

Transamerica Pyramid

Hyatt Regency

## Turning Off the Frame, Adjusting Overall Quality, and Controlling Transparency

You can make three other adjustments to your raster image: frame visibility, image quality, and image transparency.

By default, a raster image displays an outline, or a *frame*. In many instances, this frame can detract from your drawing. You can turn off image frames globally by typing **IMAGEFRAME** ↲ **0**↲. This sets the Imageframe setting to 0, which turns off the frame visibility. If it's set to 1, the frame is made visible. You can also set it to 2, which leaves the frame visible but doesn't plot it (see Figure 13.6).

**FIGURE 13.6**
A raster image with the frame on (top) and off (bottom)

Transamerica Pyramid            Hyatt Regency

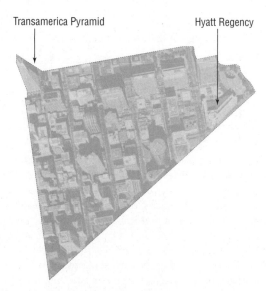

Transamerica Pyramid            Hyatt Regency

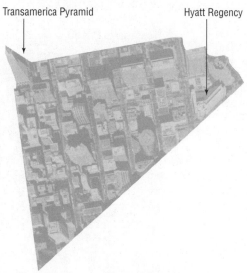

If your drawing doesn't require the highest-quality image, you can set the image quality to Draft mode. You may use Draft mode when you're tracing an image or when the image is already of a high quality. To set the image quality, enter **IMAGEQUALITY**↵ and then enter **H** for High mode (high quality) or **D** for Draft mode. In Draft mode, your drawing will regenerate faster.

High mode softens the pixels of the raster image, giving the image a smoother appearance. Draft mode displays the image in a raw, pixelated state. If you look carefully at the regions between the motorcycle and the background in the top image in Figure 13.7, you'll see that the edges of the motorcycle appear a bit jagged. In the bottom image, the High setting was used to soften the edges of the motorcycle. You may need to look closely to see the difference.

**FIGURE 13.7**
A close-up of a raster image with quality set to Draft (top) and High (bottom)

Finally, you can control the transparency of raster image files that allow transparent pixels. Some file formats, such as the CompuServe GIF 89a format, enable you to set a color in the image to be transparent (usually the background color). Most image editing programs support this format because it's a popular one used on web pages.

When you turn on the Transparency setting, objects normally obscured by the background of a raster image may show through. Enter **TRANSPARENCY**↵, and then select the raster image you want to make transparent. Press ↵, and then enter **ON** or **OFF**, depending on whether you want the image to be transparent. Unlike the Frame and Quality options, Transparency works on individual objects rather than operating globally.

**CAN'T GET TRANSPARENCY TO WORK?**

The Transparency command does not work on all types of images. As mentioned, it works with GIF files that have the background removed. You can also use a bitonal image, meaning the image must have only two colors, typically black and white. A bitonal image is also referred to as a *bitmap* image in Adobe Photoshop. It cannot be grayscale or multicolor. You can put images that do not work with the Transparency command on a layer with a transparency setting set to a value greater than 0. To use the Transparency slider, select the object, such as an image or hatch pattern, then adjust the slider to achieve the level of transparency you want. You can start at 50 and adjust downward or upward.

Note that if you want your image to print or plot with the transparency in effect, you must select the Print Transparency option in the Print - Advanced dialog box.

The Properties Inspector palette offers many of the same adjustments described in this section, and you can use it for quick access to the Transparency setting and other raster-image settings.

## The Bottom Line

**Convert paper drawings into AutoCAD files.**   AutoCAD gives you some great tools that let you convert your paper drawings into AutoCAD files. Several options are available. Depending on your needs, you'll find at least one solution that will allow you to convert your drawings quickly.

**Master It**   Describe the different methods available in AutoCAD for converting paper drawings into AutoCAD files.

**Import a raster image.**   You can use bitmap raster images as backgrounds for your CAD drawings or as underlay drawings that you can trace over.

**Master It**   Import a raster image of your choice, and use the AutoCAD drawing tools to trace over your image.

**Work with a raster image.**   Once imported, raster images can be adjusted for size, brightness, contrast, and transparency.

**Master It**   Import a raster image of your choice, and fade the image so it appears lighter and with less contrast.

# Chapter 14

# Advanced Editing and Organizing

Because you may not know all of a project's requirements when it begins, you usually base the first draft of a design on anticipated needs. As the plan goes forward, you adjust for new requirements as they arise. As more people enter the project, additional design restrictions come into play and the design is further modified. This process continues throughout the project, from the first draft to the end product.

In this chapter, you'll gain experience with some tools that will help you edit your drawings more efficiently. You'll take a closer look at Xrefs and how they may be used to help streamline changes in a drawing project. AutoCAD can be a powerful time-saving tool if used properly. This chapter examines ways to harness that power.

In this chapter, you'll learn to do the following:

◆ Use external references (Xrefs)

◆ Manage layers

## Using External References (Xrefs)

Chapter 7, "Mastering Viewing Tools, Hatches, and External References," mentioned that careful use of blocks, external references (Xrefs), and layers can help improve your productivity. In the following sections, you'll see firsthand how to use these features to help reduce design errors and speed up delivery of an accurate set of drawings. You do this by controlling layers in conjunction with blocks and Xrefs to create a common drawing database for several drawings.

In Chapter 15, "Laying Out Your Printer Output," you'll start to use Xrefs to create different floor plans for the building you worked on earlier in this book. To save some time, I've created a second one-bedroom unit plan called Unit2 that you'll use in these exercises (see Figure 14.1). You can find this new unit plan in the Chapter 14 sample files, which can be found on the companion website, www.sybex.com/go/masteringautocadmac.

**FIGURE 14.1**
The one-bedroom unit

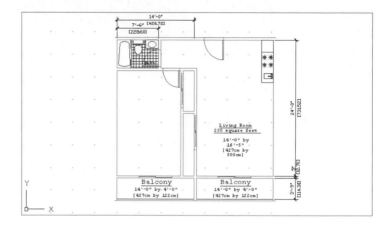

## Preparing Existing Drawings for External-Referencing

Chapter 7 discussed how you can use Xrefs to assemble one floor of the apartment. In this section, you'll explore the creation and use of Xrefs to build multiple floors, each containing slightly different sets of drawing information. By doing so, you'll learn how Xrefs enable you to use a single file in multiple drawings to save time and reduce redundancy. You'll see that by sharing common data in multiple files, you can reduce your work and keep the drawing information consistent.

You'll start by creating the files that you'll use later as Xrefs:

1. Open the Plan file. If you didn't create the Plan file, you can use the 14a-plan.dwg or 14a-plan-metric.dwg file (see Figure 14.2).

**FIGURE 14.2**
The overall plan

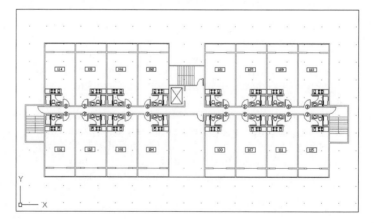

2. If they are not already, turn off the Ceiling and Flr-pat layers to get a clear, uncluttered view of the individual unit plans.

3. Use the Wblock command (enter **W**↵ at the Command prompt), and write the eight units in the corners of your plan to a file called Floor1.dwg in your Documents folder (see Figure 14.3). When you select objects for the Wblock, be sure to include the S-DOOR

door reference symbols and apartment number symbols for those units. Use 0,0 for the Wblock insertion base point. Also make sure the Delete Objects check box is selected in the Write Block dialog box before you click the Write Block button.

**FIGURE 14.3**

Units to be exported to the Floor1 file

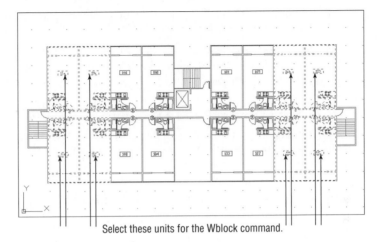

Select these units for the Wblock command.

4. Using Figure 14.4 as a guide, insert the Unit2.dwg file into the corners where the other eight units were previously. Metric users should use Unit2-metric.dwg. These files can be found in the Chapter 14 sample files available on the companion website. If you didn't create the Unit2 file earlier in this chapter, use the 14a-unit2.dwg file.

**FIGURE 14.4**

Insertion information for Unit2. Metric coordinates are shown in brackets.

Insert Unit2 at coordinate 31'-5", 104'-6" [957,3184]; x-scale factor = 1; y-scale factor = -1 (minus one).

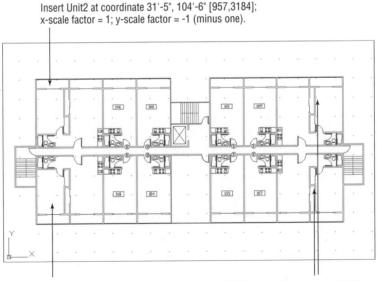

Insert Unit2 at coordinate 31'-5", 43'-8" [957,1330]; x- and y-scale factor=1.

Mirror inserted Unit2 blocks to this side.

5. After you've accurately placed the corner units, use the Wblock command to write these corner units to a file called Floor2.dwg. Again, use the 0,0 coordinate as the insertion base point for the Wblock, and make sure the Delete Objects check box is selected.

6. Choose File ➢ Save As from the menu bar to turn the remaining set of unit plans into a file called Common.dwg.

You've just created three files: Floor1, Floor2, and Common. Each file contains unique information about the building. Next, you'll use the Xref command to recombine these files for the different floor plans in your building.

## Assembling Xrefs to Build a Drawing

You'll now create composite files for each floor using Xrefs of only the files needed for the individual floors. You'll use the Attach Reference option of the Xref command to insert all the files you exported from the Plan file.

Follow these steps to create a file representing the first floor:

1. Close the Common.dwg file, create a new file, and call it Xref-1.

2. Set up this file as an architectural drawing, 8½″ × 11″ with a scale of ¹⁄₁₆″ = 1′. The upper-right corner limits for such a drawing are 2112,1632. Metric users should set up a drawing at 1:200 scale on an A4 sheet size. Your drawing area should be 4200 cm × 5940 cm. Press **Z↵ A↵** to execute the Zoom All command so your drawing area is adjusted to the window.

3. Set the Ltscale value to 192. Metric users should set it to 200.

4. Type ⌘-7 to open the Reference Manager. Click the Attach Reference tool from the Reference Manager palette or type **XA↵** to open the Select Reference File dialog box.

5. Locate and select the Common.dwg file.

6. In the Attach External Reference dialog box, make sure the Specify On-Screen check box in the Insertion Point group isn't selected. Then make sure the X, Y, and Z values in the Insertion Point group are all 0 (Figure 14.5). Because the insertion points of all the files are the same (0,0), they will fit together perfectly when they're inserted into the new files.

7. Click OK. The Common.dwg file appears in the drawing.

The drawing may appear faded. This is because AutoCAD has a feature that allows you to fade an Xref so that it is easily distinguished from other objects in your current drawing. You can change the reference-fade setting by doing the following:

1. Right-click on the drawing and select Preferences or press ⌘-, (comma). Click the Look And Feel tab. In the Transparency Controls section, locate the XRefs slider.

2. Click and drag the XRefs slider all the way to the left.

**FIGURE 14.5**
The Attach
External
Reference
dialog box

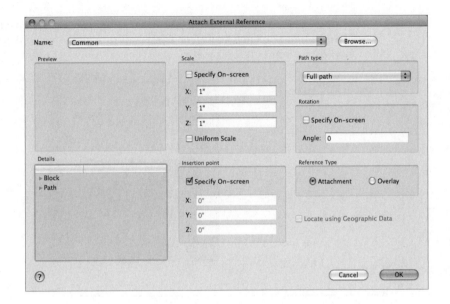

Your Xref should now appear solid. Remember the XRefs slider; you may find that you'll need it frequently when working with Xrefs.

Now continue to add some reference files:

1. Click Attach Reference from the Reference Manager, and then locate, select, and insert the `Floor1` or `Floor1-metric` file.

2. Repeat step 1 to insert the `Col-grid.dwg` or `Col-grid-metric.dwg` file as an Xref. You now have the plan for the first floor.

3. Save this file.

Next, use the current file to create another file representing a different floor:

1. Choose File ➢ Save As from the menu bar to save this file as `Xref-2.dwg`.

2. In the Reference Manager palette, select Floor1 in the list of Xrefs.

3. Right-click and select Detach from the shortcut menu. Click Yes on the alert dialog.

5. Right-click in the blank portion of the list in the Reference Manager palette, and select Insert Reference from the shortcut menu.

6. The Select Reference File dialog will open. Locate and open `Floor2.dwg`.

7. In the Attach External Reference dialog box, make sure the X, Y, and Z values in the Insertion Point group are all set to 0.

8. Click OK. The Floor2 drawing appears in place of Floor1.

Now when you need to make changes to Xref-1 or Xref-2, you can edit their individual Xref files. The next time you open Xref-1 or Xref-2, the updated Xrefs will automatically appear in their most recent forms.

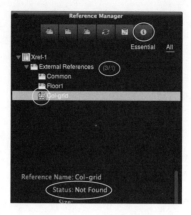

### LOCATING XREF FILES

If you move an Xref file after you insert it into a drawing, AutoCAD may not be able to find it later when you attempt to open the drawing. This is often indicated by visual clues in the Reference Manager. The icon next to the missing file will show with an exclamation mark, the external reference will now show a red number after it, indicating that there are missing Xref files, and the status in the Details group will indicate Not Found.

If you know that you'll be keeping your project files in one place, you can use the Projectname system variable in conjunction with the Application Preferences dialog box to direct AutoCAD to look in a specific location for Xref files. Here's what to do:

1. Right-click and select Preferences from the shortcut menu, press ⌘+, (comma), or enter **OP**↵.

2. Click the Application tab, and then locate and select the Project Files Search Path option.

3. Click Add and either enter a name for your project or accept the default name of Project1.

4. Click Browse and locate and select the folder where you plan to keep your Xref files.

5. Close the Application Preferences dialog box, and then enter **PROJECTNAME**↵ at the Command prompt.

6. Enter the project name you used in step 3. Save your file so it remembers this setting.

Xrefs don't need to be permanent. As you saw in the previous exercise, you can attach and detach them easily at any time. This means that if you need to get information from another file—to see how well an elevator core aligns, for example—you can temporarily attach the other file as an Xref to check alignments quickly, and then detach it when you're finished.

Think of these composite files as final plot files that are used only for plotting and reviewing. You can then edit the smaller, more manageable Xref files. Figure 14.6 illustrates the relationship of these files.

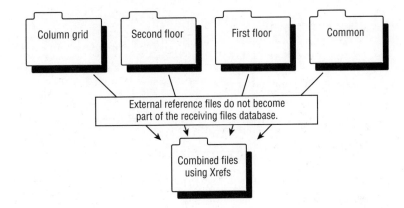

**FIGURE 14.6**
A diagram of Xref file relationships

The combinations of Xrefs are limited only by your imagination, but you should avoid multiple Xrefs of the same file in one drawing.

### UPDATING BLOCKS IN XREFS

Several advantages are associated with using Xref files. Because the Xrefs don't become part of the drawing file's database, the referencing files remain small. Also, because Xref files are easily updated, work can be split up among several people in a workgroup environment or on a network. For example, for your hypothetical apartment-building project, one person can be editing the Common file while another works on Floor1, and so on. The next time the composite Xref-1.dwg or Xref-2.dwg file is opened, it automatically reflects any new changes made in the Xref files. Let's see how to set this up:

1. Save and close the Xref-2 file, and then open the Common.dwg file.

2. Update the unit plan you edited earlier in this chapter. Click the Insert tool on the Tool Sets palette. You can also type I↵.

3. In the Insert Block dialog box, click the Browse button, and then locate and select Unit.dwg. If you can't find your Unit.dwg file, you can use 14b-unit.dwg. Click Open, and then click Insert in the Insert Block dialog box.

4. If a warning message appears, click Redefine Block.

5. At the Specify insertion point: prompt, press the Esc key.

6. Enter RE↵ to regenerate the drawing. You see the new unit plan in place of the old one (see Figure 14.7). You may also see all the dimensions and notes for each unit.

**FIGURE 14.7**
The Common file
with the revised
unit plan

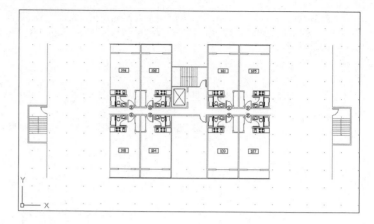

7. If the Notes layer is on, use the Layer pop-up list to turn it off.

8. Erase all the items in the empty room across the hall from the lobby.

9. Click the Insert tool on the Tool Sets palette again, and insert the utility room on the plan (utility.dwg or utility-metric.dwg); see Figure 14.8.

**FIGURE 14.8**
The utility room
inserted

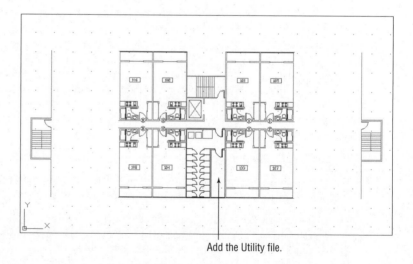

Add the Utility file.

10. You may have to move the utility block into place so that the walls all line up.

11. Save the Common file.

12. Open the Xref-1 file. You see the utility room and the typical units in their new form. Your drawing should look like the top image in Figure 14.9.

13. Open Xref-2. You see that the utility room and typical units are updated in this file as well. (See the bottom image in Figure 14.9.)

**FIGURE 14.9**
The Xref-1 and
Xref-2 files with
the units updated

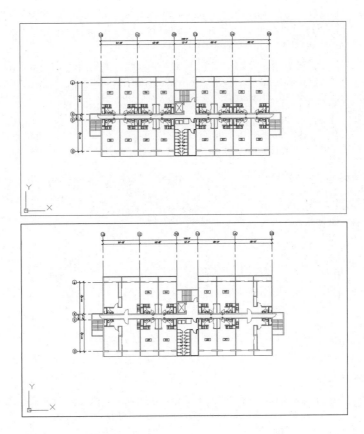

## Importing Named Elements from Xrefs

Chapter 5, "Keeping Track of Layers and Blocks," discussed how layers, blocks, linetypes, and text styles—called *named elements*—are imported along with a file that is inserted into another file. Xref files don't import named elements. You can, however, review their names and use a special command to import the ones you want to use in the current file.

---

### SAVING XREF LAYER SETTINGS

You can set the Visretain system variable to 1 to force AutoCAD to remember layer settings of Xref files.

---

AutoCAD renames named elements from Xref files by giving them the prefix of the filename from which they come. For example, the Wall layer in the Floor1 file is called Floor1|WALL in the Xref-1 file; the Toilet block is called Floor1|TOILET. You can't draw on the layer Floor1|WALL, nor can you insert Floor1|TOILET, but you can view Xref layers in the Layers palette, and you can view Xref blocks by using the Insert Block dialog box.

Next, you'll look at how AutoCAD identifies layers and blocks in Xref files, and you'll get a chance to import a layer from an Xref:

1. With the Xref-1 file open, open the Layers palette by pressing ⌘+4. Notice that the names of the layers from the Xref files are all prefixed with the filename and the vertical bar (|) character.

2. Enter **XB⏎** to open the Bind External Definitions dialog box. You see a listing of the current Xrefs. Each item shows a disclosure triangle to the left. The list box follows the Mac OS format for expandable lists (Figure 14.10).

**FIGURE 14.10**
The Bind External Definitions dialog box

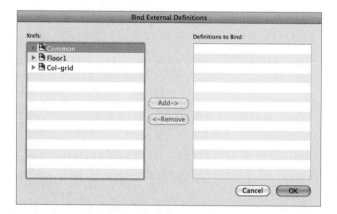

3. Click the disclosure triangle next to the Floor1 Xref item. The list expands to show the types of elements available to bind (Figure 14.11).

**FIGURE 14.11**
The expanded Floor1 list

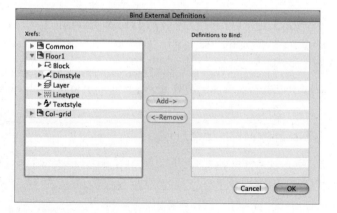

4. Click the disclosure triangle next to the Layer item. The list expands further to show the layers available for binding (Figure 14.12).

5. Locate Floor1|WALL in the list, click it, and then click the Add button. Floor1|WALL is added to the list to the right, Definitions To Bind.

**FIGURE 14.12**
The expanded
Layer list

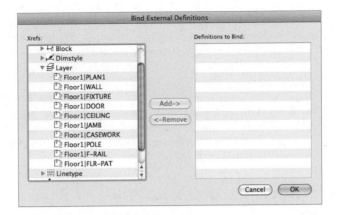

6. Click OK to bind the Floor1|WALL layer.

7. Open the Layers palette.

8. Scroll down the list and look for the Floor1|WALL layer. You won't find it. In its place is a layer called Floor1$0$WALL.

---

 **Real World Scenario**

### NESTING XREFS AND USING OVERLAYS

Xrefs can be nested. For example, if the Common.dwg file created in this chapter used the Unit.dwg file as an Xref rather than as an inserted block, you would still get the same result in the Xref-1. dwg file. That is, you would see the entire floor plan, including the unit plans, when you opened Xref-1.dwg. In this situation, Unit.dwg would be nested in the Common.dwg file, which is in turn externally referenced in the Xref-1.dwg file.

Although nested Xrefs can be helpful, take care in using Xrefs this way. For example, you might create an Xref by using the Common.dwg file in the Floor1.dwg file as a means of referencing walls and other features of the Common.dwg file. You might also reference the Common.dwg file into the Floor2.dwg file for the same reason. After you did this, however, you'd have three versions of the Common plan in the Xref-1.dwg file because each Xref would have Common.dwg attached to it. And because AutoCAD would dutifully load Common.dwg three times, Xref-1.dwg would occupy substantial computer memory, slowing your computer when you edited the Xref-1.dwg file.

To avoid this problem, use the Overlay option in the Attach External Reference dialog box. An overlaid Xref can't be nested. For example, if you use the Overlay option when inserting the Common. dwg file into the Floor1.dwg and Floor2.dwg files, the nested Common.dwg files are ignored when you open the Xref-1.dwg file, thereby eliminating the redundant occurrence of Common.dwg. In another example, if you use the Overlay option to import the Unit.dwg file into the Common.dwg file, and then attach the Common.dwg into Xref-1.dwg as an Xref, you don't see the Unit.dwg file in Xref-1.dwg. The nested Unit.dwg drawing is ignored.

As you can see, when you use Xbind to import a named item, such as the Floor1|WALL layer, the vertical bar (|) is replaced by two dollar signs surrounding a number, which is usually zero. (If for some reason the imported layer name Floor1$0$WALL already exists, the zero in that name is changed to 1, as in Floor1$1$WALL.) Other named items are renamed in the same way, using the $0$ replacement for the vertical bar.

You can also use the Bind External Definitions dialog box to bind multiple layers as well as other items from Xrefs attached to the current drawing. You can bind an entire Xref to a drawing, converting it to a simple block. By doing so, you have the opportunity to maintain unique layer names of the Xref being bound or to merge the Xref's similarly named layers with those of the current file. See Chapter 7 for details.

### Controlling the Xref Search Path

One problem AutoCAD users have encountered in the past is lost or broken links to an Xref. This occurs when an Xref file is moved from its original location or when you receive a set of drawings that includes Xrefs. The Xref links are broken because AutoCAD doesn't know where to look. Since AutoCAD 2005, you have had better control over how AutoCAD looks for Xref files.

When you insert an Xref, the Attach External Reference dialog box opens, offering you options for insertion point, scale, and rotation. This dialog box also provides the Path Type option, which enables you to select a method for locating Xrefs. You can choose from three Path Type options:

**Full Path**   Lets you specify the exact filename and path for an Xref, including the disk drive or network location. Use this option when you want AutoCAD to look in a specific location for the Xref.

**Relative Path**   Lets you specify a file location relative to the location of the current or host drawing. This option is useful when you know you'll maintain the folder structure of the host and Xref files when moving or exchanging these files. Note that because this is a relative path, this option is valid only for files that reside on the same local hard disk.

**No Path**   Perhaps the most flexible option, this tells AutoCAD to use its own search criteria to find Xrefs. When No Path is selected, AutoCAD first looks in the same folder of the host drawing; then it looks in the project search path defined in the Application tab of the Application Preferences dialog box. Last, AutoCAD looks in the Support File Search Path option, also defined in the Application tab of the Application Preferences dialog box. If you plan to send your files to a client or a consultant, you may want to use this option.

## Managing Layers

In a survey of AutoCAD users, Autodesk discovered that one of the most frequently used features in AutoCAD is the Layer command. You'll find that you turn layers on and off to display and edit the many levels of information contained in your AutoCAD files. All of the layer management tools can be found in the Format ➢ Layer Tools submenu on the menu bar, but some are also found on the Layers palette.

You can quickly revert to a previous layer setting by choosing Format ➢ Layer Tools ➢ Layer Previous. The Layer Previous tool enables you to revert to the previous layer settings without affecting other settings in AutoCAD. Note that Previous mode doesn't restore renamed or deleted layers, nor does it remove new layers.

### CHANGING THE LAYER ASSIGNMENT OF OBJECTS

There are two tools that change the layer assignments of objects: the Layer Match tool and the Change To Current Layer tool.

The *Layer Match tool* is similar to the Match Properties tool, but it's streamlined to operate only on layer assignments. After clicking this tool on the Layers palette, select the object or objects you want to change, press ↵, and then select an object whose layer you want to match.

The *Change To Current Layer tool* on the Format ➤ Layer Tools submenu on the menu bar changes an object's layer assignment to the current layer. This tool has long existed as an AutoLISP utility, and you'll find that you'll get a lot of use from it.

### CONTROLLING LAYER SETTINGS THROUGH OBJECTS

The remaining Layer tools let you make layer settings by selecting objects in the drawing. These tools are easy to use: click the tool or menu item, and then select an object.

The following list describes each tool:

**Layer Isolate/Layer Unisolate**   Layer Isolate turns off all the layers except for the layer of the selected object. Layer Unisolate restores the layer settings to the way the drawing was set before you used Layer Isolate.

**Layer Freeze**   Freezes the layer of the selected object.

**Layer Off**   Turns off the layer of the selected object.

**Layer Lock/Layer Unlock**   Locks/unlocks the layer of the selected object. A locked layer is visible but can't be edited.

**Make Object's Layer Current**   Enables you to set the current layer by selecting an object that is on the desired layer.

**Isolate To Current Viewport**   Enables you to freeze layers in all but the current viewport by selecting objects that are on the layers to be frozen. Found in the Format ➤ Layer Tools submenu on the menu bar.

**Delete**   Deletes all objects on a layer and then deletes the layer. Found in the Format ➤ Layer Tools submenu on the menu bar.

### SELECT SIMILAR AND ISOLATE OBJECT FOR EASIER EDITING

There are a few new features that can help speed up object selection. First, let's explore the Select Similar command.

Just as the name implies, Select Similar will select all objects in the drawing that are similar to the one currently selected. For example, if you wish to select all similar hatches on the drawing, Select Similar will be your best friend. This command can be invoked either before or after object selection. If you choose to use it before selecting objects, you can find the tool on the Tool Sets palette. The `Select objects or [Settings]:` prompt is displayed. Select an object, such as a line, and then press Enter. All items on the drawing that are lines and are on the same layer and color will be highlighted.

If you select an object and right-click, you'll see the Select Similar option. Click on a line, right-click, and then click Select Similar, and all the lines that are on the selected line's layer will be highlighted.

You can control how the Select Similar feature behaves by entering **SELECTSIMILAR.⌐ SE.⌐**. This opens the Select Similar Settings dialog box, which lets you set the basis for the similar selection, such as layer, color, or linetype, to name a few.

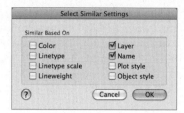

Another handy option is to isolate. If you have a set of objects, right-click, and select Isolate ➢ Isolate Objects; all but the selected objects will be made invisible. Or you can right-click and select Isolate ➢ Hide Objects to hide the selected objects. To bring back the objects that were made invisible, right-click and select Isolate ➢ End Object Isolation. If you happen to save and close a drawing that has the object isolation in effect, when you reopen the drawing, the isolated layers will be reset as if you performed the End Object Isolation command.

---

**SINGLING OUT PROXIMATE OBJECTS**

You'll sometimes need to select an object that overlaps or is very close to another object. Often in this situation you end up selecting the wrong object. To select the exact object you want, you can use the Draworder command.

You can select the overlapping object and then from the right-click menu, choose Send To Back from the Draworder flyout.

---

## The Bottom Line

**Use external references (Xrefs).**   You've seen how you can use Xrefs to quickly build variations of a floor plan that contains repetitive elements. This isn't necessarily the only way to use Xrefs, but the basic idea of how to use Xrefs is presented in the early exercises.

**Master It**   Try putting together another floor plan that contains nothing but the Unit2 plan.

**Change Layer information.**   Layers is a powerful tool used in AutoCAD drawings. You can modify a layer using various properties found in the Layers palette.

**Master It**   Modify the Ceiling layer so that it displays a very light gray line.

**Select similar objects.**   Select Similar can select alike objects. It can be invoked from the shortcut menu when objects are selected.

**Master It**   Select all the walls on the plan drawing and change them so that they are now set to the color magenta. Now reset them to their previous color.

# Chapter 15

# Laying Out Your Printer Output

Your set of drawings for the studio apartment building would probably include a larger-scale, more detailed drawing of the typical unit plan. You already have the beginnings of this drawing in the form of the Unit file.

As you've seen, the notes and dimensions you entered into the Unit file can be turned off or frozen in the Plan file so they don't interfere with the graphics of the drawing. The Unit file can be part of another drawing file that contains more detailed information about the typical unit plan at a larger scale. To this new drawing, you can add notes, symbols, and dimensions. Whenever the Unit file is altered, you update its occurrence in the large-scale drawing of the typical unit as well as in the Plan file. The units are thus quickly updated, and good coordination is ensured among all the drawings for your project.

Now, suppose you want to combine drawings that have different scales in the same drawing file—for example, the overall plan of one floor plus an enlarged view of one typical unit. You can do so using the layout views and a feature called *Paper Space*.

In this chapter, you'll learn how to do the following:

- Understand Model Space and Paper Space

- Work with Paper Space viewports

- Create odd-shaped viewports

- Understand line weights, linetypes, and dimensions in Paper Space

## Understanding Model Space and Paper Space

So far, you've looked at ways to get around in your drawing while using a single view. This single-view representation of your AutoCAD drawing is called *Model Space*. You can also set up multiple views of your drawing by using what are called *floating viewports*. You create floating viewports in layout views in what is called *Paper Space*.

To get a clear understanding of Model Space and Paper Space, imagine that your drawing is actually a full-size replica or model of the object you're drawing. Your computer screen is your window into a "room" where this model is being constructed, and the keyboard and mouse are your means of access to this room. You can control your window's position in relation to the object through the use of Pan, Zoom, View, and other display-related commands. You can also construct or modify the model by using drawing and editing commands. Think of this room as your Model Space.

You've been working on your drawings by looking through a single window into Model Space. Now, suppose you have the ability to step back and add windows with different views looking into your Model Space. The effect is as if you have several video cameras in your Model Space room, each connected to a different monitor. You can view all your windows at once on your computer screen or enlarge a single window to fill the entire screen. Further, you can control the shape of your windows and easily switch from one window to another. This is what Paper Space is like.

Paper Space lets you create and display multiple views of Model Space. Each view window, called a *viewport*, acts like an individual virtual screen. One viewport can have an overall view of your drawing, while another can be a close-up. You can also control layer visibility individually for each viewport and display different versions of the same area of your drawing. You can move, copy, and stretch viewports and even overlap them. You can set up another type of viewport, called the *tiled viewport*, in Model Space. Chapter 20, "Using Advanced 3D Features," discusses this type of viewport.

One of the most powerful features of Paper Space is the ability to print several views of the same drawing on one sheet of paper. You can also include graphic objects such as borders and notes that appear only in Paper Space. In this function, Paper Space acts much like a page-layout program such as QuarkXPress or Adobe InDesign. You can paste up different views of your drawing and then add borders, title blocks, general notes, and other types of graphic and textual data. Figure 15.1 shows the Plan drawing set up in Paper Space mode to display several views.

**FIGURE 15.1**
Different views of the same drawing in Paper Space

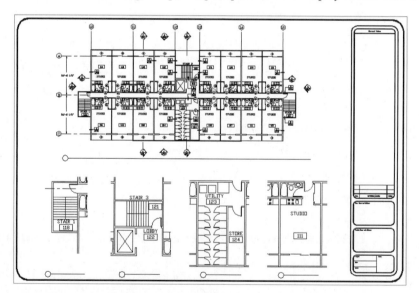

## Switching from Model Space to Paper Space

You can get to Paper Space by selecting a layout from the Layouts pop-up menu on the status bar or clicking on any of the layout thumbnails in the Show Drawings & Layouts tool on the status bar.

If you don't see the Show Drawings & Layouts or Model/Layout tools, right-click in a blank area of the status bar and click QuickView from the shortcut menu. The Show Drawings & Layouts and Model/Layout tools make up the QuickView tools.

Let's start with the basics of switching between model and Paper Space:

**1.** Open the Xref-1 file you saved from the last chapter, and ensure that your display shows the entire drawing. You can also use 15-xref1.dwg or 15-xref1-metric.dwg.

Layout1

**2.** Click the Model/Layout pop-up menu in the status bar and select Layout1. The pop-up menu is now labeled Layout1. You will see your drawing appear in a kind of page preview view (Figure 15.2).

**FIGURE 15.2**
Your drawing in a
page preview view

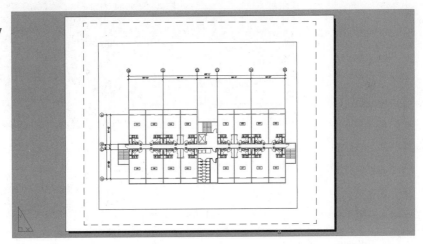

Model

**3.** Click the Model/Layout pop-up menu in the status bar and select Model to return to Model Space.

This brief exercise shows you how quickly you can shift between Model Space and a Paper Space layout by using the Model/Layout pop-up menu. The QuickView tool lets you do the same thing but offers a little more help. Try the following to see how the QuickView tool works:

**1.** Click the Show Drawings & Layouts tool in the status bar to open the QuickView dialog box. (Figure 15.3).

**2.** Double-click the thumbnail labeled Layout1. Notice that the drawing area changes to show the Paper Space of Layout1.

**3.** Click the Show Drawings & Layouts tool again, but this time double-click the thumbnail labeled Model.

If you prefer, you can use command aliases to switch between Model Space and Paper Space. Enter **TM↵ 1↵** to go to Model Space. Enter **TM↵ 0↵** to go to Paper Space.

**FIGURE 15.3**
The Quickview
dialog box

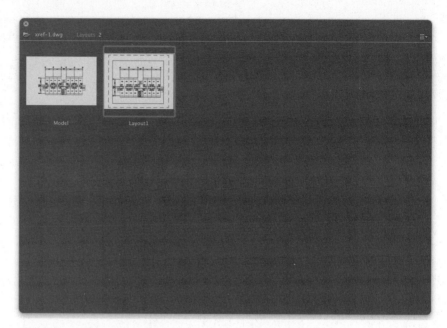

## Setting the Size of a Paper Space Layout

I mentioned that Paper Space is like a page layout program, and you saw how a Paper Space layout looks like a print preview. You can set up your layout for a specific set of printer settings, including the paper size and printer.

Let's continue our look at Paper Space by seeing how a Paper Space layout can be set up for your printer:

1. Click the Show Drawings & Layouts tool.

2. Right-click Layout1, and choose Page Setup to open the Page Setup Manager dialog box. Notice that the name of the current layout is shown in the list of current page setups (Figure 15.4).

3. Click the Modify action menu and select Edit to open the Page Setup dialog box.

   Note that if you do not have a printer configured, a warning box will appear informing you of that. Click OK to dismiss the warning dialog box.

4. Select the Letter paper-size option from the Paper Size pop-up menu. Metric users should select A4 (210 mm × 297 mm). The paper size you select here determines the shape and margin of the Paper Space layout area.

5. Select a printer from the Printer name pop-up menu.

6. Click OK to close the Page Setup dialog box, and then click Close to close the Page Setup Manager dialog box.

AutoCAD bases the Paper Space layout on the paper size and printer you specify in steps 4 and 5. The area shown in Paper Space reflects the area of the paper size you selected in step 4, and the paper margin shown by a dashed line is determined by the printer. If for some reason you need to change the paper size, repeat steps 2 through 5. You can also store the way you've set up your Paper Space layout using the Page Setup Manager dialog box you saw in step 2. See Chapter 8, "Introducing Printing and Layouts," for more on this feature.

**FIGURE 15.4**

The Page Setup Manager dialog box

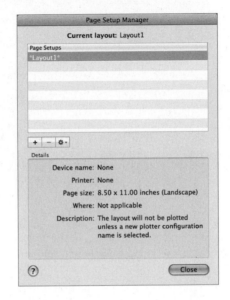

### Creating New Paper Space Viewports

As you saw in Chapter 8, the different look of the layout view tells you that you're in Paper Space. You also learned that a viewport is automatically created when you first open a layout view. The layout viewport displays an overall view of your drawing to no particular scale.

In this section, you'll work with multiple viewports in Paper Space instead of just the default single viewport you get when you open the layout view.

This first exercise shows you how to create three new viewports at once:

1. Click the viewport border to select it. The viewport border is the solid rectangle surrounding your drawing, just inside the dashed rectangle.

2. Click the Erase tool in the Tool Sets palette to erase the viewport. Your drawing disappears. Don't panic; remember that the viewport is like a window to Model Space. The objects in Model Space are still there.

3. Chose View ➤ Viewports ➤ New Viewports to open the Viewports dialog box. You can also type **VPORTS**↵. This dialog box contains a set of predefined viewport layouts (Figure 15.5). You'll learn more about the Viewports dialog box and its options in Chapter 20.

FIGURE 15.5
The Viewports
dialog box

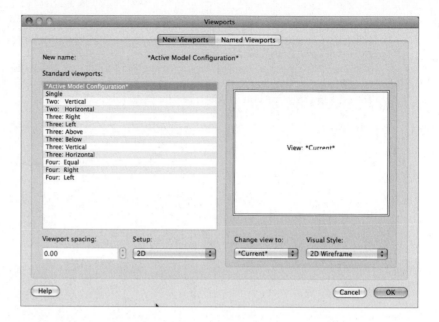

4. Click the Three: Above option in the Standard Viewports list box. The box to the right shows a sample view of the Three: Above layout you selected.

5. Click OK. The Specify first corner or [Fit] <Fit>: prompt appears.

6. Press ↵ to accept the default Fit option. The Fit option fits the viewport layout to the maximum area allowed in your Paper Space view. Three rectangles appear in the formation, as shown in Figure 15.6. Each of these is a viewport to your Model Space. The viewport at the top fills the whole width of the drawing area; the bottom half of the screen is divided into two viewports.

When you create new viewports, AutoCAD automatically fills them with the extents of your Model Space drawing. You can specify an exact scale for each viewport, as you'll see later.

Notice that the dashed line representing your paper margin has disappeared. That's because the viewports are pushed to the margin limits, thereby covering the dashed line.

You could have kept the original viewport that appeared when you first opened the Layout1 view and then added two new viewports. Completely replacing the single viewport is a bit simpler because the Viewports dialog box fits the viewports in the allowed space for you.

After you've set up a Paper Space layout, it remains part of the drawing. You may prefer to use Model Space for doing most of your drawing and then use Paper Space layouts for setting up views for printing. Changes that you make to your drawing in Model Space will automatically appear in your Paper Space layout viewports.

**FIGURE 15.6**
The newly created
viewports

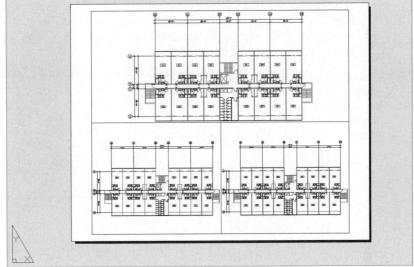

## Reaching inside Viewports

Now, suppose you need access to the objects in the viewports in order to adjust their display and edit your drawing. Try these steps:

1. Double-click inside a viewport. This gives you control over Model Space even though you're in Paper Space. (You can also enter **MS**↵ as a command alias to enter Model Space while on a layout.)

   The first thing you notice is that the UCS icon changes back to its L-shaped arrow form. It also appears in each viewport, as if you had three AutoCAD drawing windows instead of just one.

2. Move your cursor over each viewport. In one of the viewports, the cursor appears as the AutoCAD crosshair cursor, whereas in the other viewports it appears as an arrow pointer. The viewport that shows the AutoCAD cursor is the active one; you can pan, zoom, and edit objects in the active viewport.

3. Click in the lower-left viewport to activate it.

4. Click Zoom on the status bar and then type **W**↵, and place a window selection around the elevator area. You can also type **Z**↵ **W**↵.

5. Click in the lower-right viewport, and click Zoom Window to enlarge your view of a typical unit. You can also use the Pan and Zoom Realtime tools. If you don't see the UCS icon, it has been turned off. Type **UCSICON**↵ **ON**↵ to turn it on. See Chapter 20 for more on the UCS icon.

You can move from viewport to viewport even while you're in the middle of most commands. For example, you can issue the Line command, pick the start point in one viewport, go to a different viewport to pick the next point, and so on. To activate a different viewport, you click inside the viewport (see Figure 15.7).

**FIGURE 15.7**
The three viewports, each with a different view of the plan

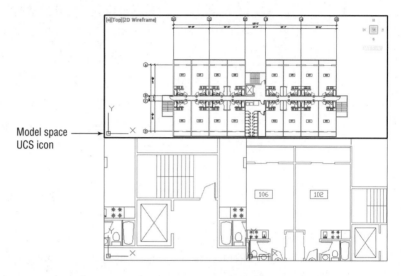

Model space  UCS icon

---

## 🌐 Real World Scenario

### SWITCHING BETWEEN VIEWPORTS

I've found that users will have a need to overlap viewports from time to time. When they do this, they are often at a loss over how to switch between the overlapping viewports, especially when one is completely surrounded by another or they are exactly the same size and in the same position. In this situation, you can move between viewports by pressing ^-R repeatedly until you get to the viewport you want.

---

You've seen how you can zoom into a viewport view, but what happens when you use the Zoom command while in Paper Space? Try the following exercise to find out:

1. Double-click an area outside the viewports to get out of Model Space.

2. Click Zoom on the status bar and then press ↵ to activate the Zoom Realtime option, and then, using your mouse, zoom in to the Paper Space view. The entire view enlarges, including the views in the viewports.

3. Right-click and choose Exit. Click Zoom on the status bar and then type **A**↵ or enter **Z**↵ **A**↵ to return to the overall view of Paper Space.

This brief exercise showed that you can use the Zoom tool in Paper Space just as you would in Model Space. All the display-related commands are available, including the Zoom Realtime command.

# Working with Paper Space Viewports

Paper Space is intended as a page-layout or composition tool. You can manipulate viewports' sizes, scale their views independently of one another, and even set layering and linetype scales independently.

Let's try manipulating the shape and location of viewports:

1. Make sure Object Snap is turned off in the status bar.

2. Make sure you're not in any viewports on the Paper Space layout. Then click the bottom edge of the lower-left viewport to expose its grips (see the top image in Figure 15.8).

**FIGURE 15.8**

Stretching, erasing, and moving viewports

Stretch the viewport grip to this location.

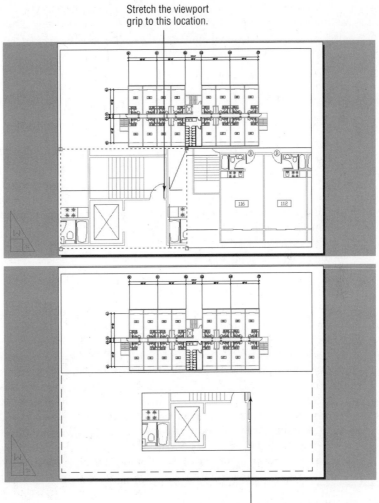

Move the viewport here.

3. Click the upper-right grip, and drag it to the location shown in the top image in Figure 15.8.

4. Press the Esc key, and erase the lower-right viewport by selecting it and clicking Erase on the Tool Sets palette or by pressing the Delete key.

5. Move the lower-left viewport so it's centered in the bottom half of the window, as shown in the bottom image in Figure 15.8.

In this exercise, you clicked the viewport edge to select it for editing. If, while in Paper Space, you attempt to click the image in the viewport, you won't select anything. Later, you'll see that you can use the osnap modes to snap to parts of the drawing image in a viewport.

Because viewports are recognized as AutoCAD objects, you can manipulate them by using all the editing commands, just as you would manipulate any other object. In the previous exercise, you moved, stretched, and erased viewports.

Next, you'll see how layers affect viewports:

1. Create a new layer called Vport.

2. In the Properties Inspector palette, change the viewport borders to the Vport layer.

3. Turn off the Vport layer. The viewport borders disappear.

4. After reviewing the results of step 3, turn the Vport layer back on.

You can assign a layer, a color, a linetype, and even a line weight to a viewport's border. If you put the viewport's border on a layer that has been turned off or frozen, that border becomes invisible, just like any other object on such a layer. Or you can put the viewport border on a non-printing layer so the border will be visible while you're editing. Making the borders invisible or putting them on a nonprinting layer is helpful when you want to compose a final sheet for printing. Even when turned off, the active viewport has a heavy border around it when you switch to Model Space, and all the viewports still display their views.

## Scaling Views in Paper Space

Paper Space has its own unit of measure. You've already seen how you're required to specify a paper size when opening a layout view to a Paper Space view. When you first enter Paper Space, regardless of the area your drawing occupies in Model Space, you're given limits that are set by the paper size you specify in the Page Setup dialog box. If you keep in mind that Paper Space is like a paste-up area that is dependent on the printer you configured for AutoCAD, this difference of scale becomes easier to comprehend. Just as you might paste up photographs and maps representing several square miles onto an 11″-×-17″ board, so can you use Paper Space to paste up views of scale drawings representing city blocks or houses on an 8½″-×-11″ sheet of paper. But in AutoCAD, you have the freedom to change the scale and size of the objects you're pasting up.

While in Paper Space, you can edit objects in Model Space through a viewport. You can then click a viewport and edit in that viewport. In this mode, objects that were created in Paper Space can't be edited. Double-click outside a viewport to go back to the Paper Space.

If you want to be able to print your drawing at a specific scale, you must indicate a scale for each viewport. Viewport scales are set in a way similar to the annotation scale in the model layout. Let's look at how to put together a layout in Paper Space and still maintain accuracy of scale:

1. Make sure you're in Paper Space. You can tell by the shape and location of the UCS icon. If it looks like a triangle in the lower-left corner of the layout view, then you are in Paper Space.

2. Click the topmost viewport's border to select it.

3. In the lower-right corner of the AutoCAD window, click the Viewport Scale pop-up menu, and select ¹⁄₃₂″ = 1′-0″. Metric users should click Custom and add a custom scale of 1:400. Then select the 1:400 scale from the Viewport Scale pop-up menu. Notice how the view in the top viewport changes.

4. Press the Esc key once to clear the selection in the viewport.

5. Click the lower viewport border.

6. Click the VP Scale pop-up menu again, and select ³⁄₁₆″ = 1′-0″. Metric users should select 1:100. The view in the viewport changes to reflect the new scale (see Figure 15.9).

**FIGURE 15.9**
Paper Space viewport views scaled to ¹⁄₃₂″ = 1′-0″ and ³⁄₁₆″ = 1′-0″ (1:400 and 1:100 for metric users)

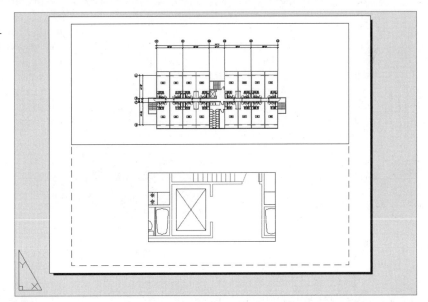

It's easy to adjust the width, height, and location of the viewports so they display only the parts of the unit you want to see. While in Paper Space, use the Stretch, Move, Scale, or Rotate command to edit any viewport border, or use the viewport's grips to edit its size and shape. The view in the viewport remains at the same scale and location while the viewport changes in size. You can move and stretch viewports with no effect on the size and location of the objects in the view. When you rotate the viewport, the view inside the viewport will also rotate.

If you need to overlay one drawing on top of another, you can overlap viewports. Use the Osnap overrides to select geometry in each viewport, even while in Paper Space. This enables you to align one viewport on top of another at exact locations.

You can also add a title block in Paper Space at a 1:1 scale to frame your viewports and then print this drawing from Paper Space at a scale of 1:1. Your print appears just as it does in Paper

Space, at the appropriate scale. Paper Space displays a dashed line to show you where the non-printable areas occur near the edge of the paper.

While you're working in Paper Space, pay close attention to the UCS icon. If it appears inside the viewing area, you are in a viewport. It's easy to pan or zoom in a viewport accidentally when you intend to pan or zoom your Paper Space view. This can cause you to lose your viewport scaling or alignment with other parts of the drawing.

One way to prevent your viewport view from being accidentally altered is to turn on Display Lock. To do this, while in Paper Space, click a viewport border. Right-click to open the shortcut menu, and then choose Display Locked ➤ Yes. After the view is locked, you can't pan or zoom within a viewport. This setting is also available in the viewport's Properties Inspector palette.

## Setting Layers in Individual Viewports

Another unique feature of Paper Space viewports is their ability to freeze layers independently. You can, for example, display the usual plan information in the overall view of a floor but show only the walls in the enlarged view of one unit.

You control viewport layer visibility through the Layers palette. You may have noticed that there are three snowflake icons for each layer listing. You're already familiar with the snowflake icon farthest to the left. This is the Freeze/Thaw icon that controls the freezing and thawing of layers globally. Several columns to the right of that icon are two icons with transparent rectangles. These icons control the freezing and thawing of layers in individual viewports. Of this pair, the one on the left controls existing viewports and the one on the right controls settings for newly created viewports. Note that in the Layers palette and the menu bar, you will see New VP Freeze and VP Freeze. VP is another way of saying *viewport*.

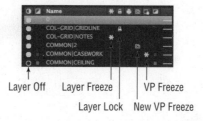

To see all of the layer options, you may need to widen the Layers palette to view all the columns or display a layer property in the list. To do so, undock the palette, and then click and drag the border of the palette. Right-click a column header and choose the properties that you want to display.

This exercise shows you firsthand how the icon for existing viewports works:

1. Double-click inside a viewport to enter Model Space.

2. Activate the lower viewport.

3. If it is not already open, open the Layers palette (⌘-4).

4. Locate the COMMON|WALL layer, and then click its name to help you isolate it.

5. Click the column labeled VP Freeze for the selected layer. You may need to widen the Layers palette to do this. If VP Freeze does not display on the Layers palette, right-click the layer header and select VP Freeze. Click the column, which looks like a transparent

rectangle under a snowflake. The icon appears in the COMMON|WALL layer, telling you that the layer is now frozen for the current viewport.

The Wall layer of the Common Xref becomes invisible in the current viewport. However, the walls remain visible in the other viewport (see Figure 15.10).

**FIGURE 15.10**

The drawing with the COMMON|WALL layer turned off in the active viewport

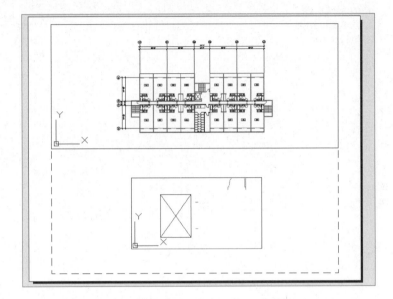

**6.** After reviewing the effects of the VP Freeze setting, go back to the Layers palette and thaw the COMMON|WALL layer by clicking the VP Freeze icon so it disappears.

**7.** Take a moment to study the drawing, and then save the Xref-1 file.

You may have noticed another column, with an identical snowflake icon next to the one you used in the previous exercise. This column controls layer visibility in any new viewports you create next rather than in existing viewports. This column might be turned off by default; if it is, right-click the column headers in the Layers palette and choose New VP Freeze.

In addition to setting the visibility of layers, you can set the other layer properties—such as color, linetype, and line weight—for each viewport. First, make sure you're in Model Space for the viewport whose layers you want to set up, and then open the Layers palette. You can set the properties for the current viewport using the VP Freeze, VP Color, VP Linetype, VP Lineweight, VP Transparency, and VP Plot Style settings for each layer (Figure 15.11).

**FIGURE 15.11**

The VP Freeze, VP Color, VP Linetype, VP Lineweight, VP Transparency and VP Plot Style columns in the Layers palette

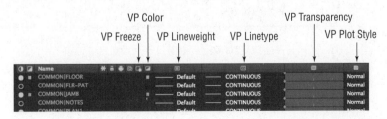

This section concludes the apartment building tutorial. Although you haven't drawn the complete building, you've learned all the commands and techniques you need to do so. Figure 15.12 shows a completed plan of the first floor. To complete your floor plans and get some practice using AutoCAD, you may want to add the symbols shown in this figure to your Plan file.

**FIGURE 15.12**
A completed floor of the apartment building

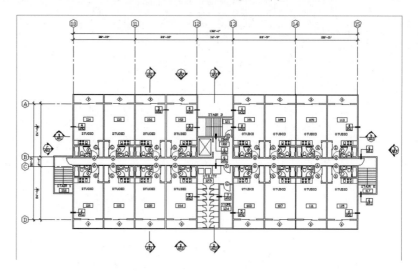

Because buildings like this one often have the same plans for several floors, the plan for the second floor can also represent the third floor. Combined with the first floor, this gives you a three-level apartment building. This project might also have a ground-level garage, which would be a separate file. You can use the Col-grid.dwg file (which can be found on the book's companion website, www.sybex.com/go/masteringautocadmac) in the new garage drawing that you create as a reference for dimensions. The other symbols can be blocks stored as files that you can retrieve in other files.

---

**MASKING OUT PARTS OF A DRAWING**

Chapter 7, "Mastering Viewing Tools, Hatches, and External References," described a method for using AutoCAD's Draworder feature to hide floor patterns under equipment or furniture in a floor layout. You can use a similar method to hide irregularly shaped areas in a Paper Space viewport. This is desirable for plotting site plans, civil plans, or floor plans that require portions of the drawing to be masked out. You may also want to mask part of a plan that is overlapped by another to expose dimension or text data.

---

## Creating and Using Multiple Paper Space Layouts

You're not limited to just one or two Paper Space layouts. You can have as many as you want, with each layout set up for a different sheet size containing different views of your drawing. You can use this feature to set up multiple drawing sheets based on a single AutoCAD drawing file. For example, suppose a client requires full sets of plans in both ⅛″ = 1′ scale and ¹⁄₁₆″ = 1″ scale. You can set up two layouts, each with a different paper size and viewport scale.

You can also set up different Paper Space layouts for the different types of drawings. A single drawing can contain the data for mechanical layout, equipment and furnishing, floor plans, and reflected ceiling plans. Although a project can require a file for each floor plan, a single file with multiple layout views can serve the same purpose.

To create new layout views, do the following:

1. Click the Show Drawings & Layouts tool in the status bar. The QuickView dialog box opens.

2. Click the menu on the upper right-hand corner of the QuickView dialog box to display the Layout options (see Figure 15.13). You can also right-click a thumbnail in the QuickView dialog box to display the options. Choose Create New Layout. The Create Layout dialog box appears with a default layout name (Layout2) for the new layout.

**FIGURE 15.13**
The Layout options

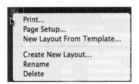

3. Click the Confirm button to add the new Layout2.

4. Double-click Layout2. The new layout appears with a single default viewport.

You've just seen how you can create a new layout using the Show Drawings & Layouts tool.

The Show Drawings & Layouts shortcut menu also includes the New Layout From Template option. The New Layout From Template option lets you create a Paper Space layout based on a layout saved in a drawing (DWG), drawing template (DWT), or DXF file. AutoCAD provides several drawing templates with standard layouts that include title blocks based on common sheet sizes.

To move a tab, simply click and drag it to where you want it to appear. Finally, if you want to duplicate, delete, or rename a layout, click the Show Drawings & Layouts tool and then right-click the layout you want to edit. You can then select the option from the shortcut menu that appears. If you select Delete, you'll see a warning message telling you that AutoCAD will permanently delete the layout you have chosen to delete. Click OK to confirm your deletion.

## Creating Odd-Shaped Viewports

In many situations, a rectangular viewport doesn't provide a view appropriate for what you want to accomplish. For example, you might want to isolate part of a floor plan that is L-shaped or circular. You can create viewports for virtually any shape you need. You can grip edit a typical rectangular viewport to change its shape into a trapezoid or other irregular four-sided polygon. You can also use the Polygonal Viewport tool to create more complex viewport shapes, as the following exercise demonstrates.

Follow these steps to set up a layout view that shows only the lower apartment units and the elevators and stairs:

1. Choose View ➢ Viewports ➢ Polygonal Viewport from the menu bar.

2. Turn on Ortho Mode from the status bar.

3. Turn off Running Osnaps, and draw the outline shown in the top portion of Figure 15.14.

4. After you finish selecting points, type **C**↵ to close the polyline. The viewport changes to conform to the new shape.

**FIGURE 15.14**
Drawing a polygon outline for a view-port

Draw this polygon outline.

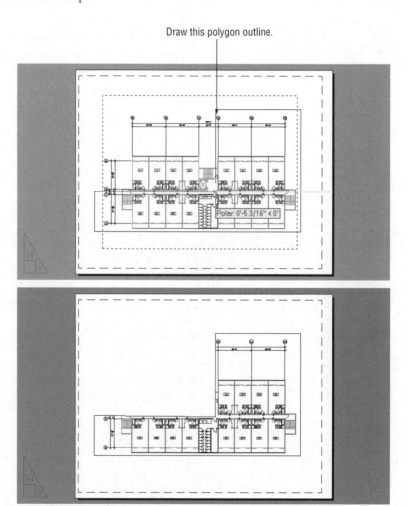

**5.** Click the viewport border to expose its grips.

**6.** Click a grip, and move it to a new location. The viewport view conforms to the new shape.

The new viewport shape gives you more flexibility in isolating portions of a drawing. This can be especially useful if you have a large project that is divided into smaller sheets. You can set up several layout views, each displaying a different portion of the plan.

What if you want a viewport that isn't rectilinear? This exercise shows you how to create a circular viewport:

**1.** Erase the viewport you just modified.

**2.** Draw a circle that roughly fills the layout.

**3.** Choose View ➤ Viewports ➤ Object from the menu bar. You can also type **-VPORTS↵ O↵** (letter *O*, not the number zero).

**4.** Click the circle. The plan appears inside the circle, as shown in Figure 15.15.

**FIGURE 15.15**
A circular viewport

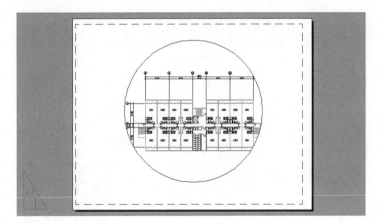

To simplify this exercise, you were asked to draw a circle as the basis for a new viewport. However, you aren't limited to circles; you can use a closed polyline or spline of any shape. (See Chapter 17, "Drawing Curves," for a detailed discussion of polylines and splines.) You can also use the Polygon tool to create a shape and then turn it into a viewport.

If you look carefully at the series of prompts for the previous exercise, you'll notice that the Object tool invokes a command-line version of the Vports command (-vports). This command-line version offers some options that the standard Vports command doesn't. The following options are available with the command-line version of Vports:

```
-vports
Specify corner of viewport or [ON/OFF/Fit/Shadeplot/Lock
Object/Polygonal/Restore/Layer/2/3/4] <Fit>:
```

You used two of the options—Polygonal and Object—in the two previous exercises.

## Understanding Line Weights, Linetypes, and Dimensions in Paper Space

The behavior of several AutoCAD features depends on whether you're in Paper Space or Model Space. The most visible of these features are line weights, linetypes, and dimensions. In the following sections, you'll take a closer look at these features and see how to use them in conjunction with Paper Space.

### Controlling and Viewing Line Weights in Paper Space

Line weights can greatly improve the readability of technical drawings. You can make important features stand out with bold line weights while keeping the noise of smaller details from overpowering a drawing. In architectural floor plans, walls are traditionally drawn with heavier lines so the outline of a plan can be easily read. Other features exist in a drawing for reference only, so they're drawn in a lighter weight than normal.

In Chapter 8, you saw how to control line weights in AutoCAD by using plot style tables. You can apply either a named plot style table or a color plot style table to a drawing. If you already have a library of AutoCAD drawings, you may want to use color plot style tables for backward compatibility. AutoCAD also enables you to assign line weights directly to layers or objects and to view the results of your line-weight settings in Paper Space.

Here's an exercise that demonstrates how to set line weights directly:

1. Open the Layers palette (⌘-4).

2. Right-click the layer list, and choose Select All.

3. Click the Lineweight column to open the Lineweight pop-up menu (Figure 15.16).

**FIGURE 15.16**
The Lineweight
pop-up menu

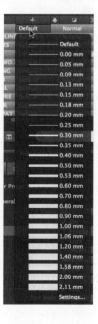

4. Select 0.13 mm from the list. You've just assigned the 0.13 mm line weight to all layers.

5. Right-click the layer list again, and choose Clear All.

6. Click the Common|WALL layer, and ⌘-click the Floor1|WALL layer to select these two layers.

7. Click the Lineweight column for either of the two selected layers to open the Lineweight pop-up menu again.

8. Select 0.40 mm from the list. You've just assigned the 0.40 mm line weight to the two selected layers.

9. Right-click the layer list and choose Clear All. Close the Layers palette or press ⌘-4.

Although you set the line weights for the layers in the drawing, you need to make a few more changes to the file settings before they're visible in Paper Space:

1. Click the Show/Hide Lineweight tool from the status bar.

2. Make sure you're in Paper Space, and then zoom in to the drawing.

3. Type **REA**↵. The lines representing the walls are now thicker, as shown in Figure 15.17.

4. After reviewing the results of this exercise, close the file.

**FIGURE 15.17**
An enlarged view of the plan with line weights displayed

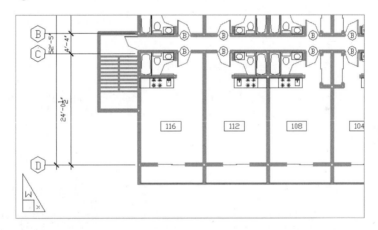

With the ability to display line weights in Paper Space, you have better control over your output. Instead of using a trial-and-error method to print your drawing and then checking your printout to see whether the line weights are correct, you can see the line weights on your screen.

This exercise showed you how to set line weights so they appear in Paper Space as they will when you print your drawing. If you normally print your drawings in black, you can go one step further and set all your layer colors to black to see how your plots will look. But you'll need to save your layer settings so you can restore the layers to their original colors. Another way to view your drawing in black and white without affecting your layer settings is to use the color plot style table described in Chapter 8.

---

**LINE WEIGHT DISPLAY SHORTCUT**

When line-weight display is turned on, you see line weights in Model Space as well as in Paper Space. Line weights can be distracting while you work on your drawing in Model Space, but you can quickly turn them off by entering **LWDISPLAY.** **OFF.** at the Command prompt. Entering **LWDISPLAY.** **ON.** turns the line-weight display back on.

---

## The Lineweight Settings Dialog Box

Another method of displaying line-weight settings is via the Lineweight Settings dialog box. Type **LW.** to open the Lineweight Settings dialog box shown in Figure 15.18.

**FIGURE 15.18**
The Lineweight
Settings dialog box

The Lineweight Settings dialog box includes some settings that were not mentioned in Chapter 8's discussion of line-weight settings. Here is a description of those settings for your reference:

**Units**  You can choose between millimeters and inches for the unit of measure for line weights. The default is millimeters.

**Default pop-up menu**  This pop-up menu lets you select the default line weight you see in the Layers palette. It's set to 0.01″ (0.25 mm) by default. You may want to lower the default line weight to 0.005″ (0.13 mm) as a matter of course because most printers these days can print lines that size and even smaller.

**Preview Scaling**  This setting lets you control just how thick line weights appear in the drawing. Move the slider to the right for thicker lines and to the left for thinner lines. This setting affects only the display on your monitor.

## Linetype Scales and Paper Space

As you've seen in previous exercises, you must carefully control drawing scales when creating viewports. Fortunately, this is easily done through the Properties Inspector palette. Although Paper Space offers the flexibility of combining images of different scale in one display, it also adds to the complexity of your task in controlling that display. Your drawing's linetype scale in particular needs careful attention.

In Chapter 5, "Keeping Track of Layers and Blocks," you saw that you had to set the linetype scale to the scale factor of the drawing in order to make the linetype visible. If you intend to print that same drawing from Paper Space, you have to set the linetype scale back to 1 to get the linetypes to appear correctly. This is because AutoCAD faithfully scales linetypes to the current unit system. Remember that Paper Space units are different from Model Space units. When you scale a Model Space image down to fit in the smaller Paper Space area, the linetypes remain scaled to the increased linetype scale settings. In the Chapter 5 example, linetypes are scaled up by a factor of 24. This causes noncontinuous lines to appear as continuous in Paper Space because you see only a small portion of a greatly enlarged noncontinuous linetype.

The Psltscale system variable enables you to determine how linetype scales are applied to Paper Space views. You can set Psltscale so the linetypes appear the same regardless of whether you view them directly in Model Space or through a viewport in Paper Space. By default, this system variable is set to 1. This causes AutoCAD to scale all the linetypes uniformly across all the viewports in Paper Space. You can set Psltscale to 0 to force the viewports to display linetypes exactly as they appear in Model Space. Psltscale is not a global setting. You must set Psltscale for each layout view that you create; otherwise, the default value of 1 will be used.

You can also control this setting in the Linetype Manager dialog box (type **LT**↵). At the bottom of the dialog, you see a check box called Use Paper Space Units For Scaling. When this check box is selected, Psltscale is set to 1. When it isn't selected, Psltscale is set to 0.

## Dimensioning in Paper Space Layouts

At times, you may find it more convenient to add dimensions to your drawing in Paper Space rather than directly on your objects in Model Space. This can be useful if you have a small project with several viewports in a layout and you want to keep dimensions aligned between viewports. You have two basic options when dimensioning Model Space objects in Paper Space. The associative dimensioning feature can make quick work of dimensions for layout views containing drawings of differing scales. Alternatively, if you prefer not to use associative dimensioning (see Chapter 11, "Using Dimensions"), you can adjust settings for individual dimension styles.

### USING ASSOCIATIVE DIMENSIONING IN PAPER SPACE

Perhaps the simplest way to dimension in Paper Space is to use the associative dimensioning feature. With this feature turned on, you can dimension Model Space objects while in a Paper Space layout. Furthermore, Paper Space dimensions of Model Space objects are automatically updated if the Model Space object is edited.

Try the following exercise to see how associative dimensioning works:

1. Click File ➢ New from the menu bar (or press ⌘-N), and use the `acad.dwt` template to create a new blank file. Metric users select use the `acadiso.dwt` template.

2. Draw a rectangle 12 units wide by 4 units high. If you're using a metric file, make the rectangle 480 units wide by 160 units high.

3. Click the Show Drawings & Layouts tool from the status bar.

4. Click the Layout1 thumbnail. Right-click and choose Page Setup.

**5.** In the Page Setup Manager dialog box, click the action menu with the icon that looks like a gear and choose Edit. Then, in the Page Setup – Layout 1 dialog box, select Letter from the Paper Size pop-up menu in the Printer/Plotter section. Metric users can pick ISO A4.

**6.** Click OK, and then close the Page Setup Manager dialog box.

Next, you'll use the rectangle you drew in Model Space to test the associative dimensioning feature in the Layout1 view:

**1.** Select the Annotation toolset from the Tool Sets palette. Click the Linear Dimension tool. Using the Endpoint osnap, dimension the bottom edge of the rectangle you drew in Model Space. The dimension shows 12.0000 (480 for metric drawings), the actual size of the rectangle.

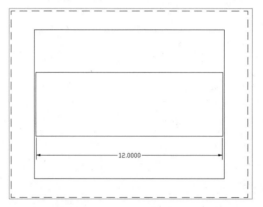

**2.** Double-click inside the viewport, and use the Zoom Realtime tool to zoom out a bit so the rectangle appears smaller in the viewport. Do not use the scroll wheel of your mouse to do this (see the next section, "Updating Associative Dimensions"). After you exit the Zoom Realtime tool, the dimension follows the new view of the rectangle.

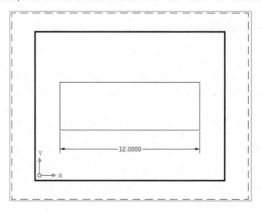

**3.** While you're in Model Space, click the rectangle, and then click the grip in the lower-left corner and drag it upward and to the right.

**4.** Click again to place the corner of the rectangle in a new location. The dimension changes to conform to the new shape.

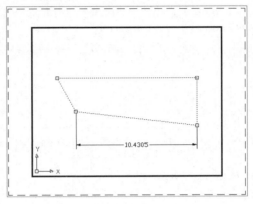

**5.** Close the drawing file without saving it. You won't need it in the future.

You've just seen how you can dimension an object in Model Space while in Paper Space. You can also dimension Model Space Xrefs in Paper Space in much the same way. The only difference is that changes to the Xref file don't automatically update dimensions made in Paper Space. You need to employ the Dimregen command to refresh Paper Space dimensions of Xref objects.

### UPDATING ASSOCIATIVE DIMENSIONS

If you use a wheel mouse to pan and zoom in a Paper Space viewport, you may need to use the Dimregen command to refresh an associative dimension. To do so, type **DIMREGEN**↵ at the Command prompt. You can also use Dimregen to refresh dimensions from drawings that have been edited in earlier versions of AutoCAD or, as mentioned already, to refresh dimensions of objects contained in external references.

### PAPER SPACE DIMENSIONING WITHOUT ASSOCIATIVE DIMENSIONING

In some situations, you may not want to use associative dimensioning although you still want to dimension Model Space objects in Paper Space. For example, you might be in an office that has different versions of AutoCAD, or you might be sharing your drawings with other offices that aren't using the latest release of AutoCAD and the use of associative dimensioning creates confusion.

To dimension Model Space objects in Paper Space without associative dimensioning, you need to have AutoCAD adjust the dimension text to the scale of the viewport from which you're dimensioning. You can have AutoCAD scale dimension values in Paper Space so they correspond to a viewport zoom-scale factor. The following steps show you how this setting is made:

**1.** Open the Dimension Style Manager dialog box by choosing Dimension ➤ Dimension Style from the menu bar, or type **DIMSTYLE**↵.

**2.** Select the dimension style you want to edit, and click the action menu with the gear icon and choose Modify.

**3.** Click the Primary Units tab.

**4.** In the Linear Dimensions group, enter the scale factor of the viewport you intend to dimension in the Scale Factor input box. For example, if the viewport is scaled to a ½″ = 1′-0″ scale, enter **24**.

**5.** Click the Apply To Layout Dimensions Only check box.

**6.** Click OK, and then click Close in the Dimension Style Manager dialog box. You're ready to dimension in Paper Space.

Remember that you can snap to objects in a Model Space viewport so you can add dimensions as you normally would in Model Space. If you're dimensioning objects in viewports of different scales, you need to set up multiple dimension styles, one for each viewport scale.

### Other Uses for Paper Space

The exercises in the preceding sections should give you a sense of how you work in Paper Space and layout views. I've given examples that reflect common uses of Paper Space. Remember that Paper Space is like a page-layout portion of AutoCAD—separate yet connected to Model Space through viewports.

You needn't limit your applications to floor plans. You can take advantage of Paper Space with interior and exterior elevations, 3D models, and detail sheets. When used in conjunction with AutoCAD's raster-import capabilities, Paper Space can be a powerful tool for creating large-format presentations.

## The Bottom Line

**Understand Model Space and Paper Space.** AutoCAD offers two viewing modes for viewing and printing your drawings. Model Space is where you do most of your work; it's the view you see when you create a new file. Layouts, also called Paper Space, are views that let you arrange the layout of your drawing, similar to how you would in a page-layout program.

**Master It** Name the method of moving from Model Space to Paper Space.

**Work with Paper Space viewports.** While in Paper Space, you can create views into your drawing using viewports. You can have several viewports, each showing a different part of your drawing.

**Master It** Explain how you can enlarge a view in a viewport.

**Create odd-shaped viewports.** Most of the time, you'll probably use rectangular viewports, but you have the option to create a viewport of any shape.

**Master It** Describe the process for creating a circular viewport.

**Understand line weights, linetypes, and dimensions in Paper Space.** You can get an accurate view of how your drawing will look on paper by making a few adjustments to AutoCAD. Your layout view will reflect how your drawing will look when printed.

**Master It** Name the dialog box used to adjust line weights and how you would access it.

# Chapter 16

# Making "Smart" Drawings with Parametric Tools

Don't let the term *parametric drawing* scare you. *Parametric* is a word from mathematics, and in the context of AutoCAD drawings, it means that you can define relationships between different objects in a drawing. For example, you can set up a pair of individual lines to stay parallel or set up two concentric circles to maintain an exact distance between each other no matter how they may be edited.

Parametric drawing is also called *constraint-based modeling*, and you'll see the word *constraint* used in the Tool Sets palette as well as the menu bar to describe sets of tools. The term *constraint* is a bit more descriptive of the tools you'll use to create parametric drawings because when you use them, you are applying a constraint upon the objects in your drawing.

In this chapter, you'll see firsthand how the parametric drawing tools work and how you might apply them to your needs.

In this chapter, you'll learn how to do the following:

◆ Use parametric drawing tools

◆ Connect objects with geometric constraints

◆ Control sizes with dimensional constraints

◆ Put constraints to use

## Why Use Parametric Drawing Tools

If you're not familiar with parametric drawing, you may be wondering what purpose it serves. With careful application of the parametric tools, you can create a drawing that you can quickly modify with just a change of a dimension or two instead of actually editing the lines that make up the drawing. Figure 16.1 shows a drawing that was set up so that the arcs and circles increase in size to an exact proportion when the overall length dimension is increased. This can save a lot of time if you're designing several parts that are similar with only a few dimensional changes.

You can also mimic the behavior of a mechanical assembly to test your ideas. The parametric drawing tools let you create linkages between objects so that if one moves, the others maintain their connection like a link in a chain. For example, you can create 3D AutoCAD models of a crankshaft and piston assembly of a car motor (see Figure 16.2) or the parallel arms of a Luxo lamp. If you move one part of the model, the other parts move in a way consistent with a real motor or lamp.

**FIGURE 16.1**
The d1 dimension in the top image was edited to change the drawing to look like the one in the lower half.

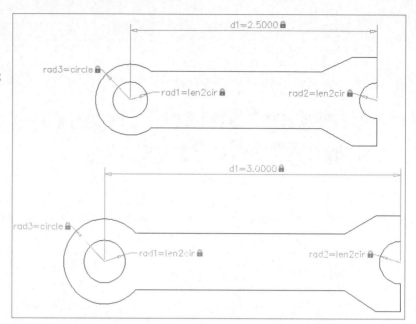

**FIGURE 16.2**
Move one part of the drawing and the other parts follow.

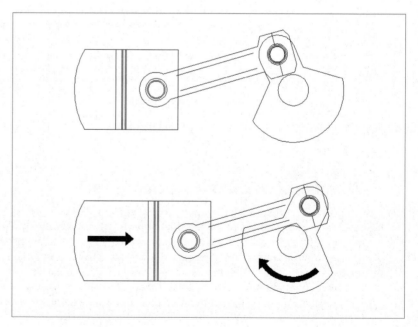

# Connecting Objects with Geometric Constraints

You'll start your exploration of parametric drawing by adding geometric constraints to an existing drawing and testing the behavior of the drawing with the constraints in place. Geometric constraints let you assign constrained behaviors to objects to limit their range of motion. Limiting motion to improve editing efficiency may seem counterintuitive, but once you've seen these tools in action, you'll see their benefits.

## Using Autoconstrain to Automatically Add Constraints

Start by opening a sample drawing and adding a few geometric constraints. The sample drawing is composed of two parallel lines connected by two arcs, as shown in Figure 16.3. These are just lines and arcs and are not polylines.

1. Open the `Parametric01.dwg` file, which can be obtained from the companion website, `www.sybex.com/go/masteringautocadmac` (Figure 16.3).

**FIGURE 16.3**
The `Parametric01` `.dwg` file containing simple lines and arcs

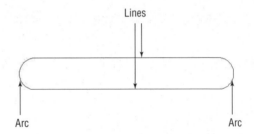

2. Click the Auto Constrain tool from the Tool Sets palette, or type **AUTOCONSTRAIN**↵.

3. Select all of the objects in the drawing, and press ↵.

You've just used the Autoconstrain command to add geometric constraints to all of the objects in the drawing. You can see a set of icons that indicate the constraints that have been applied to the objects (see Figure 16.4). The Autoconstrain command makes a "best guess" at applying constraints.

**FIGURE 16.4**
The drawing with geometric constraints added

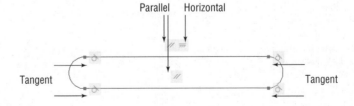

The tangent constraints that you see at the ends of the lines keep the arcs and the lines tangent to each other whenever the arcs are edited.

The parallel constraint (left) keeps the two lines parallel, and the horizontal constraint (right) keeps the lines horizontal.

There is one constraint that doesn't show an icon, but you see a clue to its existence by the small blue squares where the arcs join the lines:

1. Place your cursor on one of the blue squares.

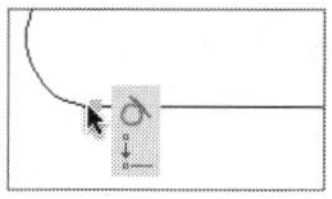

2. A new icon appears below the tangent icon. This is the Coincident icon.

The coincident constraint makes sure that the endpoints of the lines and arcs stay connected, as you'll see in the next few exercises.

## Editing a Drawing Containing Constraints

Now try editing the drawing to see firsthand how these constraints work:

1. Click the arc on the left side of the drawing (top of Figure 16.5).

2. Click the arrowhead grip to the left of the arc and move it to the left to increase the radius of the arc. The objects move in unison to maintain their geometric constraints (bottom of Figure 16.5).

3. Click again to accept the change in the arc radius.

4. Press Esc to clear the current object selection. Right-click and select Undo Grip Edit or press ⌘-Z to undo your change.

In this exercise, you saw how the tangent, parallel, horizontal, and coincident constraints worked to keep the objects together while you changed the size of one object.

**FIGURE 16.5**
Changing the radius of one arc causes the other parts of the drawing to follow because of their geometric constraints.

Click this arc.

Drag horizontally.

## Creating Constraints from Scratch

The Auto Constrain tool applied quite a few geometric constraints to the drawing. Now let's go in-depth and re-create the previous exercise. I'll explain each tool as we go along.

### THE COINCIDENT CONSTRAINT

You can either close without saving and reopen the Parametric01.dwg, which can be obtained form the companion website, or:

1. Undo all changes until you are back to the drawing before constraints were added using the Auto Constrain tool.

2. Click the Coincident tool on the Tool Sets palette, choose Parametric ➤ Geometric Constraints ➤ Coincident from the menu bar or type **GEOMCONSTRAINT**↵ **C**↵. (You can also type **GCCOINCIDENT**↵.)

3. At the Select first point or [Object/Autoconstrain] <Object>: prompt, click near the top endpoint of the left arc.

4. At the Select second point or [Object] <Object>: prompt, click the upper line at a point closest to the arc.

5. A blue square appears at the intersection of the arc and the line. As was previously mentioned, the coincident constraint makes sure the endpoints picked stay connected.

6. Click and drag the arc on the left side of the drawing and see the effect that the coincident constraint has (Figure 16.6).

**FIGURE 16.6**
The effect of the coincident constraint

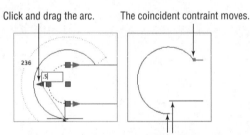

Click and drag the arc.   The coincident contraint moves.

The effect of no constraint added.

7. Choose Edit ➤ Undo from the menu bar to get the shape back to where it was.

8. Repeat steps 2 through 5 on all arc/line intersections.

### THE TANGENT CONSTRAINT

Now let's set up a constraint that will keep the arc and the line tangent:

1. Click and hold on the Coincident tool on the Tool Sets palette. A drop-down will open. Select the Tangent tool. You can also choose Parametric ➤ Geometric Constraints ➤ Tangent from the menu bar or type **GEOMCONSTRAINT**↵ **T**↵. (You can also type **GCTANGENT**↵.)

2. Select the arc and line for the first and second points as you did for the coincident constraint.

3. The Tangent icon appears next to the two objects selected.

4. Edit the arc on the left side again as you did in the previous exercises. This time the line that has the tangent constraint added maintains its tangency as you stretch the arc, as shown in Figure 16.7.

Notice that lines and arcs remain connected and tangent to each other. This is because the coincident and tangent constraints are still in effect.

---

 **Real World Scenario**

### MAINTAINING AND RELAXING CONSTRAINTS

You may have noticed that when you click the arrowhead grip of the arc that has constraints applied, you are given some choices whether you want to maintain or relax constraints. By pressing ^, you will toggle between the two options.

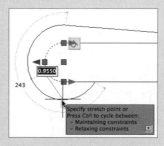

Maintaining constraints is the default action and will keep the constraint actions as they are.

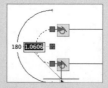

Relaxing constraints will temporarily remove the constraints attached for modification purposes. It is also a quick way of deleting any constraints attached to the object.

Let's take the Parametric01.dwg and modify the arc as we did previously:

1. Click on the left-side arc.

2. Click the arrowhead grip to the left of the arc, and drag it to the left. Notice that the lines follow along, maintaining the tangency, and the endpoints remain connected.

3. Press ^ to toggle between maintaining and relaxing constraints.

**FIGURE 16.7**
Without the hori-
zontal constraint,
both lines change
as the arc is edited.

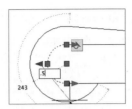

## THE PARALLEL CONSTRAINT

In the previous exercises, you have seen that when you moved the arc, the lines connecting the two arcs followed along. But what if you wanted the lines to remain parallel to each other? The parallel constraint will fix that. Let's see how it works:

1. Click and hold on the Coincident tool on the Tool Sets palette. A drop-down will open. Select the Parallel tool. You can also choose Parametric ➤ Geometric Constraints ➤ Parallel from the menu bar or type **GEOMCONSTRAINT↵ PA↵**. (You can also type **GCPARALLEL↵**.)

2. At the Select first object: prompt, click the upper line.

3. At the Select second object: prompt, click the lower line.

4. The lines are now constrained so that they cannot lose their parallelism.

5. If you stretch the arc, you will now see that the lines maintain a parallel status; the end-points will be always connected and remain tangent to the arcs.

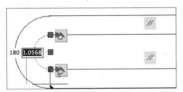

## THE HORIZONTAL CONSTRAINT

If you click on one of the lines and drag it upward or down, you will see that the lines maintain tangency and stay parallel to each other. But what if you wanted the lines to stay horizontal no matter what? Follow these steps:

1. Click and hold on the Coincident tool on the Tool Sets palette. A drop-down will open. Select the Horizontal tool. You can also choose Parametric ➤ Geometric Constraints ➤ Horizontal from the menu bar or type **GEOMCONSTRAINT↵ H↵**. (You can also type **GCHORIZONTAL↵**.)

2. At the Select an object or [2Points] <2Points>: prompt, click the upper line.

### THE CONCENTRIC CONSTRAINT

You've seen how the Auto Constrain tool applies a set of constraints to a set of objects. You have also seen some manually applied constraints. In the next exercise, you'll add a circle to the drawing and then add a few more:

1. Choose Edit ➤ Undo from the menu bar, or press ⌘-Z several times to change the drawing back to before the Horizontal constraint was added. Or, you can close the current drawing without saving and open `Parametric01a.dwg` (which is available on the companion website).

2. From the Tool Sets palette, click and hold the Linear Dimension tool. The flyout will open. Select the Radius tool, or select Draw ➤ Circle ➤ Center, Radius from the menu bar. You can also type **C**↵.

3. Click a location roughly above and to the left of the drawing, as shown in Figure 16.8. You don't need to be exact because you will use a geometric constraint to move the circle into an exact location.

4. Type **0.25**↵ for the radius of the circle.

**FIGURE 16.8**
Place the circle roughly in the location shown here.

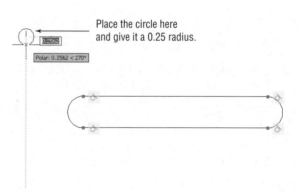

Place the circle here and give it a 0.25 radius.

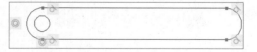

5. Click and hold on the Coincident tool on the Tool Sets palette. A drop-down will open. Select the Concentric tool. You can also choose Parametric ➤ Geometric Constraints ➤ Concentric from the menu bar or type **GEOMCONSTRAINT**↵ **CON**↵. (You can also type **GCCONCENTRIC**↵.)

6. Click the arc at the left side of the drawing, and then click the circle you just added. The circle moves to a location that is concentric to the arc, as shown in Figure 16.9.

**FIGURE 16.9**
The circle is concentric to the arc on the left side.

In this exercise, you used the geometric constraint as an editing tool to move an object into an exact location. The concentric constraint will also keep the circle inside the arc no matter where the arc moves.

---

**THE ORDER MAKES A DIFFERENCE**

When you add constraints, sometimes the order in which you add them makes an important difference. In the concentric constraint example, you selected the arc first, and then the circle. Had you selected the circle first, the arcs and lines would have moved to the circle. Instead, as you saw in the exercise, the circle moved to the inside of the arc.

---

## Using Other Geometric Constraints

You've seen firsthand how several of the geometric constraints work. For the most part, each constraint is fairly easy to understand. The tangent constraint keeps objects tangent to each other. The coincident constraint keeps the location of objects together, such as endpoints or midpoints of lines and arcs. The parallel constraint keeps objects parallel.

There are many more geometric constraints you have at your disposal. Table 16.1 gives you a concise listing of the constraints (in order of appearance in the menus) and their purposes. Note that with the exception of fix and symmetric, all of the constraints affect pairs of objects.

**TABLE 16.1:** The geometric constraints

| NAME | USE |
| --- | --- |
| Coincident | Keeps point locations of two objects together, such as the endpoints or midpoints of lines. Allowable points vary between objects and are indicated by a red circle marked with an *X* while points are being selected. |
| Collinear | Keeps lines collinear. The lines need not be connected. |
| Concentric | Keeps circles and arcs concentric. |
| Fix | Fixes a point on an object to a location in the drawing. |
| Parallel | Keeps lines parallel. |
| Perpendicular | Keeps lines or polyline segments perpendicular. |
| Horizontal | Keeps lines horizontal. |
| Vertical | Keeps lines vertical. |
| Tangent | Keeps curves, or a line and curve, tangent to each other. |
| Smooth | Maintains a smooth transition between splines and other objects. The first object selected must be a spline. You can think of this constraint as a tangent constraint for splines. |

**TABLE 16.1:** The geometric constraints *(CONTINUED)*

| NAME | USE |
| --- | --- |
| Symmetric | Maintains symmetry between two curves about an axis that is determined by a line. Before using this constraint, draw a line that you will use for the axis of symmetry. You can also use the fix, horizontal, or vertical constraint to fix the axis to a location or orientation. |
| Equal | Keeps the length of lines or polylines equal or the radius of arcs and circles equal. |

The behavior of the geometric constraints might sound simple, but you may find that they can behave in unexpected ways. With the limited space of this book, I can't give exercise examples for every geometric constraint, so I encourage you to experiment with them on your own. And have some fun with them!

## Using Constraints in the Drawing Process

Earlier you saw how the concentric constraint allowed you to move a circle into a location that's concentric to an arc. You can use other geometric constraints in a similar way. For example, you can move a line into a collinear position with another line using the collinear constraint. Or you can move a line into an orientation that's tangent to a pair of arcs or circles, as shown in Figure 16.10. The top image shows the separate line and circles and the bottom shows the objects after applying the tangent constraint. Note that while the line is tangent to the two circles, its length and orientation do not change.

**FIGURE 16.10**
You can connect two circles so that they are tangent to a line using the tangent constraint.

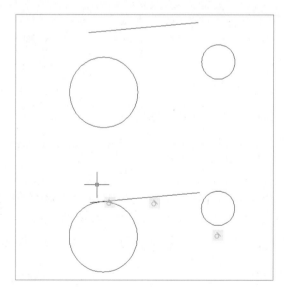

---

**ADDING CONSTRAINTS AS YOU DRAW**

In the first part of this chapter, you saw that you can add constraints to an existing drawing using the Autoconstrain command. You can also set up AutoCAD to add constraints as you draw. This feature is called Infer Constraints. You can turn Infer Constraints on or off using the Infer Constraints tool in the status bar.

If you use Infer Constraints to draw a series of lines, at the very least it will apply the coincident constraint at the end of each line segment. If you use osnaps and polar tracking, other constraints like parallel and perpendicular may be applied to objects as you draw.

---

# Controlling Sizes with Dimensional Constraints

Perhaps the heart of the AutoCAD parametric tools is the dimensional constraints. These constraints allow you to set and adjust the dimension of an assembly of parts, thereby giving you an easy way to adjust the size and even the shape of a set of objects.

For example, suppose you have a set of parts that you are drafting, each of which is just slightly different in one dimension or another. You can add geometric constraints and then add dimensional constraints, which will let you easily modify your part just by changing the value of a dimension. To see firsthand how this works, try the following exercises.

## Adding and Editing a Dimensional Constraint

In this first dimensional-constraint exercise, you'll add a horizontal dimension to the drawing you've already been working on. The drawing already has some geometric constraints that you are familiar with, so you can see how the dimensional constraints interact with the geometric constraints.

Start by adding a dimensional constraint between the two arcs:

1. Click the Aligned tool in the Tool Sets palette, or you can choose Parametrics ➢ Dimensional Constraints ➢ Aligned from the menu bar.

2. Right-click on the drawing and select Snap Overrides ➢ Center Option from the shortcut menu.

3. Place the cursor on the arc on the left side of the drawing so that the Center Osnap marker appears for the arc (Figure 16.11). Notice that the arc is highlighted as you select the center.

4. Right-click, and select Snap Overrides ➢ Center Osnap Option as you did in step 2.

5. Click the arc on the right side of the drawing (Figure 16.12).

**FIGURE 16.11**
Use the Center Osnap to select the center of the arc.

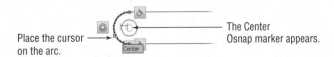

Place the cursor on the arc.

The Center Osnap marker appears.

**FIGURE 16.12**
Adding the dimensional constraint

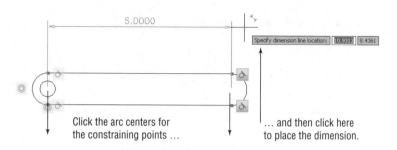

Click the arc centers for the constraining points ...

... and then click here to place the dimension.

**6.** Click a location above the drawing as shown in Figure 16.12.

**7.** At the `Dimension text` = prompt, press ⏎ to accept the current value.

The dimension constraint appears above the drawing and shows a value of d1=6.0000. The d1 is the name for that particular dimensional constraint. Each dimensional constraint is assigned a unique name, which is useful later when you want to make changes.

---

**OSNAPS ARE FORCED OFF**

In an earlier exercise, you had to select the Center Osnap from the Osnap menu. When placing dimensional constraints, you'll need to use the Osnap menu to select Center Osnaps. Running Osnaps are automatically turned off when you use the dimensional constraint tools. This is because the dimensional constraint tools use their own method of finding locations on objects.

---

Now try editing the same part by changing the dimension:

**1.** Double-click the dimension value of the dimension constraint (Figure 16.13).

**2.** Type **4.5**⏎. The part shortens to the dimension you entered.

**FIGURE 16.13**
Double-click the dimension value.

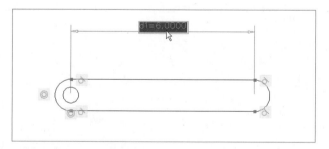

Next, add a dimension to the arc on the right side:

**1.** Click the Aligned tool from the Tool Sets palette.

**2.** Select the top endpoint of the arc on the left side (top of Figure 16.14). Do this by first hovering over the arc near the endpoint. When you see the endpoint marker, click the mouse.

3. Select the bottom endpoint of the arc in the same way.

4. Click a point to the left of the arc to place the dimension (bottom of Figure 16.14).

5. At the Dimension text = prompt, press ↵ to accept the current value.

**FIGURE 16.14**
Adding a dimensional constraint to the arc

Select the arc at this location so that the red circle appears.

Click here to place the dimension.

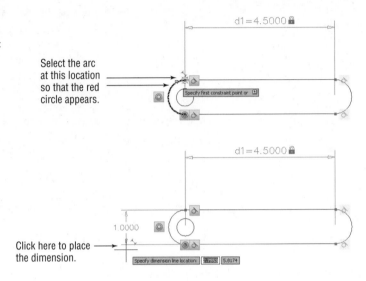

Notice that the new dimensional constraint has been given the name d2. Now try changing the size of the arc using the dimensional constraint:

1. Double-click on the dimension value of the dimensional constraint (Figure 16.15).

2. Enter 2↵. The part adjusts to the new dimension.

**FIGURE 16.15**
Adjusting the arc dimension

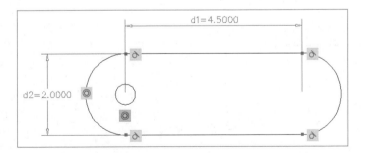

As you can see from this example, you can control the dimensions of your drawing by changing the dimensional constraint's value. This is a much faster way of making accurate changes to your drawing. Imagine what you would have to do to make these same changes if you didn't have the geometric and dimensional constraints available.

## Editing the Constraint Options

AutoCAD offers a number of controls that you can apply to the constraints feature. Choose
Parametric ➤ Constraint Settings to open the Constraint Settings dialog box (see Figure 16.16).

**FIGURE 16.16**
The Constraint
Settings dialog
box showing the
Geometric tab

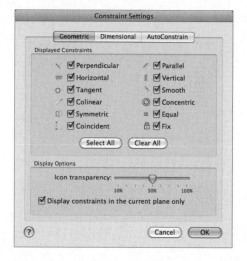

You can see that the Constraint Settings dialog box offers three tabs across the top:
Geometric, Dimensional, and AutoConstrain. The settings in the Geometric tab let you control
the display of the constraint bars, which are the constraint icons you see in the drawing when
you add constraints. You can also control the transparency of the constraint icons using the
slider near the bottom of the dialog box.

Like the Geometric tab, the Dimensional tab (Figure 16.17) gives you control over the display
of dimensional constraints. You can control the format of the text shown in the dimension and
whether dynamic constraints are displayed.

**FIGURE 16.17**
The Dimensional
tab of the Con-
straint Settings
dialog box

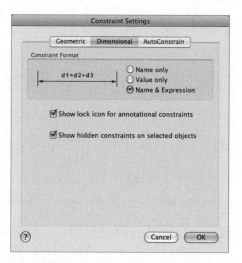

Finally, the AutoConstrain tab (Figure 16.18) gives you control over the behavior of the AutoConstrain command. You can control the priority of the constraints applied to a set of objects as well as which geometric constraints are allowed.

**FIGURE 16.18**

The AutoConstrain tab of the Constraint Settings dialog box

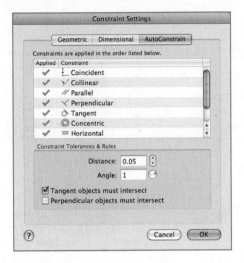

## Putting Constraints to Use

So far, you've seen some very simple applications of the parametric tools available in AutoCAD. While the parametric tools may seem simple, you can build some fairly elaborate parametric models using the geometric and dimensional constraints you've learned about here.

Besides having a drawing of a part that adjusts itself to changes in dimensional constraints, you can create assemblies that will allow you to study linkages and motion. For example, you can create a model of a piston and crankshaft from a gas engine and have the piston and crankshaft move together.

In the next exercise, you'll look at a drawing that has been set up to show just how constraints can be used to mimic the way a mechanical part behaves:

1. Open the `piston.dwg` file, which can be obtained from the companion website.

2. Click the arc in the right side of the drawing (Figure 16.19).

**FIGURE 16.19**

The piston drawing in motion

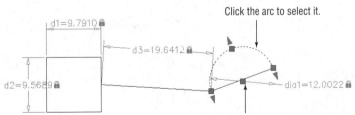

**3.** Click the center grip of the arc, and then right-click and select Rotate.

**4.** Move the cursor to rotate the arc. Notice that the "piston" that is connected to the arc with a fixed-length line follows the motion of the arc just as a piston would follow the motion of a crankshaft in a gas engine.

As you can see from this example, you can model a mechanical behavior using constraints. The piston in this drawing is a simple rectangle that has been constrained in both its height and width. A horizontal constraint has also been applied so it is capable of moving in only a horizontal direction. The line connecting the piston to the arc is constrained in its length. The coincident constraint connects it to the piston at one end and the arc at the other end. The arc itself, representing the crankshaft, uses a diameter constraint, and a fix constraint is used at its center to keep its center fixed in one location. The net result is that when you rotate the arc, each part moves in unison.

## The Bottom Line

**Use parametric drawing tools.** Parametric drawing tools enable you to create an assembly of objects that are linked to each other based on geometric or dimensional properties. With the parametric drawing tools, you can create a drawing that automatically adjusts the size of all its components when you change a single dimension.

**Master It** Name two examples given in the beginning of the chapter of a mechanical assembly that can be shown using parametric drawing tools.

**Connect objects with geometric constraints.** You can link objects together so that they maintain a particular orientation to each other.

**Master It** Name at least six of the geometric constraints available in AutoCAD.

**Control sizes with dimensional constraints.** Dimensional constraints, in conjunction with geometric constraints, let you apply dimensions to an assembly of objects to control the size of the assembly.

**Master It** Name at least four dimensional constraints.

**Put constraints to use.** Constraints can be used in a variety of ways to simulate the behavior of real objects.

**Master It** Name at least three geometric or dimensional constraints used in the `piston .dwg` file to help simulate the motion of a piston and crankshaft.

# Chapter 17

# Drawing Curves

So far in this book, you've been using basic lines, arcs, and circles to create your drawings. Now it's time to add polylines and spline curves to your repertoire. Polylines offer many options for creating forms, including solid fills and free-form curved lines. Spline curves are perfect for drawing accurate and smooth nonlinear objects.

In this chapter, you'll learn to do the following:

- ◆ Create and edit polylines
- ◆ Create a polyline spline curve
- ◆ Create and edit true spline curves
- ◆ Mark divisions on curves

## Introducing Polylines

*Polylines* are like composite line segments and arcs. A polyline may look like a series of line segments, but it acts like a single object. This characteristic makes polylines useful for a variety of applications, as you'll see in the upcoming exercises.

### Drawing a Polyline

First, to learn about the polyline, you'll begin a drawing of the top view of the joint shown in Figure 17.1.

**FIGURE 17.1**
A sketch of a
metal joint

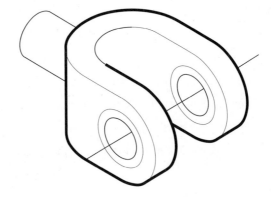

Follow these steps to draw the joint:

1. Open a new file using the acad.dwt template, and save it as Joint2d. Don't bother to make special setting changes because you'll create this drawing with the default settings.

2. From the menu bar, choose View ➢ Zoom ➢ All, or type **Z**↵ **A**↵.

3. Click the Polyline tool on the Tool Sets palette. You can also choose Draw ➢ Polyline from the menu bar or type **PL**↵.

4. At the Specify start point: prompt, enter a point at coordinate 3,3 to start your polyline.

5. At the Specify next point or [Arc/Halfwidth/Length/Undo/Width]: prompt, enter @3<0↵ to draw a horizontal line of the joint.

6. At the Specify next point or [Arc/Close/Halfwidth/Length/Undo/Width]: prompt, enter **A**↵ to continue your polyline with an arc.

---

**USING THE ARC OPTION IN THE POLYLINE COMMAND**

The Arc option enables you to draw an arc that starts from the last point you selected and then select additional options. Select the Arc option; as you move your cursor, an arc follows it in a tangential direction from the first line segment you drew. You can return to drawing line segments by entering **L**↵.

---

7. At the prompt

   Specify endpoint of arc or
   [Angle/CEnter/CLose/Direction/Halfwidth/Line/Radius/Second pt/Undo/Width]:

   enter @4<90↵ to draw a 180° arc from the last point you entered. Your drawing should now look similar to Figure 17.2.

**FIGURE 17.2**
A polyline line
and arc

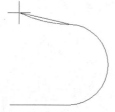

8. To continue the polyline with another line segment, enter **L**↵.

9. Enter @3<180↵. Another line segment continues from the end of the arc.

10. Press ↵ to exit the Polyline command.

You now have a sideways, U-shaped polyline that you'll use in the next exercise to complete the top view of your joint.

## Setting Polyline Options

Let's take a break from the tutorial to look at some of the Polyline prompt options that you didn't use:

**Close**   Draws a line segment from the last endpoint of a sequence of lines to the first point picked in that sequence. This works exactly like the Close option for the Line command.

**Length**   Enables you to specify the length of a line that will be drawn at the same angle as the last line entered.

**Halfwidth**   Creates a tapered line segment or an arc by specifying half its beginning and ending widths (Figure 17.3).

**FIGURE 17.3**
A tapered line segment and an arc created with Halfwidth

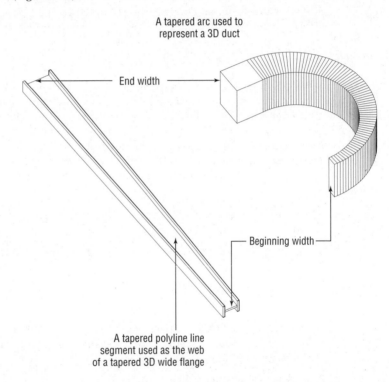

A tapered arc used to
represent a 3D duct

End width

Beginning width

A tapered polyline line
segment used as the web
of a tapered 3D wide flange

**Width**   Creates a tapered line segment or an arc by specifying the full width of the segment's beginning and ending points.

**Undo**   Deletes the last line segment drawn.

**Radius/Second pt**   The Radius and Second pt options appear when you use the Arc option to draw polyline segments. Radius lets you specify a radius for the arc and Second pt lets you specify a second point in a three-point arc.

If you want to break a polyline into simple lines and arcs, you can use the Explode tool on the Tool Sets palette, just as you would with blocks. After a polyline is exploded, it becomes a set of individual line segments or arcs.

To turn off the filling of solid polylines, enter **FILLMODE**↵ **0**↵. After changing the value of Fillmode, enter **RE**↵ to regenerate the display of the drawing.

---

**FILLETING A POLYLINE**

You can use the Fillet tool on the Tool Sets palette to fillet all the vertices of a polyline composed of straight-line segments. Click the Fillet tool or enter **F**↵, set your fillet radius by typing **R**↵ and entering a radius value, type **P**↵ to select the Polyline option, and then pick the polyline you want to fillet.

---

## Editing Polylines

You can edit polylines with many of the standard editing commands. To change the properties of a polyline, click the polyline to display its properties in the Properties Inspector palette. You can use the Stretch tool on the Tool Sets palette to move vertices of a polyline. The Trim, Extend, and Break tools on the Tool Sets palette also work with polylines.

In addition, many editing capabilities are offered only for polylines. For instance, later in this section you'll see how to smooth out a polyline by using the Fit option in the Pedit command.

In this exercise, you'll use the Offset tool on the Tool Sets palette to add the inside portion of the joint:

1. Click the Offset tool in the Tool Sets palette. You can also choose Modify ➤ Offset from the menu bar or type **O**↵.

2. At the Specify offset distance or [Through/Erase/Layer] <Through>: prompt, enter **1**↵.

3. At the Select object to offset or [Exit/Undo]<Exit>: prompt, pick the U-shaped polyline you just drew.

4. At the Specify point on side to offset or [Exit/Multiple/Undo] <Exit>: prompt, pick a point on the inside of the U shape. You'll see a concentric copy of the polyline appear (Figure 17.4).

5. Press ↵ to exit the Offset command.

**FIGURE 17.4**
The offset polyline

The concentric copy of a polyline made by choosing the Offset tool can be useful when you need to draw complex parallel curves like the ones in Figure 17.5.

**FIGURE 17.5**

Sample complex curves drawn by using offset polylines

The outside profile was drawn first; then the Offset command was used to draw the inside profile.

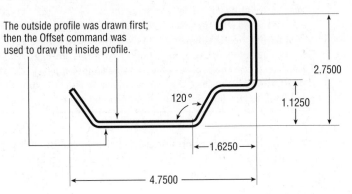

Next, complete the top view of the joint. To do this, you'll use the Pedit command:

1. Connect the ends of the polylines with two short line segments (Figure 17.6).

**FIGURE 17.6**

The polyline so far

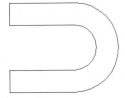

2. Choose Modify ➤ Object ➤ Polyline from the menu bar or type **PE**↵. PE is the alias for the Pedit command.

3. At the `Select polyline or [Multiple]:` prompt, pick the outermost polyline.

4. At the prompt

   ```
   Enter an option
   [Close/Join/Width/Edit vertex/Fit/Spline/Decurve/Ltype gen/Reverse/Undo]:
   ```

   enter **J**↵ for the Join option.

5. At the `Select objects:` prompt, select all the objects you've drawn so far.

6. Press ↵ to join all the objects into one polyline. It appears that nothing has happened.

7. Press ↵ again to exit the Pedit command.

8. Click the object in the drawing to expose its grips. The entire object is highlighted, indicating that all the lines have been joined into a single polyline.

---

### WHAT TO DO IF THE JOIN OPTION DOESN'T WORK

If the objects to be joined don't touch, you can use the *fuzz* join feature. Type **PE↵ M↵** to start the Pedit command with the Multiple option, select all the objects you want to join, and press ↵. If you see a convert message, enter **Y↵**. At the Enter an option [Close/Open/Join/Width/Fit/ Spline/Decurve/Ltype gen/Undo]: prompt, enter **J↵**. At the Enter fuzz distance or [Jointype]: prompt, enter a distance that approximates the size of the gap between objects. By default, AutoCAD extends the lines so they join end to end. You can use the Jointype option if you want Pedit to join segments with an additional segment.

---

By using the Width option under the Pedit command, you can change the width of a polyline. Let's change the width of your polyline to give some width to the outline of the joint. To do this, you'll use the Pedit command again, but this time you'll use a shortcut:

1. Double-click the polyline. The Pedit command starts.

2. Enter **W↵** for the Width option.

3. At the Specify new width for all segments: prompt, enter **.03↵** for the new width of the polyline.

   The line changes to the new width (Figure 17.7).

**FIGURE 17.7**
The polyline with a
new thickness

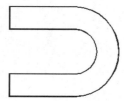

4. Press ↵ to exit the Pedit command.

5. Save this file.

In most cases, you can simply double-click on a polyline to start the Pedit command. But if you want to edit multiple polylines or if you want to convert an object or set of objects into a polyline, choose Modify ➤ Object ➤ Polyline from the menu bar or type **PE↵**.

In addition, if you have Dynamic Input turned on in the status bar, you can select the Edit Polyline options from a menu that appears at the cursor (Figure 17.8).

A third method is to select a polyline, right-click, and select Polyline from the shortcut menu. You will see many but not all of the Pedit options available.

**FIGURE 17.8**

The Edit
Polyline
options that
appear at the
cursor

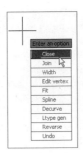

## Setting Pedit Options

Here's a brief look at a few of the Pedit command options you didn't try firsthand. Note that the names shown are from the Pedit command prompt. Items in parentheses are the option names as they appear in the polyline shortcut menu. In addition, the Edit vertex, Ltype gen, and Undo options are not available in the shortcut menu:

**Edit Vertex**    Lets you edit each vertex of a polyline individually (discussed in detail later in this chapter).

**Close**    Connects the two endpoints of a polyline with a line segment. If the polyline you selected to be edited is already closed, this option changes to Open.

**Open**    Removes the last segment added to a closed polyline.

**Width**    Sets the width of a polyline.

**Fit (Curve Fit)**    Turns polyline segments into a series of arcs.

**Spline (Spline Fit)**    The Spline option smoothes a polyline into a spline curve (discussed in detail later in this chapter).

**Decurve**    Changes a spline fit polyline into the shape it had before the Spline option was applied.

**Ltype Gen**    Controls the way noncontinuous linetypes pass through the vertices of a polyline. If you have a fitted or spline curve with a noncontinuous linetype, turn on this option.

**Reverse**    Reverses the orientation of a polyline. The orientation is based on the order in which points are selected to create the polyline. The first point picked is the beginning, or point 1, the next point is point 2, and so on. In some cases, you may want to reverse this order using the Reverse option.

**Undo**    Undoes the last Pedit option applied to a polyline.

Finally, you might notice the Polyline ➤ Edit Polyline option in the polyline right-click menu. This option starts the Pedit command without applying any of the options. You can then select the options by entering them via the keyboard.

**USING POLYLINES TO SET LINE WEIGHTS**

Typically, you would use the Lineweight feature of AutoCAD to set line weights in your drawing. In cases where the Lineweight feature will not work, you can change the thickness of regular lines and arcs by using Pedit to change them into polylines and then using the Width option to change their width. You encounter this use of polylines in some very old AutoCAD drawing files.

## Smoothing Polylines

You can create a curve in AutoCAD in many ways. If you don't need the representation of a curve to be accurate, you can use a polyline curve. In the following exercise, you'll draw a polyline curve to represent a contour on a topographical map:

1. Open the `topo.dwg` file. The top image in Figure 17.9 contains the drawing of survey data. Some of the contours have already been drawn in between the data points.

2. Zoom in to the upper-right corner of the drawing so your screen displays the area shown in the bottom image in Figure 17.9.

**FIGURE 17.9**

The `topo.dwg` file shows survey data portrayed in an AutoCAD drawing. Notice the dots indicating where elevations were taken. The actual elevation value is shown with a diagonal line from the point.

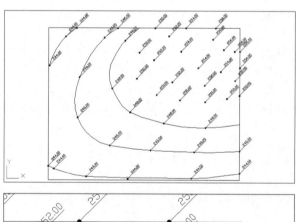

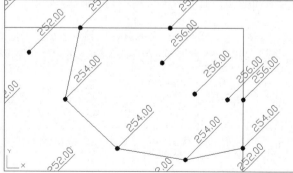

**3.** Click the Polyline tool on the Tool Sets palette. Using the Center osnap, draw a polyline that connects the points labeled 254.00. Your drawing should look like the bottom image in Figure 17.9.

**4.** Press ↵.

**5.** Next you'll convert the polyline you just drew into a smooth contour line. Double-click the contour line you just drew.

**6.** At the prompt

```
Enter an option
[Close/Join/Width/Edit vertex/Fit/Spline/Decurve/Ltype gen/Reverse/Undo]:
```

type **F↵** to select the Fit option. The polyline smoothes out into a series of connected arcs that pass through the data points.

**7.** Press ↵ to end the command.

Your contour is now complete. The Fit option under the Pedit command causes AutoCAD to convert the straight-line segments of the polyline into arcs. The endpoints of the arcs pass through the endpoints of the line segments, and the curve of each arc depends on the direction of the adjacent arc. This gives the effect of a smooth curve. Next you'll use this polyline curve to experiment with some of the editing options unique to the Pedit command.

## Editing Vertices

One of the Pedit options that I haven't yet discussed, Edit Vertex, is like a command within a command. Edit Vertex has numerous suboptions that enable you to fine-tune your polyline by giving you control over individual vertices.

To access the Edit Vertex options, follow these steps:

**1.** Turn off the Data and Border layers to hide the data points and border.

**2.** Double-click the polyline you just drew.

**3.** Type **E↵** to enter Edit Vertex mode. An X appears at the beginning of the polyline, indicating the vertex that will be affected by the Edit Vertex options.

When using Edit Vertex, you must be careful about selecting the correct vertex to be edited. Edit Vertex has 10 options. You often have to exit the Edit Vertex operation and use Pedit's Fit option to see the effect of several Edit Vertex options on a curved polyline.

### EDIT VERTEX SUBOPTIONS

After you enter the Edit Vertex mode of the Pedit command, you can perform the following functions:

♦ Break the polyline between two vertices.

♦ Insert a new vertex.

♦ Move an existing vertex.

♦ Regen the drawing to view the current shape of the polyline.

- ◆ Straighten a polyline between two vertices.
- ◆ Change the tangential direction of a vertex.
- ◆ Change the width of the polyline at a vertex.

These functions are presented in the form of the following prompt:

```
[Next/Previous/Break/Insert/Move/Regen/Straighten/Tangent/Width/eXit] <N>:
```

The following sections examine each of the options in this prompt, starting with Next and Previous.

### The Next and Previous Options

The Next and Previous options let you select a vertex for editing. When you start the Edit Vertex option, an X appears on the selected polyline to designate its beginning. As you select Next or Previous, the X moves from vertex to vertex to show which one is being edited. Let's try this:

1. Press ↵ a couple of times to move the X along the polyline. (Because Next is the default option, you only need to press ↵ to move the X.)

2. Type **P**↵ for Previous. The X moves in the opposite direction. The default option becomes Previous.

## Real World Scenario

#### WHY REVERSE A POLYLINE

One of the most frequently asked questions I receive from readers is, How can I reverse the direction of a polyline? It may seem like an odd question to someone new to AutoCAD, but reversing a polyline has quite a few uses. Perhaps the most common use is to turn a polyline that uses a complex linetype—one that includes text—right side up so that the text can be read more easily. (See Bonus Chapter 2 at www.sybex.com/go/masteringautocadmac for an example of a linetype that includes text.) If for some reason you need to reverse the direction of a polyline or spline, you can do so by using the Reverse option in the Pedit command.

### The Break Option

The Break option breaks the polyline between two vertices:

1. Position the X on one end of the segment you want to break.

2. Enter **B**↵ at the Command prompt.

3. At the `Enter an option [Next/Previous/Go/eXit] <N>:` prompt, use Next or Previous to move the X to the other end of the segment to be broken.

4. When the X is in the proper position, enter **G**↵ to break the polyline (Figure 17.10).

**FIGURE 17.10**
How the Break
option works

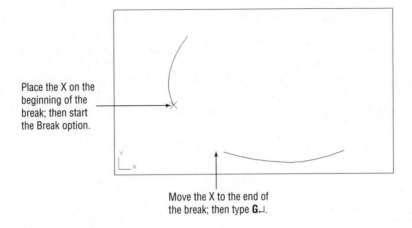

Place the X on the
beginning of the
break; then start
the Break option.

Move the X to the end of
the break; then type **G↵**.

You can also use the Break and Trim tools on the Tool Sets palette to break a polyline any-where, as you did when you drew the toilet seat in Chapter 3, "Setting Up and Using AutoCAD's Drafting Tools."

### The Insert Option

Next try the Insert option, which inserts a new vertex:

1. Type **X↵** to exit the Edit Vertex option temporarily. Then type **U↵** to undo the break.

2. Type **E↵** to return to the Edit Vertex option.

3. Press ↵ to advance the X marker to the next point.

4. Enter **I↵** to select the Insert option.

5. When the prompt Specify location for new vertex: appears, along with a rubber-banding line originating from the current X position (Figure 17.11), pick a point indicating the new vertex location. The polyline is redrawn with the new vertex.

**FIGURE 17.11**
The new vertex
location

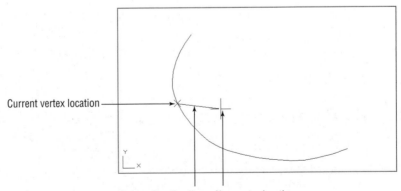

Current vertex location

Rubber-banding line    New vertex location

Notice that the inserted vertex appears between the currently marked vertex and the *next* vertex, so the Insert option is sensitive to the direction of the polyline. If the polyline is curved, the new vertex won't immediately be shown as curved. (See the first image in Figure 17.12.) You must smooth it out by exiting the Edit Vertex option and then using the Fit option, as you did to edit the site plan. (See the second image in Figure 17.12.) You can also use the Stretch tool on the Tool Sets palette to move a polyline vertex.

**FIGURE 17.12**
The polyline before and after the curve is fitted

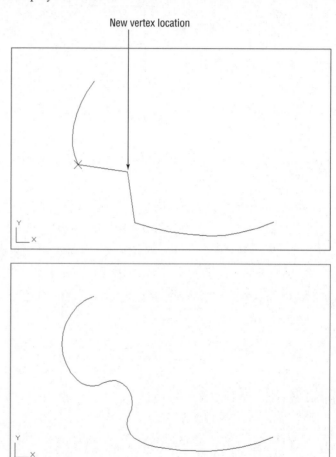

### The Move Option

In this brief exercise, you'll use the Move option to move a vertex:

1. Undo the inserted vertex by exiting the Edit Vertex option (enter **X↵**) and typing **U↵**.

2. Restart the Edit Vertex option, and use the Next or Previous option to place the X on the vertex you want to move.

3. Enter **M↵** for the Move option.

**4.** When the Specify new location for marked vertex: prompt appears, along with a rubber-banding line originating from the X (see the first image in Figure 17.13), pick the new vertex. The polyline is redrawn (see the second image in Figure 17.13). Again, if the line is curved, the new vertex appears as a sharp angle until you use the Fit option (see the final image in Figure 17.13).

You can also move a polyline vertex by using its grip.

**FIGURE 17.13**
Picking a new location for a vertex with the polyline before and after the curve is fitted

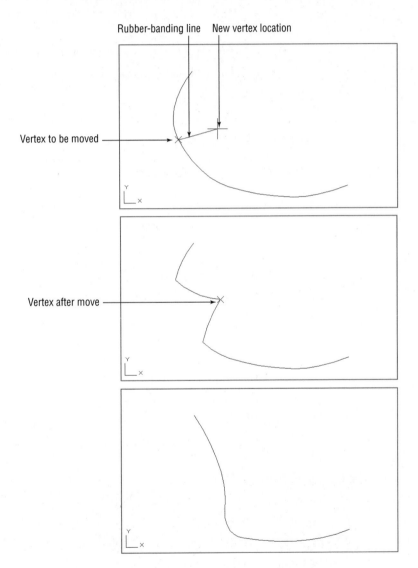

### The Regen Option

In some cases, the effect of an option does not appear in the drawing immediately. You can use the Regen option to update the display of the polyline and see any changes you've made up to that point.

### The Straighten Option

The Straighten option straightens all the vertices between two selected vertices. Using the Straighten option is a quick way to delete vertices from a polyline, as shown in the following exercise:

1. Undo the moved vertex (from the previous exercise).

2. Start the Edit Vertex option again, and select the starting vertex for the straight line.

3. Enter **S**↵ for the Straighten option.

4. At the `Enter an option [Next/Previous/Go/eXit] <N>:` prompt, move the X to the location for the other end of the straight-line segment.

5. After the X is in the proper position, enter **G**↵ for the Go option. The polyline straightens between the two selected vertices (Figure 17.14).

**FIGURE 17.14**

A polyline after straightening

Move the X here; then start the Straighten option.

Move the X here; then type **G** to straighten the polyline between the selected points.

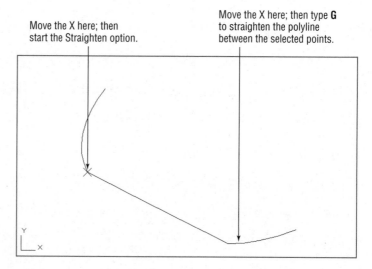

### The Tangent Option

The Tangent option alters the direction of a curve on a curve-fitted polyline:

1. Undo the straightened segment from the previous exercise.

2. Restart the Edit Vertex option, and position the X on the vertex you want to alter.

3. Enter **T**↵ for the Tangent option. A rubber-banding line appears. (See the top image in Figure 17.15.)

**4.** Point the rubber-banding line in the direction of the new tangent, and pick a point to indicate the direction of the vertex tangent. An arrow appears, indicating the new tangent direction. (See the second image in Figure 17.15.)

Don't worry if the polyline shape doesn't change. You must use Fit to see the effect of Tangent. (See the final image in Figure 17.15.)

**FIGURE 17.15**
Picking a new tangent direction

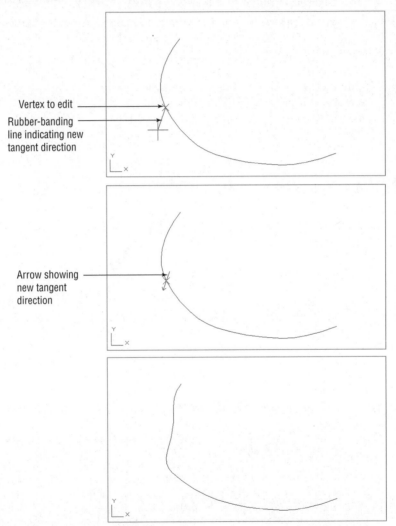

Vertex to edit

Rubber-banding line indicating new tangent direction

Arrow showing new tangent direction

### *The Width Option*

Finally, you'll try the Width option. Unlike the Pedit command's Width option, the Edit Vertex/ Width option enables you to alter the width of the polyline at any vertex. Thus you can taper or otherwise vary polyline thicknesses. Try these steps:

**1.** Undo the tangent arc from the previous exercise.

2. Return to the Edit Vertex option, and place the X at the beginning vertex of a polyline segment you want to change.

3. Type **W**⏎ to issue the Width option.

4. At the Specify starting width for next segment <0.0000>: prompt, enter a value—**12**⏎, for example—indicating the polyline width desired at this vertex.

5. At the Specify ending width for next segment <12.0000>: prompt, enter the width—**24**⏎, for example—for the next vertex.

The width of the polyline changes to your specifications (Figure 17.16).

**FIGURE 17.16**
A polyline with the width of one segment increased

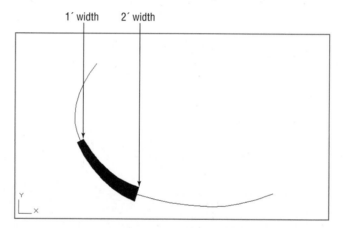

1′ width     2′ width

The Width option is useful when you want to create an irregular or curved area in your drawing that is to be filled in solid. This is another option that is sensitive to the polyline direction.

As you've seen throughout these exercises, you can use the Undo option to reverse the last Edit Vertex option used. You can also use the Exit option to leave Edit Vertex at any time. Enter **X**⏎ to display the Pedit prompt:

```
Enter an option
[Close/Join/Width/Edit vertex/Fit/Spline/Decurve/Ltype gen/Reverse/Undo]:
```

### FILLING IN SOLID AREAS

You've learned how to create a solid area by increasing the width of a polyline segment. But suppose you want to create a solid shape or a thick line. AutoCAD provides the Solid, Trace, and Donut commands to help you draw simple filled areas. The Trace command acts just like the Line command (with the added feature of allowing you to draw wide line segments). Solid lets you create solid filled areas with straight sides, and Donut draws circles with a solid width.

You can create free-form, solid-filled areas by using the Solid hatch pattern. Create an enclosed area by using any set of objects, and then use the Hatch tool to apply a solid hatch pattern to the area. See Chapter 7, "Mastering Viewing Tools, Hatches, and External References," for details on using the Hatch tool.

# Creating a Polyline Spline Curve

The Pedit command's Spline option (named after the spline tool used in manual drafting) offers you a way to draw smoother and more controllable curves than those produced by the Fit option. A polyline spline doesn't pass through the vertex points as a fitted curve does. Instead, the vertex points act as weights pulling the curve in their direction. These "weighted" vertex points are called *control vertices*. The polyline spline touches only its own beginning and end vertices. Figure 17.17 illustrates this concept.

**FIGURE 17.17**

The polyline spline curve pulled toward its control vertices

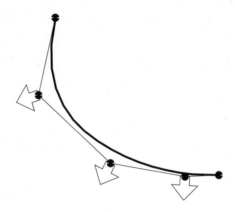

A polyline spline curve doesn't represent a mathematically true curve. See the next section, "Using True Spline Curves," to learn how to draw a more accurate spline curve.

Let's look at how using a polyline spline curve may influence the way you edit a curve:

1. Undo the width changes you made in the previous exercise.

2. To change the contour into a polyline spline curve, double-click the polyline to be curved.

3. At the `Enter an option [Close/Join/Width/Edit vertex/Fit/Spline/Decurve/ Ltype gen/Reverse/Undo]:` prompt, enter **S**↵. The polyline will turn into a spline curve. Your curve changes to look like Figure 17.18.

4. Press ↵ to exit the Pedit command.

**FIGURE 17.18**

A spline curve

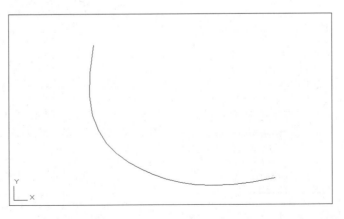

Once you apply the Spline option, your polyline takes on a smoother, more graceful appearance. It no longer passes through the points you used to define it. To see where the points went and to find out how spline curves act, do the following:

1. Click the curve. The original vertices appear as grips. (See the first image in Figure 17.19.)

2. Click the grip that is second from the top of the curve, as shown in the first image in Figure 17.19, and move the grip around. The curve follows your moves, giving you immediate feedback on how it will look.

3. Pick a point, as shown in the second image in Figure 17.19. The curve is now fixed in its new position, as shown in the bottom image of Figure 17.19.

**FIGURE 17.19**
The fitted curve changed to a spline curve, with the location of the second vertex and the new curve

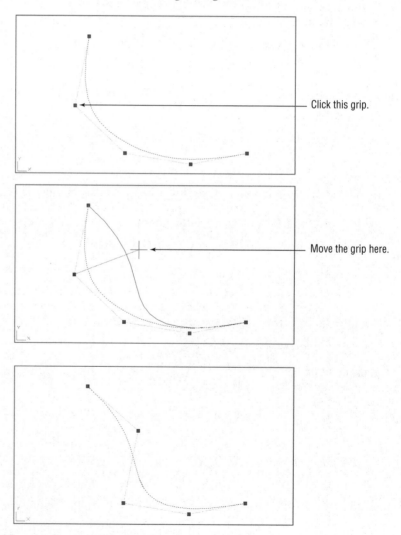

Click this grip.

Move the grip here.

**TURNING OBJECTS INTO POLYLINES AND POLYLINES INTO SPLINES**

At times, you'll want to convert regular lines, arcs, or even circles into polylines. You might want to change the width of lines or join lines to form a single object such as a boundary. Here are the steps to convert lines, arcs, and circles into polylines:

1. Choose Modify ➤ Object ➤ Polyline, or type **PE**↵ at the Command prompt.

2. At the `Select polyline or [Multiple]:` prompt, pick the object you want to convert.

3. At the prompt

      `Object selected is not a polyline. Do you want to turn it into one? <Y>:`

   press ↵. The object is converted into a polyline.

If you want to convert several objects to polylines, type **M**↵ at the `Select polyline or [Multiple]:` prompt, then select the objects you want to convert. You will see the `Convert Lines, Arcs and Splines to polylines [Yes/No]? <Y>:` prompt. Type **Y**↵, and all the selected objects are converted to polylines. You can then go on to use other Pedit options on the selected objects. If you want to convert a circle to a polyline, first break the circle (using the Break tool on the Tool Sets palette) so it becomes an arc of approximately 359°.

To turn a polyline into a true spline curve, do the following:

1. Choose Modify ➤ Object ➤ Polyline, or type **PE**↵. Select the polyline you want to convert.

2. Type **S**↵ to turn it into a polyline spline, and then press ↵ to exit the Pedit command.

3. Click the Spline tool on the Tool Sets palette or type **SPL**↵.

4. At the `Specify first point or [Method/Knots/Object]:` prompt, type **O**↵ for the Object option.

5. At the `Select spline-fit polyline:` prompt, click the polyline spline. Although it may not be apparent at first, the polyline is converted into a true spline.

You can also choose Modify ➤ Object ➤ Spline (or enter **SPE**↵) to edit a polyline spline. If you do, the polyline spline is automatically converted into a true spline.

If you know you'll always want to convert an object into a polyline when using Pedit, you can turn on the Peditaccept system variable. Enter **PEDITACCEPT**↵ at the Command prompt, and then enter **1**↵.

# Using True Spline Curves

So far, you've been working with polylines to generate spline curves. The advantage of using polylines for curves is that they can be enhanced in many ways. You can modify their width, for instance, or join several curves. But at times, you'll need a more exact representation of a curve.

The spline object, created by choosing the Spline tool on the Tool Sets palette, produces a more accurate model of a spline curve in addition to giving you more control over its shape.

The spline objects are true *Non-Uniform Rational B-Spline (NURBS)* curves. A full description of NURBS is beyond the scope of this book, but basically, NURBS are standard mathematical forms used to represent shapes.

## Drawing a True Spline

The following steps describe the process used to create a spline curve. You don't have to create them now. Make a note of this section, and refer to it when you need to draw and edit a spline. Here are the steps:

1. Choose the Spline tool on the Tool Sets palette, or type **SPL**↵.

2. At the Specify first point or [Method/Knots/Object]: prompt, select a point to start the curve. (Figure 17.20.) The prompt changes to Enter next point or [start Tangency/toLerance]:.

**FIGURE 17.20**
Start the spline curve at the first data point and then continue to select points.

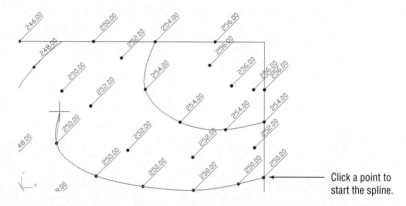

Click a point to start the spline.

3. Continue to select points until you've entered all the points you need. As you pick points, a curve appears, and it bends and flows as you move your cursor. In Figure 17.20, a Center object snap was used to select the donuts that appear as dots in the survey plan.

4. After you've selected the last point, press ↵ to exit the Spline command.

If you prefer, you can control the tangency of the spline at its first and last points. The following steps describe how the Tangency option can be used:

1. Start the spline just as before, and select the start point. At the Enter next point or [start Tangency/toLerance]: prompt, type **T**↵.

2. The prompt changes to Specify start tangent:. Also, a rubber-banding line appears from the first point of the curve to the cursor. Select a point indicating the tangency of the first point.

3. Continue to select the other points of your spline. After you've selected the last point, type **T**↵.

4. Use the cursor to indicate the tangency of the spline at the last point.

You now have a smooth curve that passes through the points you selected. These points are called the *fit points*. If you click the curve, you'll see the grips appear at the location of these fit points, and you can adjust the curve by clicking the grip points and moving them. You'll also see an arrowhead grip that appears at the beginning of the spline. If you click this arrowhead grip, you see two options: Show Fit Points and Show Control Vertices (Figure 17.21).

**FIGURE 17.21**
The Show Fit Points and Show Control Vertices options

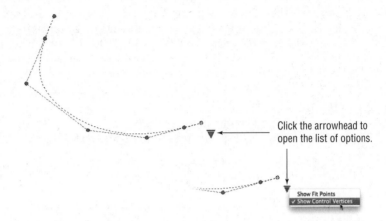

Click the arrowhead to open the list of options.

The Show Fit Points option will display the grips at the fit points, which are the points you used to draw the spline in the previous example. By default, these fit points lie on the spline, though you can adjust how close the spline follows the fit points. You can also view the control vertices, or CVs for short, which are points that control the curvature of the spline and do not lie on the spline itself (refer back to Figure 17.17). Along with the control vertices, you see a set of vectors called the *control polyline*. The control polyline helps you visualize the relationship between the CVs and the spline.

If you hover over a grip, you will see a menu that offers Stretch Fit Point, Add Fit Point, and Remove Fit Point. Stretch Fit Point enables you stretch the highlighted grip. Remove Fit Point will remove the grip. If you select Add Fit Point, you can click a point to indicate a new fit point to be added to the spline.

## Understanding the Spline Options

You may have noticed a few other options in the first Spline command prompt. When you start the Spline command, you see the Method, Knots, Degree, and Object options:

**Method** Method lets you choose between Fit and CV. The Fit option causes the spline to be drawn through the lines you select. The CV, or Control Vertices, option causes the spline to use your selected points as control vertices (refer back to Figure 17.17). Once you've drawn a spline, you can switch between fit and CV views of your polyline (Figure 17.21).

**Knots** This option is available only if Fit is chosen in the Method option discussed previously. This option offers three additional options: Chord, Square Root, and Uniform, which affect the shape of the spline as it passes through the fit point.

**Chord** The Chord option numbers the knots with decimal values.

**Square Root**    The Square Root option numbers the knots based on the square root of the chord length between consecutive knots.

**Uniform**    The Uniform option numbers the knots in consecutive integers.

**Degree**    This option is available only if CV is chosen in the Method option discussed previously. The Degree option gives you control over the number of control vectors required to create a bend in the spline. You can use the value 1, 2, or 3. The 1 value will cause the spline to produce straight lines, 2 will generate sharp curves, and 3 will generate less-sharp curves. In simple terms, the Degree value controls how closely the spline follows its control polyline.

**Object**    Object lets you convert a polyline into a spline. If the Fit option is selected under the Method option, you can convert only a spline-fitted polyline. If the CV option is selected under the Method option, you can select any polyline. With the CV Method option, the polyline will change shape so that the polyline vectors become control vectors.

Once you start to select points for the spline, you see the end Tangency, toLerance, Undo, and Close options. Table 17.1 describes these options.

**TABLE 17.1:**    The Spline command options for selecting points

| OPTION | FUNCTION |
| --- | --- |
| end Tangency | Gives you control over the tangency at the beginning and end points of the spline. |
| toLerance | Lets you control how the curve passes through the fit points. The default value of 0 causes the curve to pass through the fit points. Any value greater than 0 causes the curve to pass close to, but not through, the points. |
| Undo | Lets you undo the previous point selection in case you select the wrong point. |
| Close | Lets you close the curve into a loop. If you choose this option, you're prompted to indicate a tangent direction for the closing point. |

## Joining Splines to Other Objects

While editing drawings, you may encounter a situation where a spline has been broken into two splines and you need the broken spline to behave as a single spline. The Join command will "mend" a broken spline, or any set of splines for that matter, as long as the splines are contiguous (touching end to end).

To use the Join command, click the Join tool from the Tool Sets palette's expanded Modify panel. You can also choose Modify ➤ Join or type J↵. Select the first spline, then select the splines you want to join to the first.

Join can be used with other objects as well. You can join lines, polylines, 3D polylines, arcs, elliptical arcs, and helixes, with the following restrictions:

◆ Any of these objects can be joined to a spline, polyline, 3D polyline, or helix.

◆ Lines cannot be joined to arcs or elliptical arcs.

- ◆ Arcs cannot be joined to elliptical arcs.

- ◆ Arcs must have the same center point and radius but can have a gap between the segments you wish to join. The same is true for elliptical arcs.

- ◆ Lines must be collinear but there can be gaps between the lines to be joined.

- ◆ Unless you are joining to a polyline or 3D polyline, objects must be on the same 3D plane.

---

### SKETCHING WITH AUTOCAD

AutoCAD offers the Sketch command, which lets you do freehand drawing. If you have access to a drawing tablet, you might give the Sketch command a try. Here is a brief description of how you might use it:

1. Enter **SKETCH↵**.

2. Enter **T↵ S↵** to use a spline for your sketch object.

3. Start drawing your freehand lines. Temporary sketch lines will appear in the drawing.

4. Press ↵ when you are finished. The temporary lines will be replaces with splines.

If the spline curve doesn't look right, you may have to set the tolerance setting for the Sketch command. When using splines for sketch objects, the tolerance option sets the distance between control points for the spline. To set the spline tolerance for the Sketch command, do the following:

1. Enter **SKETCH↵**

2. Enter **L↵**, and then enter a value for the sketch tolerance. You can start by using a value that is slightly different from the default 0.5000. A lower number sets a tighter tolerance and the spline will fit closer to your temporary sketched line. A higher value "loosens" the tolerance and the spline will follow a smoother curve.

3. Start drawing your freehand lines.

If you'd like to know more about Sketch, refer to the AutoCAD Help system; it offers an excellent description of how Sketch works.

---

## Fine-Tuning Spline Curves

Spline curves are different from other types of objects, and many of the standard editing commands won't work on splines. AutoCAD offers the Splinedit command: Choose Modify ➢ Object ➢ Spline or type **SPE↵**.

### CONTROLLING THE FIT DATA OF A SPLINE

The Fit Data option of the Splinedit command lets you adjust the tangency of the beginning and endpoints, add new control points, and adjust spline tolerance settings. To get to these options, follow these steps:

1. Choose Modify ➢ Object ➢ Spline, or type **SPE↵** at the Command prompt.

2. At the Select spline: prompt, select the last spline you drew in the previous exercise.

3. At the Enter an option [Close/Join/Fit data/Edit vertex/convert to Polyline/Reverse/Undo/eXit]: prompt, type F↵ to select the Fit Data option.

4. At the [Add/Close/Delete/Move/Purge/Tangents/toLerance/eXit] <eXit>: prompt, enter the option you want to use. For example, to change the tangency of the first and last points of your spline, type T↵. You're prompted to select the tangent point of the first and last points. Table 17.2 lists the Splinedit Fit Data options and what they're for.

**TABLE 17.2:**     The Fit Data options of the Splinedit command

| OPTION | FUNCTION |
|---|---|
| Add | Lets you add more control points |
| Close | Lets you close the spline into a loop |
| Delete | Removes a control point from the spline |
| Move | Lets you move a control point |
| Purge | Deletes the fit data of the spline, thereby eliminating the Fit Data option for the purged spline |
| Tangents | Lets you change the tangency of the first and last points |
| toLerance | Controls the distance between the spline and a control point |
| eXit | Exits the Splinedit command |

If you prefer, you can double-click on a spline to start the Splinedit command instead of selecting the Edit Spline tool in the Modify panel. If you have the Dynamic Input feature turned on, you can select Splinedit options from a menu that appears at the cursor (Figure 17.22) instead of typing in an option.

**FIGURE 17.22**
The Splinedit
options

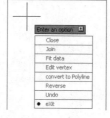

### USING GRIP OPTIONS

The Splinedit command gives you a lot of control when you want to edit a spline. But if you want to make some minor changes, you can use the shortcut menu that appears when you hover

over a grip on the spline. First, click on the spline to expose its grips, then hover over a fit point or CV. The list of options appears.

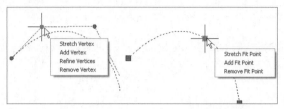

The options are slightly different depending on whether you have the fit points or CVs displayed. The options enable you to quickly add or remove a fit point or CV, and in the case of CVs, you also have the Refine Vertices option. The Refine option lets you control the pull exerted on a spline by a CV.

### WHEN CAN'T YOU USE FIT DATA?

The Fit Data option of the Splinedit command offers many ways to edit a spline. However, this option isn't available to all spline curves. When you invoke certain other Splinedit options, a spline curve loses its fit data, thereby disabling the Fit Data option. These operations are as follows:

◆ Fitting a spline to a tolerance (Spline ➢ toLerance) and moving its control vertices.

◆ Fitting a spline to a tolerance (Spline ➢ toLolerance) and opening or closing it.

◆ Refining the spline.

◆ Purging the spline of its fit data by using the Purge option of the Splinedit command. (Choose Modify ➢ Object ➢ Spline from the menu bar, or enter **Splinedit↵**, and then select the spline and enter **F↵ P↵**.)

Also note that the Fit Data option isn't available when you edit spline curves that were created from polyline splines. See the sidebar "Turning Objects into Polylines and Polylines into Splines" earlier in this chapter.

If you'd like to learn more about the Splinedit options, check the AutoCAD Help system. It offers a detailed description of how these options work.

---

**CONVERT A SPLINE INTO A POLYLINE**

AutoCAD for Mac allows you to convert a spline object into a polyline. This can be very useful when you want to edit a spline using the polyline editing tools instead of the spline editing tools. You will lose some precision in the conversion, but more often than not, this is not an issue.

To convert a spline to a polyline, double-click the spline, and then at the Enter an option prompt, type **P↵**. At the Specify a precision <10>: prompt, enter a value from 0 to 99. Note that a higher precision value may reduce the performance of AutoCAD, so use a reasonable value. You may want to experiment with different values and pick the lowest value that will still give you the results you want.

## Marking Divisions on Curves

Perhaps one of the most difficult things to do in manual drafting is to mark regular intervals on a curve. AutoCAD offers the Divide and Measure commands to help you perform this task with speed and accuracy.

You can find the Divide and Measure tools on the expanded Open Shapes panel of the Tool Sets palette, as shown in Figure 17.23. Click the arrow of the Open Shapes panel, and then click and hold the Multiple Points drop-down to display the pop-up menu.

**FIGURE 17.23**
The Divide and
Measure tools are
in the expanded
Open Shapes panel
on the Tool Sets
palette and appear
on a drop-down.

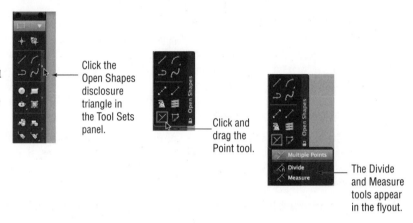

Click the Open Shapes disclosure triangle in the Tool Sets panel.

Click and drag the Point tool.

The Divide and Measure tools appear in the flyout.

The Divide and Measure commands are discussed here in conjunction with polylines, but you can use these commands on any object except blocks and text.

### Dividing Objects into Segments of Equal Length

Use the Divide command to divide an object into a specific number of equal segments. For example, suppose you need to mark off the contour you've been working on in this chapter into nine equal segments. One way to do this is to first find the length of the contour by using the List command and then sit down with a pencil and paper to figure out the exact distances between the marks. But there is another, easier way.

The Divide command places a set of point objects on a line, an arc, a circle, or a polyline, marking off exact divisions. The following exercise shows how it works:

1. Open the 17a-divd.dwg file. This file is similar to the one you've been working with in the previous exercises.

2. Click and hold the Multiple Points drop-down in the expanded Open Shapes panel of the Tool Sets palette and select Divide (Figure 17.23). You can also choose Draw ➤ Point ➤ Divide or type **DIV**↵.

3. At the Select object to divide: prompt, pick the spline contour line that shows Xs in Figure 17.24.

4. The Enter the number of segments or [Block]: prompt that appears next is asking for the number of divisions you want on the selected object. Enter **9**↵.

The Command prompt returns, and it appears that nothing has happened. But AutoCAD has placed several point objects on the contour that indicate the locations of the nine divisions you requested. To see these points more clearly, continue with the exercise.

**FIGURE 17.24**
Using the Divide command on a polyline

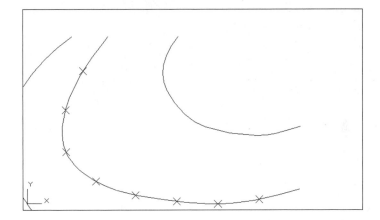

5. Choose Format ➤ Point Style from the menu bar or type **DDPTYPE**↵ to open the Point Style dialog box (Figure 17.25). You can also choose the Point Style tool in the expanded Open Shapes panel of the Tool Sets palette (Figure 17.26).

**FIGURE 17.25**
The Point Style dialog box

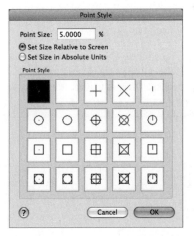

**FIGURE 17.26**
The Point Style tool
in the expanded
Open Shapes panel
of the Tool Sets
palette

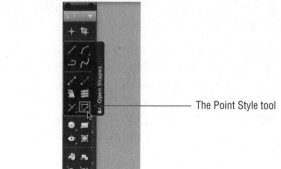

———— The Point Style tool

6. Click the X point style at the upper-right corner of the dialog box, click the Set Size Relative To Screen radio button, and then click OK.

7. If the Xs don't appear, enter **RE**↲. A set of Xs appears, showing the nine divisions (shown earlier in Figure 17.24).

You can also change the point style by changing the Pdmode system variable. When Pdmode is set to 3, the point appears as an X.

The Divide command uses *point* objects to indicate the division points. You create point objects by using the Point command. They usually appear as dots. Unfortunately, such points are nearly invisible when placed on top of other objects. But, as you've seen, you can alter their shape by using the Point Style dialog box. You can use these X points to place objects or references to break the object being divided. (The Divide command doesn't cut the object into smaller divisions.)

---

**FINDING HIDDEN NODE POINTS**

If you're in a hurry and you don't want to bother changing the shape of the point objects, you can do the following: Set Running Osnaps to Node. Then, when you're in Point Selection mode, move the cursor over the divided curve. When the cursor gets close to a point object, the Node Osnap marker appears.

---

## Dividing Objects into Specified Lengths

The Measure command acts just like Divide. However, instead of dividing an object into segments of equal length, the Measure command marks intervals of a specified distance along an object. For example, suppose you need to mark some segments exactly 5″ apart along the contour. Try the following exercise to see how the Measure command is used to accomplish this task:

1. Erase the X-shaped point objects.

2. Click and hold the Multiple Points drop-down in the expanded Open Shapes panel of the Tool Sets palette and select Measure (refer back to Figure 17.23). You can also choose Draw ➢ Point ➢ Measure or type **ME**⏎.

3. At the `Select object to measure:` prompt, pick the contour at a point closest to its bottom endpoint. You'll learn shortly why this is important.

4. At the `Specify length of segment or [Block]:` prompt, enter **60**⏎. The X points appear at the specified distance.

5. Exit without saving this file.

Bear in mind that the point you pick on the object to be measured determines where the Measure command begins measuring. In the previous exercise, for example, you picked the contour near its bottom endpoint. If you picked the top of the contour, the results would be different because the measurement would start at the top, not the bottom.

 **Real World Scenario**

**MARKING OFF INTERVALS BY USING BLOCKS INSTEAD OF POINTS**

You can also use the Block option under the Divide and Measure commands to place blocks at regular intervals along a line, a polyline, or an arc. Here's how to use blocks as markers:

1. Be sure the block you want to use is part of the current drawing file.

2. Start either the Divide or Measure command.

3. At the `Specify length of segment or [Block]:` prompt, enter **B**⏎.

4. At the `Enter name of block to insert:` prompt, enter the name of a block.

5. At the `Align block with object? [Yes/No] <Y>:` prompt, press ⏎ if you want the blocks to follow the alignment of the selected object. (Entering **N**⏎ inserts each block at a 0 angle.)

6. At the `Enter the number of segments:` prompt, or the `Specify length of segment:` prompt, enter the number or length of the segments. The blocks appear at regular intervals on the selected object.

One example of using the Block option of Divide or Measure is to place a row of sinks equally spaced along a wall. Alternatively, you might use this technique to make multiple copies of an object along an irregular path defined by a polyline. In civil-engineering projects, you can indicate a fence line by using Divide or Measure to place Xs along a polyline.

# The Bottom Line

**Create and edit polylines.**   Polylines are extremely versatile. You can use them in just about any situation in which you need to draw line work that is continuous. For this reason, you'll want to master polylines early in your AutoCAD training.

**Master It**   Draw the part shown here.

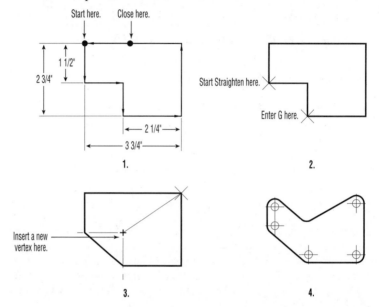

**Create a polyline spline curve.**   Polylines can be used to draw fairly accurate renditions of spline curves. This feature of polylines makes them a very useful AutoCAD object type.

**Master It**   Try drawing the outline of an object that has no or few straight lines in it, as in the file lowerfairing.jpg, which is included in the Chapter 17 sample files at www.sybex.com/go/masteringautocadmac. You can use the methods described in Chapter 13, "Copying Existing Drawings into AutoCAD," to import a raster image of your object and then trace over the image using polyline splines.

**Create and edit true spline curves.**   If you need an accurate spline curve, you'll want to use the Spline command. Spline objects offer many fine-tuning options that you won't find with polylines.

**Master It**   Try tracing over the same image from the previous Master It section, but this time use the Spline command.

**Mark divisions on curves.**   The Divide and Measure commands offer a quick way to mark off distances on a curved object. This can be a powerful resource in AutoCAD that you may find yourself using often.

**Master It**   Mark off 12 equal divisions of the spline curves you drew in the previous Master It exercise.

# Chapter 18

# Getting and Exchanging Data from Drawings

AutoCAD drawings contain a wealth of data—graphic information such as distances and angles between objects as well as precise areas and the properties of objects. However, as you become more experienced with AutoCAD, you'll also need data of a different nature. For example, as you begin to work in groups, the various settings in a drawing become important. You'll need statistics on the amount of time you spend on a drawing when you're billing computer time. As your projects become more complex, file maintenance requires a greater degree of attention. To take full advantage of AutoCAD, you'll want to exchange information about your drawing with other people and other programs.

In this chapter, you'll explore the ways in which all types of data can be extracted from AutoCAD and made available to you, your coworkers, and other programs. First you'll learn how to obtain specific data about your drawings. Then you'll look at ways to exchange data with other programs—such as word processors, desktop-publishing software, and even other CAD programs.

In this chapter, you'll learn to do the following:

◆ Find the area of closed boundaries

◆ Get general information

◆ Use the DXF file format to exchange CAD data with other programs

◆ Use AutoCAD drawings in page-layout programs

## Finding the Area of Closed Boundaries

One of the most frequently sought pieces of data you can extract from an AutoCAD drawing is the area of a closed boundary. In architecture, you want to find the area of a room or the footprint of a building. In civil engineering, you want to determine the area covered by the boundary of a property line or the area of cut for a roadway. In the following sections, you'll learn how to use AutoCAD to obtain exact area information from your drawings.

## Finding the Area of an Object

In this section, you'll practice determining the areas of regular objects. You'll start by finding the area of a simple rectangular shape, and then you'll look at methods for finding the area of more complex shapes that include curves.

First you'll determine the square-foot area of the living room and entry of your studio unit plan:

1. Start AutoCAD. Open the Unit file you created in Chapter 6, "Editing and Reusing Data To Work Efficiently," or use the 18a-unit.dwg file.

2. Zoom in to the living room and entry area so you have a view similar to Figure 18.1.

**FIGURE 18.1**
Selecting the points to determine the area of the living room and entry

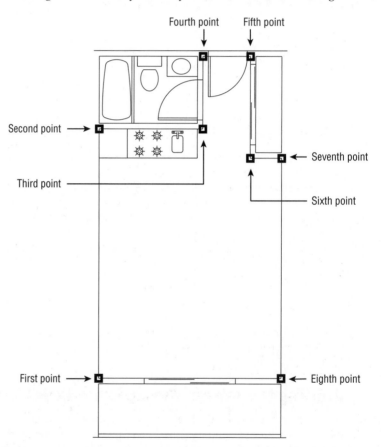

3. Choose Tools ➢ Inquiry ➢ Area from the menu bar, or type **MEA⏎ AR⏎** at the Command prompt. This starts the Measuregeom command.

4. Using the Endpoint osnap, start with the lower-left corner of the living room and select the points shown in Figure 18.1. You're indicating the boundary. Notice that as you click points, the area being calculated is indicated in green.

**5.** When you've come full circle to the eighth point shown in Figure 18.1, press ↵. You get the following message:

```
Area = 39570.00 square in. (274.7917 square ft), Perimeter = 76'-0"
```

**6.** Type **X**↵ to exit the Measuregeom command.

The number of points you can pick to define an area is limitless, so you can obtain the areas of complex shapes. Use the Blipmode feature to keep track of the points you select so you know when you come to the beginning of the point selections. Blipmode places tiny *X*s, or *blips*, on the screen each time you click a point. These blips are just visual aids and can be removed with a redraw or regen of the screen.

---

### FIND THE COORDINATE OF A POINT OR A DISTANCE IN A DRAWING

To find absolute coordinates in a drawing, use the ID command. Choose Tools ➤ Inquiry ➤ ID Point, or type **ID**↵. At the Specify point: prompt, use the Osnap overrides to pick a point; its X, Y, and Z coordinates are displayed on the Command prompt.

To find the distance between two points, choose Distance from the Inquiry submenu on the Tools menu, or type **MEA**↵ **D**↵, and then click two points. AutoCAD will display the distance in the drawing as Delta X, Delta Y, and Delta Z coordinates and as a direct distance between the selected points. The distance is also displayed in the Command prompt. You can also type **Dist**↵ and pick two points to get a simplified distance measurement.

---

## Using Hatch Patterns to Find Areas

Hatch patterns are used primarily to add graphics to your drawing, but they can also serve as a means for finding areas. You can use any hatch pattern you want because you're interested in only the area it reports back to you. You can also set up a special layer devoted to area calculations and then use this layer to add the hatch patterns for calculating areas. That way, you can turn off the hatch patterns so they don't plot, or you can turn off the Plot setting for that layer to ensure that it doesn't appear in your final output.

To practice using hatch patterns to find an area, do the following:

**1.** Set the current layer to Floor.

**2.** Turn off the Door and Fixture layers. Also make sure the Ceiling layer is turned on. You want the hatch pattern to follow the interior wall outline, so you need to turn off any objects that will affect the outline, such as the door and kitchen.

**3.** Click Hatch on the Tool Sets palette. You can also choose Draw ➤ Hatch or type **H**↵ to open the Hatch And Gradient dialog box.

---

### MEASURING BOUNDARIES THAT HAVE GAPS

If the area you're trying to measure has gaps, set the Gap Tolerance setting in the Hatch And Gradient dialog box to a value higher than the size of the gaps. If you don't see the Gap Tolerance setting, click the disclosure triangle in the lower-right corner of the Hatch And Gradient dialog box.

**4.** Click the Add: Pick Points tool. The Hatch And Gradient dialog box temporarily closes to allow you to select points in your drawing.

**5.** At the `Pick internal point or [Select objects/remove Boundaries]:` prompt, click in the interior of the unit plan. The outline of the interior is highlighted.

**6.** Press ↵ to return to the Hatch And Gradient dialog box, and click Preview (see Figure 18.2).

**7.** Right-click to complete the hatch.

**8.** Choose Tools ➢ Inquiry ➢ Area and press ↵, or type **MEA**↵ **AR**↵ **O**↵ at the Command prompt.

**9.** Click the hatch pattern you just created. Again, you get the following message:

`Total area = 39570.00 square in. (274.7917 square ft), Perimeter = 76'-0"`

**10.** Press **X**↵ to exit the command.

**FIGURE 18.2**
After you click a point on the interior of the plan to place a hatch pattern, an outline of the area is highlighted by a dotted line, and a preview of the hatch appears.

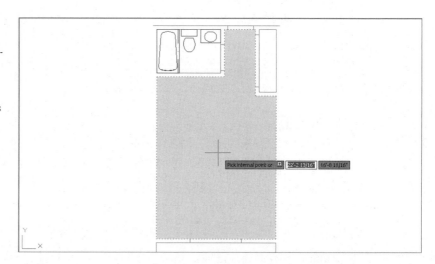

If you need to recall the last area calculation value you received, enter **'SETVAR**↵ **AREA**↵. The area is displayed in the Command Line palette. Enter **'PERIMETER**↵ to get the last perimeter calculated.

The Hatch command creates a hatch pattern that conforms to the boundary of an area. This feature, combined with the ability of the Measuregeom command to find the area of a hatch pattern, makes short work of area calculations. Another advantage of using hatch patterns is that, by default, they avoid islands within the boundary of the area you're trying to find.

The area of a hatch pattern is also reported by the Properties Inspector palette. Select the hatch pattern whose area you want to find and then right-click and select Properties. Scroll down to the bottom of the Geometry group and you'll see the Area listing for the hatch pattern you selected. You can select more than one hatch pattern and find the cumulative area of the selected hatch patterns in the Properties Inspector palette.

## Adding and Subtracting Areas with the Area Command

Hatch patterns work extremely well for finding areas, but if you find that for some reason you can't use hatch patterns, you have another alternative. You can use a command called Boundary to generate a polyline outline of an enclosed boundary and then obtain the area of the outline using the Measuregeom command options (the Distance, Angle, Area, Radius, Volume options in the Tools ➤ Inquiry submenu on the menu bar). If islands are present within the boundary, you have to use the Subtract feature of the Measuregeom command to remove the area of the island from the overall boundary area.

By using the Add and Subtract options of the Measuregeom command, you can maintain a running total of several separate areas being calculated. This gives you flexibility in finding areas of complex shapes. This section guides you through the use of these options.

For the following exercise, you'll use a flange shape that contains circles (Figure 18.3). This shape is composed of simple arcs, lines, and circles. Use these steps to see how you can keep a running tally of areas:

**FIGURE 18.3**
A flange to a
mechanical device

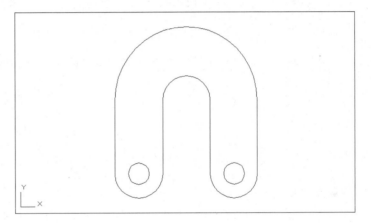

1. Exit the Unit.dwg file, and open the file Flange.dwg (see Figure 18.3). Don't bother to save changes in the Unit.dwg file.

2. Click the Boundary tool from the expanded Closed Shapes panel in the Tool Sets palette. You can also choose Draw ➤ Boundary from the menu bar or type **BO**↵ to open the Boundary Creation dialog box (Figure 18.4).

**FIGURE 18.4**
The Boundary
Creation dialog

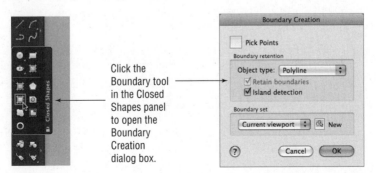

Click the
Boundary tool
in the Closed
Shapes panel
to open the
Boundary
Creation
dialog box.

3. Click Pick Points.

4. Click in the interior of the flange shape. The entire shape is highlighted, including the circle islands.

5. Press ↵. You now have a polyline outline of the shape and the circles, although it won't be obvious that polylines have been created because they're drawn over the boundary objects.

6. Continue by using the Measuregeom command's Add and Subtract options. Choose Tools ➢ Inquiry ➢ Area from the menu bar.

7. Type **A**↵ to enter Add area mode, and then type **O**↵ to select an object.

8. Click a vertical edge of the flange outline. You see the selected area highlighted in green, and the following message appears in the Command Line palette:

```
Area = 27.7080, Perimeter = 30.8496
Total area = 27.7080
```

9. Press ↵ to exit Add area mode.

10. Type **S**↵ to enter Subtract area mode, and then type **O**↵ to select an object.

11. Click one of the circles. You see the following message:

```
Total area = 0.6070, Circumference = 2.7618
Total area = 27.1010
```

This shows you the area and perimeter of the selected object and a running count of the total area of the flange outline minus the circle. You also see the area of the subtracted circle change to a different color so you can differentiate between the calculated area and the subtracted area.

12. Click the other circle. You see the following message:

```
Total area = 0.6070, Perimeter = 2.7618
Total area = 26.4940
```

Again, you see a listing of the area and perimeter of the selected object along with a running count of the total area, which now shows a value of 26.4940. This last value is the true area of the flange.

13. Press ↵ and type **X**↵ **X**↵ to exit the Measuregeom command. You can also press the Esc key to exit the command.

In this exercise, you first selected the main object outline and then subtracted the island objects. You don't have to follow this order; you can start by subtracting areas to get negative area values and then add other areas to come up with a total. You can also alternate between Add and Subtract modes, in case you forget to add or subtract areas.

You may have noticed that the Area option of the Measuregeom Command prompt offered `Specify first corner point or [Object/Add area/Subtract area/eXit]:` as the default option for both the Add and Subtract area modes. Instead of using the Object option to pick the circles, you can start selecting points to indicate a rectangular area, as you did in the first exercise in this chapter.

Whenever you press ↵ while selecting points for an area calculation, AutoCAD automatically connects the first and last points and returns the calculated area. If you're in Add or Subtract mode, you can then continue to select points, but the additional areas are calculated from the *next* point you pick.

As you can see from these exercises, it's simpler to outline an area first with a polyline wherever possible and then use the Object option to add and subtract area values of polylines.

In this example, you obtained the area of a mechanical object. However, the same process works for any type of area you want to calculate. It can be the area of a piece of property on a topographical map or the area of a floor plan. For example, you can use the Object option to find an irregular shape such as the one shown in Figure 18.5, as long as it's a closed polyline.

**FIGURE 18.5**

The site plan with an area to be calculated

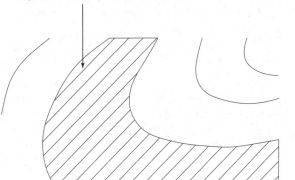

Irregular areas like the area between contours can be easily calculated using the Boundary and Area commands.

When issued through the keyboard as **MEA**↵, the Measuregeom command offers a number of other options for measuring your drawing. The options appear in the Command Line palette as `[Distance/Radius/Angle/ARea/Volume/]<Distance>` or at the cursor as a Dynamic Input option. These options are automatically selected when you click the related tool from the Inquiry submenu of the Tools menu on the menu bar. Remember that to use an option, you type the capitalized letter or letters of the option shown in the list. Table 18.1 gives you descriptions of the options and how they are used.

**TABLE 18.1:** The Measuregeom command options

| OPTION | USE |
|--------|-----|
| Distance | Returns the distance between two points. Type **D.⏎** and select two points. You can also measure cumulative distances by typing **M.⏎** after selecting the first point. |
| Radius | Returns the radius of an arc or circle. Type **R.⏎** and select an arc or circle. |
| Angle | Returns the angle of an arc or the angle between two lines. Type **A.⏎** and select the arc or two nonparallel lines. |
| Area | Returns the area of a set of points or boundary. Type **AR.⏎** to use this option. See previous exercises for instruction on the use of this option. |
| Volume | Returns the 3D volume based on an area times height. |
| Exit | Exits the current option. You can also press the Esc key. |

### Real World Scenario

#### RECORDING AREA DATA IN A DRAWING FILE

In most architectural projects, area calculations are an important part of the drawing process. As an aid in recoding area calculations, it's a good idea to create a block that contains attributes for the room number, the room area, and the date when the room area was last measured. You can then make the area and date attributes invisible so only the room number appears. The block with the attribute is then inserted into every room. Once the area of the room is discovered, it can be added to the block attribute with the Ddatte command. Such a block can be used with any drawing in which area data needs to be gathered and stored. See Chapter 12 for more on attributes. You can also use the Field object type to automatically display the area of a polyline as a text object. See Chapter 10, "Using Fields and Tables," for more on fields.

## Getting General Information

So far in this book, you've seen how to get data about the geometry of your drawings. AutoCAD also includes a set of tools that you can use to access the general state of your drawings. You can gather information about the status of current settings in a file or the time at which a drawing was created and last edited.

In the following sections, you'll practice extracting this type of information from your drawing, using the tools found in Tools ➢ Inquiry on the menu bar.

### Determining the Drawing's Status

When you work with a group of people on a large project, keeping track of a drawing's setup becomes crucial. You can use the Status command to obtain general information about the drawing you're working on, such as the base point and current mode settings. The Status command is especially helpful when you're editing a drawing someone else has worked on because you may want to identify and change settings for your own style of working. Choose Tools ➢ Inquiry ➢ Status from the menu bar to display a list like the one shown in Figure 18.6.

**FIGURE 18.6**
The Command Line palette expanded to show the results from the Status command

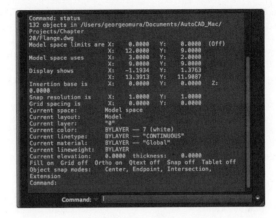

```
Command: status
132 objects in /Users/georgeomura/Documents/AutoCAD_Mac/
Projects/Chapter
20/Flange.dwg
Model space limits are X:      0.0000    Y:      0.0000   (Off)
                       X:     12.0000    Y:      9.0000
Model space uses       X:      3.0000    Y:      2.0000
                       X:      9.0000    Y:      9.0000
Display shows          X:     -1.1934    Y:      1.3763
                       X:     13.3913    Y:     11.9087
Insertion base is      X:      0.0000    Y:      0.0000   Z:
0.0000
Snap resolution is     X:      1.0000    Y:      1.0000
Grid spacing is        X:      0.0000    Y:      0.0000
Current space:        Model space
Current layout:       "g"
Current layer:        "g"
Current color:        BYLAYER --- 7 (white)
Current linetype:     BYLAYER --- "CONTINUOUS"
Current material:     BYLAYER --- "Global"
Current lineweight:   BYLAYER
Current elevation:     0.0000  thickness:      0.0000
Fill on  Grid off  Ortho on  Qtext off  Snap off  Tablet off
Object snap modes:    Center, Endpoint, Intersection,
Extension
Command:
```
Command: |

---

**USE THE STATUS COMMAND TO GET YOUR BEARINGS**

If you have problems editing a file created by someone else, the difficulty can often be attributed to a setting you aren't used to working with. If AutoCAD is acting in an unusual way, use the Status command to get a quick glimpse of the file settings before you start calling for help.

---

Table 18.2 gives a brief description of each item on the Status screen. Note that some of the items you see on the screen will vary from what is shown here, but the information applies to virtually all situations except where noted.

**TABLE 18.2:**  Items on the Status screen

| ITEM | MEANING |
| --- | --- |
| Number Objects In | The number of entities or objects in the drawing. |
| Model Space Limits Are | The coordinates of the Model Space limits. Also indicates whether limits are turned off or on. (See Chapter 3, "Setting Up and Using AutoCAD's Drafting Tools," for more details on limits.) |
| Model Space Uses | The area the drawing occupies; equivalent to the extents of the drawing. |
| **Over | If present, means that part of the drawing is outside the limit boundary. |
| Display Shows | The area covered by the current view. |

**TABLE 18.2:**     Items on the Status screen   *(CONTINUED)*

| ITEM | MEANING |
|------|---------|
| Insertion Base Is, Snap Resolution Is, and Grid Spacing Is | The current default values for these mode settings. |
| Current Space | Model Space or Paper Space. |
| Current Layout | The current layout name. |
| Current Layer | The current layer. |
| Current Color | The color assigned to new objects. |
| Current Linetype | The linetype assigned to new objects. |
| Current Material | The material assigned to new objects. |
| Current Lineweight | The current default Lineweight setting. |
| Current Elevation/Thickness | The current default Z coordinate for new objects, plus the default thickness of objects. These are both 3D-related settings. (See Chapter 19, "Creating 3D Drawings," for details.) |
| Fill, Grid, Ortho, Qtext, Snap, and Tablet | The status of these options. |
| Object Snap Modes | The current active Osnap setting. |

When you're in Paper Space, the Status command displays information regarding the Paper Space limits. See Chapter 15, "Laying Out Your Printer Output," for more on Model Space and Paper Space.

In addition to being useful in understanding a drawing file, the Status command is an invaluable tool for troubleshooting. Frequently, a technical-support person can isolate problems by using the information provided by the Status command.

## Keeping Track of Time

The Time command enables you to keep track of the time spent on a drawing for billing or analysis purposes. You can also use the Time command to check the current time and find out when the drawing was created and most recently edited. Because the AutoCAD timer uses your computer's time, be sure the time is set correctly on your Mac.

To access the Time command, enter **TIME** ↵ at the Command prompt. You get a message like the one in Figure 18.7.

**FIGURE 18.7**
The Time screen in the Command Line palette

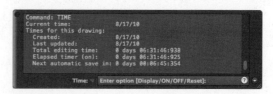

The first four lines of this message tell you the current date and time, the date and time the drawing was created, and the last time the drawing was saved.

The fifth line shows the total time spent on the drawing from the point at which the file was opened. This elapsed timer lets you time a particular activity, such as changing the width of all the walls in a floor plan or redesigning a piece of machinery. The last line tells you when the next automatic save will be.

You can turn the elapsed timer on or off or reset it by entering **ON**, **OFF**, or **RESET** at the Command prompt shown at the bottom of the message. Or press ↵ to exit the Time command.

## Getting Information from System Variables

If you've been working through this book's ongoing studio-apartment-building tutorial, you'll have noticed that I've occasionally mentioned a *system variable* in conjunction with a command. You can check the status or change the setting of any system variable while you're in the middle of another command. To do this, you type an apostrophe (') followed by the name of the system variable at the Command prompt.

For example, if you start to draw a line and suddenly decide you need to restrict your cursor movement to 45°, you can do the following:

1. At the `Specify next point or [Undo]:` prompt, enter **'SNAPANG**↵.

2. At the `>>Enter new value for SNAPANG <0>:` prompt, enter a new cursor angle. You're returned to the Line command with the cursor in its new orientation.

You can also recall information such as the last area or distance calculated by AutoCAD. Type **SETVAR**↵ **AREA**↵ to read the last area calculation. The Setvar command also lets you list all the system variables and their status as well as access each system variable individually by entering **'SETVAR**↵ **?**↵. You can then indicate which variables to list using wildcard characters such as the asterisk or question mark. For example, you can enter **g\*** to list all the system variables that start with the letter *G*.

Many system variables give you direct access to detailed information about your drawing. They also let you fine-tune your drawing and editing activities. In Appendix C, "Hardware and Software Tips," hosted on the book's accompanying website, you'll find all the information you need to familiarize yourself with the system variables. Don't feel that you have to memorize them all at once; just be aware that they're available.

## Keeping a Log of Your Activity

At times, you may find it helpful to keep a log of your activity in an AutoCAD session. A *log* is a text file containing a record of your activities. It can also contain notes to yourself or others about how a drawing is set up. Such a log can help you determine how frequently you use a particular command, or it can help you construct a macro for a commonly used sequence of commands.

The following exercise demonstrates how to save and view a detailed record of an AutoCAD session by using the Log feature:

1. Enter **LOGFILEON**↵ to turn on the Log feature.

2. Type **Status**↵ at the Command prompt.

3. Enter **LOGFILEOFF**↵ to turn off the Log feature.

4. Start a text editor.

5. With the text editor, open the log file whose name starts with Flange in the folder listed here:

```
/Users/user name/Library/Application Support/
Autodesk/local/AutoCAD Mac/R18.1/ENU/
```

This file stores the text data from the Command prompt whenever the Log File option is turned on. You must turn off the Log File option before you can view this file. Note that this location is usually a hidden one. See "Finding Hidden Folders That Contain AutoCAD Files" in Appendix B (on the book's website), "Installing and Setting Up AutoCAD for Mac," for more information.

As you can see in step 5, the log file is given the name of the drawing file from which the log is derived, with some additional numeric values. Because the Flange log file is a standard text file, you can easily send it to other members of your workgroup or print it for a permanent record.

---

### FINDING THE LOG FILE

If you can't find the log file for the current drawing, you can enter **LOGFILENAME**↵ at the Command prompt and AutoCAD will display the filename, including the full path. If you want to change the default location for the log file, open the Application Preferences dialog box and click the Application tab. Click the plus sign to the left of the Log File Location option in the list box. A listing appears showing you where the drawing log file is stored. You can then modify this setting to indicate a new location.

---

## Capturing and Saving Text Data from the Command Line Palette

If you're working in groups, it's often helpful to have a record of the status, editing time, and system variables for particular files readily available to other group members. It's also convenient to keep records of block and layer information so you can see whether a specific block is included in a drawing or what layers are normally on or off.

You can use the Clipboard to capture and save such data from the Command Line palette. The following steps show you how it's done:

1. Move the arrow cursor to the Command prompt at the bottom of the Command Line palette.

2. Right-click and choose Copy History from the shortcut menu to copy the contents of the Command Line palette to the Clipboard.

If you want to copy only a portion of the Command Line palette to the Clipboard, perform the following steps:

1. Using the I-beam text cursor, highlight the text you want to copy from the Command Line palette to the Clipboard.

2. Right-click and choose Copy from the shortcut menu. Or you can type ⌘-**C**. The high-lighted text is copied to the Clipboard.

3. Open a text-editing application, and paste the information.

You may notice four other options on the shortcut menu: Recent Commands, Paste, Paste To Command Line, and Preferences. The most recent commands are listed at the top of the shortcut menu, while additional commands are listed in the More Commands submenu. For most activities, you'll use a handful of commands repeatedly; the Recent Commands section can save you time by giving you a shortcut to those commands you use the most. The Paste options paste the first line of the contents of the Clipboard into the command line or input box of a dialog box. This can be useful for entering repetitive text or for storing and retrieving a frequently used command. Choosing Preferences opens the Application Preferences dialog box.

Items copied to the Clipboard from the Command Line palette can be pasted into dialog box input boxes. This can be a quick way to transfer layers, linetypes, or other named items from the Command Line palette into a dialog box. You can even paste text into the drawing area.

---

### RECOVERING CORRUPTED FILES

No system is perfect. Eventually, you'll encounter a file that is corrupted in some way. Two AutoCAD commands can frequently salvage a corrupted file:

**Audit**  Enables you to check a file that you can open but suspect has some problem. Audit checks the currently opened file for errors and displays the results in the Command Line palette.

**Recover**  Enables you to open a file that is so badly corrupted that AutoCAD is unable to open it in a normal way. A Select File dialog box appears in which you select a file for recovery. After you select a file, it's opened and checked for errors.

You can access these by entering them at the Command prompt. More often than not, these commands will do the job, although they aren't a panacea for all file-corruption problems. In the event that you can't recover a file even with these tools, make sure your computer is running smoothly and that other systems aren't faulty.

---

## Using the DXF File Format to Exchange CAD Data with Other Programs

AutoCAD offers many ways to share data with other programs. Perhaps the most common type of data exchange is to share drawing data with other CAD programs. In the following sections, you'll see how to export and import CAD drawings using the DXF file format.

A *Drawing Interchange Format (DXF) file* is a plain-text file that contains all the information needed to reconstruct a drawing. It's often used to exchange drawings created with other programs. Many CAD and technical drawing programs, including some 3D perspective programs, can generate or read files in DXF format. You might want to use a 3D program to view your drawing in a perspective view, or you might have a consultant who uses a different CAD program that accepts DXF files.

Be aware that not all programs that read DXF files accept all the data stored therein. Many programs that claim to read DXF files throw away much of the DXF files' information. Attributes are perhaps the most commonly ignored objects, followed by many of the 3D objects, such as meshes and 3D faces.

## Exporting and Importing DXF Files

To export your current drawing as a DXF file, follow these steps:

1. Choose File ➤ Save As from the menu bar to open the Save Drawing As dialog box.

2. Click the File Format pop-up list. You can export your drawing under a number of formats, including five DXF formats.

3. Select the appropriate DXF format, and then enter a name for your file. You don't have to include the .dxf filename extension.

4. Select a folder for the file and click Save.

In step 3, you can select any of the DXF file formats shown in the following screen shot.

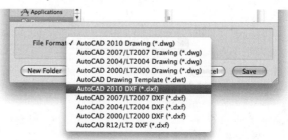

Choose the format appropriate to the program you're exporting to. In most cases, the safest choice is AutoCAD R12/LT2 DXF if you're exporting to another CAD program, although the complete functionality of the latest releases of AutoCAD won't be maintained for such files.

In addition to using the Save Drawing As dialog box, you can type **DXFOUT↵** at the Command prompt to open the Save Drawing As dialog box.

If you need to open a DXF file, you can do so by selecting DXF from the File Format pop-up list in the Select File dialog box. This is the dialog box you see when you select File ➤ Open from the menu bar. You can also use the Dxfin command:

1. Type **DXFIN↵** at the Command prompt to open the Select File dialog box.

2. Locate and select the DXF file you want to import.

3. Double-click the filename. If the drawing is large, the imported file may take several minutes to open.

# Using AutoCAD Drawings in Page-Layout Programs

As you probably know, AutoCAD is a natural for creating line art, and because of its popularity, most page-layout programs are designed to import AutoCAD drawings in one form or another. Those of you who employ page-layout software to generate user manuals or other technical documents will probably want to use AutoCAD drawings in your work. In the following sections, you'll examine ways to output AutoCAD drawings to formats that most page-layout programs can accept.

You can export AutoCAD files to page-layout software formats in two ways: by using raster export and by using vector file export.

## Exporting Raster Files

In some cases, you may need only a rough image of your AutoCAD drawing. You can export your drawing as a raster file that can be read in virtually any page-layout and word processing program. To do this, you'll use the Export feature.

1. Choose File ➢ Export from the menu bar.

2. In the Export Data dialog box, select Bitmap (*.bmp) from the File Format pop-up list.

3. Click Save.

4. You see the prompt `Select objects or <all objects and viewports>:`. Press ⏎ to export the entire drawing. As the prompt suggests, you can also select objects to export if you do not want to export the entire drawing.

The image will be exported at the resolution of your screen. Another option is to just use the Mac screen-capture feature. Press Shift-⌘-3. This produces a PNG file that can be opened by most Mac programs. The file is placed on the Desktop to make it easy to find.

If you prefer raster files in the JPEG or TIFF format, you can enter **JPGOUT⏎** or **TIFOUT⏎** to export your drawing in these formats. **PNGOUT⏎** and **BMPOUT⏎** will also work for PNG and BMP file formats.

---

### EXCHANGING FILES WITH USERS OF EARLIER RELEASES

One persistent dilemma that has plagued AutoCAD users is how to exchange files between earlier releases of the program. Remember that you can save files to earlier releases by selecting a version from the File Format pop-up list in the Save Drawing As dialog box (File ➢ Save As on the menu bar).

---

## Exporting Vector Files

If you want to have a more accurate representation of your drawing, you can use the PostScript vector format. 3D designs can be exported in the SAT format, which is associated with ACIS.

For vector-format files, DXF is the easiest to work with, and with TrueType support, DXF can preserve font information between AutoCAD and page-layout programs that support the DXF format.

The DXF file export was covered in a previous section of this chapter, so the following section will concentrate on the PostScript file format.

### POSTSCRIPT AND PDF OUTPUT

AutoCAD can export to the Encapsulated PostScript (EPS) file format. If you're using AutoCAD for the Mac, you can obtain PostScript output in two ways: You can choose File ➢ Export from the menu bar, or you can enter **PSOUT**⏎ at the Command prompt. If you choose File ➢ Export, you can use the File Format pop-up list in the Export Data dialog box to select Encapsulated PS. Another method is to install a PostScript printer driver and print your drawing to an EPS file.

As an alternative to EPS, you can "print" to an Adobe PDF file. When you get to the Print dialog box, click the PDF option to open a pop-up menu of PDF options (Figure 18.8).

**FIGURE 18.8**
The PDF options on
the Print dialog box

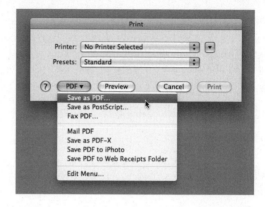

## The Bottom Line

**Find the area of closed boundaries.**   There are a number of ways to find the area of a closed boundary. The easiest way is also perhaps the least obvious.

> **Master It**   Which AutoCAD feature would you use to quickly find the area of an irregular shape like a pond or lake?

**Get general information.**   A lot of information that is stored in AutoCAD drawings can tell you about the files. You can find out how much time has been spent editing a file, for instance.

> **Master It**   What feature gives you a list of current settings and how do you get to this feature?

**Use the DXF file format to exchange CAD data with other programs.**   Autodesk created the DXF file format as a means of sharing vector drawings with other programs.

> **Master It**   Name the versions of AutoCAD you can export to using the Save As option.

**Use AutoCAD drawings in page-layout programs.**   AutoCAD drawings find their way into all types of documents, including brochures and technical manuals. Users are often asked to convert their CAD drawings into formats that can be read by page-layout software.

> **Master It**   Name some file formats, by filename extension or type, that page-layout programs can accept.

**Fix corrupted drawing files.**   At some point, you may encounter a corrupted drawing file. In some cases, the file may be so badly corrupted that AutoCAD won't open it. Fortunately, you have some options to recover a file that might otherwise be unreadable.

> **Master It**   What is the command that you can use to recover an unreadable DWG file?

# Part 4

# 3D Modeling and Imaging

# Chapter 19

# Creating 3D Drawings

Viewing an object in three dimensions gives you a sense of its true shape and form. It also helps you conceptualize your design, which results in better design decisions. In addition, using three-dimensional objects helps you communicate your ideas to those who may not be familiar with the plans, sections, and side views of your design.

A further advantage to drawing in three dimensions is that you can derive 2D drawings from your 3D models, which could take considerably more time with standard 2D drawing methods. For example, you can model a mechanical part in 3D and then quickly derive its 2D top, front, and right-side views by using the techniques discussed in this chapter.

In this chapter, you'll learn to do the following:

◆ Know the 3D modeling environment

◆ Draw in 3D using solids

◆ Create 3D forms from 2D shapes

◆ Isolate coordinates with point filters

◆ Move around your model

◆ Get a visual effect

◆ Turn a 3D view into a 2D AutoCAD drawing

## Getting to Know the 3D Modeling Environment

AutoCAD takes on a slightly different persona when you work in 3D. Your drawing area looks a little different and the Tool Sets palette can be changed to show a different set of tools. You also begin to use parts of the menu bar and drawing area that you've probably just wondered about until now. To help ease your transition into 3D, take a brief tour of the AutoCAD features you'll be using in the next several chapters.

### Getting to Know the Modeling Tool Sets Palette

Most of this book is devoted to showing you how to work in a 2D drafting environment. The tools you've been working with in the Tool Sets palette are set up to make it easy for 2D drafting.

AutoCAD also offers a set of tools designed for 3D modeling. But even with these new tools, AutoCAD behaves in the same basic way, and the AutoCAD files produced are the same regardless of whether they're 2D or 3D drawings.

To get to the 3D Modeling tools in the Tool Sets palette, you need to click the icon at the top of the Tool Sets palette and select Modeling (Figure 19.1).

**FIGURE 19.1**
The Tool Sets icon
and menu.

If you're starting a new 3D model, you'll also want to create a new file using a 3D template. Try the following to get started with 3D modeling:

1. Start AutoCAD, and then click the Tool Sets icon at the top of the Tool Sets palette and select Modeling. You'll see a new set of tools.

2. Next, to create a new 3D modeling file, choose File ➢ New from the menu bar. Select the acad3D.dwt template file and click Open. Your drawing will look similar to Figure 19.2.

**FIGURE 19.2**
The AutoCAD
3D Modeling
drawing area

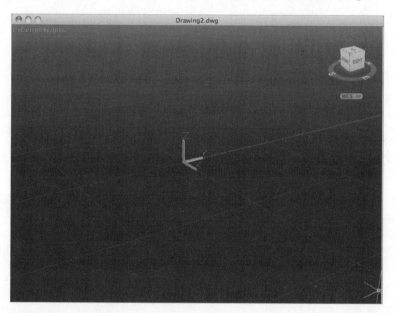

The drawing area displays the drawing in a perspective view with a dark gray background and a grid. This is really just a typical AutoCAD drawing file with a couple of setting changes. The view has been set up to be a perspective view by default, and a feature called *Visual Styles* has been set to show 3D objects as solid objects. You'll learn more about the tools you can use to adjust the appearance of your drawing's view later in this chapter. For now, let's look at the changes in the Tool Sets palette. Figure 19.3 shows the Modeling toolset and the tool groups. Note the names of the groups in the title bars to the right of each group.

**FIGURE 19.3**
The Modeling tool-
set and groups

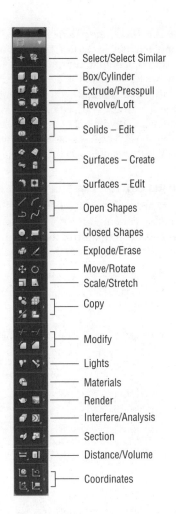

— Select/Select Similar
— Box/Cylinder
— Extrude/Presspull
— Revolve/Loft
— Solids – Edit
— Surfaces – Create
— Surfaces – Edit
— Open Shapes
— Closed Shapes
— Explode/Erase
— Move/Rotate
— Scale/Stretch
— Copy
— Modify
— Lights
— Materials
— Render
— Interfere/Analysis
— Section
— Distance/Volume
— Coordinates

At the top of the Tool Sets palette are tools for creating 3D solid primitives, which are 3D objects that can be sculpted in various ways.

Just below the 3D solid primitive tools are the solid editing tools. These tools are part of a tool group that can be expanded by clicking the disclosure triangle that appears when you hover over them.

Next are the tools for creating 3D surfaces. You can create "hollow" 3D objects of various shapes using these tools. Additional tools can be found by expanding the Surfaces – Create tool group by clicking the disclosure triangle that appears when you hover over these tools. The Surfaces – Edit tool group is located just below the Surfaces – Create tool group.

In the middle of the Tool Sets palette, you'll see the familiar Open and Closed Shapes tool groups. You can use these to help create 3D solids and surfaces. They are the same, familiar tools you've been using in the 2D environment. Many of the editing tools you have used already are also present. You'll also find the Copy and Modify tool groups. The Copy tool group includes a few tools designed for 3D editing.

Farther down the Tool Sets palette are tools for materials, rendering, and adding light sources to your 3D model. Materials, lighting, and rendering go hand in hand, and their proximity to each other will help to remind you of their close relationship.

Finally, at the very bottom of the Tool Sets palette are three more tool groups. The Coordinates tool group contains tools that give you control over your work plane, otherwise known as the User Coordinate System, or UCS. The Distance and Volume tools and Section tool group allow you to gather information about your 3D model, such as area or volume. The Section tool group contains tools that enable you to create cross sections of your 3D objects. Between the section and coordinates tools are tools that enable you to analyze and measure your model.

## Finding the 3D Options in the Menu Bar

In addition, there are commands for 3D modeling in the menu bar that don't appear in the Tool Sets palette. The View menu offers Viewports, 3D Views, Visual Styles, and Render (Figure 19.4). These options enable you to control the appearance of your model. In addition, the Orbit and Camera options give you finer control over the direction of your view.

**FIGURE 19.4**

Menu bar options for 3D modeling

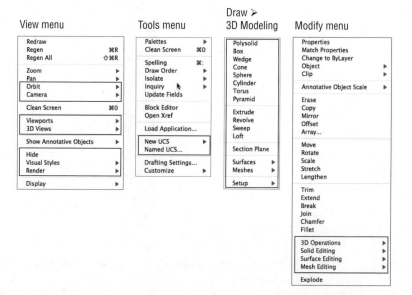

The Tools menu offers the New UCS and Named UCS options, which help to define a work plane in 3D. The Draw menu offers the 3D Modeling submenu, which contains all of the different types of 3D objects you can create in AutoCAD.

Toward the bottom of the Modify menu in the menu bar, you'll see four options that offer commands to edit 3D objects as well as commands specifically designed for solids, surfaces, and meshes, which are the three main types of 3D objects you'll work with in AutoCAD.

## Revisiting the Drawing Area Viewport Controls and ViewCube

In Chapter 1, "Exploring the AutoCAD Interface," you briefly encountered the viewport controls in the upper-left corner of the drawing area and you used the ViewCube to change your view of a

3D model of a locking clip. The ViewCube is easy to use once you've played with it a few times. It lets you go to any of the standard 3D views such as a Southwest or Northeast isometric view. You can also use the ViewCube to display a top, bottom, or side view. You can even switch between a perspective view and a parallel projection view using the ViewCube right-click menu.

The viewport controls in the upper-left corner of the drawing area enable you to control the look of your model in addition to duplicating many of the functions of the ViewCube. For example, you can go to a Northwest isometric view by clicking the Current menu option and selecting NW Isometric. (Don't do that yet. You'll get a chance to use it later on.) The Realistic menu option lets you choose from a set of different looks you can give your 3D model. These different looks, called *visual styles,* can be helpful while you work on your model. The plus sign option to the far left enables you to divide your drawing area into multiple viewports that are like separate and different views to your model.

Whenever you select an option from one of the viewport menus, the option you select is displayed in the menu. So if you were to select SW Isometric from the Current menu, the word *Current* is replaced with *SW Isometric.* For this reason, I'll give these menus fixed names for the rest of this part of the book to make it easier to identify them. Figure 19.5 identifies these menus as the Plus, 3D Views, and Visual Styles viewport menus. If you encounter these names and you forget what they refer to, come back to this figure to refresh your memory.

**FIGURE 19.5**
The Plus, 3D Views, and Visual Styles viewport menus

Now that you've been introduced to the 3D modeling features of AutoCAD, let's take a closer look. In the rest of the chapter, you'll get some hands-on experience using the Modeling toolset as well as a few other options discussed so far.

## Expanding the Status Bar for More 3D Tools

There are some hidden 3D tools that you'll begin to use in this part of the book. You may have noticed the disclosure triangle on the far right of the status bar. Click it and the status bar expands to show additional tools you'll use to create and modify 3D models (Figure 19.6).

**FIGURE 19.6**
The expanded status bar

Disclosure triangle

There are tools for lighting and various other 3D-related features. For now, just be aware that these additional tools are there. You'll be introduced to many of them throughout this part of the book.

## Drawing in 3D Using Solids

You can work with three types of 3D objects in AutoCAD: solids, surfaces, and meshes. You can treat solid objects as if they're solid material. For example, you can create a box and then remove shapes from the box as if you're carving it, as shown in Figure 19.7.

**FIGURE 19.7**
Solid modeling lets you remove or add shapes.

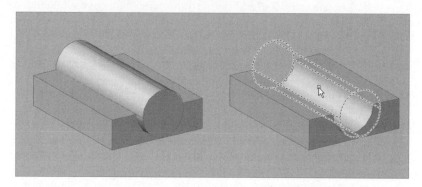

With surfaces, you create complex surface shapes by building on lines, arcs, or polylines. For example, you can quickly turn a series of curved polylines, arcs, or lines into a warped surface, as shown in Figure 19.8.

**FIGURE 19.8**
Using the Loft tool, you can use a set of 2D objects (left) to define a complex surface (right).

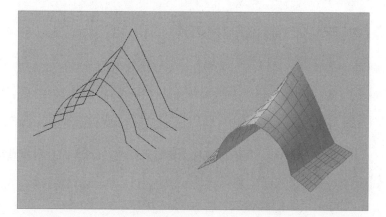

Next, you'll learn how to create a solid box and then make simple changes to it as an introduction to 3D modeling.

## Adjusting Appearances

Before you start to work on the exercise, you'll want to change the visual style to one that will make your work a little easier to visualize in the creation phase. Visual Styles offers a way to let you see your model in different styles from sketchlike to realistic. You'll learn more about Visual Styles in "Getting a Visual Effect" later in this chapter, but for now, you'll get a brief introduction by changing the style for the exercises that follow.

Choose Shades Of Gray from the Visual Styles viewport menu. You can also choose View ➤ Visual Styles ➤ Shades Of Gray from the menu bar or type **VSCURRENT**↵ **G**↵. This will give the solid objects in your model a uniform gray color and will also "highlight" the edges of the solids with a dark line so you can see them clearly.

## Creating a 3D Box

Start by creating a box using the Box tool in the Tool Sets palette:

1. Click the Box tool from Tool Sets palette. You can also choose Draw ➤ 3D Modeling ➤ Box or type **BOX**↵.

2. Click a point near the origin (0,0) of the drawing shown in Figure 19.9. Once you click, you see a rectangle follow the cursor.

3. Click another point near coordinate 20,15, as shown in Figure 19.9. As you move the cursor, the rectangle is fixed and the height of the 3D box appears.

4. Enter 4↵ for a height of 4 units for the box. You can also click to fix the height of the box.

---

**WHY THE SCREEN LOOKS DIFFERENT FROM THE PICTURES**

I'd like to point out that I have set up my display with a lighter background than the default background in AutoCAD. This is intended to help you see the various parts of the display more easily on the printed page.

In addition, when you start a 3D model using the acad3D.dwt template, the default layer 0 is set to a color that is a light blue instead of the white or black that is used in the standard acad.dwt template. The blue color is used so you can see the 3D shapes clearly when the model is displayed using a shaded visual style. If you happen to start a 3D model using the acad.dwt template, you may want to change the default layer color to something other than white or black.

**FIGURE 19.9**
Drawing a 3D
solid box

Select a location near coordinate 20,15 for the other corner.

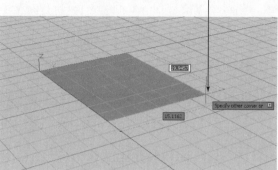

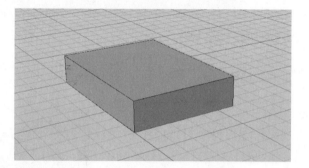

You used three basic steps in creating the box. First, you clicked one corner to establish a location for the box. Then, you clicked another corner to establish the base size. Finally, you entered a height. You use a similar set of steps to create any of the other 3D solid primitives found in the Box flyout of the Tool Sets palette. For example, for a cylinder, you select the center, then the radius, and finally the height. For a wedge, you select two corners as you did with the box, and then you select the height. You'll learn more about these 3D solid primitives in Chapter 22, "Editing and Visualizing 3D Solids."

## Editing 3D Solids with Grips

Once you've created a solid, you can fine-tune its shape by using grips:

1. Adjust your view so it looks similar to Figure 19.10, and then click the solid to select it. Grips appear on the 3D solid, as shown in the figure.

   You can adjust the location of the square grips at the base of the solid in a way that is similar to adjusting the grips on 2D objects. The arrow grips let you adjust the length of the side to which the arrows are attached. If you click an arrow grip and you have Dynamic Input turned on, a dimension appears at the cursor, as shown in Figure 19.10. You can enter a new dimension for the length associated with the selected grip, or you can click and drag the arrow to adjust the length. Remember that you can press the Tab key to shift between dimensions shown in the Dynamic Input display.

**FIGURE 19.10**
Grips appear on
3D solid.

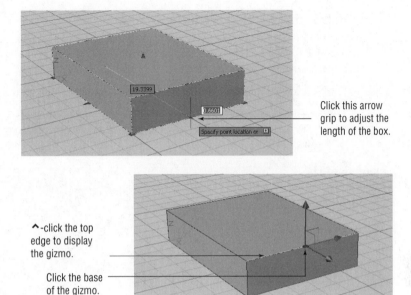

Click this arrow
grip to adjust the
length of the box.

^-click the top
edge to display
the gizmo.

Click the base
of the gizmo.

2. Click the arrow grip toward the front of the box, as shown in the top image of Figure 19.10. Now, as you move the cursor, the box changes in length.

3. Press Esc to clear the grip selection and the box selection.

You can also move individual edges by using a ^-click:

1. Hold down ^ and move the cursor over the different surfaces and edges of the box. Notice that surfaces and edges are highlighted as you do so.

2. While still holding ^, hover over the top-front edge. When it is highlighted, click it. A graphic tool called a *gizmo* appears at the midpoint of the edge, as shown in the bottom image in Figure 19.10. The gizmo has three legs pointing in the X, Y, and Z axes. It also has a grip at the base of the three legs. If your ^-click doesn't work as described, you may need to change the setting for the Legacyctrlpick system variable. At the Command prompt, enter **LEGACYCTRLPICK**⏎, and then enter **0**⏎.

3. Click the grip at the base of the gizmo, and move the cursor. The edge follows the grip.

4. Hold down ⇧, and pull the grip forward, away from the box's center. ⇧ constrains the motion in the X, Y, or Z axis.

5. Click a point to fix the edge's new position.

6. Click the Undo button to return the box to its original shape.

As you can see, you have a great deal of flexibility in controlling the shape of the box. Using ⇧ lets you constrain the motion of the grip.

## Constraining Motion with the Gizmo

You were introduced to the gizmo in the preceding exercise. This is a tool that looks like the UCS icon and appears whenever you select a 3D solid or any part of a 3D solid. Try the next exercise to see how the gizmo works:

1. ^-click the top-front edge of the box again to expose the edge's grip.

2. Place the cursor on the blue Z axis of the gizmo, but don't click. A blue line appears that extends across the drawing area, and the Z axis of the gizmo changes color, as shown in Figure 19.11.

**FIGURE 19.11**
Using the gizmo to
constrain motion

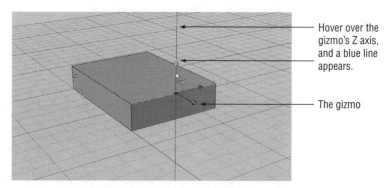

Hover over the
gizmo's Z axis,
and a blue line
appears.

The gizmo

3. Click the Z axis. Now as you move the cursor, the grip motion is constrained in the Z axis.

4. Click again to fix the location of the grip.

5. Press the Esc key to clear your grip selection.

6. Press ⌘-Z to undo the grip edit.

Here you used the gizmo to change the Z location of a grip easily. You can use the gizmo to modify the location of a single grip or the entire object.

## Rotating Objects in 3D Using Dynamic UCS

Typically, you work in what is known as the *World Coordinate System (WCS)*. This is the default coordinate system that AutoCAD uses in new drawings, but you can also create your own coordinate systems that are subsets of the WCS. A coordinate system that you create is known as a *User Coordinate System (UCS)*.

UCSs are significant in 3D modeling because they can help you orient your work in 3D space. For example, you could set up a UCS on a vertical face of the 3D box you created earlier. You could then draw on that vertical face just as you would on the drawing's WCS. Figure 19.12 shows a cylinder drawn on the side of a box. If you click the Cylinder tool, for example, and place the cursor on the side of the box, the side will be highlighted to indicate the surface to which the cylinder will be applied. In addition, if you could see the cursor in color, you would see that the blue Z axis is pointing sideways to the left and is perpendicular to the side of the box.

**FIGURE 19.12**
Drawing on the side of a box

The face is highlighted.

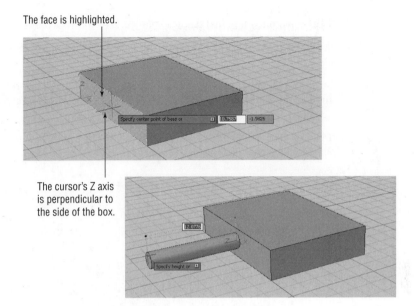

The cursor's Z axis is perpendicular to the side of the box.

The UCS has always been an important tool for 3D modeling in AutoCAD. The example just described demonstrates the Dynamic UCS, which automatically changes the orientation of the X, Y, and Z axes to conform to the flat surface of a 3D object.

You may have noticed that when you created the new 3D file using the acad3D.dwt template, the cursor looked different. Instead of the usual cross, you saw three intersecting lines. If you look carefully, you'll see that each line of the cursor is a different color. In its default configuration, AutoCAD shows a red line for the X axis, a green line for the Y axis, and a blue line for the Z axis. This mimics the color scheme of the UCS icon, as shown in Figure 19.13.

**FIGURE 19.13**
The UCS icon at the left and the cursor in 3D to the right are color matched.

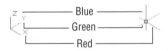

As you work with the Dynamic UCS, you'll see that the orientation of these lines changes when you point at a surface on a 3D object. The following exercise shows you how to use the Dynamic UCS to help you rotate the box about the X axis:

1. If you haven't done so already, click the disclosure triangle to the far right of the status bar to expand the status bar.

2. Be sure the Object Snap and Allow/Disallow Dynamic UCS features are turned on.

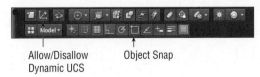

Allow/Disallow          Object Snap
Dynamic UCS

**3.** Click the Rotate tool just below the middle of the Tool Sets palette or enter **RO**↵.

**4.** At the Select objects: prompt, click the box, and then press ↵ to finish your selection.

**5.** At the Specify base point: prompt, don't click anything, but move the cursor from one surface of the box to a side of the box. As you do this, notice that the surface you point to becomes highlighted. The orientation of the cursor also changes depending on which surface you're pointing to.

**6.** Place the cursor on the left side, as shown in the top image of Figure 19.14; then ⇧-right-click your mouse and select Endpoint from the Osnap shortcut menu.

**FIGURE 19.14**
Selecting a base point, and the resulting box orientation

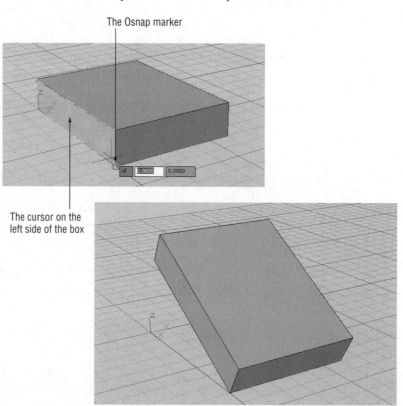

The Osnap marker

The cursor on the left side of the box

**7.** While keeping the side highlighted, place the Osnap marker on the lower-front corner of the box, as shown in the top image in Figure 19.14. Click this corner. As you move the cursor, the box rotates about the Y axis.

**8.** Enter **–30** for the rotation angle. Your box should look like the image at the bottom in Figure 19.14.

Here you saw that you can hover over a surface to indicate the plane about which the rotation is to occur. Now, suppose you want to add an object to one of the sides of the rotated box. The next section will show you another essential tool, one you can use to do just that.

**USING OBJECT SNAPS AND OSNAP TRACKING IN 3D SPACE**

If you need to place objects in precise locations in 3D, such as at endpoints or midpoints of other objects, you can do so using object snaps, just as you would in 2D. But you must take care when using osnaps where the Dynamic UCS is concerned.

In the exercise in the section "Rotating Objects in 3D Using Dynamic UCS," you were asked to make sure you placed the cursor on the side of the box that coincided with the rotational plane *before* you selected the Endpoint osnap. This ensures that the Dynamic UCS feature has selected the proper rotational plane; otherwise, the box may rotate in the wrong direction.

In some operations, you can't use osnaps in perspective mode. Osnap Tracking also doesn't work in perspective mode. Switch to a parallel projection view if you know you'll want to use osnaps. (See the section "Changing from Perspective to Parallel Projection" later in this chapter.) If you need to snap to points that are in the back of an object, switch to the 2D or 3D wireframe visual style. See the section "Getting a Visual Effect" later in this chapter for more on visual styles.

## Drawing on a 3D Object's Surface

In the rotation exercise, you saw that you can hover over a surface to indicate the plane of rotation. You can use the same method to indicate the plane on which you want to place an object. Try the following exercise to see how it's done:

1.  Click the Center, Radius tool near the middle of the Tool Sets palette or enter **C**↵.

2.  Place the cursor on the top surface of the rectangle, as indicated in the top image of Figure 19.15, and hold it there for a moment. The surface is highlighted and the cursor aligns with the angle of the top surface.

**FIGURE 19.15**
Drawing circles
on the surface
of a 3D solid

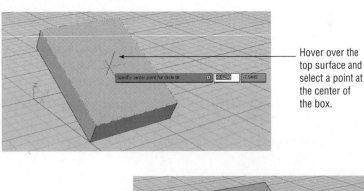

Hover over the
top surface and
select a point at
the center of
the box.

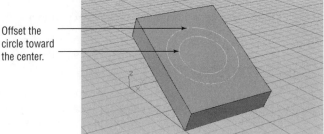

Offset the
circle toward
the center.

3. Click a point roughly at the center of the box. The circle appears on the surface, and as you move the cursor, the circle's radius follows.

4. Adjust the circle so it's roughly the same 6-unit radius as the one shown on the bottom image in Figure 19.15, and then click to set the radius. You can also enter 6↵.

5. Choose Modify ➢ Offset from the menu bar or type O↵, and offset the circle 2 units inward, as shown in the bottom image of Figure 19.15. You can use the Center osnap to indicate a direction toward the center of the circle.

---

**USING A FIXED UCS**

If you're working in a crowded area of a drawing, or if you know you need to do a lot of work on one particular surface of an object, you can create a UCS that remains in a fixed orientation until you change it instead of relying on the Dynamic UCS feature. Choose Tools ➢ New UCS ➢ Face from the menu bar, and then click the surface that defines the plane on which you want to work. The UCS aligns with the selected surface. Press ↵ to accept the face that the Face option has found, or you can use one of the options [Next/Xflip/Yflip] to move to another surface or flip the UCS. Once you've set the UCS, you won't have to worry about accidentally drawing in the wrong orientation. To return to the WCS, click World UCS from near the bottom of the Tool Sets palette. You'll learn more about the UCS in Chapter 20, "Using Advanced 3D Features."

---

This demonstrates that you can use Dynamic UCS to align objects with the surface of an object. Note that Dynamic UCS works only on flat surfaces. For example, you can't use it to place an object on the curved side of a cylinder.

## Pushing and Pulling Shapes from a Solid

You've just added a 2D circle to the top surface of the 3D box. AutoCAD offers a command that lets you use that 2D circle or any closed 2D shape to modify the shape of your 3D object. The Presspull command lets you "press" or "pull" a 3D shape to or from the surface of a 3D object. The following exercise shows how this works:

1. Make sure the Polar Tracking button in the status bar is turned on, and then enter **PRESSPULL**↵ at the Command prompt.

2. Move the cursor to the top surface of the box between both circles. (See the bottom image of Figure 19.16.)

3. With the cursor between the two circles, click the mouse. As you move the mouse, the circular area defined by the two circles moves.

4. Adjust the cursor location so the cursor is positioned below the center of the circle, as shown in the top image of Figure 19.17. Enter **3**↵ to create a 3-unit indentation, as shown in the bottom image of Figure 19.17.

You've created a circular indentation in the box by pressing the circular area defined by the two circles. You could have pulled the area upward to form a circular ridge on the box. Pressing the circle into the solid is essentially the same as subtracting one solid from another. When you press the shape into the solid, AutoCAD assumes you want to subtract the shape.

**FIGURE 19.16**
Move the cursor over different areas of the box and notice how the areas are highlighted.

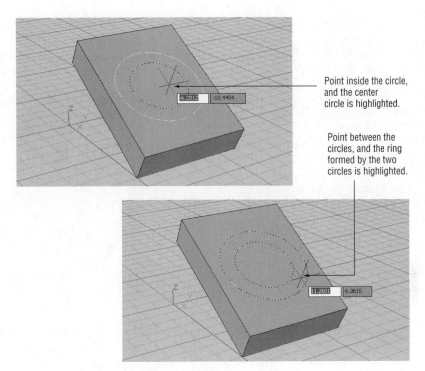

Point inside the circle, and the center circle is highlighted.

Point between the circles, and the ring formed by the two circles is highlighted.

**FIGURE 19.17**
Creating an indentation in the box using Presspull

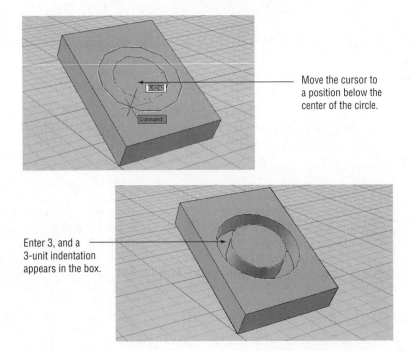

Move the cursor to a position below the center of the circle.

Enter 3, and a 3-unit indentation appears in the box.

Presspull works with any closed 2D shape, such as a circle, closed polyline, or other completely enclosed area. An existing 3D solid isn't needed. For example, you can draw two concentric circles without the 3D box and then use Presspull to convert the circles into a 3D solid ring. In the previous exercise, the solid box showed that you can use Presspull to subtract a shape from an existing solid.

As you saw in this exercise, the Presspull command can help you quickly subtract a shape from an existing 3D solid. Figure 19.18 shows some other examples of how you can use Presspull. For example, you can draw a line from one edge to another and then use Presspull to extrude the resulting triangular shape. You can also draw concentric shapes and extrude them; you can even use offset spline curves to add a trough to a solid.

**FIGURE 19.18**
Adding complex shapes using the Presspull command

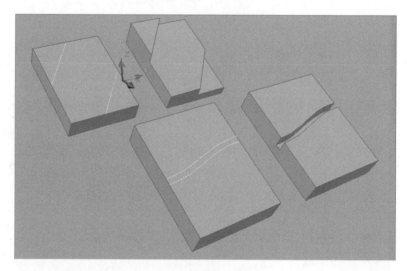

**DRAWING OUTSIDE THE SURFACE**

If you use an open 2D object such as a curved spline or line on a 3D surface, the endpoints must touch exactly on the edge of the surface before Presspull will work.

## Making Changes to Your Solid

When you're creating a 3D model, you'll hardly ever get the shape right the first time. Suppose you decide that you need to modify the shape you've created so far by moving the hole from the center of the box to a corner. The next exercise will show you how you can gain access to the individual components of a 3D solid to make changes.

The model you've been working with is composed of two objects: a box and a cylinder formed from two circles. These two components of the solid are referred to as *subobjects* of the main solid object. Faces and edges of 3D solids are also considered subobjects. When you use the Union, Subtract, and Intersect tools later on in this book, objects merge into a single solid—or at least that is how it seems at first. You can gain access to and modify the shape of the subobjects from which the shape is constructed by using ^ while clicking the solid. Try the following:

1. Place the cursor on the components of the solid you've made so far. They are highlighted as if they were one object. If you were to click it (don't do it yet), the entire object would be selected.

2. Move the cursor over the circular indentation and then press ^. As you do this, the indentation is highlighted (see the top image in Figure 19.19).

3. While still holding down ^, click the indentation. The grips for the indentation appear, as shown in the bottom image in Figure 19.19. As you may guess, you can use these grips to change the shape and location of a feature of the selected solid.

**FIGURE 19.19**
You can select subobjects of a 3D solid when you hold down ^.

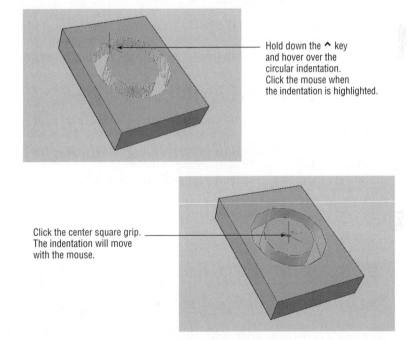

Hold down the ^ key and hover over the circular indentation. Click the mouse when the indentation is highlighted.

Click the center square grip. The indentation will move with the mouse.

4. Click the center square grip of the indentation, and move your cursor around. If you find it a bit uncontrollable, turn off Polar Tracking mode. As you move the cursor, the indentation moves with it.

5. Place the indentation in the location shown in Figure 19.20 and click. You've just moved the indentation from the center to the edge of the cylinder.

**FIGURE 19.20**
You can move the indentation to a new location using its grip.

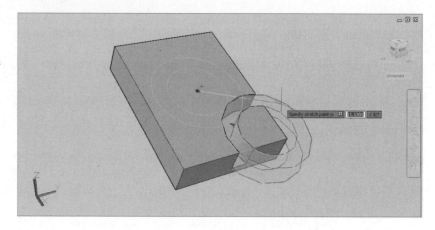

**6.** Press the Esc key to clear the selection. Exit the file and save it.

This example showed that ⌃ can be an extremely useful tool when you have to edit a solid; it allows you to select the subobjects that form your model. Once the subobjects are selected, you can move them, or you can use the arrow grips to change their size.

## Creating 3D Forms from 2D Shapes

3D solid primitives are great for creating basic shapes, but in many situations, you'll want to create a 3D form from a more complex shape. Fortunately, you can extrude 2D objects into a variety of shapes using additional 3D commands. For example, you can draw a shape like a star and then extrude it into a third dimension, as shown in Figure 19.21. Alternatively, you can use several strategically placed 2D objects to form a flowing surface like the wing of an airplane.

**FIGURE 19.21**
The closed polyline on the left can be used to construct the 3D shape on the right.

## Extruding a Polyline

You can create a 3D solid by extruding a 2D closed polyline. This is a more flexible way to create shapes because you can create a polyline of any shape and extrude it to a fairly complex form.

In the following set of exercises, you'll turn the apartment room from previous chapters into a 3D model. I've created a version of the apartment floor plan that has a few additions to make things a little easier for you. Figure 19.22 shows the file you'll use in the exercise. It's the same floor plan you've been working with in earlier chapters but with the addition of closed polylines outlining the walls.

**FIGURE 19.22**
The unit plan with closed polylines outlining the walls

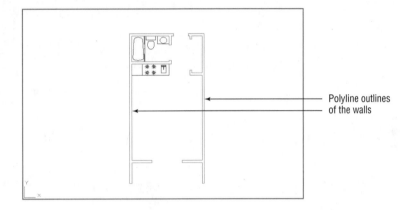

Polyline outlines of the walls

The plan isn't shaded as in the previous examples in this chapter. You can work in 3D in this display mode just as easily as in a shaded mode:

1. Open the 19-unit.dwg file. Metric users should open 21-unit-metric.dwg.

2. Choose SW Isometric from the 3D Views menu on the viewport controls (Figure 19.23). You can also type **-VIEW↵ SWISO↵**.

**FIGURE 19.23**
Selecting a view from the 3D Views menu

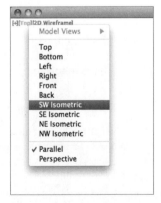

Your view now looks as if you're standing above and to the left of your drawing rather than directly above it (Figure 19.24). The UCS icon helps you get a sense of your new orientation.

**FIGURE 19.24**
A 3D view of the
unit plan

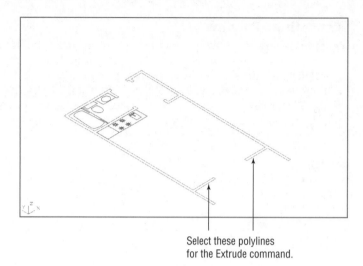

Select these polylines
for the Extrude command.

3. Click the Extrude tool in the Tool Sets palette (Figure 19.25).

**FIGURE 19.25**
Selecting the
Extrude tool
from the Tool
Sets palette

You can also enter **EXT**↵ at the Command prompt. You see the message Current wire frame density: ISOLINES=4, Closed profiles creation mode = Solid in the Command Line palette, followed by the Select objects to extrude or [MOde]: prompt.

4. Select the wall outlines shown in Figure 19.24, and then press ↵.

5. At the Specify height of extrusion or [Direction/Path/Taper angle/ Expression] <-0´-3˝>: prompt, place the cursor near the top of the drawing area and enter **8´**↵. Metric users should enter **224**↵. The walls extrude to the height you entered, as shown in Figure 19.26.

Unlike in the earlier exercise with the box, you can see through the walls because this is a 2D wireframe view. A *wireframe view* shows the volume of a 3D object by displaying the lines representing the edges of surfaces. Later in this chapter, we'll discuss how to make an object's surfaces appear opaque as they do on the box earlier in this chapter.

FIGURE 19.26
The extruded
walls

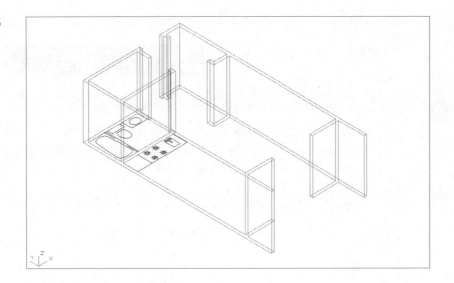

Next you'll add door headers to define the wall openings:

1. Adjust your view so you get a close look at the door shown in Figure 19.27. You can use the Pan and Zoom buttons on the status bar; you use them in this 3D view as you would in a 2D view.

**FIGURE 19.27**
Adding the door
header to the open-
ing at the balcony
of the unit plan

Select this corner… …then this corner.

Then point the cursor
downward and enter
12 for the box height.

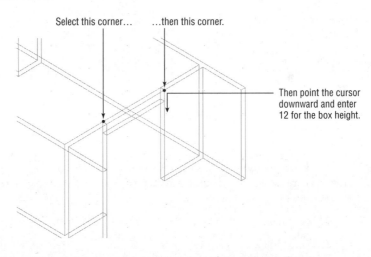

2. Turn off Dynamic UCS mode by clicking the Allow/Disallow Dynamic UCS button in the expanded status bar so it's grayed out. This helps you avoid accidentally orienting your cursor to the wall behind the door header (Figure 19.28).

**FIGURE 19.28**
Turn off
Dynamic UCS

Allow/Disallow Dynamic UCS

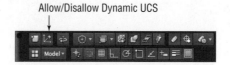

3. Click the Box tool near the top of the Tool Sets palette.

4. Use the Endpoint osnaps, and click the two points shown in Figure 19.27.

5. At the `Specify height or [2Point] <8´-0˝>:` prompt, point the cursor downward from the points you just selected, and enter **12.**↵. Metric users should enter **30.**↵. The door header appears.

6. Repeat steps 4 and 5 to draw the door headers shown in Figure 19.29.

**FIGURE 19.29**
Adding the
remaining door
headers

Add these three door headers.

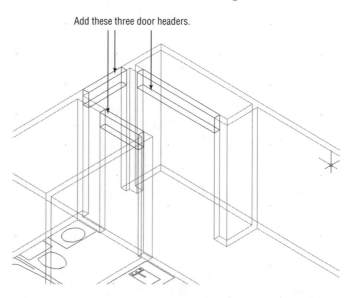

The walls and door headers give you a better sense of the space in the unit plan. To enhance the appearance of the 3D model further, you can join the walls and door headers so they appear as seamless walls and openings:

1. Zoom out so you can see the entire unit, and then click the Union tool in the Tool Sets palette (Figure 19.30). You can also enter **UNI**↵.

2. At the `Select objects:` prompt, select all the walls and headers, and then press ↵.

Now the walls and headers appear as one seamless surface without any distracting joint lines. You can really get a sense of the space of the unit plan. You'll want to explore ways of viewing the unit in 3D, but before you do that, you need to know about one more 3D modeling feature: *point filters*.

**FIGURE 19.30**

Select the Union tool.

## Isolating Coordinates with Point Filters

AutoCAD offers a method for 3D point selection that can help you isolate the X, Y, or Z coordinate of a location in 3D. Using *point filters*, you can enter an X, Y, or Z value by picking a point on the screen and telling AutoCAD to use only the X, Y, or Z value of that point or any combination of those values. For example, suppose you want to start the corner of a 3D box at the X and Y coordinates of the corner of the unit plan but you want the Z location at 3′ instead of at ground level. You can use point filters to select only the X and Y coordinates of a point and then specify the Z coordinate as a separate value. The following exercise demonstrates how this works:

1. Zoom in to the balcony door, and turn on the F-RAIL layer.

2. Click the Box tool near the top of the Tool Sets palette.

3. At the Specify first corner or [Center]: prompt, ⇧-right-click to display the Object Snap menu, and then choose Point Filters ➢ .XY. As an alternative, you can enter **.XY↵**. By doing this, you are telling AutoCAD that first you're going to specify the X and Y coordinates for this beginning point and then later indicate the Z coordinate.

   You may have noticed the .X, .Y, and .Z options on the Object Snap menu (⇧-right-click). These are the 3D point filters. By choosing one of these options as you select points in a 3D command, you can filter an X, Y, or Z value, or any combination of values, from that selected point. You can also enter filters through the keyboard.

4. At the Specify first corner or [Center]: .XY of: prompt, pick the location at the base of the wall, as shown in Figure 19.31.

5. At the (need Z): prompt, enter **36↵** (the Z coordinate). Metric users enter **92↵**. The outline of the box appears at the 36″ (or 92 cm) elevation and at the corner you selected in step 4.

6. At the Specify other corner or [Cube/Length]: prompt, ⇧-right-click to display the Object Snap menu again, and choose Point Filters ➢ .XY. Select the other endpoint indicated in Figure 19.31.

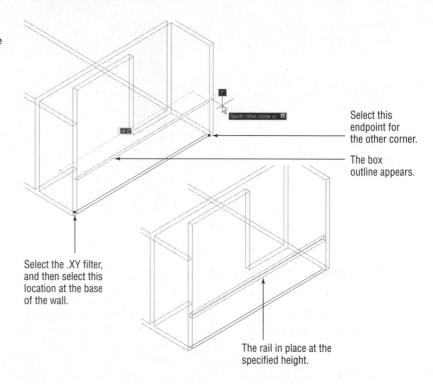

**FIGURE 19.31**
Constructing the rail using point filters

Select this endpoint for the other corner.

The box outline appears.

Select the .XY filter, and then select this location at the base of the wall.

The rail in place at the specified height.

7. At the (need Z): prompt, a temporary outline of the box appears at the 36″ height. Click the mouse to fix the base outline of the box.

8. Drag the cursor downward and enter **4↵** (**10↵** for metric users) for the height of the box. The box appears as the balcony rail.

## CONVERTING OBJECTS WITH THICKNESS INTO 3D SOLIDS

If you've worked with 3D in AutoCAD before, you probably know that you can give an object a thickness property greater than 0 to make it a 3D object. For example, a line with a thickness property greater than 0 looks like a vertical surface.

Lines with thickness

In the unit plan exercise, you can do the same for the polylines used to draw the walls. Type **CHPROP**↵ and click the wall polylines. Press ↵, type **T**↵, and type **8´** or **224 cm**. The walls appear in three dimensions. But be aware that these walls aren't 3D solids. If you zoom in to a detail of the walls, they appear hollow.

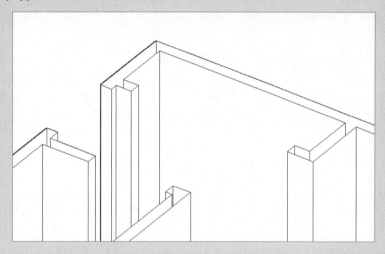

Fortunately, AutoCAD supplies a command that converts a closed polyline with thickness into a solid. Choose Modify ➢ 3D Operations ➢ Convert To Solid. You can also enter **CONVTOSOLID**↵.

Select the polyline walls; press ↵ when you've finished your selection. Once you do this, the walls become 3D solids. This operation works with any closed polyline, providing an alternate way of creating a 3D solid. If you have existing 3D models that have been produced using the Thickness property, you can use the Convert To Solid menu bar option to bring your 3D models up-to-date. The Convert To Solid option can also convert open polylines that have a width and thickness greater than 0. (See Chapter 17, "Drawing Curves," for more on polylines.)

Another menu bar option, called Convert To Surface, converts objects with thickness into 3D surface objects. You can use 3D surfaces to slice or thicken 3D solids into full 3D solids. You'll learn more about 3D surfaces in Chapter 23, "Exploring 3D Mesh and Surface Modeling."

 **Real World Scenario**

### GET TO KNOW POINT FILTERS

In my own work in 3D, point filters are a real lifesaver. They can help you locate a position in 3D when the drawing becomes crowded with objects. And since a lot of architectural models start from floor plans, you can easily "project" locations into 3D using point filters. Understanding this tool will greatly improve your ability to work in 3D.

In step 4, you selected the corner of the box, but the box didn't appear right away. You had to enter a Z value in step 5 before the outline of the box appeared. Then, in step 5, you saw the box begin at the 36″ elevation. Using point filters allowed you to place the box accurately in the drawing even though there were no features that you could snap to directly.

Now that you've gotten most of the unit modeled in 3D, you'll want to be able to look at it from different angles. Next you'll see some of the tools available to control your views in 3D.

## Moving around Your Model

AutoCAD offers a number of tools to help you view your 3D model. You've already used one to get the current 3D view. Choosing SW Isometric from the 3D Views menu on the Viewport Controls displays an isometric view from a southwest direction. You may have noticed several other isometric view options in that menu. The following sections introduce you to some of the ways you can move around in your 3D model.

### Finding Isometric and Orthogonal Views

Figure 19.32 illustrates the isometric view options you saw earlier: SE Isometric, SW Isometric, NE Isometric, and NW Isometric. The cameras represent the different viewpoint locations. You can get an idea of their location in reference to the grid and UCS icon.

**FIGURE 19.32**
The isometric viewpoints for the four isometric views available from the 3D Views menu.

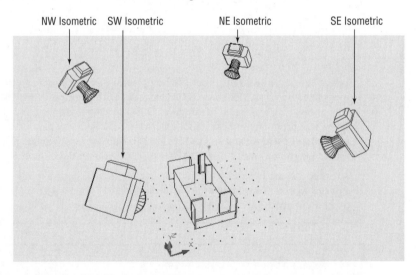

NW Isometric   SW Isometric   NE Isometric   SE Isometric

The 3D Views menu also offers another set of options: Top, Bottom, Left, Right, Front, and Back. These are orthogonal views that show the sides, top, and bottom of the model, as illustrated in Figure 19.33. In this figure, the cameras once again show the points of view.

When you use any of the view options described here, AutoCAD attempts to display the extents of the drawing. You can then use the Pan and Zoom features to adjust your view.

**FIGURE 19.33**
This diagram shows the six viewpoints of the orthogonal view options on the 3D Views menu.

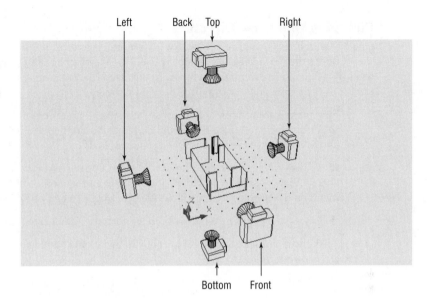

## Rotating Freely around Your Model

You may find the isometric and orthogonal views a bit restrictive. The Orbit option lets you move around your model in real time. You can fine-tune your view by clicking and dragging the mouse using this option. Try the following to see how it works:

1.  Zoom out so you see an overall view of your model.

2.  Choose View ➤ Orbit ➤ Constrained Orbit. You can also enter **3DORBIT**↵, and then right-click and select Other Navigation Modes ➤ Constrained Orbit.

3.  As you click and drag the mouse, the view revolves around your model. The cursor changes to an orbit icon to let you know you're in the middle of using the Orbit option.

4.  When you are finished, press ↵ or right-click and select Exit.

---

**CONSTRAINED ORBIT SHORTCUT**

If you have a Magic Mouse, you can hold down the ⇧ key while swiping to get the same effect as using the Orbit option.

---

If you have several objects in your model, you can select an object that you want to revolve around and then click the Orbit option. It also helps to pan your view so the object you select is in the center of the view.

When you've reached the view you want, right-click and choose Exit. You're then ready to make more changes or use another tool.

## Changing Your View Direction

One of the first tasks you'll want to do with a model is to look at it from all angles. The ViewCube is the perfect tool for this purpose. The ViewCube is a device that lets you select a view by using a sample cube. You have already seen the ViewCube in the early part of this chapter. If it is not visible in your drawing, do the following:

1. First make sure the current visual style is set to something other than 2D wireframe by selecting an option from the Visual Styles menu on the Viewport Controls in the drawing area. You can use the Shades Of Gray visual style.

2. If you don't already see the ViewCube in the upper-right corner of the drawing area, then choose View ➤ Display ➤ ViewCube ➤ On from the menu bar. You can also click the Plus menu on the Viewport Controls in the drawing area and click ViewCube.

The following list explains what you can do with the ViewCube (Figure 19.34):

◆ Click the Home icon to bring your view to the "home" position. This is helpful if you lose sight of your model.

◆ Click a corner of the cube to get an isometric-style view, or click an edge to get an "edge-on" view.

◆ You can get a top, front, right-side, or other orthogonal view just by clicking the word *Top*, *Front*, or *Right* on the ViewCube.

◆ Click and drag the N, S, E, or W label to rotate the model in the XY plane.

◆ To rotate your view of the object in 3D freely, click and drag the cube.

◆ From the icon at the bottom, select an existing UCS or create a new one from the UCS list.

**FIGURE 19.34**
The ViewCube and its options

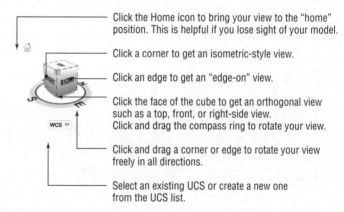

Click the Home icon to bring your view to the "home" position. This is helpful if you lose sight of your model.

Click a corner to get an isometric-style view.

Click an edge to get an "edge-on" view.

Click the face of the cube to get an orthogonal view such as a top, front, or right-side view.
Click and drag the compass ring to rotate your view.

Click and drag a corner or edge to rotate your view freely in all directions.

Select an existing UCS or create a new one from the UCS list.

You can also change from a perspective view to a parallel projection view by right-clicking the ViewCube and selecting Parallel Projection. To go from parallel projection to perspective, right-click and select Perspective or Perspective With Ortho Faces. The Perspective With Ortho Faces option works like the Perspective option except it will force a parallel projection view when you use the ViewCube to select a top, bottom, or side orthographic view.

When you are in a plan or top view, the ViewCube will look like a square, and when you hover your cursor over the cube, you'll see two curved arrows to the upper-right of the cube (Figure 19.35).

**FIGURE 19.35**
The ViewCube
top view

You can click on any of the visible corners to go to an isometric view or click the double curved arrows to rotate the view 90 degrees. The four arrowheads that you see pointing toward the cube allow you to change to an orthographic view of any of the four sides.

---

**SETTING THE HOME VIEW**

In a new file, the ViewCube's home view is similar to the SW Isometric view. To set your own home view, right-click the ViewCube and select Set Current View As Home.

---

## Changing Where You Are Looking

AutoCAD uses a camera analogy to help you set up views in your 3D model. With a camera, you have a camera location and a target, and you can fine-tune both in AutoCAD. AutoCAD also offers the Swivel option to let you adjust your view orientation. Using the Swivel option is like keeping the camera stationary while pointing in a different direction. While viewing your drawing in perspective mode, click Pan on the status bar, right-click in the drawing area, and select Other Navigation Modes ➤ Swivel. (Remember that you need to right-click the ViewCube and select Perspective for the perspective mode or choose Perspective from the 3D Views menu on the Viewport control.)

At first, the Swivel option might seem just like the Pan command. But in the 3D world, Pan actually moves both the camera and the target in unison. Using Pan is a bit like pointing a camera out the side of a moving car. If you don't keep the view in the camera fixed on an object, you are panning across the scenery. Using the Swivel option is like standing on the side of the road and turning the camera to take in a panoramic view.

To use the Swivel option, do the following:

1. While in a perspective view, click the Pan tool in the status bar.

2. Right-click in the drawing area, and choose Other Navigation Modes ➤ Swivel. You can also type **3DSWIVEL⏎** at the Command prompt or choose View ➤ Camera ➤ Swivel.

3. Click and drag in the drawing to swivel your point of view.

4. When you have the view you want, right-click and select Exit.

If you happen to lose your view entirely, you can press ⌘-Z to return to your previous view and start over. You can also click the Zoom button in the status bar, and then right-click and select Previous.

## Changing from Perspective to Parallel Projection

When you create a new drawing using the acad3D.dwt template, you're automatically given a perspective view of the file. If you need a more schematic parallel projection style of view, you can get one from the ViewCube's right-click shortcut menu (Figure 19.36). You can return to a perspective view by using the same shortcut menu shown in the figure.

**FIGURE 19.36**
The Perspective Projection and Parallel Projection options

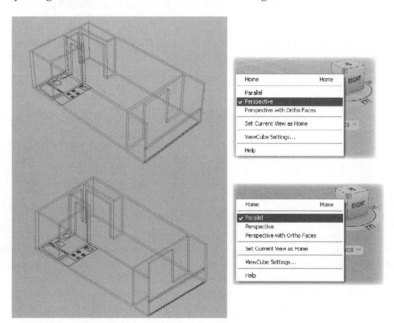

## Getting a Visual Effect

3D models are extremely useful in communicating your ideas to others, but sometimes you find that the default appearance of your model isn't exactly what you want. If you're only in a schematic design stage, you may want your model to look more like a sketch instead of a finished product. Conversely, if you're trying to sell someone on a concept, you may want a realistic look that includes materials and even special lighting.

AutoCAD provides a variety of ways to help you get a visual style, from a simple wireframe to a fully rendered image complete with chrome and wood. In the following sections, you'll get a preview of what is available to control the appearance of your model. In Chapter 21, "Rendering 3D Drawings," you'll get an in-depth look at rendering and camera features that allow you to produce views from hand-sketched "napkin" designs to finished renderings.

## Using Visual Styles

In the earlier tutorials in this chapter, you drew a box that appeared to be solid. When you then opened an existing file to extrude the unit plan into the third dimension, you worked in a wireframe view. These views are known as *visual styles* in AutoCAD. You used the default 3D visual style called Realistic when you drew the box. The unit plan used the default 2D Wireframe visual style that is used in the AutoCAD Classic style of drawing.

Sometimes, it helps to use a different visual style, depending on your task. For example, the 2D Wireframe visual style in your unit plan model can help you visualize and select things that are behind a solid. AutoCAD includes several shaded view options that can bring out various features of your model. Try the following exercises to explore some of the other visual styles:

**1.** Click the Visual Styles menu on the Viewport Controls in the drawing area (Figure 19.37). You can also find the list in the menu bar under View ➢ Visual Styles.

**FIGURE 19.37**
The Visual Styles menu on the Viewport Controls

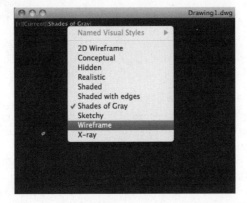

**2.** Select Wireframe. You can also enter **VSCURRENT↵ W↵**. Your model appears as a transparent wireframe object with a gray background.

**3.** To get to the shaded view of your model, choose Realistic or Shades Of Gray from the Visual Styles menu or enter **VSCURRENT↵ R↵** or **VSCURRENT↵ G↵**.

You may have noticed a few other visual style options. Figure 19.38 shows a few of those options as they're applied to a sphere. 2D Wireframe and Wireframe may appear the same, but Wireframe uses a perspective view and a background color, whereas 2D Wireframe uses a parallel projection view and no background color. Figure 19.39 shows the 3D room in the Sketchy visual style.

**FIGURE 19.38**
Visual styles applied to a sphere

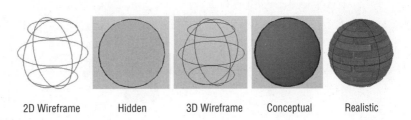

2D Wireframe    Hidden    3D Wireframe    Conceptual    Realistic

**FIGURE 19.39**
The Sketchy visual style applied to the 3D room

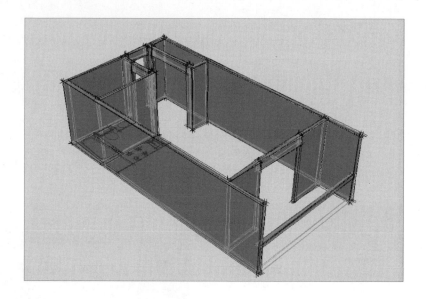

## Creating a Visual Style

You can create your own visual style, though it is not an easy or straightforward process. You will need to use a set of system variables to set up a visual style, then use the VSSAVE command to save the visual style system variable settings.

If you feel adventurous and would like to try creating a visual style, you can study the visual style system variables in the AutoCAD for Mac Help website. Choose Help ➢ AutoCAD Help, and then when you get to the AutoCAD for Mac Help page, choose Command Reference ➢ System Variables. On the System Variables page, click V System Variables. Study the system variable whose name begins with *VS*.

Creating a visual style using the system variables may seem a bit primitive, but it is likely that a much easier method using a graphical interface, such as the one found in the Windows version, will appear in later versions of AutoCAD for Mac.

## Turning a 3D View into a 2D AutoCAD Drawing

Many architectural firms use AutoCAD 3D models to study their designs. After a specific part of a design is modeled and approved, they convert the model into 2D elevations, ready to plug in to their elevation drawing.

If you need to convert your 3D models into 2D line drawings, you can use the Flatshot tool in the Section tool group.

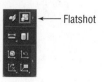

Flatshot

Set up your drawing view, and then click the Flatshot tool in the Tool Sets palette or enter **Flatshot⏎** at the Command prompt to open the Flatshot dialog box (Figure 19.40).

**FIGURE 19.40**

The Flatshot
dialog box

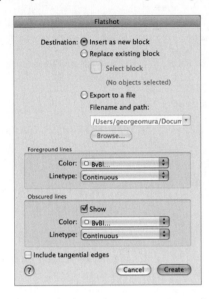

Select the options you want to use for the 2D line drawing, and then click Create. Depending on the options you select, you'll be prompted to select an insertion point or indicate a location for an exported drawing file. The 2D line drawing will be placed on the plane of the current UCS, so if you are viewing your model in a 3D view but you are in the world UCS, the 2D line drawing will appear to be projected onto the XY plane.

Flatshot offers the ability to place the 2D version of your model in the current drawing as a block, to replace an existing block in the current drawing, or to save the 2D version as a DWG file. Table 19.1 describes the Flatshot options in more detail.

**TABLE 19.1:**     Flatshot options

| OPTION | WHAT IT DOES |
| --- | --- |
| **Destination** | |
| Insert As New Block | Inserts the 2D view in the current drawing as a block. You're prompted for an insertion point, a scale, and a rotation. |
| Replace Existing Block | Replaces an existing block with a block of the 2D view. You're prompted to select an existing block. |
| Select Block | If Replace Existing Block is selected, lets you select a block to be replaced. A warning is shown if no block is selected. |

**TABLE 19.1:**     Flatshot options   *(CONTINUED)*

| OPTION | WHAT IT DOES |
|---|---|
| Export To A File | Exports the 2D view as a drawing file. |
| Filename And Path | Displays the location for the export file. Click the Browse button to specify a location. |
| **Foreground Lines** | |
| Color | Sets the overall color for the 2D view. |
| Linetype | Sets the overall linetype for the 2D view. |
| **Obscured Lines** | |
| Show | Displays hidden lines. |
| Color | If Show is turned on, sets the color for hidden lines. |
| Linetype | If Show is turned on, sets the linetype for hidden lines. The Current Linetype Scale setting is used for linetypes other than continuous. |
| Include Tangential Edges | Displays edges for curved surfaces. |

One very useful feature of Flatshot is that it can create a 2D drawing that displays the hidden lines of a 3D mechanical drawing. Turn on the Show option, and then select a linetype such as Hidden for obscured lines to produce a 2D drawing like the one shown in Figure 19.41.

**FIGURE 19.41**
A sample of a 2D drawing generated from a 3D model using Flatshot. Note the dashed lines showing the hidden lines of the view.

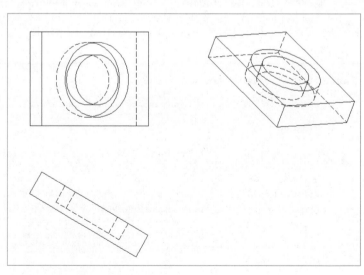

---

### 🌐 Real World Scenario

#### THINGS TO WATCH OUT FOR WHEN EDITING 3D OBJECTS

You can use the Move and Stretch commands on 3D objects to modify their Z coordinate values—but you have to be careful with these commands when editing in 3D. Here are a few tips that I've picked up while working on various 3D projects:

◆ If you want to move a 3D solid using grips, you need to select the square grip at the bottom center of the solid. The other grips move only the feature associated with the grip, like a corner or an edge. Once that bottom grip is selected, you can switch to another grip as the base point for the move by doing the following: After selecting the base grip, right-click, select Base Point from the shortcut menu, and click the grip you want to use.

◆ The Scale command will scale an object's Z coordinate value as well as the standard X coordinate and Y coordinate. Suppose you have an object with an elevation of 2 units. If you use the Scale command to enlarge that object by a factor of 4, the object will have a new elevation of 2 units times 4, or 8 units. If, on the other hand, that object has an elevation of 0, its elevation won't change because 0 times 4 is still 0. You can use the 3dscale command to restrict the scaling of an object to a single plane.

◆ You can also use the Array, Mirror, and Rotate commands (on the Tool Sets palette) on 3D solid objects, but these commands don't affect their Z coordinate values. Z coordinates can be specified for base and insertion points, so take care when using these commands with 3D models.

◆ Using the Move, Stretch, and Copy commands (on the Tool Sets palette) with osnaps can produce unpredictable and unwanted results. As a rule, it's best to use point filters when selecting points with osnap overrides. For example, to move an object from the endpoint of one object to the endpoint of another on the same Z coordinate, invoke the .XY point filter at the Specify base point: and Specify second point: prompts before you issue the Endpoint override. Proceed to pick the endpoint of the object you want; then, enter the Z coordinate or pick any point to use the current default Z coordinate.

◆ When you create a block, it uses the currently active UCS to determine its own local coordinate system. When that block is later inserted, it orients its own coordinate system with the current UCS. (The UCS is discussed in more detail in Chapter 20.)

## The Bottom Line

**Know the 3D modeling environment.**   When you work in 3D, you need a different set of tools from those for 2D drafting. AutoCAD offers the Modeling toolset on the Tool Sets palette, which provides the tools you need to create 3D models.

**Master It**   Name some of the tool groups that are unique to the Modeling toolset on the Tool Sets palette.

**Draw in 3D using solids.** AutoCAD offers a type of object called a 3D solid that lets you quickly create and edit shapes.

**Master It** What does the Presspull command do?

**Create 3D forms from 2D shapes.** The Modeling toolset offers a set of basic 3D shapes, but other commands enable you to create virtually any shape you want from 2D drawings.

**Master It** Name the command that lets you change a closed 2D polyline into a 3D solid.

**Isolate coordinates with point filters.** When you're working in 3D, selecting points can be a complicated task. AutoCAD offers point filters to let you specify the individual X, Y, and Z coordinates of a location in space.

**Master It** What does the .XY point filter do?

**Move around your model.** Getting the view you want in a 3D model can be tricky.

**Master It** Where is the menu that lets you select a view from a list of predefined 3D views?

**Get a visual effect.** At certain points in your model making, you'll want to view your 3D model with surface colors and even material assignments. AutoCAD offers several ways to do this.

**Master It** What are the steps to take to change the view from Wireframe to Realistic?

**Turn a 3D view into a 2D AutoCAD drawing.** Sometimes, it's helpful to convert a 3D model view into a 2D representation. AutoCAD offers the Flatshot command, which quickly converts a 3D view into a 2D line drawing.

**Master It** What type of object does Flatshot create?

# Chapter 20

# Using Advanced 3D Features

AutoCAD for Mac's extended set of tools, menu options, and commands for working with 3D drawings let you create 3D objects with few limitations on shape and orientation. This chapter focuses on the use of these features, which help you easily generate 3D forms and view them in both perspective and orthogonal modes.

In this chapter, you'll learn to do the following:

- ◆ Master the User Coordinate System
- ◆ Understand the UCS options
- ◆ Use viewports to aid in 3D drawing
- ◆ Create complex 3D surfaces
- ◆ Create spiral forms
- ◆ Create surface models
- ◆ Move objects in 3D space

## Setting Up AutoCAD for This Chapter

Before you start, I'd like you to set up AutoCAD in a way that will make your work a little easier. You'll use the Modeling Tool Sets panel you were introduced to in Chapter 19, "Creating 3D Drawings." To do so, follow these steps:

1. Start AutoCAD.

2. Click the Tool Sets icon at the top of the Tool Sets palette.

3. Make sure Modeling is selected. You'll see the modeling tools appear.

In Chapter 19, you started a new 3D model using a template set up for 3D modeling. Here you'll start to work with the default 2D drawing. Now you're ready to get to work.

# Mastering the User Coordinate System

The User Coordinate System (UCS) enables you to define a custom coordinate system in 2D and 3D space. You've been using a default UCS, called the *World Coordinate System (WCS)*, all along. By now, you're familiar with the L-shaped icon in the lower-left corner of the AutoCAD screen containing a small square and the letters *X* and *Y*. The square indicates that you're currently in the WCS; the *X* and *Y* indicate the positive directions of the X and Y axes. WCS is a global system of reference from which you can define other UCSs.

It may help to think of these AutoCAD UCSs as different drawing surfaces, or two-dimensional planes. You can have several UCSs at any given time. By setting up these different UCSs, you can draw as you would in the WCS in 2D yet draw a 3D image.

Suppose you want to draw a house in 3D with doors and windows on each of its sides. You can set up a UCS for each of the sides, and then you can move from UCS to UCS to add your doors and windows (Figure 20.1). In each UCS, you draw your doors and windows as you would in a typical 2D drawing. You can even insert elevation views of doors and windows that you created in other drawings.

**FIGURE 20.1**

Different UCSs in a 3D drawing

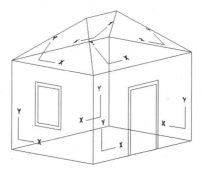

In this chapter, you'll experiment with several views and UCSs. All the commands you'll use are available from the Tools menu on the menu bar and at the command line. Many are also available from the bottom of the Tool Sets palette in the Coordinates tool group (Figure 20.2).

**FIGURE 20.2**

The Coordinates tool group

World UCS ⟶ ⟵ Previous UCS
X/Y/Z ⟶ ⟵ View/Object/Face
UCS ⟶ ⟵ 3-Point UCS
Define UCS Origin ⟶ ⟵ Z-Axis Vector
UCS Icon Properties ⟶ ⟵ Manage UCS

## Defining a UCS

In the first set of exercises, you'll create a 3D model of the Barcelona chair, which is a fairly well-known chair design. In creating this chair, you'll be exposed to the UCS as well as to some of the other 3D capabilities available in AutoCAD:

1. Open the `barcelona1.dwg` file. (Barcelona is the model name of the real-life version of the chair.) Metric users should open `barcelona1_metric.dwg`. This file contains two rectangles that you'll use to create a chair.

**2.** Select SW Isometric from the 3D Views menu on the Viewport Controls (Figure 20.3). You can also type **V↵ SWISO↵**. This gives you a 3D view from the lower-left side of the rectangles, as shown in the bottom image in Figure 20.4. Zoom out a bit to give yourself some room to work.

**3.** Select the two rectangles.

**FIGURE 20.3**
The SW Isometric from the 3D Views menu on the Viewport Controls

**FIGURE 20.4**
The chair seat and back in the Plan (top) and Isometric (bottom) views

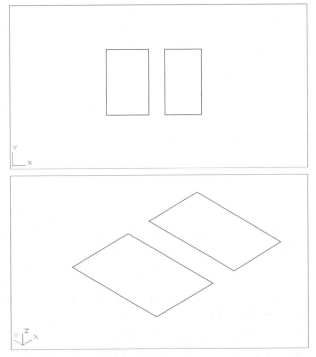

**4.** In the upper part of the Tool Sets palette, click the Extrude tool.

**5.** Position the cursor so that the direction of extrusion is upward, and then enter **3↵** for a height of 3″. Metric users should make the height 7.6 cm.

Notice that the UCS icon appears in the same plane as the current coordinate system. The icon will help you keep track of which coordinate system you're in. Now you can see the chair components as 3D objects.

Next, you'll define a UCS that is aligned with one side of the seat:

1. Click the Manage UCS tool from the Coordinates tool group of the Tool Sets palette (refer back to Figure 20.2) or type **UCSMAN**↵ to open the UCS dialog box (Figure 20.5).

2. Select the Orthographic tab to view a set of predefined UCSs.

3. Select Front in the list box. Figure 20.5 shows the orientation of the Front UCS.

**FIGURE 20.5**
The six predefined
UCS orientations

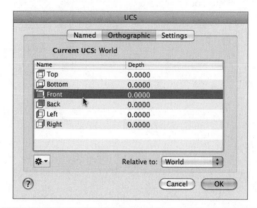

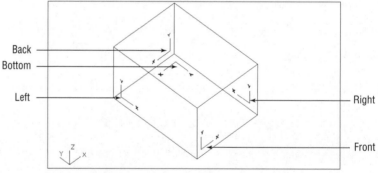

The WCS serves as the top view.

4. Click the Options action menu and choose Set Current from the menu to make the Front UCS current.

5. Click OK to close the dialog box.

The Orthographic tab of the UCS dialog box offers a set of predefined UCSs for each of the six standard orthographic projection planes. Figure 20.5 shows these UCSs in relation to the WCS. You may notice that there is no top view. The World Coordinate System (WCS) can be used in place of a top view.

Because a good part of 3D work involves drawing in these orthographic planes, AutoCAD supplies the ready-made UCS orientations for quick access. But you aren't limited to these six orientations. If you're familiar with mechanical drafting, you'll see that the orthographic UCSs correspond to the typical orthographic projections used in mechanical drafting. If you're an architect, you'll recognize that the Front, Left, Back, and Right UCSs correspond to the south, west, north, and east elevations of a building.

Before you continue building the chair model, you'll move the UCS to the surface on which you'll be working. Right now, the UCS has its origin located in the same place as the WCS origin.

You can move a UCS so that its origin is anywhere in the drawing where it's needed:

1. Choose Tools ➤ New UCS ➤ Origins on the menu bar or type **UCS**↵ **O**↵.

2. Use the Endpoint osnap and click the bottom-front corner of the chair seat, as shown in Figure 20.6. The UCS icon moves to indicate its new origin's location.

**FIGURE 20.6**
Setting up a UCS

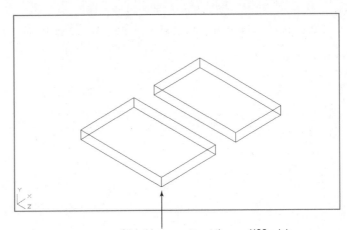

Click this corner to set the new UCS origin.

You just created a new UCS based on the Front UCS you selected from the UCS dialog box. Now, as you move your cursor, the origin of the UCS icon corresponds to a 0,0 coordinate. Although you have a new UCS, the WCS still exists; you can always return to it when you need to.

## Saving a UCS

After you've gone through the work of creating a UCS, you may want to save it, especially if you think you'll come back to it later. Here's how to save a UCS:

1. Choose Manage UCS from the Coordinates tool group of the Tool Sets palette. You can also choose Tools ➤ Named UCS on the menu bar or type **UCSMAN**↵ to open the UCS dialog box.

2. Make sure the Named tab is selected, and then highlight the Unnamed option in the Current UCS list box.

3. Click on the word *Unnamed*. The item changes to allow editing.

**4.** Type **3DSW↵** for the name of your new UCS.

**5.** Click OK to exit the dialog box.

Your UCS is now saved with the name 3DSW. You can recall it from the UCS dialog box or by using other methods that you'll learn about later in this chapter.

## Working in a UCS

Next, you'll arrange the seat and back and draw the legs of the chair. Your UCS is oriented so that you can easily adjust the orientation of the chair components. As you work through the next exercise, notice that although you're manipulating 3D objects, you're really using many of the same tools and commands you've used to edit 2D objects.

Follow these steps to adjust the seat and back and to draw legs:

**1.** Click the seat back to expose its grips. The seat back is the box to the right.

**2.** Click the bottom grip, as shown in the first image in Figure 20.7.

**FIGURE 20.7**
Moving the components of the chair into place

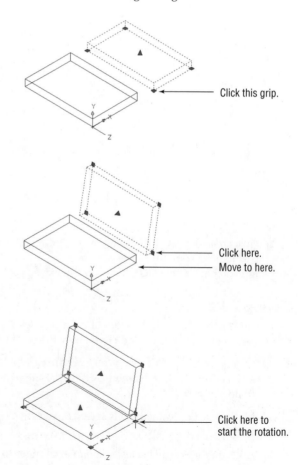

Click this grip.

Click here.
Move to here.

Click here to
start the rotation.

3. Right-click the mouse to open the Grip Edit shortcut menu.

4. Choose Rotate from the menu. The seat back now rotates with the movement of the cursor. It rotates in the plane of the new UCS you created earlier.

5. Type 80↵ to rotate the seat back 80°. Your view looks like the second image in Figure 20.7.

6. Click the bottom grip, as shown in the second image in Figure 20.7.

7. Right-click the mouse again and choose Move.

8. Using the Endpoint osnap, click the top corner of the chair seat to join the chair back to the seat, as shown in the second image in Figure 20.7.

9. Click the chair seat to add it to the selection; then click the bottom-corner grip of the seat, as shown in the third image in Figure 20.7.

10. Right-click and choose Rotate from the Grip Edit shortcut menu.

11. Enter –10↵ to rotate both the seat and back minus 10°. Press the Esc key to clear the grips. Your chair looks like Figure 20.8.

**FIGURE 20.8**
The chair after rotating and moving the components

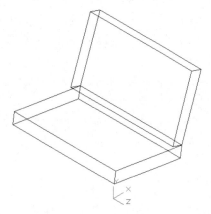

The new UCS orientation enabled you to use the grips to adjust the chair seat and back. All the grip rotation in the previous exercise was confined to the plane of the new UCS. Mirroring and scaling will also occur in relation to the current UCS.

## Building 3D Parts in Separate Files

As you work in 3D, your models will become fairly complex. When your model becomes too crowded for you to see things clearly, it helps to build parts of the model and then import them instead of building everything in one file. In the next set of exercises, you'll draw the legs of the chair and then import them to the main chair file to give you some practice in the procedure.

I've prepared a drawing called legs.dwg, which consists of two polylines that describe the shape of the legs. I did this to save you some tedious work that isn't related to 3D modeling.

You'll use this file as a starting point for the legs, and then you'll import the legs into the barcelona1.dwg file:

1. Open the legs.dwg file. Metric users should open the legs_metric.dwg file. The file consists of two polyline splines that are in the shape of one set of legs. You'll turn these simple lines into 3D solids.

2. Choose Modify ➤ Object ➤ Polyline from the menu bar or type **PE.↵**.

3. At the Select polyline or [Multiple]: prompt, enter **M.↵** to select multiple polylines. Then select the two polylines, and press ↵.

4. At the Enter an option [Close/Open/Join/Width/Fit/Spline/Decurve/Ltype gen/ Reverse/Undo]: prompt, enter **W.↵**.

5. At the Specify new width for all segments: prompt, enter **0.5.↵** to give the polylines a width of 0.5″. Metric users should enter **1.27.↵**.

6. Press ↵ to exit the Pedit command.

Next, you need to change the Thickness property of the two polylines to make them 2″ or 5 cm wide. You'll use the Chprop command to do this:

1. With the two polylines selected, enter **CHPROP.↵**.

2. Enter **T.↵** for the Thickness option and enter **2.↵.↵** to set their thickness to 2. Metric users should set their thickness to 5 cm.

3. Choose Modify ➤ 3D Operations ➤ Convert to Solid on the menu bar or enter **CONVTOSOLID.↵** at the Command prompt.

4. Select the two polylines, and then press ↵. The lines become 3D solids.

5. Click the Union tool in the upper part of the Tool Sets palette. You can also type **UNION.↵**.

6. Select the two legs, and press ↵. The two legs are now a single 3D solid, as shown in Figure 20.9.

**FIGURE 20.9**
The polylines con-
verted to 3D solids

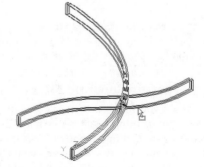

As you've just seen, you can convert polylines that have both a width and a thickness into 3D solids. Thickness is another property both open and closed 2D objects have in common, and it is a property that can be edited through the Chprop command. Now you're ready to add the legs to the rest of the chair:

1. Click in the barcelona1 drawing, and choose View ➢ Zoom ➢ Extents to get an overall view of the chair so far.

2. Click in the legs drawing, select the legs, right-click, and select Clipboard ➢ Copy.

3. Click in the barcelona1 drawing, right-click, and choose Clipboard ➢ Paste. The leg appears in the drawing.

4. Click to place the legs in the barcelona1 drawing. You don't need to be precise about placing the legs; you can move them into position next.

5. Use the Move tool on the Tool Sets palette to move the legs so the endpoint of the horizontal leg joins the chair seat, as shown in Figure 20.10.

**FIGURE 20.10**

Cut and paste the legs from the legs drawing to the barcelona1 drawing and align the leg with the chair seat and back.

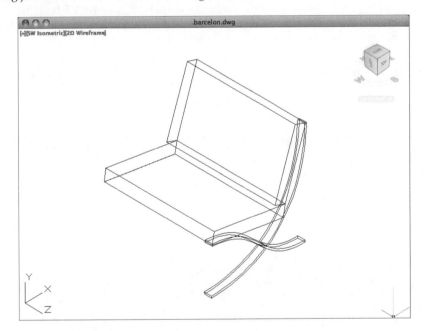

6. Save and close the `legs.dwg` file.

In these last few exercises, you worked on the legs of the chair in a separate file and then imported them into the main chair file using the Clipboard. By working on parts in separate files, you can keep your model organized and more manageable. You may have also noticed that although the legs were drawn in the WCS, they were inserted in the 3DSW UCS that you created earlier. This shows you that imported objects are placed in the current UCS. The same would have happened if you inserted an Xref or another file.

# Understanding the UCS Options

You've seen how to select a UCS from a set of predefined UCSs. You can frequently use these preset UCSs and make minor adjustments to them to get the exact UCS you want.

You can define a UCS in other ways. You can, for example, use the surface of your chair seat to define the orientation of a UCS. In the following sections, you'll be shown the different ways you can set up a UCS. Learning how to move effortlessly between UCSs is crucial to mastering the creation of 3D models, so you'll want to pay special attention to the command options shown in these examples.

Note that these examples are for your reference. You can try them out on your own model. Figure 20.2, shown earlier, will help you locate the tools mentioned in this section.

## CONTROLLING THE UCS ICON

If the UCS icon isn't behaving as described in this chapter's exercises, chances are that its settings have been altered. You can control the behavior of the UCS icon through the Ucsicon command. Type **UCSICON.⏎** to view the options available in the Command Line palette. They are [ON/OFF/ All/Noorigin/Origin/Properties].

The options for the Ucsicon command affect the way the UCS icon behaves. The ON/OFF options control whether the UCS icon is displayed or not. The All option causes changes to the UCS icon to appear in all viewports. The Noorigin/Origin option determines whether the UCS icon appears at the origin of the drawing or if it is kept in the lower-left corner of the drawing at all times. The Properties option opens the UCS Icon dialog box.

If you have multiple viewports set up in a drawing, you can set these options independently for each viewport. As mentioned, the All option forces the setting changes to apply in all viewports.

Another tool for controlling the UCS icon is the UCS Icon dialog box. To open it, click UCS Icon Properties tool from the Coordinates tool group on the Tool Sets palette (see Figure 20.2) or enter **UCSICON.⏎ P.⏎**.

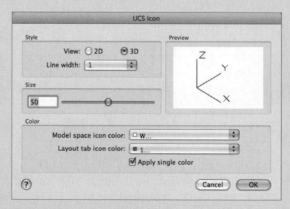

Using this dialog box, you can fine-tune the appearance of the UCS icon, including its size and color. The 2D radio button in the Style group changes the UCS icon to the old-style UCS icon used in earlier Windows releases of AutoCAD.

## UCS Based on Object Orientation

You can define a UCS based on the orientation of an object. This is helpful when you want to work on a predefined object to fill in details on its surface plane. The following steps are for information only and aren't part of the tutorial. You can try this at another time when you aren't working through an exercise.

Follow these steps to define a UCS this way:

1. Click and hold the View tool in the Coordinates tool group of the Tool Sets palette and release when the cursor is over the Object tool. You can also choose Tools ➤ New UCS ➤ Object from the menu bar or type **UCS↵ OB↵**.

2. At the `Select object to align UCS:` prompt, pick the object that you want to use to define the UCS. For example, you could click a 3D solid that you want to edit. The UCS icon shifts to reflect the new coordinate system's orientation. Figure 20.11 shows an example of using the OB (Object) option to select the edge of the chair back.

**FIGURE 20.11**
Using the Object option of the UCS command to locate a UCS

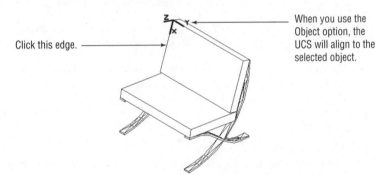

Click this edge. ⎯⎯⎯⎯⎯⎯⎯⎯⎯⎯→

When you use the Object option, the UCS will align to the selected object.

When you create a UCS using the Object option, the location of the UCS origin and its orientation depend on how the selected object was created. Table 20.1 describes how an object can determine the orientation of a UCS.

---

**TABLE 20.1:** Effects of objects on the orientation of a UCS

| OBJECT TYPE | UCS ORIENTATION |
|---|---|
| Arc | The center of the arc establishes the UCS origin. The X axis of the UCS passes through the pick point on the arc. |
| Circle | The center of the circle establishes the UCS origin. The X axis of the UCS passes through the pick point on the circle. |
| Dimension | The midpoint of the dimension text establishes the UCS origin. The X axis of the UCS is parallel to the X axis that was active when the dimension was drawn. |
| Face (of a 3D solid) | The origin of the UCS is placed on a quadrant of a circular surface or on the corner of a polygonal surface. |

**TABLE 20.1:**     Effects of objects on the orientation of a UCS   *(CONTINUED)*

| OBJECT TYPE | UCS ORIENTATION |
| --- | --- |
| Line | The endpoint nearest the pick point establishes the origin of the UCS, and the XZ plane of the UCS contains the line. |
| Point | The point location establishes the UCS origin. The UCS orientation is arbitrary. |
| 2D polyline | The starting point of the polyline establishes the UCS origin. The X axis is determined by the direction from the first point to the next vertex. |
| 3D polyline | Returns the message `This object does not define a coordinate system.` |
| Spline | The UCS is created with its XY plane parallel to the XY plane of the UCS that was current when the spline was created. |
| Solid | The first point of the solid establishes the origin of the UCS. The second point of the solid establishes the X axis. |
| Trace | The direction of the trace establishes the X axis of the UCS, and the beginning point sets the origin. |
| 3D Face | The first point of the 3D Face establishes the origin. The first and second points establish the X axis. The plane defined by the 3D Face determines the orientation of the UCS. |
| Shapes, text, blocks, attributes, and attribute definitions | The insertion point establishes the origin of the UCS. The object's rotation angle establishes the X axis. |

## UCS Based on Offset Orientation

At times, you may want to work in a UCS that has the same orientation as the current UCS but is offset. For example, you might be drawing a building that has several parallel walls offset with a sawtooth effect (Figure 20.12).

 You can easily hop from one UCS to a new, parallel UCS by using the UCS Origin option. Click Define UCS Origin from the Coordinates tool group. You can also choose Tools ➢ New UCS ➢ Origin on the menu bar or type **UCS↵ O↵**. At the `Specify new origin point <0,0,0>:` prompt, pick the new origin for your UCS.

Another UCS option, called Move, will move an existing, named UCS to a new location and keep its original orientation. You won't find the UCS Move option on any tool group or menu bar, but you can use it by entering **UCS↵ M↵** at the Command prompt.

The steps in the following section are for information only and aren't part of the tutorial. You can try this at another time when you aren't working through an exercise.

**FIGURE 20.12**
Using the Origin
option to shift
the UCS

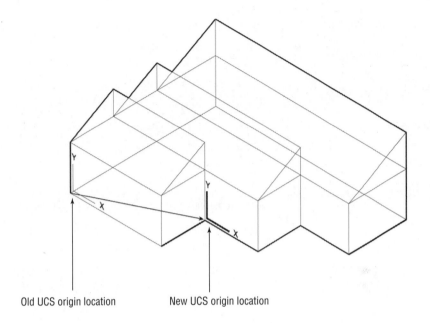

Old UCS origin location          New UCS origin location

## UCS Rotated around an Axis

Suppose you want to change the orientation of the X, Y, or Z axis of a UCS. You can do so by using the X, Y, or Z flyout on the Tool Sets palette's Coordinates tool group (Figure 20.13). These are perhaps among the most frequently used UCS options.

**FIGURE 20.13**
The X, Y and Z fly-
out in the Tool Sets
palette's Coordi-
nates tool group.

Click and hold
the X tool to
open the flyout.

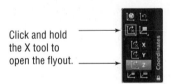

1. Click and hold the X tool from the Coordinates tool group of the Tool Sets palette and release the cursor over Z from the flyout. You can also choose Tools ➢ New UCS ➢ Z on the menu bar or type **UCS.⏎ Z.⏎**. This enables you to rotate the current UCS around the Z axis.

2. At the Specify rotation angle about Z axis <90>: prompt, press ⏎ to accept the default of 90°. The UCS icon rotates about the Z axis to reflect the new orientation of the current UCS (Figure 20.14).

Similarly, the X and Y options enable you to rotate the UCS about the current X and Y axis, respectively, just as you did for the Z axis earlier. The X and Y tools are helpful in orienting a UCS to an inclined plane. For example, if you want to work on the plane of a sloped roof of a building, you can first use the Set UCS Origin tool to align the UCS to the edge of a roof, and then use the X icon to rotate the UCS to the angle of the roof slope, as shown in Figure 20.15. Note that the default is 90°, so you only have to press ⏎ to rotate the UCS 90°, but you can also enter a rotation angle.

**FIGURE 20.14**
Rotating the UCS
about the Z axis

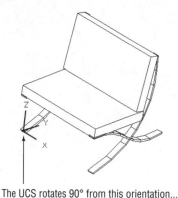 

The UCS rotates 90° from this orientation...          ...to this orientation.

**FIGURE 20.15**
Moving a UCS to
the plane of a slop-
ing roof

Slope of roof

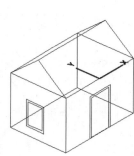 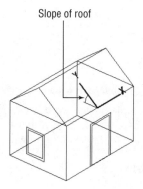

Finally, you align the Z axis between two points using the Z-Axis Vector option. This is useful when you have objects in the drawing that you can use to align the Z axis. Here are the steps:

1. Click the Z-Axis Vector tool in the Coordinates tool group of the Tool Sets palette, or type **UCS↵ ZA↵**.

2. At the `Specify new origin point or [Object]<0,0,0>:` prompt, press ↵ to accept the default, which is the current UCS origin, or you can select a new origin.

3. At the following prompt, select another point to indicate the Z axis orientation:

   `Specify point on positive portion of Z-axis <0´-0˝, 0´-0˝, 0´-1˝>:`

   Figure 20.16 shows the resulting UCS if you use the bottom of the barcelona1 chair leg to define the Z axis.

Because your cursor location is in the plane of the current UCS, it's best to pick a point on an object by using either osnap overrides or coordinate filters.

**FIGURE 20.16**
Picking points
for the Z-Axis
Vector icon

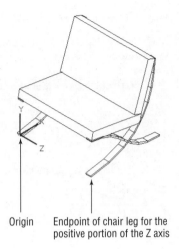

Origin      Endpoint of chair leg for the
            positive portion of the Z axis

### Orienting a UCS in the View Plane

Finally, you can define a UCS in the current view plane. This points the Z axis toward the user. This is useful if you want to switch quickly to the current view plane for editing or for adding text to a 3D view.

Click the View tool from the Coordinates tool group of the Tool Sets palette. You can also choose Tools ➤ New UCS ➤ View on the menu bar or type **UCS↵ V↵**. The UCS icon changes to show that the UCS is aligned with the current view.

AutoCAD uses the current UCS origin point for the origin of the new UCS. By defining a view as a UCS, you can enter text to label your drawing, just as you would in a technical illustration. Text entered in a plane created this way appears normal.

You've finished your tour of the UCS command. Set the UCS back to the WCS by clicking the World UCS tool in the Tool Sets palette's Coordinates tool group, and save the `barcelona1.dwg` file.

You've explored every option in creating a UCS, except one. In the section "Creating a Curved 3D Surface" later in this chapter, you'll learn about the 3-Point option for creating a UCS. This is the most versatile method for creating a UCS, but it's more involved than some of the other UCS options.

### Saving a UCS with a View

AutoCAD has the ability to save a UCS with a view. Type **V↵ E↵ U↵**. The prompt Save current UCS with saved views? [Yes/No]: appears. The default setting is Yes, which saves the current UCS along with a saved view so that when the view is restored, the UCS is also restored with it.

## Using Viewports to Aid in 3D Drawing

In Chapter 15, "Laying Out Your Printer Output," you worked extensively with AutoCAD's floating viewports in Paper Space. In this section, you'll use *tiled* viewports to see your 3D model from several sides at the same time. This is helpful in both creating and editing 3D drawings because it enables you to refer to different portions of the drawing without having to change views.

Tiled viewports are created directly in Model Space, as you'll see in the following exercise:

1. Choose View ➤ Viewports ➤ New Viewports on the menu bar or type **VPORTS**↵ to open the Viewports dialog box (Figure 20.17).

**FIGURE 20.17**
The Viewports dialog box

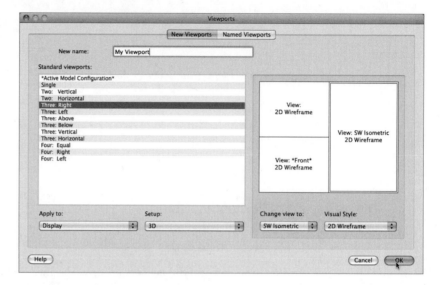

2. Make sure the New Viewports tab is selected, and then select Three: Right from the Standard Viewports list on the left. The window on the right changes to display a sample of the viewport configuration. It shows three rectangles, which represent the viewports, arranged with two on the left and one larger one to the right. Each rectangle is labeled as Current; this tells you that the current view will be placed in each viewport.

3. Open the Setup pop-up menu at the bottom of the dialog box, and select 3D. The labels in the viewport sample change to indicate Top, Front, and SE Isometric. This is close to the arrangement you want, but you need to make one more adjustment. The viewport to the right, SE Isometric, shows the back side of the chair. You want an SW Isometric view in this window.

4. Click the SE Isometric viewport sample. The sample viewport border changes to a double border to indicate that it's selected.

5. Open the Change View To pop-up menu just below the sample viewports, and select SW Isometric. The label in the selected viewport changes to let you know that the view will now contain the SW Isometric view. The Change View To list contains the standard four isometric views and the six orthogonal views. By clicking a sample viewport and selecting an option from the Change View To pop-up menu, you can arrange your viewport views nearly any way you want.

6. Click the upper-left viewport sample to highlight it, and then select Top from the Change View To pop-up menu.

7. To name this viewport arrangement, enter **My Viewport** in the New Name input box.

8. Click OK. Your display changes to show three viewports arranged as they were indicated in the Viewports dialog box (Figure 20.18).

**FIGURE 20.18**

Three viewports, each displaying a different view

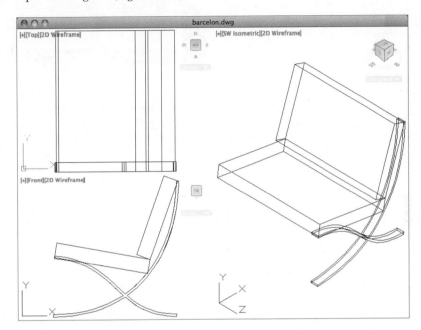

You've set up your viewports. Let's check to see that your viewport arrangement was saved:

1. Choose View ➢ Viewports ➢ Named Viewports from the menu bar to open the Viewports dialog box again.

2. Make sure the Named Viewports tab is selected. My Viewport is listed in the Named Viewports list. If you click it, a sample view of your viewport arrangement appears on the right.

3. After you've reviewed the addition to the Named Viewports list, close the dialog box.

Now, take a close look at your viewport setup. The UCS icon in the orthogonal views in the two left viewports is oriented to the plane of the view. AutoCAD enables you to set up a different UCS for each viewport. The top view uses the WCS because it's in the same plane as the WCS. The side view has its own UCS, which is parallel to its view. The isometric view to the right retains the current UCS.

Look at the 3D Views menu on the Viewport Controls for each viewport. Notice that they show the view name for each view: Top, Front, and SW Isometric. You can change these settings individually for each viewport.

Another Viewports dialog box option you haven't tried yet is the Apply To pop-up menu in the New Viewports tab (Figure 20.19).

**FIGURE 20.19**
The Apply To
pop-up menu

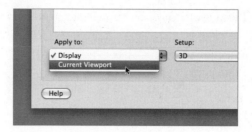

This pop-up menu shows two options: Display and Current Viewport. When Display is selected, the option you choose from the Standard Viewports pop-up menu applies to the overall display. When Current Viewport is selected, the option you select applies to the selected viewport in the sample view in the right side of the dialog box. You can use the Current Viewport option to build multiple viewports in custom arrangements.

You have the legs for one side of the chair. The next step is to mirror those legs for the other side:

1. Click the top view of the chair in the upper-left viewport.

2. Turn on Polar Tracking in the Status Bar palette, and then click the Mirror tool in the Copy tool group of the Tool Sets palette (Figure 20.20). You can also choose Modify ➢ Mirror from the menu bar or type **MI**↵.

**FIGURE 20.20**
The Mirror tool
in the Copy tool
group

Mirror

3. In the upper-left viewport, click the 3D solid representing the chair legs, and then press ↵.

4. At the `Specify first point of mirror line:` prompt, use the Midpoint osnap and select the midpoint of the chair seat, as shown in Figure 20.21.

**FIGURE 20.21**
Mirroring the legs
from one side to
another

Click the midpoint
of this edge.

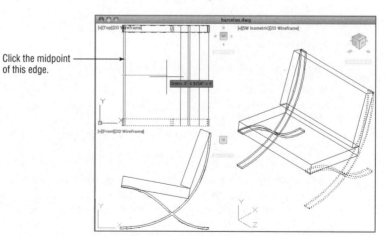

5. At the Specify second point of mirror line: prompt, pick any location to the right of the point you selected so the rubber-banding line is exactly horizontal.

6. Press ↵ at the Erase source objects? [Yes/No] <N>: prompt. The legs are mirrored to the opposite side of the chair. Your screen should look similar to Figure 20.21.

Your chair is complete. Let's finish by getting a better look at it:

1. Click the viewport to the right, showing the SW Isometric view.

2. Choose View ➢ Viewports ➢ New Viewports, and select Single from the Standard Viewports list and click OK. You can also enter **-VPORTS↵** (with a hyphen) **SI↵**.

3. Use the Zoom button on the Status Bar palette to adjust your view so that it looks similar to Figure 20.22.

**FIGURE 20.22**
The chair in 3D with hidden lines removed

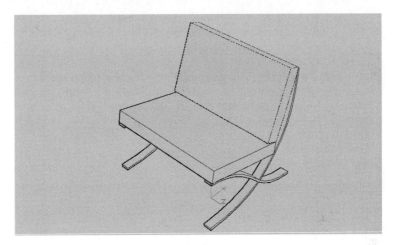

4. Click the Visual Styles menu on the Viewport Controls (Figure 20.23) and select Shades Of Gray to get a view similar to Figure 20.22. Note that your background may appear much darker.

**FIGURE 20.23**
The Visual Styles menu on the Viewport Controls

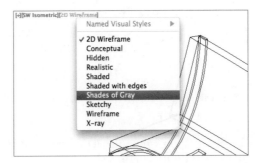

5. Exit the file. You can save if you like or close without saving in case you want to do the exercise again.

## Creating Complex 3D Surfaces

In the previous example, you drew a chair composed of objects that were mostly straight lines or curves with a thickness. All the forms in that chair were defined in planes perpendicular to one another. For a 3D model such as this, you can get by using the orthographic UCSs. At times, however, you'll want to draw objects that don't fit so easily into perpendicular or parallel planes. In the following sections, you'll create more-complex forms by using some of AutoCAD's other 3D commands.

### Laying Out a 3D Form

In this next group of exercises, you'll draw a butterfly chair. This chair has no perpendicular or parallel planes to work with, so you'll start by setting up some points that you'll use for reference only. This is similar in concept to laying out a 2D drawing. As you progress through the drawing construction, notice how the reference points are established to help create the chair. You'll also construct some temporary 3D lines to use for reference. These temporary lines will be your layout. These points will define the major UCSs needed to construct the drawing. The main point is to show you some of the options for creating and saving UCSs.

To save time, I've created the 2D drawing that you'll use to build your 3D layout. This drawing consists of two rectangles that are offset by 4″ (10 mm for metric users). To make it more interesting, they're also off center from each other (Figure 20.24).

**FIGURE 20.24**
Setting up a layout
for a butterfly chair

The first thing you'll need to do is set up the drawing for the layout:

1. Open the butterfly1.dwg file.

2. Click SW Isometric from the 3D Views menu on the Viewport Controls (Figure 20.25) or type V↵ **SWISO**↵. This gives you a view from the lower-left side of the rectangles.

**FIGURE 20.25**

The SW Isometric option in the 3D View menu

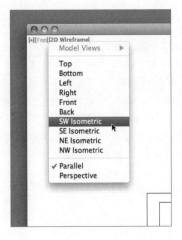

**3.** Zoom out so the rectangles occupy about a third of the drawing area window.

Now you need to move the outer rectangle in the Z axis so its elevation is 30″ (76 cm for metric users):

**1.** Click the outer rectangle, and then click one of its grips.

**2.** Right-click to open the Grip Edit shortcut menu.

**3.** Choose Move, and then enter @0,0,30↵; metric users should enter **@0,0,76**↵. This tells AutoCAD to move the rectangle a 0 distance in both the X and Y axes and 30″ (or 76 cm) in the Z axis.

**4.** Pan your view downward so it looks similar to Figure 20.26.

**FIGURE 20.26**

The finished chair layout

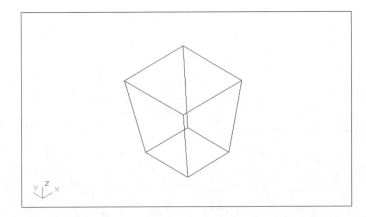

**5.** Use the Line tool near the middle of the Tool Sets palette to draw lines from the corners of the bottom square to the corners of the top square. Use the Endpoint osnap to select the exact corners of the squares. Your model should look like Figure 20.26. This is the layout for your chair—not the finished product.

As an alternate method in step 3, after choosing Move from the Grip Edit shortcut menu, you can turn on Ortho mode and point the cursor vertically so it shows –Z in the coordinate readout. Then enter **30↵**, or **76↵** for metric users.

## Using a 3D Polyline

Now you'll draw the legs for the butterfly chair by using a 3D polyline. This is a polyline that can be drawn in 3D space. Here are the steps:

1. Click 3D Polyline from the expanded Open Shapes tool group in the Tool Sets palette (Figure 20.27). You can also choose Draw ➤ 3D Polyline on the menu bar, or type **3P↵**.

**FIGURE 20.27**
The 3D Polyline tool in the Open Shapes tool group

2. At the Specify start point of polyline: prompt, pick a series of points, as shown in Figure 20.28 (top), by using the Endpoint and Midpoint osnaps. Use the Close option to close the series of lines.

**FIGURE 20.28**
Using 3D polylines to draw the legs of the butterfly chair

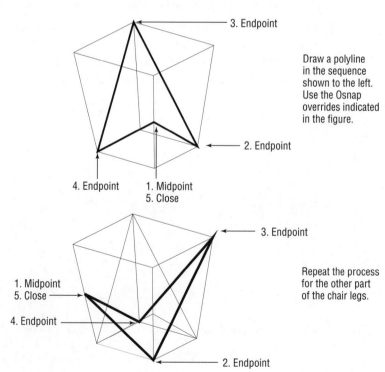

3. Draw another 3D polyline in the mirror image of the first (see the lower image in Figure 20.28).

4. Erase the connecting vertical lines that make up the frame, but keep the rectangles. You'll use them later.

All objects, with the exception of lines and 3D polylines, are restricted to the plane of your current UCS. Two other legacy 3D objects, 3D Faces and 3D meshes, are also restricted. You can use the Pline command to draw polylines in only one plane, but you can use the 3DPoly command to create a polyline in three dimensions. 3DPoly objects can't, however, be given thickness or width.

## Creating a Curved 3D Surface

Next, you'll draw the seat of the chair. The seat of a butterfly chair is usually made of canvas, and it drapes from the four corners of the chair legs. You'll first define the perimeter of the seat by using arcs, and then you'll use the Loft tool to form the shape of the draped canvas. The Loft tool creates a surface based on four objects defining the edges of that surface. In this example, you'll use arcs to define the edges of the seat.

To draw the arcs defining the seat edges, you must first establish the UCSs in the planes of those edges. In the previous example, you created a UCS for the side of the chair before you could draw the legs. In the same way, you must create a UCS defining the planes that contain the edges of the seat.

Because the UCS you want to define isn't orthogonal, you'll need to use the three-point method. This lets you define the plane of the UCS based on three points:

1. Click the 3-Point UCS tool from the expanded Coordinates tool group in the Tool Sets palette. You can also choose Tools ➤ New UCS ➤ 3 Point on the menu bar or type **UCS↵ 3↵**. This option enables you to define a UCS based on three points that you select. Remember, it helps to think of a UCS as a drawing surface situated on the surface of the object you want to draw or edit.

2. At the Specify new origin point <0,0,0>: prompt, use the Endpoint osnap to pick the bottom of the chair leg to the far left, as shown in the left image of Figure 20.29. This is the origin point of your new UCS.

3. At the Specify point on positive portion of X-axis: prompt, use the Endpoint osnap to pick the bottom of the next leg to the right of the first one, as shown in the left image in Figure 20.29.

**FIGURE 20.29**
Defining and saving three UCSs

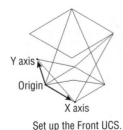

Set up the Front UCS.

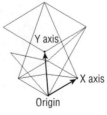

Set up the Side UCS.

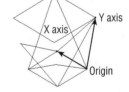

Set up the Back UCS.

4. At the Specify point on positive-Y portion of the UCS XY plane: prompt, pick the top corner of the butterfly chair seat, as shown in the left image in Figure 20.29. The UCS icon changes to indicate your new UCS.

5. Now that you've defined a UCS, you need to save it so that you can return to it later. Click the Manage UCS tool from the expanded Coordinates tool group of the Tool Sets palette. You can also choose Tools ➤ Named UCS on the menu bar or type UC↲ to open the UCS dialog box.

6. With the Named tab selected, double-click the Unnamed item in the list box.

7. Enter **FRONT**↲.

8. Click OK to exit the UCS dialog box.

You've defined and saved a UCS for the front side of the chair. As you can see from the UCS icon, this UCS is at a non-orthogonal angle to the WCS. Continue by creating UCSs for two more sides of the butterfly chair using the 3-Point UCS option:

1. Define a UCS for the side of the chair, as shown in the middle image in Figure 20.29. Use the UCS dialog box to rename this UCS Side, just as you did for Front in steps 5 through 8 in the previous exercise. Remember that you renamed the unnamed UCS.

2. Repeat these steps for a UCS for the back of the chair, named Back. Use the right image in Figure 20.29 for reference.

3. Open the UCS dialog box again; in the Named tab, highlight Front.

4. Click the Option action menu and choose Set Current. Then click OK. This activates Front as the current UCS.

5. Click the Start, End, Direction tool from the 3-Point Arc tool flyout on the Tool Sets palette (Figure 20.30).

**FIGURE 20.30**
The Start, End, Direction tool in the 3-Point flyout.

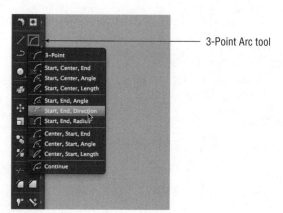

3-Point Arc tool

6. Draw the arc defining the front edge of the chair (Figure 20.31). Use the Endpoint Osnap override to pick the top endpoints of the chair legs as the endpoints of the arc. (If you need help with the Arc command, refer to the section "Using the Layout" in Chapter 3, "Setting Up and Using AutoCAD's Drafting Tools.")

**FIGURE 20.31**
Drawing the front and back seat edge using arcs and a polyline spline

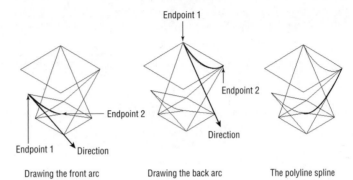

Drawing the front arc        Drawing the back arc        The polyline spline

7. Repeat steps 3 through 6 for the UCS named Back—each time using the top endpoints of the legs for the endpoints of the arc.

8. Restore the UCS for the side, but instead of drawing an arc, use the Polyline tool and draw a polyline spline similar to the one in Figure 20.31. If you need help with polyline splines, see Chapter 17, "Drawing Curves."

Next, you'll mirror the side-edge spline to the opposite side. This will save you from having to define a UCS for that side:

1. Click the World UCS tool on the Coordinates tool group of the Tool Sets palette to restore the WCS. You do this because you want to mirror the arc along an axis that is parallel to the plane of the WCS. Remember that you must use the coordinate system that defines the plane in which you want to work.

2. Click the polyline you drew for the side of the chair (the one drawn on the Side UCS).

3. Click the Midpoint grip of the arc in the Side UCS; then right-click and choose Mirror from the shortcut menu.

4. Enter **C↵** to select the Copy option.

5. Enter **B↵** to select a new base point for the mirror axis.

6. At the Specify base point: prompt, use the Midpoint override to pick the midpoints of the rectangle at the bottom of the model. Refer to Figure 20.32 for help. The polyline should mirror to the opposite side, and your chair should look like Figure 20.33.

7. Press the Esc key to clear the grips.

**FIGURE 20.32**
Set your UCS to World, and then mirror the arc that defines the side of the chair seat.

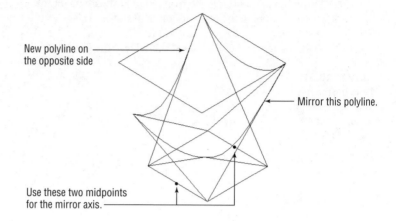

New polyline on the opposite side

Mirror this polyline.

Use these two midpoints for the mirror axis.

**FIGURE 20.33**
Your butterfly chair so far

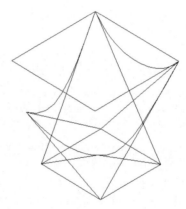

Finally, let's finish this chair by adding the mesh representing the chair seat:

1. Click the Loft tool from the upper part of the Tool Sets palette. You can also choose Draw ➢ 3D Modeling ➢ Loft from the menu bar or enter **LOFT**↵ at the Command prompt.

2. Click the arc at the front of the layout.

3. Click the arc at the back of the layout, and then press ↵ to finish your selection of cross sections.

4. Enter **G**↵ for the Guides option. You'll use the two polylines as guides.

5. Select the two polylines on the sides of the layout, and then press ↵ to complete your selection. Your chair begins to take form, as shown in Figure 20.34.

**FIGURE 20.34**
The butterfly
chair so far

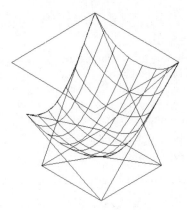

6. Choose File ➤ Save on the menu bar to save the chair so far.

You've got the beginnings of a butterfly chair with the legs drawn in schematically and the seat as a 3D surface. You can add some detail by using a few other tools and commands, as you'll see in the next set of exercises.

## Converting the Surface into a Solid

In the previous example, you used the Loft tool to create a 3D surface. Once you have a surface, you can convert it to a solid to perform other modifications.

You'll want to round the corners of the seat surface to simulate the way a butterfly chair hangs off its frame. You'll also round the corners of the frame and turn the frame into a tubular form. Start by rounding the seat surface. This will involve turning the surface into a solid so you can use solid editing tools to get the shape you want:

1. Click the Thicken tool in the expanded Solids – Edit tool group of the Tool Sets palette (Figure 20.35). You can also choose Modify ➤ 3D Operations ➤ Thicken on the menu bar or enter **Thicken**↵ at the Command prompt.

**FIGURE 20.35**
The Thicken tool
in the Solids – Edit
tool group

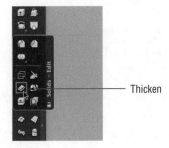

Thicken

2. Select the seat surface, and press ↵ to finish your selection.

3. At the `Specify thickness <0´-0˝>:` prompt, enter **0.01**↵, or **0.025**↵ for metric users.

The seat surface appears to lose its webbing, but it has just been converted to a very thin 3D solid.

## Shaping the Solid

The butterfly chair is in a fairly schematic state. The corners of the chair are sharply pointed, whereas a real butterfly chair would have rounded corners. In this section, you'll round the corners of the seat with a little help from the original rectangles you used to form the layout frame.

First, you'll use the Fillet command to round the corners of the rectangles. Then, you'll use the rounded rectangles to create a solid from which you'll form a new seat:

1. Choose the Fillet tool from the lower portion of the Tool Sets palette, or enter **F**↵ at the Command prompt.

2. Enter **R**↵ for the fillet radius option.

3. Enter **3**↵ to set the radius. Metric users enter **7.5**↵.

4. Enter **P**↵ for the Polyline option.

5. Select the top rectangle, as shown in Figure 20.36. The polyline corners become rounded.

**FIGURE 20.36**
Round the corners of the rectangles with the Fillet command.

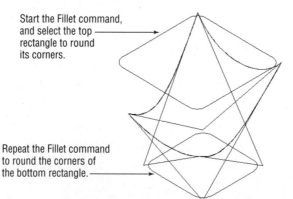

Start the Fillet command, and select the top rectangle to round its corners.

Repeat the Fillet command to round the corners of the bottom rectangle.

6. Press ↵ to repeat the Fillet command.

7. Enter **P**↵ to use the Polyline option, and then click the bottom rectangle as shown in Figure 20.36. Now both polylines have rounded corners.

Next, create a 3D solid from the two rectangles using the Loft tool:

1. Click the Loft tool near the top of the Tool Sets palette, or enter **LOFT**↵.

2. Select the two rectangles and press ↵ to finish your selection.

3. Press ↵ again to exit the Loft command. The rectangles join to form a 3D solid (Figure 20.37).

**FIGURE 20.37**
The lofted rect-
angles form a 3D
solid.

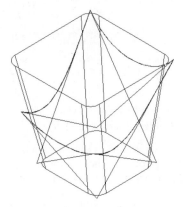

## Finding the Interference between Two Solids

In the next exercise, you'll use a tool that is intended to find the interference between two solids. This is useful if you're working with crowded 3D models and you need to check whether objects may be interfering with each other. For example, a mechanical designer might want to check to make sure duct locations aren't passing through a structural beam.

You'll use Interference Checking as a modeling tool to obtain a shape that is a combination of two solids: the seat and the rectangular solid you just created. Here are the steps:

1. Click the Interference Checking tool near the bottom of the Tool Sets palette. You can also choose Modify ➢ 3D Operations ➢ Interference Checking on the menu bar or type **INTERFERE**↵.

2. At the Select first set of objects or [Nested selection/Settings]: prompt, select the chair seat solid, and then press ↵.

3. At the Select second set of objects or [Nested selection/checK first set] <checK>: prompt, click the rectangular solid you created in the previous exercise and press ↵. The Interference Checking dialog box appears (Figure 20.38), and the drawing temporarily changes to a view similar to the Realistic visual style.

**FIGURE 20.38**

Checking for interference

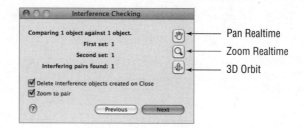

The view shows the interference of the two solids in red. Notice that the corners are rounded on the red interference.

4. In the Interference Checking dialog box, turn off the Delete Interference Objects Created On Close option and click Close. The display returns to the wireframe view. If you look carefully at the seat corners, you see a new solid overlaid on the seat (Figure 20.39).

5. Delete the rectangular solid and the original seat, as shown in Figure 20.39.

**FIGURE 20.39**

The interference solid appears on top of the original seat.

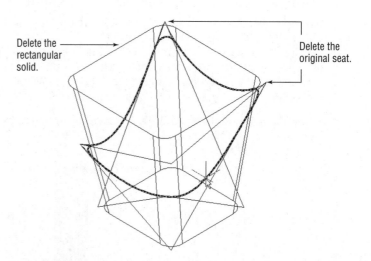

As mentioned earlier, the Interference Checking tool is intended to help you find out whether objects are colliding in a 3D model; as you've just seen, though, it can be an excellent modeling tool that can help you derive a form that you may not otherwise have the ability to create.

A number of other options are available when you're using the Interference Checking tool. Table 20.2 lists the options in the Interference Checking dialog box.

**TABLE 20.2:** Interference Checking dialog box options

| OPTION | WHAT IT DOES |
| --- | --- |
| First Set | Specifies the number of objects in the first set of selected objects |
| Second Set | Specifies the number of objects in the second set of selected objects |
| Interfering Pairs Found | Indicates the number of interferences found |
| Delete Interference Objects Created On Close | Deletes the interference object after the dialog box is closed |
| Zoom To Pair | Zooms to the interference object while you're using the Previous and Next options |
| Previous | Highlights the previous interference object |
| Next | Highlights the next interference object if multiple objects are present |
| Pan Realtime | Closes the dialog box to allow you to use Pan Realtime |
| Zoom Realtime | Closes the dialog box to allow you to use Zoom Realtime |
| 3D Orbit | Closes the dialog box to allow you to use 3D Orbit |

The prompt for the Interference command also showed some options. The prompt in step 2 shows `Nested selection/Settings`. The `Nested selection` option lets you select objects that are nested in a block or an Xref. The `Settings` option opens the Interference Settings dialog box (Figure 20.40).

**FIGURE 20.40**
Settings for interference

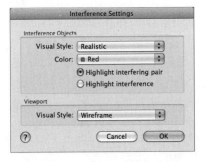

This dialog box offers settings for the temporary display of interference objects while you're using the Interference command. Table 20.3 lists the options for this dialog box.

**TABLE 20.3:**    Interference Settings dialog box options

| OPTION | WHAT IT DOES |
| --- | --- |
| Visual Style | Controls the visual style for interference objects |
| Color | Controls the color for interference objects |
| Highlight Interfering Pair | Highlights the interfering objects |
| Highlight Interference | Highlights the resulting interference objects |
| Visual Style | Controls the visual style for the drawing while displaying the interference objects |

## Creating Tubes with the Sweep Tool

One more element needs to be taken care of before your chair is complete. The legs are currently simple lines with sharp corners. In this section, you'll learn how you can convert lines into 3D tubes. To make it more interesting, you'll add rounded corners to the legs.

Start by rounding the corners on the lines you've created for the legs:

1. Use the Explode tool near the middle of the Tool Sets palette to explode the 3D polyline legs into simple lines.

2. Choose the Fillet tool from the Tool Sets palette, or enter **F↵** at the Command prompt.

3. Enter **R↵** to set the fillet radius.

4. Enter **2↵** for the radius. Metric users should enter **5↵**

5. Enter **M↵** to select multiple pairs of lines, and then select pairs of lines to fillet their corners.

6. When all the corners are rounded, press ↵ to exit the Fillet command.

7. Delete the two polyline splines you used to form the sides of the seat. Your drawing should look like Figure 20.41.

The chair is almost complete, but the legs are just wireframes. Next you'll give them some thickness by turning them into tubes. Start by creating a set of circles. You'll use the circles to define the diameter of the tubes:

1. Draw a ⅜″ (19 mm) radius circle in the location shown in Figure 20.41. Don't worry if your location is a little off; the placement of the circle isn't important.

2. Use the Array command to make 15 copies of the circle. In Figure 20.41, a 4-×-4 array is used with the default 1″ spacing. Metric users should use a spacing of about 30 mm.

**FIGURE 20.41**
Drawing the circles
for the tubes

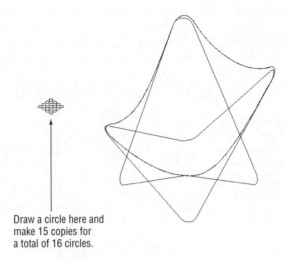

Draw a circle here and
make 15 copies for
a total of 16 circles.

Now you're ready to form the tubes:

1. Click and hold the Revolve flyout from the Tool Sets palette and release the cursor over the Sweep tool (Figure 20.42). You can also Choose Draw ➤ 3D Modeling ➤ Sweep on the menu bar or enter **SWEEP**↵ at the Command prompt.

**FIGURE 20.42**
The Sweep tool in
the Revolve flyout
of the Tool Sets
palette

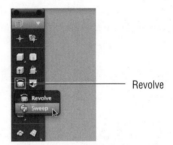

Revolve

2. At the `Select objects to sweep or [MOde]:` prompt, click one of the circles you just created. It doesn't matter which circle you use because they're identical. Press ↵ when you're finished.

3. At the `Select sweep path or [Alignment/Base point/Scale/Twist]:` prompt, select one of the lines or fillet arcs that make up the legs.

4. Press ↵ to repeat the Sweep command, and then repeat steps 2 and 3 for each part of the leg segments, including the fillet arcs.

5. Continue with step 4 until all the lines and arcs in the legs have been converted into tubes.

6. Change the color of the solid representing the seat to cyan, and then select the Realistic visual style from the Visual Styles menu on the Viewport Controls. Your drawing will look similar to the first image in Figure 20.43, which shows a perspective view. The second image is the chair with some materials assigned to its parts and a slight adjustment to the seat location.

7. Close the file. You can save it or, if you intend to repeat the exercise, close and do not save.

**FIGURE 20.43**
A perspective view and a rendered view of the butterfly chair with tubes for legs

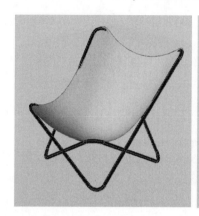 

## Using Sweep to Create Complex Forms

Although you used circles with the Sweep command to create tubes, you can use almost any closed or open shape. Figure 20.44 shows some examples of closed shapes you can use with the Sweep command.

**FIGURE 20.44**
You can use most closed shapes with the Sweep command.

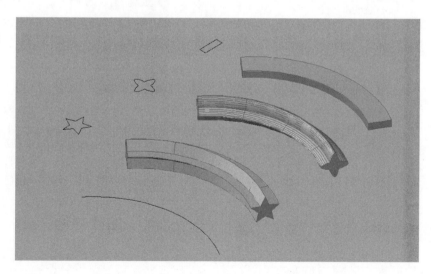

In step 3 of the previous exercise, you may have noticed some command-line options. These options offer additional control over the way Sweep works. Here is a rundown on how they work:

**Alignment**   This option lets you determine whether the object to sweep is automatically set perpendicular to the sweep path. By default, this option is set to Yes, which means the object to sweep is set perpendicular to the path. If set to No, Sweep assumes the current angle of the object, as shown in Figure 20.45.

**FIGURE 20.45**

Alignment lets you set the angle between the object to sweep and the sweep path.

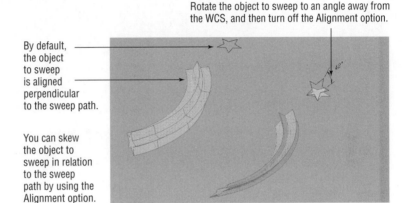

By default, the object to sweep is aligned perpendicular to the sweep path.

Rotate the object to sweep to an angle away from the WCS, and then turn off the Alignment option.

You can skew the object to sweep in relation to the sweep path by using the Alignment option.

**Base point**   By default, Sweep uses the center of the object to sweep as the location to align with the path, as shown in Figure 20.46. Base Point lets you set a specific location on the object.

**FIGURE 20.46**

Using the Base Point option

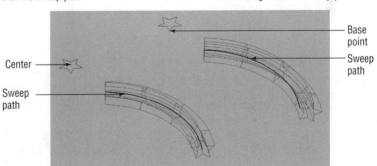

By default, the center of the object to sweep is aligned with the sweep path.

With the Base Point option, you can select a location on the object to sweep that will align with the sweep path.

Center

Sweep path

Base point

Sweep path

**Scale**   You can have Sweep scale the sweep object from one end of the path to the other to create a tapered shape, as shown in Figure 20.47. This option requires a numeric scale value.

**FIGURE 20.47**
Scale lets you scale the object to sweep as it's swept along the path.

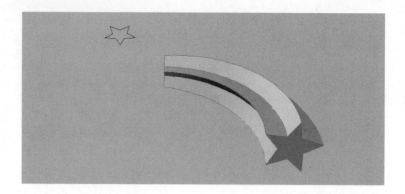

**Twist**   You can have the object to sweep twist along the path to form a spiral shape, as shown in Figure 20.48. This option requires a numeric value in the form of degrees of rotation.

**FIGURE 20.48**
You can have the object to sweep twist along the path to create a spiral effect.

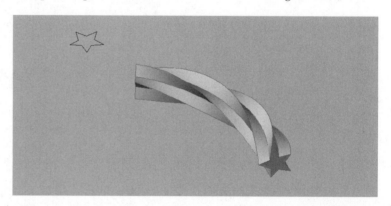

These options are available as soon as you select the sweep object and before you select the path object. You can use any combination of options you need. For example, you can apply the Twist and Scale options together, as shown in Figure 20.49.

**FIGURE 20.49**
The Scale and Twist options applied together

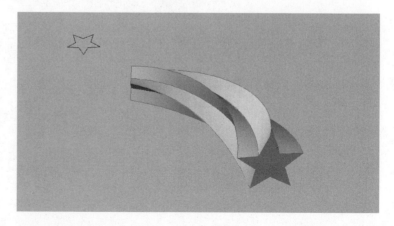

## Creating Spiral Forms

You can use the Sweep tool in conjunction with the Helix tool to create a spiral form, such as a spring or the threads of a screw. You've already seen how the Sweep tool works. Try the following to learn how the Helix tool works firsthand.

In this exercise, you'll draw a helicoil thread insert. This is a device used to repair stripped threads; it's basically a coiled steel strip that forms internal and external threads. Here are the steps:

1. Open the Helicoil.dwg file. This is a standard AutoCAD drawing containing a closed polyline in a stretched octagon shape.

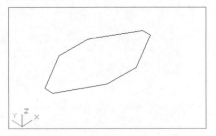

This is the cross section of the helicoil thread, and you'll use it as an object to sweep after you've created a helix.

2. Click the Helix tool from the Open Shapes tool group of the Tool Sets palette. You can also choose Draw ➤ Helix on the menu bar or type **HELIX**↵.

You see the following prompt:

```
Number of turns = 3.0000  Twist=CCW
Specify center point of base:
```

3. Pick a point roughly in the center of the view. A rubber-banding line appears along with a circle.

4. At the Specify base radius or [Diameter] <1.0000>: prompt, enter **0.375**↵.

5. At the Specify top radius or [Diameter] <0.3750>: prompt, press ↵ to accept the default, which is the same as the value you entered in step 4.

6. At the Specify helix height or [Axis endpoint/Turns/turn Height/tWist] <1.0000>: prompt, enter **T**↵ to use the Turns option.

7. At the Enter number of turns <3.0000>: prompt, enter **15**↵ to create a helix with 15 turns total.

8. At the Specify helix height or [Axis endpoint/Turns/turn Height/tWist] <1.0000>: prompt, press ↵ to accept the default height of 1. The helix appears as a spiral drawn to the dimensions you've just specified for diameter, turns, and height (Figure 20.50).

**FIGURE 20.50**
The helix and the helicoil after using Sweep

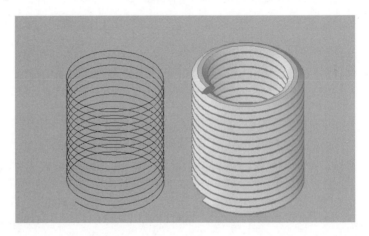

In step 6, you used the Turns option to specify the total number of turns in the helix. You also have other options that give you control over the shape of the helix. Figure 20.51 shows you the effects of the Helix command options. You may want to experiment with them on your own to get familiar with Helix.

**FIGURE 20.51**
The Helix command options

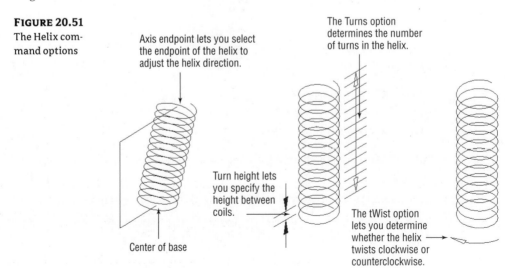

Axis endpoint lets you select the endpoint of the helix to adjust the helix direction.

The Turns option determines the number of turns in the helix.

Turn height lets you specify the height between coils.

The tWist option lets you determine whether the helix twists clockwise or counterclockwise.

Center of base

**EDIT A HELIX WITH THE PROPERTIES INSPECTOR**

If you find that you've created a helix with the wrong settings, you don't have to erase and re-create it. You can use the Properties Inspector palette to make adjustments to any of the helix options presented in Figure 20.51, even after a helix has been created. Select the helix, right-click, and choose Properties. Look in the Geometry category of the Properties Inspector palette for the helix settings.

Now, use the Sweep tool to complete the helicoil:

1. Click the Sweep tool from the Revolve flyout in the Tool Sets palette, or enter **SWEEP**↵ at the Command prompt.

2. Select the thread cross section in the lower-left corner of the drawing, and then press ↵.

3. Select the helix. After a moment, the helicoil appears.

4. To see the helicoil more clearly, choose the Realistic option from the Visual Styles menu on the Viewport Controls, and then change the helicoil to the helicoil layer.

5. Close and save the file. If you intend to repeat this exercise, close but don't save.

If the space between the coils is too small for the cross section, you may get an error message. If you get an error message at step 3, make sure you created the helix exactly as specified in the previous exercise. You may also try increasing the helix height.

In step 3, instead of selecting the sweep path, you can select an option to apply to the object to sweep. For example, by default, Sweep aligns the object to sweep at an angle that is perpendicular to the path and centers the object to sweep. See "Using Sweep to Create Complex Forms" earlier in this chapter.

## Creating Surface Models

In an earlier exercise, you used the Loft command to create the seat of a butterfly chair. In this section, you'll return to the Loft command to explore some of its other uses. This time, you'll use it to create a 3D model of a hillside based on a set of site-contour lines. You'll also see how you can use a surface created from the Loft command to slice a solid into two pieces, imprinting the solid with the surface shape.

**Real World Scenario**

**ARCHITECTURAL APPLICATIONS FOR THE HELIX TOOL**

The helix example given here is a device often used to repair spark plug threads that have been stripped, but the helix can be used in other applications besides mechanical modeling. You might use a helix to draw a circular ramp for a parking garage. Instead of multiple turns, you would use a single rotation or a half rotation. The radius of the helix would be much larger, to accommodate the width of a car.

**OLD VERSUS NEW SURFACES**

If you've used earlier Windows releases of AutoCAD to create 3D models, you've probably used surface modeling to create some of your 3D objects. If you open an old drawing file that contains those 3D surfaces, you'll see that they are called polygon meshes. You can convert those older mesh objects into new surface objects by choosing Modify ➤ 3D Operations ➤ Convert To Surface on the menu bar. If you prefer to use the older 3D surface modeling tools like Revsurf and Rulesurf, they are still available, though they now create mesh surfaces. You will learn more about mesh modeling in Chapter 23, "Exploring 3D Mesh and Surface Modeling."

Start by creating a 3D surface using the Loft command:

1. Open the contour.dwg file.

2. Click the Loft tool from the Tool Sets palette.

3. Select each brown contour in consecutive order from right to left or left to right. It doesn't matter whether you start at the left end or the right end, but you must select the contours in order.

4. When you're finished selecting all the contours, press ↵ and wait a moment. AutoCAD requires a bit of time to calculate the surface. Once it does, you see the surface applied over the contour lines (Figure 20.52).

**FIGURE 20.52**
Creating a 3D surface from contour lines

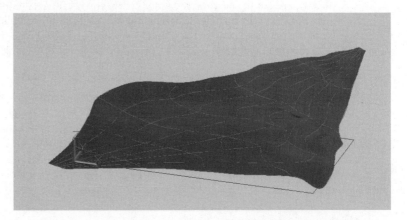

5. At the Enter an option [Guides/Path/Cross sections only/Settings] <Cross sections only>: prompt, press ↵ to exit the Loft command.

Once the loft surface has been placed, you can make adjustments to the way the loft is generated by using the arrow grip that appears when you select the surface:

1. Click the surface to select it.

**2.** Click the arrowhead that appears by the surface. This is known as a multifunction grip.

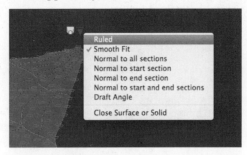

**3.** Select the Ruled option from the menu. The surface changes slightly to conform to the new Ruled surface option (Figure 20.53).

**FIGURE 20.53**
The surface with
the Ruled option
selected

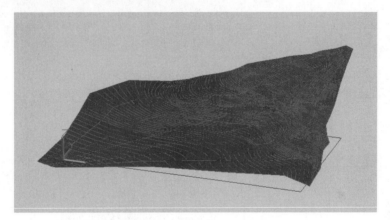

In the butterfly chair exercise, you used the Guides option of the Loft command. This allowed you to use the polyline curves to guide the loft shape from the front arc to the back arc. In this exercise, you didn't use the command options and went straight to the multifunction grip menu. The Ruled option that you used in step 3 generates a surface that connects the cross sections in a straight line.

## Slicing a Solid with a Surface

In the `barcelona1.dwg` chair example, you converted a surface into a solid using the Thicken command. Next, you'll use a surface to create a solid in a slightly different way. This time, you'll use the surface to slice a solid into two pieces. This will give you a form that is more easily read and understood as a terrain model:

**1.** Click the Extrude tool from the Tool Sets palette.

**2.** Select the large rectangle below the contours, and press ↵. The rectangle turns into a box whose height follows your cursor.

**3.** Move the cursor upward so the box looks similar to the one in Figure 20.54. Then click the mouse to fix the box's height.

**FIGURE 20.54**
The box extruded through the contours

You may have noticed that as you raised the box height, you could see how it intersected the contour surface. Next you'll slice the box into two pieces:

**1.** Click the Slice tool from the expanded Solids – Edit tool group in the Tool Sets palette (Figure 20.55).

**FIGURE 20.55**
The Slice tool

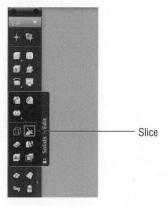

Slice

**2.** At the Select objects to slice: prompt, select the box and press ↵.

**3.** At the Specify start point of slicing plane or [planar Object/Surface/Zaxis/ View/XY/YZ/ZX/3points] <3points>: prompt, enter **S**↵ to use the Surface option.

**4.** At the Select a surface: prompt, select the contour surface.

5. At the `Select solid to keep or [keep Both sides] <Both>:` prompt, click the part of the box that is below the surface. The top part of the box disappears, and you see the surface once again.

6. Delete the contour surface and the contour lines. The box remains with an imprint of the surface, as shown in Figure 20.56.

**FIGURE 20.56**
The box with the contour surface imprinted

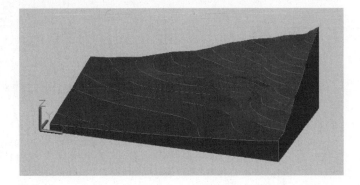

In step 3, you saw a prompt that offered a variety of methods for slicing the box. The Surface option allowed you to slice the box using an irregular shape, but most of the other options let you slice a solid by defining a plane or a series of planar objects.

## Finding the Volume of a Cut

A question I hear frequently from civil engineers is, How can I find the volume of earth from an excavated area? This is often referred to as a *cut* from a *cut and fill* operation. To do this, you first have to create the cut shape. Next, you use the Interfere command to find the intersection between the cut shape and the contour surface. You can then find the volume of the cut shape using one of AutoCAD's inquiry commands. The following exercise demonstrates how this is done.

Suppose that the contour model you've just created represents a site where you'll excavate a rectangular area for a structure. You want to find the amount of earth involved in the excavation. A rectangle has been placed in the contour drawing representing such an area:

1. Select Wireframe from the Visual Styles menu on the Viewport Controls. This allows you to see the excavation rectangle more clearly.

2. Click the Extrude tool in the Tool Sets palette.

3. Select the rectangle shown in Figure 20.57. If the rectangle is not highlighted, press ⇧-spacebar until it is.

4. Click to select the rectangle and press ↵.

5. Extrude the rectangle to the height of 10′.

**FIGURE 20.57**
Selecting the rect-
angle representing
the excavation area

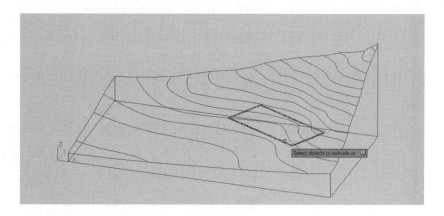

Here you used the Selection Cycling feature to help you select the rectangle, which is over-lapped by the contour solid. Selection Cycling lets you determine the object you are about to select by highlighting an object that overlaps another object. If the highlighted object is not cor-rect, you can press ⇧-spacebar and AutoCAD will highlight the next object it thinks you might want to select, thereby filtering out other objects nearby that might be selected accidentally. Once the object you want to select is highlighted, click in the drawing area.

With the excavation rectangle in place, you can use the Interfere command to find the volume of the excavation:

1. Click the Interference Checking tool near the bottom of the Tool Sets palette.

2. At the `Select first set of objects or [Nested selection/Settings]:` prompt, click the contour and press ↵.

3. At the `Select second set of objects or [Nested selection/checK first set] <checK>:` prompt, select the box and press ↵. The Interference Checking dialog box appears.

4. In the Interference Checking dialog box, turn off the Delete Interference Objects Created On Close option, and click Close.

5. Delete the box you used to represent the excavation area. The remaining shape contains the volume of the excavation.

6. Type **MASSPROP**↵.

7. At the `Select objects:` prompt, select the excavation solid, as shown in Figure 20.58, and then right-click and select Enter. The Command Line palette displays the properties of the excavation area. At the top, you see the volume of the selected solid in cubic inches (Figure 20.59).

8. At the `Write analysis to a file? [Yes/No] <N>:` prompt, you can press ↵ to exit the command or enter **Y**↵ to save the information to a text file.

**FIGURE 20.58**
The 3D solid representing the excavation

**FIGURE 20.58**
The 3D solid representing the excavation

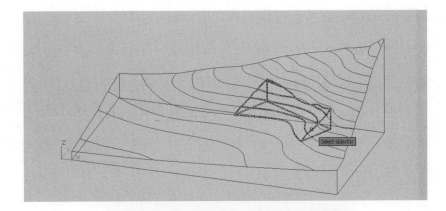

**FIGURE 20.59**
The Command Line palette expanded to show the mass and volume information from the Massprop command

## Understanding the Loft Command

As you've seen from the exercises in this chapter, the Loft command lets you create just about any shape you can imagine, from a simple sling to the complex curves of a contour map. If your loft cross sections are a set of closed objects like circles or closed polygons, the resulting object is a 3D solid instead of a surface when the Mode option is set to solid. Setting Mode to Surface causes the Loft command to create a surface instead of a 3D solid when lofting closed objects.

The order in which you select the cross sections is important because Loft will follow your selection order to create the surface or solid. For example, Figure 20.60 shows a series of circles used for a lofted solid. The circles are identical in size and placement, but the order of selection is different. The solid on the left was created by selecting the circles in consecutive order from bottom to top, creating an hourglass shape. The solid on the right was created by selecting the two larger circles first from bottom to top; the smaller, intermediate circle was selected last. This selection order created a hollowed-out shape with sides that are more vertical.

**FIGURE 20.60**
The order in which you select the cross sections affects the result of the Loft command.

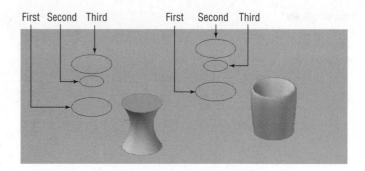

In addition to the selection order, several other settings affect the shape of a solid created by the Loft command. In the contour-map example, you selected the Ruled option from a multifunction grip after you had completed the Loft command. You can also set the Ruled option through the Loft Settings dialog box (Figure 20.61). This dialog box appears during the Loft command when you select the Settings option after you've selected a set of cross sections.

**FIGURE 20.61**
Loft Settings:
Smooth Fit

You can radically affect the way the Loft command forms a surface or a solid through the options in this dialog box, so it pays to understand what those settings do. Take a moment to study the following sections, which describe the Loft Settings dialog box options.

### RULED AND SMOOTH FIT

The Ruled option connects the cross sections with straight surfaces, as shown in the sample on the left in Figure 20.62.

The Smooth Fit option connects the cross sections with a smooth surface. It attempts to make the best smooth transitions between the cross sections, as shown on the right in Figure 20.62.

**FIGURE 20.62**
Samples of a ruled loft at left and a smooth-fit loft on the right

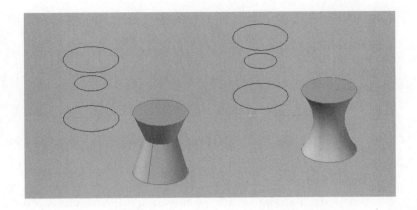

## NORMAL TO

Normal To is a set of four options presented in a pop-up menu. To understand what this option does, you need to know that *normal* is a mathematical term referring to a direction that is perpendicular to a plane, as shown in Figure 20.63. In these options, *Normal* refers to the direction the surface takes as it emerges from a cross section.

**FIGURE 20.63**
A normal is a direction perpendicular to a plane.

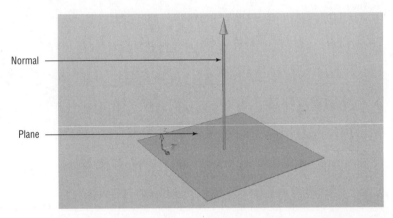

Normal

Plane

   If you use the All Cross Sections option, the surfaces emerge in a perpendicular direction from all the cross sections, as shown in the first image in Figure 20.64. If you use the End Cross Section option, the surface emerges in a direction that is perpendicular to just the end cross section, as shown in the second image in Figure 20.64. The Start Cross Section option causes the surface to emerge in a direction perpendicular to the start cross section. The Start And End Cross Sections option combines the effect of the Start Cross Section and End Cross Section options.

**FIGURE 20.64**
Samples of
the Normal To
options applied
to the same set
of cross sections

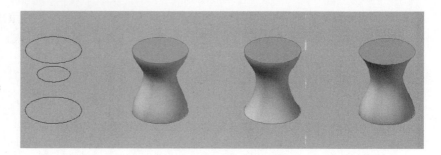

### DRAFT ANGLES

The Draft Angles option affects only the first and last cross sections. This option generates a smooth surface with added control over the start and end angle. Unlike the Normal To option, which forces a perpendicular direction to the cross sections, Draft Angles allows you to set an angle for the surface direction. For example, if you set Start Angle to a value of 0, the surface will bulge outward from the start cross section, as shown in the first image of Figure 20.65.

**FIGURE 20.65**
The Draft
Angles options

Likewise, an End Angle setting of 0 will cause the surface to bulge at the end cross section (see the second image in Figure 20.65).

The Start and End Magnitude settings let you determine a relative strength of the bulge. The right image in Figure 20.65 shows a draft angle of 0 and magnitude of 50 for the last cross section.

### CLOSE SURFACE OR SOLID

The Close Surface Or Solid option is available only when the Smooth Fit option is selected. It causes the first and last cross section objects to be connected so the surface or solid loops back from the last to the first cross section. Figure 20.66 shows the cross sections at the left, a smooth version in the middle, and a smooth version with the Close Surface Or Solid option turned on on the right. The Close Surface Or Solid option causes the solid to become a tube.

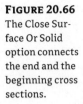

**FIGURE 20.66**
The Close Surface Or Solid option connects the end and the beginning cross sections.

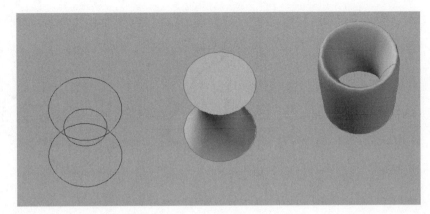

# Moving Objects in 3D Space

AutoCAD provides three menu bar options specifically designed for moving objects in 3D space: 3D Align, 3D Move, and 3D Rotate. You can find all three commands in the Modify ➤ 3D Operations submenu on the menu bar. These options help you perform some of the most common moves associated with 3D editing.

## Aligning Objects in 3D Space

In mechanical drawing, you often create the parts in 3D and then show an assembly of the parts. The 3D Align command can greatly simplify the assembly process. The following steps show how to use 3D Align to line up two objects at specific points:

1. Open the `Align.dwg` file from the Chapter 20 sample files found at www.sybex.com/go/masteringautocadmac.

2. Click the 3D Align tool just below the middle of the Tool Sets palette. You can also choose Modify ➤ 3D Operations ➤ 3D Align on the menu bar or type **3DALIGN↵**.

3. At the `Select objects:` prompt, select the 3D wedge-shaped object and press ↵. (The *source object* is the object you want to move.)

4. At the `Specify base point or [Copy]:` prompt, pick a point on the source object that is the first point of an alignment axis, such as the center of a hole or the corner of a surface. For the Align drawing, use the upper-left corner of the wedge.

5. At the `Specify second point or [Continue] <C>:` prompt, pick a point on the source object that is the second point of an alignment axis, such as another center point or other corner of a surface. For this example, select the other top corner of the wedge.

6. At the `Specify third source point or [Continue] <C>:` prompt, you can press ↵ if two points are adequate to describe the alignment. Otherwise, pick a third point on the source object that, along with the first two points, best describes the surface plane you want aligned with the destination object. Pick the lower-right corner of the wedge shown in Figure 20.67.

**FIGURE 20.67**
Aligning two 3D
objects

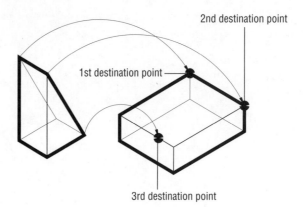

2nd destination point

1st destination point

3rd destination point

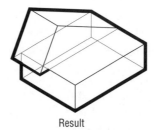

Result

7. At the Specify first destination point: prompt, pick a point on the destination object to which you want the first source point to move. (The *destination object* is the object with which you want the source object to align.) This is the top corner of the rectangular shape. (See the first destination point in Figure 20.67.)

8. At the Specify second destination point or [eXit] <X>: prompt, pick a point on the destination object indicating how the first and second source points are to align in relation to the destination object. (See the second destination point in Figure 20.67.)

9. You're prompted for a third destination point. Pick a point on the destination object that, along with the previous two destination points, describes the plane with which you want the source object to be aligned. (See the third destination point in Figure 20.67.) The source object will move into alignment with the destination object.

## Using the 3D Move command

In Chapter 19, you saw how you can use a gizmo to help restrain the motion of an object in the X, Y, or Z axis. AutoCAD offers a 3D Move command specifically designed for 3D editing that includes a gizmo to restrain motion.

You don't need to perform these steps as an exercise. You can try the command on your own when you need to use it.

Here's how it works:

1. Choose Modify ➤ 3D Operations ➤ 3D Move on the menu bar. You can also enter **3DMOVE**↵.

2. Select the object or set of objects you want to move, and press ↵. The Move gizmo appears on the object (Figure 20.68).

**FIGURE 20.68**
The Move gizmo

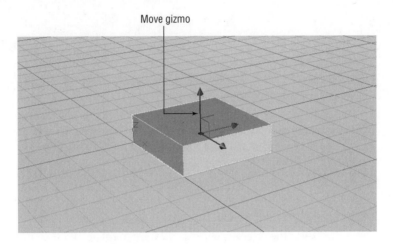

Move gizmo

3. Point to the X, Y, or Z axis of the Move gizmo but don't click it. As you hover over an axis, a motion axis vector appears indicating the direction your object will move if you click the axis, as shown in Figure 20.69.

**FIGURE 20.69**
An axis vector
appears when you
hover over an axis
of the gizmo.

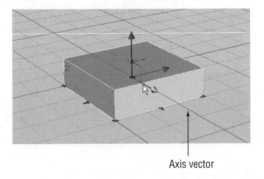

Axis vector

4. Click an axis while the vector appears and then enter a distance along the axis, or click a point to complete the move.

Alternatively, in step 3, you can hover over and click a plane indicator on the gizmo to restrain the motion along one of the planes defined by two of the axes (Figure 20.70).

Plane indicator

**FIGURE 20.70**
Hover over the plane indicator to restrain the motion along a plane.

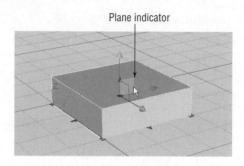

Plane indicator

## Rotating an Object in 3D

The 3D Rotate command is another command that is like an extension of its 2D counterpart. With 3D Rotate, a Rotate gizmo appears that restrains the rotation about the X, Y, or Z axis.

You don't need to perform these steps as an exercise. You can try the command on your own when you need to use it.

Here's how it works:

1. Choose Modify ➢ 3D Operations ➢ 3D Rotate on the menu bar. You can also enter **3DROTATE**⏎.

2. Select the object or objects you want to rotate and then press ⏎. The Rotate gizmo appears on the object (Figure 20.71).

**FIGURE 20.71**
The Rotate gizmo

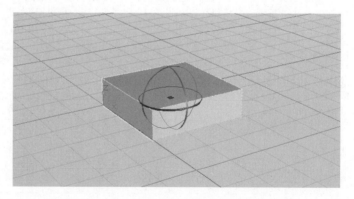

3. At the `Specify a base point:` prompt, you can select a point about which the selected objects are to be rotated. The gizmo will move to the point you select.

4. Point to the colored circle that represents the axis of rotation for your objects. A vector appears, representing the axis of rotation. When you're happy with the selected axis, click the mouse.

5. At the `Specify angle start point or type an angle:` prompt, you can enter an angle value or click a point. You can use the ⇧ key or Ortho mode to restrain the direction to 90°.

**6.** If you click a point in step 5, you will see the `Specify angle end point:` prompt. Enter an angle value or click another point for the rotation angle.

You can also just select one of the circles in step 3 instead of selecting a base point. If you do this, then the selected object begins to rotate. You don't have to select a start and end angle.

---

### USING 3DMIRROR AND 3DARRAY

Two Tool Sets palette tools, 3D Mirror and 3D Array, are 3D versions of the Mirror and Array tools. They work in a way that's similar to how the standard Mirror and Array tools work, with a slight difference.

3D Mirror begins by asking you to select objects. Then you're asked to specify a mirror plane instead of a mirror axis. You can define a plane using the default three points, or you can use one of the seven other options: `Object/Last/Zaxis/View/XY/YZ/ZX`. By using a plane instead of an axis, you can mirror an object or set of objects anywhere in 3D space. One way to visualize this is to imagine holding a mirror up to your 3D model. The mirror is your 3D plane, and the reflected image is the mirrored version of the object. Imagine tilting the mirror to various angles to get a different mirror image. In the same way, you can tilt the plane in the 3D Mirror tool to mirror an object in any number of ways.

3D Array works like the command-line version of the Array command and offers the same prompts with a couple of additions. If you choose to do a rectangular array, you're prompted for the usual row and column numbers, along with the number of levels for the third dimension. You're also prompted for the distance between rows, columns, and levels.

For the Polar option of 3D Array, you are prompted for the number of items to array, the direction, the angle to fill, and whether to rotate the arrayed objects, just as with the standard Array command. In addition to being asked for a point to indicate the center of the array, you're prompted to select two points to indicate an axis of rotation. The axis can be defined in any direction in 3D space, so your array can be tilted from the current UCS. One way to visualize this is to think of a bicycle wheel with the array axis as the axle of the wheel and the array objects as the spokes. You can align the axle in any direction and the array of spokes will be perpendicular to the axle.

---

# The Bottom Line

**Master the User Coordinate System.**  The User Coordinate System (UCS) is a vital key to editing in 3D space. If you want to master 3D modeling, you should become familiar with this feature.

**Master It**   Name some of the predefined UCS planes.

**Understand the UCS options.**  You can set up the UCS orientation for any situation. It isn't limited to the predefined settings.

**Master It**   Give a brief description of some of the ways you can set up a UCS.

**Use viewports to aid in 3D drawing.** In some 3D modeling operations, it helps to have several different views of the model through the Viewports feature.

**Master It** Name some of the predefined standard viewports offered in the Viewports dialog box.

**Create complex 3D surfaces.** You aren't limited to straight, flat surfaces in AutoCAD. You can create just about any shape you want, including curved surfaces.

**Master It** What tool did you use in this chapter's chair exercise to convert a surface into a solid?

**Create spiral forms.** Spiral forms frequently occur in nature, so it's no wonder that we often use spirals in our own designs. Spirals are seen in screws, stairs, and ramps as well as in other man-made forms.

**Master It** Name the commands or tools used in the example in the section "Creating Spiral Forms," and name two elements that are needed to create a spiral.

**Create surface models.** You can create a 3D surface by connecting a series of lines that define a surface contour. You can create anything from a 3D landscape to a car fender using this method.

**Master It** What is the tool or command used to convert a series of open objects into a 3D surface?

**Move objects in 3D space.** You can move objects in 3D space using tools that are similar to those for 2D drafting. But when it comes to editing objects, 3D modeling is much more complex than 2D drafting.

**Master It** What does the Rotate gizmo do?

# Chapter 21

# Rendering 3D Drawings

In this chapter, you'll learn how to use rendering tools in AutoCAD to produce rendered still images of your 3D models. With these tools, you can add materials and control lighting. You also have control over the reflectance and transparency of objects.

In this chapter, you'll learn to do the following:

◆ Simulate the sun

◆ Create effects using materials and lights

◆ Control your render quality

◆ Print your renderings

## Testing the Waters

Before we get into the main tutorial in this chapter, let's first take a peek at what's possible with AutoCAD's rendering tools. This first exercise will give you a chance to learn how you can quickly see a rendered view of a 3D model and how you can easily add materials to objects.

The first file you'll work with in this section is simply a collection of primitive shapes in a random arrangement. First, you'll use the Render command to view the file without any materials, and then you'll add a few materials to get familiar with the Material Browser and see how it can be used to create a more lifelike rendering. Start by opening a sample file and render it as is:

1. First, turn on the Selection Cycling system variable by entering **SELECTIONCYCLING**↵ **2**↵. You'll need it in some of the later exercises.

2. Make sure Modeling is selected in the Tool Sets palette.

3. Next, open the Material Browser by choosing View ➢ Render ➢ Materials Browser (Figure 21.1).

4. Open the `Rendering_example_raw.dwg` file.

5. Click the Render tool in the lower part of the Tool Sets palette (Figure 21.2).

6. The Render window opens and takes a moment to produce the rendered view (Figure 21.3).

**FIGURE 21.1**
The Material
Browser

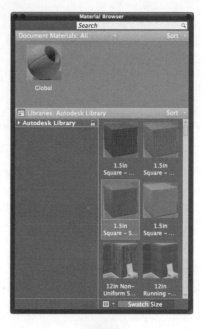

**FIGURE 21.2**
The Render icon
in the Tool Sets
palette

**FIGURE 21.3**
The Render win-
dow with the ren-
dered view

All of the objects in the view are rendered using the default Global material.
Now try adding a material to the sphere:

1. Take a look at the Material Browser in Figure 21.4. Click the disclosure triangle to the left of the Autodesk Library option. This opens a list of material categories.

**FIGURE 21.4**

The Material Browser with the expanded Autodesk Library option

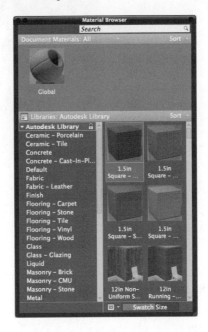

2. Scroll down the categories list and select Metal. A set of materials is displayed in the panel to the right of the list.

3. In the list on the right, click Brass – Polished. Brass – Polished appears at the top of the Material Browser.

4. Click the sphere in the drawing and then click the Brass – Polished icon. You'll notice that the sphere changes color to indicate its new material.

5. Click the Render tool again to see the result.

You now see that the sphere appears to be made of polished brass in the rendered view. In this exercise, you applied a material by clicking and dragging it to an object.
Now add a few more materials using a slightly different method:

1. Click the cylinder to the far left of the drawing area to select it.

2. In the Material Browser, scroll down the list of materials on the right-side panel to locate Chrome – Polished.

3. Click Chrome – Polished to apply it to the cylinder.

4. Next, click the foreground of the 3D model to select the rectangle that defines the "ground," as shown in Figure 21.5.

**FIGURE 21.5**
Click the fore-
ground surface to
select it.

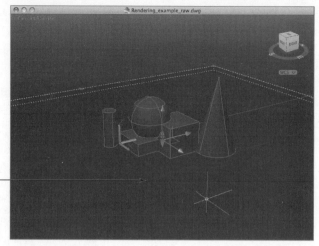

Click the
foreground
to select the
"ground"
plane.

5. Back in the Material Browser, scroll the list on the left-hand side to locate and select Fabric.

6. In the panel to the right, locate and select Plaid 1. This applies the Plaid 1 material to the "ground."

7. Click the Render tool again.

8. Once you've had a chance to look at the rendering, close the Rendering_example_raw. dwg file without saving it.

After rendering the view in step 7, you could see the Plaid 1 material of the foreground reflected in the brass sphere and chrome cylinder (Figure 21.6). The added materials give the rendered view a more realistic appearance.

**FIGURE 21.6**
The rendered view
with additional
materials

This brief introduction to materials and rendering shows you some of the potential of these tools. In the rest of the chapter, you'll get an in-depth view of the many ways you can control the appearance of rendered views from your 3D models.

## Creating a Quick-Study Rendering

Throughout the rest of this chapter, you'll work with a 3D model that was created using AutoCAD's 3D modeling tools. The model is of two buildings on a street corner. You'll start by using the default rendering settings to get a quick view of what you have to start with:

1. Open the facade.dwg file.

2. Click the Render tool near the bottom of the Tool Sets palette.

3. The Render window appears, and you see the rendering generated in the Render window display (Figure 21.7).

**FIGURE 21.7**
The Render window with your first rendered view of the building

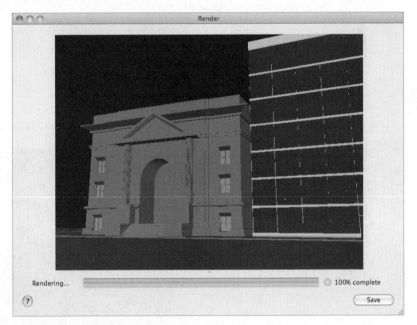

## Simulating the Sun

AutoCAD allows you to create several types of light sources. If you don't add a light source, AutoCAD uses two default lighting sources that have no particular direction or characteristic. The rendering you just did uses the default lighting to show your model.

You can add a point light that behaves like a lightbulb, a spotlight, or a directed light that behaves like a distant light source such as the sun. AutoCAD also offers a sunlight option that can be set for the time of the year and the hour of the day. This sunlight option is especially important for shadow studies in architectural models.

## Setting Up the Sun

Let's add the sun to the model to give a better sense of the building's form and relationship to its site. Start by making sure the sun is set for your location:

**1.** Click the Sun Status button in the expanded Status Bar palette (Figure 21.8).

**FIGURE 21.8**

The Sun Status button in the expanded Status Bar palette

You may see a message box warning you that the default lighting must be turned off when other lights are used. Click Turn Off The Default Lighting.

**2.** Make sure nothing is selected in the drawing and then click All near the top of the Properties Inspector palette.

**3.** Scroll down the list to the Sun and Sky category. Notice that you have quite a few options that let you control the sun's intensity and shadow effects (Figure 21.9).

**FIGURE 21.9**

The Sun properties in the Properties Inspector palette

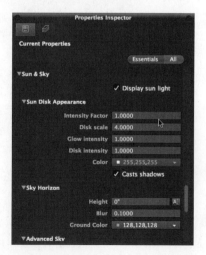

**4.** Click the Render tool in the Tool Sets palette. The Render window appears and begins to create a new rendering with the sunlight option turned on.

Now that you've added the sun, you can see the shadows that the sunlight casts. You can turn off the shadows for the sun if you prefer, but they're on by default.

---

**USING DISTANT LIGHTS**

As you begin to use the lights in AutoCAD, you'll come across the distant light. A distant light is like a cross between a point light and a spotlight and is similar to the sun in AutoCAD. The sun is a point source of light, but it's so far away that its rays are essentially parallel. A distant light behaves in a similar way. It has a point location, yet its light rays are parallel.

When you click the distant-light tool in the expanded Lights tool group in the Tool Sets palette, you are asked for a light location and direction. You can use object snaps to accurately place the location and direction of a distant light to control things like shadows and light reflection. Note that when you turn on the Lightingunits system variable described later in this chapter (in the section entitled "Using the Sun and Sky Simulation"), you are prompted to disable distant lights.

---

# Creating Effects Using Materials and Lights

Up to now, we've talked about only two light sources: a distant light and the sun. Two other light sources are available to help simulate light: point-light sources and spotlights. The following sections will show you some examples of how to use these types of light sources, along with some imagination, to perform any number of visual tricks.

The office building on the right half of the rendering is still a bit cold looking. It's missing a sense of activity. You may notice that when you look at glass office buildings, you can frequently see the ceiling lights from the exterior of the building—provided the glass isn't too dark. In a subtle way, those lights lend a sense of life to a building.

## Adding Glass to the Windows

The glass parts of the model are rendered in the color of their layer. You can add a glass material to make them appear more like glass in a building.

Earlier in this chapter, you added metal and fabric materials to a sample model. The process is the same for glass:

1. If the Material Browser isn't open, open it now by choosing View ➤ Render ➤ Materials Browser on the menu bar.

2. If the Autodesk Library is blank, click the disclosure triangle to the left to expand the list.

3. Scroll down the list and select Glass glazing. The list to the right shows several sample glass types.

4. Scroll down the list to the right and click Light Bronze Reflective. The sample of Light Bronze Reflective appears at the top of the Material Browser.

5. In the drawing window, select the blue box representing the glass (Figure 21.10).

**FIGURE 21.10**
Selecting the object representing glass in the model

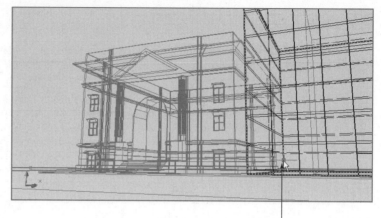

Click the blue box in the drawing.

6. Click the Light Bronze Reflective sample at the top of the Material Browser. This applies the material to the selected object.

7. Click the Render tool in the Tool Sets palette. The building to the right now appears to be made of glass (Figure 21.11).

**FIGURE 21.11**
The building rendered with the sun turned on and a glass material added

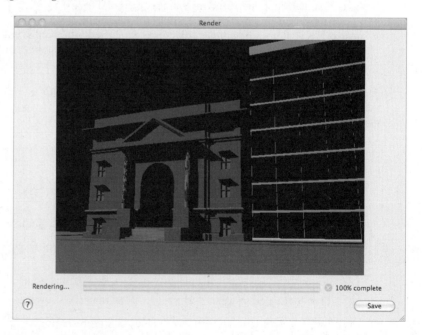

## Adding a Self-Illuminated Material

With the Light Bronze Reflective material assigned to the glass, you begin to see a little of the interior. To help improve the image, you'll add some ceiling lights to the office building. I've already supplied the lights in the form of square 3D Faces arrayed just at the ceiling level of each floor, as shown in Figure 21.12. In this section, you'll learn how to make the ceiling lights appear illuminated.

The ceiling lights appear as squares.

**FIGURE 21.12**

The 3D Face squares representing ceiling light fixtures

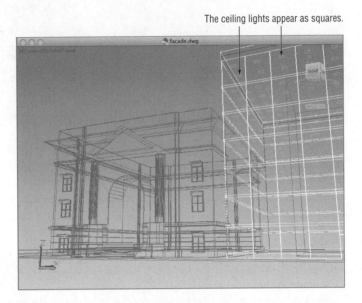

Follow these steps to assign a reflective white material to the ceiling fixtures:

1. In the Material Browser, select Glass from the Autodesk Library list.

2. In the icon list to the right, scroll down until you see Light Bulb – On and click it.

3. In the Layers palette, right-click the Clglite layer and select Isolate Selected Layer.

4. Select all of the remaining cyan rectangles in the view.

5. Click the Light Bulb – On thumbnail in the top portion of the Material Browser to assign that material to the cyan rectangles.

6. In the Layers palette, turn all of the layers back on.

7. Render your view. The lights appear in the ceiling of each of the floors (Figure 21.13).

In the previous exercise, you added a self-illuminated material that, when assigned to an object, appears to glow. You then added this material to the ceiling lights in the model. This self-illuminated material doesn't actually produce light in the model, however. To do that, you'll have to add light objects such as a distant lights or spotlights.

**FIGURE 21.13**
The lights appear in the ceilings of the building to the right.

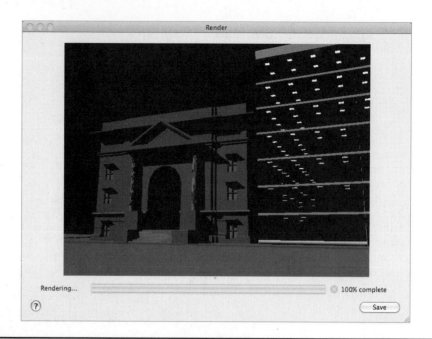

## USING PROCEDURAL MAPS

*Procedural maps* are texture maps that are derived mathematically rather than from a bitmap image. The advantage of a procedural map is that it gives a more natural representation of a material. For example, if you cut a notch out of a box that uses a wood procedural map, the notch appears correctly with the appropriate wood grain. Do the same for a box that uses a bitmap texture map and the grain doesn't appear correctly. With a bitmap texture map, the same image is placed on all four sides of the box, so cuts don't show the grain properly.

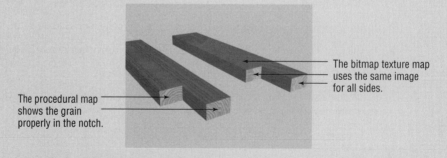

The procedural map shows the grain properly in the notch.

The bitmap texture map uses the same image for all sides.

AutoCAD offers several types of procedural maps. You can select them from the Material Browser for materials such as ceramic, concrete, masonry, plastic, stone, and wood.

## Using the Sun and Sky Simulation

You can set up AutoCAD to simulate realistic lighting effects in exterior views. Earlier in this chapter, you added a distant light to approximate the light bouncing off the ground. AutoCAD's

Sun and Sky Simulation feature offers a more accurate rendition of reflected light that takes into account the light bouncing off neighboring buildings and surfaces. To see how this feature works, try the following exercise:

1. At the Command prompt, enter **Lightingunits**↵.

2. At the Enter new value for LIGHTINGUNITS <0>: prompt, enter **2**.

If you have a drawing that uses distant lights, you may see a warning message asking if you want to disable distant lights. Leave them enabled by selecting Allow Distant Lights.

By changing the Lightingunits setting, you turn on the Photometric Lighting feature in AutoCAD. The Photometric Lighting feature gives you finer control over the intensity of the lights you add to your model. The Lightingunits system variable can be set to 0 (generic units), 1 (international units), or 2 (American units). When you are in a perspective view and Lightingunits is set to 1 or 2, you can turn on the Sun and Sky Simulation feature.

This next exercise demonstrates how the Sun and Sky Simulation feature works:

1. Click the Sky Status pop-up menu in the Status Bar palette and select the Sky Background And Illumination option.

2. The background of your main view changes.

3. Click the Render tool. After a minute or two, you get a finished rendering. Your model renders using the current Sun settings. The shadows on the center building are more realistic and show more detail of the building (Figure 21.14).

**FIGURE 21.14**
The rendering with the Sky Background And Illumination feature turned on

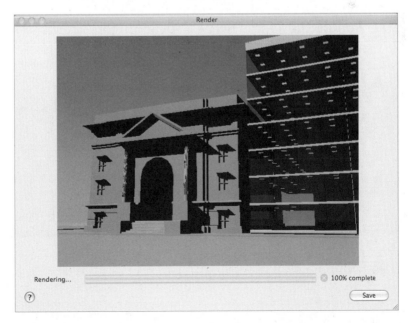

You can further refine your image by adjusting the brightness of the sun and sky. Here's how:

1. Press the Esc key to make sure nothing is selected.

2. Click the All option near the top of the Properties Inspector palette.

3. Scroll down to the Sun & Sky category (see Figure 21.15).

**FIGURE 21.15**
Click the All option and adjust the Sun & Sky category.

4. Change the Intensity Factor setting to 2. This has the effect of brightening the sun.

5. Render the view again.

This time, the rendering is brighter and has more contrast.

## Simulating a Night Scene with Spotlights

*Spotlights* are lights that can be directed and focused on a specific area. They're frequently used to provide emphasis and are usually used for interior views or product presentations. In this exercise, you'll set up a night view of the Facade model by using spotlights to illuminate the facade.

You'll start by setting up a view to help place the spotlights. You'll save this view because you'll be going back to it several times:

1. Select SE Isometric from the 3D Views menu on the viewport controls.

2. Right-click the ViewCube and select Parallel (Figure 21.16).

3. Adjust your view so it looks similar to Figure 21.17.

4. Save this view by typing **View**⏎ **S**⏎ **SE Isometric Wireframe**⏎.

**FIGURE 21.16**
Select Parallel from the View-Cube's shortcut menu.

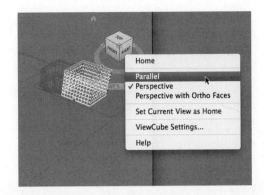

**FIGURE 21.17**
Set up your view to look similar to this, and then add the spotlight.

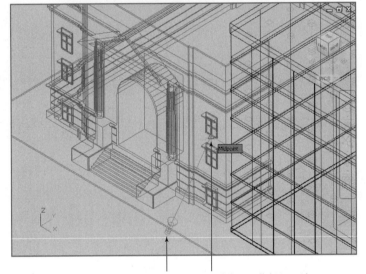

Place the spotlight here...        ...and the spotlight target here.

Now you're ready to add the lights:

1. Click the Spotlight tool from the lower part of the Tool Sets palette (Figure 21.18), or enter **Spotlight.**⏎ at the Command prompt.

**FIGURE 21.18**
Click the Spotlight tool from the Tool Sets palette.

2. At the `Specify source location <0,0,0>:` prompt, click the point shown in Figure 21.17. Don't use osnaps because you don't want the light to be placed accidentally below the ground plane. You don't have to be exact, but the idea is to place the spotlight in front of the windows on the right side of the entrance to the building.

3. At the `Specify target location <0,0,-10>:` prompt, use the Midpoint osnap and select the bottom of the windowsill of the upper window, as shown in Figure 21.17. You see the prompt

```
Enter an option to change
[Name/Intensity/Status/Hotspot/Falloff/shadoW/Attenuation/Color/eXit] <eXit>:
```

4. Press ↵ to accept the default settings. You can always change the optional settings for the light through the Properties Inspector palette.

5. Copy the spotlight you just created to the location shown in Figure 21.19. You can use the spotlight target to copy from the midpoint of one window sill to the other.

**FIGURE 21.19**
Copy the spotlight to this location.

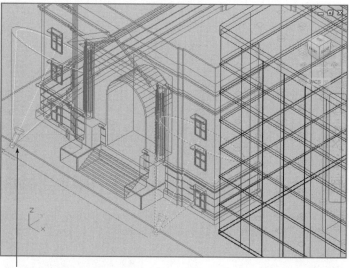

Copy the spotlight to this location.

6. You're trying to produce a nighttime rendering, so turn off the sun by clicking the Sun Status button in the expanded Status Bar palette.

7. Return to the original view by choosing Model Views ➤ Temp from the 3D Views menu in the viewport controls.

8. Turn off the Lightingunits system variable by typing **LIGHTINGUNITS**↵ **0**↵.

9. Click the Render tool in the Tool Sets palette to see the results of your spotlight addition. Your rendering will look similar to Figure 21.20.

**FIGURE 21.20**
The rendered view
of the model with
the spotlights

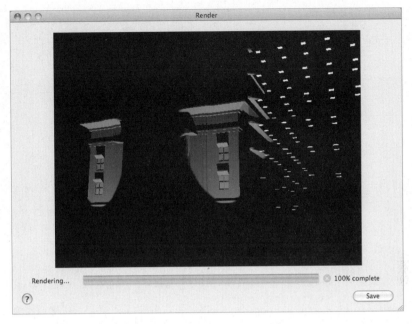

## Adding a Point Light

A few things still need to be added to improve this rendering. You can adjust the spotlight so it casts light over a wider area. You can also add a light in the entrance so it isn't quite so dark. The next section will show you how to make adjustments to your spotlight. First, you'll add a point light to obtain a different lighting effect:

1. Return to the view you used to add the spotlights by choosing SE Isometric Wireframe from the 3D Views menu in the viewport controls.

2. Click the Point tool from the lower part of the Tool Sets palette (Figure 21.21) or enter **Pointlight**↵.

**FIGURE 21.21**
Click the Point
tool from the
Tool Sets palette.

3. At the Specify source location <0,0,0>: prompt, ⇧-right-click and select Center from the Object Snap shortcut menu. Then select the arch over the entrance, as shown in Figure 21.22, to place the point light.

**FIGURE 21.22**
Select the center of the arch.

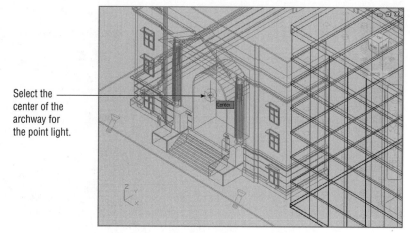

Select the center of the archway for the point light.

4. At the prompt

```
Enter an option to change [Name/Intensity/Status/shadoW/
Attenuation/Color/eXit] <eXit>:
```

press ↵ to accept the default settings for the point light.

5. The point light appears as a spherical glyph in the archway of the building.

6. Click the Render tool in the Tool Sets palette. Your rendering will look similar to Figure 21.23.

**FIGURE 21.23**
The rendered view of the model with the spotlights modified and the point light added

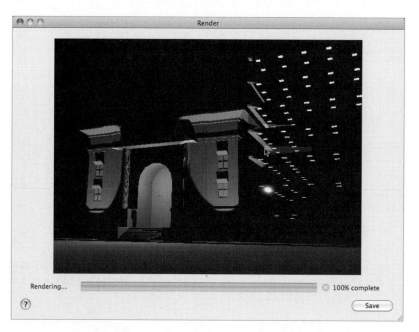

## Editing Lights

You've added the point light. Before you see the results in a rendering, you'll also change the spread of the spotlights. In this exercise, you'll edit the properties of the spotlight. Not all lights have the same properties, but the basic process for editing all lights is the same:

1. ⇧-click the two spotlights to select them.

2. Click Essentials in the Properties Inspector palette. You'll see that there are a number of settings available, including Intensity Factor. You can adjust these settings to control the lights (Figure 21.24).

**FIGURE 21.24**
Light adjustment options in the Properties Inspector palette

Notice that there is one red and one yellow light cone for each spotlight. The cones also have an arrowhead at each of four locations around the widest part of the cone. These are the hotspot and falloff cones. They help you visualize the size of the hotspot and falloff of the light from each spotlight. Next, adjust the falloff of both spotlights to soften their effect on the view:

1. Click the arrowhead at the spotlight cone to the right (Figure 21.25). A text box appears that reflects the angle of the falloff for the spotlight.

2. Type 90.⏎. The cone changes shape to become wider.

3. Repeat steps 1 and 2 for the spotlight to the left.

**FIGURE 21.25**
Click the arrowhead on the spotlight cone shown here.

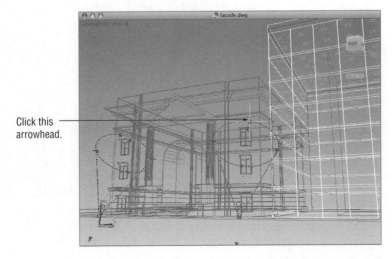

Click this arrowhead.

**4.** Render the view. Now the spotlights have a softer effect (Figure 21.26).

**FIGURE 21.26**
The model rendered with the falloff adjusted to 90 degrees

In step 2, you saw a list of options for the spotlight. Many of these options are available when you first insert the light; they appear as command-line options. Often, it's easier to place the light first and then play with the settings.

**FIGURE 21.27**
The hotspot and falloff of a spotlight at the top produce the lighting shown at the bottom.

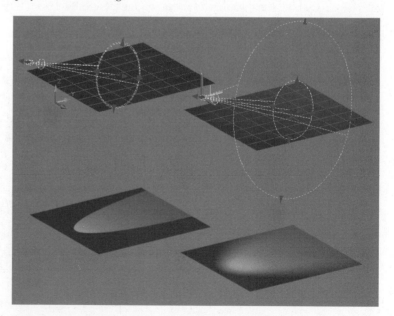

In this example, you adjusted the spotlight's falloff. By increasing the falloff angle, you broadened the spread of the light cast by the spotlight and also made the transition from light to dark appear smoother, as shown in Figure 21.27. The hotspot can also be adjusted to a narrow beam or a wide swath.

Many other light properties are available to you in the Properties Inspector palette. Table 21.1 describes them.

**TABLE 21.1:** Some of the properties available for lights

| PROPERTY | DESCRIPTION |
| --- | --- |
| **General** | |
| Name | Shows the name of the light |
| Type | Sets the type of light |
| On/Off Status | Shows whether light is on or off |
| Hotspot Angle | Sets the spotlight hotspot angle |
| Falloff Angle | Sets the spotlight falloff angle |
| Intensity Factor | Sets the light intensity |
| Filter Color | Sets the secondary light color simulating a color filter over a lamp |
| Plot Glyph | Allows the light glyph to be plotted |
| Glyph Display | Controls the display of the light glyph |
| **Attenuation** | |
| Type | Type of attenuation: Inverse Linear, Inverse Square, or None |
| Use Limits | Lets you turn on attenuation limits |
| Start Limit Offset | If Use Limits is on, sets the distance to the beginning of attenuation |
| End Limit Offset | If Use Limits is on, sets the distance to the end of attenuation |
| **Rendered Shadow Details** | |
| Type | Lets you select between sharp and soft shadow edges |
| Map Size | When shadow maps are used, lets you determine the size of the shadow map in pixels |
| Softness | When shadow maps are used, determines the softness of shadows |

**IMPROVING THE SMOOTHNESS OF CIRCLES AND ARCS**

Here is an issue that readers are constantly asking me about. You may notice that at times, when you're using the Render, Hide, or Shade tool, the edge of solids or region arcs appears segmented rather than curved. This may be fine for producing layouts or backgrounds for hand-rendered drawings, but for final prints, you want arcs and circles to appear as smooth curves. You can adjust the accuracy of arcs in your hidden, rendered, or shaded views through a setting in the Application Preferences dialog box.

You can modify the Smoothness For 3D Printing/Rendering setting in the Document Settings tab of the Application Preferences dialog box to improve the smoothness of arcs. Its default value is 0.5, but you can increase it to as high as 10 to smooth out faceted curves. In the facade.dwg model, you can set Smoothness For 3D Printing/Rendering to 1.5 to render the archway in the entry as a smooth arc instead of a series of flat segments. You can also adjust this setting by using the Facetres system variable.

## Controlling Render Quality

Once you've rendered your model, you may find that you need to make some changes to the rendered image. You can always export the image to another program like Photoshop, to "dress up" the image and adjust lighting and contrast. There are a few things you can do within AutoCAD as well.

One feature you can use to improve the overall sharpness of your rendering is the Renderquality setting. So far, the renderings of the building have been a bit jagged. You can create a smoother image by typing **RENDERQUALITY↵ 5↵**. This sets the Renderquality setting to its maximum value of 5. You can use a range from –3 to 5, with -3 being the lowest quality. With Renderquality set to 5, you will see smoother edges and more detail in your renderings.

If your rendered image is too dark or you want to bump up the contrast, the Properties Inspector palette offers the Brightness, Contrast, and Midtone settings under the Render category. You can find these settings at the bottom of the Properties Inspector palette when you click the All button. Make sure you do not have anything selected in your drawing before you click All.

## Printing Your Renderings

When you've decided that your rendering is perfect, you can print a copy directly from AutoCAD. Through a layout view, you can also put together presentations that include 2D floor plans and elevations with your rendering on a single sheet. Alternatively, you can have several renderings on one sheet.

Try the following to set up a layout view to render the 3D model in both a rendered view and a hidden-line view:

1. Click the Show Drawings And Layouts button in the Status Bar palette and then choose Layout1.

2. Click the viewport border to expose its grips, and then use a grip to make the viewport smaller so it's about half the height of the Paper Space layout. Keep the height-to-width proportions of the viewport as close to the original as possible.

3. Double-click inside the viewport and then select Model Views ➤ Temp from the 3D Views menu on the viewport controls.

4. Make sure the Sun Status button in the expanded Status Bar palette is on.

5. Double-click outside the viewport, and then copy the viewport so you have an identical viewport near the original (Figure 21.28).

**FIGURE 21.28**
The preview with duplicate views

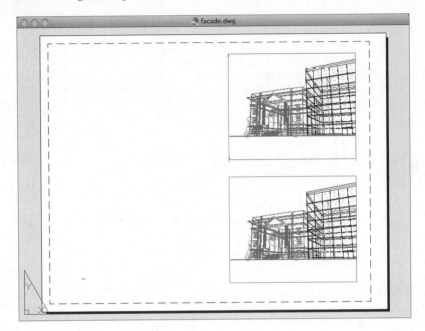

Now you're ready to set up the viewport to render the views in specific ways. For example, you can set one viewport to render as a fully rendered view while rendering another viewport as a hidden-line view:

1. Click the border of the top viewport, right-click, and choose Shade Plot ➤ Rendered.

2. Click the border of the lower viewport, right-click, and choose Shade Plot ➤ Hidden.

3. Choose File ➤ Print on the menu bar.

4. Choose a printer name for the Printer pop-up menu, and then click Preview. After a moment, you see a preview of your plot showing a fully rendered view in the top viewport and a hidden-line view in the lower viewport (Figure 21.29).

You can add viewports to include floor plans and elevations if needed. Another option is to add isometric views with labels that point out drawing features.

You also have control over the quality of the rendered viewport. Choose File ➤ Page Setup Manager on the menu bar. The Page Setup Manager dialog box opens. Click the Gear icon just below the Current Layout list, and choose Edit to open the Page Setup dialog box. Next, click the Advanced button. You can use the 3D Viewports group to select from a pair of viewport-quality settings (Figure 21.30).

**FIGURE 21.29**
The final comparison rendering

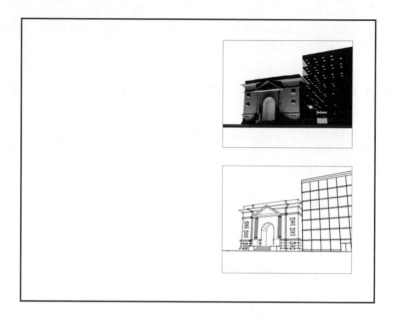

**FIGURE 21.30**
Select a quality setting from the Quality pop-up menu.

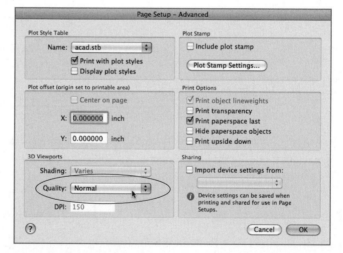

You can choose from Draft, Preview, Normal, Presentation, Maximum, and Custom. Custom enables the DPI setting, allowing you to control the resolution of your output. These options are described in detail in Chapter 8, "Introducing Printing and Layouts," so I won't go into detail here. Just remember that the options are available to help you get the most from your rendered printer output.

**Real World Scenario**

### GETTING A SKETCH PRESENTATION WITH VISUAL STYLES

One of the most interesting issues I've encountered while creating 3D presentations of buildings is that, quite often, architects do not want a realistic rendering of their designs. The reason is that a realistic rendering gives the impression that the design is already "set in stone" or has progressed to a more advanced level than it actually has.

So although this chapter has focused on getting a realistic rendering of your model, frequently you'll want to show your model in a less realistic view. This is especially true in the early stages when you don't want to give the impression that you've created a finished design. There are several visual styles you can use to this end.

You can print visual styles from either the model or named layout view. If you choose a layout view to print a visual style, select the viewport border, and select As Displayed from the Shade Plot drop-down list. Then select the visual style you want to use for your print from the Viewport Visual Styles drop-down list inside the viewport.

## The Bottom Line

**Simulate the sun.** One of the most practical uses of AutoCAD's rendering feature is to simulate the sun's location and resulting shadows. You can generate shadow studies for any time of the year in any location on the earth.

   **Master It** How do you get to the sun properties?

**Create effects using materials and lights.** You can use materials and lights together to control the appearance of your model.

   **Master It** Name the part of the example model in this chapter that was used to show how a material can appear to glow.

**Control your render quality.** AutoCAD offers a few features to give you some control over the quality of your rendering. The default rendering settings allow you to view your rendering at a level good enough to gauge how it will look.

   **Master It** Name the two features discussed in this chapter that allow you to control the quality of your renderings.

**Print your renderings.** You can save your rendered views as bitmap files using the Render window. If you prefer, you can also have AutoCAD include a rendering in a layout. You can include different renderings of the same file in a single layout.

   **Master It** Give a general description of the process for setting up a rendered viewport in a layout.

# Chapter 22

# Editing and Visualizing 3D Solids

In the previous 3D chapters, you spent some time becoming familiar with the AutoCAD 3D modeling features. In this chapter, you'll focus on 3D solids and how they're created and edited. You'll also learn how you can use some special visualization tools to show your 3D solid in a variety of ways.

You'll create a fictitious mechanical part to explore some of the ways you can shape 3D solids. This will also give you a chance to see how you can turn your 3D model into a standard 2D mechanical drawing. In addition, you'll learn about the 3D solid editing tools that are available through the Tool Sets palette and the menu bar.

In this chapter, you'll learn to do the following:

◆ Understand solid modeling

◆ Create solid forms

◆ Create complex solids

◆ Edit solids

◆ Streamline the 2D drawing process

◆ Visualize solids

## Understanding Solid Modeling

Solid modeling is a way of defining 3D objects as solid forms. When you create a 3D model by using solid modeling, you start with the basic forms of your model—cubes, cones, and cylinders, for example. These basic solids are called *primitives*. Then, using more of these primitives, you begin to add to or subtract from your basic forms.

For example, to create a model of a tube, you first create two solid cylinders, one smaller in diameter than the other. You then align the two cylinders so that they're concentric and tell AutoCAD to subtract the smaller cylinder from the larger one. The larger of the two cylinders becomes a tube whose inside diameter is that of the smaller cylinder, as shown in Figure 22.1. Several primitives are available for modeling solids in AutoCAD (Figure 22.2).

You can join these shapes—polysolid, box, wedge, cone, sphere, cylinder, pyramid, and donut (or *torus*)—in one of four ways to produce secondary shapes. The first three, demonstrated in Figure 22.3 using a cube and a cylinder as examples, are called *Boolean operations*. (The name comes from the nineteenth-century mathematician George Boole.)

The three Boolean operations are as follows:

**Intersection** Uses only the intersecting region of two objects to define a solid shape

**Subtraction** Uses one object to cut out a shape in another

**Union** Joins two primitives so they act as one object

The fourth option, *interference*, lets you find exactly where two or more solids coincide in space—similar to the results of a union. The main difference between interference and union is that interference enables you to keep the original solid shapes, whereas union discards the original solids, leaving only their combined form. With interference, you can have AutoCAD either show you the shape of the coincident space or create a solid based on the shape of the coincident space.

Joined primitives are called *composite solids*. You can join primitives to primitives, composite solids to primitives, and composite solids to other composite solids.

Now let's look at how you can use these concepts to create models in AutoCAD.

**FIGURE 22.1**
Creating a tube
by using solid
modeling

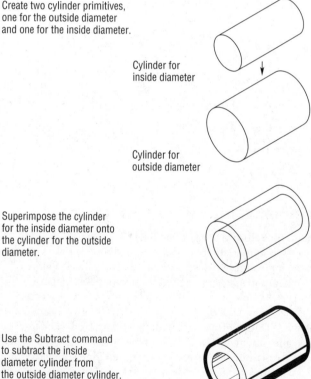

Create two cylinder primitives, one for the outside diameter and one for the inside diameter.

Cylinder for inside diameter

Cylinder for outside diameter

Superimpose the cylinder for the inside diameter onto the cylinder for the outside diameter.

Use the Subtract command to subtract the inside diameter cylinder from the outside diameter cylinder.

**FIGURE 22.2**
The solid primitives

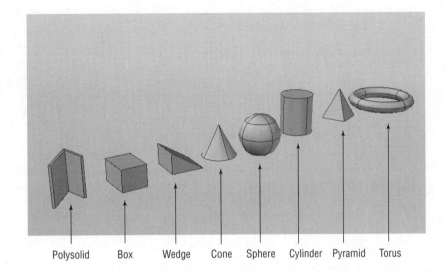

Polysolid  Box  Wedge  Cone  Sphere  Cylinder  Pyramid  Torus

**FIGURE 22.3**
The intersection, subtraction, and union of a cube and a cylinder

A solid box and a solid cylinder are superimposed.

The intersection of the primitives creates a solid cylinder with the ends skewed.

The cylinder subtracted from the box creates a hole in the box.

The union of the two primitives creates a box with two round pegs.

---

**EXERCISE EXAMPLES ARE "UNITLESS"**

To simplify the exercises in this chapter, the instructions don't specify inches or centimeters. This way, users of both the metric and Imperial measurement systems can use the exercises without having to read through duplicate information.

---

## Creating Solid Forms

In the following sections, you'll begin to draw the object shown later in the chapter in Figure 22.18. In the process, you'll explore the creation of solid models by creating primitives and then setting up special relationships between them.

Primitives are the basic building blocks of solid modeling. At first, it may seem limiting to have only eight primitives to work with, but consider the varied forms you can create with just a few two-dimensional objects. Let's begin by creating the basic mass of your steel bracket.

First, prepare your drawing for the exercise:

1. Open the file called Bracket.dwg. This file contains some objects that you'll use in the first half of this chapter to build a 3D solid shape.

2. Make sure the Tool Sets palette shows the Modeling tool set.

3. Close the Material Browser if it is open.

### Joining Primitives

In this section, you'll merge the two box objects. First, you'll move the new box into place. Then you'll join the two boxes to form a single solid:

1. Click the Move tool, pick the smaller of the two boxes, and then press ↵.

2. Use the Midpoint osnap, and pick the middle of the front edge of the smaller box, as shown in the top image in Figure 22.4.

3. Use the Midpoint osnap to pick the middle of the bottom edge of the larger box, as shown in the bottom image in Figure 22.4.

4. Click the Union tool in the upper part of the Tool Sets palette, or type **UNI**↵.

**FIGURE 22.4**
Moving the
smaller box

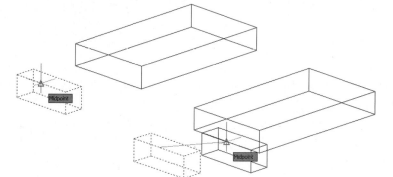

**5.** Click both boxes and press ↵. Your drawing now looks like Figure 22.5.

**FIGURE 22.5**
The two boxes
joined

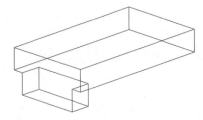

As you can see in Figure 22.5, the form has joined to appear as one object. It also acts like one object when you select it. You now have a composite solid made up of two box primitives.

Now let's place some holes in the bracket. In this next exercise, you'll discover how to create negative forms to cut portions out of a solid:

**1.** Turn on the layer called Cylinder. Two cylinder solids appear in the model, as shown in Figure 22.6. These cylinders are 1.5 units tall.

**FIGURE 22.6**
The cylinders
appear when the
Cylinder layer is
turned on.

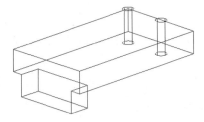

**2.** Click and hold the Union tool in the Tool Sets palette and click the Subtract tool from the flyout (Figure 22.7), or type **SU**↵.

**FIGURE 22.7**
The Subtract tool
on the Union flyout

**3.** At the Select solids, surfaces, and regions to subtract from… Select objects: prompt, pick the composite solid of the two boxes and press ↵.

**4.** At the Select solids, surfaces, and regions to subtract… Select objects: prompt, click the two cylinders and press ↵. The cylinders are subtracted from the bracket.

**5.** To temporarily view the solid with hidden lines removed, choose View ➤ Hide. You see a hidden-line view of the solid, similar to the one shown in Figure 22.8.

**FIGURE 22.8**

The bracket so far, with hidden lines removed

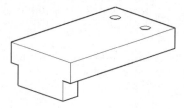

As you learned in the earlier chapters in Part 4, Wireframe views, such as the one in the previous exercise, are somewhat difficult to decipher. Until you use the Hide command (View ➢ Hide), you can't be sure that the subtracted cylinders are in fact holes. Using the Hide command frequently will help you keep track of what's going on with your solid model. You can also use a visual style like Hidden or Shades Of Gray.

You may also have noticed in step 4 that even though the cylinders were taller than the opening they created, they worked fine to remove part of the rectangular solid. The cylinders were 1.5 units tall, not 1 unit, which is the thickness of the bracket. Having drawn the cylinders taller than needed, you saw that when AutoCAD performed the subtraction, it ignored the portion of the cylinders that didn't affect the bracket. AutoCAD always discards the portion of a primitive that isn't used in a subtract operation.

---

### USING 3D SOLID OPERATIONS ON 2D DRAWINGS

You can apply some of the features described in this chapter to 2D drafting by taking advantage of AutoCAD's region object. *Regions* are two-dimensional objects to which you can apply Boolean operations.

The following illustration shows how a set of closed polyline shapes can be quickly turned into a drawing of a wrench using regions. The shapes at the top of the figure are first converted into regions using the Region tool on the Closed Shapes tool group. Next, the shapes are aligned, as shown in the middle of the image. Finally, the circles and rectangle are joined with the Union command (type **UNI↵**); then, the hexagonal shapes are subtracted from the combined shape (type **SU↵**). You can use the Region.dwg sample file if you'd like to experiment.

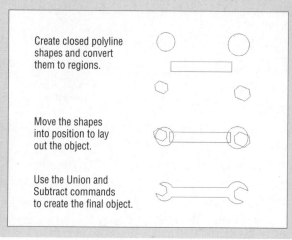

Create closed polyline shapes and convert them to regions.

Move the shapes into position to lay out the object.

Use the Union and Subtract commands to create the final object.

You can use regions to generate complex surfaces that may include holes or unusual bends.

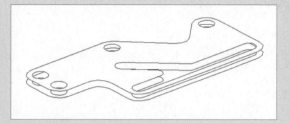

Keep in mind the following:

◆ Regions act like surfaces; when you remove hidden lines, objects behind the regions are hidden.

◆ You can explode regions to edit them. However, exploding a region causes the region to lose its surfacelike quality, and objects no longer hide behind its surface(s).

◆ You can ⌃-click the edge of a region to edit a region's shape.

## Creating Complex Solids

As you learned earlier, you can convert a polyline into a solid by using the Extrude tool on the Tool Sets palette. This process lets you create more-complex shapes than the built-in primitives. In addition to the simple straight extrusion you've already tried, you can extrude shapes into curved paths or you can taper an extrusion.

### Tapering an Extrusion

Let's look at how you can taper an extrusion to create a fairly complex solid with little effort:

1. Turn on the Taper layer. A rectangular polyline appears. This rectangle has its corners rounded to a radius of 0.5 using the Fillet command.

2. Click the Extrude tool near the top of the Tool Sets palette, or enter **EXT**↵ at the Command prompt.

3. At the `Select objects to extrude or [MOde]:` prompt, pick the polyline on the Taper layer and press ↵.

4. At the `Specify height of extrusion or [Direction/Path/Taper angle/Expression]:` prompt, enter **T**↵.

5. At the `Specify angle of taper for extrusion or [Expression] <0>:` prompt, enter **4**↵.

6. At the `Specify height of extrusion or [Direction/Path/Taper angle/Expression]:` prompt, point the cursor upward and enter **3**↵. The extruded polyline looks like Figure 22.9.

**FIGURE 22.9**
The extruded
polyline

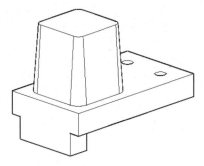

7. Join the part you just created with the original solid. Click the Union tool on the Tool Sets palette or type **UNI**↵.

8. Click the extruded part and the composite solid just below it. Press ↵ to complete your selection.

In step 5, you can indicate a taper for the extrusion. Specify a taper in terms of degrees from the Z axis, or enter a negative value to taper the extrusion outward. You can also press ↵ to accept the default of 0° to extrude the polyline without a taper.

---

**WHAT ARE ISOLINES?**

You may have noticed the message in the Command Line palette that reads as follows:
```
Current wire frame density: ISOLINES=4
```
This message tells you the current setting for the Isolines system variable. This variable controls the way curved objects, such as cylinders and holes, are displayed. A setting of 4 causes a cylinder to be represented by four lines with a circle at each end. You can see this in the holes that you created for the Bracket model in the previous exercise. You can change the Isolines setting by entering **ISOLINES**↵ at the Command prompt. You then enter a value for the number of lines to use to represent surfaces. This setting is also controlled by the Contour Lines Per Surface option in the Document Settings tab of the Application Preferences dialog box.

---

## Sweeping a Shape on a Curved Path

As you'll see in the following exercise, the Sweep command lets you extrude virtually any polyline shape along a path defined by a polyline, an arc, or a 3D polyline. At this point, you've created the components needed to do the extrusion. Next, you'll finish the extruded shape:

1. Turn on the Path layer. This layer contains the circle you'll extrude and the polyline path, which looks like an S, as shown in Figure 22.10.

2. Click the Sweep tool from the Revolve flyout, or type **SWEEP**↵. Click the circle, and then press ↵.

**FIGURE 22.10**
**FIGURE 22.10**
Hidden-line view
showing parts of
the drawing you'll
use to create a
curved extrusion

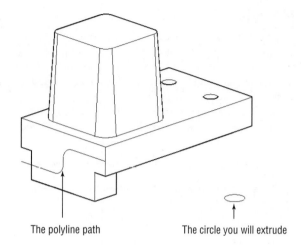

The polyline path         The circle you will extrude

3. At the Select sweep path or [Alignment/Base point/Scale/Twist]: prompt, click
   the polyline curve.

4. AutoCAD generates a solid tube that follows the path. The tube may not look like a tube
   because AutoCAD draws extruded solids such as this with four lines showing their profile.

5. Click the Subtract tool from the Union flyout on the Tool Sets palette or type **SU**↵, and
   then select the composite solid.

6. Press ↵. At the Select objects: prompt, click the curved solid you just created and
   press ↵. The curved solid is subtracted from the square solid.

7. Choose View ➤ Hide. Your drawing looks like Figure 22.11.

**FIGURE 22.11**
The solid after sub-
tracting the curve

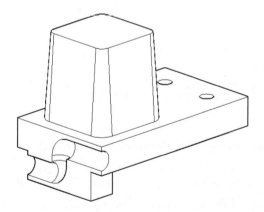

In this exercise, you used a curved polyline for the extrusion path, but you can use any type
of 2D or 3D polyline, as well as a line or arc, for an extrusion path.

## Revolving a Polyline

When your goal is to draw a circular object, you can use the Revolve tool in the Tool Sets palette to create a solid that is *revolved*, or swept in a circular path. Think of Revolve's action as similar to a lathe that lets you carve a shape from an object on a spinning shaft. In this case, the object is a polyline, and rather than carve it, you define the profile and then revolve the profile around an axis.

In the following exercise, you'll draw a solid that will form a slot in the tapered solid. A 2D polyline that is the profile of the slot has been created for you. You'll simply use cut and paste to bring the polyline into the bracket drawing:

1. Select 2D Wireframe from the Visual Styles menu on the Viewport Controls.

2. Zoom in to the top of the tapered box so you have a view similar to Figure 22.12.

**FIGURE 22.12**
An enlarged view
of the top of the
tapered box and
pasted polyline

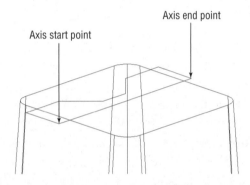

Axis start point

Axis end point

3. Turn on the Revolve layer. This layer contains a closed polyline that you'll use to create a cylindrical shape.

4. Click the Revolve tool on the Tool Sets palette, or type **REV.↵** at the Command prompt.

5. At the `Select objects to revolve or [MOde]:` prompt, pick the polyline on the top of the tapered surface and press ↵.

6. When you see the prompt
   `Specify axis start point or define axis by [Object/X/Y/Z] <Object>:`

   use the Endpoint osnap override and pick the beginning corner endpoint of the polyline you just added, as shown in Figure 22.12.

7. At the `Specify axis endpoint:` prompt, pick the axis endpoint indicated in Figure 22.12.

8. At the `Specify angle of revolution or [STart angle/Reverse/eXpression] <360>:` prompt, press ↵ to sweep the polyline a full 360°. The revolved form appears, as shown in Figure 22.13.

**FIGURE 22.13**
The revolved
polyline

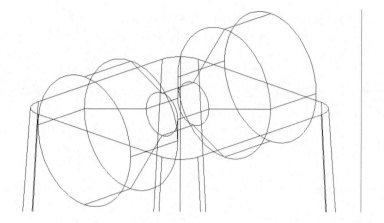

You just created a revolved solid that will be subtracted from the tapered box to form a slot in the bracket. However, before you subtract it, you need to make a slight change in the orientation of the revolved solid:

1. Choose Modify ➤ 3D Operations ➤ 3D Rotate on the menu bar, or type **3DROTATE**↵. You see the following prompt:

```
Current positive angle in UCS: ANGDIR=counterclockwise ANGBASE=0
Select objects:
```

2. Select the revolved solid and press ↵.

3. At the `Specify base point:` prompt, use the Midpoint osnap and click the right side edge of the top surface, as shown in Figure 22.14.

**FIGURE 22.14**
Selecting the
points to rotate the
revolved solid in
3D space

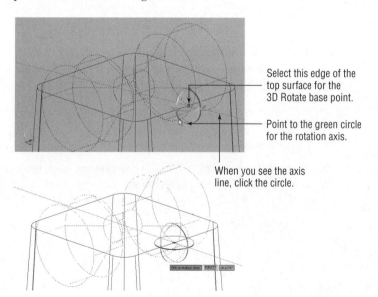

Select this edge of the
top surface for the
3D Rotate base point.

Point to the green circle
for the rotation axis.

When you see the axis
line, click the circle.

4. At the `Pick a rotation axis:` prompt, point to the green rotation grip. When you see a green line appear along the Y axis, click the mouse.

5. At the `Specify angle start point or type an angle:` prompt, enter **-5↵** for a minus 5 degrees rotation. The solid rotates 5° about the Y axis.

6. Click the Subtract tool from the Union flyout, or type **SU↵**. Click the tapered box, and then press ↵.

7. At the `Select objects:` prompt, click the revolved solid and press ↵. Your drawing looks like Figure 22.15.

**FIGURE 22.15**
The composite solid

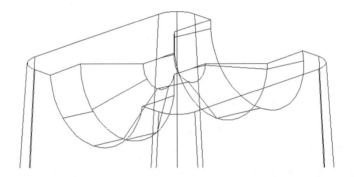

## Editing Solids

Basic solid forms are fairly easy to create. Refining those forms requires some special tools. In the following sections, you'll learn how to use familiar 2D editing tools, as well as some new tools, to edit a solid. You'll also be introduced to the Slice tool, which lets you cut a solid into two pieces.

### Splitting a Solid into Two Pieces

One of the more common solid-editing tools you'll use is the Slice tool. As you may guess from its name, Slice enables you to cut a solid into two pieces. The following exercise demonstrates how it works:

1. Choose View ➢ Zoom ➢ All to get an overall view of your work so far.

2. Click the Slice tool from the Solids – Edit tool group (Figure 22.16), or type **SL↵**.

3. At the `Select objects to slice:` prompt, click the model and press ↵. Note that if you need to, you could select more than one solid at this prompt. The Slice command would then slice all the solids through the plane indicated in steps 4 and 5. For now, you're just selecting one solid.

**FIGURE 22.16**
The Slice tool on the Solids – Edit tool group

4. At the prompt
   ```
   Specify start point of slicing plane or
   [planar Object/Surface/Zaxis/View/XY/YZ/ZX/
   3points] <3points>:
   ```

   type **XY**⏎. This lets you indicate a slice plane parallel to the XY plane.

5. At the `Specify a point on the XY-plane <0,0,0>:` prompt, type **0,0,0.5**⏎. This places the slice plane at the Z coordinate of 0.5 units. You can also use the Midpoint osnap and pick any vertical edge of the rectangular base of the solid. If you want to delete one side of the sliced solid, you can indicate the side you want to keep by clicking it in step 6 instead of entering **B**⏎.

6. At the `Specify a point on desired side or [keep Both sides]:` prompt, type **B**⏎ to keep both sides of the solid. AutoCAD divides the solid horizontally, one-half unit above the base of the part as shown in Figure 22.17.

**FIGURE 22.17**
The solid sliced through the base

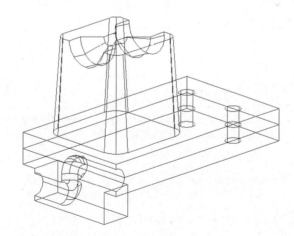

In step 4, you saw a number of options for the Slice command. You may want to make note of those options for future reference. Table 22.1 provides a list of the options and their purposes.

**TABLE 22.1:**     Slice command options

| OPTION | PURPOSE |
| --- | --- |
| planar Object | Lets you select an object to define the slice plane. |
| Surface | Lets you select a surface object to define the shape of a slice (see Chapter 20, "Using Advanced 3D Features"). |
| Zaxis | Lets you select two points defining the Z axis of the slice plane. The two points you pick are perpendicular to the slice plane. |
| View | Generates a slice plane that is perpendicular to your current view. You're prompted for the coordinate through which the slice plane must pass— usually a point on the object. |
| XY/YZ/ZX | Pick one of these to determine the slice plane based on the X, Y, or Z axis. You're prompted to pick a point through which the slice plane must pass. |
| 3points | The default setting; lets you select three points defining the slice plane. Normally, you pick points on the solid. |

## Rounding Corners with the Fillet Tool

Your bracket has a few sharp corners that you may want to round in order to give it a more realistic appearance. You can use the Tool Sets palette's Fillet and Chamfer tools to add these rounded corners to your solid model:

1. Click the Fillet tool in the middle of the lower half of the Tool Sets palette or type **F**⏎.

2. At the Select first object or [Undo/Polyline/Radius/Trim/Multiple]: prompt, pick the edge indicated in the first image in Figure 22.18.

3. At the Enter fillet radius or [Expression] <0.5000>: prompt, type **0.2**⏎.

4. At the Select an edge or [Chain/Radius]: prompt, type **C**⏎ for the Chain option. Chain lets you select a series of solid edges to be filleted.

5. Select one of the other seven edges at the base of the tapered form and press ⏎.

6. Type **HIDE**⏎ to get a quick look at your model in a hidden line view, as shown in the second image in Figure 22.18.

As you saw in step 4, Fillet acts a bit differently when you use it on solids. The Chain option lets you select a set of edges instead of just two adjoining objects.

**FIGURE 22.18**
Filleting solids

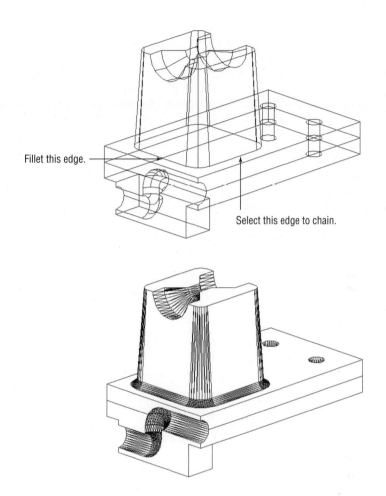

Fillet this edge.

Select this edge to chain.

## Chamfering Corners with the Chamfer Tool

Now let's try chamfering a corner. To practice using Chamfer, you'll add a countersink to the cylindrical hole you created in the first solid:

1. Type **REGEN**↵ to return to a wireframe view of your model.

2. Click the Chamfer tool (Figure 22.19), which is next to the Fillet tool on the Tool Sets palette, or type **Cha**↵.

**FIGURE 22.19**
Click the Chamfer tool.

**3.** At the prompt

`Select first line or [Undo/Polyline/Distance/Angle/Trim/mEthod/Multiple]:`

pick the edge of the hole, as shown in Figure 22.20. Notice that the top surface of the solid is highlighted and that the prompt changes to `Enter surface selection option [Next/OK (current)] <OK>:`. The highlighting indicates the base surface, which will be used as a reference in step 5. (You could also type **N**↵ to choose the other adjoining surface, the inside of the hole, as the base surface.)

**FIGURE 22.20**
Picking the edge to chamfer

Select the edge of this hole.

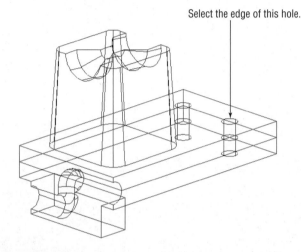

**4.** Press ↵ to accept the current highlighted face.

**5.** At the `Specify base surface chamfer distance or [Expression] <0.1250>:` prompt, type **0.125**↵. This indicates that you want the chamfer to have a width of 0.125 across the highlighted surface.

**6.** At the `Specify other surface chamfer distance or [Expression] <0.2000>:` prompt, type **0.2**↵.

**7.** At the `Select an edge or [Loop]:` prompt, click the top edges of both holes, and then press ↵. When the Chamfer command has completed its work, your drawing looks like Figure 22.21.

**8.** After reviewing the work you've done here, save the `Bracket.dwg` file.

The Loop option in step 7 lets you chamfer the entire circumference of an object. You don't need to use it here because the edge forms a circle. The Loop option is used when you have a rectangular or other polygonal edge you want to chamfer.

**FIGURE 22.21**
The chamfered edges

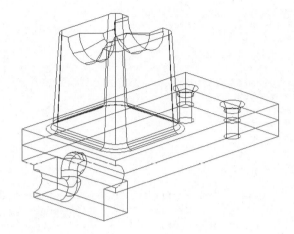

## Using the Solid Editing Tools

You've added some refinements to the Bracket model by using standard AutoCAD editing tools. There is a set of tools that is specifically geared toward editing solids. You already used the Union and Subtract tools found in the Solids – Edit tool group. In the following sections, you'll explore some of the other tools in that tool group.

You don't have to perform the exercises, but reviewing them will show you what's available. When you're more comfortable working in 3D, you may want to come back and experiment with the file called solidedit.dwg shown in the figures in the following sections.

---

**PARALLEL PROJECTION NEEDED FOR SOME FEATURES**

Many of the features discussed in these sections work only in a parallel projection view. You can switch to a parallel projection view by choosing the 2D Wireframe visual style, or, if you have the ViewCube turned on, right-click the ViewCube and select Parallel. You can also choose Parallel from the 3D Views menu on the Viewport Controls.

---

### MOVING A SURFACE

You can move any flat surface of a 3D solid by choosing Modify ➤ Solid Editing ➤ Move Faces. When you choose this option, you're prompted to select faces. Because you can select only the edge of two joining faces, you must select an edge and then use the Remove option to remove one of the two selected faces from the selection set (Figure 22.22). Once you've made your selection, press ↵. You can then specify a distance for the move.

After you've selected the surface you want to move, Move Faces acts just like the Move command: You select a base point and a displacement. Notice how the curved side of the model extends its curve to meet the new location of the surface. This shows you that AutoCAD attempts to maintain the geometry of the model when you make changes to the faces.

**FIGURE 22.22**

To select the vertical surface to the far right of the model, click the edge and then use the Remove option to remove the top surface from the selection.

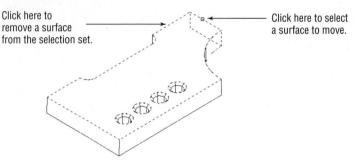

Click here to remove a surface from the selection set.

Click here to select a surface to move.

Move Faces also lets you move entire features, such as the hole in the model. In Figure 22.23, one of the holes has been moved so that it's no longer in line with the other three. This was done by selecting the countersink and the hole while using the Move Faces option.

**FIGURE 22.23**

Selecting a surface to offset

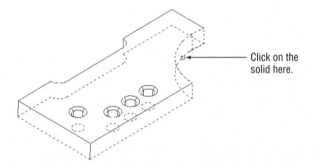

Click on the solid here.

If a solid's History setting is enabled, you can ^-click on its surface to expose the surface's grip. You can then use the grip at the center of the surface to move the surface.

### OFFSETTING A SURFACE

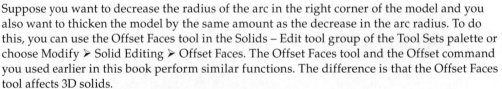

Suppose you want to decrease the radius of the arc in the right corner of the model and you also want to thicken the model by the same amount as the decrease in the arc radius. To do this, you can use the Offset Faces tool in the Solids – Edit tool group of the Tool Sets palette or choose Modify ➢ Solid Editing ➢ Offset Faces. The Offset Faces tool and the Offset command you used earlier in this book perform similar functions. The difference is that the Offset Faces tool affects 3D solids.

When you click the Offset Faces tool or choose Modify ➢ Solid Editing ➢ Offset Faces, you're prompted to select faces. As with the Move Faces option, you must select an edge that will select two faces. If you want to offset only one face, you must use the Remove option to remove one of the faces. In Figure 22.23, an edge is selected. Figure 22.24 shows the effect of the Offset Faces tool when both faces are offset.

**FIGURE 22.24**
The model after offsetting the curved and bottom surfaces

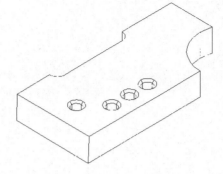

### DELETING A SURFACE

Now suppose you've decided to eliminate the curved part of the model. You can delete a surface by choosing Modify ➤ Solid Editing ➤ Delete Faces from the menu bar. Once again, you're prompted to select faces. Typically, you'll want to delete only one face, such as the curved surface in the example model. You use the Remove option to remove the adjoining face that you don't want to delete before finishing your selection of faces to remove.

When you attempt to delete surfaces, keep in mind that the surface you delete must be recoverable by other surfaces in the model. For example, you can't remove the top surface of a cube, expecting it to turn into a pyramid. That would require the sides to change their orientation, which isn't allowed in this operation. You can, on the other hand, remove the top of a box with tapered sides. Then, when you remove the top, the sides converge to form a pyramid.

### ROTATING A SURFACE

All the surfaces of the model are parallel or perpendicular to each other. Imagine that your design requires two sides to be at an angle. You can change the angle of a surface by choosing Modify ➤ Solid Editing ➤ Rotate Faces on the menu bar.

As with the prior solid-editing tools, you're prompted to select faces. You must then specify an axis of rotation. You can either select a point or use the default of selecting two points to define an axis of rotation, as shown in Figure 22.25. Once the axis is determined, you can specify a rotation angle. Figure 22.26 shows the result of rotating the two front-facing surfaces 4°.

**FIGURE 22.25**
Defining the axis of rotation

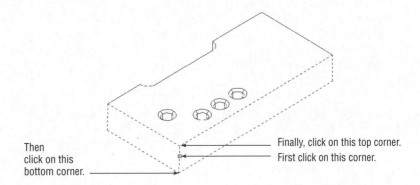

Then click on this bottom corner.

Finally, click on this top corner.
First click on this corner.

**FIGURE 22.26**
The model
after rotating
two surfaces

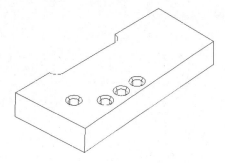

### TAPERING A SURFACE

In an earlier exercise, you saw how to create a new tapered solid by using the Extrude command. But what if you want to taper an existing solid? Here's what you can do.

The Taper Faces tool from the Solids – Edit tool group prompts you to select faces. You can select faces, as described for the previously discussed solid-editing tools, using the Remove or Add option (Figure 22.27). Press ↵ when you finish your selection, and then indicate the axis from which the taper is to occur. In the model example in Figure 22.27, select two corners defining a vertical axis. Finally, enter the taper angle. Figure 22.28 shows the model tapered at a 4° angle.

**FIGURE 22.27**
Selecting the
surfaces to taper
and indicating
the direction of
the taper

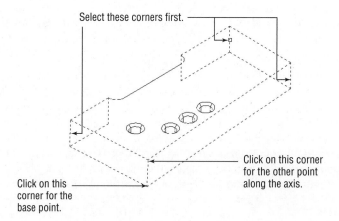

Select these corners first.

Click on this corner for the other point along the axis.

Click on this corner for the base point.

**FIGURE 22.28**
The model after
tapering the sides

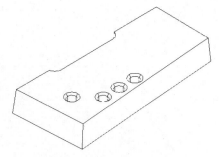

### EXTRUDING A SURFACE

You've used the Extrude tool to create two of the solids in the Bracket model. The Extrude tool requires a closed polyline as a basis for the extrusion. As an alternative, the Solids – Edit tool group offers the Extrude Faces tool, which extrudes a surface of an existing solid.

When you click the Extrude Faces tool from the Solids – Edit tool group or type **SOLIDEDIT↵ F↵ E↵**, you see the `Select faces or [Undo/Remove]:` prompt. Select an edge or a set of edges or use the Remove or Add option to select the faces you want to extrude. Press ↵ when you've finished your selection, and then specify a height and taper angle. Figure 22.29 shows the sample model with the front surface extruded and tapered at a 45° angle. You can extrude multiple surfaces simultaneously if you need to by selecting them.

**FIGURE 22.29**
The model with a surface extruded and tapered

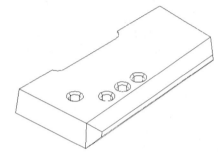

Aside from those features, the Extrude Faces tool works just like the Extrude command.

### TURNING A SOLID INTO A SHELL

In many situations, you'll want your 3D model to be a hollow mass rather than a solid mass. The Shell option on the menu bar lets you convert a solid into a shell.

When you choose Modify ➤ Solid Editing ➤ Shell, or type **SOLIDEDIT↵ B↵ S↵**, you're prompted to select a 3D solid. You're then prompted to remove faces. At this point, you can select an edge of the solid to indicate the surface you want removed. The surface you select is completely removed from the model, exposing the interior of the shell. For example, if you select the front edge of the sample model shown in Figure 22.30, the top and front surfaces are removed from the model, revealing the interior of the solid, as shown in Figure 22.31. After selecting the surfaces to remove, you can enter a shell offset distance.

**FIGURE 22.30**
Selecting the edge to be removed

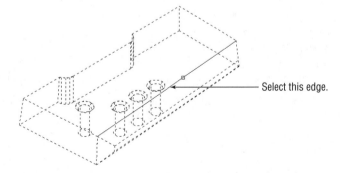

Select this edge.

**FIGURE 22.31**
The solid model
after using the
Shell option

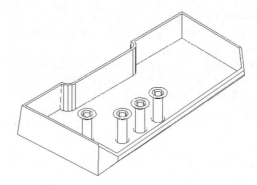

The shell thickness is added to the outside surface of the solid. When you're constructing your solid with the intention of creating a shell, you need to take this into account.

### COPYING FACES AND EDGES

At times, you may want to create a copy of a surface of a solid to analyze its area or to produce another part that mates to that surface. The Modify ➤ Solid Editing ➤ Copy Faces option creates a copy of any surface on your model. The copy it produces is a type of object called a *region*.

The copies of the surfaces are opaque and can hide objects behind them when you perform a hidden-line removal (type **HIDE**↵).

Another menu bar option that is similar to Copy Faces is Copy Edges, which can be found by choosing Modify ➤ Solid Editing ➤ Copy Edges. Instead of selecting surfaces as in the Copy Faces tool, you select all the edges you want to copy. The result is a series of simple lines representing the edges of your model. This option can be useful if you want to convert a solid into a set of 3D Faces. The Copy Edges option creates a framework onto which you can add 3D Faces.

### ADDING SURFACE FEATURES

If you need to add a feature to a flat surface, you can do so with the Modify ➤ Solid Editing ➤ Imprint Edges option. An added surface feature can then be colored using the Modify ➤ Solid Editing ➤ Color Faces option or extruded using the Presspull tool near the top of the Tool Sets palette. This feature is a little more complicated than some of the other solid-editing tools, so you may want to try the following exercise to see firsthand how it works.

You'll start by inserting an object that will be the source of the imprint. You'll then imprint the main solid model with the object's profile:

1. Choose Insert ➤ Block from the menu bar to open the Insert Block dialog box, or type **I**↵.

2. Click Browse, and then locate the `imprint.dwg` sample file and select it.

3. In the Insert Block dialog box, make sure the Explode Block check box is selected.

4. Click Insert, then enter **0,0**↵ for the insertion point and press ↵ to finish inserting the block. The block appears in the middle of the solid.

5. Choose Modify ➤ Solid Editing ➤ Imprint Edges or type **IMPRINT**↵.

**6.** Click the main solid model.

**7.** Click the inserted solid.

**8.** At the `Delete the source object [Yes/No]<N>:` prompt, enter **Y↵↵**.

You now have an outline of the intersection between the two solids imprinted on the top surface of your model. The imprint is really a set of edges that have been added to the surface of the solid. To help the imprint stand out, try the following steps to change its color:

**1.** Choose Modify ➤ Solid Editing ➤ Color Faces, or type **SOLIDEDIT↵ F↵ L↵**.

**2.** Click the imprint from the previous exercise. The imprint and the entire top surface are highlighted.

**3.** At the `Select faces or [Undo/Remove/ALL]:` prompt, type **R↵**; then click the outer edge of the top surface to remove it from the selection set.

**4.** Press ↵ to open the Color Palette dialog box.

**5.** Click the red color sample in the dialog box, and then click OK. The imprint is now red.

**6.** Press ↵ twice to exit the command.

**7.** To see the full effect of the Color Faces option, choose the Conceptual or Realistic visual style from the Visual Styles menu in the Viewports Control.

If you want to remove an imprint from a surface, ⌃-click the imprint and press the Delete key.

### SEPARATING A DIVIDED SOLID

While editing solids, you can end up with two separate solid forms that were created from one solid, as shown in Figure 22.32. Even though the two solids appear separated, they act like a single object. In these situations, AutoCAD offers the Modify ➤ Solid Editing ➤ Separate option. Choose this option or type **SOLIDEDIT↵ B↵ P↵** and select the solid that has been separated into two forms.

**FIGURE 22.32**
When the tall, thin solid is subtracted from the larger solid, the result is two separate forms, yet they still behave as a single object.

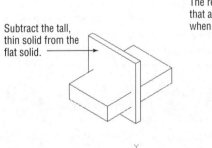

Subtract the tall, thin solid from the flat solid.

The result is two forms that act like a single object when selected.

Separate will separate the two forms into two distinct solids.

**USING THE COMMAND LINE FOR SOLID EDITING**

The solid-editing tools are options of a single AutoCAD command called Solidedit. If you prefer to use the keyboard, here are some tips on using the Solidedit command. When you first enter **SOLIDEDIT↵** at the Command prompt, you see the following prompt:

```
Enter a solids editing option [Face/Edge/Body/Undo/eXit] <eXit>:
```

You can select the Face, Edge, or Body option to edit the various parts of a solid. If you select Face, you see the following prompt:

```
Enter a face editing option [Extrude/Move/Rotate/Offset/Taper/
Delete/Copy/coLor/mAterial/Undo/eXit] <eXit>:.
```

The options from this prompt produce the same results as their counterparts on the Solid Editing panel.

If you select Edge at the first prompt, you see the following prompt:

```
Enter an edge editing option [Copy/coLor/Undo/eXit] <eXit>:.
```

The Copy option lets you copy a surface, and the coLor option lets you add color to a surface.

If you select Body from the first prompt, you see the following prompt:

```
Enter a body editing option [Imprint/seParate solids/Shell/
cLean/Check/Undo/eXit] <eXit>:.
```

These options also perform the same functions as their counterparts on the Solids – Edit tool group or the Modify ➤ Solid Editing menu option. As you work with this command, you can use the Undo option to undo the last Solidedit option you used without exiting the command.

Figure 22.32 is included in the sample figures at www.sybex.com/go/masteringautocadmac under the name Separate example.dwg. You can try the Separate option in this file on your own.

Through some simple examples, you've seen how each of the solid-editing tools works. You aren't limited to using these tools in the way they were demonstrated in this chapter, and this book can't anticipate every situation you might encounter as you create solid models. These examples are intended as an introduction to these tools, so feel free to experiment with them. You can always use the Undo option to backtrack in case you don't get the results you expect.

This concludes your tour of the solid-editing tools. Next you'll learn how to use 3D solid models to generate 2D working drawings quickly.

**FINDING THE PROPERTIES OF A SOLID**

All this effort to create a solid model isn't designed just to create a pretty picture. After your model is drawn and built, you can obtain information about its physical properties.

You can find the volume, the moment of inertia, and other physical properties of your model by using the Massprop command. These properties can also be recorded as a file on disk, so you can modify your model without worrying about losing track of its original properties.

To find the mass properties of a solid, enter **MASSPROP↵**, and then follow the prompts.

# Streamlining the 2D Drawing Process

Using solids to model a part—such as with the bracket and Solidedit examples in this chapter—may seem a bit exotic, but there are definite advantages to modeling in 3D, even if you only want to draw the part in 2D as a page in a set of manufacturing specs.

The exercises in the following sections show you how to generate a typical mechanical drawing from your 3D model quickly by using Paper Space and the solid-editing tools. You'll also examine techniques for dimensioning and including hidden lines.

 **Real World Scenario**

### ARCHITECTURAL ELEVATIONS FROM 3D SOLIDS

If your application is architecture and you've created a 3D model of a building by using solids, you can use the tools described in the following sections to generate 2D elevation drawings from your 3D solid model.

You might use solid models to generate 2D line drawings of elevations. Such line drawings can be "rendered" in a 2D drawing program like Adobe Photoshop or Illustrator. Be aware that such drawings will not be as accurate as those drawn from scratch, but they are fine for the early stages of a design project.

## Drawing Standard Top, Front, and Right-Side Views

One of the most common types of mechanical drawings is the *orthogonal projection*. This style of drawing shows separate top, front, and right-side views of an object. Sometimes a 3D image is added for clarity. You can derive such a drawing in a few minutes using the Flatshot tool described in Chapter 19 (see the section "Turning a 3D View into a 2D AutoCAD Drawing").

With Flatshot, you can generate the standard top, front, and right-side orthogonal projection views, which you can further enhance with dimensions, hatch patterns, and other 2D drawing features. Follow these steps:

1. In the Bracket.dwg file, open the 3D Views menu on the Viewport Controls, and then click on an orthogonal projection view from the list, such as Top, Left, or Right (Figure 22.33). You can also use the View ➢ 3D Views submenu on the menu bar or the ViewCube to select an orthogonal view. See Chapter 19 for more on the ViewCube.

2. Click the Flatshot tool near the bottom of the Tool Sets palette or type **FLATSHOT**↵.

3. In the Flatshot dialog box (Figure 22.34), select the options you want and click Create. See Table 19.1 in Chapter 19 for the Flatshot options.

If you select Insert As New Block in the Flatshot dialog box, you're prompted to select an insertion point to insert the block that is the 2D orthogonal view of your model. By default, the view is placed in the same plane as your current view, as shown in Figure 22.35. Once you've created all your views, you can move them to a different location in your drawing so you can create a set of layout views to your 2D orthogonal views, as shown in Figure 22.36. You can also place the orthogonal view blocks on a separate layer and then, for each layout viewport, freeze the layer of the 3D model so that only the 2D views are displayed.

**FIGURE 22.33**
The 3D Views
menu on the View-
port Controls

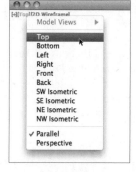

**FIGURE 22.34**
The Flatshot
dialog box

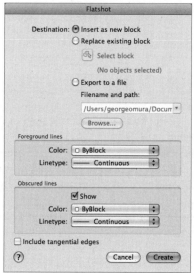

**FIGURE 22.35**
The 2D orthogonal
views shown in
relation to the
3D model

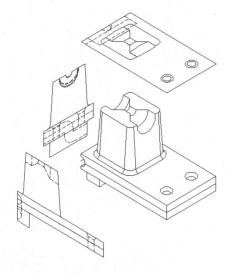

**FIGURE 22.36**
**FIGURE 22.36**
You can use
a layout to
arrange a set of
views created
by Flatshot.
Dimensions,
notes, and a title
block can be
added to com-
plete the layout.

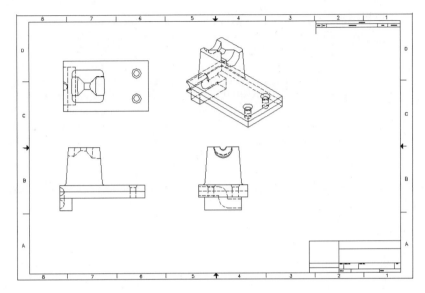

If your model changes and you need to update the orthogonal views, you can repeat the steps listed here. However, instead of selecting Insert As New Block in the Flatshot dialog box, select Replace Existing Block to update the original orthogonal view blocks. If you want, you can include an isometric view to help communicate your design more clearly.

### Set Up Standard Views in a Layout Viewport

To set up a layout viewport to display a view, like a top or right-side view of a 3D model, double-click inside the viewport and then select a view from the 3D Views menu on the Viewport Controls. To set the scale of a viewport, click the viewport border (double-click outside the viewport if you cannot select its border) and then select a scale from the VP Scale pop-up menu on the Status Bar palette. If you'd like to refresh your memory on layouts in general, refer to Chapter 15, "Laying Out Your Printer Output."

## Adding Dimensions and Notes in a Layout

Although I don't recommend adding dimensions in Paper Space for architectural drawings, it may be a good idea for mechanical drawings such as the one in this chapter. By maintaining the dimensions and notes separate from the actual model, you keep these elements from getting in the way of your work on the solid model. You also avoid the confusion of having to scale the text and dimension features properly to ensure that they will plot at the correct size. See Chapter 9, "Adding Text to Drawings," and Chapter 11, "Using Dimensions," for a more detailed discussion of notes and dimensions.

As long as you set up your Paper Space work area to be equivalent to the final print size, you can set dimension and text to the sizes you want when you print. If you want text ¼″ high, you set your text styles to be ¼″ high.

To include dimensions, make sure you're in a layout view, and then use the dimension commands in the normal way. However, you need to make sure full associative dimensioning is turned on. Type **DIMASSOC⏎ 2⏎** to turn on associative dimensioning or **DIMASSOC⏎ 1⏎** to turn it off. Dimassoc is the system variable that controls associative dimensioning. With associative dimensioning turned on, dimensions in a layout view display the true dimension of the object being dimensioned, regardless of the scale setting of the viewport.

If you don't have the associative dimensioning option turned on and your viewports are set to a scale other than 1 to 1, you have another option: You can set the Overall Scale option in the New or Modify Dimension Style dialog box to a proper value. The following steps show you how:

1. Click the Show Drawings & Layouts button in the Status Bar palette, and then select the Model layout for your drawing.

2. Choose Format ➢ Dimension Style from the menu bar to open the Dimension Style Manager.

3. Make sure you've selected the style you want to edit, and then click the Options action menu and choose Modify to open the Modify Dimension Style dialog box.

4. Click the Primary Units tab.

5. In the Scale Factor input box in the Linear Dimensions group, enter the value by which you want your Paper Space dimensions multiplied. For example, if your Paper Space views are scaled at one-half the actual size of your model, enter **2** in this box to multiply your dimensions' values by two.

6. Click the Apply To Layout Dimensions Only check box. This ensures that your dimension is scaled only while you're adding dimensions in Paper Space. Dimensions added in Model Space aren't affected.

7. Click OK to close the Modify Dimension Style dialog box, and then click Close in the Dimension Style Manager.

You've had to complete a lot of steps to get the final drawing, but compared with drawing these views by hand, you undoubtedly saved a great deal of time. In addition, as you'll see later in this chapter, what you have is more than just a 2D drafted image. With what you created, further refinements are now easy.

## Using Visual Styles with a Viewport

In Chapter 19, you saw how you can view your 3D model using visual styles. A visual style can give you a more realistic representation of your 3D model, and it can show off more of the details, especially on rounded surfaces. You can also view and plot a visual style in a layout view. To do this, you make a viewport active and then turn on the visual style you want to use for that viewport. The following exercise gives you a firsthand look at how this is done:

1. Back in the Bracket.dwg drawing, click the Show Drawings & Layouts button in the Status Bar palette and double-click the Layout1 thumbnail.

2. Double-click inside the viewport with the isometric view of the model to switch to Model Space.

3. Select Conceptual from the Visual Styles menu on the Viewport Controls (Figure 22.37).

**FIGURE 22.37**

The Visual Styles menu on the View-port Controls

The view may appear a bit dark because of the black color setting for the object. You can change the color to a lighter one such as cyan or blue to get a better look.

4. Double-click outside the isometric viewport to return to Paper Space.

If you have multiple viewports in a layout, you can change the visual style of one viewport without affecting the other viewports. This can help others visualize your 3D model more clearly.

You'll also want to know how to control the hard-copy output of a shaded view. For this, you use the shortcut menu:

1. Click the isometric view's viewport border to select it.

2. Right-click to open the shortcut menu, and select the Shade Plot option to display a set of Shade Plot options (Figure 22.38).

3. Take a moment to study the menu, and then click As Displayed.

**FIGURE 22.38**

The Shade Plot submenu

The As Displayed option prints the viewport as it appears in the drawing area. You use this option to print the currently displayed visual style. Wireframe sets the viewport to a Wireframe view. Hidden sets the viewport to a hidden-line view similar to the view you see when you use the Hide command. At the bottom of the menu is the Rendered option, which sets the view to use AutoCAD's Render feature when printing, described in Chapter 21, "Rendering 3D Drawings." You can use the Rendered option to print ray-traced renderings of your 3D models.

Remember these options on the shortcut menu as you work on your drawings and when you print. They can be helpful in communicating your ideas, but they can also get lost in the array of tools that AutoCAD offers.

## Visualizing Solids

If you're designing a complex object, sometimes it helps to be able to see it in ways that you couldn't in the real world. AutoCAD offers two visualization tools that can help others understand your design ideas.

If you want to show off the internal workings of a part or an assembly quickly, you can use the X-ray effect, which can be found in the Visuals Styles menu on the Viewport Controls.

Figure 22.39 shows an isometric view of the bracket using the Vsfaceopacity system variable, which also gives an X-ray-like appearance to your model. The Realistic visual style combined with the Vsfaceopacity system variable gives this effect. The color of the bracket has also been changed to a light gray to help visibility. You can see the internal elements as if the object were semitransparent. The Vsfaceopacity works with any 3D visual style, although it works best with a style that shows some of the surface features (such as the Conceptual or Realistic visual style).

To use it, enter **VSFACEOPACITY**, and then enter a value for the opacity. You can start with 50 and adjust from there. The default value is –60 for an opaque object.

**FIGURE 22.39**
The bracket displayed using a Realistic visual style and the X-ray effect of the Vsfaceopacity command.

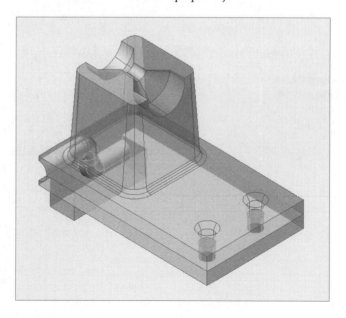

Another tool to help you visualize the internal workings of a design is the Sectionplane command. This command creates a plane that defines the location of a cross section. A section plane can also do more than just show a cross section. Try the following exercise to see how it works:

1. In the Bracket file, click Model in the Status Bar palette, select Model from the pop-up menu, and then change the color of layer 0 to a light gray so you can see the bracket more clearly when using the Realistic visual style.

2. Select Realistic from the Visual Styles menu on the Viewport Controls.

3. Make sure that the Object Snap and Object Snap Tracking toggles are turned off in the Status Bar palette. This will allow you to point to surfaces on the model while using the Sectionplane command.

4. Adjust your view so it looks similar to Figure 22.40.

5. Click the Section Plane tool near the bottom of the Tool Sets palette. You can also enter **SECTIONPLANE⏎** at the Command prompt. You'll see the following prompt:

```
Select face or any point to locate
section line or [Draw section/Orthographic]:
```

6. Click the front plane of the bracket, as shown in Figure 22.40. A plane appears on that surface.

**FIGURE 22.40**
Adding the section plane to your bracket

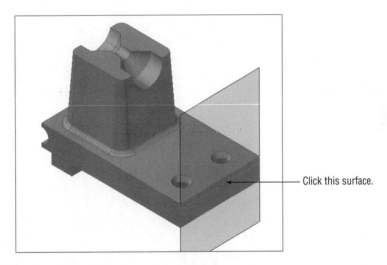

Click this surface.

You can move the section plane object along the solid to get a real-time view of the section it traverses. To do this, you need to turn on the Live Section feature. To check whether Live Section is turned on, do the following:

1. Click the section plane, and then right-click. If you see a check mark by the Activate Live Sectioning option, then you know it's on. If you don't see a check mark, then choose Activate Live Sectioning to turn it on.

**2.** Click the red axis on the Move gizmo, as shown in Figure 22.41. The axis turns yellow to indicate that it is active and you see a red vector appear. If you don't see the gizmo, make sure you are in the Realistic visual style.

**FIGURE 22.41**
Moving the surface plane across the bracket

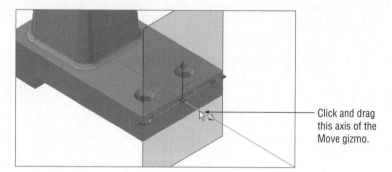

Click and drag this axis of the Move gizmo.

**3.** Move the cursor slowly toward the back of the bracket.

**4.** When the section plane is roughly in the middle of the tapered portion of the bracket, click the mouse to fix the plane in place. You should have a view similar to Figure 22.42.

**FIGURE 22.42**
The surface plane fixed at a location

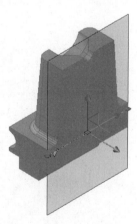

Now you see only a portion of the bracket behind the section plane plus the cross section of the plane, as shown in Figure 22.43. You can have the section plane display the front portion as a ghosted image by doing the following:

**1.** With the section plane selected (you should still see its Move gizmo), right-click and choose Live Section Settings. In the Section Settings dialog box, under the Cut-Away Geometry category, click Show. Click OK. The front portion of the bracket appears in red (Figure 22.43).

**2.** Press the Esc key to remove the section plane from the current selection. The cut-away geometry remains in view.

**FIGURE 22.43**

The front portion of the bracket is displayed with the Show Cut-Away Geometry option turned on.

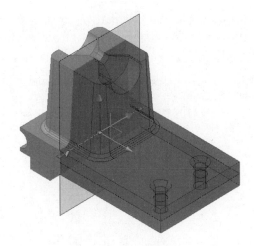

You can double-click on the section plane to toggle between a solid view and a cut-away view of the geometry. This toggles the Active Live Sectioning option.

You can also add a jog in the section plane to create a more complex section cut. Here's how it's done:

1. Select the section plane.

2. Right-click, and choose Add Jog To Section.

3. At the `Specify a point on the section line to add jog:` prompt, use the Nearest object snap to select a point on the section plane line (Figure 22.44).

**FIGURE 22.44**

Moving the jog in the section plane

Use the Nearest osnap and click the section line here to create the jog.

Click this grip to move the back portion of the section plane.

Move the plane to this location.

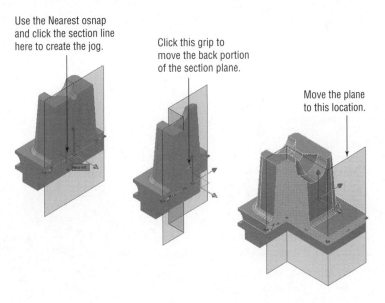

**4.** Click the grip on the back portion of the section plane, as shown in Figure 22.44, and drag it toward the right so the jog looks similar to the third panel in the figure.

**5.** Press the Esc key to get a clear view of the new section.

As you can see from this example, you can adjust the section using the grips on the section plane line. You can use the Nearest osnap to select a point anywhere along the section line to a jog. Click and drag the endpoint grips to rotate the section plane to an angle.

You may have also noticed another arrow in the section plane (Figure 22.45).

**FIGURE 22.45**
The arrow presents additional options for the section plane.

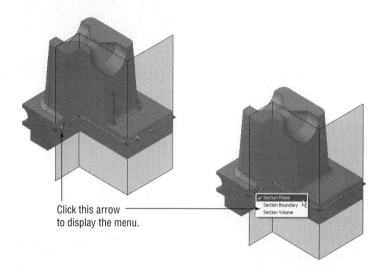

Click this arrow to display the menu.

When you click the downward-pointing arrow, you see three options for visualizing the section boundary: Section Plane, Section Boundary, and Section Volume.

By using these other settings, you can start to include sections through the sides, back, top, or bottom of the solid. For example, if you click the Section Boundary option, another boundary line appears with grips (Figure 22.46). To see it clearly, you may have to press Esc and then select the section plane again. You can then manipulate these grips to show section cuts along those boundaries.

**FIGURE 22.46**
Another boundary line appears with grips when you click the Section Boundary option.

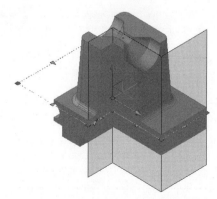

The Section Volume option displays the boundary of a volume along with grips at the top and bottom of the volume (Figure 22.47). These grips allow you to create a cut plane from the top or bottom of the solid.

**FIGURE 22.47**
The boundaries shown using the Section Volume option

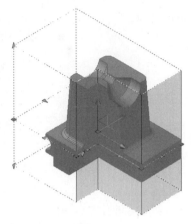

Finally, you can get a copy of the solid that is behind or in front of the section plane. Right-click the section plane, and choose Generate 2D/3D Section to open the Generate Section/Elevation dialog box. Click the Hide Advanced Settings disclosure triangle to expand the dialog box and display more options (Figure 22.48).

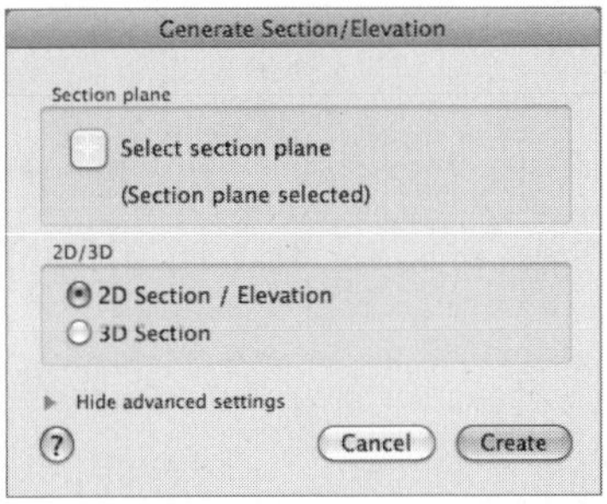

**FIGURE 22.48**
The Generate Section/Elevation dialog box

If you select 2D Section/Elevation, a 2D image of the section plane is inserted in the drawing in a manner similar to the insertion of a block. You're asked for an insertion point, an X and Y scale, and a rotation angle.

The 3D Section option creates a copy of the portion of the solid that is bounded by the section plane or planes, as shown in Figure 22.49.

---

**USING A SECTION PLANE IN AN ARCHITECTURAL MODEL**

If your application is architectural, you can use a section plane and the 2D Section/Elevation option to get an accurate elevation drawing. Instead of placing the section plane inside the solid, move it away from the solid model and use the 2D Section/Elevation option.

**FIGURE 22.49**
A copy of the solid minus the section area is created using the 3D Section option of the Generate Section/Elevation dialog box.

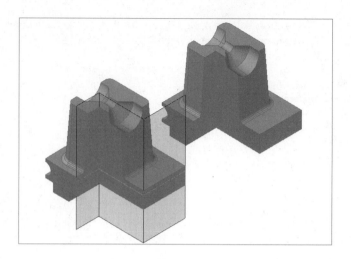

You can access more detailed settings for the 2D Section/Elevation, 3D Section, and Section Settings options by clicking the Hide Advanced Settings disclosure triangle at the bottom of the Generate Section/Elevation dialog box (Figure 22.50). The Section Settings button near the bottom opens the Section Settings dialog box, which lists the settings for the section feature.

**FIGURE 22.50**
The Generate Section/Elevation dialog box

Disclosure triangle ⎯⎯⎯⎯⎯⎯

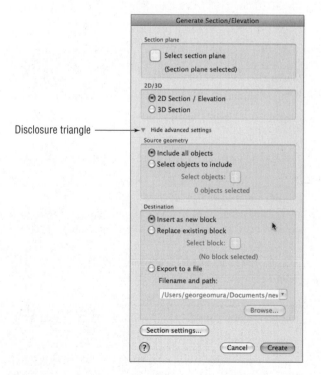

If you create a set of orthogonal views in a layout, the work you do to find a section is also reflected in the layout views (Figure 22.51).

**FIGURE 22.51**
A set of orthogonal views in a layout

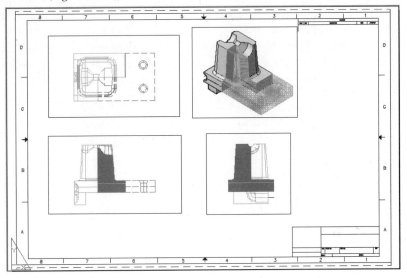

## TAKING ADVANTAGE OF STEREOLITHOGRAPHY

A discussion of solid modeling wouldn't be complete without mentioning stereolithography. This is one of the most interesting technological wonders that has appeared as a by-product of 3D computer modeling. *Stereolithography* is a process that generates physical reproductions of 3D computer solid models. Special equipment converts your AutoCAD-generated files into a physical model.

This process offers the mechanical designer a method for rapidly prototyping designs directly from AutoCAD drawings, though applications don't have to be limited to mechanical design. Architects can take advantage of this process too. My own interest in Tibetan art led me to create a 3D AutoCAD model of a type of statue called a Zola, shown here. I sent this model to a service to have it reproduced in resin.

AutoCAD supports stereolithography through the Export and Stlout commands. These commands generate an STL file, which can be used with a *Stereolithograph Apparatus (SLA)* to generate a model. You must first create a 3D solid model in AutoCAD. Then you can use the Export Data dialog box to export your drawing in the STL format. Choose File ➢ Export from the menu bar, and make sure the File Format pop-up menu shows Lithography (*.stl) before you click the Save button.

The AutoCAD 3D solids are translated into a set of triangular-faceted meshes in the STL file. You can use the Smoothness For 3D Printing/Rendering setting in the Document Settings tab of the Application Preferences dialog box to control the fineness of these meshes. See Chapter 21 for more information on this setting.

## The Bottom Line

**Understand solid modeling.** Solid modeling lets you build 3D models by creating and joining 3D shapes called solids. There are several built-in solid shapes called primitives, and you can create others using the Extrude tool.

**Master It** Name some of the built-in solid primitives available in AutoCAD.

**Create solid forms.** You can use Boolean operations to sculpt 3D solids into the shape you want. Two solids can be joined to form a more complex one, or you can remove one solid from another.

**Master It** Name the three Boolean operations you can use on solids.

**Create complex solids.** Besides the primitives, you can create your own shapes based on 2D polylines.

**Master It** Name three tools that let you convert closed polylines and circles into 3D solids.

**Edit solids.** Once you've created a solid, you can make changes to it using the solid-editing tools offered on the Solids – Edit tool group or the Modify ➢ Solid Editing submenu on the menu bar.

**Master It** Name at least four of the tools found on the Solids – Edit tool group.

**Streamline the 2D drawing process.** You can create 3D orthogonal views of your 3D model to create standard 2D mechanical drawings.

**Master It** What is the name of the tool in the Tool Sets palette that lets you create a 2D drawing of a 3D model?

**Visualize solids.** In addition to viewing your 3D model in a number of different orientations, you can view it as if it were transparent or cut in half.

**Master It** What is the name of the command that lets you create a cut view of your 3D model?

# Chapter 23

# Exploring 3D Mesh and Surface Modeling

AutoCAD has always offered tools that allowed users to construct fairly complex 3D models. With the solid-modeling tools, you can even model some very organic forms. But there are some types of forms that require a type of modeling known as *mesh modeling*. Mesh modeling enables you to create smooth, curved volumes by manipulating faces that make up an object's surface.

With mesh modeling, you can quickly create curved shapes that are difficult or even impossible to create by other means. AutoCAD also offers the ability to convert a mesh model into a 3D solid so that you can perform Boolean operations.

AutoCAD for Mac introduces a set of 3D surface modeling tools that extend its ability to produce and edit curved, organic forms. In this chapter, you'll get a chance to explore many of the current features of mesh modeling through a series of exercises, and you'll be introduced to the new surface modeling tools. You'll also learn how you can convert a mesh or 3D surface into a solid. You'll start by creating a simple shape as an introduction, and then you'll move on to a more complex form.

In this chapter you'll learn to do the following:

◆ Create a simple 3D mesh

◆ Edit faces and edges

◆ Create complex meshes

◆ Convert meshes to solids

◆ Understand 3D surfaces

◆ Edit 3D surfaces

## Creating a Simple 3D Mesh

As an introduction to the mesh modeling features in AutoCAD, you'll draw a simple box and then smooth the box. This first exercise will show you some of the basic mesh modeling tools and what types of control you can exert on a model. Follow these steps:

1. Create a new file using the acad3D.dwt or acadiso3D.dwt template. Choose File ➢ New from the menu bar, or press ⌘-N.

2. At the Select Template dialog box, select the acad3D.dwt template (metric users can select acadiso3D.dwt) and then click Open.

3. From the Tool Sets button, select Modeling.

4. Choose the Shaded With Edges visual style from the Visual Styles menu on the Viewport Controls. This will give you a close approximation of the appearance of meshes you'll see in the figures shown in this book.

## Creating a Mesh Primitive

Meshes are similar to solids in that they start from what is called a *primitive*. You may recall that 3D solid primitives are predetermined shapes from which you can form more complex shapes. The mesh primitives are very similar to the 3D solid primitives you learned about in Chapter 19, "Creating 3D Drawings," and Chapter 22, "Editing and Visualizing 3D Solids." You can see the different mesh primitives that are available by choosing Draw ➢ 3D Modeling ➢ Meshes ➢ Primitives from the menu bar or by typing **MESH↵**.

In the next exercise, you'll use the mesh box primitive to start building your seat cushion:

1. Type **MESH↵ B↵**.

2. At the Specify first corner or [Center]: prompt, enter **0,0↵** to start the mesh at the drawing origin.

3. You'll want a mesh that is 21 units in the X axis by 32 units in the Y axis, so at the Specify other corner or [Cube/Length]: prompt, enter **21,32↵** (metric users can type **533.4,812.8↵**).

4. At the Specify height or [2Point]: prompt, place your cursor anywhere above the base of the mesh and enter **4↵** for a 4-inch height (metric users can enter 101.6). You now have a basic shape for your mesh (see Figure 23.1).

**FIGURE 23.1**
The mesh box primitive

You've just created a mesh box, but you have several other mesh primitives at your disposal. When you typed the Mesh command, you saw the cylinder, cone, sphere, pyramid, wedge, and torus primitive options. When creating your model, consider which of these primitives will best suit your needs.

## Understanding the Parts of a Mesh

Before you go any further, you'll want to understand the structure of a mesh. Notice that each side is divided into nine panels, or *faces* as they are called in AutoCAD. You can edit these faces to change the shape and contour of your mesh. You can also control the number of faces that a mesh will display, which will be covered in the section "Editing Faces and Edges" later in this chapter.

Figure 23.2 shows the names of the different parts of a simple mesh: the vertex, the edge, and the face. These three parts are called subobjects of the mesh, and you can move their position in the mesh to modify a mesh's shape.

**FIGURE 23.2**
The subobjects of a mesh

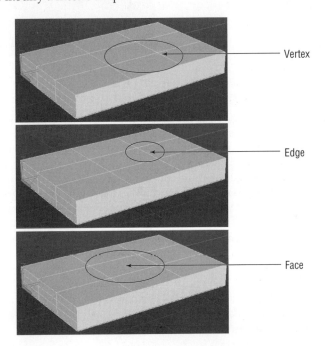

Vertex

Edge

Face

To help you select different subobjects on a mesh, the Subobject Selection Filter submenu (located on the right-click shortcut menu) offers the Filter flyout, which shows the No Filter tool by default. You'll use this flyout in many of the exercises in this chapter.

## Smoothing a Mesh

One of the main features of a mesh is its ability to become a smooth, curved object. Right now your cushion has sharp edges, but you can round the corners using the Smooth tools.

Try modifying the mesh to smooth its corners:

1. Click the rectangular mesh to select it.

2. Type **MESHSMOOTHMORE**⏎ (or choose Modify ➤ Mesh Editing ➤ Smooth More from the menu bar). The edges of the mesh become faceted and smoother in appearance.

3. Repeat the **MESHSMOOTHMORE** command. The mesh becomes smoother still (see Figure 23.3).

**FIGURE 23.3**
The mesh after applying the Smooth More tool twice

4. Now type **MESHSMOOTHLESS**⏎, select the object, and press ⏎ (or choose Modify ➤ Mesh Editing ➤ Smooth Less from the menu bar). The mesh becomes less smooth.

5. Press Esc to clear the selection.

---

**DON'T FORGET THE RIGHT-CLICK MENU**

The Smooth More and Smooth Less options are also available on the right-click shortcut menu.

---

As you can see from this exercise, you can smooth a mesh using the Smooth More tool. The more times you apply it to a mesh, the smoother your mesh becomes. The number of faces of the mesh determines how Smooth More affects the mesh. The fewer the faces, the broader the application of smoothness.

When you apply the Smooth More tool to a mesh, the faces of the mesh become faceted. This simulates the smooth appearance. If you look closely at a mesh that has only one or two levels of smoothing applied, you can see the facets.

## Editing Faces and Edges

The shape you created earlier demonstrates one of the main features of meshes. In this section, you'll create a model of a surfboard to see how you can push and pull the subobjects of a mesh to create a form.

You'll start with the same form, a box shape, but this time you'll modify some of the parameters that define the box's structure. You can control the number of faces that a mesh primitive will have before it is created. The following exercise introduces you to the tools and methods used to edit meshes.

**KNOW THE VIEWCUBE**

Throughout the following exercise, you'll make heavy use of the ViewCube. Make sure you are familiar with how it works. If you need a refresher, see Chapter 19.

Start by creating a new drawing and setting up the parameters for the mesh.

1. Choose File ➤ New from the menu bar (or press ⌘-N), select acad3D.dwt, and then click Open. Metric users can select the acadiso3D.dwt file.

2. Choose the Shaded With Edges visual style from the Visual Styles menu on the Viewport Controls.

3. Type **DIVMESHBOXWIDTH**↵ **4**↵. This sets the mesh division for the box width to four faces instead of the default three.

4. Type **DIVMESHBOXLENGTH**↵ **4**↵. This sets the mesh division for the box mesh length to four faces instead of the default three.

5. Finally, type **DIVMESHBOXHEIGHT**↵ **1**↵. This sets the mesh division for the box mesh height to one face instead of the default three.

The parameters you change alter the number of faces on mesh primitives that you create, including the box primitive in the next exercise. You'll see the results in the next set of steps:

1. Type **MESH**↵ **B**↵ to create a primitive mesh box.

2. At the Specify first corner or [Center]: prompt, type **0,0**↵ to start the corner at the origin of the drawing.

3. At the Specify other corner or [Cube/Length]: prompt, enter **50,30**↵ to create a 50″-×-30″ base for the box. Metric users can enter **1270,762**↵.

4. At the Specify height or [2Point] prompt, point the cursor in the positive Z direction and then enter **3.5**↵ for a 3.5 units thickness. Metric users enter **88.9**↵.

5. Center the box in your view.

6. Click the mesh box to select it. On the Properties Inspector palette, click the Smoothness drop-down list in the Geometry group. Select Level 4. Your mesh box is now smoothed again as it was originally. Your model should look similar to Figure 23.4.

**FIGURE 23.4**
The mesh box

---

**WHAT DOES THE SMOOTH MESH TOOL DO?**

The Smooth Mesh option on the menu bar (Draw ➢ 3D Modeling ➢ Meshes ➢ Smooth Mesh) is not intended to work on meshes. Instead, it converts 3D objects other than meshes into mesh objects. You can convert a solid into a mesh, for example, using this tool. 3D surfaces can also be converted, and it even works on region objects that are technically not 3D objects.

You might be tempted to convert a mesh to a solid, edit it, and then turn it back into a mesh. Although this can be done, we don't recommend it. You'll find that your model becomes too unwieldy to work with.

---

## Stretching Faces

You now have the basis for the surfboard, though it might seem like an odd shape for a surfboard. Next you'll start to form the surfboard by manipulating the faces and edges of the mesh. Start by pulling two sides of the mesh to give it a shape more like a surfboard:

1. Use the ViewCube and Pan tools to adjust your view so it looks similar to Figure 23.5. This view will allow you to easily select and "pull" some of the faces that will become the front and back of the surfboard.

2. Click on the box and then right-click. From the shortcut menu, select Subobject Selection Filter ➢ Edge.

3. Notice the mesh lines. This will help you see where to place the selection window in the next step.

4. Hold down ⌃ and then click and drag a crossing selection window over the middle faces at the front edge of the box, as shown in Figure 23.5. The faces are highlighted, and you see the XYZ gizmo.

5. Place your cursor on the red X axis of the gizmo.

**FIGURE 23.5**
Hold down the ⌃ key and place a crossing selection window as shown here.

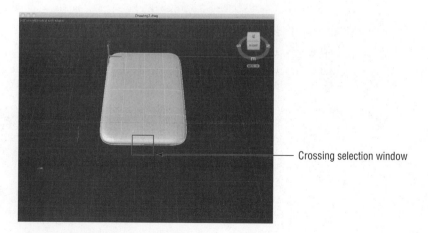

———— Crossing selection window

6. When the red axis extension line appears, click and drag the gizmo downward in the positive X direction. The mesh begins to elongate.

7. When your mesh looks similar to Figure 23.6, click your mouse button.

8. Press Esc twice to remove the faces from the current selection and remove the current selection filter.

**FIGURE 23.6**
Click and drag the gizmo when you see the red axis extension.

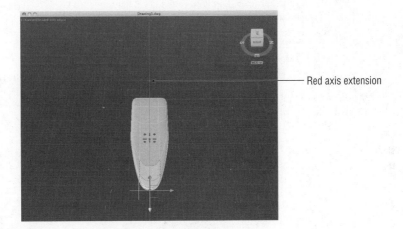

Red axis extension

The portion of the mesh you "pull" out will become the front. Next, do the same for the back of the surfboard:

1. Use the Pan tool to adjust your view so it looks similar to Figure 23.7. This view will allow you to easily select and "pull" some of the faces that will become the back of the surfboard.

2. Click on the box mesh to expose its mesh lines again.

**FIGURE 23.7**
Hold down ^ and place a crossing selection window as shown here.

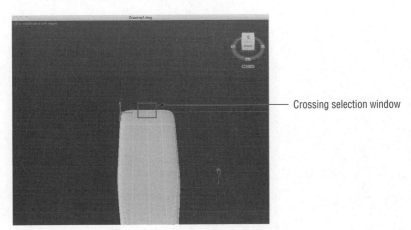

Crossing selection window

3. Hold down ^ and then place a crossing selection window over the middle faces at the back edge of the box as shown in Figure 23.7. The faces are highlighted, and you see the XYZ gizmo.

4. Place your cursor on the red X axis of the gizmo, and when the red axis extension line appears, click and drag the gizmo upward in the negative X direction.

5. When your mesh looks similar to Figure 23.8, click your mouse button.

6. Press Esc to remove the faces from the current selection.

7. Click the Home tool on upper-left side of the ViewCube to get a better view of your mesh so far (see Figure 23.9).

**FIGURE 23.8**
Adjust the mesh to look similar to this one.

**FIGURE 23.9**
The mesh so far

## Moving an Edge

The surfboard needs a sharper point at the front. Instead of moving the faces as you've already done, you can move an edge to give the front a more pointed shape. The next set of steps will show you how to do this:

1. Using the ViewCube, adjust your view so you have a close-up of the front tip of the surf-board, as shown in Figure 23.10.

2. Click on the mesh and then right-click. Choose Subobject Selection Filter ➢ Edge from the shortcut menu.

3. Hover over the front edge until you see the edge line, and then click the edge, as shown in Figure 23.10. The XYZ gizmo appears.

4. Hover over the X axis of the gizmo, and when the red extension line appears, click and drag the X axis downward along the positive X direction.

5. When it looks similar to Figure 23.11, click the mouse button.

**FIGURE 23.10**
Click the front-center edge shown here.

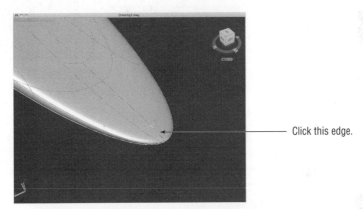

Click this edge.

**FIGURE 23.11**
Pull the front edge so that the mesh looks similar to this image.

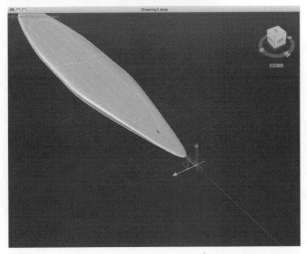

Next, give the front of the mesh a slight curve by adjusting the Z axis of the front edge:

1. Hover over the Z axis of the gizmo, and when the blue axis extension line appears, click and drag the Z axis downward in the negative Z direction.

2. When it looks similar to Figure 23.12, click the mouse button.

**FIGURE 23.12**
Move the front edge downward in the Z axis.

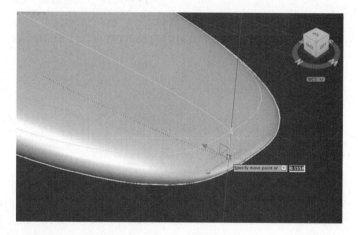

3. Press the Esc key to clear your edge selection.

4. Click the Home tool in the ViewCube to return to the home view.

I asked you to adjust the edge downward because you'll want to have a bottom view of your surfboard. This will enable you to add fins to the board without having to flip the mesh over.

---

**FINE-TUNE THE MESH**

You might notice that the surfboard has a slight trough down the middle after you move the front edge downward. You can remove that trough and add some additional curvature to the board by moving the two edges on the side of the mesh toward the front.

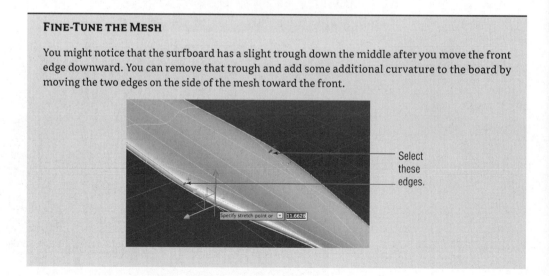

Select these edges.

You can click edges with the Edge subobject filter selected. Once you have these edges selected, use the blue Z axis on the gizmo to move them down to eliminate the trough.

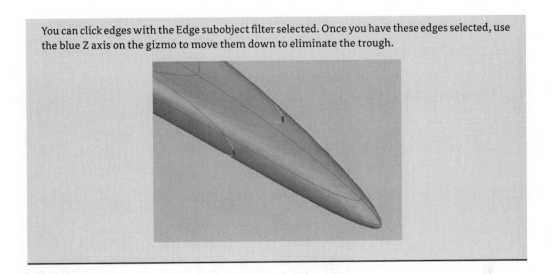

## Adding More Faces

The surfboard is still missing some fins. You could model some fins as separate meshes and then later join them to the surfboard. You can also use the MESHREFINE command to add more edges and then use those edges as the basis for your fins. The following exercise will show how this is done:

1. Adjust your view so it looks similar to Figure 23.13.

2. Click on the mesh and then right-click and select Face from the Subobject Selection Filter.

3. Click the faces shown in Figure 23.13.

**FIGURE 23.13**
Select the faces to refine.

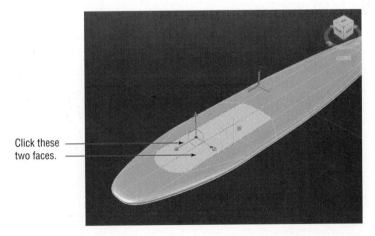

Click these two faces.

4. Right-click and select Refine Mesh from the shortcut menu. The selected faces will be subdivided into smaller faces and edges, as shown in Figure 23.14. (You can also type **MESHREFINE**.⏎.)

**FIGURE 23.14**
The refined faces

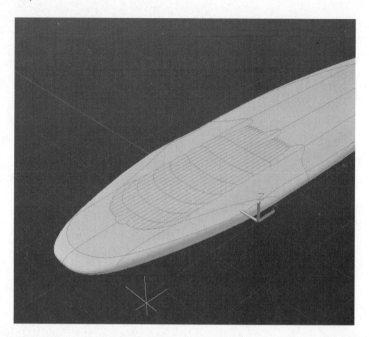

### UNDERSTANDING HOW REFINE MESH WORKS

You have some control over the number of faces that Refine Mesh creates through the level of smoothness applied to a mesh. If you reduce the smoothness of a mesh, the Refine Mesh tool will produce fewer faces. If you increase the smoothness, Refine Mesh will produce more faces—four more per facet, to be precise.

To understand how this works, you have to take a closer look at how the Smooth More tool works. Each time you apply the Smooth More tool to a mesh, every face of the mesh is divided into four facets. These facets aren't actually faces, but they divide a face in such a way as to simulate a rounded surface. The Refine Mesh tool further divides each of these facets into four faces. You can see this division clearly if you apply Refine Mesh to a face in a mesh that has only one level of smoothness applied.

The next step in creating the fins is to edit some of the newly created edges:

1. Zoom into the surfboard so your view looks similar to Figure 23.15.

2. Click on the mesh and then right-click and select Edge from the Subobject Selection Filter flyout.

3. Click the edges shown in Figure 23.15.

**FIGURE 23.15**
Select the edges for the fins.

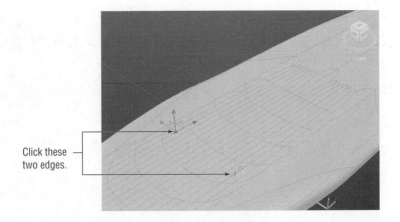

Click these two edges.

4. Hover over the Z axis on the gizmo so that the axis extension appears, and then click and drag the Z axis upward in the positive Z direction. If you run out of room at the top of the window, move the Z axis as far as you can with one click and drag, and then repeat the Z axis move.

5. Adjust the edges so they look similar to those in Figure 23.16, and then click the mouse button.

6. Adjust the X axis of the gizmo toward the back of the surfboard so the fins look similar to how they look in Figure 23.17.

**FIGURE 23.16**
Adjust the edges to create the fins.

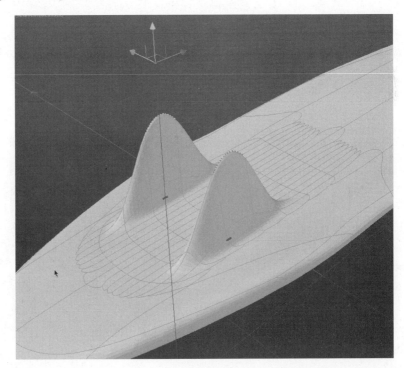

**FIGURE 23.17**
Adjust the fins toward the back of the surfboard.

7. Press the Esc key to clear your selection of mesh edges.

## Rotating an Edge

The fins still aren't quite the right shape. They are a bit too broad at the base. The next exercise shows you how to rotate an edge to further adjust the shape of the fins:

1. With the Edge subobject filter still selected, click the back edge of the fins as shown in Figure 23.18.

**FIGURE 23.18**
Click and drag the green circle on the Rotate gizmo.

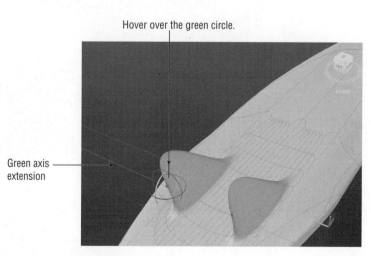

Hover over the green circle.

Green axis extension

**2.** Right-click over the gizmo, and choose Rotate (see Figure 23.19).

**FIGURE 23.19**
Select the Rotate
gizmo tool.

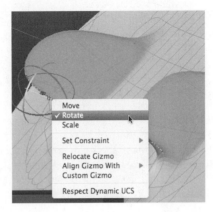

**3.** Hover over the green circle of the Rotate gizmo in the location shown in Figure 23.19 until you see the green axis extension, and then click and drag the mouse to rotate the edge. Adjust the rotation of the edge so that the fins look similar to those in Figure 23.20, and then release the mouse button.

**FIGURE 23.20**
The finished
surfboard

**4.** Press the Esc key to clear your selection.

**5.** Use the Home tool on the ViewCube to get an overall view of the surfboard (see Figure 23.20).

In this exercise, you switched from the Move gizmo to the Rotate gizmo. You can also use the Scale gizmo to scale a face or edge.

This may not be the most accurate rendition of a surfboard (our apologies if you are a surfer), but the general shape of the surfboard has given you a chance to explore many of the features of the Mesh toolset.

---

**CHANGING THE GIZMO ON-THE-FLY**

In addition to the right-click menu, you can change the current gizmo using the Gizmo drop-down list on the expanded status bar. You can also set the orientation of the gizmo through the Gizmo shortcut menu, which will allow you to move subobjects in directions other than perpendicular to the face or edge. You can orient the gizmo to the WCS, the current UCS, or a face on a mesh through the Align Gizmo With option on the shortcut menu (refer back to Figure 23.19).

---

## Adding a Crease

The Add Crease tool can help you fine-tune your mesh shapes. It does exactly what it says. It can introduce a crease in your otherwise smooth mesh shape. The Add Crease tool does this in two ways: It can flatten a face or remove the smoothing around an edge.

In the following exercises, you'll use the surfboard one more time to experiment with the Add Crease tool. First you'll see how you can add a sharp point to the surfboard:

1.  Adjust your view of the surfboard so you can see the front point, as shown in Figure 23.21. Turn off the grid so you can see the shape clearly.

**FIGURE 23.21**
Set up your view. Select the front edge of the surfboard.

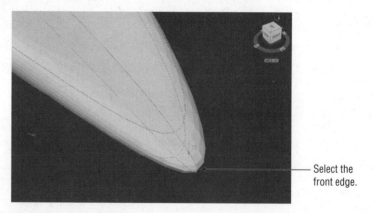

Select the front edge.

2.  Type **CREASE**↵ (or choose Modify ➢ Mesh Editing ➢ Crease from the menu bar). At the `Select mesh subobjects to crease:` prompt, select a face from the front as shown in Figure 23.21 and press Enter.

3.  At the `Specify crease value [Always]<Always>:` press Enter.

You can see from this exercise that the front edge of the surfboard is now quite sharp since it no longer has any smoothness, as shown in Figure 23.22.

**FIGURE 23.22**
The surfboard
after applying
Add Crease tool

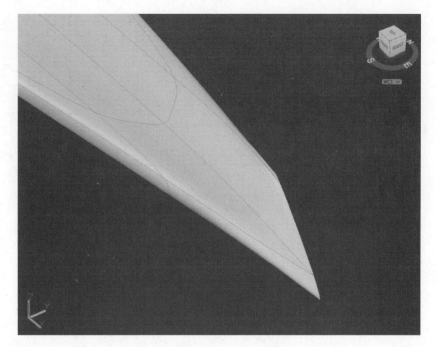

The surfboard is grossly deformed, but you can see how the side faces have now become flat and the edges of the face form a crease. You could use the Add Crease tool to sharpen the edge of the fins. This would also have the effect of making the fins thinner.

## Splitting and Extruding a Mesh Face

There are two more tools that can be a great aid in editing your meshes: Split Face and Extrude Face. The Split Face tool will split a face into two faces. The Extrude Face tool behaves like the Extrude Face tool you have seen for 3D solids. Both of these tools are a bit tricky to use, so they bear a closer look.

To use the Split Face tool, you first select a mesh face, then select two points, one on each side of the face. The following exercise shows how it works:

1. Open the `SplitMesh.dwg` sample file from the Chapter 23 folder, which can be obtained at `www.sybex.com/go/masteringautocadmac`. This file contains a simple mesh box that has been smoothed.

2. Type **MESHSPLIT**↵ (or choose Modify ➤ Mesh Editing ➤ Split Face from the menu bar).

3. Click the face shown in Figure 23.23.

4. Move the cursor to the left edge of the face until you see a knife icon appear next to the cursor.

5. Click roughly in the middle of the edge.

**FIGURE 23.23**
Select this face.

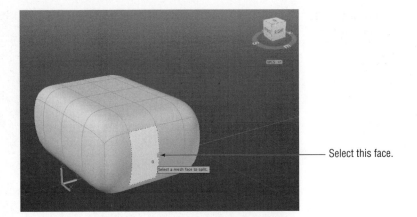

— Select this face.

**6.** Move the cursor along the right edge of the face. You'll see some temporary lines giving you a preview of the location of the split (see Figure 23.24).

**FIGURE 23.24**
Selecting the
points for the split

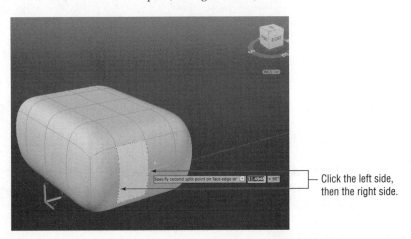

— Click the left side,
then the right side.

**7.** Move the cursor roughly in the middle of the right edge. The face changes temporarily to show you how it will look when it is divided into two faces.

**8.** Click the mouse button. The shape of the mesh changes to accommodate the new face.

As you can see, Split Face is not a precision tool, but if you don't like the location of the split, you can move the newly created edge using one of the gizmos.

Next, let's look at the Extrude Face tool. At first, you might think that the Extrude Face tool is redundant since you can use the Move gizmo to move a face in a direction away from the mesh, as you saw in an earlier exercise. Using the Extrude Face tool is different from moving a face because it isolates the movement to the selected face as much as possible. To see how this works, try the following:

**1.** Type **MESHEXTRUDE**↵ (or choose Modify ➤ Mesh Editing ➤ Extrude Face from the menu bar) and then click the face as indicated in Figure 23.25. Press ↵.

**FIGURE 23.25**
Select this face.

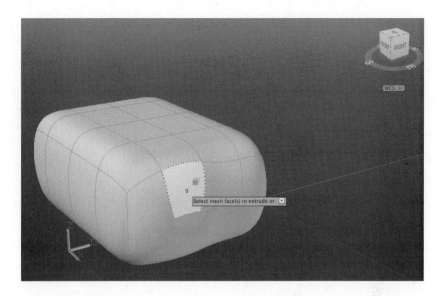

**2.** Click and drag the Z axis in the positive direction. When the mesh looks similar to Figure 23.26, click to finish the move. The smoothness of the side is maintained as you pull the face.

**FIGURE 23.26**
The moved and extruded face

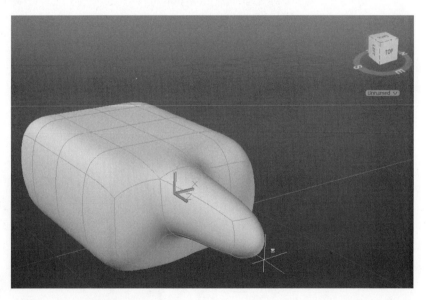

You can see from this example that the Extrude Face tool confines the deformation of the mesh to only the face you select. Note that you can select multiple faces for the extrusion.

🌐 **Real World Scenario**

**USING SPLIT MESH FACE AND ADD CREASE TOGETHER**

In a "usability study" conducted by Autodesk, the product designers gave an example of how to add a crease to the top surface of a computer mouse model. In that example, the Add Crease tool and the Split Face tool were used together. First, a new edge was created using the Split Face tool, and then the Add Crease tool was applied to the newly created edge to form the crease. Using these two tools together in this way, you can add a crease just about anywhere on a mesh.

## Creating Complex Meshes

So far, you've been working with mesh volumes, but the Mesh submenu on the Draw menu offers four tools that let you create a variety of complex meshes. These are the *revolved*, *edge*, *ruled*, and *tabulated surfaces*. They are the latest incarnation of some of the earliest 3D tools offered by AutoCAD, and they work exactly like the old features they replace. But just like the mesh volumes you've been working with, the mesh surfaces can be quickly smoothed, and their subobjects can be edited using the gizmos you learned about in this and earlier chapters. The following sections give a little more detail about these tools and how they are used.

The following instructions are for your reference only and you are not required to do them as exercises. But if you like, you can try them out on the `SurfaceMeshSamples.dwg` file provided with the sample drawings for this chapter located on the book's companion website.

### Revolved Mesh

To create a revolved mesh, you need a profile to revolve and a line that acts as an axis of revolution (see Figure 23.27). The profile can be any object, but a polyline or spline is usually used.

**FIGURE 23.27**
The Revolved Surface tool

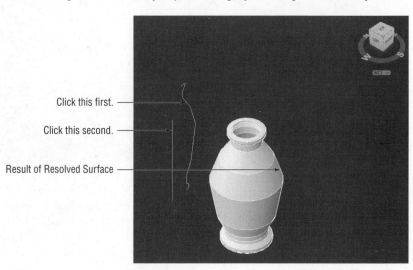

Click this first. ————

Click this second. ————

Result of Resolved Surface ————

To create a revolved mesh, follow these steps:

1. Type **REVSURF**↵.

2. At the `Select objects to revolve:` prompt, select the first object, as shown in Figure 23.27. This is known as the Profile. Then press ↵ and select the axis object.

3. At the `Specify object that defines the axis or revolution:` prompt, press ↵ and select the second object, as shown in Figure 23.27. This is known as the axis object.

4. At the `Specify start angle <0>:` prompt, enter the angle of rotation for the surface, or just press ↵ to accept the default angle of 360°. As you might infer from the prompt, you can create a revolved surface that is not completely closed.

---

### GETTING SMOOTHER SURFACES

The mesh surfaces will appear faceted when you first create them. Typically, the revolved, ruled, and tabulated surfaces will have 6 faces. The edge surface will have an array of 36 faces. You can increase the number of faces that are generated by these tools by changing the Surftab1 and Surftab2 settings. Surftab1 will increase the faces generated by the revolved, ruled, and tabulated surface tools. Surftab1 and Surftab2 can be used to increase the faces of an edge surface.

To use the Surftab settings, type **SURFTAB1**↵ or **SURFTAB2**↵ and enter a numeric value. The value you enter will be the number of faces generated by these surface mesh tools. Don't get carried away; an increase in the number of faces will also increase the size of your file. Besides, you can always use the Smooth More tool to smooth out the appearance of these surface objects.

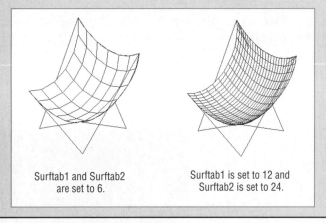

Surftab1 and Surftab2       Surftab1 is set to 12 and
    are set to 6.              Surftab2 is set to 24.

---

## Edge Mesh

In Chapter 22 you learned how to draw a butterfly chair that has the shape of a draped fabric seat. Before the newer 3D modeling tools were introduced, the Edge Surface tool (see Figure 23.28) was used in that butterfly chair example. This tool is a bit trickier to use only because the objects defining the surface must be selected in sequential order. In other words, you can't randomly select the objects.

**FIGURE 23.28**
Results of using the
Edge Surface tool

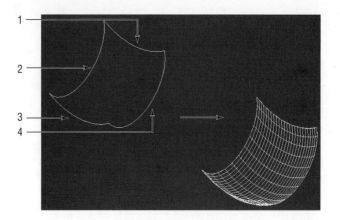

Here's how it works:

1. Type **EDGESURF↵**.

2. Select the four objects that are the edges of the surface you want to create. Make sure you select the objects in clockwise or counterclockwise order. Don't select them "crosswise."

## Ruled Mesh

The Ruled Mesh tool creates a surface mesh from two 2D objects such as lines, arc, polylines, or splines. This is perhaps the simplest mesh tool to use since you only have to click two objects to form a mesh (Figure 23.29). But like Edge Mesh, it has a tricky side. You'll want to click the same side of each object unless you want the surface to twist as shown in Figure 23.30.

To create a ruled mesh, take the following steps:

1. Type **RULESURF↵**.

2. Click two objects that are not on the same XY plane. The mesh is created between the objects.

**FIGURE 23.29**
The finished ruled
surface

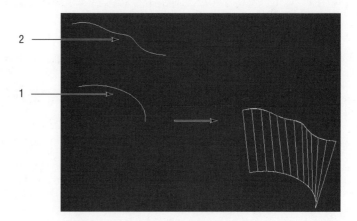

**FIGURE 23.30**
Where you click on objects affects the outcome.

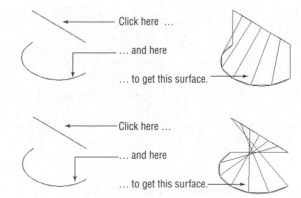

**Tabulated Mesh**

The Tabulated Mesh tool is like an extrude tool for surfaces (see Figure 23.31). Chapter 19, "Creating 3D Drawings," showed you how you can use the Extrude tool to create a 3D solid from a closed polygon. The Extrude tool will also work on open polygons, lines, and arcs, but it will extrude the object in only a perpendicular direction. The Tabulated Surface tool lets you "extrude" an object in a direction you control with a line. The line can point in any direction in space.

**FIGURE 23.31**
The Tabulated Surface

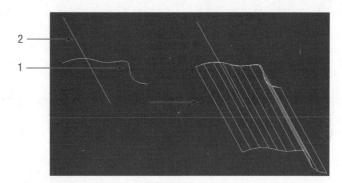

Here's how to use it:

**1.** Type **TABSURF↵**.

**2.** Select the object that defines the profile of your mesh.

**3.** Click the object that defines the direction for the surface.

As with the other surface mesh tools, the point at which you select objects will affect the way the object is generated. For the tabulated mesh, the direction of the mesh depends on where you click the line that defines the surface direction.

---

**CONVERTING MESHES TO SOLIDS**

I mentioned earlier that you can convert a mesh to a solid. In doing so, you can take advantage of the many solid-editing tools available in AutoCAD. The Boolean tools can be especially useful in editing meshes that have been turned into solids.

The conversion process is fairly simple using the tools in the right-click shortcut menu when you pick a mesh or type **CONVTOSOLID**↵ and then select the mesh or meshes you want to convert. Press ↵ to complete the process. The Convert To Surface tool (**CONVTOSURFACE**↵) works in much the same way, but it creates a surface object instead of a solid.

---

## Understanding 3D Surfaces

So far in this book, you've worked with 3D solids and meshes. A third type of 3D object, called a *surface*, completes AutoCAD's set of 3D modeling tools to make AutoCAD for Mac a complete 3D modeling application in its own right.

When you click the Tool Sets button on the Tool Sets palette and choose Modeling, you'll see the tools you'll need to work with surface modeling. You can also see more of them via Draw ➢ 3D Modeling ➢ Surfaces and Modify ➢ Surface Editing on the menu bar.

You can see quite a few tools that we haven't covered so far. These surface creation tools work in the same way the mesh tools work. In fact, they are the essentially the same tools. They just use a different command option to create a surface instead of a solid. The big difference is that to create a solid, you need to start with a closed polyline. With the surface version of the Loft, Sweep, Extrude, and Revolve tools, you can start with an open spline, polyline, or other object. And even if you do use a closed object, such as a circle or closed polyline, you will still get a 3D surface instead of a solid (see Figure 23.32).

**FIGURE 23.32**
A circle extruded using the solid Extrude and the surface Extrude

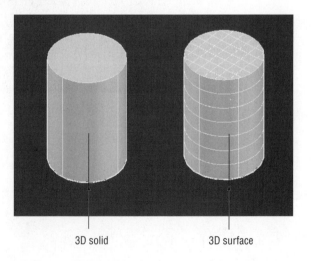

3D solid          3D surface

Two additional surface creation tools are the Surface Network and Planar Surface tools. Here's a brief description of each:

**Surface Network tool**   The Surface Network tool (Figure 23.33) lets you create a surface from several curves.

**FIGURE 23.33**
Creating a surface
with the Surface
Network tool

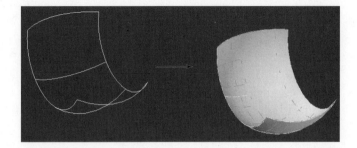

**Planar Surface tool**   With the Planar Surface tool, you can create a flat surface either by selecting two points to indicate a rectangular surface or by selecting a closed 2D object to create a flat surface with an irregular boundary, as shown in Figure 23.34.

**FIGURE 23.34**
Creating a planar
surface

Click the Planar Surface tool and click a point, and then click
and drag for the second point to create a rectangular surface.

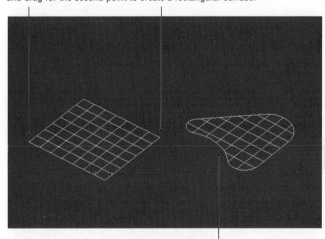

Click the Planar Surface tool and press ↵, and then
select a closed 2D shape such as a circle or a polyline.

## Editing Surfaces

Surface objects have a unique set of editing tools that allow you to create fairly detailed models. Some tools, like Surface Fillet and Surface Trim (see Figure 23.35), offer the same function as their 2D drawing counterparts. The following list includes a description of each tool. They are discussed in more detail later in this section.

**Surface Extrude**   The Surface Extrude tool will allow you to take a 2D object and turn it into a 3D object.

**Surface Trim**   The Surface Trim tool lets you trim one or several surfaces to other surfaces. You can also type **SURFTRIM**.

**Surface Untrim**   Surface Untrim does exactly what it says. It reverses a trim operation. You can also type **SURFUNTRIM**.

**Surface Fillet**   With the Surface Fillet tool, you can join one surface to another with an intermediate rounded surface (see Figure 23.35).

**Offset**   Surface Offset, like the Surface Trim tool, mimics its 2D counterpart. It will create a new surface that is parallel to the original. When you start the Surface Offset tool from the Surfaces – Create tool group and select a surface, you'll see arrows indicating the direction of the offset. You can type **F↵** to flip the direction of the offset. Enter a distance for the offset and press ↵ to create the offset surface (see Figure 23.36). You can also type **SURFOFFSET**.

**FIGURE 23.35**
Using the Surface Fillet and Surface Trim tools

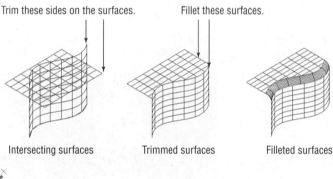

Trim these sides on the surfaces.   Fillet these surfaces.

Intersecting surfaces     Trimmed surfaces     Filleted surfaces

**FIGURE 23.36**
Using the Surface Offset tool

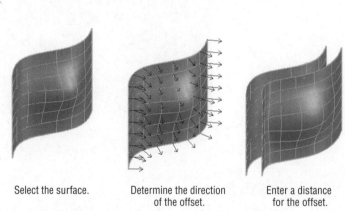

Select the surface.     Determine the direction of the offset.     Enter a distance for the offset.

**Blend**   Surface Blend will connect two surfaces with an intermediate surface. You can also type **SURFBLEND**.

**Patch**    Surface Patch will close an open surface like the end of a tube. Surface Patch also lets you control whether the closing "patch" is flat or curved, as shown in Figure 23.37. You can also type **SURFPATCH**.

There are two other surface editing tools to make mention of. They are Surface Extend and Surface Sculpt. Although I won't go into great detail, they are shown for your reference. The following includes a description of each tool:

**Surface Extend**    The Surface Extend tool simply enables you to extend the edge of a surface beyond its current location. Unlike its 2D equivalent, it does not extend a surface to another surface object, though you could extend beyond a surface and then use the Surface Trim tool. You can also type **SURFEXTEND**.

**Surface Sculpt**    The Surface Sculpt tool is like a super trim. You can align several surfaces to completely enclose a volume (left image in Figure 23.38), then use the Surface Sculpt tool to trim all of the surfaces at once into a completely closed 3D shape (right image in Figure 23.38). By default, the new object is a solid.

**FIGURE 23.37**
The Surface Patch tool can create a flat or rounded patch over a open surface.

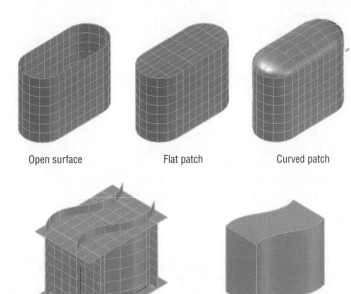

Open surface          Flat patch          Curved patch

**FIGURE 23.38**
The Surface Sculpt tool creates a container-like shape from several surfaces.

## Using Extrude, Surface Trim, Surface Untrim, and Fillet

Now that you have an overview of the basic surface modeling tools, try the following set of exercises to see firsthand how they work.

## USING THE EXTRUDE TOOL

Start with the Extrude tool on two basic shapes:

1. Open the Surfaces1.dwg file, which can be obtained at www.sybex.com/go/masteringautocadmac. Note that the visual style shown on the Viewport Controls is set to 2D Wireframe.

2. Choose Extrude from the Surfaces – Create tool group on the Tool Sets palette.

3. At the Select objects to extrude or [MOde]: prompt, type **MO↵ SU↵**. This will create an extruded surface.

3. Click the circle in the drawing, and then press ↵. A surface appears and its length changes as you move the cursor.

4. Adjust the surface height to 5 units so it looks similar to Figure 23.39.

5. Click Extrude again and extrude the arc horizontally 5 units so it looks similar to the extrusion in Figure 23.39.

**FIGURE 23.39**
Extrude the circle and arc (left image) 5 units to look like the image on the right.

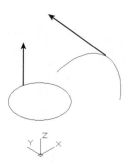 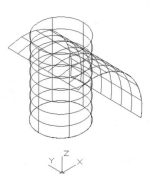

## USING THE SURFACE TRIM AND SURFACE UNTRIM TOOLS

The Surface Trim tool is similar to the 2D Trim tool except there is the additional step at the beginning where you have to select the object you intend to trim. Let's try it:

1. Click Surface Trim from the Surfaces – Edit tool group on the Tool Sets palette.

2. Click both the cylinder and the extruded arc surface, and then press ↵. This first step selects the objects to trim.

3. Click both objects again and then press ↵. This time you're selecting the objects to trim to. You want to trim the top of the cylinder to the arc and the arc to the cylinder.

4. Finally, click the cylinder near the top edge to indicate what part you want to trim. Also click the extruded arc surface anywhere outside of the cylinder. Your surfaces should look like the right image in Figure 23.40.

**FIGURE 23.40**
Trimming the surfaces

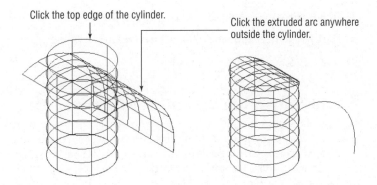

Click the top edge of the cylinder.

Click the extruded arc anywhere outside the cylinder.

The Surface Untrim tool will revert your trimmed object back to its original shape. To do this, follow these steps:

1. Click the Surface Untrim tool from the Surfaces – Edit tool group on the Tool Sets palette.

2. Click the top edge of the cylinder and press ↵. The arc is back to its original extruded shape.

Go ahead and perform the Surface Trim operation on the arc again. You'll need this shape for the next exercise.

Notice that the original arc you used to extrude the arc surface is still there. You'll use that a little later in this chapter.

### USING THE SURFACE FILLET TOOL

Now try out the Surface Fillet tool:

1. Click the Surface Fillet tool from the Surfaces – Edit tool group on the Tool Sets palette.

2. Click the top surface as it is shown inside the cylinder and then click the cylinder. The two surfaces are filleted, as shown in Figure 23.41.

**FIGURE 23.41**
Using the Surface Fillet tool

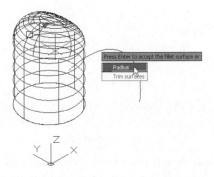

Press Enter to accept the fillet surface or
Radius
Trim surfaces

3. The prompt Press Enter to accept the fillet surface or [Radius/Trim surface]: appears. Type **R**↵ to enter a different radius.

4. Type **0.5**↵. The radius changes. You still have the opportunity to change the radius again.

5. Type **R**↵ and then type **0.2**↵. The radius changes again.

6. Press ↵ to finish the fillet.

## Using Surface Offset, Surface Blend, and Surface Patch

As mentioned earlier, a few of the tools on the Tool Sets palette are a bit like editing tools. Surface Offset, Surface Blend, and Surface Patch create new surfaces that use existing surfaces as their basis. Surface Offset creates a new surface that is parallel to an existing one and is similar to the 2D Offset command. Surface Blend is a bit like the Surface Fillet tool in that it will join two surfaces with an intermediate surface. Surface Patch will create a surface that closes an open-ended surface.

To get a better idea of how these three tools work, try the following set of exercises.

### USING THE SURFACE OFFSET TOOL

Start by creating a parallel copy of an existing surface using the Surface Offset tool:

1. Open the Patch1.dwg sample file which can be obtained from the Chapter 23 sample folder on the book's companion website.

2. Click the Surface Offset tool from the Surfaces – Create tool group on Tool Sets palette.

3. Click the surface in the drawing and then press ↵. You see a set of arrows appear as shown in the left image of Figure 23.42.

**FIGURE 23.42**
Using the Surface
Offset tool

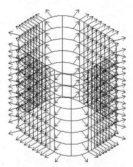 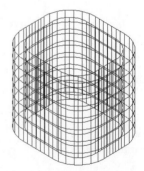

4. Type **F**↵. The arrows now point in the opposite direction.

5. Type **F**↵ again to return the arrows to their previous direction, facing outward.

6. Enter **0.5**↵ for the offset distance. The offset surface appears around the original surface as shown in the right image of Figure 23.42.

The arrows play an important role in helping you visualize the result of your offset, so instead of picking a direction, you adjust the direction of the arrows.

### USING THE SURFACE BLEND TOOL

Now try the Surface Blend tool:

1. Use the Move command to move the outer surface vertically in the Z axis roughly 5 units. Remember that you can hold down the ⇧ key to restrain the cursor to the Z axis. If you see the Surface Associativity message, click Continue. You'll learn more about associativity later in this chapter.

2. Adjust your view so you can see both surfaces, and then click the Surface Blend tool from the Surfaces – Create tool group on the Tool Sets palette.

3. Select the eight edges along the top of the lower surface as shown in Figure 23.43. When you're sure you've selected all of the edges, press ↵.

4. Select the eight edges along the bottom of the upper surface as shown in Figure 23.43. When you're sure you've selected all of the edges, press ↵. A new, preview surface appears that joins the upper and lower surfaces.

**FIGURE 23.43**
Selecting the edges
for the Surface
Blend tool

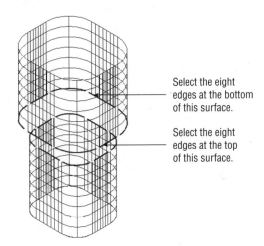

Select the eight edges at the bottom of this surface.

Select the eight edges at the top of this surface.

In steps 3 and 4, if you cannot pick more than one edge at a time, make sure you have the system variable PICKADD set to 1.

5. You might notice a couple of grip arrowheads that appear along the top and bottom edge of the new blend surface. Click one of them and a menu appears offering three options: Position, Tangent, and Curvature (Figure 23.44).

6. Click Curvature on one of the grips.

7. Click Curvature on the other grip to blend the surface.

The Surface Blend tool offers a number of options that control the shape of the blend surface. You saw three options available from the grip arrowhead. The options are available even after you have placed the surface. You can click on the surface to expose the grip arrowheads.

In addition, the Surface Blend tool offers two command options: CONtinuity and Bulge magnitude. Table 23.1 describes these features and their functions.

**FIGURE 23.44**
Using the grip arrowhead to adjust the blend surface

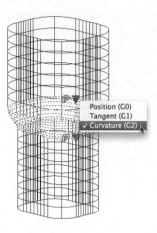

### USING THE SURFACE PATCH TOOL

Now let's take a look at the Surface Patch tool. The Surface Patch tool lets you close the end of a surface with another surface. You can add a flat or curved surface as you'll see in the next exercise. Try adding a patch surface to the top of the upper surface in the `Patch1.dwg` model:

1. Pan your view so you can clearly see the top of the surface model as shown in the left image in Figure 23.45.

2. Click the Surface Patch tool from the Surfaces – Create tool group on the Tool Sets palette.

3. Select the eight edges of the surface as shown in Figure 23.45.

4. Press ↵ when you are sure you've selected all of the edges. The patch surface appears.

5. Click the grip arrowhead that appears along the edge of the patch and select Tangent. The surface is now curved.

**FIGURE 23.45**
Adding the patch surface to the end of the model

Select the top edges

6. Press ↵ to finish the patch surface.

7. To get a better view of the surface, select the Shaded With Edges option from the Visual Styles menu in the Viewport Controls.

You may have noticed that the grip arrowhead options in step 5 were similar to the grip options you saw for the Surface Blend tool. The Surface Patch tool offers an additional command option called CONStrain geometry. Table 23.1 describes these options.

**TABLE 23.1:**      The Surface Blend and Surface Patch options

| OPTION | FUNCTION |
| --- | --- |
| (G0) Position | Causes the surface to connect without any blending curvature. |
| (G1) Tangent | Causes the surface to blend with direction. |
| (G2) Curvature | Causes the surface to blend with direction and similar curvature or rate of change in surface direction. |
| CONtinuity | Controls how smoothly the surfaces flow into each other. |
| Bulge magnitude | Allows you to adjust the amount of bulge or curvature in the blend surface. Values can be between 0 and 1. |
| CONStrain geometry (Surfpatch command) | Offers additional guide curves to control the patch surface. |

## Understanding Associativity

Surface Associativity is a feature that is on by default, and its function is similar to the Associative feature of hatches (see Chapter 7, "Mastering Viewing Tools, Hatches, and External References," for more on hatches). You may recall that when you create a 2D hatch pattern with the hatch Associative feature turned on, the hatch's shape will conform to any changes made to the boundary used to enclose the hatch pattern.

Surface Associativity in surface modeling works in a similar way, only instead of a hatch pattern conforming to changes in a boundary, the surface conforms to changes in the shapes that are used to create them. For example, if you were to make changes to the arc that you used to extrude the arc surface, the arc surface and the trimmed cylinder would also follow the changes.

### USING ASSOCIATIVITY TO EDIT A SURFACE MODEL

Rather than try to explain any further, let's try it out so you can see firsthand how associativity works:

1. Return to the Surfaces1.dwg file and click the arc to expose its grips.

2. Click the square grip at the arc's left endpoint and drag it downward along the Z axis. When it is roughly in the position shown in Figure 23.46, click again to fix the grip's location. The shape of the surface model changes to conform to the new shape of the arc.

**FIGURE 23.46**
Adjusting the
shape of the arc

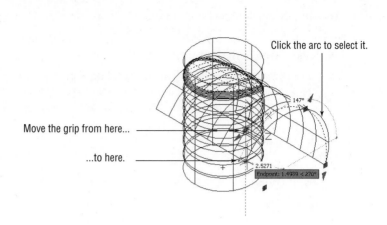

Click the arc to select it.

Move the grip from here...

...to here.

3. Zoom into the top of the surface model so you have a view similar to Figure 23.47.

**FIGURE 23.47**
Adjusting the fillet
radius

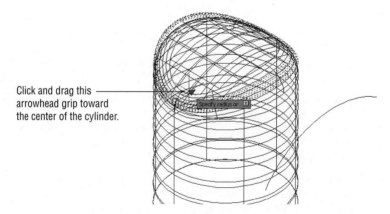

Click and drag this
arrowhead grip toward
the center of the cylinder.

4. Click the filleted portion of the surface. An arrowhead grip appears.

5. Click the arrowhead grip. Another arrowhead grip appears.

6. Click this arrowhead grip and slowly drag it toward the center of the cylinder.
   Notice that the radius of the fillet changes as you move the grip.

7. Click to fix the fillet radius to its new size.

8. Press the Esc key to clear your selection.

### USING ARROWHEAD GRIPS TO EDIT A SURFACE

You've just seen the Surface Associativity feature in action. You can also change the shape of
the circle used to extrude the cylinder to modify the surface model's diameter. There are additional hidden grips that allow you to adjust the shape of the surfaces directly. For example, you

can modify the taper of the cylinder using an arrowhead grip that you can turn on through the Properties Inspector palette, as shown in these steps:

1. Click the cylindrical part of the surface model.

2. In the Properties Inspector palette, scroll down to the bottom until you get to the Surface Associativity category. Make sure All is selected in the Properties Inspector palette before you can see the Surface Associativity category.

3. Click the check box next to Show Associativity. You now see the circle at the base of the cylinder in a bold outline.

4. At the top of the cylinder, click and drag the right-pointing arrowhead grip to the right. As you do this, you see the dynamic display showing you an angle (see the left image in Figure 23.48).

5. Position the arrowhead grip so that the angle shows 6°, and then click to fix the grip in place. The cylinder is now tapered and the top surface conforms to the new shape, as shown in the right image in Figure 23.48.

**FIGURE 23.48**
Changing the taper
of the cylinder

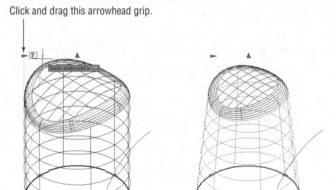

Click and drag this arrowhead grip.

Surface Associativity can be very useful, but in order to take full advantage of this feature, you will want to plan your model construction carefully. In addition, Surface Associativity can limit some editing and creation functions. For example, the Surface Fillet tool may not work on a complex surface model with associativity turned on but will when the associativity is turned off for the objects involved.

### TURNING OFF OR REMOVING ASSOCIATIVITY

You can turn off or remove associativity for an object through the Properties Inspector palette. Select the object, and then in the Properties Inspector palette, scroll down to the Surface Associativity category (see Figure 23.49). This category offers two options: Maintain Associativity and Show Associativity. The Maintain Associativity option offers Yes, Remove, and None options.

**FIGURE 23.49**
The Surface Associativity panel in the Properties Inspector palette

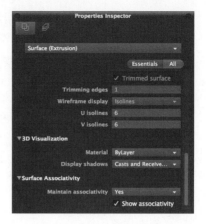

You can select Remove to remove associativity altogether or select None to limit the associativity to the set of objects currently associated with the surface model. Once you change this setting, you can't return to a previous setting except with an Undo.

---

### CONSTRAINTS, SURFACES, AND ASSOCIATIVITY

In Chapter 16, "Making "Smart" Drawings with Parametric Tools," you learned that you can add constraints to objects to control their behavior. With Surface Associativity turned on, you can extrude constrained objects and the resulting surface will also follow the constraints of the source 2D objects. But remember that if you use constraints with 3D surfaces in this way, you need to carefully plan the way you build your model to make efficient use of constraints.

---

## Editing with Control Vertices

So far you've been creating *procedural surfaces*, which are surfaces that allow you to take advantage of associativity. AutoCAD also allows you to create *NURBS surfaces*. You may recall that splines are also NURBS, so you might think of a NURBS surface as a kind of 3D surface spline. Splines allow you to move, add, or subtract control vertices, or CVs, and you can control the way the CVs "pull" on the curve of the spline. Likewise, NURBS surfaces allow you to add or remove CVs and adjust the direction and force of the CVs.

There are two ways to create a NURBS surface. You can turn on the NURBS Creation option by typing **SURFACEMODELINGMODE↵ 1↵** and then go about creating your 3D surfaces. Any 3D surface you create with this option turned on will be a NURBS surface.

### CONVERTING A SURFACE TO A NURBS SURFACE

You can convert an existing surface to a NURBS surface by typing **CONVTONURBS↵**. This tool also converts 3D solids and meshes. To use it, follow these steps:

1. Open the CVedit1.dwg sample file, which can be obtained from the book's companion website.

2. Make sure the NURBS option is on by typing **SURFACEMODELINGMODE↵ 1↵**.

3. Click the Extrude tool from the Surfaces – Create tool group on the Tool Sets palette.

4. Type **MO↵ SU↵** to create an extruded surface.

5. Select the spline and press ↵.

6. Point the cursor upward and type **6↵** to make the extruded surface 6 units in the Z axis.

7. Select the NURBS surface.

8. In the Surface Associativity category in the Properties Inspector palette, select Maintain Associativity and None.

### Exposing CVs to Edit a NURBS Surface

You've just created a NURBS surface. You can expose the CVs for the surface using the Show CV tool. Try the following to view and edit the CVs.

1. Select the NURBS surface.

2. In the Geometry category in the Properties Inspector palette, click the CV Hull check box. The CVs appear for the surface.

3. Click the CV as shown in Figure 23.50.

**FIGURE 23.50**
Exposing the CVs

Click and drag this CV along the Y axis.

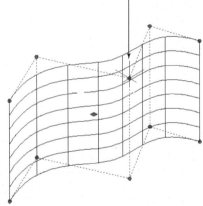

4. Move the CV in the Y axis and notice how the surface deforms. The top edge moves with the CV, while the bottom edge maintains its shape.

5. Press the Esc key twice to clear your selection.

In this exercise, you saw how you can gain access to the CVs of a NURBS surface to make changes to the shape. Right now, the CVs are located only at the top and bottom of the surface, but you can add more CVs to give you more control over the shape of the surface.

### Adding CVs to a NURBS Surface

The next exercise shows you how you can add additional CVs through the Rebuild option:

1. Click the surface to select it and then right-click and select NURBS Editing ➤ Rebuild. The Rebuild Surface dialog box appears (see Figure 23.51). You can also type **CVREBUILD**↵ or choose Modify ➤ Surface Editing ➤ NURBS Surface Editing➤ Rebuild.

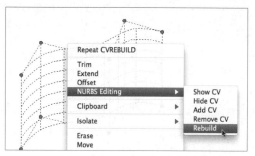

**FIGURE 23.51**
The Rebuild Surface dialog box

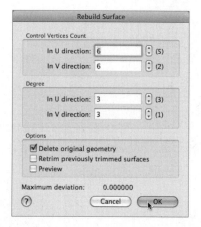

2. In the Control Vertices Count group of the Rebuild Surface dialog box, make sure the In U Direction option is set to 8 and the In V Direction option is set to 7.

   The U direction is along the horizontal curve, while the V direction is along the straight, vertical curve. If you count the CVs in each row or column, you'll see that they match the values you entered for U and V.

3. Click OK. Now you see that many more CVs are available.

Now if you were to move a CV, the surface is able to deform along the Z axis, where it remained a straight line before.

**WHAT ARE THE U AND V DIRECTIONS?**

While working in 3D, you'll see references to the U and V directions. You can think of these as the X and Y axes of a 3D surface. There is also a W direction, which corresponds to the Z axis, or the normal direction to a surface.

The Rebuild Surface dialog box offers a number of other options you'll want to know about. Table 23.2 gives you a rundown.

**TABLE 23.2:** The Rebuild Surfaces dialog box options

| OPTION | PURPOSE |
| --- | --- |
| **CONTROL VERTICES COUNT** | |
| In U Direction | Sets the number of CVs in the U direction |
| In V Direction | Sets the number of CVs in the V direction |
| **Degree** | |
| In U Direction | Sets the number of CVs available per span in the U direction |
| In V Direction | Sets the number of CVs available per span in the V direction |
| **Options** | |
| Delete Original Geometry | Determines whether the original geometry is retained or not |
| Retrim Previously Trimmed Surfaces | Determines whether trimmed surfaces are retained from the original surface |
| **Maximum Deviation** | Displays the maximum deviation between the original and rebuilt surface |

Two other tools in the NURBS Editing shortcut menu allow you to either add or remove a set of CVs. The Add CV tool lets you place a row or column of CVs. The Remove CV tool will remove a row or column of CVs. Both options allow you to toggle between the U and V directions for the addition or removal by typing **D**↵.

The Add CV and Remove CV tools can be useful when you want to fine-tune the curvature of a surface. Where you want a "tighter" curve, you can add more CVs to an area of the surface. You can then move the CVs in the selected area to increase the curvature. To smooth out the curvature of an area, remove the CVs.

## Editing with the 3D Edit Bar

You've seen how a NURBS surface can be set up to add additional CVs, which in turn allow you to adjust the shape of the surface. But the CVs by themselves allow you to adjust their pull on the surface only by moving the CVs closer to or farther away from the surface.

The 3D Edit bar gives you more control over the behavior of individual CVs. With the 3D Edit bar, you can change the strength and direction of the "pull" exerted by a CV.

Try the following exercise to see firsthand how the 3D Edit bar works:

1. Type **3DEDITBAR**↵.

2. Select the NURBS surface. Now as you move the cursor across the surface, you see two red lines that follow the U and V directions of the surface (see Figure 23.52).

**FIGURE 23.52**
The 3D Edit bar's U and V directions are shown by two red lines.

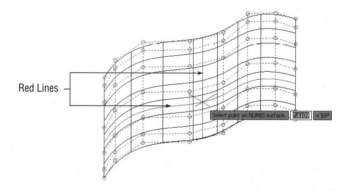

Red Lines

3. Click the point shown in Figure 23.52. A Move gizmo appears along with two other features called the magnitude handle and the expansion grip (see Figure 23.53).

**FIGURE 23.53**
The magnitude handle and expansion grip

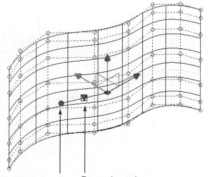

Magnitude handle    Expansion grip

The Move gizmo gives you a bit more control over the location of the CV since it allows you to isolate movement in the X, Y, or Z direction. The expansion grip lets you change the tangency of the CV, while the magnitude grip lets you control the strength of the CV.

Try the following steps to see how these two features work:

1. Click the expansion grip. Notice that the Move gizmo switches to the location of the expansion grip.

2. Hover over the green Y axis of the gizmo, and when you see the green Y axis vector, click and drag the mouse. Notice how the surface warps as you move the mouse. If you look carefully at the 3D Edit bar, you see that it pivots around the new location of the expansion grip, the CV location.

3. Press the Esc key to release the Y axis, and then click the expansion grip. The Move gizmo returns to its original location at the CV.

4. Now click the magnitude handle and move it horizontally. You see that the surface is "pulled" in both directions of the U axis of the surface.

5. Press the Esc key to release the magnitude handle.

6. Right-click on the 3D Edit bar and select V Tangent Direction. Notice that the magnitude handle changes its orientation so that it is aligned to the V direction of the surface.

7. Click and drag the magnitude handle to see how it affects the surface.

8. Press the Esc key twice to exit the 3D Edit bar.

As you can see from this exercise, the 3D Edit bar gives you much more control over a CV than you would have otherwise. You also saw the shortcut menu for the 3D Edit bar (see Figure 23.54) in step 6. The shortcut menu allows you to change the direction of the magnitude grip, but it also lets you switch the position of the Move gizmo and the expansion grip with the Move Point Location and Move Tangent Direction options. The Relocate Base Point option enables you to move to a different CV location. Table 23.3 includes descriptions of these options.

**FIGURE 23.54**
The 3D Edit bar's
shortcut menu

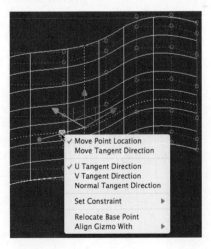

**TABLE 23.3:**     The 3D Edit bar's right-click menu options

| OPTION | PURPOSE |
| --- | --- |
| Move Point Location | Places the Move gizmo at the CV location |
| Move Tangent Direction | Places the Move gizmo at the expansion grip location to allow adjustment to the tangent direction of the CV |
| U Tangent Direction | Aligns the magnitude grip to the surface's U direction |
| V Tangent Direction | Aligns the magnitude grip to the surface's V direction |
| Normal Tangent Direction | Aligns the magnitude grip to a direction that is normal (perpendicular) to the surface |
| Set Constraint | Constrains changes to the tangency in a specific direction such as X, Y, or Z or in a plane defined by a pair of axes |
| Relocate Base Point | Moves the CV Edit bar to a different location on the surface |
| Align Gizmo With | Aligns the gizmo with the world or current UCS or with a face on the surface |

**USING THE 3D OBJECT SNAPS**

You may have noticed the 3D Object Snap button in the status bar when it is expanded.

This tool works in a way that is similar to how the Object Snap button you've used in earlier chapters works. When the 3D Object Snap button is on, you can snap to geometry on 3D objects. If you right-click this button, you'll see the list of locations you can snap to.

You can think of the 3D Object Snap button as an extension of the standard set of object snaps that allow you to pick locations on 3D solids, meshes, and surfaces. Right-click on the 3D Object Snap button and choose Settings and you will see the Drafting Settings dialog box open to the 3D Object Snap tab. There you can choose which 3D object snap you want to appear as the default when this tool is turned on.

### Making Holes in a Surface with the Project Geometry Tool

Eventually, you'll need to place an opening in a surface, so AutoCAD offers the Project Geometry tool. This tool allows you to project a closed 2D object's shape onto a 3D surface. For example, if you want to place a circular hole in the surface you edited in the previous exercise, you would draw a circle parallel to that surface and then use the Surface Projection UCS tool.

Try the following exercise to see how the Project Geometry tool works:

1. From the Layers palette, turn on the Circle layer. A circle appears in the drawing.

2. Type **UCS↵** and then type **OB↵**. This lets you align the UCS to an object.

3. Click the circle to align the UCS to the circle.

4. Type **SURFACEAUTOTRIM↵ 1↵** to turn Autotrim on.

5. Type **PROJECTGEOMETRY↵ PRO↵ U↵**.

6. Click the circle and press ↵.

7. Click the surface. The circle is projected onto the surface and the area inside the projected circle is trimmed (Figure 23.55).

**FIGURE 23.55**
The circle projected onto the surface

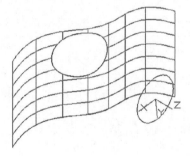

In this exercise, you aligned the UCS to the circle. The Project Geometry tool you used in step 5 projected the circle in the Z axis of this new UCS that is aligned with the circle.

The other two Project Geometry options use different criteria to project geometry. The View option will project geometry along the line of sight. If you had used this tool in the previous exercise, the projected circle and opening would appear directly behind the circle from your current view. The Points (or Vector) option projects geometry along a vector that you indicate with two points. You can use the 3D object snaps to select points on the geometry and the surface.

## Visualizing Curvature: Understanding the Surface Analysis Tools

In addition to the surface editing tools, AutoCAD offers several surface analysis options. These options offer some visual aids to help you see the curvature of your surface's models more clearly. They can be found under the Analysis tool group on the Tool Sets palette and are called Zebra Analysis, Draft Analysis, and Curvature Analysis.

Zebra Analysis displays stripes that allow you to better visualize how the curvature of surfaces blend. The smoother the stripes, the better the transition between surfaces.

Curvature Analysis displays colors to indicate the direction and amount of curvature in a surface. A negative curvature is a saddle shape and displays a blue color. A positive curvature, or bowl shape, displays in red.

Draft Analysis displays colors to help you determine draft angles. Draft angles are often used in the design of objects that are to be cast from a mold and are important in allowing the cast object to be easily removed from the mold.

The Analysis Options tool opens the Analysis Options dialog box, which enables you to control the way the different analysis tools are displayed. You must use a visual style other than Wireframe.

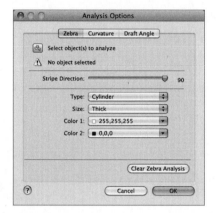

## The Bottom Line

**Create a simple 3D mesh.**   Mesh modeling allows you to create more organic 3D forms by giving you unique smoothing and editing tools. You can start your mesh model by creating a basic shape using the mesh primitives.

> **Master It**   Name at least six mesh primitives available on the Primitives submenu under Draw ➢ 3D Modeling ➢ Meshes on the menu bar.

**Edit faces and edges.**   The ability to edit faces and edges is essential to creating complex shapes with mesh objects.

> **Master It**   Name the tool that is used to divide a face into multiple faces.

**Create mesh surfaces.**   The Mesh primitives let you create shapes that enclose a volume. If you just want to model a smooth, curved surface in 3D, you might find the surface mesh tools helpful.

> **Master It**   How many objects are needed to use the Edge Surface tool?

**Convert meshes to solids.** You can convert a mesh into a 3D solid to take advantage of many of the solid-editing tools available in AutoCAD.

**Master It** Name at least two tools you can use on a solid that you cannot use on a mesh.

**Understand 3D surfaces.** 3D surfaces can be created using some of the same tools you use to create 3D solids.

**Master It** Name at least two tools you can use to create both 3D solids and 3D surfaces.

**Edit 3D surfaces.** AutoCAD offers a wide range of tools that are unique to 3D surfaces.

**Master It** Name at least four tools devoted to CV editing.

# Appendix A

# The Bottom Line

Each of The Bottom Line sections in the chapters suggest exercises to deepen skills and understanding. Sometimes there is only one possible solution, but often you are encouraged to use your skills and creativity to create something that builds on what you know and lets you explore one of many possible solutions.

## Chapter 1: Exploring the AutoCAD Interface

**Use the AutoCAD application.**    AutoCAD is a typical Windows graphics program that makes use of the menu bar and tools. If you've used other graphics programs, you'll see at least a few familiar tools.

**Master It**   Name the components of the AutoCAD application you can use to select a function.

**Solution**   AutoCAD offers the menu bar, the Tool Sets palette, and the status bar.

**Get a closer look with the Zoom command.**   The Zoom command is a common tool in graphics programs. It enables you to get a closer look at a part of your drawing or to expand your view to see the big picture.

**Master It**   Name at least two ways of zooming into a view.

**Solution**   Choose options from the Zoom tool from the status bar or right-click and click Zoom from the shortcut menu.

**Save a file as you work.**   Nothing is more frustrating than having a power failure cause you to lose hours of work. It's a good idea to save your work frequently. AutoCAD offers an Automatic Save feature that can be a lifesaver if you happen to forget to save your files.

**Master It**   How often does the AutoCAD Automatic Save feature save your drawing?

**Solution**   Automatic Save saves a copy of a drawing every 10 minutes by default. This interval can be modified by the user.

**Make changes and open multiple files.**   As with other Mac applications, you can have multiple files open and exchange data between them.

**Master It**   With two drawings open, how can you copy parts of one drawing into the other?

**Solution**   Use the standard Copy and Paste features of the Mac OS. Select the parts you want to copy, right-click, select Clipboard, and then Copy. In the other drawing, right-click in the drawing area, select Clipboard, and then Paste.

# Chapter 2: Creating Your First Drawing

**Specify distances with coordinates.** One of the most basic skills you need to learn is how to indicate exact distances through the keyboard. AutoCAD uses a simple annotation system to indicate distance and direction.

**Master It** What would you type to indicate a relative distance of 14 units at a 45° angle?

**Solution** @14<45

**Interpret the cursor modes and understand prompts.** AutoCAD's cursor changes its shape depending on the command that is currently active. These different cursor modes can give you a clue regarding what you should be doing.

**Master It** Describe the Point Selection cursor and the Object Selection cursor.

**Solution** The Point Selection cursor is a simple crosshair. The Object Selection cursor is a small square.

**Select objects and edit with grips.** Grips are small squares or arrowheads that appear at key points on the object when they're selected. They offer a powerful way to edit objects.

**Master It** How do you select multiple grips?

**Solution** Hold down ⇧ while clicking the grips.

**Use Dynamic Input.** Besides grips, objects display their dimensional properties when selected. These dimensional properties can be edited to change an object's shape.

**Master It** How do you turn on Dynamic Input? And once it's on, what key lets you shift between the different dimensions of an object?

**Solution** The Dynamic Input button on the AutoCAD status bar turns Dynamic Input on and off. When an object is selected, you can move between the dimensional properties by pressing the Tab key.

**Get help.** AutoCAD's Help window is thorough in its coverage of AutoCAD's features. New and experienced users alike can often find answers to their questions through the Help window, so it pays to become familiar with it.

**Master It** What keyboard key do you press for context-sensitive help?

**Solution** Function-F1.

**Display data in the Command Line palette.** AutoCAD offers the Command Line palette, which keeps a running account of the commands you use. This can be helpful in retrieving input that you've entered when constructing your drawing.

**Master It** Name a command that displays its results in the Command Line palette.

**Solution** The List command.

**Display the properties of an object.** The Properties Inspector palette is one of the most useful sources for drawing information. Not only does it list the properties of an object, it lets you change the shape, color, and other properties of objects.

**Master It** How do you open the Properties Inspector palette for a particular object?

**Solution** Select the object whose properties you want to view. Right-click the object and select Properties.

# Chapter 3: Setting Up and Using AutoCAD's Drafting Tools

**Set up a work area.**   A blank AutoCAD drawing offers few clues about the size of the area you're working with, but you can get a rough idea of the area shown in the drawing window.

**Master It**   Name two ways to set up the area of your work.

**Solution**   You can use the Limits command to define the work area, otherwise known as the limits of the drawing. You can also draw a rectangle that is the size of your work area.

**Explore the drawing process.**   To use AutoCAD effectively, you'll want to know how the different tools work together to achieve an effect. The drawing process often involves many cycles of adding objects and then editing them.

**Master It**   Name the tool that causes the cursor to point in an exact horizontal or vertical direction.

**Solution**   Polar Tracking. Ortho mode can also perform this function.

**Plan and lay out a drawing.**   If you've ever had to draw a precise sketch with just a pencil and pad, you've probably used a set of lightly drawn guidelines to lay out your drawing first. You do the same thing in AutoCAD, but instead of lightly drawn guidelines, you can use any object you want. In AutoCAD, objects are easily modified or deleted, so you don't have to be as careful when adding guidelines.

**Master It**   What is the name of the feature that lets you select exact locations on objects?

**Solution**   Object Snap, or osnap.

**Use the AutoCAD modes as drafting tools.**   The main reason for using AutoCAD is to produce precise technical drawings. AutoCAD offers many tools to help you produce a drawing with the precision you need.

**Master It**   What dialog box lets you set both the grid and snap spacing?

**Solution**   The Drafting Settings dialog box.

# Chapter 4: Organizing Objects with Blocks and Groups

**Create and insert a block.**   If you have a symbol that you use often in a drawing, you can draw it once and then turn it into an AutoCAD block. A block can be placed in a drawing multiple times in any location, like a rubber stamp. A block is stored in a drawing as a block definition, which can be called up at any time.

**Master It**   Name the dialog box used to create a block from objects in a drawing, and also name the tool to open this dialog box.

**Solution**   The Define Block dialog box can be opened using the Create tool.

**Modify a block.**   Once you've created a block, it isn't set in stone. One of the features of a block is that you can change the block definition and all the copies of the block are updated to the new definition.

**Master It**   What is the name of the tool used to "unblock" a block?

**Solution**   You can use the Explode tool to break a block down to its component objects. Once this is done, you can modify the objects and then redefine the block.

**Understand the annotation scale.** In some cases, you'll want to create a block that is dependent on the drawing scale. You can create a block that adjusts itself to the scale of your drawing through the annotation scale. When the annotation scale feature is turned on for a block, the block can be set to appear at the correct size depending on the scale of your drawing.

**Master It** What setting in the Define Block dialog box turns on the annotation scale feature, and how do you set the annotation scale of a block?

**Solution** The Annotative option in the Define Block dialog box turns on the annotation scale feature. You can set the scales for a block by selecting the block, right-clicking, and selecting Object Scale ➢ Add/Delete Scales.

**Group objects.** Blocks can be used as a tool to group objects together, but blocks can be too rigid for some grouping applications. AutoCAD offers groups, which are collections of objects that are similar to blocks but aren't as rigidly defined.

**Master It** How are groups different from blocks?

**Solution** Objects in a group can be easily edited by turning groups off with the ⌐⌐ -A keyboard shortcut. Also, unlike blocks, groups don't have a single definition that's stored in the drawing and defines the group's appearance. You can copy a group, but each copy is independent of the other groups.

## Chapter 5: Keeping Track of Layers and Blocks

**Organize information with layers.** Layers are perhaps the most powerful feature in AutoCAD. They help to keep drawings well organized, and they give you control over the visibility of objects. They also let you control the appearance of your drawing by setting colors, line weights, and linetypes.

**Master It** Describe the process of creating a layer.

**Solution** Click the Plus icon at the bottom left of the Layers palette. Type the name for your new layer.

**Control layer visibility.** When a drawing becomes dense with information, it can be difficult to edit. If you've organized your drawing using layers, you can reduce its complexity by turning off layers that aren't important to your current session.

**Master It** Describe two methods for hiding a layer.

**Solution** In the Layers palette, select a layer, and click the Freeze icon for the layer. You can also select the layer from the Layers palette list and then click the Freeze option in the Properties Inspector palette.

**Keep track of blocks and layers.** At times, you may want a record of the layers or blocks in your drawing. You can create a list of layers using the log-file feature in AutoCAD.

**Master It** How do you turn on the log-file feature?

**Solution** Type **LOGFILEMODE**⌐ **1**⌐.

# Chapter 6: Editing and Reusing Data to Work Efficiently

**Create and use templates.**   If you find that you're using the same settings repeatedly when you create a new drawing file, you can set up an existing file the way you like and save it as a template. You can then use your saved template for any new drawings you create.

> **Master It**   Describe the method for saving a file as a template.

> **Solution**   After setting up a blank drawing with the settings you use most frequently, choose Save As from the menu bar. In the Save Drawing As dialog box, choose AutoCAD Drawing Template (*.dwt) from the File Format drop-down list, give it a name, and click Save. In the command line, specify whether the template is English or metric and then enter a descriptive name to save the template.

**Copy an object multiple times.**   Many tools in AutoCAD allow you to create multiple copies. The Array command offers a way to create circular copies or row and column copies.

> **Master It**   What names are given to the two types of arrays in the Array dialog box?

> **Solution**   Rectangular and polar.

**Develop your drawing.**   When laying down simple line work, you'll use a few tools frequently. The exercises in the early part of this book showed you some of these commonly used tools.

> **Master It**   What tool can you use to join two lines end to end?

> **Solution**   Fillet.

**Find an exact distance along a curve.**   AutoCAD offers some tools that allow you to find an exact distance along a curve.

> **Master It**   Name the two tools you can use to mark off exact distances along a curve.

> **Solution**   Measure and Divide.

**Change the length of objects.**   You can accurately adjust the length of a line or arc in AutoCAD using a single command.

> **Master It**   What is the command alias for the command that changes the length of objects?

> **Solution**   The command is **LEN**.

**Create a new drawing by using parts from another drawing.**   You can save a lot of time by reusing parts of drawings. The Export command can help.

> **Master It**   True or false: The Export command saves only blocks as drawing files.

> **Solution**   False. You can use Export with any type of object or set of objects in a drawing.

# Chapter 7: Mastering Viewing Tools, Hatches, and External References

**Assemble the parts.**   Technical drawings are often made up of repetitive parts that are drawn over and over. AutoCAD makes quick work of repetitive elements in a drawing, as shown in the first part of this chapter.

**Master It**   What is the object used as the basic building block for the unit plan drawing in the beginning of this chapter?

**Solution**   Blocks of a typical unit plan are used to build a floor plan of an apartment building.

**Take control of the AutoCAD display.**   Understanding the way the AutoCAD display works can save you time, especially in a complex drawing.

**Master It**   Name the command used to save views in AutoCAD. Describe how to recall a saved view.

**Solution**   The View command allows you to save views. You can recall views by typing **VIEW↵ R↵**.

**Use hatch patterns in your drawings.**   Patterns can convey a lot of information at a glance. You can show the material of an object, or you can indicate a type of view, like a cross section, by applying hatch patterns.

**Master It**   How do you open the Hatch And Gradient dialog box?

**Solution**   Choose Hatch from the Tool Sets palette, choose Draw ➢ Hatch from the menu bar, or type **HATCH↵**.

**Understand the boundary hatch options.**   The boundary hatch options give you control over the way hatch patterns fill an enclosed area.

**Master It**   Describe an island as it relates to boundary hatch patterns.

**Solution**   An island is a bounded area in the area to be hatched.

**Use external references.**   External references are drawing files that you've attached to the current drawing to include as part of the drawing. Because external references aren't part of the current file, they can be worked on at the same time as the referencing file.

**Master It**   Describe how drawing files are attached as external references.

**Solution**   Open the Reference Manager palette (⌘-7), click the Attach Reference tool at the upper left, and then locate and select the file you want to attach.

# Chapter 8: Introducing Printing and Layouts

**Print a plan.**   Unlike other types of documents, AutoCAD drawings can end up on nearly any size sheet of paper. To accommodate the range of paper sizes, the AutoCAD printer settings are fairly extensive and give you a high level of control over your output.

**Master It**   Name a few of the settings available in the Print dialog box.

**Solution**   Paper Size, Orientation, and Printer/Plotter Name are a few of the settings available in the Print dialog box.

**Understanding the print settings.**   The print settings in AutoCAD offer a way to let you set up how a drawing will be printed.

**Master It**   Where would you find the setting to print upside down?

**Solution**   The Print Upside Down setting is in the Print – Advanced dialog box, located in the Print Options group.

**Use layout views for WYSIWYG printing.**  The layout views show you what your print output will look like before you actually print.

**Master It**  True or false: Layout views give you limited control over the appearance of your drawing printouts.

**Solution**  False.

# Chapter 9: Adding Text to Drawings

**Prepare a drawing for text.**  AutoCAD offers an extensive set of features for adding text to a drawing, but you need to do a little prep work before you dive in.

**Master It**  Name two things you need to do to prepare a drawing for text.

**Solution**  Set up a layer for your text. Create a text style for your drawing.

**Set the annotation scale and add text.**  Before you start to add text, you should set the annotation scale for your drawing. Once this is done, you can begin to add text.

**Master It**  In a sentence or two, briefly describe the purpose of the annotation scale feature. Name the tool you use to add text to a drawing.

**Solution**  The annotation scale feature converts your text size to the proper height for the scale of your drawing. To add text to a drawing, use the Mtext tool.

**Explore text formatting in AutoCAD.**  Because text styles contain font and text-size settings, you can usually set up a text style and then begin to add text to your drawing. For those special cases where you need to vary text height and font or other text features, you can use the Text Editor visor of the text editor.

**Master It**  What text formatting tool can you use to change text to boldface type?

**Solution**  The Bold button.

**Add simple single-line text objects.**  In many situations, you need only a single word or a short string of text. AutoCAD offers the single line text object for these instances.

**Master It**  Describe the methods for starting the single-line text command.

**Solution**  Click the Single Line text icon in the Tool Sets palette. Enter **DT**⏎ at the command prompt.

**Use the Check Spelling feature.**  It isn't uncommon for a drawing to contain the equivalent of several pages of text, and the likelihood of having misspelled words can be high. AutoCAD offers the Check Spelling feature to help you keep your spelling under control.

**Master It**  What option do you select in the Check Spelling dialog box when it finds a misspelled word and you want to accept the suggestion it offers?

**Solution**  Change.

**Find and replace text.**  A common activity when editing technical drawings is finding and replacing a word throughout a drawing.

**Master It**  True or false: The Find And Replace feature in AutoCAD works very differently than the find-and-replace feature in other programs.

**Solution**  False.

# Chapter 10: Using Fields and Tables

**Use fields to associate text with drawing properties.**   Fields are a special type of text object that can be linked to object properties. They can help to automate certain text-related tasks.

**Master It**   Name two uses for fields that you learned about in the first part of this chapter.

**Solution**   Fields can be used to update text that labels a block. They can also be used to update text and report the area enclosed by a polyline.

**Add tables to your drawing.**   The Tables feature can help you make quick work of schedules and other tabular data that you want to include in a drawing.

**Master It**   What is the name of the visor that appears when you click the Table tool?

**Solution**   Text Editor.

**Edit the table line work.**   Because tables include line work to delineate their different cells, AutoCAD gives you control over table borders and lines.

**Master It**   How do you get to the Cell Border Properties dialog box?

**Solution**   Select the cell or cells in the table, and in the Properties Inspector palette, select Border Style from the Cells category.

**Add formulas to cells.**   Tables can function like spreadsheets by allowing you to add formulas to cells.

**Master It**   What type of text object lets you add formulas to cells?

**Solution**   Field.

**Export tables.**   The Table feature allows you to export the text from a table to a CSV file that can be imported into a Microsoft Excel spreadsheet.

**Master It**   Describe how to export a table from AutoCAD into an Excel spreadsheet.

**Solution**   Click to highlight the table. From the Table visor, choose the Export tool. In the Export Data dialog box, choose a name and a location for the file. Click Save. In Excel, choose File ➢ Open from the menu bar. In the Files Of Type pop-up menu, select All Files. Locate the file and click Open.

# Chapter 11: Using Dimensions

**Understand the components of a dimension.**   Before you start to dimension with AutoCAD, it helps to become familiar with the different parts of a dimension. This will help you set up your dimensions to fit the style of dimensions that you need.

**Master It**   Name a few of the dimension components.

**Solution**   Dimension line, dimension text, extension line, and arrow.

**Create a dimension style.**   As you become more familiar with technical drawing and drafting, you'll learn that there are standard formats for drawing dimensions. Arrows, text size, and even the way dimension lines are drawn are all subject to a standard format. Fortunately,

AutoCAD offers dimension styles that let you set up your dimension format once and then call up that format whenever you need it.

**Master It**   What is the name of the dialog box that lets you manage dimension styles, and how do you open it?

**Solution**   The Dimension Style Manager is the name of the dialog box. You can open it by choosing Format ➤ Dimension Style on menu bar.

**Draw linear dimensions.**   The most common dimension you'll use is the linear dimension. Knowing how to place a linear dimension is a big first step in learning how to dimension in AutoCAD.

**Master It**   Name the three locations you're asked for when placing a linear dimension.

**Solution**   First extension line origin, second extension line origin, and dimension line location.

**Edit dimensions.**   Dimensions often change in the course of a project, so you should know how to make changes to dimension text or other parts of a dimension.

**Master It**   How do you start the command to edit dimension text?

**Solution**   Enter **ED**↵ at the Command prompt.

**Dimension non-orthogonal objects.**   Not everything you dimension will use linear dimensions. AutoCAD offers a set of dimension tools for dimensioning objects that aren't made up of straight lines.

**Master It**   Name some of the types of objects for which a linear dimension isn't appropriate.

**Solution**   Arc and angle between two lines. Linear dimensions can be used for circles in certain situations.

**Add a note with a leader arrow.**   In addition to dimensions, you'll probably add lots of notes with arrows pointing to features in a design. AutoCAD offers the multileader for this purpose.

**Master It**   What two types of objects does the multileader combine?

**Solution**   Leader lines (arrowhead and line) and text.

**Apply ordinate dimensions.**   When accuracy counts, ordinate dimensions are often used because they measure distances that are similar to coordinates from a single feature.

**Master It**   What AutoCAD feature that isn't strictly associated with dimensions do you use for ordinate dimensions?

**Solution**   UCS.

**Add tolerance notation.**   Mechanical drafting often requires the use of special notation to describe tolerances. AutoCAD offers some predefined symbols that address the need to include tolerance notation in a drawing.

**Master It**   How do you open the Geometric Tolerance dialog box?

**Solution**   Click Tolerance from the expanded Dimensions tool group, choose Dimension ➤ Tolerance on the menu bar, or type **TOL**↵.

## Chapter 12: Using Attributes

**Create attributes.** Attributes are a great tool for storing data with drawn objects. You can include as little or as much data as you like in an AutoCAD block.

> **Master It** What is the name of the object you must include in a block to store data?

> **Solution** Attribute definition.

**Edit attributes.** The data you include in a block is easily changed. You may have several copies of a block, each of which must contain its own unique sets of data.

> **Master It** What is the simplest way to gain access to a block's attribute data?

> **Solution** Double-click the block to open the Enhanced Attribute Editor.

## Chapter 13: Copying Existing Drawings into AutoCAD

**Convert paper drawings into AutoCAD files.** AutoCAD gives you some great tools that let you convert your paper drawings into AutoCAD files. Several options are available. Depending on your needs, you'll find at least one solution that will allow you to convert your drawings quickly.

> **Master It** Describe the different methods available in AutoCAD for converting paper drawings into AutoCAD files.

> **Solution** The methods are scaling directly from a drawing, scanning and converting with a third-party program, and scanning to a raster file that can then be imported into AutoCAD to be traced over.

**Import a raster image.** You can use bitmap raster images as backgrounds for your CAD drawings or as underlay drawings that you can trace over.

> **Master It** Import a raster image of your choice, and use the AutoCAD drawing tools to trace over your image.

> **Solution** From the Reference Manager, click Attach Reference to open the Select Reference File dialog box, or type **ATTACH**↵ in the Command Line palette. Change the File Format drop-down list to All Image Files. Locate and select the raster image file you want to import. Click Open to open the Attach Image dialog box, and then click OK. Specify an insertion point and scale factor.

**Work with a raster image.** Once imported, raster images can be adjusted for size, brightness, contrast, and transparency.

> **Master It** Import a raster image of your choice, and fade the image so it appears lighter and with less contrast.

> **Solution** Click a raster image's border. In the Properties Inspector palette's Image Adjust section, click and drag the Fade slider to the right. The raster image appears faded.

# Chapter 14: Advanced Editing and Organizing

**Use external references (Xrefs).**   You've seen how you can use Xrefs to quickly build variations of a floor plan that contains repetitive elements. This isn't necessarily the only way to use Xrefs, but the basic idea of how to use Xrefs is presented in the early exercises.

**Master It**   Try putting together another floor plan that contains nothing but the Unit2 plan.

**Solution**   Replace the eight studio units in the Common.dwg file with four of the Unit2 plans.

**Change Layer information.**   Layers is a powerful tool used in AutoCAD drawings. You can modify a layer using various properties found in the Layers palette.

**Master It**   Modify the Ceiling layer so that it displays a very light gray line.

**Solution**   In the Layers palette, select the Ceiling layer. Click the color swatch and click Select Color. The Color palette will open. Select the index color 9, or type **9** in the space provided.

**Select similar objects.**   Select Similar can select alike objects. It can be invoked from the shortcut menu when objects are selected.

**Master It**   Select all the walls on the plan drawing and change them so that they are now set to the color magenta. Now reset them to their previous color.

**Solution**   Click on a wall, and right-click. Choose the Select Similar option in the shortcut menu. In the Properties Inspector palette, select the color swatch and choose Magenta. Press Esc. To reset the color back, select a wall, use the Select Similar option, and change the color swatch to Bylayer.

# Chapter 15: Laying Out Your Printer Output

**Understand Model Space and Paper Space.**   AutoCAD offers two viewing modes for viewing and printing your drawings. Model Space is where you do most of your work; it's the view you see when you create a new file. Layouts, also called Paper Space, are views that let you arrange the layout of your drawing, similar to how you would in a page-layout program.

**Master It**   Name the method of moving from Model Space to Paper Space.

**Solution**   You can use the Show Drawing & Layouts tool in the status bar to display the model and layout preview panels.

**Work with Paper Space viewports.**   While in Paper Space, you can create views into your drawing using viewports. You can have several viewports, each showing a different part of your drawing.

**Master It**   Explain how you can enlarge a view in a viewport.

**Solution**   You can double-click inside a viewport and then use the Zoom tool to enlarge the view.

**Create odd-shaped viewports.**   Most of the time, you'll probably use rectangular viewports, but you have the option to create a viewport of any shape.

**Master It**   Describe the process for creating a circular viewport.

**Solution**   In Paper Space, draw a circle. Next, choose View ➢ Viewports ➢ Object from the menu bar.

**Understand line weights, linetypes, and dimensions in Paper Space.**   You can get an accurate view of how your drawing will look on paper by making a few adjustments to AutoCAD. Your layout view will reflect how your drawing will look when printed.

**Master It**   Name the dialog box used to adjust line weights and how you would access it.

**Solution**   The Lineweight Settings dialog box. You can access it by typing **LW**↵ or via the Lineweight drop-down list in the Layers palette.

# Chapter 16: Making "Smart" Drawings with Parametric Tools

**Use parametric drawing tools.**   Parametric drawing tools enable you to create an assembly of objects that are linked to each other based on geometric or dimensional properties. With the parametric drawing tools, you can create a drawing that automatically adjusts the size of all its components when you change a single dimension.

**Master It**   Name two examples given in the beginning of the chapter of a mechanical assembly that can be shown using parametric drawing tools.

**Solution**   The examples are a crankshaft and piston and a Luxo lamp.

**Connect objects with geometric constraints.**   You can link objects together so that they maintain a particular orientation to each other.

**Master It**   Name at least six of the geometric constraints available in AutoCAD.

**Solution**   The constraints are coincident, collinear, concentric, fix, parallel, perpendicular, horizontal, vertical, tangent, smooth, symmetric, and equal.

**Control sizes with dimensional constraints.**   Dimensional constraints, in conjunction with geometric constraints, let you apply dimensions to an assembly of objects to control the size of the assembly.

**Master It**   Name at least four dimensional constraints.

**Solution**   The dimensional constraints are linear, horizontal, vertical, aligned, radius, diameter, and angular.

**Put constraints to use.**   Constraints can be used in a variety of ways to simulate the behavior of real objects.

**Master It**   Name at least three geometric or dimensional constraints used in the `piston.dwg` file to help simulate the motion of a piston and crankshaft.

**Solution**   The geometric constraints used were horizontal, parallel, fix, and coincident. The dimensional constraints used were horizontal, vertical, aligned, and diameter.

# Chapter 17: Drawing Curves

**Create and edit polylines.** Polylines are extremely versatile. You can use them in just about any situation in which you need to draw line work that is continuous. For this reason, you'll want to master polylines early in your AutoCAD training.

**Master It** Draw the part shown here.

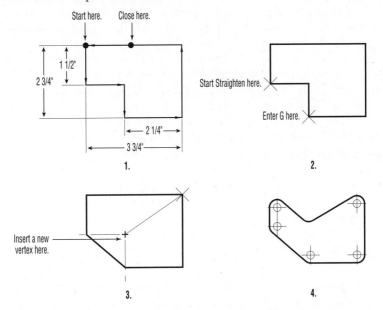

**Solution** There are many ways to create this drawing. Use these instructions as guidelines, but keep in mind that this is not the only way to create the drawing:

1. Open a new file called PART14 using the acad.dwt template. Set the Snap spacing to 0.25, and be sure Snap mode is on. Use the Pline command to draw the object shown in step 1 of the drawing shown here. Start at the upper-left corner, and draw in the direction indicated by the arrows. Use the Close option to add the last line segment.

2. Start the Pedit command, select the polyline, and then type **E**↵ to issue the Edit Vertex option. Press ↵ until the X mark moves to the first corner, as shown here. Enter **S**↵ for the Straighten option.

   At the Enter an option prompt, press ↵ twice to move the X to the other corner shown in step 2 of the drawing. Press **G**↵ for Go to straighten the polyline between the two selected corners.

3. Press ↵ three times to move the X to the upper-right corner, and then enter **I**↵ for Insert. Pick a point as shown in step 3 of the drawing. The polyline changes to reflect the new vertex. Enter **X**↵ to exit the Edit Vertex option, and then press ↵ to exit the Pedit command.

4. Start the Fillet command, use the Radius option to set the fillet radius to 0.30, and then use the Polyline option and select the polyline you just edited. All the corners become rounded to the 0.30 radius. Add the 0.15 radius circles as shown in step 4 of the drawing, and exit and save the file.

**Create a polyline spline curve.** Polylines can be used to draw fairly accurate renditions of spline curves. This feature of polylines makes them a very useful AutoCAD object type.

**Master It** Try drawing the outline of an object that has no or few straight lines in it, as in the file `lowerfairing.jpg`, which is included in the Chapter 17 sample files at www. sybex.com/go/masteringautocadmac. You can use the methods described in Chapter 13, "Copying Existing Drawings into AutoCAD," to import a raster image of your object and then trace over the image using polyline splines.

**Solution** Import a raster image by using the Attach Reference tool in the Reference Manager. Use the Polyline command to trace over the image. Use short, straight polyline segments while you trace. After you place each polyline, double-click it and select the Spline option. Once you change the line to a spline curve, it may shift away from the original line you traced over. Click the polyline, and then adjust the grips so the line fits over the raster image.

**Create and edit true spline curves.** If you need an accurate spline curve, you'll want to use the Spline command. Spline objects offer many fine-tuning options that you won't find with polylines.

**Master It** Try tracing over the same image from the previous Master It section, but this time use the Spline command.

**Solution** Import a raster image by using the Attach Reference tool in the Reference Manager. Use the Spline command to trace over the image. As you draw the spline, select control points that are closer together for tighter curves. The closer the control points are, the tighter you can make the curve. Notice that, unlike with a polyline spline, you don't have to readjust the curve after it's been placed.

**Mark divisions on curves.** The Divide and Measure commands offer a quick way to mark off distances on a curved object. This can be a powerful resource in AutoCAD that you may find yourself using often.

**Master It** Mark off 12 equal divisions of the spline curves you drew in the previous Master It exercise.

**Solution** Choose Divide from the Multiple Points drop-down in the expanded Open Shapes tool group's panel of the Tool Sets palette, select the spline, and then enter **12.**↵ If you don't see the points that mark off the divisions, type **DDPTYPE**↵, select the X point style, and click OK.

## Chapter 18: Getting and Exchanging Data from Drawings

**Find the area of closed boundaries.** There are a number of ways to find the area of a closed boundary. The easiest way is also perhaps the least obvious.

**Master It**   Which AutoCAD feature would you use to quickly find the area of an irregular shape like a pond or lake?

**Solution**   Hatch.

**Get general information.**   A lot of information that is stored in AutoCAD drawings can tell you about the files. You can find out how much time has been spent editing a file, for instance.

**Master It**   What feature gives you a list of current settings and how do you get to this feature?

**Solution**   You can open the Status command by choosing Tools ➢ Inquiry ➢ Status from the menu bar.

**Use the DXF file format to exchange CAD data with other programs.**   Autodesk created the DXF file format as a means of sharing vector drawings with other programs.

**Master It**   Name the versions of AutoCAD you can export to using the Save As option.

**Solution**   2010, 2007, 2004, 2002, and R12.

**Use AutoCAD drawings in page-layout programs.**   AutoCAD drawings find their way into all types of documents, including brochures and technical manuals. Users are often asked to convert their CAD drawings into formats that can be read by page-layout software.

**Master It**   Name some file formats, by filename extension or type, that page-layout programs can accept.

**Solution**   PDF (.pdf), EPS (.eps), BMP (.bmp), and PNG (.png).

**Fix corrupted drawing files.**   At some point, you may encounter a corrupted drawing file. In some cases, the file may be so badly corrupted that AutoCAD won't open it. Fortunately, you have some options to recover a file that might otherwise be unreadable.

**Master It**   What is the command that you can use to recover an unreadable DWG file?

**Solution**   Recover.

# Chapter 19: Creating 3D Drawings

**Know the 3D modeling environment.**   When you work in 3D, you need a different set of tools from those for 2D drafting. AutoCAD offers the Modeling toolset on the Tool Sets palette, which provides the tools you need to create 3D models.

**Master It**   Name some of the tool groups that are unique to the Modeling toolset on the Tool Sets palette.

**Solution**   Solids – Create, Solids – Edit, Surfaces – Create, Surfaces – Edit, Render, Lights, Materials, Analysis, Section, and Coordinates.

**Draw in 3D using solids.**   AutoCAD offers a type of object called a 3D solid that lets you quickly create and edit shapes.

**Master It**   What does the Presspull command do?

**Solution**   Presspull lets you press or pull a 3D solid shape from another 3D solid. It can also be used to press or pull a closed 2D object drawn on the surface of a solid.

**Create 3D forms from 2D shapes.** The Modeling toolset offers a set of basic 3D shapes, but other commands enable you to create virtually any shape you want from 2D drawings.

**Master It** Name the command that lets you change a closed 2D polyline into a 3D solid.

**Solution** Extrude.

**Isolate coordinates with point filters.** When you're working in 3D, selecting points can be a complicated task. AutoCAD offers point filters to let you specify the individual X, Y, and Z coordinates of a location in space.

**Master It** What does the .XY point filter do?

**Solution** The .XY point filter lets you select an X,Y coordinate, after which you can specify a Z coordinate as a separate value.

**Move around your model.** Getting the view you want in a 3D model can be tricky.

**Master It** Where is the menu that lets you select a view from a list of predefined 3D views?

**Solution** The 3D Views menu of the Viewport Controls is in the drawing area; it offers predefined 3D viewpoints. You can also choose View ➤ 3D Views from the menu bar.

**Get a visual effect.** At certain points in your model making, you'll want to view your 3D model with surface colors and even material assignments. AutoCAD offers several ways to do this.

**Master It** What are the steps to take to change the view from Wireframe to Realistic?

**Solution** Click the Visual Styles viewport menu, and select Realistic.

**Turn a 3D view into a 2D AutoCAD drawing.** Sometimes, it's helpful to convert a 3D model view into a 2D representation. AutoCAD offers the Flatshot command, which quickly converts a 3D view into a 2D line drawing.

**Master It** What type of object does Flatshot create?

**Solution** A block or drawing file.

# Chapter 20: Using Advanced 3D Features

**Master the User Coordinate System.** The User Coordinate System (UCS) is a vital key to editing in 3D space. If you want to master 3D modeling, you should become familiar with this feature.

**Master It** Name some of the predefined UCS planes.

**Solution** Front, Back, Left, Right, Top, Bottom.

**Understand the UCS options.** You can set up the UCS orientation for any situation. It isn't limited to the predefined settings.

**Master It** Give a brief description of some of the ways you can set up a UCS.

**Solution** Object orientation, selection of three points, rotation about an axis, selection of a Z-axis direction, and selection of the view plane.

**Use viewports to aid in 3D drawing.** In some 3D modeling operations, it helps to have several different views of the model through the Viewports feature.

**Master It** Name some of the predefined standard viewports offered in the Viewports dialog box.

**Solution** Two: Vertical; Two: Horizontal; Three: Right; Three: Left; Three: Above; Three: Below; Three: Vertical; Three: Horizontal; Four: Equal; Four: Right; and Four: Left.

**Create complex 3D surfaces.** You aren't limited to straight, flat surfaces in AutoCAD. You can create just about any shape you want, including curved surfaces.

**Master It** What tool did you use in this chapter's chair exercise to convert a surface into a solid?

**Solution** The Thicken tool.

**Create spiral forms.** Spiral forms frequently occur in nature, so it's no wonder that we often use spirals in our own designs. Spirals are seen in screws, stairs, and ramps as well as in other man-made forms.

**Master It** Name the commands or tools used in the example in the section "Creating Spiral Forms," and name two elements that are needed to create a spiral.

**Solution** The commands are Helix and Sweep. A helix and a profile are needed.

**Create surface models.** You can create a 3D surface by connecting a series of lines that define a surface contour. You can create anything from a 3D landscape to a car fender using this method.

**Master It** What is the tool or command used to convert a series of open objects into a 3D surface?

**Solution** Loft.

**Move objects in 3D space.** You can move objects in 3D space using tools that are similar to those for 2D drafting. But when it comes to editing objects, 3D modeling is much more complex than 2D drafting.

**Master It** What does the Rotate gizmo do?

**Solution** It lets you graphically determine the axis of rotation for an object being rotated.

# Chapter 21: Rendering 3D Drawings

**Simulate the sun.** One of the most practical uses of AutoCAD's rendering feature is to simulate the sun's location and resulting shadows. You can generate shadow studies for any time of the year in any location on the earth.

**Master It** How do you get to the sun properties?

**Solution** Make sure nothing is selected in the drawing and then click the All button in the Properties Inspector palette.

**Create effects using materials and lights.** You can use materials and lights together to control the appearance of your model.

**Master It**   Name the part of the example model in this chapter that was used to show how a material can appear to glow.

**Solution**   Light bulb material.

**Control your render quality.**   AutoCAD offers a few features to give you some control over the quality of your rendering. The default rendering settings allow you to view your rendering at a level good enough to gauge how it will look.

**Master It**   Name the two features discussed in this chapter that allow you to control the quality of your renderings.

**Solution**   The Renderquality setting and the Properties Inspector palette.

**Print your renderings.**   You can save your rendered views as bitmap files using the Render window. If you prefer, you can also have AutoCAD include a rendering in a layout. You can include different renderings of the same file in a single layout.

**Master It**   Give a general description of the process for setting up a rendered viewport in a layout.

**Solution**   Create a viewport, and then set up the view you want for the viewport using the 3D Views menu in the viewport controls. Select the viewport's border, right-click, and select a Shade Plot menu option.

## Chapter 22: Editing and Visualizing 3D Solids

**Understand solid modeling.**   Solid modeling lets you build 3D models by creating and joining 3D shapes called solids. There are several built-in solid shapes called primitives, and you can create others using the Extrude tool.

**Master It**   Name some of the built-in solid primitives available in AutoCAD.

**Solution**   Box, wedge, cone, sphere, cylinder, pyramid, torus, and polysolid.

**Create solid forms.**   You can use Boolean operations to sculpt 3D solids into the shape you want. Two solids can be joined to form a more complex one, or you can remove one solid from another.

**Master It**   Name the three Boolean operations you can use on solids.

**Solution**   Intersection, subtraction, and union.

**Create complex solids.**   Besides the primitives, you can create your own shapes based on 2D polylines.

**Master It**   Name three tools that let you convert closed polylines and circles into 3D solids.

**Solution**   Extrude, Revolve, and Sweep.

**Edit solids.**   Once you've created a solid, you can make changes to it using the solid-editing tools offered on the Solids – Edit tool group or the Modify ➤ Solid Editing submenu on the menu bar.

**Master It**   Name at least four of the tools found on the Solids – Edit tool group.

**Solution**   The tools found on the Solids - Edit tool group are Union, Subtract, Intersect, Slice, Thicken, Extract Edges, Taper Faces, Extrude Faces, Offset Faces.

**Streamline the 2D drawing process.**   You can create 3D orthogonal views of your 3D model to create standard 2D mechanical drawings.

**Master It**   What is the name of the tool in the Tool Sets palette that lets you create a 2D drawing of a 3D model?

**Solution**   Flatshot.

**Visualize solids.**   In addition to viewing your 3D model in a number of different orientations, you can view it as if it were transparent or cut in half.

**Master It**   What is the name of the command that lets you create a cut view of your 3D model?

**Solution**   Sectionplane.

# Chapter 23: Exploring 3D Mesh and Surface Modeling

**Create a simple 3D mesh.**   Mesh modeling allows you to create more organic 3D forms by giving you unique smoothing and editing tools. You can start your mesh model by creating a basic shape using the mesh primitives.

**Master It**   Name at least six mesh primitives available on the Primitives submenu under Draw ➢ 3D Modeling ➢ Meshes on the menu bar.

**Solution**   The mesh primitives are box, cone, sphere, pyramid, wedge, torus, and cylinder.

**Edit faces and edges.**   The ability to edit faces and edges is essential to creating complex shapes with mesh objects.

**Master It**   Name the tool that is used to divide a face into multiple faces.

**Solution**   The Mesh Refine tool.

**Create mesh surfaces.**   The Mesh primitives let you create shapes that enclose a volume. If you just want to model a smooth, curved surface in 3D, you might find the surface mesh tools helpful.

**Master It**   How many objects are needed to use the Edge Surface tool?

**Solution**   Four.

**Convert meshes to solids.**   You can convert a mesh into a 3D solid to take advantage of many of the solid-editing tools available in AutoCAD.

**Master It**   Name at least two tools you can use on a solid that you cannot use on a mesh.

**Solution**   Union, Subtract, Intersect, Interfere, any of the edge- or face-editing tools on the Tool Sets palette.

**Understand 3D surfaces.**   3D surfaces can be created using some of the same tools you use to create 3D solids.

**Master It** Name at least two tools you can use to create both 3D solids and 3D surfaces.

**Solution** Any of the following: Loft, Sweep, Extrude, and Revolve.

**Edit 3D surfaces.** AutoCAD offers a wide range of tools that are unique to 3D surfaces.

**Master It** Name at least four tools devoted to CV editing.

**Solution** Any of the following: 3D Edit bar, Convert To NURBS, Show CV, Hide CV, Surface Rebuild (Rebuild), Add CV Surface CV (or just CV Add), and Remove CV (or CV Remove).

# Index

**Note to the Reader:** Throughout this index **boldfaced** page numbers indicate primary discussions of a topic. *Italicized* page numbers indicate illustrations.